Portfolio Management
Study Sessions 12-15

CFA® PROGRAM CURRICULUM • VOLUME 5

LEVEL III
2008

PEARSON

Custom
Publishing

Printed in the United States of America

10 9 8 7 6 5 4 3 2

ISBN 0-536-34531-7

2006160842

AG/JS

Please visit our web site at *www.pearsoncustom.com*

PEARSON CUSTOM PUBLISHING
501 Boylston Street, Suite 900, Boston, MA 02116
A Pearson Education Company

CONTENTS

HOW TO USE THE CFA PROGRAM CURRICULUM

Congratulations on passing Level II of the Chartered Financial Analyst (CFA®) Program. This exciting and rewarding program of study reflects your desire to become a serious investment professional. You are participating in a program noted for its high ethical standards and the breadth of knowledge, skills, and abilities it develops. Your commitment to the CFA Program should be educationally and professionally rewarding.

The credential you seek is respected around the world as a mark of accomplishment and dedication. Each level of the program represents a distinct achievement in professional development. Successful completion of the program is rewarded with membership in a prestigious global community of investment professionals. CFA charterholders are dedicated to life-long learning and maintaining currency with the ever-changing dynamics of a challenging profession.

The CFA examination measures your degree of mastery of the assigned CFA Program curriculum. Effective study and preparation based on that curriculum are keys to your success on the examination.

Curriculum Development

The CFA Program curriculum is grounded in the practice of the investment profession. CFA Institute regularly conducts a practice analysis survey of investment professionals around the world to determine the knowledge, skills, and abilities that are relevant to the profession. The survey results define the Candidate Body of Knowledge (CBOK™), an inventory of knowledge and responsibilities expected of the investment management professional at the level of a new CFA charterholder. The survey also determines how much emphasis each of the major topic areas receives on the CFA examinations.

A committee made up of practicing charterholders, in conjunction with CFA Institute staff, designs the CFA Program curriculum to deliver the CBOK to candidates. The examinations, also written by practicing charterholders, are designed to allow you to demonstrate your mastery of the CBOK as set forth in the CFA Program curriculum. As you structure your personal study program, you should emphasize mastery of the CBOK and the practical application of that knowledge. For more information on the practice analysis, CBOK, and development of the CFA Program curriculum, please visit www.cfainstitute.org/toolkit.

Organization

The Level III CFA Program curriculum is organized into two topic areas. Each topic area begins with a brief statement of the material and the depth of knowledge expected.

Each topic area is then divided into one or more study sessions. These study sessions—18 sessions in the Level III curriculum—should form the basic structure of your reading and preparation.

Each study session includes a statement of its structure and objective, and is further divided into specific reading assignments. The outline on the inside front cover of each volume illustrates the organization of these 18 study sessions.

The reading assignments are the basis for all examination questions, and are selected or developed specifically to teach the CBOK. These readings are drawn from textbook chapters, professional journal articles, research analyst reports, CFA Program-commissioned content, and cases. Many readings include problems and solutions as well as appendices to help you learn.

Reading-specific Learning Outcome Statements (LOS) are listed in the pages introducing each study session as well as at the beginning of each reading. These LOS indicate what you should be able to accomplish after studying the reading. We encourage you to review how to properly use LOS, and the descriptions of commonly used LOS "command words," at www.cfainstitute.org/toolkit. The command words signal the depth of learning you are expected to achieve from the reading. You should use the LOS to guide and focus your study, as each examination question is based on an assigned reading and one or more LOS. However, the readings provide context for the LOS and enable you to apply a principle or concept in a variety of scenarios. It is important to study the whole of a required reading.

Features of the Curriculum

- ▶ **Required vs. Optional Segments** - You should read all of the pages for an assigned reading. In some cases, however, we have reprinted an entire chapter or article and marked those parts of the reading that are not required as "optional." The CFA examination is based only on the required segments, and the optional segments are included only when they might help you to better understand the required segments (by seeing the required material in its full context). When an optional segment begins, you will see an icon and a solid vertical bar in the outside margin that will continue until the optional segment ends, accompanied by another icon. *Unless the material is specifically marked as optional, you should assume it is required.* Keep in mind that the optional material is provided strictly for your convenience and will not be tested. You should rely on the required segments and the reading-specific LOS in preparing for the examination.

- ▶ **Problems/Solutions** - *All questions and problems in the readings as well as their solutions (which are provided in an appendix at the end of each volume) are required material.* When appropriate, we have included problems after the readings to demonstrate practical application and reinforce your understanding of the concepts presented. The questions and problems are designed to help you learn these concepts. Many of the questions are in the same style and format as the actual CFA examination and will give you test-taking experience in that format. Examination questions that come from a past CFA examination are marked with the CFA logo in the margin.

  For your benefit, we have also made available the last three years' LIII essay questions and solutions. Please visit www.cfainstitute.org/toolkit to review these resources.

- ▶ **Margins** - The wide margins in each volume provide space for your note-taking.

- ▶ **Two-color Format** - To enrich the visual appeal and clarity of the exhibits, tables, and text, the curriculum is printed in a two-color format.

- ▶ **Six-volume Structure** - For portability of the curriculum, the material is spread over six volumes.

- ▶ **Glossary and Index** - For your convenience, we have printed a comprehensive glossary and index in each volume. Throughout the curriculum, a **bolded blue** word in a reading denotes a term defined in the glossary.

Designing Your Personal Study Program

Create a Schedule - An orderly, systematic approach to examination preparation is critical. You should dedicate a consistent block of time every week to reading and studying. Complete all reading assignments and the associated problems and solutions in each study session. Review the LOS both before and after you study each reading to ensure that you have mastered the applicable content and can demonstrate the knowledge, skill, or ability described by the LOS and the assigned reading.

CFA Institute estimates that you will need to devote a minimum of 10–15 hours per week for 18 weeks to study the assigned readings. Allow a minimum of one week for each study session, and plan to complete them all at least 30–45 days prior to the examination. This schedule will allow you to spend the final four to six weeks before the examination reviewing the assigned material and taking multiple online sample examinations.

At CFA Institute, we believe that candidates need to commit to a minimum of 250 hours reading and reviewing the curriculum, and taking online sample examinations, to master the material. This recommendation, however, may substantially underestimate the hours needed for appropriate examination preparation depending on your individual circumstances, relevant experience, and academic background.

You will undoubtedly adjust your study time to conform to your own strengths and weaknesses, and your educational and professional background. You will probably spend more time on some study sessions than on others. You should allow ample time for both in-depth study of all topic areas and additional concentration on those topic areas for which you feel least prepared.

Candidate Preparation Toolkit - We have created the online toolkit to provide a single comprehensive location for resources and guidance for candidate preparation. In addition to in-depth information on study program planning, the CFA Program curriculum, and the online sample examinations, the toolkit also contains curriculum errata, printable study session outlines, sample examination questions, and more. Errata identified in the curriculum are corrected and listed periodically in the errata listing in the toolkit. We encourage you to use the toolkit as your central preparation resource during your tenure as a candidate. Visit the toolkit at www.cfainstitute.org/toolkit.

Online Sample Examinations - After completing your study of the assigned curriculum, use the CFA Institute online sample examinations to measure your knowledge of the topics and to improve your examination-taking skills. After each question, you will receive immediate feedback noting the correct response and indicating the assigned reading for further study. The sample examinations are designed by the same people who create the actual CFA examinations, and reflect the question formats, topics, and level of difficulty of the actual CFA examinations, in a timed environment. Aggregate data indicate that the CFA examination pass rate was higher among candidates who took one or more online sample examinations than among candidates who did not take the online sample examinations. For more information on the online sample examinations, please visit www.cfainstitute.org/toolkit.

Preparatory Providers - After you enroll in the CFA Program, you may receive numerous solicitations for preparatory courses and review materials. Although preparatory courses and notes may be helpful to some candidates, you should view these resources as *supplements* to the assigned CFA Program curriculum. The CFA examinations reference only the CFA Institute assigned curriculum—no preparatory course or review course materials are consulted or referenced.

Before you decide on a supplementary prep course, do some research. Determine the experience and expertise of the instructors, the accuracy and currency of their content, the delivery method for their materials, and the provider's claims of success. Most importantly, make sure the provider is in compliance with the CFA Institute Prep Provider Guidelines Program. Three years of prep course products can be a significant investment, so make sure you're getting a sufficient return. Just remember, there are no shortcuts to success on the CFA examinations. Prep products can enhance your learning experience, but the CFA curriculum is the key to success. For more information on the Prep Provider Guidelines Program, visit www.cfainstitute.org/cfaprog/resources/prepcourse.html.

SUMMARY

Every question on the CFA examination is based on specific pages in the required readings and on one or more LOS. Frequently, an examination question is also tied to a specific example highlighted within a reading or to a specific end-of-reading question/problem and its solution. To make effective use of the curriculum, please remember these key points:

1. All pages printed in the Custom Curriculum are required reading for the examination except for occasional sections marked as optional. You may read optional pages as background, but you will not be tested on them.

2. All questions/problems printed at the end of readings and their solutions in the appendix to each volume are required study material for the examination.

3. Make appropriate use of the CFA Candidate Toolkit, the online sample examinations, and preparatory courses and review materials.

4. Commit sufficient study time to cover the 18 study sessions, review the materials, and take sample examinations.

Feedback

At CFA Institute, we are committed to delivering a comprehensive and rigorous curriculum for the development of competent, ethically grounded investment professionals. We rely on candidate and member feedback as we work to incorporate content, design, and packaging improvements. You can be assured that we will continue to listen to your suggestions. Please send any comments or feedback to curriculum@cfainstitute.org. Ongoing improvements in the curriculum will help you prepare for success on the upcoming examinations, and for a lifetime of learning as a serious investment professional.

PORTFOLIO MANAGEMENT

STUDY SESSIONS

Study Session 17   Portfolio Management in a Global Context
Study Session 18   Global Investment Performance Standards

This Volume includes Study Sessions 12–15.

TOPIC LEVEL LEARNING OUTCOME

The candidate should be able to construct an appropriate investment policy statement and asset allocation, formulate strategies for managing, monitoring, and rebalancing the investment portfolio, and interpret performance relative to benchmarks and present investment returns in a manner consistent with Global Investment Performance Standards (GIPS®).

STUDY SESSION 12
RISK MANAGEMENT

Effective risk management identifies, assesses, and controls numerous sources of risk, both financial and non-market related, in an effort to achieve the highest possible level of reward for the risks incurred. With the increasingly complex nature of investment management firms and investment portfolios, sophisticated risk management techniques have been developed to provide analysts with the necessary tools to properly measure the varying facets of risk.

The reading in this study session describes a framework for risk management, focusing on the concepts and tools for measuring and managing market risk and credit risk.

READING ASSIGNMENT

Reading 37   Risk Management

LEARNING OUTCOMES

Reading 37: Risk Management
The candidate should be able to:

a. compare and contrast the main features of the risk management process, risk governance, risk reduction, and an enterprise risk management system;

b. recommend and justify the risk exposures an analyst should report as part of an enterprise risk management system;

c. evaluate the strengths and weaknesses of a company's risk management processes and the possible responses to a risk management problem;

d. evaluate a company's or a portfolio's exposures to financial and non-financial risk factors;

e. interpret and compute value at risk (VAR) and explain its role in measuring overall and individual position market risk;

f. compare and contrast the analytical (variance–covariance), historical, and Monte Carlo methods for estimating VAR and discuss the advantages and disadvantages of each;

3

g. discuss the advantages and limitations of VAR and its extensions, including cash flow at risk, earnings at risk, and tail value at risk;

h. compare and contrast alternative types of stress testing and discuss the advantages and disadvantages of each;

i. evaluate the credit risk of an investment position, including forward contract, swap, and option positions;

j. demonstrate the use of risk budgeting, position limits, and other methods for managing market risk;

k. demonstrate the use of exposure limits, marking to market, collateral, netting arrangements, credit standards, and credit derivatives to manage credit risk;

l. compare and contrast the Sharpe ratio, risk-adjusted return on capital, return over maximum drawdown, and the Sortino ratio as measures of risk-adjusted performance;

m. demonstrate the use of VAR and stress testing in setting capital requirements.

RISK MANAGEMENT
by Don M. Chance, Kenneth Grant, and John Marsland

LEARNING OUTCOMES

The candidate should be able to:

a. compare and contrast the main features of the risk management process, risk governance, risk reduction, and an enterprise risk management system;

b. recommend and justify the risk exposures an analyst should report as part of an enterprise risk management system;

c. evaluate the strengths and weaknesses of a company's risk management processes and the possible responses to a risk management problem;

d. evaluate a company's or a portfolio's exposures to financial and non-financial risk factors;

e. interpret and compute value at risk (VAR) and explain its role in measuring overall and individual position market risk;

f. compare and contrast the analytical (variance–covariance), historical, and Monte Carlo methods for estimating VAR and discuss the advantages and disadvantages of each;

g. discuss the advantages and limitations of VAR and its extensions, including cash flow at risk, earnings at risk, and tail value at risk;

h. compare and contrast alternative types of stress testing and discuss the advantages and disadvantages of each;

i. evaluate the credit risk of an investment position, including forward contract, swap, and option positions;

j. demonstrate the use of risk budgeting, position limits, and other methods for managing market risk;

k. demonstrate the use of exposure limits, marking to market, collateral, netting arrangements, credit standards, and credit derivatives to manage credit risk;

l. compare and contrast the Sharpe ratio, risk-adjusted return on capital, return over maximum drawdown, and the Sortino ratio as measures of risk-adjusted performance;

m. demonstrate the use of VAR and stress testing in setting capital requirements.

Managing Investment Portfolios: A Dynamic Process, Third Edition, John L. Maginn, Donald L. Tuttle, Jerald E. Pinto, and Dennis W. McLeavey, editors. Copyright © 2007 by CFA Institute. Reprinted with permission.

5

1 INTRODUCTION

Investment is an intrinsically risky activity. Indeed, risk taking is an innate characteristic of human activity and as old as humankind itself. Without risk, we have little possibility of reward. We thus need to treat risk management as a critical component of the investment process. Specifically, with regard to both individual investments and entire portfolios, we should examine and compare the full spectrum of risks and expected returns to ensure that to the greatest extent possible the exposures we assume are at all times justified by the rewards we can reasonably expect to reap. Proper identification, measurement, and control of risk are key to the process of investing, and we put our investment objectives at risk unless we commit appropriate resources to these tasks.

A portfolio manager must be familiar with risk management not only as it relates to portfolio management but also as it relates to managing an enterprise, because a portfolio manager is a responsible executive in an enterprise (his investment firm). He must also understand the risks and risk management processes of companies in which he invests. The risk management framework presented in this reading is an inclusive one, applicable to the management of both enterprise and portfolio risk.

Although portfolio managers and enterprises may occasionally hedge their risks or engage in other risk-reducing transactions, they should not, and indeed cannot, restrict their activities to those that are risk free, as discussed in more detail later. The fact that these entities engage in risky activities raises a number of important questions:

▶ What is an effective process for identifying, measuring, and managing risk?
▶ Which risks are worth taking on a regular basis, which are worth taking on occasion, and which should be avoided altogether?
▶ How can our success or lack of success in risk taking be evaluated?
▶ What information should be reported to investors and other stakeholders concerning the risk of an enterprise or a portfolio?

The answers to these questions and many others collectively define the process of *risk management*. Over the course of this reading, we endeavor to explain this process and some of its most important concepts. Consistent with the book's focus on portfolio management, this reading concentrates on managing risks arising from transactions that are affected by interest rates, stock prices, commodity prices, and exchange rates. We also survey the other risks that most enterprises face and illustrates the discussion from a variety of perspectives. The reading is organized as follows. Section 2 defines and explains a risk management framework. Section 3 discusses what constitutes good risk management. Sections 4, 5, and 6 discuss the individual steps in the risk management process, and we conclude with a summary.

RISK MANAGEMENT AS A PROCESS   2

We can formally define risk management as follows:

> Risk management is a process involving the identification of exposures to risk, the establishment of appropriate ranges for exposures (given a clear understanding of an entity's objectives and constraints), the continuous measurement of these exposures (either present or contemplated), and the execution of appropriate adjustments whenever exposure levels fall outside of target ranges. The process is continuous and may require alterations in any of these activities to reflect new policies, preferences, and information.

This definition highlights that risk management should be a *process*, not just an activity. A process is continuous and subject to evaluation and revision. Effective risk management requires the constant and consistent monitoring of exposures, with an eye toward making adjustments, whenever and wherever the situation calls for them.[1] Risk management in its totality is all at once a proactive, anticipative, and reactive process that continuously monitors and controls risk.

Exhibit 1 illustrates the *practical application of the process* of risk management as it applies to a hypothetical business enterprise. We see at the top that the company faces a range of financial and nonfinancial risks; moving down the exhibit, we find

EXHIBIT 1	Risk Management Process: The Practice of Risk Management

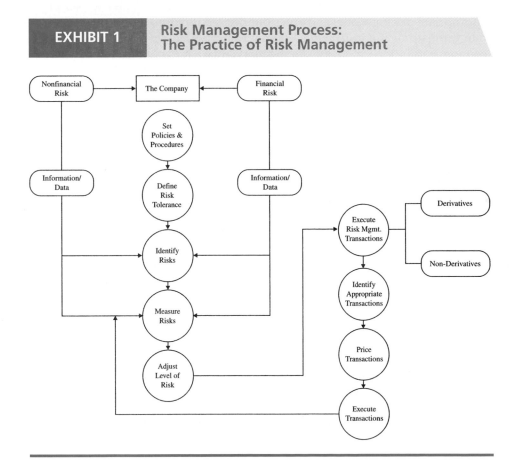

---

[1] For brevity, we often refer to an exposure to risk or risk exposure (the state of being exposed to or vulnerable to a risk) as simply an *exposure*.

that the company has responded to this challenge by establishing a series of risk management policies and procedures. First, it defines its risk tolerance, which is the level of risk it is willing and able to bear.[2] It then identifies the risks, drawing on all sources of information, and attempts to measure these risks using information or data related to all of its identified exposures. The process of risk measurement can be as simple as Exhibit 1 illustrates, but more often than not it involves expertise in the practice of modeling and sometimes requires complex analysis. Once the enterprise has built effective risk identification and measurement mechanisms, it is in a position to adjust its risk exposures, wherever and whenever exposures diverge from previously identified target ranges. These adjustments take the form of risk-modifying transactions (broadly understood to include the possible complete transfer of risk). The execution of risk management transactions is itself a distinct process; for portfolios, this step consists of trade identification, pricing, and execution. The process then loops around to the measurement of risk and continues in that manner, and to the constant monitoring and adjustment of the risk, to bring it into or maintain it within the desired range.

In applying the risk management process to portfolio management, managers must devote a considerable amount of attention to measuring and pricing the risks of financial transactions or positions, particularly those involving derivatives. Exhibit 2 illustrates this process of pricing and measuring risk, expanding on the detail given in Exhibit 1. In Exhibit 2, we see at the top that in pricing the transaction, we first identify the source(s) of uncertainty. Then we select the appropriate pricing model and enter our desired inputs to derive our most accurate estimate of the instrument's model value (which we hope reflects its true economic value). Next, we look to the marketplace for an indication of where we can actually execute the transaction. If the execution price is "attractive" (i.e., the market will buy the instrument from us at a price at or above, or sell it to us at a price at or below, the value indicated by our model), it fits our criteria for acceptance; if not, we should seek an alternative transaction. After executing the transaction, we would then return to the process of measuring risk.

Our discussion of Exhibit 1 highlighted that risk management involves adjusting levels of risk to appropriate levels, not necessarily eliminating risk altogether. It is nearly impossible to operate a successful business or investment program without taking risks. Indeed, a company that accepted no risk would not be an operating business. Corporations take risks for the purpose of generating returns that increase their owners' wealth. Corporation owners, the shareholders, risk their capital with the same objective in mind. *Companies that succeed in doing the activities they should be able to do well, however, cannot afford to fail overall because of activities in which they have no expertise.* Accordingly, many companies hedge risks that arise from areas in which they have no expertise or comparative advantage. In areas in which they do have an edge (i.e., their primary line of business), they tend to hedge only tactically. They hedge when they think they have sufficient information to suggest that a lower risk position is appropriate. They manage risk, increasing it when they perceive a competitive advantage and decreasing it when they perceive a competitive disadvantage. In essence, they attempt to efficiently allocate risk. Similarly, portfolio managers attempt to efficiently use risk to achieve their return objectives.

We have illustrated that risk management involves far more than risk reduction or hedging (one particular risk-reduction method). Risk management is a general practice that involves risk modification (e.g., risk reduction or risk

---

[2] An enterprise may have different risk tolerances for different types of risk in a manner that does not readily permit averaging, so we should view risk tolerance in this context as potentially multidimensional.

EXHIBIT 2	Risk Management Process: Pricing and Measuring Risk

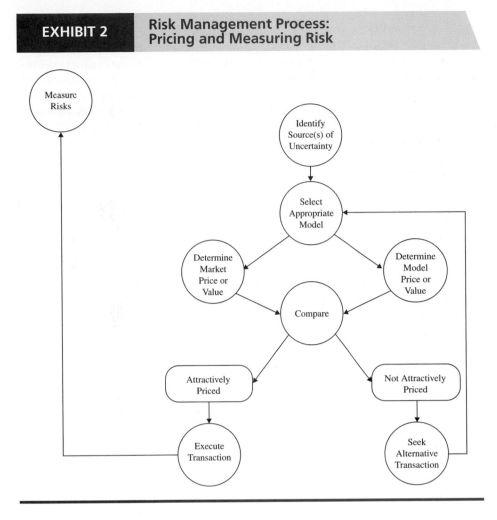

expansion) as deemed necessary and appropriate by the custodians of capital and its beneficial owners.

For the risk management process to work, managers need to specify thoughtfully the business processes they use to put risk management into practice. We refer to these processes collectively as risk governance, the subject of the next section.

RISK GOVERNANCE   3

Senior management is ultimately responsible for *every* activity within an organization. Their involvement is thus essential for risk management to succeed. The process of setting overall policies and standards in risk management is called **risk governance**. Risk governance involves choices of governance structure, infrastructure, reporting, and methodology. The quality of risk governance can be judged by its transparency, accountability, effectiveness (achieving objectives), and efficiency (economy in the use of resources to achieve objectives).

Risk governance begins with choices concerning governance structure. Organizations must determine whether they wish their risk management efforts to be centralized or decentralized. Under a centralized risk management system, a company has a single risk management group that monitors and ultimately controls all of the organization's risk-taking activities. By contrast, a decentralized system places risk management responsibility on individual business unit managers. In a decentralized approach, each unit calculates and reports its exposures independently. Decentralization has the advantage of allowing the people closer to the actual risk taking to more directly manage it. Centralization permits economies of scale and allows a company to recognize the offsetting nature of distinct exposures that an enterprise might assume in its day-to-day operations. For example, suppose one subsidiary of a company buys from Japan and another subsidiary sells to Japan, with both engaged in yen-denominated transactions. Each subsidiary would perceive some foreign exchange exposure. From a centralized viewpoint, however, these risks have offsetting effects, thereby reducing the overall need to hedge.

Moreover, even when exposures to a single risk factor do not directly offset one another, enterprise-level risk estimates may be lower than those derived from individual units because of the risk-mitigating benefits of diversification. For example, one corporate division may borrow U.S. dollars at five-year maturities, and another division may fund its operation by issuing 90-day commercial paper. In theory, the corporation's overall sensitivity to rising interest rates may be less than the sum of that reported by each division, because the five-year and 90-day rate patterns are less than perfectly correlated.

In addition, centralized risk management puts the responsibility on a level closer to senior management, where we have argued it belongs. It gives an overall picture of the company's risk position, and ultimately, the overall picture is what counts. This centralized type of risk management is now called **enterprise risk management** (ERM) or sometimes firmwide risk management because its distinguishing feature is a firmwide or across-enterprise perspective.[3] In ERM, an organization must consider each risk factor to which it is exposed—both in isolation and in terms of any interplay among them.

Risk governance is an element of **corporate governance** (the system of internal controls and procedures used to manage individual companies). As risk management's role in corporate governance has become better appreciated, the importance of ERM has risen proportionately. Indeed, for risk-taking entities (this means nearly the entire economic universe), it is contradictory to suggest that an organization has sound corporate governance without maintaining a clear and continuously updated understanding of its exposures at the enterprise level. Senior managers who have an adequate understanding of these factors are in a superior governance position to those who do not, and over time this advantage is almost certain to accrue to the bottom line. Therefore, the risk management system of a company that chooses a **decentralized risk management** approach requires a mechanism by which senior managers can inform themselves about the enterprise's overall risk exposures.

At the enterprise level, companies should control not only the sensitivity of their earnings to fluctuations in the stock market, interest rates, foreign exchange rates, and commodity prices, but also their exposures to credit spreads and default risk, to gaps in the timing match of their assets and liabilities, and to operational/systems failures, financial fraud, and other factors that can affect corporate profitability and even survival.

---

[3] The Committee of Sponsoring Organizations of the Treadway Commission defines ERM as follows: "Enterprise risk management is a process, effected by an entity's board of directors, management, and other personnel, applied in strategy setting and across the enterprise, designed to identify potential events that may affect the entity, and manage risk to be within its risk appetite, to provide reasonable assurance regarding the achievement of entity objectives" (2004, p. 2).

> ## EXAMPLE 1
>
> ### Some Risk Governance Concerns of Investment Firms
>
> Regardless of the risk governance approach chosen, effective risk governance for investment firms demands that the trading function be separated from the risk management function. An individual or group that is independent of the trading function must monitor the positions taken by the traders or risk takers and price them independently. The risk manager has the responsibility for monitoring risk levels for all portfolio positions (as well as for portfolios as a whole) and executing any strategies necessary to control the level of risk. To do this, the risk manager must have timely and accurate information, authority, and independence from the trading function. That is not to say that the trading function will not need its own risk management expertise in order to allocate capital in an optimal fashion and maximize risk-adjusted profit. Ideally, the risk manager will work with the trading desks in the development of risk management specifications, such that everyone in the organization is working from a common point of reference in terms of measuring and controlling exposures.
>
> Effective risk governance for an investment firm also requires that the back office be fully independent from the front office, so as to provide a check on the accuracy of information and to forestall collusion. (The **back office** is concerned with transaction processing, record keeping, regulatory compliance, and other administrative functions; the **front office** is concerned with trading and sales.) Besides being independent, the back office of an investment firm must have a high level of competence, training, and knowledge because failed trades, errors, and oversights can lead to significant losses that may be amplified by leverage. The back office must effectively coordinate with external service suppliers, such as the firm's **global custodian**. The global custodian effects **trade settlement** (completion of a trade wherein purchased financial instruments are transferred to the buyer and the buyer transfers money to the seller), safekeeping of assets, and the allocation of trades to individual custody accounts. Increasingly, financial institutions are seeking risk reduction with cost efficiencies through **straight-through processing** (STP) systems that obviate manual and/or duplicative intervention in the process from trade placement to settlement.

An effective ERM system typically incorporates the following steps:

1. Identify each *risk factor* to which the company is exposed.
2. Quantify each exposure's size in money terms.
3. Map these inputs into a risk estimation calculation.[4]
4. Identify overall risk exposures as well as the contribution to overall risk deriving from each risk factor.
5. Set up a process to report on these risks periodically to senior management, who will set up a committee of division heads and executives to determine capital allocations, risk limits, and risk management policies.
6. Monitor compliance with policies and risk limits.

---

[4] For example, using Value at Risk or another of the concepts that we will discuss later.

Steps 5 and 6 help enormously in allowing an organization to quantify the magnitude and distribution of its exposures and in enabling it to use the ERM system's output to more actively align its risk profile with its opportunities and constraints on a routine, periodic basis.

As a final note, effective ERM systems always feature centralized data warehouses, where a company stores all pertinent risk information, including position and market data, in a technologically efficient manner. Depending on the organization's size and complexity, developing and maintaining a high-quality data warehouse can require a significant and continuing investment. In particular, the process of identifying and correcting errors in a technologically efficient manner can be enormously resource intensive—especially when the effort requires storing historical information on complex financial instruments. It is equally clear, however, that the return on such an investment can be significant.

4   IDENTIFYING RISKS

As indicated above, economic agents of all types assume different types of exposures on a near-continuous basis. Moreover, these risk exposures take very different forms, each of which, to varying extents, may call for customized treatment. Effective risk management demands the separation of risk exposures into specific categories that reflect their distinguishing characteristics. Once a classification framework is in place, we can move on to the next steps in the risk management process: identification, classification, and measurement.

Although the list is far from exhaustive, many company (or portfolio) exposures fall into one of the following categories: market risk (including interest rate risk, exchange rate risk, equity price risk, commodity price risk); credit risk; liquidity risk; operational risk; model risk; settlement risk; regulatory risk; legal/contract risk; tax risk; accounting risk; and sovereign/political risk. These risks may be grouped into financial risks and nonfinancial risks as shown in Exhibit 3.[5] **Financial risk** refers to all risks derived from events in the external financial markets; **nonfinancial risk** refers to all other forms of risk.

EXHIBIT 3	The Sources of Risk

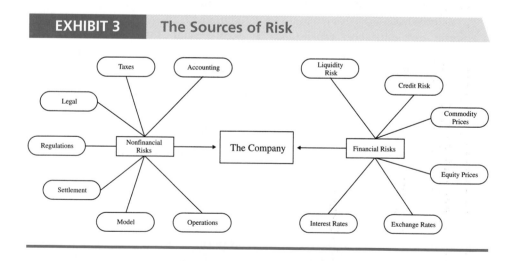

---

[5] A notable risk that could be included in a comprehensive listing (particularly as pertains to commercial enterprises) is business risk, defined by Ross, Westerfield, and Jordan (1993, p. 527) as "the equity risk that comes from the nature of the firm's operating activities." For example, the risk for a hotel business that arises from variability in room occupancy rates would be classified as business risk. In a later section on other risks, we also discuss two types of risks related to netting.

Example 2 illustrates a simple analysis of risk exposures. In the example, we have detailed the subtypes of market risk; each one may pose unique issues of measurement and management.

EXAMPLE 2

An Analysis of Risk Exposures

Liam McNulty is the risk manager for a large multinational agricultural concern, Agripure. The company grows its own corn, wheat, and soybeans but pays large sums to third parties for pesticides, fertilizer, and other supplies. For this, it must borrow heavily to finance its purchases. Customers typically purchase Agripure's goods on credit. Moreover, Agripure buys and sells its products and raw materials worldwide, often transacting in the domestic currency of its customers and suppliers. Finally, to finance its own expansion, Agripure intends to issue stock.

Recommend and justify the risk exposures that McNulty should report as part of an enterprise risk management system for Agripure.

Solution: McNulty should report on the following risk exposures:

- ► Market risk, including these subtypes:
  - ► Commodity price risk, because Agripure has exposures in raw materials and finished products.
  - ► Foreign exchange risk, because it buys and sells products worldwide, often transacting in the home currency of the entity on the other side of the transaction.
  - ► Equity market risk, because Agripure's expansion financing is affected by the price it receives for its share issuance.
  - ► Interest rate risk, because Agripure has exposures in financing its raw material purchases and because its customers typically purchase their goods on credit.
- ► Credit risk, because Agripure's customers typically purchase their goods on credit.
- ► Operational risk, because as an agricultural producer Agripure is subject to weather-related risk (an external event).

In the following sections, we discuss each of these risks in detail.

4.1 Market Risk

Market risk is the risk associated with interest rates, exchange rates, stock prices, and commodity prices. It is linked to supply and demand in various marketplaces. Although we may distinguish among interest rate risk, currency risk, equity market risk, and commodity risk when discussing measurement and management issues, for example, these subtypes all have exposure to supply and demand. Much of the evolution that has taken place in the field of risk management has emanated from a desire to understand and control market risks, and we will have a good deal to say about this topic throughout the balance of this reading.

One set of market risk takers with special requirements for market risk are defined-benefit (DB) pension funds, which manage retirement assets generally under strict regulatory regimes. Pension fund risk management necessarily concerns itself with funding the stream of promised payments to pension plan participants. Therefore, a DB plan must measure its market exposures not purely on the basis of its assets but also in terms of the risks of pension assets in relation to liabilities. Other investors as well can have strong asset/liability management concerns.[6] This has important implications for exposure measurement, risk control, capital allocation and risk budgeting, which we will address later.

4.2 Credit Risk

Apart from market risk, credit risk is the primary type of financial risk that economic agents face. **Credit risk** is the risk of loss caused by a counterparty or debtor's failure to make a promised payment. This definition reflects a traditional binary concept of credit risk, by and large embodied by default risk (i.e., the risk of loss associated with the nonperformance of a debtor or counterparty). For the last several years, however, credit markets have taken on more and more of the characteristics typically associated with full-scale trading markets. As this pattern has developed, the lines between credit risk and market risk have blurred as markets for credit derivatives have developed.[7] For example, the holder of a traded credit instrument could suffer a loss as a result of a short-term supply–demand imbalance without the underlying probability of default changing. Some subset of market participants often suffers losses whether credit is improving or deteriorating because it is now quite easy to take long and short positions in credit markets. Finally, note that pricing conventions for credit typically take the form of spreads against market benchmarks, for example, government bond yields or swap rates.[8] Thus when a given credit instrument is said to be priced at 150 over, it typically means that the instrument can be purchased to yield 150 basis points over the rate on the market benchmark (e.g., the government bond with the same maturity).

Until the era of OTC derivatives, credit risk was more or less exclusively a concern in the bond and loan markets. Exchange-traded derivatives are guaranteed against credit loss. Over-the-counter derivatives, however, contain no explicit credit guaranty and, therefore, subject participants to the threat of loss if their counterparty fails to pay.

Before OTC derivatives became widely used, bond portfolio managers and bank loan officers were the primary credit risk managers. They assessed credit risk in a number of ways,[9] including the qualitative evaluation of corporate fundamentals through the review of financial statements, the calculation of credit scores, and by relying on consensus information that was and still is widely available for virtually every borrower. The synthesis of this "credit consensus" resides with rating agencies and credit bureaus, which were historically, and to some extent still are, the primary sources of information on credit quality. The proliferation and complexity of financial instruments with credit elements in the OTC

[6] See the readings on institutional investors and asset allocation in particular.

[7] A **credit derivative** is a contract in which one party has the right to claim a payment from another party in the event that a specific credit event occurs over the life of the contract.

[8] A **swap rate** is the interest rate applicable to the pay-fixed-rate side of an interest rate swap. See Chance (2003) to review the basics of swaps.

[9] Credit risk in the more general context of fixed-income securities is discussed in more detail in Fabozzi (2004a), Chapter 15. Many of the principles of credit risk analysis for fixed-income securities also apply to derivatives.

derivatives market, however, has placed new demands on the understanding of credit risk. Indeed, the need to better understand credit risk has led to significant progress in developing tools to measure and manage this risk.

4.3 Liquidity Risk

Liquidity risk is the risk that a financial instrument cannot be purchased or sold without a significant concession in price because of the market's potential inability to efficiently accommodate the desired trading size.[10] In some cases, the market for a financial instrument can dry up completely, resulting in a total inability to trade an asset. This risk is present in both initiating and liquidating transactions, for both long and short positions, but can be particularly acute for liquidating transactions—especially when such liquidation is motivated by the need to reduce exposures in the wake of large losses. Those wishing to sell securities under these circumstances can find the market bereft of buyers at prices acceptable to the seller, particularly in periods of unusually high market stress. Perhaps less frequently, short sellers in need of covering losing positions are at risk to short squeezes. This situation is often exacerbated by the fact that for most cash instruments, short sellers establish positions by borrowing the securities in question from brokerage firms and other entities that typically can require the securities to be returned with little or no advance warning. Although derivatives can be used to effectively sell an asset or liquidate a short position, they often will not help in managing liquidity risk. If the underlying is illiquid, there is a good possibility that the universe of associated derivative instruments may also be illiquid.

For traded securities, the size of the **bid–ask spread** (the spread between the bid and ask prices), stated as a proportion of security price, is frequently used as an indicator of liquidity.[11] When markets are illiquid, dealers expect to sell at relatively high prices and buy at relatively low prices to justify their assumption of exposure to liquidity risk. However, bid–ask quotations apply only to specified, usually small size, trades, and are thus an imprecise measure of liquidity risk. Other, more complex measures of liquidity have been developed to address the issue of trading volume. For example, Amihud's (2002) illiquidity ratio measures the price impact per $1 million traded in a day, expressed in percentage terms. Note, however, that no explicit transaction volume is available for many OTC instruments. Less formally, one of the best ways to measure liquidity is through the monitoring of transaction volumes, with the obvious rule of thumb being that the greater the average transaction volume, the more liquid the instrument in question is likely to be. Historical volume patterns, however, may not repeat themselves at times when the liquidity they imply is most needed.

Liquidity risk is a serious problem and often is difficult to observe and quantify. It is not always apparent that certain securities are illiquid: Some that are liquid when purchased (or sold short) can be illiquid by the time they are sold (or repurchased to cover short positions). Valuation models rarely encompass this liquidity risk in estimating fair value. Those models that do attempt to incorporate transaction costs do so in a nonformulaic manner. Of course, these problems typically reach their apex when the markets themselves are under

---

[10] Liquidity has been used in various senses. For example, **funding risk** (the risk that liabilities funding long asset positions cannot be rolled over at reasonable cost) has sometimes been referred to as a type of liquidity risk; liquidity in this sense relates to the availability of cash. One would still distinguish between market liquidity risk (discussed in the reading) and funding liquidity risk.

[11] For example, see Amihud and Mendelson (1986). We must state the bid–ask spread as a proportion of stock price to control for differences in securities' prices.

stress and the need for liquidity is most acute. Liquidity assessments that fail to consider the problems that might arise during periods of market stress are incomplete from a risk management perspective. For all of these reasons, liquidity risk is one of the more complex aspects of risk management.

We now turn our attention to nonfinancial risks, starting with operational risk.

4.4 Operational Risk

Operational risk, sometimes called operations risk, is the risk of loss from failures in a company's systems and procedures or from external events. These risks can arise from computer breakdowns (including bugs, viruses, and hardware problems), human error, and events completely outside of companies' control, including "acts of God" and terrorist actions.

Computer failures are quite common, but the development of backup systems and recovery procedures has reduced their impact in recent years. Technology bugs and viruses are potentially quite risky but have become more manageable with the proper personnel, software, and systems. Even the smallest business has learned to back up files and take them off the premises. Larger businesses have much more extensive computer risk management practices.

Human failures include the typically manageable unintentional errors that occur in every business, along with more critical and potentially disastrous incidences of willful misconduct.

EXAMPLE 3

An Operational Risk for Financial Services Companies: The Rogue Trader

Among the more prominent examples of operational risk for financial service companies is that of the so-called rogue trader: an individual who has either assumed an irresponsibly high level of risk, engaged in unauthorized transactions, or some combination of the two. The risks associated with this type of activity increase the longer it goes undetected, and often the very lack of controls that creates the opportunity for a rogue trader in the first place renders it difficult to quickly determine that a problem exists. In some extreme cases, such as an incident that occurred in the Singapore office of Barings Bank, a rogue trader can cause an entire organization to fold. The incidence of high-profile rogue trading episodes has multiplied since the early 1990s, but in nearly all of these episodes, the problem's major source was a lack of rudimentary corporate controls and oversight.[12]

Our definition of operational risk includes losses from external events. Insurance typically covers damage from fires, floods and other types of natural disasters, but insurance provides only cash compensation for losses. If a flood destroys the trading room of a bank, the monies recovered likely will not come close to paying for the loss of customers who may take their trading business

---

[12] For more on the subject of operational risk in financial services companies, see Marshall (2001).

elsewhere. Hence, most companies have backup facilities they can activate in such cases. The 1993 World Trade Center bombing in New York City led many companies to establish backup systems in the event of another terrorist attack, which sadly took place on a greater scale eight years later. The speed with which trading enterprises, including the New York Stock Exchange, domiciled inside or near the World Trade Center reestablished full-scale operations after such a devastating attack is but one indication of the increased importance placed on operational risk management by these enterprises.

In some cases, companies manage operational risk by using insurance contracts, which involves a transfer of risk. A few types of derivative contracts even pay off for operational losses, but the market for these has not fully developed. These instruments are essentially insurance contracts. Most companies manage operational risk, however, by monitoring their systems, taking preventive actions, and having a plan in place to respond if such events occur.

4.5 Model Risk

Model risk is the risk that a model is incorrect or misapplied; in investments, it often refers to valuation models. Model risk exists to some extent in any model that attempts to identify the fair value of financial instruments, but it is most prevalent in models used in derivatives markets.

Since the development of the seminal Black–Scholes–Merton option pricing model, both derivatives and derivative pricing models have proliferated.[13] The development of so many models has brought model risk to prominence. If an investor chooses an inappropriate model, misinterprets the results, or uses incorrect inputs, the chance of loss increases at the same time that control over risk is impaired. Therefore, investors must scrutinize and objectively validate all models they use.

4.6 Settlement (Herstatt) Risk

The payments associated with the purchase and sale of cash securities such as equities and bonds, along with cash transfers executed for swaps, forwards, options, and other types of derivatives, are referred to collectively as settlements. The process of settling a contract involves one or both parties making payments and/or transferring assets to the other. We define settlement risk as the risk that one party could be in the process of paying the counterparty while the counterparty is declaring bankruptcy.[14]

Most regulated futures and options exchanges are organized in such a way that they themselves (or a closely affiliated entity) act as the central counterparty to all transactions. This facility usually takes the form of a clearing house, which is backed by large and credible financial guarantees. All transactions on the exchange take place between an exchange member and the central counterparty, which removes settlement risk from the transaction. The possibility always exists, however, that the exchange member is acting in an agency capacity and/or that its end client fails to settle. Clearly in these circumstances, the responsibility falls to the exchange member to make good and bear any loss on the trade.

---

[13] See Chance (2003).

[14] Note that settlement can also fail because of operational problems even when the counterparty is creditworthy; the risk in that case would be an operational risk.

OTC markets, including those for bonds and derivatives, do not rely on a clearing house. Instead, they effect settlement through the execution of agreements between the actual counterparties to the transaction. With swaps and forward contracts, settlements take the form of two-way payments. Two-way payments create the problem that one party could be in the process of paying its counterparty while that counterparty is declaring bankruptcy and failing to make its payment. Netting arrangements, used in interest rate swaps and certain other derivatives, can reduce settlement risk. In such arrangements, the financial instrument is periodically marked to market (under an agreed-upon methodology) and the "loser" pays the "winner" the difference for the period. This mechanism reduces the magnitude of any settlement failures to the net payment owed plus the cost of replacing the defaulted contract. Transactions with a foreign exchange component, however (e.g., currency forwards and currency swaps, but also spot trades), do not lend themselves to netting. Furthermore, such contracts often involve two parties in different countries, increasing the risk that one party will be unaware that the other party is declaring bankruptcy. The risk has been called Herstatt risk because of a famous incident in 1974 when Bank Herstatt failed at a time when counterparties were sending money to it.

Fortunately, bankruptcy does not occur often. Furthermore, through continuously linked settlement (CLS) in which payments on foreign exchange contracts are executed simultaneously, this risk has been even further mitigated.[15]

4.7 Regulatory Risk

Regulatory risk is the risk associated with the uncertainty of how a transaction will be regulated or with the potential for regulations to change. Equities (common and preferred stock), bonds, futures, and exchange-traded derivatives markets usually are regulated at the federal level, whereas OTC derivative markets and transactions in alternative investments (e.g., hedge funds and private equity partnerships) are much more loosely regulated. Federal authorities in most countries take the position that these latter transactions are private agreements between sophisticated parties, and as such should not be regulated in the same manner as publicly traded markets. Indeed, in some circumstances, unsophisticated investors are excluded altogether from participating in such investments.

With regard to derivatives, companies that are regulated in other ways may have their derivatives business indirectly regulated. For example, in the United States, banks are heavily regulated by federal and state banking authorities, which results in indirect regulation of their derivatives business. Beyond these de facto restrictions, however, in most countries, the government does not regulate the OTC derivatives business.[16]

Regulation is a source of uncertainty. Regulated markets are always subject to the risk that the existing regulatory regime will become more onerous, more restrictive, or more costly. Unregulated markets face the risk of becoming regulated, thereby imposing costs and restrictions where none existed previously. Regulatory risk is difficult to estimate because laws are written by politicians and regulations are written by civil servants; laws, regulations, and enforcement activities may change with changes in political parties and regulatory personnel. Both the regulations and their enforcement often reflect attitudes and philosophies

---

[15] The execution takes place in a five-hour window (three hours in Asia Pacific), representing the overlapping business hours of different settlement systems. For more information, see www.cls-group.com.

[16] Of course, contract law always applies to any such transaction.

that may change over time. Regulatory risk and the degree of regulation also vary widely from country to country.

Regulatory risk often arises from the arbitrage nature of derivatives and structured transactions. For example, a long position in stock accompanied by borrowing can replicate a forward contract or a futures contract. Stocks are regulated by securities regulators, and loans are typically regulated by banking oversight entities. Forward contracts are essentially unregulated. Futures contracts are regulated at the federal level in most countries, but not always by the same agency that regulates the stock market. Equivalent combinations of cash securities and derivatives thus are not always regulated in the same way or by the same regulator. Another example of inconsistent or ambiguous regulatory treatment might arise from a position spanning different geographic regions, such as the ownership of a NASDAQ-listed European-domiciled technology company in a European stock portfolio.

4.8 Legal/Contract Risk

Nearly every financial transaction is subject to some form of contract law. Any contract has two parties, each obligated to do something for the other. If one party fails to perform or believes that the other has engaged in a fraudulent practice, the contract can be abrogated. A dispute would then likely arise, which could involve litigation, especially if large losses occur. In some cases, the losing party will claim that the counterparty acted fraudulently or that the contract was illegal in the first place and, therefore, should be declared null and void. The possibility of such a claim being upheld in court creates a form of **legal/contract risk**: the possibility of loss arising from the legal system's failure to enforce a contract in which an enterprise has a financial stake.

Derivative transactions often are arranged by a dealer acting as a principal. The legal system has upheld many claims against dealers, which is not to say that the dealer has always been in the wrong but simply that dealers have sometimes put themselves into precarious situations. Dealers are indeed often advisors to their counterparties, giving the impression that if the dealer and counterparty enter into a contract, the counterparty expects the contract to result in a positive outcome. To avoid that misunderstanding, dealers may go to great lengths to make clear that they are the opposite party, not an advisor. Dealers also write contracts more carefully to cover the various contingencies that have been used against them in litigation. But a government or regulator might still take the legal view that a dealer has a higher duty of care for a less experienced counterparty. Contract law is in most circumstances federally or nationally governed. As such, the added possibility exists in arbitrage transactions that different laws might apply to each side of the transaction, thus adding more risk.

4.9 Tax Risk

Tax risk arises because of the uncertainty associated with tax laws. Tax law covering the ownership and transaction of financial instruments can be extremely complex, and the taxation of derivatives transactions is an area of even more confusion and uncertainty. Tax rulings clarify these matters on occasion, but on other occasions, they confuse them further. In addition, tax policy often fails to keep pace with innovations in financial instruments. When this happens, investors are left to guess what type and level of taxation will ultimately apply, creating the risk that they have guessed wrongly and could later be subject to back taxes. In some cases, transactions that appear upfront to be exempt from taxation could later be found to be taxable, thereby creating a future expense that was unanticipated (and perhaps impossible to anticipate) at the time that the transaction was executed. We noted, in discussing regulatory risk, that equivalent combinations of financial instruments are not always regulated the same way. Likewise, equivalent combinations of financial instruments are not always subject to identical tax treatment. This fact creates a tremendous burden of inconsistency and confusion, but on occasion the opportunity arises for arbitrage gains, although the tax authorities often quickly close such opportunities.

Like regulatory risk, tax risk is affected by the priorities of politicians and regulators. Many companies invest considerable resources in lobbying as well as hiring tax experts and consultants to control tax risk.

4.10 Accounting Risk

Accounting risk arises from uncertainty about how a transaction should be recorded and the potential for accounting rules and regulations to change. Accounting statements are a key, if not primary, source of information on publicly traded companies. In the United States, accounting standards are established primarily by the Financial Accounting Standards Board (FASB). Legal requirements in the area of accounting are enforced for publicly traded companies by federal securities regulators and by the primary stock exchange associated with the security. Non-U.S. domiciled companies that raise capital in the United States are also subject to these standards and laws. The law demands accurate accounting statements, and inaccurate financial reporting can subject corporations and their principals to civil and criminal litigation for fraud. In addition, the market punishes companies that do not provide accurate accounting statements, as happened for Enron and its auditor Arthur Andersen.

The International Accounting Standards Board (IASB) sets global standards for accounting. The FASB and the IASB have been working together toward convergence of accounting standards worldwide with 2005 targeted for harmonization. Historically, accounting standards have varied from country to country, with some countries requiring a higher level of disclosure than others.

EXAMPLE 4

Accounting Risk: The Case of Derivative Contracts

Accounting for derivative contracts has raised considerable confusion. When confusion occurs, companies run the risk that the accounting treatment for transactions could require adjustment, which could possibly lead to a need to restate earnings. Earnings restatements are almost always embarrassing for a company, because they suggest either a desire to hide information, the company's failure to fully understand material elements of its business, or some combination of the two. Restatements are very detrimental to corporate valuations because they cause investors to lose confidence in the accuracy of corporate financial disclosures. Beyond that, if negligence or intent to mislead was involved, the company could face civil and criminal liabilities as well.

Confusion over the proper accounting for derivatives gives rise to accounting as a source of risk. As with regulatory and tax risk, sometimes equivalent combinations of derivatives are not accounted for uniformly. The accounting profession typically moves to close such loopholes, but it does not move quickly and certainly does not keep pace with the pace of innovation in financial engineering, so problems nearly always remain.

The IASB in IAS 39 (International Accounting Standard No. 39) requires the inclusion of derivatives and their associated gains and losses on financial statements, as does the FASB in SFAS 133 (Statement of Financial Accounting Standard No. 133). These rulings contain some areas of confusion and inconsistency, however, affording considerable room for interpretation.[17]

Most companies deal with accounting risk by hiring personnel with the latest accounting knowledge. In addition, companies lobby and communicate actively with accounting regulatory bodies and federal regulators in efforts to modify accounting rules in a desired direction and to make them clearer. Companies have tended to fight rules requiring more disclosure, arguing that disclosure per se is not always beneficial and can involve additional costs. A trade-off exists between the rights of corporations to protect proprietary information from competitors and the need to adequately inform investors and the public. This controversy is unlikely to go away, suggesting that accounting risk will always remain.

4.11 Sovereign and Political Risks

Although they are covered indirectly above in areas such as regulatory, accounting, and tax risk, we can also isolate, and to a certain extent evaluate, the risks associated with changing political conditions in countries where portfolio managers may choose to assume exposure. Although this topic merits more discussion than can reasonably be devoted in this space, we can broadly define two types of exposures.

Sovereign risk is a form of credit risk in which the borrower is the government of a sovereign nation. Like other forms of credit risk, it has a current and a potential component, and like other forms, its magnitude has two components: the likelihood of default and the estimated recovery rate. Of course, the task of evaluating sovereign risk is in some ways more complex than that of evaluating other types of credit exposure because of the additional political component involved. Like other types of borrowers, debtor nations have an asset/liability/cash flow profile that competent analysts can evaluate. In addition to this profile, however, lenders to sovereigns (including bondholders) must consider everything from the country's willingness to meet its credit obligations (particularly in unstable political environments) to its alternative means of financing (seeking help from outside entities such as the International Monetary Fund, imposing capital controls, etc.) and other measures it might take, such as currency devaluation, to stabilize its situation.

The presence of sovereign risk is real and meaningful, and perhaps the most salient example of its deleterious effects can be found in Russia's 1998 default. This episode represented the first time in many decades that a nation of such

---

[17] Gastineau, Smith, and Todd (2001) provides excellent information on accounting for derivatives in the United States.

size and stature failed to meet its obligations to its lenders. Moreover, although the country was experiencing considerable trauma at that time—in part as the result of a contagion in emerging markets—it is abundantly clear that Russia was *unwilling* rather than *unable* to meet these obligations. The end result was a global financial crisis, in which investors lost billions of dollars and the country's robust development arc was slowed down for the better part of a decade.

Political risk is associated with changes in the political environment. Political risk can take many forms, both overt (e.g., the replacement of a pro-capitalist regime with one less so) and subtle (e.g., the potential impact of a change in party control in a developed nation), and it exists in every jurisdiction where financial instruments trade.

4.12 Other Risks

Companies face nonfinancial and financial risks other than those already mentioned. ESG risk is the risk to a company's market valuation resulting from environmental, social, and governance factors. Environmental risk is created by the operational decisions made by the company managers, including decisions concerning the products and services to offer and the processes to use in producing those products and services. Environmental damage may lead to a variety of negative financial and other consequences. Social risk derives from the company's various policies and practices regarding human resources, contractual arrangements, and the workplace. Liability from discriminatory workplace policies and the disruption of business resulting from labor strikes are examples of this type of risk. Flaws in corporate governance policies and procedures increase governance risk, with direct and material effects on a company's value in the marketplace.

One little-discussed but very large type of risk that some investment companies face is that of performance netting risk, often referred to simply as netting risk. Performance netting risk, which applies to entities that fund more than one strategy, is the potential for loss resulting from the failure of fees based on net performance to fully cover contractual payout obligations to individual portfolio managers that have positive performance when other portfolio managers have losses and when there are asymmetric incentive fee arrangements with the portfolio managers. The problem is best explained through an example.

Consider a hedge fund that charges a 20 percent incentive fee of any positive returns and funds two strategies equally, each managed by independent portfolio managers (call them Portfolio Managers A and B). The hedge fund pays Portfolio Managers A and B 10 percent of any gains they achieve. Now assume that in a given year, Portfolio Manager A makes $10 million and Portfolio Manager B loses the same amount. The net incentive fee to the hedge fund is zero because it has generated zero returns. Unless otherwise negotiated, however (and such clauses are rare), the hedge fund remains obligated to pay Portfolio Manager A $1 million. As a result, the hedge fund company has incurred a loss, despite breaking even overall in terms of returns.[18] Note that the asymmetric nature of incentive fee contracts (i.e., losses are not penalized as gains are rewarded) plays a critical role in creating the problem the hedge fund faces. Because such arrangements are effectively a call option on a percentage of profits, in some circumstances they may provide an incentive to take excessive risk (the value of a call option is positively related to the underlying's volatility). Nevertheless, such arrangements are widespread.

---

[18] The asymmetric nature of the incentive fee contract (currently typical for hedge funds) plays a critical role in this example; were the arrangement symmetric, with negative returns penalized as positive returns are rewarded, the issue discussed would disappear.

Performance netting risk occurs only in multistrategy, multimanager environments and only manifests itself when individual portfolio managers within a jointly managed product generate actual losses over the course of a fee-generating cycle—typically one year. Moreover, an investment entity need not be flat or down on the year to experience netting-associated losses. For any given level of net returns, its portion of fees will by definition be higher if all portfolio managers generate no worse than zero performance over the period than they would if some portfolio managers generate losses. As mentioned earlier, an asymmetric incentive fee contract must exist for this problem to arise.

Performance netting risk applies not just to hedge funds but also to banks' and broker/dealers' trading desks, commodity trading advisors, and indeed, to any environment in which individuals have asymmetric incentive fee arrangements but the entity or unit responsible for paying the fees is compensated on the basis of net results. Typically this risk is managed through a process that establishes absolute negative performance thresholds for individual accounts and aggressively cuts risk for individual portfolio managers at performance levels at, near, or below zero for the period in question.[19]

Distinct from performance netting risk, settlement netting risk (or again, simply netting risk) refers to the risk that a liquidator of a counterparty in default could challenge a netting arrangement so that profitable transactions are realized for the benefit of creditors.[20] Such risk is mitigated by netting agreements that can survive legal challenge.

MEASURING RISK   5

Having spent some time identifying some of the major sources of risk, both financial and nonfinancial, we now turn our attention toward the measurement of those risks. In particular, we look at some techniques for measuring market risk and credit risk. Subsequently, we briefly survey some of the issues for measuring nonfinancial risk, a very difficult area but also a very topical one—particularly after the advent of the Basel II standards on risk management for international banks, which we will discuss.

5.1 Measuring Market Risk

Market risk refers to the exposure associated with actively traded financial instruments, typically those whose prices are exposed to the changes in interest rates, exchange rates, equity prices, commodity prices, or some combination thereof.[21]

Over the years, financial theorists have created a simple and finite set of statistical tools to describe market risk. The most widely used and arguably the most important of these is the standard deviation of price outcomes associated with an underlying asset. We usually refer to this measure as the asset's volatility, typically represented by the Greek letter sigma (σ). Volatility is often an adequate description of portfolio risk, particularly for those portfolios composed of instruments

---

[19] For more information on this topic, see Grant (2004).

[20] See http://www.foa.co.uk/documentation/netting/index.jsp.

[21] The definition of market risk given here is the one used in the practice of risk management. The term market risk, however, is often used elsewhere to refer to the risk of the market as a whole, which is usually known as systematic risk. In this reading, we define market risk as risk management professionals do.

with linear payoffs.[22] In some applications, such as indexing, volatility relative to a benchmark is paramount. In those cases, our focus should be on the volatility of the deviation of a portfolio's returns in excess of a stated benchmark portfolio's returns, known as **active risk**, **tracking risk**, **tracking error volatility**, or by some simply as **tracking error**.

As we will see shortly, the volatility associated with individual positions, in addition to being a very useful risk management metric in its own right, can be combined with other simple statistics, such as correlations, to form the building blocks for the portfolio-based risk management systems that have become the industry standard in recent years. We cover these systems in the next section of this reading.

A portfolio's exposure to losses because of market risk typically takes one of two forms: sensitivity to adverse movements in the value of a key variable in valuation (primary or first-order measures of risk) and risk measures associated with *changes in* sensitivities (secondary or second-order measures of risk). Primary measures of risk often reflect linear elements in valuation relationships; secondary measures often take account of curvature in valuation relationships. Each asset class (e.g., bonds, foreign exchange, equities) has specific first- and second-order measures.

Let us consider measures of primary sources of risk first. For a stock or stock portfolio, **beta** measures sensitivity to market movements and is a linear risk measure. For bonds, **duration** measures the sensitivity of a bond or bond portfolio to a small parallel shift in the yield curve and is a linear measure, as is **delta** for options, which measures an option's sensitivity to a small change in the value of its underlying. These measures all reflect the expected change in price of a financial instrument for a unit change in the value of another instrument.

Second-order measures of risk deal with the change in the price sensitivity of a financial instrument and include convexity for fixed-income portfolios and gamma for options. **Convexity** measures how interest rate sensitivity changes with changes in interest rates.[23] **Gamma** measures the delta's sensitivity to a change in the underlying's value. Delta and gamma together capture first- and second-order effects of a change in the underlying.

For options, two other major factors determine price: volatility and time to expiration, both first-order or primary effects. Sensitivity to volatility is reflected in **vega**, the change in the price of an option for a change in the underlying's volatility. Most early option-pricing models (e.g., the Black–Scholes–Merton model) assume that volatility does not change over the life of an option, but in fact, volatility does generally change. Volatility changes are sometimes easy to observe in markets: Some days are far more volatile than others. Moreover, new information affecting the value of an underlying instrument, such as pending product announcements, will discernibly affect volatility. Because of their nonlinear payoff structure, options are typically very responsive to a change in volatility. Swaps, futures, and forwards with linear payoff functions are much less sensitive to changes in volatility. Option prices are also sensitive to changes in time to expiration, as measured by **theta**, the change in price of an option associated with a one-day reduction in its time to expiration.[24] Theta, like vega, is a risk that is associated exclusively with options. Correlation is a source of risk for certain types of options—for example, options on more than one

---

[22] The contrast is with instruments such as options that have nonlinear or piecewise linear payoffs. See Chance (2003) for more on the payoff functions of options.

[23] Convexity is covered in some detail in Fabozzi (2004a), Chapter 7.

[24] For more information on theta, see Chance (2003).

underlying (when the correlations between the underlyings' returns constitute a risk variable).[25]

Having briefly reviewed traditional notions of market risk measurement, we introduce a new topic, one that took the industry by storm: value at risk.

5.2 Value at Risk

During the 1990s, value at risk—or VAR, as it is commonly known—emerged as the financial service industry's premier risk management technique.[26] JPMorgan (now JPMorgan Chase) developed the original concept for internal use but later published the tools it had developed for managing risk (as well as related information).[27] Probably no other risk management topic has generated as much attention and controversy as has value at risk. In this section, we take an introductory look at VAR, examine an application, and look at VAR's strengths and limitations.

VAR is a probability-based measure of loss potential for a company, a fund, a portfolio, a transaction, or a strategy. It is usually expressed either as a percentage or in units of currency. Any position that exposes one to loss is potentially a candidate for VAR measurement. VAR is most widely and easily used to measure the loss from market risk, but it can also be used—subject to much greater complexity—to measure the loss from credit risk and other types of exposures.

We have noted that VAR is a probability-based measure of loss potential. This definition is very general, however, and we need something more specific. More formally: **Value at risk** is an estimate of the loss (in money terms) that we expect to be exceeded with a given level of probability over a specified time period.[28]

Readers are encouraged to think very carefully about the implications of this definition, which has a couple of important elements. First, we see that VAR is an estimate of the loss that we expect to be exceeded. Hence, it measures a minimum loss. The actual loss may be much worse without necessarily impugning the VAR model's accuracy. Second, we see that VAR is associated with a given probability. Say the VAR is €10,000,000 at a probability of 5 percent for a given time period. All else equal, if we lower the probability from 5 percent to 1 percent, the VAR will be larger in magnitude because we now are referring to a loss that we expect to be exceeded with only a 1 percent probability. Third, we see that VAR has a time element and that as such, VARs cannot be compared directly unless they share the same time interval. There is a big difference among potential losses that are incurred daily, weekly, monthly, quarterly, or annually. Potential losses over longer periods should be larger than those over shorter periods, but in most instances, longer time periods will not increase exposure in a linear fashion.

Consider the following example of VAR for an investment portfolio: *The VAR for a portfolio is $1.5 million for one day with a probability of 0.05.* Recall what this statement says: *There is a 5 percent chance that the portfolio will lose at least $1.5 million in a single day.* The emphasis here should be on the fact that *the $1.5 million loss is a minimum.* With due care, it is also possible to describe VAR as a maximum: The

---

[25] For more information, see Chance (2003).

[26] The terminology "Value-at-Risk" is expressed in different ways. For example, sometimes hyphens are used and sometimes it is just written as "Value at Risk." Sometimes it is abbreviated as VAR and sometimes as VaR. Those who have studied econometrics should be alert to the fact that the letters VAR also refer to an estimation technique called Vector Autoregression, which has nothing to do with Value at Risk. We shall use the abbreviation "VAR."

[27] RiskMetrics Group has now spun off from JPMorgan and is an independent company. See www.riskmetrics.com.

[28] In the terminology of statistics, VAR with an x percent probability for a given time interval represents the xth percentile of the distribution of outcomes (ranked from worst to best) over that time period.

probability is 95 percent that the portfolio will lose no more than $1.5 million in a single day. We see this equivalent perspective in the common practice of stating VAR using a confidence level: For the example just given, we would say that *with 95 percent confidence* (or *for a 95 percent confidence level*), *the VAR for a portfolio is $1.5 million for one day*.[29] We prefer to express VAR in the form of a minimum loss with a given probability. This approach is a bit more conservative, because it reminds us that the loss could be worse.[30]

5.2.1 Elements of Measuring Value at Risk

Although VAR has become an industry standard, it may be implemented in several forms, and establishing an appropriate VAR measure requires the user to make a number of decisions about the calculation's structure. Three important ones are picking a probability level, selecting the time period over which to measure VAR, and choosing the specific approach to modeling the loss distribution.[31]

The probability chosen is typically either 0.05 or 0.01 (corresponding to a 95 percent or 99 percent confidence level, respectively). The use of 0.01 leads to a more conservative VAR estimate, because it sets the figure at the level where there should be only a 1 percent chance that a given loss will be worse that the calculated VAR. The trade-off, however, is that the VAR risk estimate will be much larger with a 0.01 probability than it will be for a 0.05 probability. In the above example, we might have to state that the VAR is $2.1 million for one day at a probability of 0.01. The risk manager selects 0.01 or 0.05; no definitive rule exists for preferring one probability to the other. For portfolios with largely linear risk characteristics, the two probability levels will provide essentially identical information. However, the tails of the loss distribution may contain a wealth of information for portfolios that have a good deal of optionality or nonlinear risks, and in these cases risk managers may need to select the more conservative probability threshold.

The second important decision for VAR users is choosing the time period. VAR is often measured over a day, but other, longer time periods are common. Banking regulators prefer two-week period intervals. Many companies report quarterly and annual VARs to match their performance reporting cycles. Investment banks, hedge funds, and dealers seem to prefer daily VAR, perhaps because of the high turnover in their positions. Regardless of the time interval selected, the longer the period, the greater the VAR number will be because the magnitude of potential losses varies directly with the time span over which they are measured. The individual or individuals responsible for risk management will choose the time period.

Once these primary parameters are set, one can proceed to actually obtain the VAR estimate. This procedure involves another decision: the choice of technique. The basic idea behind estimating VAR is to identify the probability distribution characteristics of portfolio returns. Consider the information in Exhibit 4, which is a simple probability distribution for the return on a portfolio over a specified time period. Suppose we were interested in the VAR at a probability of 0.05. We would add up the probabilities for the class intervals until we reached a cumulative probability of 0.05. Observe that the probability is 0.01 that the

---

[29] This would be referred to as 95% one-day VAR.

[30] For a long position, the maximum possible loss is the entire value of the portfolio. For a short position, or a portfolio with both long and short positions, it is impossible to state the maximum possible loss because at least in theory, a short faces the possibility of unlimited losses.

[31] As we will learn in this section, users can select from three basic VAR methodologies, each of which uses a slightly different algorithm to estimate exposure.

EXHIBIT 4	Sample Probability Distribution of Returns on a Portfolio

Return on Portfolio	Probability
Less than −40%	0.010
−40% to −30%	0.010
−30% to −20%	0.030
−20% to −10%	0.050
−10% to −5%	0.100
−5% to −2.5%	0.125
−2.5% to 0%	0.175
0% to 2.5%	0.175
2.5% to 5%	0.125
5% to 10%	0.100
10% to 20%	0.050
20% to 30%	0.030
30% to 40%	0.010
Greater than 40%	0.010
	1.000

portfolio will lose at least 40 percent, 0.01 that the portfolio will lose between 30 percent and 40 percent, and 0.03 that the portfolio will lose between 20 percent and 30 percent. Thus, the probability is 0.05 that the portfolio will lose at least 20 percent. Because we want to express our risk measure in units of money, we would then multiply 20 percent by the portfolio's initial market value to obtain VAR. The VAR for a probability of 0.01 would be 40 percent multiplied by the market value. From a confidence-level perspective, we estimate with 99 percent confidence that our portfolio will lose no more than 40 percent of its value over the specified time period.

Exhibit 4 offers a simplified representation of the information necessary to estimate VAR. This method for calculating VAR is rather cumbersome, and the information is not always easy to obtain. As such, the industry has developed a set of three standardized methods for estimating VAR: the analytical or variance–covariance method, the historical method, and the **Monte Carlo simulation method**. We will describe and illustrate each of these in turn.

5.2.2 The Analytical or Variance–Covariance Method

The analytical or variance–covariance method begins with the assumption that portfolio returns are normally distributed. Recall from your study of portfolio management that a normal distribution can be completely described by its expected value and standard deviation.

Consider the standard normal distribution, a special case of the normal distribution centered on an expected value of zero and having a standard deviation of 1.0. We can convert any outcome drawn from a nonstandard normal distribution to a standard normal value by taking the outcome of interest, subtracting its mean, and dividing the result by its standard deviation. The resulting value then conforms to the standard normal distribution.[32] With the standard normal distribution, 5 percent of possible outcomes are likely to be smaller than -1.65.[33] Therefore, to calculate a 5 percent VAR for a portfolio (i.e., VAR at a probability of 0.05), we would estimate its expected return and subtract 1.65 times its estimated standard deviation of returns. So, the key to using the analytical or variance–covariance method is to estimate the portfolio's expected return and standard deviation of returns. An example follows.[34]

Suppose the portfolio contains two asset classes, with 75 percent of the money invested in an asset class represented by the S&P 500 Index and 25 percent invested in an asset class represented by the NASDAQ Composite Index.[35] Recall that a portfolio's expected return is a weighted average of the expected returns of its component stocks or asset classes. A portfolio's variance can be derived using a simple quadratic formula that combines the variances and covariances of the component stocks or asset classes. For example, assume that μ_S and μ_N are the expected returns of the S&P 500 and NASDAQ, respectively; σ_S and σ_N are their standard deviations; and ρ is the correlation between the two asset classes. The expected return, μ_P, and variance, σ_P^2, of the combined positions are given as

$$\mu_P = w_S\mu_S + w_N\mu_N$$

$$\sigma_P^2 = w_N^2\sigma_S^2 + w_N^2\sigma_N^2 + 2\rho w_S w_N \sigma_S \sigma_N$$

where w indicates the percentage allocated to the respective classes. The portfolio's standard deviation is just the square root of its variance. Exhibit 5 provides estimates of the portfolio's expected value and standard deviation using actual numbers, where we obtain μ_P of 0.135 and σ_P of 0.244.

EXHIBIT 5	Estimating the Expected Return and Standard Deviation of a Portfolio Combining Two Asset Classes		
	S&P 500	**NASDAQ**	**Combined Portfolio**
Percentage invested (w)	0.75	0.25	1.00
Expected annual return (μ)	0.12	0.18	0.135[a]
Standard deviation (σ)	0.20	0.40	0.244[b]
Correlation (ρ)	0.90		

[a] Expected return of portfolio: $\mu_P = w_S\mu_S + w_N\mu_N = 0.75(0.12) + 0.25(0.18) = 0.135$

[b] Standard deviation of portfolio:

$$\sigma_P^2 = w_S^2\sigma_S^2 + w_N^2\sigma_N^2 + 2\rho w_S w_N \sigma_S \sigma_N$$
$$= (0.75)^2(0.20)^2 + (0.25)^2(0.40)^2 + 2(0.90)(0.75)(0.25)(0.20)(0.40) = 0.0595$$
$$\sigma_P = (\sigma_P^2)^{1/2} = (0.0595)^{1/2} = 0.244$$

---

[32] For example, suppose you were interested in knowing the probability of obtaining a return of -15 percent or less when the expected return is 12 percent and the standard deviation is 20 percent. You would calculate the standard normal value, called a "z", as $(-0.15 - 0.12)/0.20 = -1.35$. Then you would look up this value in a table or use a spreadsheet function, such as Microsoft Excel's "=normsdist()" function. In this case, the probability is 0.0885.

[33] See DeFusco, McLeavey, Pinto, and Runkle (2004), pp. 255–56.

[34] For more detailed information, see DeFusco et al. (2004), Chapter 11.

[35] The extension to three or more classes is relatively straightforward once one knows how to calculate the variance of a portfolio of more than two assets. We shall focus here on the two-asset-class case.

Note that the example provided above is quite simplistic, involving only two assets, and thus only two variances and one covariance. As such, the calculation of portfolio variance is relatively manageable. As the number of instruments in the portfolio increases, however, the calculation components expand dramatically and the equation quickly becomes unwieldy. The important thing to remember is that in order to derive the variance for a portfolio of multiple financial instruments, all we require are the associated variances and covariances, along with the ability to calculate their quadratic relationship.

If we are comfortable with the assumption of a normal distribution and the accuracy of our estimates of the expected returns, variances, and correlations, we can confidently use the analytical-method estimate of VAR. Exhibit 6 illustrates the calculation of this estimate. VAR is first expressed in terms of the return on the portfolio. With an expected return of 0.135, we move 1.65 standard deviations along the x-axis in the direction of lower returns. Each standard deviation is 0.244. Thus we would obtain $0.135 - 1.65(0.244) = -0.268$.[36] At this point, VAR could be expressed as a loss of 26.8 percent. We could say that there is a 5 percent chance that the portfolio will lose at least 26.8 percent in a year. It is also customary to express VAR in terms of the portfolio's currency unit. Therefore, if the portfolio is worth \$50 million, we can express VAR as $\$50,000,000(0.268) = \$13.4$ million.

This figure is an annual VAR. If we prefer a daily VAR, we can adjust the expected return to its daily average of approximately $0.135/250 = 0.00054$ and the standard deviation to its daily value of $0.244/\sqrt{250} = 0.01543$, which are

EXHIBIT 6	Annual VAR for a Portfolio with Expected Return of 0.135 and Standard Deviation of 0.244

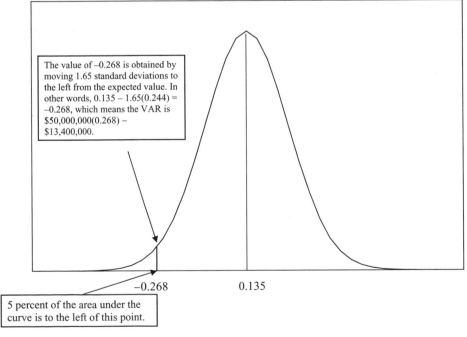

The value of −0.268 is obtained by moving 1.65 standard deviations to the left from the expected value. In other words, $0.135 - 1.65(0.244) = -0.268$, which means the VAR is $\$50,000,000(0.268) - \$13,400,000$.

−0.268   0.135

5 percent of the area under the curve is to the left of this point.

[36] The reader can confirm that 1.65 and 2.33 standard deviations give the correct VAR at the 5 percent and 1 percent probability levels, respectively, using the Microsoft Excel function "=normsdist()".

based on the assumption of 250 trading days in a year and statistical independence between days. Then the daily VAR is $0.00054 - 1.65(0.01543) = -0.0249$. On a dollar basis, the daily VAR is $\$50,000,000(0.0249) = \$1.245$ million.

For a 1 percent VAR, we would move 2.33 standard deviations in the direction of lower returns. Thus the annual VAR would be $0.135 - 2.33(0.244) = -0.434$ or $\$50,000,000(0.434) = \$21.7$ million. The daily VAR would be $0.00054 - 2.33(0.01543) = -0.035$ or $\$50,000,000(0.035) = \$1.75$ million.

Some approaches to estimating VAR using the analytical method assume an expected return of zero. This assumption is generally thought to be acceptable for daily VAR calculations because expected daily return will indeed tend to be close to zero. Because expected returns are typically positive for longer time horizons, shifting the distribution by assuming a zero expected return will result in a larger projected loss, so the VAR estimate will be greater. Therefore, this small adjustment offers a slightly more conservative result and avoids the problem of having to estimate the expected return, a task typically much harder than that of estimating associated volatility. Another advantage of this adjustment is that it makes it easier to adjust the VAR for a different time period. For example, if the daily VAR is estimated at $\$100,000$, the annual VAR will be $\$100,000\sqrt{250} = \$1,581,139$. This simple conversion of a shorter-term VAR to a longer-term VAR (or vice versa) does not work, however, if the average return is not zero. In these cases, one would have to convert the average return and standard deviation to the different time period and compute the VAR from the adjusted average and standard deviation.

EXAMPLE 5

VAR with Different Probability Levels and Time Horizons

Consider a portfolio consisting of stocks as one asset class and bonds as another. The expected return on the portfolio's stock portion is 12 percent, and the standard deviation is 22 percent. The expected return on the bond portion is 5 percent, and the standard deviation is 7 percent. All of these figures are annual. The correlation between the two asset classes is 0.15. The portfolio's market value is $\$150$ million and is allocated 65 percent to stocks and 35 percent to bonds. Determine the VAR using the analytical method for the following cases:

1. a 5 percent yearly VAR

2. a 1 percent yearly VAR

3. a 5 percent weekly VAR

4. a 1 percent weekly VAR

Solutions: First, we must calculate the annual portfolio expected return and standard deviation. Using S to indicate stocks and B to indicate bonds, we have

$$\mu_P = w_S\mu_S + w_B\mu_B = 0.65(0.12) + 0.35(0.05) = 0.0955$$
$$\sigma_P^2 = w_S^2\sigma_S^2 + w_B^2\sigma_B^2 + 2\rho w_S w_B \sigma_S \sigma_B$$
$$= (0.65)^2(0.22)^2 + (0.35)^2(0.07)^2 + 2(0.15)(0.65)(0.35)(0.22)(0.07)$$
$$= 0.0221$$
$$\sigma_P = \sqrt{0.0221} = 0.1487$$

1. For a 5 percent yearly VAR, we have $\mu_P - 1.65\sigma_P = 0.0955 - 1.65(0.1487) = -0.1499$. Then the VAR is $150,000,000(0.1499) = \$22.485$ million.

2. For a 1 percent yearly VAR, we have $\mu_P - 2.33\sigma_P = 0.0955 - 2.33(0.1487) = -0.251$. Then the VAR is $150,000,000(0.251) = \$37.65$ million.

3. For weekly VAR, we adjust the expected return to $0.0955/52 = 0.00184$ and the standard deviation to $0.1487/\sqrt{52} = 0.02062$. The 5 percent weekly VAR is then $\mu_P - 1.65\sigma = 0.00184 - 1.65(0.02062) = -0.03218$. Then the VAR is $150,000,000(0.03218) = \$4.827$ million.

4. The 1 percent weekly VAR is $\mu_P - 2.33\sigma_P = 0.00184 - 2.33(0.02062) = -0.0462$. Then the VAR is $150,000,000(0.0462) = \$6.93$ million.

The analytical or variance–covariance method's primary advantage is its simplicity. Its primary disadvantage is its reliance on several simplifying assumptions, including the normality of return distributions. In principle, there is no reason why the calculation demands a normal distribution, but if we move away from the normality assumption, we cannot rely on variance as a complete measure of risk. Distributions can deviate from normality because of skewness and kurtosis. Skewness is a measure of a distribution's deviation from the perfect symmetry (the normal distribution has a skewness of zero). A positively skewed distribution is characterized by relatively many small losses and a few extremes gains and has a long tail on its right side. A negatively skewed distribution is characterized by relatively many small gains and a few extreme losses and has a long tail on its left side. When a distribution is positively or negatively skewed, the variance–covariance method of estimating VAR will be inaccurate.

In addition, many observed distributions of returns have an abnormally large number of extreme events. This quality is referred to in statistical parlance as leptokurtosis but is more commonly called the property of fat tails.[37] Equity markets, for example, tend to have more frequent large market declines than a normal distribution would predict. Therefore, using a normality assumption to estimate VAR for a portfolio that features fat tails could understate the actual magnitude and frequency of large losses. VAR would then fail at precisely what it is supposed to do: measure the risk associated with large losses.

A related problem that surfaces with the analytical or variance–covariance method is that the normal distribution assumption is inappropriate for portfolios that contain options. The return distributions of options portfolios are often far from normal. Remember that a normal distribution has an unlimited upside and an unlimited downside. Call options have unlimited upside potential, as in a normal distribution, but their downside is a fixed value (the call's premium) and the distribution of call returns is highly skewed. Put options have a large but limited upside and a fixed downside (the put's premium), and the distribution of put returns is also highly skewed. In the same vein, covered calls and protective puts have return distributions that are sharply skewed in one direction or the other.

---

[37] See DeFusco, McLeavey, Pinto, and Runkle (2004), Chapter 5.

Therefore, when portfolios contain options, the assumption of a normal distribution to estimate VAR presents a significant problem. One common solution is to estimate the option's price sensitivity using its delta. Recall that delta expresses a linear relationship between an option's price and the underlying's price (i.e., Delta = Change in option price/Change in underlying). A linear relationship lends itself more easily to treatment with a normal distribution. That is, a normally distributed random variable remains normally distributed when multiplied by a constant. In this case, the constant is the delta. The change in the option price is assumed to equal the change in the underlying price multiplied by the delta. This trick converts the normal distribution for the return on the underlying into a normal distribution for the option return. As such, the use of delta to estimate the option's price sensitivity for VAR purposes has led some to call the analytical method (or variance–covariance method) the **delta-normal method**. The use of delta is appropriate only for small changes in the underlying, however. As an alternative, some users of the delta-normal method add the second-order effect, captured by gamma. Unfortunately, as these higher-order effects are added, the relationship between the option price and the underlying's price begins to approximate the true nonlinear relationship. At that point, using a normal distribution becomes completely inappropriate. Therefore, using the analytical method could cause problems if a portfolio has options or other financial instruments that do not follow the normal distribution. Moreover, it is often difficult, if not impossible, to come up with a single second-order estimate that both is accurate and fits seamlessly into a variance/covariance VAR model.

5.2.3 The Historical Method

Another widely used VAR methodology is the **historical method**. Using historical VAR, we calculate returns for a given portfolio using actual daily prices from a user-specified period in the recent past, graphing these returns into a histogram. From there, it becomes easy to identify the loss that is exceeded with a probability of 0.05 (or 0.01 percent, if preferred).

Consider the portfolio we have been examining, consisting of 75 percent invested in the S&P 500 and 25 percent invested in the NASDAQ Composite Index. Exhibit 7, a histogram, shows the daily returns on this portfolio for a recent calendar year. First, we note that the distribution is similar, but by no means identical, to that of a normal distribution. This portfolio has a few more returns slightly lower than the midpoint of the return sample than it would if its distribution were perfectly normal. With the historical method, however, we are not constrained to using the normal distribution. We simply collect the historical data and identify the return below which 5 (or 1) percent of returns fall. Although we could attempt to read this number from the histogram, it is much easier to simply rank-order the returns and determine the VAR figure from the sorted returns and the portfolio's dollar value.

The year examined here contains 248 returns. Having 5 percent of the returns in the distribution's lower tail would mean that about 12 return observations should be less than the VAR estimate. Thus the approximate VAR figure would be indicated by the 12th-worst return. A rank ordering of the data reveals that the 12th-worst return is −0.0294. For a $50,000,000 portfolio, the one-day VAR would thus be 0.0294($50,000,000) = $1.47 million.[38]

---

[38] Technically, the VAR would fall between the 12th- and 13th-worst returns. Using the 13th-worst return gives a more conservative VAR. Alternatively, we might average the 12th- and 13th-worst returns.

EXHIBIT 7	Historical Daily Returns on a Portfolio Invested 75 Percent in S&P 500 and 25 Percent in NASDAQ

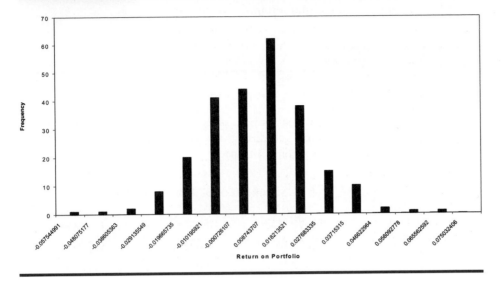

The historical method is also sometimes called the **historical simulation method**. This term is somewhat misleading because the approach involves not a *simulation* of the past returns but rather what *actually happened* in the past. In this context, note that a portfolio that an investor might have held in the past might not be the same as the one that investor will have in the future. When using the historical method, one must always keep in mind that the purpose of the exercise is to apply *historical* price changes to the *current* portfolio.[39] In addition, instruments such as bonds and most derivatives behave differently at different times in their lives, and any accurate historical VAR calculation must take this into account by adjusting current bond/derivative pricing parameters to simulate their current characteristics across the period of analysis. For example, a historical VAR calculation that goes back one year for a portfolio that contains bonds that mature in the year 2027 should actually use otherwise identical bonds maturing in 2026 as proxies; these bonds are the most accurate representations of the current risk profile because they would have presented themselves one year ago in time. When a company uses a different portfolio composition to calculate its historical VAR than the one it actually had in the past, it may be more appropriate to call the method a historical simulation.

The historical method has the advantage of being **nonparametric** (i.e., involving minimal probability-distribution assumptions), enabling the user to avoid any assumptions about the type of probability distribution that generates returns. The disadvantage, however, is that this method relies completely on events of the past, and whatever distribution prevailed in the past might not hold in the future. In particular, periods of unusually large negative returns, such as the 23 percent one-day decline in the Dow Jones Industrial Average on

---

[39] For example, in the two-asset portfolio we illustrated here, the weights were 75 percent S&P 500 and 25 percent NASDAQ. If the company were going forward with a different set of weights, it would obviously need to use the weights it planned to use in the future when calculating the VAR by the historical method.

19 October 1987, might be questionable as an assumption for the future. This problem applies to the other types of VAR methodologies as well, however, including the analytical method and Monte Carlo simulation, both of which derive their inputs, more often than not, entirely from the historical prices associated with the securities contained in the portfolio.

EXAMPLE 6

Calculating VAR Using the Historical Method

For simplicity, we use a one-stock portfolio. Exhibit 8 shows the 40 worst monthly returns on IBM stock during the last 20 years, in descending order, as of 2003 (minus signs omitted):

EXHIBIT 8	IBM Stock: Worst Monthly Returns		
0.17867	0.07237	0.05031	0.03372
0.17505	0.07234	0.04889	0.02951
0.17296	0.07220	0.04697	0.02905
0.16440	0.07126	0.04439	0.02840
0.10655	0.07064	0.04420	0.02584
0.09535	0.06966	0.04173	0.02508
0.09348	0.06465	0.04096	0.02270
0.08236	0.06266	0.03633	0.02163
0.08065	0.06204	0.03626	0.02115
0.07779	0.05304	0.03464	0.01976

For both calculations below, assume the portfolio value is $100,000.

1. Calculate a 5 percent monthly VAR using the historical method.

2. Calculate a 1 percent monthly VAR using the historical method.

Solutions: First, we note that during the last 20 years, there were 240 monthly returns. We see here only the worst 40 returns. Therefore, although we lack the entire distribution of returns, we do have enough to calculate the VAR.

1. Out of 240 returns, the 5 percent worst are the 12 worst returns. Therefore, the historical VAR would be about the 12th-worst return. From the exhibit, we see that this return is −0.07234. So, the one-month VAR is 0.07234($100,000) = $7,234.

2. The 1 percent worst returns are 2.4 returns. We would probably use the second-worst return, which is −0.17505. The VAR is 0.17505($100,000) = $17,505. Alternatively, we might average the second- and third-worst returns to obtain (−0.17505 + −0.17296)/2 = −0.17401. Then the one-month VAR would be 0.17401($100,000) = $17,401.

The excerpt from The Goldman Sachs Group, Inc., annual report that follows in Example 7 shows how this investment firm reports its VAR. We see that Goldman Sachs reports average values for 5 percent daily VAR for its fiscal year using a variation of the historical simulation method. Goldman Sachs reports on VAR for interest rate, equity, currency, and commodity products, as well as for its overall trading positions (total VAR). Total VAR is less than the sum of the individual VARs because the risks of Goldman Sachs' positions in the various products are less than perfectly correlated. The diversification effect reported in the table in Example 7 equals the difference between the sum of the individual VARs and total VAR. For example, for 2005, the diversification effect is \$37 + \$34 + \$17 + \$26 − \$70 = −\$44.

EXAMPLE 7

Value at Risk and the Management of Market Risk at Goldman Sachs

The following excerpt is from the 2005 Annual Report of Goldman Sachs:

> VaR is the potential loss in value of Goldman Sachs' trading positions due to adverse market movements over a defined time horizon with a specified confidence level.
>
> For the VaR numbers reported below, a one-day time horizon and a 95% confidence level were used. This means that there is a 1 in 20 chance that daily trading net revenues will fall below the expected daily trading net revenues by an amount at least as large as the reported VaR. Thus, shortfalls from expected trading net revenues on a single trading day greater than the reported VaR would be anticipated to occur, on average, about once a month. Shortfalls on a single day can exceed reported VaR by significant amounts. Shortfalls can also accumulate over a longer time horizon such as a number of consecutive trading days.
>
> The VaR numbers below are shown separately for interest rate, equity, currency and commodity products, as well as for our overall trading positions. The VaR numbers in each risk category include the underlying product positions and related hedges that may include positions in other product areas. For example, the hedge of a foreign exchange forward may include an interest rate futures position, and the hedge of a long corporate bond position may include a short position in the related equity.
>
> The modeling of the risk characteristics of our trading positions involves a number of assumptions and approximations. While management believes that these assumptions and approximations are reasonable, there is no standard methodology for estimating VaR, and different assumptions and/or approximations could produce materially different VaR estimates.
>
> We use historical data to estimate our VaR and, to better reflect current asset volatilities, we generally weight historical data to give greater importance to more recent observations. Given its reliance on historical data, VaR is most effective in estimating risk exposures in markets in which there are no sudden fundamental

changes or shifts in market conditions. An inherent limitation of VaR is that the distribution of past changes in market risk factors may not produce accurate predictions of future market risk. Different VaR methodologies and distributional assumptions could produce a materially different VaR. Moreover, VaR calculated for a one-day time horizon does not fully capture the market risk of positions that cannot be liquidated or offset with hedges within one day. Changes in VaR between reporting periods are generally due to changes in levels of exposure, volatilities and/or correlations among asset classes.

The following table sets forth the daily VaR:

Average daily VaR[a] (in millions)

Risk categories	Year Ended November		
	2005	2004	2003
Interest rates	$37	$36	$38
Equity prices	34	32	27
Currency rates	17	20	18
Commodity prices	26	20	18
Diversification effect[b]	(44)	(41)	(43)
Total	$70	$67	$58

[a] During the second quarter of 2004, we began to exclude from our calculation other debt portfolios that cannot be properly measured in VaR. The effect of excluding these portfolios was not material to prior periods and, accordingly, such periods have not been adjusted. For a further discussion of the market risk associated with these portfolios, see "—Other Debt Portfolios" below. [This matter is not reproduced in this excerpt]

[b] Equals the difference between total VaR and the sum of the VaRs for the four risk categories. This effect arises because the four market risk categories are not perfectly correlated.

Our average daily VaR increased to $70 million in 2005 from $67 million in 2004. The increase was primarily due to higher levels of exposure to commodity prices, equity prices and interest rates, partially offset by reduced exposures to currency rates, as well as reduced volatilities, particularly in interest rate and equity assets.

Our average daily VaR increased to $67 million in 2004 from $58 million in 2003, primarily due to higher levels of exposure to equity prices, currency rates and commodity prices, partially offset by reduced exposures to interest rates, as well as reduced volatilities, particularly in interest rates and equity assets.

The Annual Report continues with a table giving other information about VAR, including high and low daily values.

Source: Goldman Sachs 2005 Annual Report, pp. 50–52.

The next section addresses the third method of estimating VAR, Monte Carlo simulation.

5.2.4 The Monte Carlo Simulation Method

The third approach to estimating VAR is Monte Carlo simulation. In general, Monte Carlo simulation produces random outcomes so we can examine what might happen given a particular set of risks. It is used widely in the sciences as well as in business to study a variety of problems. In the financial world in recent years, it has become an extremely important technique for measuring risk. Monte Carlo simulation generates random outcomes according to an assumed probability distribution and a set of input parameters. We can then analyze these outcomes to gauge the risk associated with the events in question. When estimating VAR, we use Monte Carlo simulation to produce random portfolio returns. We then assemble these returns into a summary distribution from which we can determine at which level the lower 5 percent (or 1 percent, if preferred) of return outcomes occur. We then apply this figure to the portfolio value to obtain VAR.

Monte Carlo simulation uses a probability distribution for each variable of interest and a mechanism to randomly generate outcomes according to each distribution. Our goal here is to gain a basic understanding of the technique and how to use it. Therefore, we illustrate it without explaining the full details of how to generate the random values.

Suppose we return to the example of our $50 million portfolio invested 75 percent in the S&P 500 and 25 percent in the NASDAQ Composite Index. We assume, as previously, that this portfolio should have an annual expected return of 13.5 percent and a standard deviation of 24.4 percent. We shall now conduct a Monte Carlo simulation using the normal distribution with these parameters. Keep in mind that in practice, one advantage of Monte Carlo simulation is that it does not require a normal distribution, but the normal distribution is often used and we shall stay with it for illustrative purposes.

We use a random number generator to produce a series of random values, which we then convert into a normally distributed stream of outcomes representing a rate of return for this portfolio over a period of one year. Suppose the first value it produces is a return of −21.87 percent. This rate corresponds to an end-of-year portfolio value of $39.07 million. The second random return it produces is −4.79 percent, which takes the portfolio value to $47.61 million.[40] The third random return it produces is 31.38 percent, which makes the portfolio value $65.69 million. We continue this process a large number of times, perhaps several thousand or even several million. To keep the simulation to a manageable size for illustrative purposes, we generate only 300 outcomes.

Exhibit 9 shows the histogram of portfolio outcomes. Notice that even though we used a normal distribution to generate the outcomes, the resulting distribution does not look entirely normal. Of course, we should be surprised if it did because we used only 300 random outcomes, a relatively small sample.

To obtain the point in the lower tail that 5 percent of the outcomes exceed, we rank order the data and find the 15th-lowest outcome, which is a portfolio value of $34.25 million, corresponding to a loss of $15.75 million. This value is higher than the annual VAR estimated using the analytical method ($13.4 million). These two values would be identical (or nearly so) if we had employed a

---

[40] The random outcomes are independent, not sequential. Each outcome thus represents a return relative to the full initial portfolio value of $50 million.

EXHIBIT 9	Simulated Values after One Year for a Portfolio Invested 75 Percent in S&P 500 and 25 Percent in NASDAQ

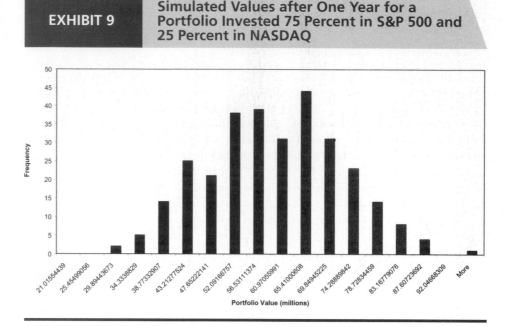

sufficiently large sample size in the Monte Carlo simulation so that the sample VAR would converge to the true population VAR.

In Monte Carlo simulation, we can make any distributional assumption that we believe is appropriate. In many practical applications, it is inappropriate to assume a normal return distribution. In particular, for many derivatives dealers, the problems in managing the risk of these instruments are compounded by the fact that an extremely large number of random variables may affect the value of their overall position. These variables are often not normally distributed, and furthermore, they often interact with each other in complex ways. Monte Carlo simulation is often the only practical means of generating the information necessary to manage the risk. With tens of thousands of transactions on the books of most dealers, however, Monte Carlo simulation can require extensive commitments of computer resources.

5.2.5 *"Surplus at Risk": VAR as It Applies to Pension Fund Portfolios*

You will recall from earlier points in our discussion that pension funds face a slightly different set of challenges in the measurement of market exposures, primarily because of the fact that the assets must fund pension obligations whose present value is itself subject to interest rate risk and other risks.[41] The difference between the value of the pension fund's assets and liabilities is referred to as the **surplus**, and it is this value that pension fund managers seek to enhance and protect. If this surplus falls into negative territory, the plan sponsor must contribute funds to make up the deficit over a period of time that is specified as part of the fund's plan.

In order to reflect this set of realities in their risk estimations, pension fund managers typically apply VAR methodologies not to their portfolio of assets but

---

[41] An example of a defined benefit pension plan's obligation is the promise is to pay, for each year of service, a certain percentage of a vested participant's average salary in their final five years of service; this promise may include cost-of-living adjustments.

to the surplus. To do so, they simply express their liability portfolio as a set of short securities and calculate VAR on the net position. VAR handles this process quite elegantly, and once this adjustment is made, all three VAR methodologies can be applied to the task.

5.3 The Advantages and Limitations of VAR

Although value at risk has become the industry standard for risk assessment, it also has widely documented imperfections. VAR can be difficult to estimate, and different estimation methods can give quite different values. VAR can also lull one into a false sense of security by giving the impression that the risk is properly measured and under control. VAR often underestimates the magnitude and frequency of the worst returns, although this problem often derives from erroneous assumptions and models. As we discuss later, VAR for individual positions does not generally aggregate in a simple way to portfolio VAR. Also, VAR fails to incorporate positive results into its risk profile, and as such, it arguably provides an incomplete picture of overall exposures.

Users of VAR should routinely test their system to determine whether their VAR estimates prove accurate in predicting the results experienced over time. For example, if daily VAR at 0.05 is estimated at $1 million, then over a reasonable period of time, such as a year, a loss of at least $1 million should be exceeded approximately $250(0.05) = 12.5$ days. If the frequency of losses equal to or greater than this amount is markedly different, then the model is not accomplishing its objectives. This process of comparing the number of violations of VAR thresholds with the figure implied by the user-selected probability level is part of a process known as **backtesting**. It is extremely important to go through this exercise, ideally across multiple time intervals, to ensure that the VAR estimation method adopted is reasonably accurate. For example, if the VAR estimate is based on daily observations and targets a 0.05 probability, then in addition to ensuring that approximately a dozen threshold violations occur during a given year, it is also useful to check other, shorter time intervals, including the most recent quarter (for which, given 60-odd trading days, we would expect approximately three VAR exceptions—i.e., losses greater than the calculated VAR), and the most recent month (20 observations, implying a single VAR exception). Note that the results should not be expected to precisely match the probability level predictions but should at a minimum be of similar magnitude. If the results vary much from those that the model predicts, then users must examine the reasons and make appropriate adjustments.

An accurate VAR estimate can also be extremely difficult to obtain for complex organizations. In the simple example we used previously, VAR was driven solely by the large- and small-cap U.S. stocks. For a large international bank, however, the exposures might be to a variety of domestic and international interest rate markets, numerous exchange rates, perhaps some equity markets, and even some commodity markets. A bank could have exposure to literally thousands of risks. Consolidating the effects of these exposures into a single risk measure can be extremely difficult. Nonetheless, most large banks manage to do so and, generally, do an excellent job of managing their risk.

VAR has the attraction of quantifying the potential loss in simple terms and can be easily understood by senior management. Regulatory bodies have taken note of VAR as a risk measure, and some require that institutions provide it in their reports. In the United States, the Securities and Exchange Commission now requires publicly traded companies to report how they are managing financial risk. VAR is one acceptable method of reporting that information.

Another advantage of VAR is its versatility. Many companies use VAR as a measure of their capital at risk. They will estimate the VAR associated with a particular activity, such as a line of business, an individual asset manager, a subsidiary, or a division. Then, they evaluate performance, taking into account the VAR associated with this risky activity. In some cases, companies allocate capital based on VAR. For example, a pension fund might determine its overall acceptable VAR and then inform each asset class manager that it can operate subject to its VAR not exceeding a certain amount. The manager's goal is to earn the highest return possible given its VAR allocation. This activity is known as risk budgeting; we cover it in more detail in a later section.

In summary, VAR has notable advantages and disadvantages. Controversy and criticism have surrounded it.[42] Nevertheless, if a risk manager uses VAR with full awareness of its limitations, he should definitely gain useful information about risk. Even if VAR gives an incorrect measure of the loss potential, the risk manager can take this risk measurement error into account when making the key overall decisions—provided, of course, that the magnitude of the error can be measured and adjusted for with some level of precision, e.g., through back testing a VAR method against historical data. The controversy remains, but VAR as a risk measure is unlikely to ever be completely rejected. It should not, however, be used in isolation. VAR is often paired with stress testing, discussed in a subsequent section. Remember too that no risk measure can precisely predict future losses. It is important to ensure that the inputs to the VAR calculation are as reliable as possible and relevant to the current investment mix.

5.4 Extensions and Supplements to VAR

Risk managers have developed several useful extensions and supplements to VAR. In this section, we review several of the more noteworthy.

A key concern to risk managers is the evaluation of the portfolio effect of a given risk. The ability to isolate the effect of a risk, particularly in complex portfolios with high correlation effects, is very important. We can use incremental VAR (IVAR) to investigate the effect. **Incremental VAR** measures the incremental effect of an asset on the VAR of a portfolio by measuring the difference between the portfolio's VAR while including a specified asset and the portfolio's VAR with that asset eliminated.[43] We can also use IVAR to assess the incremental effect of a subdivision on an enterprise's overall VAR. Although IVAR gives an extremely limited picture of the asset's or portfolio's contribution to risk, it nonetheless provides useful information about how adding the asset will affect the portfolio's overall risk as reflected in its VAR.

Some variations of VAR are **cash flow at risk** (CFAR) and **earnings at risk** (EAR). CFAR and EAR measure the risk to a company's cash flow or earning, respectively, instead of its market value as in the case of VAR. CFAR is the minimum cash flow loss that we expect to be exceeded with a given probability over a

---

[42] A well-known critic of VAR has likened its use to flying an aircraft with a potentially flawed altimeter. With an altimeter, a pilot may think he knows the correct altitude. Without an altimeter, the pilot will look out the window. Of course, this argument presumes that there are no clouds below. The probability of hitting trees or a mountain is the joint probability that the aircraft is too low and that the altimeter gives a false signal, which is less than the simple probability that the aircraft is too low. Aware of the potential for the altimeter to be flawed, the pilot will also seek information from other sources, which themselves are less than 100 percent accurate. So will the risk manager when using VAR. Both will gauge the risk against their tolerance for risk and take appropriate action. We look at some of these other sources of risk information in the next section.

[43] For more details, see Crouhy, Galai, and Mark (2001), Chapter 6.

specified time period. EAR is defined analogously to CFAR but measures risk to accounting earnings. CFAR and EAR can be used when a company (or portfolio of assets) generates cash flows or profits but cannot be readily valued in a publicly traded market, or when the analyst's focus is on the risk to cash flow and earnings, for example, in a valuation. CFAR and EAR can complement VAR's perspective on risk.

Another useful tool to supplement VAR is the **tail value at risk** (TVAR), also known as the **conditional tail expectation**. TVAR is defined as the VAR plus the expected loss in excess of VAR, when such excess loss occurs. For example, given a 5 percent daily VAR, TVAR might be calculated as the average of the worst 5 percent of outcomes in a simulation.

VAR developed initially as a measure for market risk, which is the risk associated with the primary market forces of interest rates, exchange rates, stock prices, and commodity prices. With some difficulty, VAR can be extended to handle credit risk, the risk that a counterparty will not pay what it owes. More-recent extensions of VAR have tended to focus on modeling assets with non-normal underlying distributions. The use of conditional normal distribution based on different regimes is a very intriguing concept, but the mathematics used in this area can be daunting.[44]

5.5 Stress Testing

Managers often use stress testing (a term borrowed from engineering) to supplement VAR as a risk measure. The main purpose of VAR analysis is to quantify potential losses under normal market conditions. Stress testing, by comparison, seeks to identify unusual circumstances that could lead to losses in excess of those typically expected. Clearly, different scenarios will have attached probabilities of occurring that vary from the highly likely to the almost totally improbable. It is, therefore, the natural complement to VAR analysis. Two broad approaches exist in stress testing: scenario analysis and stressing models.

5.5.1 Scenario Analysis

Scenario analysis is the process of evaluating a portfolio under different states of the world. Quite often it involves designing scenarios with deliberately large movements in the key variables that affect the values of a portfolio's assets and derivatives.

One type of scenario analysis, that of **stylized scenarios**, involves simulating a movement in at least one interest rate, exchange rate, stock price, or commodity price relevant to the portfolio. These movements might range from fairly modest changes to quite extreme shifts. Many practitioners use standard sets of stylized scenarios to highlight potentially risky outcomes for the portfolio. Some organizations have formalized this process; for example, the Derivatives Policy Group recommends its members look at the following seven scenarios:

► parallel yield curve shifting by ±100 basis points (1 percentage point)
► yield curve twisting by ±25 basis points[45]
► each of the four combinations of the above shifts and twists

---

[44] For an extremely entertaining tour of some of the pitfalls of traditional risk analysis and some solutions, see Osband (2002).

[45] A twist is a nonparallel movement in the yield curve. An example of a twist is a 25-bp increase in short rates and no change in long rates, which would result in a flattening of the yield curve.

▶ implied volatilities changing by ±20 percent from current levels

▶ equity index levels changing by ±10 percent

▶ major currencies moving by ±6 percent and other currencies by ±20 percent

▶ swap spread changing by ±20 basis points

In 1988, the Chicago Mercantile Exchange introduced a system call SPAN to calculate collateral requirements based on their members' total portfolios of futures and options. The objective of this system was to stress portfolios under a variety of scenarios. SPAN has become a very popular system among futures and options exchanges worldwide to set margin requirements. It offers a very useful, generalized form of scenario analysis that combines elements of VAR with some specified overlay based on real-world observation of the relationship among financial instruments.

Scenario analysis is a very useful enhancement to VAR, enabling those interested in risk analysis to identify and analyze specific exposures that might affect a portfolio. The results, of course, are only as good as implied by the accuracy of the scenarios devised. One problem with the stylized scenario approach is that the shocks tend to be applied to variables in a sequential fashion. In reality, these shocks often happen at the same time, have much different correlations than normal, or have some causal relationship connecting them.

Another approach to scenario analysis involves using **actual extreme events** that have occurred in the past. Here, we might want to put our portfolio through price movements that simulate the stock market crash of October 1987; the collapse of Long-Term Capital Management in 1998; the technology stock bubble of the late 1990s; the abrupt bursting of said bubble, beginning in the spring of 2000; or the market reaction to the terrorist attacks of 11 September 2001. This type of scenario analysis might be particularly useful if we think that the occurrence of extreme market breaks has a higher probability than that given by the probability model or historical time period being used in developing the VAR estimate. Stress testing of actual extreme events forces one to direct attention to these outcomes.

We might also create scenarios based on **hypothetical events**—events that have never happened in the markets or market outcomes to which we attach a small probability. These types of scenarios are very difficult to analyze and may generate confusing outcomes, so it is important to carefully craft hypothetical analyses if they are to generate information that adds value to the risk management processes.

Having devised a series of appropriate scenarios, the next step in the process is to apply them to the portfolio. The key task here is to understand the instruments' sensitivities to the underlying risk factors being stressed. This process is often a complex one that demands an understanding of the portfolio's risk parameters such that we can make appropriate approximations from standardized risk characteristics such as betas, deltas, gammas, duration, and convexity. Market liquidity is often a consideration also, especially when the underlying valuation models for assets assume arbitrage-free pricing, which assumes the ability to transact in any quantity. In addition, liquidity often dries up completely in a market crisis.

5.5.2 Stressing Models

Given the difficulty in estimating the sensitivities of a portfolio's instruments to the scenarios we might design, another approach might be to use an existing model and apply shocks and perturbations to the model inputs in some mechanical way. This approach might be considered more scientific because it emphasizes a range of possibilities rather than a single set of scenarios, but it will be more computationally demanding. It is also possible to glean some idea of the likelihood of different scenarios occurring.

The simplest form of stressing model is referred to as **factor push**, the basic idea of which to is to push the prices and risk factors of an underlying model in the most disadvantageous way and to work out the combined effect on the portfolio's value. This exercise might be appropriate for a wide range of models, including option-pricing models such as Black–Scholes–Merton, multifactor equity risk models, and term structure factor models. But factor push also has its limitations and difficulties—principally the enormous model risk that occurs in assuming the underlying model will function in an extreme risk climate.

Other approaches include **maximum loss optimization**—in which we would try to optimize mathematically the risk variable that will produce the maximum loss—and **worst-case scenario analysis**—in which we can examine the worst case that we actually expect to occur.

Overall stress testing is a valuable complement to VAR analysis and can highlight weaknesses in risk management procedures.

5.6 Measuring Credit Risk

Credit risk is present when there is a positive probability that one party owing money to another will renege on the obligation (i.e., the counterparty could default). If the defaulting party has insufficient resources to cover the loss or the creditor cannot impose a claim on any assets the debtor has that are unrelated to the line of business in which the credit was extended, the creditor can suffer a loss.[46] A creditor might be able to recover some of the loss, perhaps by having the debtor sell assets and pay the creditors a portion of their claim.

Credit losses have two dimensions: the likelihood of loss and the associated amount of loss (reflecting, of course, the amount of credit outstanding and the associated recovery rate). The likelihood of loss is a probabilistic concept: In every credit-based transaction, a given probability exists that the debtor will default. When a default does occur, however, creditors are often able to recover at least a portion of their investment, and as such, it is necessary and appropriate to assess the magnitude of this recovery (i.e., the recovery rate) in order to fully understand the risk profile of the credit dynamic. In relation to data on market risk, the amount of information available on credit losses is much smaller. Credit losses occur infrequently, and as such, the empirical data set from which to draw exposure inferences is quite limited. Although some statistical data are available, historical recovery rates can be unreliable. It can be hard to predict what an asset could be sold for in bankruptcy proceedings, and claims are not always paid in the order specified by bankruptcy law.

In the risk management business, exposure must often be viewed from two different time perspectives. We must assess first the risk associated with immediate credit events and second the risk associated with events that may happen later. With respect to credit, the risk of events happening in the immediate future is called **current credit risk** (or, alternatively, **jump-to-default risk**); it relates to the risk that amounts due at the present time will not be paid. For example, some risk exists that the counterparty could default on an interest or swap payment due immediately. Assuming, however, that the counterparty is solvent and that it will make the current payment with certainty, the risk remains

---

[46] The personal assets of a corporation's owners are shielded from creditors by the principle of limited liability, which can also apply to certain partnerships. The law supporting limited liability is a fundamental one in most societies and supports the notion that default is a right. Indeed, option-pricing theory has been used to value this right as the option that it actually is.

that the entity will default at a later date. This risk is called **potential credit risk**, and it can differ quite significantly from current credit risk; the relationship between the two is a complex one. A company experiencing financial difficulties at present could, with sufficient time, work out its problems and be in better financial condition at a later date. Regardless of which risk is greater, however, a creditor must assess credit risk at different points in time. In doing so, the creditor must understand how different financial instruments have different patterns of credit risk, both across instruments and across time within a given instrument. This point will be discussed later in this section.

Another element of credit risk, which blends current and potential credit risk, is the possibility that a counterparty will default on a current payment to a different creditor. Most direct lending or derivative-based credit contracts stipulate that if a borrower defaults on any outstanding credit obligations, the borrower is in default on them all (this is known as a **cross-default provision**). Creditors stipulate this condition as one means of controlling credit exposure; in particular, it allows them to act quickly to mitigate losses to counterparties unable to meet any of their obligations. For example, suppose Party A owes Party B, but no payments are due for some time. Party A, however, currently owes a payment to Party C and is unable to pay. A is, therefore, in default to Party C. Depending on what actions C takes, A may be forced into bankruptcy. If so, then B's claim simply goes into the pool of other claims on A. In that case, A has technically defaulted to B without actually having a payment due.

In a previous section, we discussed how VAR is used to measure market risk. VAR is also used, albeit with greater difficulty, to measure credit risk. This measure is sometimes called **credit VAR**, default VAR, or credit at risk. Like ordinary VAR, it reflects the minimum loss with a given probability during a period of time. A company might, for example, quote a credit VAR of €10 million for one year at a probability of 0.05 (or a confidence level of 95 percent). In other words, the company has a 5 percent chance of incurring default-related losses of at least €10 million in one year. Note that credit VAR cannot be separated from market VAR because credit risk arises from gains on market positions held. Therefore, to accurately measure credit VAR, a risk manager must focus on the upper tail of the distribution of market returns, where the return to the position is positive, in contrast to market risk VAR, which focuses on the lower tail. Suppose the 5 percent upper tail of the market risk distribution is €5 million. The credit VAR can be roughly thought of as €5 million, but this thinking assumes that the probability of loss is 100 percent and the net amount recovered in the event of a loss is zero. Further refinements incorporating more-accurate measures of the default probability and recovery rate should lead to a lower and more accurate credit VAR. In addition, the explosion of volume and liquidity in the credit derivatives market has vastly increased the amount of information available to risk managers with respect to the problem of understanding how the marketplace values credit risk on a real-time basis. Nevertheless, estimating credit VAR is more complicated than estimating market VAR because credit events are rare and recovery rates are hard to estimate. Credit risk is less easily aggregated than market risk; the correlations between the credit risks of counterparties must be considered.

In the next sections, we present the perspective of option pricing theory on credit risk and the measurement of credit risk exposures for certain derivative contracts.

5.6.1 Option-Pricing Theory and Credit Risk

Option theory enables us to better understand the nature of credit risk. In this section, we will see that the stock of a company with leverage can be viewed as a call option • on its assets. This approach will lead to the result that a bond with

EXHIBIT 10	Payoffs to the Suppliers of Capital to the Company			

		Payoffs at Time T	
Source of Capital	Market Value at Time 0	$A_T < F$	$A_T \geq F$
Bondholders	B_0	A_T	F
Stockholders	S_0	0	$A_T - F$
Total	$B_0 + S_0 = A_0$	A_T	A_T

credit risk can be viewed as a default-free bond plus an implicit short put option written by the bondholders for the stockholders.

Consider a company with assets with a market value of A_0 and debt with a face value of F. The debt is in the form of a single zero-coupon bond due at time T. The bond's market value is B_0. Thus the stock's market value is

$$S_0 = A_0 - B_0$$

At time T, the assets will be worth A_T and the company will owe F. If $A_T \geq F$, the company will pay off its debt, leaving the amount $A_T - F$ for the stockholders. Thus S_T will be worth $A_T - F$. If the assets' value is insufficient to pay off the debt ($A_T < F$), the stockholders will discharge their obligation by turning over the assets to the bondholders. Thus the bondholders will receive A_T, which is less than their claim of F, and the stockholders will receive nothing. The company is, therefore, bankrupt. Exhibit 10 illustrates these results by showing the payoffs to the two suppliers of capital.

Notice that the payoffs to the stockholders resemble those of a call option in which the underlying is the assets, the exercise price is F, and the option expires at time T, the bond maturity date. Indeed, the stock of a company with a single zero-coupon bond issue is a call option on the assets.

To better understand the nature of stock as a call option, let us recall the concept of **put–call parity**,[47] where $p_0 + S_0 = c_0 + X/(1 + r)^T$. The put price plus the underlying price equals the call price plus the present value of the exercise price. So, working this through for our own problem, we find the correspondences shown in Exhibit 11.

EXHIBIT 11	Equity as a Call Option on the Value of a Company	
Variable	Traditional Framework	Current Framework
Underlying	S_0 (stock)	A_0 (value of assets)
Exercise price	X	F (face value of bond)
Time to expiration	T	T (maturity of bond)
Risk-free rate	r	r
Call price	c_0	S_0 (value of stock)
Put price	p_0	p_0

---

[47] See Chance (2003), Chapter 4.

Note the last line. We see that in the traditional framework, there is a put option, which we know is an option to sell the underlying at a fixed price. In fact, we know from put-call parity that $p_0 = c_0 - S_0 + X/(1 + r)^T$. The put is equivalent to a long call, a short position in the underlying stock, and a long position in a risk-free bond with face value equal to the exercise price. In the current framework, the standard expression of put-call parity is $p_0 + A_0$ (put plus underlying) $= S_0 + F/(1 + r)^T$ (stock plus present value of bond principal). Turning this expression around and reversing the order of the put and bond, we obtain

$$A_0 = S_0 + F/(1 + r)^T - p_0$$

Noting, however, that by definition the asset value, A_0, equals the stock's market value, S_0, plus the bond's market value, B_0,

$$A_0 = S_0 + B_0$$

we see that the bond's market value must be equivalent to

$$B_0 = F/(1 + r)^T - p_0$$

The first term on the right-hand side is equivalent to a default-free zero-coupon bond paying F at maturity. The second term is a short put. The bondholders' claim, which is subject to default, can thus be viewed as a default-free bond and a short put on the assets. In other words, the bondholders have implicitly written the stockholders a put on the assets. From the stockholders' perspective, this put is their right to fully discharge their liability by turning over the assets to the bondholders, even though those assets could be worth less than the bondholders' claim. In legal terminology, this put option is called the stockholders' right of limited liability.

The existence of this implicit put option is the difference between a default-free bond and a bond subject to default. This approach to understanding credit risk forms the basis for models that use option-pricing theory to explain credit risk premiums, probabilities of default, and the valuation of companies that use leverage. In practice, the capital structures of most companies are more complex than the one used here, but practical applications of model variants appear in the financial industry.

5.6.2 The Credit Risk of Forward Contracts

Recall that forward contracts involve commitments on the part of each party. No cash is due at the start, and no cash is paid until expiration, at which time one party owes the greater amount to the other. The party that owes the larger amount could default, leaving the other with a claim of the defaulted amount. Each party assumes the other's credit risk. Prior to expiration, no current credit risk exists, because no current payments are owed, but there is potential credit risk in connection with the payments to be made at expiration. Current credit risk arises when the contract is at its expiration. Below we will examine how potential credit risk changes during the life of the contract as the value of the underlying changes.

From the perspective of a given party, a forward contract's market value can be easily calculated as the present value of the amount owed to the party minus the present value of the amount it owes. So, the market value at a given time reflects the potential credit risk. This is another reason why the calculation of market value is important: It indicates the amount of a claim that would be subject to loss in the event of a default.

For example, look at a forward contract that expires in one year. The underlying asset price is $100 and the risk-free interest rate is 5 percent. We can determine that the forward price is $100(1.05) = $105. We could then assume that three months later, the asset price is $102. We can determine that the long forward contract's value at that time is $102 − $105/(1.05)^{0.75} = $0.7728. This is the value to the long because the contract is a claim on the asset, which is currently worth $102, and an obligation to pay $105 for it in nine months. To the holder of the long position, this contract is worth $0.7728, and to the holder of the short position, it is worth −$0.7728.

Which party bears the potential credit risk? The long's claim is positive; the short's claim is negative. Therefore, the long currently bears the credit risk. As it stands right now, the value of the long's claim is $0.7728. No payment is currently due, and hence no current credit risk exists, but the payments that are due later have a present value of $0.7728. Actual default may or may not occur at expiration. Moreover, at expiration, the amount owed is unlikely to be this same amount. In fact, if the spot price falls enough, the situation will have turned around and the long could owe the short the greater amount. Nonetheless, in assessing the credit risk three months into the contract, the long's claim is $0.7728. This claim has a probability of not being paid and also has the potential for recovery of a portion of the loss in the event of default. If the counterparty declares bankruptcy before the contract expires, the claim of the non-defaulting counterparty is the forward contract's market value at the time of the bankruptcy, assuming this value is positive. So, if the short declares bankruptcy at this time, the long has a claim worth $0.7728. If the long declares bankruptcy, the long holds an asset worth $0.7728.

5.6.3 The Credit Risk of Swaps

A swap is similar to a series of forward contracts. The periodic payments associated with a swap imply, however, that credit risk will be present at a series of points during the contract's life. As with forward contracts, the swap's market value can be calculated at any time and reflects the present value of the amount at risk for a credit loss (i.e., the potential credit risk).

Consider, for example, the case of a plain vanilla interest rate swap with a one-year life and quarterly payments at LIBOR. Using the term structure, we can determine that the swap has a fixed rate of 3.68 percent, leading to quarterly fixed payments of $0.0092 per $1 notional principal. We then can move forward 60 days into the life of the swap and, with a new term structure, we can determine that the swap's market value is $0.0047 per $1 notional principal. To the party that is long (i.e., paying fixed and receiving floating), the swap has a positive market value. To the counterparty, which pays floating and receives fixed, the claim has a market value of −$0.0047.

As with a forward contract, the market value indicates the present value of the payments owed to the party minus the present value of the payments the party owes. Only 60 days into the life of a swap with quarterly payments, no payment is due for 30 more days. Thus there is no current credit risk. There is, however, potential credit risk. The market value of $0.0047 represents the amount that is at risk of loss for default. Of course, if default occurs, it will be at a later date when the amount will probably be different. Moreover, the market value could reverse its sign. At this time, the amount owed by the short to the long is greater, but at a later date, the amount owed by the long to the short could be greater. As with forward contracts, if the party to which the value is negative defaults, the counterparty has a claim of that value. If the party to which the value is positive defaults, the defaulting party holds an asset with the positive market value. Also, the counterparty could default to someone else, thereby being forced to declare bankruptcy before a payment on this swap is due. In that case, the swap's market value at that time is either the claim of the creditor or the asset held by the bankrupt party in bankruptcy proceedings.

The credit risk of swaps can vary greatly across product types within this asset class and over a given swap's lifetime. For interest rate and equity swaps, the potential credit risk is largest during the middle period of the swap's life. During the beginning of a swap's life, typically we would assume that the credit risk is small because, presumably, the involved counterparties have performed sufficient current credit analysis on one another to be comfortable with the arrangement or otherwise they would not engage in the transaction. At the end of the life of the swap, the credit risk is diminished because most of the underlying risk has been amortized through the periodic payment process. There are fewer payments at the end of a swap than at any other time during its life; hence, the amount a party can lose because of a default is smaller. This leaves the greatest exposure during the middle period, a point at which 1) the credit profile of the counterparties may have changed for the worse and 2) the magnitude and frequency of expected payments between counterparties remain material. One exception to this pattern involves currency swaps, which often provide for the payment of the notional principal at the beginning and at the end of the life of the transaction. Because the notional principal tends to be a large amount relative to the payments, the potential for loss caused by the counterparty defaulting on the final notional principal payment is great. Thus, whereas interest rate swaps have their greatest credit risk midway during the life of the swap, currency swaps have their greatest credit risk between the midpoint and the end of the life of the swap.

5.6.4 *The Credit Risk of Options*

Forward contracts and swaps have bilateral default risk. Although only one party will end up making a given payment, each party could potentially be the party owing the net amount. Options, on the other hand, have unilateral credit risk. The buyer of an option pays a cash premium at the start and owes nothing more unless, under the buyer's sole discretion, he decides to exercise the option. Once the premium is paid, the seller assumes no credit risk from the buyer. Instead, credit risk accrues entirely to the buyer and can be quite significant. If the buyer exercises the option, the seller must meet certain terms embedded in the contract. If the option is a call, the seller must deliver the underlying or pay an equivalent cash settlement. If the option is a put, the seller must accept delivery of the underlying and pay for it or meet these obligations in the form of cash payments. If the seller fails to fulfill her end of the obligation, she is in default. Like forward contracts, European options have no payments due until expiration. Hence, they have no current credit risk until expiration, although significant potential credit risk exists.

Consider a European call option for which the underlying security has a price of 52.75 and a standard deviation of 0.35. The exercise price is 50, the risk-free rate is 4.88 percent continuously compounded, and the option expires in nine months. Using the Black–Scholes–Merton model, we find that the value of the option is 8.5580. The holder thus has potential credit risk represented by a present claim of 8.5580. This amount can be thought of as the amount that is at risk, even though at expiration the option will probably be worth a different amount. In fact, the option might even expire out of the money, in which case it would not matter if the short were bankrupt. If the short declares bankruptcy before expiration, the long has a claim on the value of the option under bankruptcy law.

If the option were American, the value could be greater. Moreover, with American options, current credit risk could arise if the option holder decides to exercise the option early. This alternative creates the possibility of the short defaulting before expiration.

EXAMPLE 8

Calculating Credit Risk Exposures

Calculate the amount at risk of a credit loss in the following situations:

1. A U.S. party goes long a forward contract on €1 denominated in dollars in which the underlying is the euro. The original term of the contract was two years, and the forward rate was $0.90. The contract now has 18 months or 1.5 years to maturity. The spot or current exchange rate is $0.862. The U.S. interest rate is 6 percent, and the euro interest rate is 5 percent. The interest rates are based on discrete compounding/discounting. At the point when the contract has 1.5 years remaining, the value of the contract to the long per $1 notional principal equals the spot exchange rate, $0.862, discounted at the international interest rate for 1.5 years, minus the forward rate, $0.90, discounted at the domestic interest rate for 1.5 years:[48]

$$\frac{\$0.862}{(1.05)^{1.5}} - \frac{\$0.90}{(1.06)^{1.5}} = -\$0.0235$$

Evaluate the credit risk characteristics of this situation.

2. Consider a plain vanilla interest rate swap with two months to go before the next payment. Six months after that, the swap will have its final payment. The swap fixed rate is 7 percent, and the upcoming floating payment is 6.9 percent. All payments are based on 30 days in a month and 360 days in a year. Two-month LIBOR is 7.250 percent, and eight-month LIBOR is 7.375 percent. The present value factors for two and eight months can be calculated as follows:

$$\frac{1}{1 + 0.0725(60/360)} = 0.9881$$

$$\frac{1}{1 + 0.07375(240/360)} = 0.9531$$

The next floating payment will be 0.069(180/360) = 0.0345. The present value of the floating payments (plus hypothetical notional principal) is 1.0345(0.9881) = 1.0222. Given an annual rate of 7 percent, the fixed payments will be 0.07(180/360) = 0.035.

---

[48] See Chance (2003), pp. 58–59.

> The present value of the fixed payments (plus hypothetical notional principal) is, therefore, 0.035(0.9881) + 1.035(0.9531) = 1.0210.
> Determine the amount at risk of a credit loss and state which party currently bears the risk. Assume a $1 notional principal.
>
> 3. A dealer has sold a call option on a stock for $35 to an investor. The option is currently worth $46, as quoted in the market. Determine the amount at risk of a credit loss and state which party currently bears the risk.
>
> **Solution to 1:** The position has a negative value to the long, so the credit risk is currently borne by the short. From the short's point of view, the contract has a value of $0.0235 per $1 notional principal. No payments are due for 18 months, but the short's claim on the long is worth $0.0235 more than the long's claim on the short. Therefore, this amount is the current value of the amount at risk for a credit loss. Of course, the amount could, and probably will, change over the life of the contract. The credit risk exposure might even shift to the other party.
>
> **Solution to 2:** The market value of the swap to the party paying fixed and receiving floating is 1.0222 − 1.0210 = 0.0012. This value is positive to the party paying fixed and receiving floating; thus this party currently assumes the credit risk. Of course, the value will change over the life of the swap and may turn negative, meaning that the credit risk is then assumed by the party paying floating and receiving fixed.
>
> **Solution to 3:** All of the credit risk is borne by the investor (the owner of the call), because he will look to the dealer (the seller) for the payoff if the owner exercises the option. The current value of the amount at risk is the market price of $46.

Derivatives' credit risk can be quite substantial, but this risk is considerably less than that faced by most lenders. When a lender makes a loan, the interest and principal are at risk. The loan principal corresponds closely to the notional principal of most derivative contracts. With the exception of currency swaps, the notional principal is never exchanged in a swap. Even with currency swaps, however, the risk is much smaller than on a loan. If a counterparty defaults on a currency swap, the amount owed to the defaulting counterparty serves as a type of collateral because the creditor is not required to pay it to the defaulting party. Therefore, the credit risk on derivative transactions tends to be quite small relative to that on loans. On forward and swap transactions, the netting of payments makes the risk extremely small relative to the notional principal and to the credit risk on a bond or loan of equivalent principal.

5.7 Liquidity Risk

One of the implicit assumptions in risk management with VAR is that positions can be liquidated when they approach or move outside pre-agreed risk limits. In practice, some assets are far more liquid than others and practitioners will often liquidity-adjust VAR estimates accordingly. Wide bid–ask spreads in proportion to price are an obvious measure of the cost of trading an illiquid instrument or underlying security. But some instruments simply trade very infrequently at any price—a far more complex problem, because infrequently quoted prices often give the statistical illusion of low or lower volatility. This dynamic is counterintuitive, because we would expect instruments that are illiquid to have a higher bid–ask spread and higher volatilities.

A famous case of underestimating liquidity risk is the failure of the hedge fund Long-Term Capital Management (LTCM) in 1998. LTCM was set up by a group of bond traders and academics and was engaged in arbitrage or relative value trading on world fixed-income markets through the use of the swap market. The total equity in the fund peaked at around $5 billion, but this amount was leveraged around 25 times (perhaps substantially more when the full impact of derivatives is considered). The BIS estimated that the notional value of the swaps entered into by LTCM was around 2.4 percent of the entire world swap market. LTCM failed to appreciate the market moves that would occur when it attempted to liquidate positions, particularly those in illiquid, emerging, fixed-income markets. The New York Federal Reserve was forced to act for fear of a global financial crisis and organized a consortium of 14 international banks to manage the assets of the fund. In the end, and after substantial financial help, LTCM's investors lost more than 90 percent of their equity.

5.8 Measuring Nonfinancial Risks

Nonfinancial risks are intrinsically very difficult to measure. Indeed, some of the nonfinancial exposures we have discussed, such as regulatory risk, tax risk, legal risk, and accounting risk, could easily be thought of as not measurable in any precise mathematical way. They are unlike market risk and the VAR concept because we usually lack an observable distribution of losses related to these factors.

Some of these risks could be thought of as more suitable for insurance than measurement and hedging. Like a flood that occurs every 50 years, they might well affect a large number of instruments or contracts. Here, it is possible to learn from best practice in the insurance industry. Insurance companies usually have sufficient assets and are capitalized to withstand these uncertain events. Where it is possible to model a source of risk, actuaries often use techniques like extreme value theory, but even these techniques are only as good as the historical data on which they are based.

5.8.1 Operational Risk

Until a few years ago, the subject of operational risk received little attention, and ideas about actually measuring operational risk were practically unheard of. But a number of well-publicized losses at financial institutions, ranging from a breakdown of internal systems to rogue employees and in some cases employee theft, have put operational risk justifiably into the forefront.

Furthermore, the explicit mention of operational risk requirements in the Basel II banking regulations has created real advantages for banks that can credibly measure their operational risks. This, in turn, has led to an explosion in the academic literature relating to the measurement of operational risk and its role in enterprise risk systems.

EXAMPLE 9

Basel II—A Brief Overview

The Basel banking regulations apply only to large international banks, but national governments use them as a guideline in formulating their own financial laws and regulations, so the regulations have much more widespread importance. In January 2001, the Basel Committee on Banking Supervision issued a proposal for a New Basel Capital Accord that would replace the 1988 Capital Accord. This first accord, "Basel I," was widely criticized for being too inflexible in applying an across-the-board 8 percent capital adequacy ratio that made no discrimination between a well risk-managed bank and one that was not.[49]

The Basel II proposal incorporates three mutually reinforcing pillars that allow banks and supervisors to evaluate properly the various risks that banks face:

► Pillar 1: Capital Requirements
► Pillar 2: Supervisory Review
► Pillar 3: Market Discipline

The first pillar of Basel II moves away from a blanket, one-size-fits-all approach and allows banks to develop their own mathematically based financial models. Once these internally developed techniques have been successfully demonstrated to the regulators, banks are able to progress to higher levels of risk management that within the accord are offset by reduced regulatory capital charges. Key to these higher levels of risk management are advanced systems for managing credit risk and operational risk.

The second pillar, supervisory review, requires banks to meet Basel-recommended operational risk requirements that have been tailored by their host country. "Risky" banks, whose risk management systems score lowly in the areas of market risk and operational risk, face penalties. Better-risk-managed banks will have major competitive advantages over rivals, in that, all else equal, they are likely to be subject to reduced capital requirements per unit of risk.

The third pillar says that banks must fulfill the Basel requirements for transparency and disclosing company data. A key point here is that banks must reveal more detail about their profits and losses, which may lead to a supervisory authority reviewing risk systems and changing the capital allocation under the first pillar.

---

[49] A **capital adequacy ratio** is a measure of the adequacy of capital in relation to assets. The purpose of capital is to absorb unanticipated losses with sufficient margin to permit the entity to continue as a going concern. Basel I specified a capital adequacy ratio as a percent of the credit-risk-weighted assets on the bank's balance sheet, where bank assets were divided into four broad categories. For more details, see Saunders and Cornett (2003).

MANAGING RISK 6

Having established methods for the identification and measurement of risk, we turn our attention to a critical stage of any solid risk management program: that of *managing* risk. The key components, which by now should be somewhat intuitive to you, are as follows:

▶ An effective risk governance model, which places overall responsibility at the senior management level, allocates resources effectively and features the appropriate separation of tasks between revenue generators and those on the control side of the business.

▶ Appropriate systems and technology to combine information analysis in such a way as to provide timely and accurate risk information to decision makers.

▶ Sufficient and suitably trained personnel to evaluate risk information and articulate it to those who need this information for the purposes of decision making.

A recent advertisement for the RiskMetrics Group (www.riskmetrics.com) identified the following nine principles of effective risk management:

▶ There is no return without risk. Rewards go to those who take risks.

▶ Be transparent. Risk should be fully understood.

▶ Seek experience. Risk is measured and managed by people, not mathematical models.

▶ Know what you don't know. Question the assumptions you make.

▶ Communicate. Risk should be discussed openly.

▶ Diversify. Multiple risks will produce more consistent rewards.

▶ Show discipline. A consistent and rigorous approach will beat a constantly changing strategy.

▶ Use common sense. It is better to be approximately right than to be precisely wrong.

▶ Return is only half the equation. Decisions should be made only by considering the risk and return of the possibilities.

Risk management is in so many ways just good common business sense. It is quite remarkable, however, that commonsense rules are violated so easily and so often. But that problem is not unique to risk management.

Currently, two professional organizations are devoted to risk management. The Global Association of Risk Professionals (GARP) and the Professional Risk Managers' International Association (PRMIA) are actively involved in promoting knowledge in the field of risk management. You may wish to visit their Web sites at www.garp.com and www.prmia.org.

With these principles in mind, in the following section, we will discuss the various components of a well-adapted risk-control program.

6.1 Managing Market Risk

Let us assume we have correctly identified the sources of market risk that affect our business. Further assume that we have decided on an appropriate way to measure market risk and successfully deployed the systems we need to monitor our positions and measure our risk in a timely way. The result is an appropriate firmwide VAR estimate and associated breakdown by business area. Now we must ask ourselves the following questions: How do we know how much risk is acceptable for us to take? What is the overall exposure assumption capacity for the enterprise, and how close to full capacity should we run? We already know that VAR is not a measure of the maximum possible loss but only a probabilistic guide to the minimum loss we might expect with a certain frequency over a certain time frame.

Our **enterprise risk management** system will be incomplete without a well-thought-out approach to setting appropriate **risk tolerance** levels and identifying the proper corrective behavior to take if our actual risks turn out to be significantly higher or lower than is consistent with our risk tolerance. Note here that in many circumstances, it could cause as many problems to take too little risk as to take too much risk. As we noted at the beginning of this reading, companies are in business to take risk and taking too little risk will more than likely reduce the possible rewards; it could even make the company vulnerable to takeover. In a more extreme scenario, insufficient risk-taking may lead to situations in which the expected return stands little chance of covering variable (let alone fixed) costs.

Corrective behavior in the case of excessive market risk will almost always result in the need for additional hedging or the scaling back of tradable positions. Quite often, however, liquidity and other factors will prevent perfect hedging, perhaps exacerbating risk concerns rather than mitigating them.

6.1.1 Risk Budgeting

In recent years, companies and portfolio managers have begun to implement a new approach to risk management called **risk budgeting**. It focuses on questions such as, "Where do we want to take risk?" and "What is the efficient allocation of risk across various units of an organization or investment opportunities?" Risk budgeting is relevant in both an organizational and a portfolio management context.

To take an organizational perspective first, risk budgeting involves establishing objectives for individuals, groups, or divisions of an organization that take into account the allocation of an acceptable level of risk. As an example, the foreign exchange (FX) trading desk of a bank could be allocated capital of €100 million and permitted a daily VAR of €5 million. In other words, the desk is granted a budget, expressed in terms of allocated capital and an acceptable level of risk, expressed in euro amounts of VAR. In variations on this theme, instead of using VAR units an organization might allocate risk based on individual transaction size, the amount of working capital needed to support the portfolio, or the amount of losses acceptable for any given time period (e.g., one month). In any case, the innovation here is that the enterprise allocates risk capital before the fact in order to provide guidance on the acceptable amount of risky activities that a given unit can undertake.

A well-run risk-taking enterprise manages these limits carefully and constantly monitors their implementation. Any excesses are reported to management immediately for corrective action. Under this type of regime, management can compare the profits generated by each unit with the amount of capital and risk employed. So, to continue our example from above, say the FX trading desk made a quarterly profit of €20 million from its allocation. The bank's fixed-income trading desk was allocated capital of €200 million and permitted a daily

VAR of €5 million; the fixed-income trading desk made €25 million in quarterly trading profits. We note that the allocated daily VARs for the two business areas are the same, so each area has the same risk budget, and that the fixed-income desk generated better returns on the VAR allocation, but worse on the allocation of actual capital, than did the FX desk. (The FX desk shows a €20/€100 = 20% return on capital versus €25/€200 = 12.5% for the fixed-income desk.) This type of scenario is quite common and highlights the complexities of the interaction between risk management and capital allocation. Risk and capital are finite resources that must be allocated carefully.

The sum of risk budgets for individual units will typically exceed the risk budget for the organization as a whole because of the impacts of diversification. Returning to our example, let us assume that for the enterprise in question, its FX and bond trading desks engage in activities that are only weakly correlated. In this case, our present allocation of capital and risk might make perfect sense. For example, the daily VAR of the two business areas combined might be €7 million (i.e., 70 percent of the combined risk allocation for the two desks), for which we again generate a total quarterly profit of €20,000,000 + €25,000,000 = €45 million.

Alternatively, say the two business areas are very highly correlated (their correlation coefficient equals 1) and their combined daily VAR is €5,000,000 + €5,000,000 = €10 million (i.e., 100 percent of the aggregate VAR allocation across desks). The combined profit is still €20,000,000 + €25,000,000 = €45 million. Under these circumstances—and particularly if the bank's management believes that the correlations will remain strong—management might consider closing down the fixed-income desk to generate 0.20(€100,000,000 + €200,000,000) = €60 million of returns on the (€2,000,000)(€5,000,000) = €10 million of VAR. Contrast this strategy with that of closing down the foreign exchange trading desk and allocating all of the capital and risk to the bond trading desk, which would produce 0.125(€200,000,000 + €100,000,000) = €37.5 million in profit for the €10 million in VAR, representing a lower return on both capital and VAR.

A risk-budgeting perspective has also been applied to allocating funds to portfolio managers. Consider an active investor who wants to allocate funds optimally to several domestic and nondomestic equity and fixed-income investment managers. Such an investor might focus on tracking risk as the primary risk measure and decide on an overall maximum acceptable level for it, such as 200 basis points. The expected information ratio (IR) for each manager is one possible measure of each manager's ability to add value, considering the managers in isolation.[50] In this application, however, it is appropriate for the investor to adjust each manager's IR to eliminate the effect of asset class correlations; such correlation-adjusted IRs will capture each manager's incremental ability to add value in a portfolio context. Using such correlation-adjusted IRs, we can determine the optimal tracking risk allocation for each investment manager (which, intuitively, is positively related to his correlation-adjusted IR).[51]

Through these two examples, we edge toward some understanding of risk-adjusted performance measures, which we will discuss in greater detail later in the reading. The point about risk budgeting is that it is a comprehensive methodology that empowers management to allocate capital and risk in an optimal way to the

---

[50] The information ratio is active return divided by active risk; it measures active return per unit of active risk.

[51] See Waring, Whitney, Pirone, and Castile (2000) and references therein for further reading.

most profitable areas of a business, taking account of the correlation of returns in those business areas.

It once again bears mention that for many portfolio managers, risk budget allocations should be measured in relation to risk to the surplus—that is, the difference between the values of assets and liabilities.

EXAMPLE 10

A Fund Management Company and Risk Budgeting

We can readily illustrate the methodology and underlying economics of risk budgeting with the example of a fund management company. We choose, for this example, a multistrategy hedge fund, because although mutual funds and other types of institutional money managers certainly face similar risk management issues, they are often bound by strict guidelines that tie their risk budgeting to factors such as the performance of a benchmark index and other mandated fund management protocols. For example, the Vanguard family of mutual funds offers a wide range of indexed mutual funds. These funds' associated risk budgets are very narrowly defined, as the managers are called on at all times to track the underlying index very closely in terms of securities held, associated portfolio weightings, and so forth. As investor funds flow in and out of these securities, portfolio managers execute trades that do little more than reestablish this replication balance. Of course, many institutional fund products allow for much broader deviations from market benchmarks; in most cases, however, risk budgeting will be constrained by certain principles associated with benchmarking.

Hedge funds with multiple portfolio managers (as well as, in some cases, the proprietary trading divisions of banks and broker/dealers) have many fewer risk constraints than indexed mutual funds; they have more freedom, therefore, in establishing risk budgets. Because of the absolute return (as opposed to benchmark-driven) nature of their performance, and because of issues such as performance netting risk covered earlier in this reading, it is very much in their interest to ensure that each portfolio in the enterprise operates within a well-conceived risk budget framework. Included among the critical components of such a program might be the following:

▶ **Performance Stopouts** A performance stopout is the maximum amount that a given portfolio is allowed to lose in a period (e.g., a month or a year).

▶ **Working Capital Allocations** Most funds will allocate a specific amount of working capital to each portfolio manager, both as a means of enforcing risk disciplines and also to ensure the ability to fund all operations.

▶ **VAR Limits** Discussed above.

▶ **Scenario Analysis Limits** The risk manager of the fund company may establish risk limits based on the scenario analysis discussed in the preceding section. Under such an approach, the portfolio manager would be compelled to construct a portfolio such that under speci-

fied scenarios, it did not produce losses greater than certain predetermined amounts.

▶ **Risk Factor Limits** Portfolio managers may be subject to limits on
individual risk factors, as generated by a VAR analysis (e.g., VAR
exposure to a certain risk cannot exceed, say, $X or X%) or driven
by linear (e.g., duration, beta) or nonlinear (e.g., convexity, gamma)
risk estimation methodologies.

▶ **Position Concentration Limits** Many risk managers seek to enforce
diversification by mandating a specific maximum amount for individual positions.

▶ **Leverage Limits** A maximum amount of leverage in the portfolio
may be specified.

▶ **Liquidity Limits** To help manage liquidity exposure, large funds will
often also set position limits as a specified maximum percentage of
daily volume, float, or open interest.

Of course, other types of limits are imposed on portfolio managers
in a multistrategy environment, and by the same token, the risk-budgeting strategy of a given enterprise may include only a subset of the examples provided immediately above. Nevertheless, some subset of these
limit structures is present in nearly every multistrategy fund vehicle,
and it is difficult to imagine an effective risk control system that does not
set limits.

6.2 Managing Credit Risk

It is important that creditors do a good job of measuring and controlling credit
risk. Estimating default probabilities is difficult because of the infrequency of
losses for many situations where credit risk exists. Moreover, credit losses differ
considerably from losses resulting from market moves. Credit is a one-sided risk.
If Party B owes Party A the amount of £1,000, B will end up paying A either
£1,000 or some amount ranging from zero to £1,000. A's rate of return is certainly not normally distributed and not even symmetric. All of the risk is downside. Thus credit risk is not easily analyzed or controlled using such measures as
standard deviation and VAR. Creditors need to regularly monitor the financial
condition of borrowers and counterparties. In addition, they can use the risk
management techniques for credit discussed below.

6.2.1 Reducing Credit Risk by Limiting Exposure

Limiting the amount of exposure to a given party is the primary means of managing credit risk. Just as a bank will not lend too much money to one entity, neither will a party engage in too many derivatives transactions with one
counterparty. Exactly how much exposure to a given counterparty is "too much"
is still not easy to quantify. Experienced risk managers often have a good sense of
when and where to limit their exposure, and they make extensive use of quantitative credit exposure measures to guide them in this process. Banks have regulatory constraints on the amount of credit risk they can assume, which are
specified in terms of formulas.

6.2.2 Reducing Credit Risk by Marking to Market

One device that the futures market uses to control credit risk is marking tradable positions to market. The OTC derivatives market also uses **marking to market** to deal with credit risk: Some OTC contracts are marked to market periodically during their lives. Recall that a forward contract or swap has a market value that is positive to one party and negative to another. When a contract calls for marking to market, the party for which the value is negative pays the market value to the party for which the value is positive. Then the fixed rate on the contract is recalculated, taking into account the new spot price, interest rate, and time to expiration.

Recall that we examined a one-year forward contract with an initial forward price of $105. Three months later, when the asset price was $102, its value was $0.7728 to the long. If the contract were marked to market at that time, the short would pay the long $0.7728. Then, the two parties would enter into a new contract expiring in nine months with a new forward price, which would be $102(1.05)^{0.75} = $105.80.

EXAMPLE 11

Repricing a Forward Contract

Consider a one-year forward contract established at a rate of $105. The contract is four months into its life. The spot price is $108, the risk-free rate is 4.25 percent, and the underlying makes no cash payments. The two parties decided at the start that they will mark the contract to market every four months. The market value of the contract is $108 − $105/(1.0425)^{8/12} = $5.873. Determine how the cash flows and resets would work under these circumstances.

Solution: The contract is positive to the long, so the short pays the long $5.873. The parties then reprice the contract. The new price is $108(1.0425)^{8/12} = $111.04. At this point, the forward price is reset to $111.04. The parties will then mark to market again at the eight-month point and reset the forward price. This price will then stay in force until expiration.

OTC options usually are not marked to market because their value is always positive to one side of the transaction. Of course, one party of the option certainly bears credit risk, but marking to market is usually done only with contracts with two-way credit risk. Option credit risk is normally handled by collateral.

6.2.3 Reducing Credit Risk with Collateral

The posting of collateral is a widely accepted credit exposure mitigant in both lending and derivatives transactions. One very prominent example of its use comes from futures markets, which require that all market participants post margin collateral. Beyond this, many OTC derivative markets have collateral posting provisions, with the collateral usually taking the form of cash or highly liquid, low-risk securities. A typical arrangement involves the routine, periodic posting of values sufficient to cover mark-to-market deficiencies. To illustrate, if a given derivatives contract has a positive value to Party A and a negative value to Party B, then Party B owes more than Party A, and Party B must put collateral into an account designated for this purpose. As the contract's market value changes, the amount of collateral that must be maintained will vary, increasing as the market value increases and vice versa. At some point, if the market value of the transaction changes sign (i.e., goes from positive to negative for one of the participants), the collateral position will typically reverse itself, with the entity previously posting collateral seeing a release of these assets and the other participant in the transaction experiencing a collateral obligation. In addition to market values, collateral requirements are sometimes also based on factors such as participants' credit ratings.

6.2.4 Reducing Credit Risk with Netting

One of the most common features used in two-way contracts with a credit risk component, such as forwards and swaps, is netting. This process, which we have already briefly discussed, involves the reduction of all obligations owed between counterparties into a single cash transaction that eliminates these liabilities. For example, if a payment is due and Party A owes more to Party B than B owes to A, the difference between the amounts owed is calculated and Party A pays the net amount owed. This procedure, called **payment netting**, reduces the credit risk by reducing the amount of money that must be paid. If Party A owes €100,000 to Party B, which owes €40,000 to A, then the net amount owed is €60,000, which A owes to B. Without netting, B would need to send €40,000 to A, which would send €100,000 to B. Suppose B was in the process of sending its €40,000 to A but was unaware that A was in default and unable to send the €100,000 to B. If the €40,000 is received by A, B might be unable to get it back until the bankruptcy court decides what to do, which could take years. Using netting, only the €60,000 owed by A to B is at risk.

In the examples we have seen so far, netting is applied on the payment date. The concept of netting can be extended to the events and conditions surrounding a bankruptcy. Suppose A and B are counterparties to a number of derivative contracts. On some of the contracts, the market value to A is positive, while on others, the market value to B is positive. If A declares bankruptcy, the parties can use netting to solve a number of problems. If A and B agree to do so before the bankruptcy, they can net the market values of *all* of their derivative contracts to determine one overall value owed by one party to another. It could well be the case that even though A is bankrupt, B might owe more to A than A owes to B. Then, rather than B being a creditor to A, A's claim on B becomes one of A's remaining assets. This process is referred to as **closeout netting**.

During this bankruptcy process, netting plays an important role in reducing a practice known in the financial services industry as cherry picking, which in this case would involve a bankrupt company attempting to enforce contracts that are favorable to it while walking away from those that are unprofitable. In our example, without netting, A could default on the contracts in which it owes more to B than B owes to A, but B could be forced to pay up on those contracts in which it owes more to A than A owes to B.

To be supported through the bankruptcy process, however, netting must be recognized by the legal system and works best when each party's rights and obligations are specified at the time before or contemporaneous to the executions of transactions. Most, but not all, legal jurisdictions recognize netting.

6.2.5 Reducing Credit Risk with Minimum Credit Standards and Enhanced Derivative Product Companies

As noted above, the first line of defense against credit risk is limiting the amount of business one party engages in with another. An important and related concept is to ensure that all credit-based business is undertaken with entities that have adequate levels of credit quality. The historical standard measures for such credit quality come from rating agencies such as Moody's Investors Service and Standard & Poor's. Some companies will not do business with an enterprise unless its rating from these agencies meets a prescribed level of credit quality. This practice can pose a problem for some **derivatives dealers**, most of which engage in other lines of business that expose them to a variety of other risks; for example, banks are the most common derivatives dealers. To an end user considering engaging in a derivative contract with a dealer, the potential for the dealer's other business to cause the dealer to default is a serious concern. Banks, in particular, are involved in consumer and commercial lending, which can be quite risky. In the United States, for example, we have seen banking crises involving bad loans to the real estate industry and underdeveloped countries.

The possibility that bad loans will cause a bank to default on its derivatives transactions is quite real, and credit ratings often reflect this possibility. In turn, ratings are a major determinant in business flows for banks that act as dealers. Hence, many derivatives dealers have taken action to control their exposure to rating downgrades. One such action is the formation of a type of subsidiary that is separate from the dealer's other activities. These subsidiaries are referred to as **enhanced derivatives products companies** (EDPCs), sometimes known as **special purpose vehicles** (SPVs). These companies are usually completely separate from the parent organization and are not liable for the parent's debts. They tend to be very heavily capitalized and are committed to hedging all of their derivatives positions. As a result of these features, these subsidiaries almost always receive the highest credit quality rating by the rating agencies. In the event that the parent goes bankrupt, the EDPC is not liable for the parent company's debts; if the EDPC goes under, however, the parent is liable for an amount up to its equity investment and may find it necessary to provide even more protection. Hence, an EDPC would typically have a higher credit rating than its parent. In fact, it is precisely for the purpose of obtaining the highest credit rating, and thus the most favorable financing terms with counterparties, that banks and broker dealers go through the expense of putting together EDPCs.

6.2.6 Transferring Credit Risk with Credit Derivatives

Another mechanism for managing credit risk is to transfer it to another party. Credit derivatives provide mechanisms for such transfers. Credit derivatives include such contracts as credit default swaps, total return swaps, credit spread options, and credit spread forwards. These transactions are typically customized, although the wording of contract provisions is often standardized. In a **credit default swap**, the protection buyer pays the protection seller in return for the right to receive a payment from the seller in the event of a specified credit event. In a **total return swap**, the protection buyer pays the total return on a reference obligation (or basket of reference obligations) in return for floating-rate payments. If the reference obligation has a credit event, the total return on the reference obligation should fall; the total return should also fall in the event of an increase in interest rates, so the protection seller (total return receiver) in this contract is actually exposed to both credit risk and interest rate risk. A **credit spread option** is an option on the yield spread of a reference obligation and over a referenced benchmark (such as the yield on a specific default-free security of the same maturity); by contrast, a **credit spread forward** is a forward contract on a yield spread. Credit derivatives may be used not only to eliminate credit risk but also to assume credit risk. For example, an investor may be well positioned to assume a credit risk because it is uncorrelated with other credit risks in her portfolio.[52]

6.3 Performance Evaluation

In order to maximize risk-adjusted return through the capital allocation process, we must measure performance against risks assumed and budgeted at both the business unit or substrategy level and enterprise or overall portfolio level. All business activities should be evaluated against the risk taken, and a considerable body of knowledge has developed concerning the evaluation of investment performance from a risk-adjusted perspective. Traditional approaches, which take into account return against a risk penalty, are now used in other areas of business activity besides portfolio management. Some banks and service providers have developed sophisticated performance evaluation systems that account for risk, and they have marketed these systems successfully to clients. Risk-adjusted performance, as measured against sensible benchmarks, is a critically important capital allocation tool because it allows for the comparison of results in terms of homogenous units of exposure assumption. Absent these measurement tools, market participants with high risk profiles are likely to be given higher marks for positive performance than they arguably deserve because they derive more from increased exposure assumption than they do from superior portfolio management methodologies. Furthermore, most investment professionals are compensated on the basis of the performance of their portfolios, trading positions, or investment ideas, and it is appropriate to judge performance in risk-adjusted terms.

Following is a list of standard methodologies for expressing return in units of exposure assumption:

▶ **Sharpe Ratio** The seminal measure for risk-adjusted return, the Sharpe Ratio has become the industry standard. The traditional definition of this measure is as follows:[53]

$$\text{Sharpe ratio} = \frac{\text{Mean portfolio return} - \text{Risk-free rate}}{\text{Standard deviation of portfolio return}}$$

The basic idea, therefore, is entirely intuitive: The Sharpe ratio is the mean return earned in excess of the risk-free rate per unit of volatility or total risk. By subtracting a risk-free rate from the mean return, we can isolate the performance associated with risk-taking activities. One elegant outcome of the calculation is that a portfolio engaging in

---

[52] For more information on credit derivatives, see Fabozzi (2004b), Chapter 9, and Chance (2003), Chapter 9.

[53] This traditional definition of the Sharpe ratio can be directly linked to the capital market line and related capital market theory concepts (see Elton, Gruber, Brown, and Goetzmann, 2003). Sharpe (1994), however, defines the Sharpe ratio as a general construct using the mean excess return in relation to a benchmark in the numerator and the standard deviation of returns in excess of the benchmark in the denominator (see the discussion of the information ratio in the reading on evaluating portfolio performance for an illustration of this usage). Using the risk-free rate as the benchmark, the numerator would be as given in the text but the denominator would be the standard deviation of returns in excess of the risk-free rate (which, in practice, would infrequently result in significant discrepancies).

"zero risk" investment, such as the purchase of Treasury bills for which the expected return is precisely the risk-free rate, earns a Sharpe ratio of exactly zero.

The Sharpe ratio calculation is the most widely used method for calculating risk-adjusted return. Nevertheless, it can be inaccurate when applied to portfolios with significant nonlinear risks, such as options positions. In part for these reasons, alternative risk-adjusted return methodologies have emerged over the years, including the following.

▶ **Risk-Adjusted Return on Capital (RAROC)** This concept divides the expected return on an investment by a measure of capital at risk, a measure of the investment's risk that can take a number of different forms and can be calculated in a variety of ways that may have proprietary features. The company may require that an investment's expected RAROC exceed a RAROC benchmark level for capital to be allocated to it.[54]

▶ **Return over Maximum Drawdown (RoMAD)** Drawdown, in the field of hedge fund management, is defined as the difference between a portfolio's maximum point of return (known in industry parlance as its "high-water" mark), and any subsequent low point of performance. *Maximum* drawdown is the largest difference between a high-water and a subsequent low. Maximum drawdown is a preferred way of expressing the risk of a given portfolio—particularly as associated track records become longer—for investors who believe that observed loss patterns over longer periods of time are the best available proxy for actual exposure.

Return over maximum drawdown is simply the average return in a given year that a portfolio generates, expressed as a percentage of this drawdown figure. It enables investors to ask the following question: Am I willing to accept an occasional drawdown of X percent in order to generate an average return of Y percent? An investment with $X = 10$ percent and $Y = 15$ percent (RoMAD = 1.5) would be more attractive than an investment with $X = 40$ percent and $Y = 10$ percent (RoMAD = 0.25).

▶ **Sortino Ratio** One school of thought concerning the measurement of risk-adjusted returns argues, with some justification, that portfolio managers should not be penalized for volatility deriving from outsized positive performance. The Sortino ratio adopts this perspective. The numerator of the Sortino ratio is the return in excess of the investor's minimum acceptable return (MAR). The denominator is the downside deviation using the MAR as the target return.[55] **Downside deviation** computes volatility using only rate of return data points below the MAR. Thus the expression for the Sortino ratio is

Sortino ratio = (Mean portfolio return − MAR)/Downside deviation

If the MAR is set at the risk-free rate, the Sortino ratio is identical to the Sharpe ratio, save for the fact that it uses downside deviation instead of the standard deviation in the denominator. A side-by-side comparison of rankings of portfolios according to the Sharpe and Sortino ratios can provide a sense of whether outperformance may be affecting assessments of risk-adjusted performance. Taken together, the two ratios can tell a more

---

[54] For more information on RAROC, see Saunders and Cornett (2003).

[55] Downside deviation, the term usually used in presenting the Sortino ratio, could also be called a target semideviation (using MAR as the target).

detailed story of risk-adjusted return than either will in isolation, but the Sharpe ratio is better grounded in financial theory and analytically more tractable. Furthermore, departures from normality of returns can raise issues for the Sortino ratio as much as for the Sharpe ratio.

These approaches are only a subset of the methodologies available to investors wishing to calculate risk-adjusted returns. Each approach has both its merits and its drawbacks. Perhaps the most important lesson to bear in mind with respect to this mosaic is the critical need to understand the inputs to any method, so as to be able to interpret the results knowledgeably, with an understanding of their possible limitations.

6.4 Capital Allocation

In addition to its unquestionable value in the task of capital preservation, risk management has become a vital, if not central, component in the process of allocating capital across units of a risk-taking enterprise. The use of inputs, such as volatility/correlation analysis, risk-adjusted return calculations, scenario analysis, etc., provides the allocators of risk capital with a much more informed means of arriving at the appropriate conclusions on how best to distribute this scarce resource. The risk management inputs to the process can be used in formal, mathematical, "optimization" routines, under which enterprises input performance data into statistical programs that will then offer appropriate capital allocation combinations to make efficient use of risk. Quantitative output may simply serve as background data for qualitative decision-making processes. One way or another, however, risk management has become a vital input into the capital allocation process, and it is fair to describe this development as positive from a systemic perspective.

As part of the task of allocating capital across business units, organizations must determine how to measure such capital. Here there are multiple methodologies, and we will discuss five of them in further detail:

1. **Nominal, Notional, or Monetary Position Limits** Under this approach, the enterprise simply defines the amount of capital that the individual portfolio or business unit can use in a specified activity, based on the actual amount of money exposed in the markets. It has the advantage of being easy to understand, and, in addition, it lends itself very nicely to the critical task of calculating a percentage-based return on capital allocated. Such limits, however, may not capture effectively the effects of correlation and offsetting risks. Furthermore, an individual may be able to work around a nominal position using other assets that can replicate a given position. For these reasons, although it is often useful to establish notional position limits, it is seldom a *sufficient* capital allocation method from a risk control perspective.

2. **VAR-Based Position Limits** As an alternative or supplement to notional limits, enterprises often assign a VAR limit as a proxy for allocated capital. This approach has a number of distinct advantages, most notably the fact that it allocates capital in units of estimated exposure and thus acts in greater harmony with the risk control process. This approach has potential problems as well, however. Most notably, the limit regime will be only as effective as the VAR calculation itself; when VAR is cumbersome, less than completely accurate, not well understood by traders, or some combination of the above, it is difficult to imagine it providing rational results from a capital

allocation perspective. In addition, the relation between overall VAR and the VARs of individual positions is complex and can be counterintuitive.[56] Nevertheless, VAR limits probably have an important place in any effective capital allocation scheme.

3. **Maximum Loss Limits** Irrespective of other types of limit regimes that it might have in place, it is crucial for any risk-taking enterprise to establish a maximum loss limit for each of its risk-taking units. In order to be effective, this figure must be large enough to enable the unit to achieve performance objectives but small enough to be consistent with the preservation of capital. This limit must represent a firm constraint on risk-taking activity. Nevertheless, even when risk-taking activity is generally in line with policy, management should recognize that extreme market discontinuities can cause such limits to be breached.

4. **Internal Capital Requirements** Internal capital requirements specify the level of capital that management believes to be appropriate for the firm. Some regulated financial institutions, such as banks and securities firms, typically also have regulatory capital requirements that, if they are higher, overrule internal requirements. Traditionally, internal capital requirements have been specified heuristically in terms of the capital ratio (the ratio of capital to assets). Modern tools permit a more rigorous approach. If the value of assets declines by an amount that exceeds the value of capital, the firm will be insolvent. Say a 0.01 probability of insolvency over a one-year horizon is acceptable. By requiring capital to equal at least one-year aggregate VAR at the 1 percent probability level, the capital should be adequate in terms of the firm's risk tolerance. If the company can assume a normal return distribution, the required amount of capital can be stated in standard deviation units (e.g., 1.96 standard deviations would reflect a 0.025 probability of insolvency). A capital requirement based on aggregate VAR has an advantage over regulatory capital requirements in that it takes account of correlations. Furthermore, to account for extraordinary shocks, we can stress test the VAR-based recommendation.

5. **Regulatory Capital Requirements** In addition, many institutions (e.g., securities firms and banks) must calculate and meet regulatory capital requirements. Wherever and whenever this is the case, it of course makes sense to allocate this responsibility to business units. Meeting regulatory capital requirements can be a difficult process, among other reasons because such requirements are sometimes inconsistent with rational capital allocation schemes that have capital preservation as a primary objective. Nevertheless, when regulations demand it, firms must include regulatory capital as part of their overall allocation process.

Depending on such factors as the type of enterprise, its corporate culture, fiduciary obligations, etc., the most effective approach to capital allocation probably involves a combination of most, if not all, of the above methodologies. The trick, of course, is to combine the appropriate ones in a rational and consistent manner that creates the proper incentives for balance between the dual objectives of profit maximization and capital preservation.

---

[56] For example, one cannot add the VAR of individual positions to obtain a conservative measure (i.e., maximum) of overall VAR because it is possible for the sum of the VARs to be greater than the VAR of the combined positions.

6.5 Psychological and Behavioral Considerations

Over the past several years, a body of research has emerged that seeks to model the behavioral aspects of portfolio management. This concept has important implications for risk management for two reasons. First, risk takers may behave differently at different points in the portfolio management cycle, depending on such factors as their recent performance, the risk characteristics of their portfolios, and market conditions. Second, and on a related note, risk management would improve if these dynamics could be modeled.

Although the topic merits more discussion than we can possibly include in this context, the main factor to consider from a risk management perspective is the importance of establishing a risk governance framework that anticipates the points in a cycle when the incentives of risk takers diverge from those of risk capital allocators. One prominent example (although by no means the only one) occurs when portfolio managers who are paid a percentage of their profits in a given year fall into a negative performance situation. The trader's situation does not deteriorate from a compensation perspective with incremental losses at this point (i.e., the trader is paid zero, no matter how much he loses), but of course the organization as a whole suffers from the trader's loss. Moreover, the risks at the enterprise level can be nonlinear under these circumstances because of concepts of netting risk covered earlier in this reading. These and other behavioral issues can be handled best by risk control and governance processes that contemplate them. One such example is limit setting, which can, with some thought, easily incorporate many of these issues.[57]

---

[57] Those interested in studying these topics further may wish to refer to Grant (2004) and Kiev (2002).

SUMMARY

Financial markets reward competence and knowledge in risk management and punish mistakes. Portfolio managers must therefore study and understand the discipline of successful risk management. In this reading, we have introduced basic concepts and techniques of risk management and made the following points:

▶ Risk management is a process involving the identification of the exposures to risk, the establishment of appropriate ranges for exposures, the continuous measurement of these exposures, and the execution of appropriate adjustments to bring the actual level and desired level of risk into alignment. The process involves continuous monitoring of exposures and new policies, preferences, and information.

▶ Typically, risks should be minimized wherever and whenever companies lack comparative advantages in the associated markets, activities, or lines of business.

▶ Risk governance refers to the process of setting risk management policies and standards for an organization. Senior management, which is ultimately responsible for all organizational activities, must oversee the process.

▶ Enterprise risk management is a centralized risk management system whose distinguishing feature is a firmwide or across-enterprise perspective on risk.

▶ Financial risk refers to all risks derived from events in the external financial markets. Nonfinancial risk refers to all other forms of risk. Financial risk includes market risk (risk related to interest rates, exchange rates, stock prices, and commodity prices), credit risk, and liquidity risk. The primary sources of nonfinancial risk are operations risk, model risk, settlement risk, regulatory risk, legal risk, tax risk, and accounting risk.

▶ Traditional measures of market risk include linear approximations such as beta for stocks, duration for fixed income, and delta for options, as well as second-order estimation techniques such as convexity and gamma. For products with option-like characteristics, techniques exist to measure the impact of changes in volatility (vega) and the passage of time (theta). Sensitivity to movements in the correlation among assets is also relevant for certain types of instruments.

▶ Value at risk (VAR) estimates the minimum loss that a party would expect to experience with a given probability over a specified period of time. Using the complementary probability (i.e., 100 percent minus the given probability stated as a percent), VAR can be expressed as a maximum loss at a given confidence level. VAR users must make decisions regarding appropriate time periods, confidence intervals, and specific VAR methodologies.

▶ The analytical or variance–covariance method can be used to determine VAR under the assumption that returns are normally distributed by subtracting a multiple of the standard deviation from the expected return, where the multiple is determined by the desired probability level. The advantage of the method is its simplicity. Its disadvantages are that returns are not normally distributed in any reliable sense and that the method does not work well when portfolios contain options and other derivatives.

▶ The historical method estimates VAR from data on a portfolio's performance during a historical period. The returns are ranked, and VAR is obtained by determining the return that is exceeded in a negative sense

5 percent or 1 percent (depending on the user's choice) of the time. The historical method has the advantage of being simple and not requiring the assumption of a normal distribution. Its disadvantage is that accurate historical time-series information is not always easily available, particularly for instruments such as bonds and options, which behave differently at different points in their life spans.

▶ Monte Carlo simulation estimates VAR by generating random returns and determining the 5 percent or 1 percent (depending on the user's choice) worst outcomes. It has the advantages that it does not require a normal distribution and can handle complex relationships among risks. Its disadvantage is that it can be very time consuming and costly to conduct the large number of simulations required for accuracy. It also requires the estimation of input values, which can be difficult.

▶ VAR can be difficult to estimate, can give a wide range of values, and can lead to a false sense of security that risk is accurately measured and under control. VAR for individual positions do not generally aggregate in a simple way to portfolio VAR. VAR also puts all emphasis on the negative outcomes, ignoring the positive outcomes. It can be difficult to calculate VAR for a large complex organization with many exposures. On the other hand, VAR is a simple and easy-to-understand risk measure that is widely accepted. It is also adaptable to a variety of uses, such as allocating capital.

▶ Incremental VAR measures the incremental effect of an asset on the VAR of a portfolio. Cash flow at risk and earnings at risk measure the risk to a company's cash flow or earnings instead of market value, as in the case of VAR. Tail value at risk is VAR plus the expected loss in excess of VAR, when such excess loss occurs. Stress testing is another important supplement to VAR.

▶ Credit risk has two dimensions, the probability of default and the associated recovery rate.

▶ Credit risk in a forward contract is assumed by the party to which the market value is positive. The market value represents the current value of the claim that one party has on the other. The actual payoff at expiration could differ, but the market value reflects the current value of that future claim.

▶ Credit risk in swaps is similar to credit risk in forward contracts. The market value represents the current value of the claim on the future payments. The party holding the positive market value assumes the credit risk at that time. For interest rate and equity swaps, credit risk is greatest near the middle of the life of the swap. For currency swaps with payment of notional principal, credit risk is greatest near the end of the life of the swap.

▶ Credit risk in options is one-sided. Because the seller is paid immediately and in full, she faces no credit risk. By contrast, the buyer faces the risk that the seller will not meet her obligations in the event of exercise. The market value of the option is the current value of the future claim the buyer has on the seller.

▶ VAR can be used to measure credit risk. The interpretation is the same as with standard VAR, but a credit-based VAR is more complex because it must interact with VAR based on market risk. Credit risk arises only when market risk results in gains to trading. Credit VAR must take into account the complex interaction of market movements, the possibility of default, and recovery rates. Credit VAR is also difficult to aggregate across markets and counterparties.

► Risk budgeting is the process of establishing policies to allocate the finite resource of risk capacity to business units that must assume exposure in order to generate return. Risk budgeting has also been applied to allocation of funds to investment managers.

► The various methods of controlling credit risk include setting exposure limits for individual counterparties, exchanging cash values that reflect mark-to-market levels, posting collateral, netting, setting minimum credit, using special-purpose vehicles that have higher credit ratings than the companies that own them, and using credit derivatives.

► Among the measures of risk-adjusted performance that have been used in a portfolio context are the Sharpe ratio, risk-adjusted return on capital, return over maximum drawdown, and the Sortino ratio. The Sharpe ratio uses standard deviation, measuring total risk as the risk measure. Risk-adjusted return on capital accounts for risk using capital at risk. The Sortino ratio measures risk using downside deviation, which computes volatility using only rate-of-return data points below a minimum acceptable return. Return over maximum drawdown uses maximum drawdown as a risk measure.

► Methods for allocating capital include nominal position limits, VAR-based position limits, maximum loss limits, internal capital requirements, and regulatory capital requirements.

PRACTICE PROBLEMS FOR READING 37

1. Discuss the difference between centralized and decentralized risk management systems, including the advantages and disadvantages of each.

2. Stewart Gilchrist follows the automotive industry, including Ford Motor Company. Based on Ford's 2003 annual report, Gilchrist writes the following summary:

   Ford Motor Company has businesses in several countries around the world. Ford frequently has expenditures and receipts denominated in non-U.S. currencies, including purchases and sales of finished vehicles and production parts, subsidiary dividends, investments in non-U.S. operations, etc. Ford uses a variety of commodities in the production of motor vehicles, such as non-ferrous metals, precious metals, ferrous alloys, energy, and plastics/resins. Ford typically purchases these commodities from outside suppliers. To finance its operations, Ford uses a variety of funding sources, such as commercial paper, term debt, and lines of credit from major commercial banks. The company invests any surplus cash in securities of various types and maturities, the value of which are subject to fluctuations in interest rates. Ford has a credit division, which provides financing to customers wanting to purchase Ford's vehicles on credit. Overall, Ford faces several risks. To manage some of its risks, Ford invests in fixed-income instruments and derivative contracts. Some of these investments do not rely on a clearing house and instead effect settlement through the execution of bilateral agreements.

   Based on the above discussion, recommend and justify the risk exposures that should be reported as part of an Enterprise Risk Management System for Ford Motor Company.

3. NatWest Markets (NWM) was the investment banking arm of National Westminster Bank, one of the largest banks in the United Kingdom. On 28 February 1997, NWM revealed that a substantial loss had been uncovered in its trading books. During the 1990s, NatWest was engaged in trading interest rate options and swaptions on several underlying currencies. This trading required setting appropriate prices of the options by the traders at NatWest. A key parameter in setting the price of an interest rate option is the implied volatility of the underlying asset—that is, the interest rate on a currency. In contrast to other option parameters that affect the option prices, such as duration to maturity and exercise price, implied volatility is not directly observable and must be estimated. Many option pricing models imply that the implied volatility should be the same for all options on the same underlying, irrespective of their exercise price or maturity. In practice, however, implied volatility is often observed to have a curvilinear relationship with the option's moneyness (i.e., whether the option is out of the money, at the money, or in the money), a relationship sometimes called the *volatility smile*. Implied volatility tended to be higher for out-of-the-money options than for at-the-money options on the same underlying.

   NWM prices on certain contracts tended to consistently undercut market prices, as if the out-of-the money options were being quoted at implied volatilities that were too low. When trading losses mounted in an interest rate option contract, a trader undertook a series of off-market-price transactions between the options portfolio and a swaptions portfolio to transfer the losses to a type of contract where losses were easier to conceal. A subsequent investigation revealed that the back office did not independently value the trading positions in question and that lapses in trade reconciliation had occurred.

What type or types of risk were inadequately managed in the above case?

4. Sue Ellicott supervises the trading function at an asset management firm. In conducting an in-house risk management training session for traders, Ellicott elicits the following statements from traders:

► Trader 1: "Liquidity risk is not a major concern for buyers of a security as opposed to sellers."

► Trader 2: "In general, derivatives can be used to substantially reduce the liquidity risk of a security."

Ellicott and the traders then discuss two recent cases of a similar risk exposure in an identical situation that one trader (Trader A) hedged and another trader (Trader B) assumed as a speculation. A participant in the discussion makes the following statement concerning the contrasting treatment:

► Trader 3: "Our traders have considerable experience and expertise in analyzing the risk, and this risk is related to our business. Trader B was justified in speculating on the risk within the limits of his risk allocation."

State and justify whether each trader's statement is correct or incorrect.

5. A large trader on the government bond desk of a major bank loses €20 million in a year, in the process reducing the desk's overall profit to €10 million. Senior management, on looking into the problem, determines that the trader repeatedly violated his position limits during the year. They also determine that the bulk of the loss took place in the last two weeks of the year, when the trader increased his position dramatically and experienced 80 percent of his negative performance. The bank dismisses both the trader and his desk manager. The bank has an asymmetric incentive compensation contract arrangement with its traders.

A. Discuss the performance netting risk implications of this scenario.

B. Are there any reasons why the timing of the loss is particularly significant?

C. What mistakes did senior management make? Explain how these errors can be corrected.

6. Ford Credit is the branch of Ford Motor Company that provides financing to Ford's customers. For this purpose, it obtains funding from various sources. As a result of its interest rate risk management process, including derivatives, Ford Credit's debt reprices faster than its assets. This situation means that when interest rates are rising, the interest rates paid on Ford Credit's debt will increase more rapidly than the interest rates earned on assets, thereby initially reducing Ford Credit's pretax net interest income. The reverse will be true when interest rates decline.

Ford's annual report provides a quantitative measure of the sensitivity of Ford Credit's pretax net interest income to changes in interest rates. For this purpose, it uses interest rate scenarios that assume a hypothetical, instantaneous increase or decrease in interest rates of 1 percentage point across all maturities. These scenarios are compared with a base case that assumes that interest rates remain constant at existing levels. The differences between the scenarios and the base case over a 12-month period represent an estimate of the sensitivity of Ford Credit's pretax net interest income. This sensitivity as of year-end 2003 and 2002 is as follows:

	Pretax Net Interest Income Impact Given a One Percentage Point Instantaneous *Increase* in Interest Rates (in millions)	Pretax Net Interest Income Impact Given a One Percentage Point Instantaneous *Decrease* in Interest Rates (in millions)
December 31, 2003	($179)	$179
December 31, 2002	($153)	$156

Source: Annual Report of Ford Motor Company, 2003.

Describe the strengths and weaknesses of the interest rate risk analysis presented in the foregoing table.

7. A. An organization's risk management function has computed that a portfolio held in one business unit has a 1 percent weekly value at risk (VAR) of £4.25 million. Describe what is meant in terms of a minimum loss.

B. The portfolio of another business unit has a 99 percent weekly VAR of £4.25 million (stated using a confidence limit approach). Describe what is meant in terms of a maximum loss.

8. Each of the following statements about VAR is true *except:*

A. VAR is the loss that would be exceeded with a given probability over a specific time period.

B. Establishing a VAR involves several decisions, such as the probability and time period over which the VAR will be measured and the technique to be used.

C. VAR will be larger when it is measured at 5 percent probability than when it is measured at 1 percent probability.

D. VAR will be larger when it is measured over a month than when it is measured over a day.

9. Suppose you are given the following sample probability distribution of annual returns on a portfolio with a market value of $10 million.

Return on Portfolio	Probability
Less than −50%	0.005
−50% to −40%	0.005
−40% to −30%	0.010
−30% to −20%	0.015
−20% to −10%	0.015
−10% to −5%	0.165
−5% to 0%	0.250
0% to 5%	0.250
5% to 10%	0.145
10% to 20%	0.075
20% to 30%	0.025
30% to 40%	0.020
40% to 50%	0.015
Greater than 50%	0.005
	1.000

Based on this probability distribution, determine the following:

A. 1 percent yearly VAR

B. 5 percent yearly VAR

10. An analyst would like to know the VAR for a portfolio consisting of two asset classes: long-term government bonds issued in the United States and long-term government bonds issued in the United Kingdom. The expected monthly return on U.S. bonds is 0.85 percent, and the standard deviation is 3.20 percent. The expected monthly return on U.K. bonds, in U.S. dollars, is 0.95 percent, and the standard deviation is 5.26 percent. The correlation between the U.S. dollar returns of U.K. and U.S. bonds is 0.35. The portfolio market value is $100 million and is equally weighted between the two asset classes. Using the analytical or variance–covariance method, compute the following:

A. 5 percent monthly VAR

B. 1 percent monthly VAR

C. 5 percent weekly VAR

D. 1 percent weekly VAR

11. You invested $25,000 in the stock of Dell Computer Corporation in early 2002. You have compiled the monthly returns on Dell's stock during the 1997–2001 period, as given below.

1997	1998	1999	2000	2001
0.2447	0.1838	0.3664	−0.2463	0.4982
0.0756	0.4067	−0.1988	0.0618	−0.1627
−0.0492	−0.0313	0.0203	0.3216	0.1743
0.2375	0.1919	0.0077	−0.0707	0.0215
0.3443	0.0205	−0.1639	−0.1397	−0.0717
0.0439	0.1263	0.0744	0.1435	0.0735
0.4561	0.1700	0.1047	−0.1090	0.0298
−0.0402	−0.0791	0.1942	−0.0071	−0.2061
0.1805	0.3150	−0.1434	−0.2937	−0.1333
−0.1729	−0.0038	−0.0404	−0.0426	0.2941
0.0507	−0.0716	0.0717	−0.3475	0.1647
−0.0022	0.2035	0.1861	−0.0942	−0.0269

Using the historical method, compute the following:

A. 5 percent monthly VAR

B. 1 percent monthly VAR

12. Consider a $10 million portfolio of stocks. You perform a Monte Carlo simulation to estimate the VAR for this portfolio. You choose to perform this simulation using a normal distribution of returns for the portfolio, with an expected annual return of 14.8 percent and a standard deviation of 20.5 percent. You generate 700 random outcomes of annual return for this portfolio, of which the worst 40 outcomes are given below.

−0.400	−0.320	−0.295	−0.247
−0.398	−0.316	−0.282	−0.233
−0.397	−0.314	−0.277	−0.229
−0.390	−0.310	−0.273	−0.226
−0.355	−0.303	−0.273	−0.223
−0.350	−0.301	−0.261	−0.222
−0.347	−0.301	−0.259	−0.218
−0.344	−0.300	−0.253	−0.216
−0.343	−0.298	−0.251	−0.215
−0.333	−0.296	−0.248	−0.211

Using the above information, compute the following:

A. 5 percent annual VAR

B. 1 percent annual VAR

13. **A.** A firm runs an investment portfolio consisting of stocks as well as options on stocks. Management would like to determine the VAR for this portfolio and is thinking about which technique to use. Discuss a problem with using the analytical or variance–covariance method for determining the VAR of this portfolio.

   B. Describe a situation in which an organization might logically select each of the three VAR methodologies.

14. An organization's 5 percent daily VAR shows a number fairly consistently around €3 million. A backtest of the calculation reveals that, as expected under the calculation, daily portfolio losses in excess of €3 million tend to occur about once a month. When such losses do occur, however, they typically are more than double the VAR estimate. The portfolio contains a very large short options position.

   A. Is the VAR calculation accurate?

   B. How can the VAR figure best be interpreted?

   C. What additional measures might the organization take to increase the accuracy of its overall exposure assessments?

15. Indicate which of the following statements about credit risk is (are) false, and explain why.

   A. Because credit losses occur often, it is easy to assess the probability of a credit loss.

   B. One element of credit risk is the possibility that the counterparty to a contract will default on an obligation to another (i.e., third) party.

   C. Like the buyer of a European-style option, the buyer of an American-style option faces no current credit risk until the expiration of the option.

16. Ricardo Colón, an analyst in the investment management division of a financial services firm, is developing an earnings forecast for a local oil services company. The company's income is closely linked to the price of oil. Furthermore, the company derives the majority of its income from sales to the United States. The economy of the company's home country depends significantly on export oil sales to the United States. As a result, movements in world oil prices in U.S. dollar terms and the U.S. dollar value of the home country's currency are strongly positively correlated. A decline in oil prices would reduce the company's sales in U.S. dollar terms, all else being equal. On the other hand, the appreciation of the home country's currency relative to the U.S. dollar would reduce the company's sales in terms of the home currency.

   According to Colón's research, Raúl Rodriguez, the company's chief risk officer, has made the following statement:

   > "The company has rejected hedging the market risk of a decline in oil prices by selling oil futures and hedging the currency risk of a depreciation of the U.S. dollar relative to our home currency by buying home currency futures in U.S. markets. We have decided that a more effective risk management strategy for our company is to not hedge either market risk or currency risk."

   A. State whether the company's decision to not hedge market risk was correct. Justify your answer with one reason.

   B. State whether the company's decision to not hedge currency risk was correct. Justify your answer with one reason.

   C. Critique the risk management strategy adopted.

17. Tony Smith believes that the price of a particular underlying, currently selling at $96, will increase substantially in the next six months, so he purchases a European call option expiring in six months on this underlying. The call option has an exercise price of $101 and sells for $6.

　A. How much is the current credit risk, if any?

　B. How much is the current value of the potential credit risk, if any?

　C. Which party bears the credit risk(s), Tony Smith or the seller?

18. Following are four methods for calculating risk-adjusted performance: the Sharpe ratio, risk-adjusted return on capital (RAROC), return over maximum drawdown (RoMAD), and the Sortino ratio. Compare and contrast the measure of risk that each method uses.

Questions 19–24 relate to Monika Kreuzer

Monika Kreuzer chairs the risk management committee for DGI Investors, a European money management firm. The agenda for the 1 June committee meeting includes three issues concerning client portfolios:

1. Estimating a new value at risk (VAR) for the Stimson Industries portfolio.
2. Answering questions from Kalton Corporation managers.
3. Revising the VAR for Muth Company given new capital market expectations.

1. VAR for Stimson Industries DGI currently provides a 5 percent yearly VAR on the equity portfolio that it manages for Stimson. The €50 million portfolio has an expected annual return of 9.6 percent and an annual standard deviation of 18.0 percent. With a standard normal distribution, 5 percent of the possible outcomes are 1.65 standard deviations or more below the mean. Using the analytical (variance–covariance) method for calculating VAR, DGI estimates the 5 percent yearly VAR to be €10.05 million. Assuming that monthly returns are independent, committee member Eric Stulz wants to estimate a 5 percent *monthly* VAR for Stimson's portfolio.

Stulz asks his fellow committee members for feedback on the following statements about VAR in a report he is preparing for Stimson Industries:

1. "VAR is the loss that would be exceeded with a given probability over a specific time period."
2. "Establishing a VAR involves several decisions, such as the probability and time period over which the VAR will be measured and the technique to be used."
3. "A portfolio's VAR will be larger when it is measured at a 5 percent probability than when it is measured at a 1 percent probability."
4. "A portfolio's VAR will be larger when it is measured over a month than when it is measured over a day."

2. Questions from Kalton Corporation Managers Kalton Corporation has two large derivatives positions with a London securities house. The first position is a long forward currency contract to buy pounds at €1.4500. The current exchange rate is €1.4000 per pound. The second position is a long put position on the DJ Euro STOXX Index with a strike price of 305.00. The current closing price of the index is 295.00. A Kalton manager has written, "I am concerned about the risks of these two large positions. Who is bearing the credit risks, Kalton Corporation or the counterparty (the London securities house)?" Kreuzer suggests that DGI reply: "Kalton Corporation is bearing the credit risk of the currency forward contract, but the London securities house is bearing the credit risk of the put option on the DJ Euro STOXX Index."

Because they believe that the credit risk in corporate bonds is going to decline, Kalton Corporation managers have decided to increase Kalton's credit risk exposure in corporate bonds. They have asked Kreuzer and the risk management committee to recommend derivatives positions to accomplish this change.

3. **Revising the VAR for Muth Company** Kreuzer provides a variety of statistics to Muth, for whom DGI manages a portfolio composed of 50 percent in Asia-Pacific equities and 50 percent in European equities. One of the statistics that Kreuzer supplies Muth is a 5 percent monthly VAR estimate based on the analytical (variance–covariance) method. Kreuzer is concerned that changes in the market outlook will affect Muth's risk. DGI is updating its capital market expectations, which will include (1) an increase in the expected return on Asia-Pacific equities and (2) an increase in the correlation between Asia-Pacific equities and European equities. Kreuzer comments: "Considered independently, and assuming that other variables are held constant, each of these changes in capital market expectations will increase the monthly VAR estimate for the Muth portfolio."

Kreuzer also discusses the limitations and strengths of applying VAR to the Muth portfolio. She states that: "One of the advantages of VAR is that the VAR of individual positions can be simply aggregated to find the portfolio VAR." Kreuzer also describes how VAR can be supplemented with performance evaluation measures, such as the Sharpe ratio. She states: "The Sharpe ratio is widely used for calculating a risk-adjusted return, although it can be an inaccurate measure when applied to portfolios with significant options positions."

---

19. The monthly VAR that Stulz wants to estimate for the Stimson portfolio is *closest* to:

2006 exam

    A. €0.8 million.
    B. €2.1 million.
    C. €2.9 million.
    D. €3.9 million.

20. Regarding the four statements in the report that Stulz is preparing for Stimson Industries, the statement that is *incorrect* is:

2006 exam

    A. statement #1.
    B. statement #2.
    C. statement #3.
    D. statement #4.

21. Regarding Kalton's two derivatives positions, is Kreuzer correct about which party is bearing the credit risk of the currency forward contract and the put option on the DJ Euro STOXX Index, respectively?

2006 exam

	Currency Forward Contract	Put Option on the DJ Euro STOXX Index
A.	No	No
B.	No	Yes
C.	Yes	No
D.	Yes	Yes

22. To make the desired change in Kalton's credit risk exposure in corporate bonds, Kreuzer could recommend that Kalton take a position as a:

A. seller in a credit default swap.

B. buyer in a credit default swap.

C. buyer of a credit spread call option.

D. buyer of a put option on a corporate bond.

23. Is Kreuzer correct in predicting the independent effects of the increase in the expected return and the increase in the correlation, respectively, on the calculated VAR of the Muth portfolio?

	Effect of Increase in the Expected Return	Effect of Increase in the Correlation
A.	No	No
B.	No	Yes
C.	Yes	No
D.	Yes	Yes

24. Are Kreuzer's statements about an advantage of VAR and about the Sharpe ratio, respectively, correct?

	Statement about an Advantage of VAR	Statement about the Sharpe Ratio
A.	No	No
B.	No	Yes
C.	Yes	No
D.	Yes	Yes

STUDY SESSION 13
RISK MANAGEMENT APPLICATIONS OF DERIVATIVES

This study session addresses risk management strategies using forwards and futures, option strategies, floors and caps, and swaps. Collectively referred to as derivatives, these investment vehicles can be employed for a variety of risk management purposes, including modification of portfolio duration and beta, implementation of changes in asset allocation, and synthesis of cash market instruments. Derivatives strategies have proven useful to both investors and borrowers, which accounts for their broad appeal. A growing number of security types now have embedded derivatives, and portfolio managers must be able to account for their effect on the return/risk profile of the security. After completing Study Session 13, the candidate will better understand the advantages and disadvantages of derivative strategies, including the difficulties in creating and maintaining a dynamic hedge.

READING ASSIGNMENTS

Reading 38   Risk Management Applications of Forward and Futures Strategies
Reading 39   Risk Management Applications of Option Strategies
Reading 40   Risk Management Applications of Swap Strategies

LEARNING OUTCOMES

Reading 38: Risk Management Applications of Forward and Futures Strategies

The candidate should be able to:

a. demonstrate the use of equity futures contracts to achieve a target beta for a stock portfolio and calculate and interpret the number of futures contracts required;

b. construct a synthetic stock index fund using cash and stock index futures (equitizing cash);

c. create synthetic cash by selling stock index futures against a long stock position;

d. demonstrate the use of equity and bond futures to adjust the allocation of a portfolio between equity and debt;

e. demonstrate the use of futures to adjust the allocation of a portfolio across equity sectors and to gain exposure to an asset class in advance of actually committing funds to the asset class;

f. discuss the three types of exposure to exchange rate risk and demonstrate the use of forward contracts to reduce the risk associated with a future transaction (receipt or payment) in a foreign currency;

g. explain the limitations to hedging the exchange rate risk of a foreign market portfolio and discuss two feasible strategies for managing such risk.

Reading 39: Risk Management Applications of Option Strategies

The candidate should be able to:

a. determine and interpret the value at expiration, profit, maximum profit, maximum loss, breakeven underlying price at expiration, and general shape of the graph for the major option strategies (bull spread, bear spread, butterfly spread, collar, straddle, box spread);

b. determine the effective annual rate for a given interest rate outcome when a borrower (lender) manages the risk of an anticipated loan using an interest rate call (put) option;

c. determine the payoffs for a series of interest rate outcomes when a floating rate loan is combined with (1) an interest rate cap, (2) an interest rate floor, or (3) an interest rate collar;

d. explain why and how a dealer delta hedges an option portfolio, why the portfolio delta changes, and how the dealer adjusts the position to maintain the hedge;

e. identify the conditions in which a delta-hedged portfolio is affected by the second-order gamma effect.

Reading 40: Risk Management Applications of Swap Strategies

The candidate should be able to:

a. demonstrate how an interest rate swap can be used to convert a floating-rate (fixed-rate) loan to a fixed-rate (floating-rate) loan;

b. calculate and interpret the duration of an interest rate swap;

c. explain the impact to cash flow risk and market value risk when a borrower converts a fixed-rate loan to a floating-rate loan;

d. determine the notional principal value needed on an interest rate swap to achieve a desired level of duration in a fixed-income portfolio;

e. explain how a company can generate savings by issuing a loan or bond in its own currency and using a currency swap to convert the obligation into another currency;

f. demonstrate how a firm can use a currency swap to convert a series of foreign cash receipts into domestic cash receipts;

g. explain how equity swaps can be used to diversify a concentrated equity portfolio, provide international diversification to a domestic portfolio, and alter portfolio allocations to stocks and bonds;

h. demonstrate the use of an interest rate swaption (1) to change the payment pattern of an anticipated future loan and (2) to terminate a swap.

RISK MANAGEMENT APPLICATIONS OF FORWARD AND FUTURES STRATEGIES

by Don M. Chance

LEARNING OUTCOMES

The candidate should be able to:

a. demonstrate the use of equity futures contracts to achieve a target beta for a stock portfolio and calculate and interpret the number of futures contracts required;

b. construct a synthetic stock index fund using cash and stock index futures (equitizing cash);

c. create synthetic cash by selling stock index futures against a long stock position;

d. demonstrate the use of equity and bond futures to adjust the allocation of a portfolio between equity and debt;

e. demonstrate the use of futures to adjust the allocation of a portfolio across equity sectors and to gain exposure to an asset class in advance of actually committing funds to the asset class;

f. discuss the three types of exposure to exchange rate risk and demonstrate the use of forward contracts to reduce the risk associated with a future transaction (receipt or payment) in a foreign currency;

g. explain the limitations to hedging the exchange rate risk of a foreign market portfolio and discuss two feasible strategies for managing such risk.

INTRODUCTION 1

In preceding readings, we examined the characteristics and pricing of forwards, futures, options, and swaps. On occasion, we made reference to possible ways in which these instruments could be used. In Readings 38, 39, and 40, we examine more specifically the strategies and applications that are commonly used with these instruments. Here in Reading 38, we focus on forward and futures contracts. These instruments are quite similar. Both involve commitments for one

OPTIONAL SEGMENT BEGINS

party to buy and the other to sell an underlying instrument at a future date at a price agreed on at the start of the contract. The underlying instrument might be an interest payment, a bond, a stock, or a currency. Forward contracts are customized agreements between two parties: The terms are agreed on by both parties in a formal legal contract that exists in an environment outside of regulatory constraints. Each party is subject to potential default on the part of the other. Futures contracts, on the other hand, are standardized instruments created on a **futures exchange**, protected against credit losses by the clearinghouse, and subject to federal regulatory oversight.

In this reading, we examine a number of scenarios in which parties facing risk management problems use forward and futures contracts to alter the risk of their positions. In some situations we use forwards and in others we use futures. For cases in which either would suffice, we pick the instrument that is most commonly used in that type of situation. Although we shall not devote a great deal of space up front to justifying why we picked the instrument we did, we shall provide some discussion of this point in Section 6.

After completing this reading, you may be surprised to observe that we do not cover an important class of derivative strategies, those that are called *arbitrage.* This omission is not because they are not important enough to cover or that they are not risk management strategies; in fact, we have *already* covered them. When we covered the pricing of forwards, futures, options, and swaps, we explained how these instruments are priced by combining the underlying and risk-free bonds to replicate the derivative or by combining a long position in the underlying and a short position in the derivative to replicate a risk-free position. From there we obtained a formula that gives us the correct price of the derivative. An arbitrage profit is possible if the derivative is not priced according to the formula. We have already looked at how those strategies are executed. We should not expect to encounter arbitrage opportunities very often in practice. They are quickly captured by derivatives trading firms, which themselves cannot expect to be able to *consistently* claim such opportunities before they disappear.[1]

Businesses make products and provide services as they attempt to increase shareholder wealth. In doing so, they face a variety of risks. Managing risk lies at the heart of what companies do. All companies specialize in managing the risk of whatever market their primary business is in: Airlines deal with the risk associated with the demand for air travel, software companies deal with the risk associated with the demand for new computer programs, movie companies deal with the

---

[1] Suppose market participants assume that arbitrage opportunities are so infrequent and difficult to capture before they are gone that no one monitors market prices looking for arbitrage opportunities. Then these arbitrage opportunities will begin to occur more frequently. A market in which arbitrage opportunities are rare, and therefore prices are fair and accurate, is ironically a market in which participants believe they can indeed uncover and exploit arbitrage opportunities. Thus, an arbitrage-free market requires disbelievers.

risk associated with the demand for their films. But these companies also deal with other risks, such as the risk of interest rates and exchange rates. Usually these companies take calculated risks in their primary lines of business and avoid risks they do not feel qualified to take, such as interest rate risk and exchange rate risk. Naturally this approach involves a practice called **hedging**.

Hedging involves taking a market position to protect against an undesirable outcome. Suppose a company has a strong belief that interest rates will increase. It engages in a forward rate agreement (FRA) transaction to lock in the rate on a loan it will take out at a later date. This position protects the company from the undesirable outcome of an increase in interest rates, but it also prevents the company from enjoying any decline in rates. In that sense, the position is as much a speculative position as if a speculator had made the following prediction: *We believe that interest rates will rise to an unacceptable level, and we intend to trade on that basis to make money.* By engaging in the FRA to hedge this outcome, the company trades to make a profit from its FRA that will help offset any increase in the interest rate on its future loan. But by locking in a rate, it forgoes the possibility of benefiting from a decline in interest rates. The company has made a bet that rates will rise. If they fall, the company has lost the bet and lost money on its FRA that offsets the benefit of the lower interest rate on this loan planned for a later date.

In this reading we shall not overindulge in the use of the term hedging. We shall say that companies do more than hedge: *They manage risk.* They carefully consider scenarios and elect to adjust the risk they face to a level they feel is acceptable. In many cases, this adjustment will involve the reduction of risk; in some cases, however, the scenario will justify increasing the company's risk. In all cases, the company is just altering the risk from its current level to the level the company desires. And that is what managing risk is all about.

This reading is divided into five main parts. Sections 2 and 3 focus on the management of interest rate and equity market risk, respectively. Section 4 combines interest rate and equity risk management applications by looking at how investors can manage an asset portfolio using futures. Section 5 looks at the management of foreign currency risk. In Section 6 we examine the general question of whether to use forwards or futures to manage risk, and in Section 7 we look at a few final issues.

STRATEGIES AND APPLICATIONS FOR MANAGING INTEREST RATE RISK

2

Almost every business borrows money from time to time. A company borrowing at a fixed rate may think it is immune to interest rate risk, but that is not the case. Risk arises from the possibility that interest rates can increase from the time the company decides to take the loan to the time it actually takes the loan. Most companies make plans to borrow based on their cash needs at specific future dates. The rates they pay on these loans are important determinants of their future cash needs, as reflected in their planned interest payments. Exposure to interest rate risk is, therefore, a major concern. Failing to manage interest rate risk can hinder the planning process, as well as result in unexpected demands on cash necessitated by unexpectedly higher interest payments.

2.1 Managing the Interest Rate Risk of a Loan Using an FRA

There are several situations in which a company might want to manage the interest rate risk of a loan. The two we look at here involve a company planning to take out a loan at a later date. In one situation, the loan has a single interest rate and a single interest payment. In another situation, a company takes out a floating-rate loan in which the interest rate is reset periodically.

2.1.1 Single-Payment Loan

Exhibit 1 presents the case of Global BioTechnology (GBT), which determines that it will need to borrow money at a later date at a rate of LIBOR plus 200 basis points. Fearing an increase in interest rates between now and the day it takes out the loan, it enters into a long position in an FRA. The FRA has a fixed rate, called the FRA rate. If the underlying rate at expiration is above the FRA rate, GBT as the holder of the long position will receive a lump sum of cash based on the difference between the FRA rate and the market rate at that time. This payment will help offset the higher rate GBT would be paying on its loan. If the rate in the market falls below the FRA rate, however, GBT will end up paying the counterparty, which will offset the lower rate GBT will be paying on its loan. The end result is that GBT will pay approximately a fixed rate, the FRA rate.

EXHIBIT 1	Using an FRA to Lock in the Rate on a Loan

Scenario (15 April)

Global BioTechnology (GBT) is a U.S. corporation that occasionally undertakes short-term borrowings in U.S. dollars with the rate tied to LIBOR. To facilitate its cash flow planning, it uses an FRA to lock in the rate on such loans as soon as it determines that it will need the money.

On 15 April, GBT determines that it will borrow $40 million on 20 August. The loan will be repaid 180 days later on 16 February, and the rate will be at LIBOR plus 200 basis points. Because GBT believes that interest rates will increase, it decides to manage this risk by going long an FRA. An FRA will enable it to receive the difference between LIBOR on 20 August and the FRA rate quoted by the dealer on 15 April. The quoted rate from the dealer is 5.25 percent. GBT wants to lock in a 7.25 percent rate: 5.25 percent plus 200 basis points.

Action

GBT confirms that it will borrow $40 million at LIBOR plus 200 basis points on 20 August. GBT goes long an FRA at a rate of 5.25 percent to expire on 20 August with the underlying being 180-day LIBOR.

(Exhibit continued on next page . . .)

EXHIBIT 1	(continued)

Scenario (20 August)

At contract expiration, 180-day LIBOR is 6 percent.

Outcome and Analysis

The FRA payoff is given by the general formula:

Notional principal $\times$

$$\left[\frac{\left(\begin{array}{c} \text{Underlying rate} \\ \text{at expiration} \end{array} - \text{Forward contract rate} \right)\left(\dfrac{\text{Days in underlying rate}}{360} \right)}{1 + \text{Underlying rate}\left(\dfrac{\text{Days in underlying rate}}{360} \right)} \right]$$

or $40,000,000 \times \left[\dfrac{(0.06 - 0.0525)\,(180/360)}{1 + 0.06\,(180/360)} \right] = \$145,631$

GBT receives this amount in cash. Therefore, to obtain $40 million in cash, it has to borrow $40,000,000 - \$145,631 = \$39,854,369$ at LIBOR plus 200 basis points, $0.06 + 0.02 = 0.08$, or 8 percent.

On 16 February GBT pays back $39,854,369[1 + 0.08(180/360)] = \$41,448,544$. So, it effectively pays a rate of

$$\left(\frac{\$41,448,544}{\$40,000,000} - 1 \right)\left(\frac{360}{180} \right) = 0.0724$$

The net effect is that GBT receives $40 million on 20 August and pays back $41,448,544 on 16 February, a rate of 7.24 percent. This rate was effectively locked in on 15 April at the FRA rate of 5.25 percent plus the 200 basis points GBT pays over LIBOR.

Shown below are the results for possible LIBORs on 20 August of 2 percent, 4 percent, . . ., 10 percent.

LIBOR on 20 August	FRA Payoff	Amount Borrowed	LIBOR + 200 bps Loan Rate	Amount Repaid on 16 February	Effective Loan Rate
0.02	−$643,564	$40,643,564	0.04	$41,456,435	0.0728
0.04	−245,098	40,245,098	0.06	41,452,451	0.0726
0.06	145,631	39,854,369	0.08	41,448,544	0.0724
0.08	528,846	39,471,154	0.10	41,444,712	0.0722
0.10	904,762	39,095,238	0.12	41,440,952	0.0720

In this problem, the FRA rate is 5.25 percent. In the exhibit, we described an outcome in which the underlying rate, 180-day LIBOR, is 6 percent. GBT ends up paying $6\% + 2\% = 8\%$ on the loan, but the FRA pays off an amount sufficient to reduce the effective rate to 7.24 percent. Note the table at the end of the exhibit showing other possible outcomes. In all cases, the rate GBT pays is approximately the FRA rate of 5.25 percent plus 200 basis points. This rate is not precisely 7.25 percent, however, because of the way in which the FRA is constructed to pay off at expiration. When LIBOR on 20 August is above 5.25 percent, the FRA payoff on that day reduces the amount that has to be borrowed at LIBOR plus 200 basis points. This reduction works to the advantage of GBT. Conversely, when rates are below 5.25 percent, the amount that must be borrowed increases but that amount is borrowed at a lower rate. Thus, there is a slight asymmetric effect of a few basis points that prevents the effective loan rate from precisely equaling 7.25 percent.

In a similar manner, a lender could lock in a rate on a loan it plans to make by going short an FRA. Lenders are less inclined to do such transactions, however, because they cannot anticipate the exact future borrowing needs of their customers. In some cases, banks that offer credit lines at floating rates might wish to lock in lending rates using FRAs. But because the choice of whether to borrow is the borrower's and not the lender's, a lender that uses an FRA is taking considerable risk that the loan will not even be made. In that case, the lender would do better to use an option so that, in the worst case, it loses only the option premium.

EXAMPLE 1

ABTech plans to borrow $10 million in 30 days at 90-day LIBOR plus 100 basis points. To lock in a borrowing rate of 7 percent, it purchases an FRA at a rate of 6 percent. This contract would be referred to as a 1×4 FRA because it expires in one month (30 days) and the underlying Eurodollar matures four months (120 days) from now. Thirty days later, LIBOR is 7.5 percent. Demonstrate that ABTech's effective borrowing rate is 7 percent if LIBOR in 30 days is 7.5 percent.

Solution: If LIBOR is 7.5 percent at the expiration of the FRA in 30 days, the payoff of the FRA is

Notional principal $\times$

$$
\left[\frac{\left(\begin{array}{c} \text{Underlying rate} \\ \text{at expiration} \end{array} - \text{Forward contract rate} \right) \left(\dfrac{\text{Days in underlying rate}}{360} \right)}{1 + \text{Underlying rate} \left(\dfrac{\text{Days in underlying rate}}{360} \right)} \right]
$$

which is

$$
\$10,000,000 \times \left[\frac{(0.075 - 0.06)(90/360)}{1 + 0.075(90/360)} \right] = \$36,810
$$

Because this amount is a cash inflow, ABTech will not need to borrow a full $10,000,000. Instead, it will borrow $10,000,000 − $36,810 = $9,963,190.

The amount it will pay back in 90 days is

$$
\$9,963,190[1 + (0.075 + 0.01)(90/360)] = \$10,174,908
$$

The effective rate is, therefore,

$$\left(\frac{\$10,174,908}{\$10,000,000} - 1\right)\left(\frac{360}{90}\right) \approx 0.07$$

ABTech borrows at LIBOR plus 100 basis points. Therefore, using an FRA, it should be able to lock in the FRA rate (6 percent) plus 100 basis points, which it does.

2.1.2 Floating-Rate Loan

In the example above, the loan involved only a single payment and, therefore, we had only one setting of an interest rate to worry about. Many loans are **floating-rate loans**, meaning that their rates are reset several times during the life of the loan. This resetting of the rate poses a series of risks for the borrower.

Suppose a corporation is taking out a two-year loan. The rate for the initial six months is set today. The rate will be reset in 6, 12, and 18 months. Because the current rate is already in place, there is nothing the corporation can do to mitigate that risk.[2] It faces, however, the risk of rising interest rates over the remaining life of the loan, which would result in higher interest payments.

One way to control this risk is to enter into a series of FRA transactions with each component FRA tailored to expire on a date on which the rate will be reset. This strategy will not lock in the *same* fixed rate for each semiannual period, but different rates for each period will be locked in. Another alternative would be to use futures. For example, for a LIBOR-based loan, the Eurodollar futures contract would be appropriate. Nonetheless, the use of futures to manage this risk poses significant problems. One problem is that the Eurodollar futures contract has expirations only on specific days during the year. The Chicago Mercantile Exchange offers contract expirations on the current month, the next month, and a sequence of months following the pattern of March, June, September, and December. Thus, it is quite likely that no contracts would exist with expirations that align with the later payment reset dates. The Eurodollar futures contract expires on the second London business day before the third Wednesday of the month. This date might not be the exact day of the month on which the rate is reset. In addition, the Eurodollar futures contract is based only on the 90-day Eurodollar rate, whereas the loan rate is pegged to the 180-day rate. Although many dealer firms use the Eurodollar futures contract to manage the risk associated with their over-the-counter derivatives, they do so using sophisticated techniques that measure and balance the volatility of the futures contract to the volatility of their market positions. Moreover, they adjust their positions rapidly in response to market movements. Without that capability, borrowers who simply need to align their interest rate reset dates with the dates on which their derivatives expire can do so more easily with swaps. We shall cover how this is done in Reading 40. Nevertheless, an understanding of how FRAs are used will help with an understanding of this application of swaps.

---

[2] If a corporation were planning to take out a floating-rate loan at a later date, it would also be concerned about the first interest rate and might attempt to lock in that rate. In the example used here, we placed the company in a situation in which it already knows its initial rate and, therefore, is worried only about the remaining rate resets.

2.2 Strategies and Applications for Managing Bond Portfolio Risk

In Section 2.1, we dealt with the risk associated with short-term borrowing interest rates, which obviously affects short-term borrowers and lenders. The risk associated with longer-term loans primarily takes the form of bond market risk. Here we shall take a look at a firm managing a government bond portfolio, that is, a lending position. The firm can manage the risk associated with interest rates by using futures on government bonds. In the next three sections, we explore how to measure the risk of a bond portfolio, measure the risk of bond futures, and balance those risks.

2.2.1 Measuring the Risk of a Bond Portfolio

The sensitivity of a bond to a general change in interest rates is usually captured by assuming that the bond price changes in response to a change in its yield, which is driven by the general level of rates. The responsiveness of a bond price to a yield change is captured in two ways: duration and basis point value.[3]

Duration is a measure of the size and timing of the cash flows paid by a bond. It quantifies these factors by summarizing them in the form of a single number, which is interpreted as an average maturity of the bond. To speak in terms of an average maturity of a bond of a given specific maturity sounds somewhat strange, but remember that a coupon bond is really just a combination of zero-coupon bonds.[4] The average maturity of these component zero-coupon bonds is the duration. The average is not an ordinary average but a weighted average, with the weights based on the present values of the respective cash payments on the bonds. Hence, the weights are not equal, and the large principal repayment places the greatest emphasis on the final payment.

Suppose the bond price is B, the yield is y_B, and Macaulay duration is DUR_B. Then the relationship between the change in the bond price and its yield is given as

$$\Delta B \approx -DUR_B B \frac{\Delta y_B}{1 + y_B}$$

where the Greek symbol Δ indicates "change in" and where the overall relationship is shown as an approximation ($\approx$). For this relationship to be exact requires that the yield change be very small.[5] The left-hand side, ΔB, is the change in the bond price. The negative sign on the right-hand side is consistent with the inverse relationship between the bond price and its yield.[6]

A somewhat simplified version of the above equation is

$$\Delta B \approx -MDUR_B B \Delta y_B$$

---

[3] Readers may first wish to review some fixed-income securities material. See especially Chapter 7 of *Fixed Income Analysis for the Chartered Financial Analyst Program*, Frank J. Fabozzi (Frank J. Fabozzi Associates, 2000).

[4] This analogy comes about because the coupons and final principal on a bond can be viewed as zero-coupon bonds, each maturing on the date on which a coupon or the final principal is paid. The value of a coupon or the final principal is analogous to the face value of a zero-coupon bond. In the U.S. Treasury bond market, companies buy coupon bonds and sell claims on the individual coupons and principal, which are referred to as Treasury strips.

[5] If the yield change is not sufficiently small, it may be necessary to incorporate second-order effects, which are captured by a bond's convexity.

[6] The above relationship is based on annual coupons. If the coupons are paid semiannually, then $1 + y_B$ should be $1 + y_B/2$. In this case, the duration will be stated as the number of semiannual, rather than annual, periods.

where $MDUR_B = DUR_B/(1 + y_B)$. $MDUR_B$ is called the **modified duration** and is just an adjustment of the duration for the level of the yield. We shall use the relationship as captured by the modified duration.[7]

As an example, suppose the bond price is $922.50, modified duration is 5.47 years, and the yield increases by 15 basis points. Then the price change should be approximately

$$\Delta B \approx -5.47(\$922.50)(0.0015) = -\$7.57$$

In response to a 15 basis point increase in yield, the bond price should decrease by approximately $7.57. So the new bond price would be predicted to be $922.50 − $7.57 = $914.93.

The relationship between the bond price and its yield is sometimes stated another way. We often speak in terms of the change in the bond price for a 1 basis point change in yield. This value is sometimes referred to as **basis point value** (or BPV), **present value of a basis point** (or PVBP), or **price value of a basis point** (again PVBP). We refer to this concept as PVBP, defined as

$$PVBP_B \approx MDUR_B B(0.0001)$$

The multiplication by 0.0001 enables PVBP to capture how much the bond price changes for a 1 basis point change. In the example above, the PVBP for our bond is

$$PVBP_B \approx (5.47)(\$922.50)(0.0001) = \$0.5046$$

So for a 1 basis point change, the bond price would change by approximately $0.5046. Accordingly, a 15 basis point change produces a price change of $15(\$0.5046) = \$7.57$. Both duration and PVBP measure the same thing, however, and we shall use only duration.

Duration and PVBP are usually thought of with respect to individual bonds, but in practice, they are typically used at the portfolio level. Hence, we should care more about the duration of a bond portfolio than about the duration of an individual bond. With respect to yield, we do not usually speak in terms of the yield of a bond portfolio, but in this case we must. A given bond portfolio can be thought of as a series of cash flows that can be captured in terms of a representative bond. Thus, we might describe this bond as a bond portfolio with a market value of $922.5 million, a modified duration of 5.47 years, and a portfolio yield that is a complex weighted average of the yields on the component bonds of the portfolio. The portfolio yield can change by a certain number of basis points. That yield change is a weighted average of the yield changes on the component bonds. Given such a yield change, the bond portfolio value will change in an approximate manner according to the duration formula shown above.

The way a bond price changes according to a yield change indicates its responsiveness to interest rates. Given a bond futures contract, we can also measure its sensitivity to interest rate changes.

2.2.2 Measuring the Risk of Bond Futures

Having measured the responsiveness of a bond portfolio to an interest rate change, we now need to measure the responsiveness of a futures contract to an

---

[7] The duration before dividing by $1 + y_B$ is sometimes called the **Macaulay duration**, to distinguish it from the modified duration. It is named for Frederick Macaulay, one of the economists who first derived it.

interest rate change. Most bond futures, contracts are based on a hypothetical benchmark bond. The Chicago Board of Trade's U.S. Treasury bond futures contract is based on a 6 percent bond with at least 15 years from the futures expiration to maturity or the first call date. Even though the benchmark bond has a 6 percent coupon, any bond meeting the maturity requirement can be delivered. At any time, a single bond exists that the holder of the short position would find optimal to deliver if current conditions continued. That bond is called the **cheapest to deliver** and can be thought of as the bond on which the futures contract is based. In other words, the cheapest to deliver bond is the underlying. The responsiveness of the futures contract to an interest rate change is equivalent to the responsiveness of that bond on the futures expiration day to an interest rate change.

We can think of this concept as the responsiveness of the underlying bond in a forward context. This responsiveness can be measured as that bond's modified duration on the futures expiration and, as such, we can use the price sensitivity formula to capture the sensitivity of the futures contract to a yield change. Accordingly, we shall, somewhat loosely, refer to this as the implied duration of the futures contract, keeping in mind that what we mean is the duration of the underlying bond calculated as of the futures expiration. Moreover, we also mean that the underlying bond has been identified as the cheapest bond to deliver and that if another bond takes its place, the duration of that bond must be used. We use the term *implied* to emphasize that a futures contract does not itself have a duration but that its duration is implied by the underlying bond. In addition to the duration, we also require an **implied yield** on the futures, which reflects the yield on the underlying bond implied by pricing it as though it were delivered at the futures contract expiration.

Hence, we can express the sensitivity of the futures price to a yield change as

$$\Delta f \approx -\text{MDUR}_f f \,\Delta y_f \tag{38-1}$$

where MDUR_f is the implied modified duration of the futures, f is the futures price, and Δy_f is the basis point change in the implied yield on the futures.

Now that we have a measure of the responsiveness of a bond portfolio and the responsiveness of a bond futures contract to interest rate changes, we should be able to find a way to balance the two to offset the risk.

2.2.3 Balancing the Risk of a Bond Portfolio against the Risk of Bond Futures

We now make the simple assumption that a single interest rate exists that drives all interest rates in the market. We assume that a 1 basis point change in this interest rate will cause a 1 basis point change in the yield on the bond portfolio and a 1 basis point change in the implied yield on the futures. We will relax that assumption later. For now, consider a money manager who holds a bond portfolio of a particular market value and will not be adding to it or removing some of it to balance the risk. In other words, the manager will not make any transactions in the actual bonds themselves. The manager can, however, trade any number of futures contracts to adjust the risk. Let N_f be the number of futures contracts traded. To balance the risk, suppose we combine the change in the value of the bond portfolio and the change in the value of N_f futures and set these equal to zero: $\Delta B + N_f \Delta f = 0$. Solving for N_f produces $N_f = -\Delta B/\Delta f$. Substituting our formulas for ΔB and Δf, we obtain

$$N_f = -\left(\frac{\text{MDUR}_B}{\text{MDUR}_f}\right)\left(\frac{B}{f}\right)\left(\frac{\Delta y_B}{\Delta y_f}\right) = -\left(\frac{\text{MDUR}_B}{\text{MDUR}_f}\right)\left(\frac{B}{f}\right)$$

where we assume that $\Delta y_B/\Delta y_f = 1$; or in other words, the bond portfolio yield changes one-for-one with the implied yield on the futures.[8]

Now let us go back to the major simplifying assumption we made. We assumed that an interest rate change occurs in the market and drives the yield on the bond and the implied yield on the futures one-for-one. In reality, this assumption is unlikely to hold true. Suppose, for example, the rate driving all rates in the United States is the overnight Fed funds rate.[9] If this rate changes by 1 basis point, not all rates along the term structure are likely to change by 1 basis point. What actually matters, however, is not that all rates change by the same amount but that the yield on the bond portfolio and the implied yield on the futures change by the same amount for a 1 basis point change in this rate. If that is not the case, we need to make an adjustment.

Suppose the yield on the bond portfolio changes by a multiple of the implied yield on the futures in the following manner:

$$\Delta y_B = \beta_y \Delta y_f \qquad \text{(38-2)}$$

We refer to the symbol β_y as the **yield beta**. It can be more or less than 1, depending on whether the bond yield is more sensitive or less sensitive than the implied futures yield. If we take the formula we previously obtained for ΔB, substitute $\beta_y \Delta y_f$ where we previously had Δy_B, and use this new variation of the formula in the formula $N_f = -\Delta B/\Delta f$, we obtain

$$N_f = -(MDUR_B/MDUR_f)(B/f)\beta_y \qquad \text{(38-3)}$$

This is the more general formula, because $\beta_y = 1.0$ is just the special case we assumed at the start.

We can modify Equation 38-3 so that it gives us the number of futures contracts needed to change our portfolio's modified duration to meet a target. What we have done so far *completely* balances the risk of the futures position against the risk of the bond portfolio, eliminating the risk. In the practice of risk management, however, we might not always want to eliminate the risk; we might want to adjust it only a little. At some times we might even want to increase it.

The risk of the overall bond portfolio reflects the duration of the bonds and the duration of the futures. Suppose we consider a target overall modified duration of the portfolio, $MDUR_T$. This amount is our desired overall modified duration. Because the portfolio consists of bonds worth B and futures, which have zero value, the overall portfolio value is B.[10] Now we introduce the notion of a dollar duration, which is the duration times the market value. The target dollar duration of our portfolio is set equal to the dollar duration of the bonds we hold and the dollar duration of the futures contracts:

$$B(MDUR_T) = B(MDUR_B) + f(MDUR_f)N_f$$

---

[8] Technically, this equation is the ratio of two approximate formulas, but we remove the approximation symbol from this point onward.

[9] The overnight Fed funds rate is the rate that banks charge each other to borrow and lend excess reserves for one night.

[10] Recall that futures contracts have value through the accumulation of price changes during a trading day. At the end of the day, all gains and losses are paid out through the marking-to-market process and the value then goes back to zero. We assume we are at one of those points at which the value is zero.

Solving for N_f, we obtain

$$N_f = \left(\frac{MDUR_T - MDUR_B}{MDUR_f}\right)\left(\frac{B}{f}\right)$$

Observe that if we wish to increase the modified duration from $MDUR_B$ to something higher, then $MDUR_T$ is greater than $MDUR_B$ and the overall sign of N_f will be positive, so we buy futures. This relationship should make sense: Buying futures would add volatility and increase duration. If we wish to reduce the modified duration from $MDUR_B$ to something lower, then $MDUR_T$ will be less than $MDUR_B$ and the sign of N_f will be negative, meaning that we need to sell futures. Selling futures would reduce duration and volatility. In the extreme case in which we want to eliminate risk completely, we want $MDUR_T$ to equal zero. In that case, the above formula reduces to the original one we obtained earlier in this section for the case of completely eliminating risk. In a similar manner, if the bond and futures yields do not change one-for-one, we simply alter the above formula to

$$N_f = \left(\frac{MDUR_T - MDUR_B}{MDUR_f}\right)\left(\frac{B}{f}\right)\beta_y \qquad \text{(38-4)}$$

to incorporate the yield beta.

Now we explore how to use what we have learned in this section.

2.2.4 Managing the Risk of a Government Bond Portfolio

A money manager can use Equation 38-4 to determine the number of futures contracts to buy or sell to adjust the duration of a portfolio. Such a transaction might be done in anticipation of a strong or weak market in bonds over a temporary period of time. In Exhibit 2, we illustrate the case of a pension fund that wants to increase the portfolio duration. We see that the futures transaction was successful in increasing the duration but not as precisely as planned. In fact, even without doing the futures transaction, the portfolio duration was not exactly as the company had believed. Duration is not an exact measure, nor does the bond price change occur precisely according to the duration formula.[11]

| EXHIBIT 2 | Using Bond Futures to Manage the Risk of a Bond Portfolio |

Scenario (7 July)

A portion of the pension fund of United Energy Services (UES) is a portfolio of U.S. government bonds. On 7 July, UES obtained a forecast from its economist that over the next month, interest rates are likely to make a significant unexpected decline. Its portfolio manager would like to take a portion of the bond portfolio and increase the duration to take advantage of this forecasted market movement.

Specifically, UES would like to raise the duration on $75 million of bonds from its current level of 6.22 to 7.50. Both of these duration and all durations used in this problem are modified durations. UES has identified an appropriate

(Exhibit continued on next page . . .)

---

[11] For this reason, we stated that the bond price change, given the duration and yield change, is *approximately* given by the formula in the text.

EXHIBIT 2   (continued)

Treasury bond futures contract that is currently priced at $82,500 and has an implied modified duration of 8.12. UES has estimated that the yield on the bond portfolio is about 5 percent more volatile than the implied yield on the futures. Thus, the yield beta is 1.05.

Action

To increase the duration, UES will need to buy futures contracts. Specifically, the number of futures contracts UES should use is

$$N_f = \left(\frac{MDUR_T - MDUR_B}{MDUR_f}\right)\left(\frac{B}{f}\right)\beta_y$$

$$= \left(\frac{7.50 - 6.22}{8.12}\right)\left(\frac{\$75,000,000}{\$82,500}\right)1.05 = 150.47$$

Because fractional contracts cannot be traded, UES will buy 150 contracts.

Scenario (6 August)

The implied yield on the futures has decreased by 35 basis points, and the futures price has now moved to $85,000.[12] The yield on the bond portfolio has decreased by 40 basis points, and the portfolio has increased in value by $1,933,500.

Outcome and Analysis

The profit on the futures transaction is found by multiplying the number of futures contracts by the difference between the new price and the old price:

Profit on futures contract = N_f(New futures price − Old futures price)

In this case, the profit on the futures contract is $150(\$85,000 - \$82,500) = \$375,000$. Thus, the overall gain is $1,933,500 + $375,000 = $2,308,500.

How effective was the transaction? To answer this question, we compare the *ex post* duration to the planned duration. The purpose was to increase the duration from 6.22 to a planned 7.50. The return on the portfolio was

$$\frac{\$1,933,500}{\$75,000,000} = 0.0258$$

or 2.58 percent without the futures transaction, and

$$\frac{\$2,308,500}{\$75,000,000} = 0.0308$$

or 3.08 percent with the futures transaction. What does this set of calculations imply about the portfolio's *ex post* duration? Recall that duration is a measure of the

(Exhibit continued on next page . . .)

---

[12] In the examples in this reading, bond futures prices move to a new level in the course of the scenario. These new futures prices come from the cost-of-carry model (assuming there is no mispricing in the market).

EXHIBIT 2   (continued)

percentage change in portfolio value with respect to a basis point change in yield. The *ex post* duration[13] of the portfolio can be measured by dividing the percentage change in portfolio value by the 40 basis point change in the portfolio yield:

$$\frac{0.0258}{0.0040} = 6.45$$

without the futures transaction and

$$\frac{0.0308}{0.0040} = 7.70$$

with the futures transaction. UES came fairly close to achieving its desired increase in duration using futures.

In the example here, the fund increased its modified duration during a time when interest rates fell and the bond portfolio value increased. It leveraged itself to take advantage of a favorable outlook. Not all such decisions work out so well. Suppose in this example the economist had a different forecast, and as a result, UES wanted to eliminate all interest rate risk. So let us rework the problem under the assumption that the fund put on a full hedge, thereby reducing the modified duration to zero.

With $\text{MDUR}_T = 0$, the number of futures contracts would be

$$N_f = \left(\frac{0 - 6.22}{8.12}\right)\left(\frac{\$75,000,000}{\$82,500}\right)1.05 = -731.19$$

Thus, the fund would sell 731 contracts. The profit from the futures transaction[14] would be $-731(\$85,000 - \$82,500) = -\$1,827,500$. The overall transaction earned a profit of $\$1,933,500 - \$1,827,500 = \$106,000$, a gain of

$$\frac{\$106,000}{\$75,000,000} = 0.0014$$

or 0.14 percent. Thus, shorting the futures contracts virtually wiped out all of the gain from the decrease in interest rates. Our *ex ante* objective was to reduce the modified duration to zero. The *ex post* modified duration, however, turned out to be

$$\frac{0.0014}{0.0040} = 0.35$$

Thus, the modified duration was reduced almost to zero.

---

[13] Of course, the *ex post* duration without the futures transaction is not exactly 6.22 because duration is an inexact measure, and the actual bond price change may not be precisely what is given by the modified duration formula.

[14] Notice that in calculating the profit from a futures transaction, we multiply the number of futures contracts by the futures price at the close of the strategy minus the original futures price. It is important to maintain the correct sign for the number of futures contracts. This formulation always results in a positive number for N_f times the futures selling price and a negative number for N_f times the futures buying price, which should make sense. Of course, as previously noted, we also ignore the marking-to-market feature of futures contracts.

EXAMPLE 2

Debt Management Associates (DMA) offers fixed-income portfolio management services to institutional investors. It would like to execute a duration-changing strategy for a €100 million bond portfolio of a particular client. This portfolio has a modified duration of 7.2. DMA plans to change the modified duration to 5.00 by using a futures contract priced at €120,000, which has an implied modified duration of 6.25. The yield beta is 1.15.

A. Determine how many futures contracts DMA should use and whether it should buy or sell futures.

B. Suppose that the yield on the bond has decreased by 20 basis points at the horizon date. The bond portfolio increases in value by 1.5 percent. The futures price increases to €121,200. Determine the overall gain on the portfolio and the *ex post* modified duration as a result of the futures transaction.

Solution to A: The appropriate number of futures contracts is

$$N_f = \left(\frac{5 - 7.2}{6.25}\right)\left(\frac{100,000,000}{120,000}\right)1.15 = -337.33$$

So DMA should sell 337 contracts.

Solution to B: The value of the bond portfolio will be €100,000,000(1.015) = €101,500,000. The profit on the futures transaction is −337(€121,200 − 120,000) = −€404,400; a loss of €404,400. Thus, the overall value of the position is €101,500,000 − €404,400 = €101,095,600, a return of approximately 1.1 percent. The bond yield decreases by 20 basis points and the portfolio gains 1.1 percent. The *ex post* modified duration would be 0.0110/0.0020 = 5.50.

Changing the duration—whether increasing it, reducing it partially, or reducing it all the way to zero—is an inexact process. More importantly, however, risk management by adjusting duration is only a means of implementing a strategy in response to an outlook. No one can guarantee that the outlook will not be wrong.

2.2.5 Some Variations and Problems in Managing Bond Portfolio Risk

In the examples used here, the bond portfolio consisted of government bonds. Of course, corporate and municipal bonds are widely held in bond portfolios. Unfortunately, there is no corporate bond futures contract.[15] A municipal bond futures contract exists in the United States, based on an index of municipal

---

[15] There have been attempts to create futures contracts on corporate bonds, but these contracts have not been successful in generating enough trading volume to survive.

bonds, but its volume is relatively light and the contract may not be sufficiently liquid for a large-size transaction.[16] Government bond futures contracts tend to be relatively liquid. In fact, in the United States, different contracts exist for government securities of different maturity ranges, and most of these contracts are relatively liquid.

If one uses a government bond futures to manage the risk of a corporate or municipal bond portfolio, there are some additional risks to deal with. For instance, the relationship between the yield change that drives the futures contract and the yield change that drives the bond portfolio is not as reliable. The yield on a corporate or municipal bond is driven not only by interest rates but also by the perceived default risk of the bond. We might believe that the yield beta is 1.20, meaning that the yield on a corporate bond portfolio is about 20 percent more volatile than the implied yield that drives the futures contract. But this relationship is usually estimated from a regression of corporate bond yield changes on government bond yield changes. This relationship is less stable than if we were running a regression of government bond yield changes on yield changes of a different government bond, the one underlying the futures.

In addition, corporate and municipal bonds often have call features that can greatly distort the relationship between duration and yield change and also make the measurement of duration more complicated. For example, when a bond's yield decreases, its price should increase. The duration is meant to show approximately how much the bond's price should increase. But when the bond is callable and the yield enters into the region in which a call becomes more likely, its price will increase by far less than predicted by the duration. Moreover, the call feature complicates the measurement of duration itself. Duration is no longer a weighted-average maturity of the bond.

Finally, we should note that corporate and municipal bonds are subject to default risk that is not present in government bonds. As the risk of default changes, the yield spread on the defaultable bond relative to the default-free government bond increases. This effect further destabilizes the relationship between the bond portfolio value and the futures price so that duration-based formulas for the number of futures contracts tend to be unreliable.

It is tempting to think that if one wants to increase (decrease) duration and buys (sells) futures contracts, that at least the transaction was the right type even if the number of futures contracts is not exactly correct. The problem, however, is that changes in the bond portfolio value that are driven by changes in default risk or the effects of call provisions will not be matched by movements in the futures contract. The outcome will not always be what is expected.

Another problem associated with the modified duration approach to measuring and managing bond portfolio risk is that the relationship between duration and yield change used here is an instantaneous one. It captures *approximately* how a bond price changes in response to an immediate and very small yield change. As soon as the yield changes or an instant of time passes, the duration changes. Then the number of futures contracts required would change. Thus, the positions described here would need to be revised. Most bond portfolio managers do not perform these kinds of frequent adjustments, however, and simply accept that the transaction will not work precisely as planned.

We should also consider the alternative that the fund could adjust the duration by making transactions in the bonds themselves. It could sell relatively

---

[16] In the Commodity Futures Trading Commission's fiscal year 2001, the Chicago Board of Trade's municipal bond futures contract traded about 1,400 contracts a day. Each contract is worth about $100,000 of municipal bonds. Thus, the average daily volume amounts to about $140 million of municipal bonds—not a very large amount relative to the size of the municipal bond market.

low-duration bonds and buy relatively high-duration bonds to raise the duration to the desired level. There is still no guarantee, however, that the actual duration will be exactly as desired. Likewise, to reduce the duration to zero, the fund could sell out the entire bond portfolio and place the proceeds in cash securities that have low duration. Reducing the duration to essentially zero would be easier to do than increasing it, because it would not be hard to buy bonds with essentially zero duration. Liquidating the entire portfolio, however, would be quite a drastic thing to do, especially given that the fund would likely remain in that position for only a temporary period.

Raising the duration by purchasing higher-duration bonds would be a great deal of effort to expend if the position is being altered only temporarily. Moreover, the transaction costs of buying and selling actual securities are much greater than those of buying and selling futures.

In this reading, we shall consider these adjustments as advanced refinements that one should understand before putting these types of transactions into practice. Although we need to be aware of these technical complications, we shall ignore them in the examples here.

Now let us take a look at managing risk in the equity market.

STRATEGIES AND APPLICATIONS FOR MANAGING EQUITY MARKET RISK

3

Even though interest rates are volatile, the stock market is even more volatile. Hence, the risk associated with stock market volatility is greater than that of bond market volatility. Fortunately, the stock market is generally more liquid than the bond market, at least compared with long-term and corporate and municipal bonds. The risk associated with stock market volatility can be managed relatively well with futures contracts. As we have previously noted, these contracts are based on stock market indices and not individual stocks. Although futures on individual stocks are available, most diversified investors manage risk at the portfolio level, thereby preferring futures on broad-based indices. Accordingly, this will be our focus in this reading. We look more specifically at the risk of managing individual stocks when we study option strategies in Reading 39.

3.1 Measuring and Managing the Risk of Equities

Futures provide the best way to manage the risk of diversified equity portfolios. Although the standard deviation, or volatility, is a common measure of stock market risk, we prefer a measure that more accurately reflects the risk of a diversified stock portfolio. One reason for this preference is that we shall use futures that are based on broadly diversified portfolios. The most common risk measure of this type is the **beta**,[17] often denoted with the Greek symbol β. Beta is an important factor in capital market and asset pricing theory and, as we see here, it plays a major role in risk management. Although you may have encountered beta elsewhere, we shall take a quick review of it here.

---

[17] At this point, we must distinguish this beta from the yield beta. When we use the term "yield beta," we mean the relationship of the yield on the instrument being hedged to the implied yield on the futures. When we use the term "beta" without a modifier, we mean the relationship of a stock or portfolio to the market.

Beta measures the relationship between a stock portfolio and the market portfolio, which is an abstract hypothetical measure of the portfolio containing *all* risky assets, not just stocks. The market portfolio is the most broadly diversified portfolio of all. We know, however, that it is impossible to identify the composition of the true market portfolio. We tend to use proxies, such as the S&P 500 Index, which do not really capture the true market portfolio. Fortunately, for the purposes of risk management, precision in the market portfolio does not matter all that much. Obviously there are no futures contracts on the true market portfolio; there can be futures contracts only on proxies such as the S&P 500. That being the case, it is appropriate to measure the beta of a portfolio relative to the index on which the futures is based.

Beta is a relative risk measure. The beta of the index we use as a benchmark is 1.0. Ignoring any asset-specific risk, an asset with a beta of 1.10 is 10 percent more volatile than the index. A beta of 0.80 is 20 percent less volatile than the index. Beta is formally measured as

$$\beta = \frac{\text{cov}_{SI}}{\sigma_I^2}$$

where cov_{SI} is the covariance between the stock portfolio and the index and σ_I^2 is the variance of the index. Covariance is a measure of the extent to which two assets, here the portfolio and the index, move together.[18] If the covariance is positive (negative), the portfolio and the index tend to move in the same (opposite) direction. By itself, the magnitude of the covariance is difficult to interpret, but the covariance divided by the product of the standard deviations of the stock and the index produces the familiar measure called the correlation coefficient. For beta, however, we divide the covariance by the variance of the index and obtain a measure of the volatility of the portfolio relative to the market.

It is important to emphasize that beta measures only the portfolio volatility relative to the index. Thus, it is a measure only of the risk that cannot be eliminated by diversifying a portfolio. This risk is called the systematic, nondiversifiable, or market risk. A portfolio that is not well diversified could contain additional risk, which is called the nonsystematic, diversifiable, or asset-specific risk.[19] Systematic risk is the risk associated with broad market movements; nonsystematic risk is the risk unique to a company. An example of the former might be a change in interest rates by the Federal Reserve; an example of the latter might be a labor strike on a particular company. Because it captures only systematic risk, beta may seem to be a limited measure of risk, but the best way to manage nonsystematic risk, other than diversification, is to use options, as we do in Reading 39. At this point, we focus on managing systematic or market risk.

As a risk measure, beta is similar to duration. Recall that we captured the dollar risk by multiplying the modified duration by the dollar value of the portfolio. For the bond futures contract, we multiplied its implied modified duration by the futures price. We called this the dollar-implied modified duration. In a similar manner, we shall specify a dollar beta by multiplying the beta by the dollar value of the portfolio. For the futures, we shall multiply its beta by the futures price, f. For the futures contract, beta is often assumed to be 1.0, but that is not exactly the case, so we will specify it as β_f. The dollar beta of the futures contract is $\beta_f f$. The dollar beta of the stock portfolio is written as $\beta_S S$, where β_S is the beta of the stock portfolio and S is the market value of the stock portfolio.

---

[18] More specifically, the covariance measures the extent to which the *returns* on the stock and the index move together.

[19] We also sometimes use the term "idiosyncratic risk."

If we wish to change the beta, we specify the desired beta as a target beta of β_T. Because the value of the futures starts off each day as zero, the dollar beta of the combination of stock and futures if the target beta is achieved is $\beta_T S$.[20] The number of futures we shall use is N_f, which is the unknown that we are attempting to determine. We set the target dollar beta to the dollar beta of the stock portfolio and the dollar beta of N_f futures:

$$\beta_T S = \beta_S S + N_f \beta_f f$$

We then solve for N_f and obtain

$$N_f = \left(\frac{\beta_T - \beta_S}{\beta_f}\right)\left(\frac{S}{f}\right)$$

(38-5)

Observe that if we want to increase the beta, β_T will exceed β_S and the sign of N_f will be positive, which means that we must buy futures. If we want to decrease the beta, β_T will be less than β_S, the sign of N_f will be negative, and we must sell futures. This relationship should make sense: Selling futures will offset some of the risk of holding the stock. Alternatively, buying futures will add risk as $\beta_T > \beta_S$ and $N_f > 0$.

In the special case in which we want to completely eliminate the risk, β_T would be zero and the formula would reduce to

$$N_f = -\left(\frac{\beta_S}{\beta_f}\right)\left(\frac{S}{f}\right)$$

In this case, the sign of N_f will always be negative, which makes sense. To hedge away all of the risk, we definitely need to sell futures.

In the practical implementation of a stock index futures trade, we need to remember that stock index futures prices are quoted on an order of magnitude the same as that of the stock index. The actual futures price is the quoted futures price times a designated multiplier. For example, if the S&P 500 futures price is quoted at 1225, the multiplier of $250 makes the actual futures price $1225(\$250) = \$306{,}250$. This amount would be the value of f in the above formulas. In some situations, the futures price will simply be stated, as for example $306,250. In that case, we can assume the price is quoted as $f = \$306{,}250$ and the multiplier is 1.

We also need to remember that the futures contract will hedge only the risk associated with the relationship between the portfolio and the index on which the futures contract is based. Thus, for example, a portfolio consisting mostly of small-cap stocks should not be paired with a futures contract on a large-cap index such as the S&P 500. Such a transaction would manage only the risk that large-cap stocks move with small-cap stocks. If any divergence occurs in the relationship between these two sectors, such as large-cap stocks going up and small-cap stocks going down, a transaction designed to increase (decrease) risk could end up decreasing (increasing) risk.

Recall also that dividends can interfere with how this transaction performs. Index futures typically are based only on price indices; they do not reflect the

---

[20] Recall that the market value of the portfolio will still be the same as the market value of the stock, because the value of the futures is zero. The futures value becomes zero whenever it is marked to market, which takes place at the end of each day. In other words, the target beta does not appear to be applied to the value of the futures in the above analysis because the value of the futures is zero.

payment and reinvestment of dividends. Therefore, dividends will accrue on the stocks but are not reflected in the index. This is not a major problem, however, because dividends in the short-term period covered by most contracts are not particularly risky.

3.2 Managing the Risk of an Equity Portfolio

To adjust the beta of an equity portfolio, an investment manager could use Equation 38-5 to calculate the number of futures contracts needed. She can use the formula to either increase or decrease the portfolio's systematic risk. The manager might increase the beta if she expects the market to move up, or decrease the beta if she expects the market to move down. Also, the betas of equity portfolios change constantly by virtue of the market value of the portfolio changing.[21] Therefore, futures can be used to adjust the beta from its actual level to the desired level.

Exhibit 3 illustrates the case of a pension fund that wants to increase its equity portfolio beta during a period in which it expects the market to be strong. It increases its beta from 0.90 to 1.10 by purchasing 29 futures contracts. Betas, however, are notoriously difficult to measure. We see after the fact that the beta actually was increased to 1.15. As long as we buy (sell) futures contracts, however, we will increase (decrease) the beta.

EXHIBIT 3	Using Stock Index Futures to Manage the Risk of a Stock Portfolio

Scenario (2 September)

BB Holdings (BBH) is a U.S. conglomerate. Its pension fund generates market forecasts internally and receives forecasts from an independent consultant. As a result of these forecasts, BBH expects the market for large-cap stocks to be stronger than it believes everyone else is expecting over the next two months.

Action

BBH decides to adjust the beta on $38,500,000 of large-cap stocks from its current level of 0.90 to 1.10 for the period of the next two months. It has selected a futures contract deemed to have sufficient liquidity; the futures price is currently $275,000 and the contract has a beta of 0.95. The appropriate number of futures contracts to adjust the beta would be

$$N_f = \left(\frac{\beta_T - \beta_S}{\beta_f}\right)\left(\frac{S}{f}\right) = \left(\frac{1.10 - 0.90}{0.95}\right)\left(\frac{\$38,500,000}{\$275,000}\right) = 29.47$$

So it buys 29 contracts.

(Exhibit continued on next page . . .)

---

[21] Consider, for example, a portfolio in which $3 million is invested in stock with a beta of 1.0 and $1 million is invested in cash with a beta of 0.0 and a rate of 5 percent. The equity market weight is, therefore, 0.75, and the overall beta is $1.0(0.75) + 0.0(0.25) = 0.75$. Now suppose the following year, the stock increases by 20 percent. Then the stock value will be $3.6 million and the cash balance will be $1.05 million. The overall portfolio value will be $4.65 million, so the equity market weight will be $3.6/4.65 = 0.77$. Thus, 77 percent of the portfolio will now have a beta of $1.0(0.77)$, and the overall beta will have drifted upward to 0.77.

EXHIBIT 3   (continued)

Scenario (3 December)

The market as a whole increases by 4.4 percent. The stock portfolio increases to $40,103,000. The stock index futures contract rises to $286,687.50,[22] an increase of 4.25 percent.

Outcome and Analysis

The profit on the futures contract is $29(\$286{,}687.50 - \$275{,}000.00) = \$338{,}937.50$. The rate of return for the stock portfolio is

$$\frac{\$40{,}103{,}000}{\$38{,}500{,}000} - 1 = 0.0416$$

or 4.16 percent. Adding the profit from the futures gives a total market value of $\$40{,}103{,}000.00 + \$338{,}937.50 = \$40{,}441{,}937.50$. The rate of return for the stock portfolio is

$$\frac{\$40{,}441{,}937.50}{\$38{,}500{,}000.00} - 1 = 0.0504$$

or 5.04 percent. Because the market went up by 4.4 percent and the overall gain was 5.04 percent, the effective beta of the portfolio was

$$\frac{0.0504}{0.044} = 1.15$$

Thus, the effective beta is quite close to the target beta of 1.10.

Of course, be aware that increasing the beta increases the risk. Therefore, if the beta is increased and the market falls, the loss on the portfolio will be greater than if beta had not been increased. Decreasing the beta decreases the risk, so if the market rises, the portfolio value will rise less. As an example, consider the outcome described in Exhibit 3. Suppose that instead of being optimistic, the fund manager was very pessimistic and wanted to decrease the beta to zero. Therefore, the target beta, β_T, is 0.0. Then the number of futures contracts would be

$$N_f = \left(\frac{0.0 - 0.90}{0.95}\right)\frac{\$38{,}500{,}000}{\$275{,}000.00} = -132.63$$

So the fund sells 133 futures. Given the same outcome as in Exhibit 3, the profit on the futures contracts would be

$$-133(\$286{,}687.50 - \$275{,}000.00) = -\$1{,}554{,}437.50$$

---

[22] In the examples in this reading, stock futures prices move to a new level in the course of the scenario. These new futures prices come from the cost-of-carry model (assuming there is no mispricing in the market).

There would be a loss of more than \$1.5 million on the futures contracts. The market value of the stock after it moved up was \$40,103,000, but with the futures loss, the market value is effectively reduced to \$40,103,000.00 − \$1,554,437.50 = \$38,548,562.50. This is a return of

$$\frac{\$38,548,562.50}{\$38,500,000.00} - 1 = 0.0013$$

Thus, the effective beta is

$$\frac{0.0013}{0.044} = 0.030$$

The beta has been reduced almost to zero. This reduction costs the company virtually all of the upward movement, but such a cost is to be expected if the beta were changed to zero.

EXAMPLE 3

Equity Analysts Inc. (EQA) is an equity portfolio management firm. One of its clients has decided to be more aggressive for a short period of time. It would like EQA to move the beta on its \$65 million portfolio from 0.85 to 1.05. EQA can use a futures contract priced at \$188,500, which has a beta of 0.92, to implement this change in risk.

A. Determine the number of futures contracts EQA should use and whether it should buy or sell futures.

B. At the horizon date, the equity market is down 2 percent. The stock portfolio falls 1.65 percent, and the futures price falls to \$185,000. Determine the overall value of the position and the effective beta.

Solution to A: The number of futures contracts EQA should use is

$$N_f = \left(\frac{1.05 - 0.85}{0.92}\right)\left(\frac{\$65,000,000}{\$188,500}\right) = 74.96$$

So EQA should buy 75 contracts.

Solution to B: The value of the stock portfolio will be \$65,000,000(1 − 0.0165) = \$63,927,500. The profit on the futures transaction is 75(\$185,000 − \$188,500) = −\$262,500. The overall value of the position is \$63,927,500 − \$262,500 = \$63,665,000.

Thus, the overall return is $\frac{\$63,665,000}{\$65,000,000} - 1 = -0.0205$

Because the market went down by 2 percent, the effective beta is 0.0205/0.02 = 1.025.

3.3 Creating Equity out of Cash

Stock index futures are an excellent tool for creating synthetic positions in equity, which can result in significant transaction cost savings and preserve liquidity. In this section, we explore how to create a synthetic index fund and how to turn cash into synthetic equity.

The relationship between a futures or forward contract and the underlying asset is determined by a formula that relates the risk-free interest rate to the dividends on the underlying asset. Entering into a hypothetical arbitrage transaction in which we buy stock and sell futures turns an equity position into a risk-free portfolio. In simple terms, we say that

Long stock + Short futures = Long risk-free bond

We can turn this equation around to obtain[23]

Long stock = Long risk-free bond + Long futures

If we buy the risk-free bonds and buy the futures, we replicate a position in which we would be buying the stock. This synthetic replication of the underlying asset can be a very useful transaction when we wish to construct a synthetic stock index fund, or when we wish to convert into equity a cash position that we are required to maintain for liquidity purposes. Both of these situations involve holding cash and obtaining equity market exposure through the use of futures.

3.3.1 Creating a Synthetic Index Fund

A **synthetic index fund** is an index fund position created by combining risk-free bonds and futures on the desired index. Suppose a U.S. money manager would like to offer a new product, a fund on an index of U.K. stock as represented by the Financial Times Stock Exchange (FTSE) 100 Index. The manager will initiate the fund with an investment of £100 million. In other words, the U.S. money manager would offer clients an opportunity to invest in a position in British stock with the investment made in British pounds.[24] The manager believes the fund is easier to create synthetically using futures contracts.

To create this synthetic index fund, we need to know several more pieces of information. The dividend yield on the U.K. stocks is 2.5 percent, and the FTSE 100 Index futures contract that we shall use expires in three months, has a quoted price of £4,000, and has a multiplier of £10.[25] The U.K. risk-free interest

---

[23] We turn the equation around by noting that to remove a short futures position from the left-hand side, we should buy futures. If we add a long futures position to the left-hand side, we have to add it to the right-hand side.

[24] If you are wondering why U.S. investors would like to invest in a position denominated in British pounds rather than dollars, remember that the currency risk can be a source of diversification. Adding a position in the U.K. equity market provides one tier of diversification, while adding the risk of the dollar/pound exchange rate adds another tier of diversification, especially because the exchange rate is likely to have a low correlation with the U.S. stock market.

[25] Recall that the multiplier is a number multiplied by the quoted futures price to obtain the actual futures price. In this section, accurately pricing the futures contract is important to the success of these strategies. For example, assume the S&P 500 is at 1,000 and the multiplier is $250, so the full price is $(1,000)($250) = $250,000$. We wish to trade a futures contract priced at f, where f is based on the index value of 1,000 grossed up by the risk-free rate and reduced by the dividends. It is far easier to think of f in terms of its relationship to S without the multiplier. In one case, however, we shall let the multiplier be 1, so you should be able to handle either situation.

rate is 5 percent.[26] When the futures contract expires, it will be rolled over into a new contract.

To create this synthetic index fund, we must buy a certain number of futures. Let the following be the appropriate values of the inputs:

V = amount of money to be invested, £100 million

f = futures price, £4,000

T = time to expiration of futures, 0.25

δ = dividend yield on the index, 0.025

r = risk-free rate, 0.05

q = multiplier, £10

We would like to replicate owning the stock and reinvesting the dividends. How many futures contracts would we need to buy and add to a long bond position? We designate N_f as the required number of futures contracts and $N_f{}^*$ as its rounded-off value.

Now observe that the payoff of $N_f{}^*$ futures contracts will be $N_f{}^*q(S_T - f)$. This equation is based on the fact that we have $N_f{}^*$ futures contracts, each of which has a multiplier of q. The futures contracts are established at a price of f. When it expires, the futures price will be the spot price, S_T, reflecting the convergence of the futures price at expiration to the spot price.

The futures payoff can be rewritten as $N_f{}^*qS_T - N_f{}^*qf$. The minus sign on the second term means that we shall have to pay $N_f{}^*qf$. The (implied) plus sign on the first term means that we shall receive $N_f{}^*qS_T$. Knowing that we buy $N_f{}^*$ futures contracts, we also want to know how much to invest in bonds. We shall call this V* and calculate it based on $N_f{}^*$. Below we shall show how to calculate $N_f{}^*$ and V*. If we invest enough money in bonds to accumulate a value of $N_f{}^*qf$, this investment will cover the amount we agree to pay for the FTSE: $N_f{}^* \times q \times f$. The present value of this amount is $N_f{}^*qf/(1 + r)^T$.

Because the amount of money we start with is V, we should have V equal to $N_f{}^*qf/(1 + r)^T$. From here we can solve for $N_f{}^*$ to obtain

$$N_f{}^* = \frac{V(1 + r)^T}{qf} \qquad \text{(rounded to an integer)} \qquad \text{(38-6)}$$

But once we round off the number of futures, we do not truly have V dollars invested. The amount we actually have invested is

$$V^* = \frac{N_f{}^*qf}{(1 + r)^T} \qquad \text{(38-7)}$$

We can show that investing V* in bonds and buying $N_f{}^*$ futures contracts at a price of f is equivalent to buying $N_f{}^*q/(1 + \delta)^T$ units of stock.

As noted above, if we have bonds maturing to the value $N_f{}^*qf$, we have enough cash on hand to pay the obligation of $N_f{}^*qf$ on our futures contract. The

---

[26] It might be confusing as to why we care about the U.K. interest rate and not the U.S. interest rate. This transaction is completely denominated in pounds, and the futures contract is priced in pounds based on the U.K. dividend yield and interest rate. Hence, the U.K. interest rate plays a role here, and the U.S. interest rate does not.

futures contract will pay us the amount $N_f{*}qS_T$. If we had actually purchased units of stock, the reinvestment of dividends into new units means that we would end up with the equivalent of $Nf{*}q$ units, and means that we implicitly started off with $N_f{*}q/(1 + \delta)^T$ units.

In short, this transaction implies that we synthetically start off with $N_f{*}q/(1 + \delta)^T$ units of stock, collect and reinvest dividends, and end up with $N_f{*}q$ units. We emphasize that all of these transactions are synthetic. We do not actually own the stock or collect and reinvest the dividends. We are attempting only to replicate what would happen if we actually owned the stock and collected and reinvested the dividends.

Exhibit 4 illustrates this transaction. The interest plus principal on the bonds is a sufficient amount to buy the stock in settlement of the futures contract, so the fund ends up holding the stock, as it originally wanted.

EXHIBIT 4   Constructing a Synthetic Index Fund

Scenario (15 December)

On 15 December, a U.S. money manager for a firm called Strategic Money Management (SMM) wants to construct a synthetic index fund consisting of a position of £100 million invested in U.K. stock. The index will be the FTSE 100, which has a dividend yield of 2.5 percent. A futures contract on the FTSE 100 is priced at £4,000 and has a multiplier of £10. The position will be held until the futures expires in three months, at which time it will be renewed with a new three-month futures. The U.K. risk-free rate is 5 percent. Both the risk-free rate and the dividend yield are stated as annually compounded figures.

Action

The number of futures contracts will be

$$N_f = \frac{V(1 + r)^T}{qf} = \frac{£100,000,000(1.05)^{0.25}}{£10(4,000)} = 2,530.68$$

Because we cannot buy fractions of futures contracts, we round N_f to $N_f{*} = 2,531$. With this rounding, we are actually synthetically investing

$$\frac{2,531(£10)4,000}{(1.05)^{0.25}} = £100,012,622$$

in stock. So we put this much money in risk-free bonds, which will grow to £100,012,622$(1.05)^{0.25}$ = £101,240,000. The number of units of stock that we have effectively purchased at the start is

$$\frac{N_f{*}q}{(1 + \delta)^T} = \frac{2,531(10)}{(1.025)^{0.25}} = 25,154.24$$

If the stock had actually been purchased, dividends would be received and reinvested into additional shares. Thus, the number of shares would grow to $25,154.24(1.025)^{0.25} = 25,310$.

(Exhibit continued on next page . . .)

> **EXHIBIT 4**   **(continued)**
>
> *Scenario (15 March)*
>
> The index is at S_T when the futures expires.
>
> *Outcome and Analysis*
>
> The futures contracts will pay off the amount
>
> $$\text{Futures payoff} = 2{,}531(£10)(S_T - £4{,}000) = £25{,}310 S_T - £101{,}240{,}000$$
>
> This means that the fund will pay £101,240,000 to settle the futures contract and obtain the market value of 25,310 units of the FTSE 100, each worth S_T. Therefore, the fund will need to come up with £101,240,000, but as noted above, the money invested in risk-free bonds grows to a value of £101,240,000.
>
> SMM, therefore, pays this amount to settle the futures contracts and effectively ends up with 25,310 units of the index, the position it wanted in the market.

There are a few other considerations to note. One is that we rounded according to the usual rules of rounding, going up if the fraction is 0.5 or greater. By rounding up, we shall have to invest more than V in bonds. If we rounded down, we shall invest less than V. It does not really matter whether we always round up on 0.5 or greater, but that is the rule we shall use here. It should also be noted that this transaction does not capture the dividends that would be earned if one held the underlying stocks directly. The yield of 2.5 percent is important in the computations here, but the fund does not earn these dividends. All this transaction does is capture the performance of the index. Because the index is a price index only and does not include dividends, this synthetic replication strategy can capture only the index performance without the dividends.[27] Another concern that could be encountered in practice is that the futures contract could expire later than the desired date. If so, the strategy will still be successful if the futures contract is correctly priced when the strategy is completed. Consistent with that point, we should note that any strategy using futures will be effective only to the extent that the futures is correctly priced when the position is opened and also when it is closed. This point underscores the importance of understanding the pricing of futures contracts.

3.3.2 Equitizing Cash

The strategy of combining risk-free bonds and futures is used not only to replicate an index; it is also used to take a given amount of cash and turn it into an equity position while maintaining the liquidity provided by the cash. This type of transaction is sometimes called **equitizing cash**. Consider an investment fund that has a large cash balance. It would like to invest in equity but either is not allowed to do so or cannot afford to take the risk that it might need to liquidate a large amount of stock in a short period of time, which could be difficult to do or might result in significant losses. Nonetheless, the fund is willing to take the

---

[27] The values of some stock indices, called total return indices, include reinvested dividends. If a futures contract on the total return index is used, then the strategy would capture the dividends. Doing so would, however, require a few changes to the formulas given here.

risk of equity market exposure provided it can maintain the liquidity. The above transaction can be altered just slightly to show how this is done.

Suppose the fund in Exhibit 4 is actually a U.K. insurance company that has about £100 million of cash invested at the risk-free rate. It would like to gain equity market exposure by investing in the FTSE 100 index. By policy, it is allowed to do so, provided that it maintains sufficient liquidity. If it engages in the synthetic index strategy described above, it maintains about £100 million invested in cash in the form of risk-free bonds and yet gains the exposure to about £100 million of U.K. stock. In the event that it must liquidate its position, perhaps to pay out insurance claims, it need only liquidate the U.K. risk-free bonds and close out the futures contracts. Given the liquidity of the futures market and the obvious liquidity of the risk-free bond market, doing so would be relatively easy.

There is one important aspect of this problem, however, over which the fund has no control: the pricing of the futures. Because the fund will take a long position in futures, the futures contract must be correctly priced. If the futures contract is overpriced, the fund will pay too much for the futures. In that case, the risk-free bonds will not be enough to offset the excessively high price effectively paid for the stock. If, however, the futures contract is underpriced, the fund will get a bargain and will come out much better.

Finally, we should note that these strategies can be illustrated with bond futures to gain bond market exposure, but they are more commonly implemented using stock index futures to gain equity market exposure.

EXAMPLE 4

Index Advantage (INDEXA) is a money management firm that specializes in turning the idle cash of clients into equity index positions at very low cost. INDEXA has a new client with about $500 million of cash that it would like to invest in the small-cap equity sector. INDEXA will construct the position using a futures contract on a small-cap index. The futures price is 1,500, the multiplier is $100, and the contract expires in six months. The underlying small-cap index has a dividend yield of 1 percent. The risk-free rate is 3 percent per year.

A. Determine exactly how the cash can be equitized using futures contracts.

B. When the futures contract expires, the index is at S_T. Demonstrate how the position produces the same outcome as an actual investment in the index.

Solution to A: INDEXA should purchase

$$N_f = \frac{\$500,000,000(1.03)^{0.5}}{\$100(1,500)} = 3,382.96$$

futures contracts. Round this amount to $N_f^* = 3,383$. Then invest

$$\frac{3,383(\$100)(1,500)}{(1.03)^{0.5}} = \$500,005,342$$

in risk-free bonds paying 3 percent interest. Note that this is not exactly an initial investment of $500 million, because one cannot purchase fractions of futures contracts. The bonds will grow to a value of $500,005,342(1.03)^{0.5}$ = $507,450,000. The number of units of stock effectively purchased through the use of futures is

$$\frac{N_f{}^*q}{(1 + \delta)^T} = \frac{3,383(100)}{(1.01)^{0.5}} = 336,621.08$$

If 336,621.08 shares were actually purchased, the accumulation and reinvestment of dividends would result in there being $336,621.08(1.01)^{0.5} =$ 338,300 shares at the futures expiration.

Solution to B: At expiration, the payoff on the futures is

$$3,383(100)(S_T - 1500) = 338,300 S_T - \$507,450,000$$

In other words, to settle the futures, INDEXA will owe $507,450,000 and receive the equivalent of 338,300 units of stock worth S_T.

3.4 Creating Cash out of Equity

Because we have the relation Long stock + Short futures = Long risk-free bonds, we should be able to construct a synthetic position in cash by selling futures against a long stock position. Indeed we have already done a similar transaction when we sold futures to reduce the stock portfolio beta to zero. Therefore, if we wish to sell stock, we can do so by converting it to synthetic cash. This move can save transaction costs and avoid the sale of large amounts of stock at a single point in time.

Suppose the market value of our investment in stock is V, and we would like to create synthetic cash roughly equivalent to that amount. We shall sell futures, with the objective that at the horizon date, we shall have $V(1 + r)^T$. Money in the amount of V will have grown in value at the risk-free rate. Each unit of the index is priced at S. The number of units of the index we shall effectively convert to cash would appear to be (V/S), but because of reinvested dividends, we actually end up with $(1 + \delta)^T$ units of stock for every unit we start with. Hence, the number of units we are effectively converting to cash is $(V/S)(1 + \delta)^T$.

As in the example of the synthetic index fund, we shall again have a problem in that the number of futures contracts must be rounded off to an integer. Keeping that in mind, the payoff of the futures contracts will be $qN_f{}^*(S_T - f) = qN_f{}^*S_T - qN_f{}^*f$. If the number of units of stock is $(V/S)(1 + \delta)^T$, then the value of the overall position (long stock plus short futures) will be $(V/S)(1 + \delta)^T S_T + qN_f{}^*S_T - qN_f{}^*f$. Because we are trying to convert to risk-free bonds (cash), we need to find a way to eliminate the S_T term. We just solve for the value of $N_f{}^*$ that will cause the first two terms to offset.[28] We obtain a previous equation, Equation 38-6

$$N_f{}^* = -\frac{V(1 + r)^T}{qf} \qquad \text{(rounded to an integer)}$$

----

[28] In order to get this solution, we must take the result that $f = S(1 + r)^T/(1 + \delta)^T$ and turn it around so that $S = f(1 + \delta)^T/(1 + r)^T$ to find the value of S.

As usual, the minus sign means that N_f^* is less than zero, which means we are selling futures. Because of rounding, the amount of stock we are actually converting is

$$V^* = \frac{-N_f^* qf}{(1 + r)^T}$$ **(38-8)**

Therefore, if we use N_f^* futures contracts, we have effectively converted stock worth V^* to cash. This will not be the exact amount of stock we own, but it will be close. As in the case of the synthetic index fund, reinvestment of dividends means that the number of units of stock will be $-N_f^* q/(1 + \delta)^T$ at the start and $-N_f^* q$ when the futures expires. In Exhibit 5, we illustrate the application of this strategy for a pension fund that would like to convert $50 million of stock to synthetic cash.

EXHIBIT 5	Creating Synthetic Cash

Scenario (2 June)

The pension fund of Interactive Industrial Systems (IIS) holds a $50 million portion of its portfolio in an indexed position of the Nasdaq 100, which has a dividend yield of 0.75 percent. It would like to convert that position to cash for a two-month period. It can do this using a futures contract on the Nasdaq 100, which is priced at 1484.72, has a multiplier of $100, and expires in two months. The risk-free rate is 4.65 percent.

Action

The fund needs to use

$$N_f = \frac{-V(1 + r)^T}{qf} = -\frac{\$50,000,000(1.0465)^{2/12}}{\$100(1484.72)} = -339.32$$

futures contracts. This amount should be rounded to $N_f^* = -339$. Because of rounding, the amount of stock synthetically converted to cash is really

$$\frac{-N_f^* q}{(1 + r)^T} = \frac{339(\$100)(1484.72)}{(1.0465)^{2/12}} = \$49,952,173$$

This amount should grow to $\$49,952,173(1.0465)^{2/12} = \$50,332,008$. The number of units of stock is

$$\frac{-N_f^* q}{(1 + \delta)^T} = \frac{339(\$100)}{(1.0075)^{2/12}} = 33,857.81$$

at the start, which grows to $33,857.81(1.0075)^{2/12} = 33,900$ units when the futures expires.

Scenario (4 August)

The stock index is at S_T when the futures expires.

(Exhibit continued on next page . . .)

EXHIBIT 5	(continued)

Outcome and Analysis

The payoff of the futures contract is

$$-339(\$100)(S_T - 1484.72) = -\$33,900S_T + \$50,332,008$$

As noted, dividends are reinvested and the number of units of the index grows to 33,900 shares. The overall position of the fund is

Stock worth $33,900S_T$
Futures payoff of $-33,900S_T + \$50,332,008$

or an overall total of $50,332,008. This is exactly the amount we said the fund would have if it invested $49,952,173 at the risk-free rate of 4.65 percent for two months. Thus, the fund has effectively converted a stock position to cash.

EXAMPLE 5

Synthetics Inc. (SYNINC) executes a variety of synthetic strategies for pension funds. One such strategy is to enable the client to maintain a liquid balance in cash while retaining exposure to equity market movements. A similar strategy is to enable the client to maintain its position in the market but temporarily convert it to cash. A client with a $100 million equity position wants to convert it to cash for three months. An equity market futures contract is priced at $325,000, expires in three months, and is based on an underlying index with a dividend yield of 2 percent. The risk-free rate is 3.5 percent.

A. Determine the number of futures contracts SYNINC should trade and the effective amount of money it has invested in risk-free bonds to achieve this objective.

B. When the futures contracts expire, the equity index is at S_T. Show how this transaction results in the appropriate outcome.

Solution to A: First note that no multiplier is quoted here. The futures price of $325,000 is equivalent to a quoted price of $325,000 and a multiplier of 1.0. The number of futures contracts is

$$N_f = -\frac{\$100,000,000(1.035)^{0.25}}{\$325,000} = -310.35$$

Rounding off, SYNINC should sell 310 contracts. This is equivalent to selling futures contracts on stock worth

$$\frac{310(\$325,000)}{(1.035)^{0.25}} = \$99,887,229$$

and is the equivalent of investing \$99,887,229 in risk-free bonds, which will grow to a value of $\$99,887,229(1.035)^{0.25} = \$100,750,000$. The number of units of stock being effectively converted to cash is (ignoring the minus sign)

$$\frac{N_f * q}{(1 + \delta)^T} = \frac{310(1)}{(1.02)^{0.25}} = 308.47$$

The accumulation and reinvestment of dividends would make this figure grow to $308.47(1.02)^{0.25} = 310$ units when the futures expires.

Solution to B: At expiration, the profit on the futures is $-310(S_T - \$325,000) = -310S_T + \$100,750,000$. That means SYNINC will have to pay $310S_T$ and will receive \$100,750,000 to settle the futures contract. Due to reinvestment of dividends, it will end up with the equivalent of 310 units of stock, which can be sold to cover the amount $-310S_T$. This will leave \$100,750,000, the equivalent of having invested in risk-free bonds.

You might be wondering about the relationship between the number of futures contracts given here and the number of futures contracts required to adjust the portfolio beta to zero. Here we are selling a given number of futures contracts against stock to effectively convert the stock to a risk-free asset. Does that not mean that the portfolio would then have a beta of zero? In Section 3.2, we gave a different formula to reduce the portfolio beta to zero. These formulas do not appear to be the same. Would they give the same value of N_f? In the example here, we sell the precise number of futures to completely hedge the stock portfolio. The stock portfolio, however, has to be identical to the index. It cannot have a different beta. The other formula, which reduces the beta to zero, is more general and can be used to eliminate the systematic risk on any portfolio. Note, however, that only systematic risk is eliminated. If the portfolio is not fully diversified, some risk will remain, but that risk is diversifiable, and the expected return on that portfolio would still be the risk-free rate. If we apply that formula to a portfolio that is identical to the index on which the futures is based, the two formulas are the same and the number of futures contracts to sell is the same in both cases.[29]

Finally, we should note that we could have changed the beta of the portfolio by making transactions in individual securities. To raise (lower) the beta we could sell (buy) low-beta stocks and buy (sell) high-beta stocks. Alternatively, we could do transactions in the portfolio itself and the risk-free asset. To reduce the beta to zero, for example, we could sell the entire portfolio and invest the money in the risk-free asset. To increase the beta, we could reduce any position we hold in the risk-free asset, even to the point of borrowing by issuing the risk-free asset.[30] In this reading, we illustrate how these transactions can be better executed using derivatives, which have lower transaction costs and generally greater liquidity. There is no guarantee that either approach will result in the portfolio having the exact beta

---

[29] A key element in this statement is that the futures beta is the beta of the underlying index, multiplied by the present value interest factor using the risk-free rate. This is a complex and subtle point, however, that we simply state without going into the mathematical proof.

[30] Students of capital market theory will recognize that the transactions we describe in this paragraph are those involving movements up and down the capital market line, which leads to investors finding their optimal portfolios. This kind of trading activity in turn leads to the well-known capital asset pricing model.

the investor desired. Betas are notoriously difficult to measure. But executing the transactions in derivatives provides an attractive alternative to having to make a large number of transactions in individual securities. In light of the fact that many of these adjustments are intended to be only temporary, it makes far more sense to do the transactions in derivatives than to make the transactions in the underlying securities, provided that one is willing to keep re-entering positions upon contract expirations.

4   ASSET ALLOCATION WITH FUTURES

It has been widely noted that the most important factor in the performance of an asset portfolio is the allocation of the portfolio among asset classes. In this book, we do not develop techniques for determining the best allocation among asset classes any more than we attempt to determine what beta to set as a target for our stock portfolio or what duration to set as a target for our bond portfolio. We focus instead on how derivative strategies can be used to implement a plan based on a market outlook. As we saw previously in this reading, we can adjust the beta or duration effectively with lower cost and greater liquidity by using stock index or bond futures. In this section, we look at how to allocate a portfolio among asset classes using futures.

4.1 Adjusting the Allocation among Asset Classes

Consider the case of a $300 million portfolio that is allocated 80 percent ($240 million) to stock and 20 percent ($60 million) to bonds. The manager wants to change the allocation to 50 percent ($150 million) stock and 50 percent ($150 million) bonds. Therefore, the manager wants to reduce the allocation to stock by $90 million and increase the allocation to bonds by $90 million. The trick, however, is to use the correct number of futures contracts to set the beta and duration to the desired level. To do this, the manager should sell stock index futures contracts to reduce the beta on the $90 million of stock from its current level to zero. This transaction will effectively convert the stock to cash. She should then buy bond futures contracts to increase the duration on the cash from its current level to the desired level.

Exhibit 6 presents this example. The manager sells 516 stock index futures contracts and buys 742 bond futures contracts. Two months later, the position is worth $297,921,622. As we show, had the transactions been done by selling stocks and buying bonds, the portfolio would be worth $297,375,000, a difference of only about 0.2 percent relative to the original market value. Of course, the futures transactions can be executed in a more liquid market and with lower transaction costs.

Exhibit 7 shows a variation of this problem in which a portfolio management firm wants to convert a portion of a bond portfolio to cash to meet a liquidity requirement and another portion to a higher duration. On the portion it wants to convert to cash, it sells 104 futures contracts. This is the correct amount to change the duration to 0.25, the approximate duration of a short-term money market instrument. It then buys 33 futures contracts to raise the duration on the other part of the portfolio. The net is that it executes only one transaction of 71 contracts, and the end result is a portfolio worth $3,030,250 at the end of the period. Had the transactions been done by selling and buying securities, the portfolio would have been worth $3,048,000, or about the same amount. Another question we shall examine is whether this strategy actually meets the liquidity requirement.

EXHIBIT 6	Adjusting the Allocation between Stocks and Bonds

Scenario (15 November)

Global Asset Advisory Group (GAAG) is a pension fund management firm. One of its funds consists of $300 million allocated 80 percent to stock and 20 percent to bonds. The stock portion has a beta of 1.10 and the bond portion has a duration of 6.5. GAAG would like to temporarily adjust the asset allocation to 50 percent stock and 50 percent bonds. It will use stock index futures and bond futures to achieve this objective. The stock index futures contract has a price of $200,000 (after accounting for the multiplier) and a beta of 0.96. The bond futures contract has an implied modified duration of 7.2 and a price of $105,250. The yield beta is 1. The transaction will be put in place on 15 November, and the horizon date for termination is 10 January.

Action

The market value of the stock is 0.80($300,000,000) = $240,000,000. The market value of the bonds is 0.20($300,000,000) = $60,000,000. Because it wants the portfolio to be temporarily reallocated to half stock and half bonds, GAAG needs to change the allocation to $150 million of each.

Thus, GAAG effectively needs to sell $90 million of stock by converting it to cash using stock index futures and buy $90 million of bonds by using bond futures. This would effectively convert the stock into cash and then convert that cash into bonds. Of course, this entire series of transactions will be synthetic; the actual stock and bonds in the portfolio will stay in place.

Using Equation 38-5, the number of stock index futures, denoted as N_{sf}, will be

$$N_{sf} = \left(\frac{\beta_T - \beta_S}{\beta_f}\right)\frac{S}{f_s}$$

where β_T is the target beta of zero, β_S is the stock beta of 1.10, β_f is the futures beta of 0.96, S is the market value of the stock involved in the transaction of $90 million, and f_s is the price of the stock index futures, $200,000. We obtain

$$N_{sf} = \left(\frac{0. - 1.10}{0.96}\right)\frac{\$90,000,000}{\$200,000} = -515.63$$

Rounding off, GAAG sells 516 contracts.

Using Equation 38-4, the number of bond futures, denoted as N_{bf}, will be

$$N_{bf} = \left(\frac{MDUR_T - MDUR_B}{MDUR_f}\right)\frac{B}{f_b}$$

where $MDUR_T$ is the target modified duration of 6.5, $MDUR_B$ is the modified duration of the existing bonds, $MDUR_f$ is the implied modified duration of the futures (here 7.2), B is the market value of the bonds of $90 million, and f_b is the bond futures price of $105,250. The modified duration of the existing bonds is the modified duration of a cash position. The sale of stock index futures provides $90 million of synthetic cash that is now converted into bonds using bond

(Exhibit continued on next page . . .)

███ **EXHIBIT 6**   (continued) ███

futures. Because no movement of actual cash is involved in these futures market transactions, the modified duration of cash is effectively equal to zero. We obtain

$$N_{bf} = \left(\frac{6.5 - 0.0}{7.2}\right)\left(\frac{\$90,000,000}{\$105,250}\right) = 771.97$$

So GAAG buys 772 contracts.

Scenario (10 January)

During this period, the stock portion of the portfolio returns −3 percent and the bond portion returns 1.25 percent. The stock index futures price goes from $200,000 to $193,600, and the bond futures price increases from $105,250 to $106,691.

Outcome and Analysis

The profit on the stock index futures transaction is −516($193,600 − $200,000) = $3,302,400. The profit on the bond futures transaction is 772($106,691 − $105,250) = $1,112,452. The total profit from the futures transaction is, therefore, $3,302,400 + $1,112,452 = $4,414,852. The market value of the stocks and bonds will now be

    Stocks: $240,000,000(1 − 0.03) = $232,800,000
    Bonds: $60,000,000(1.0125)   = $ 60,750,000
    Total: $293,550,000

Thus, the total portfolio value, including the futures gains, is $293,550,000 + $4,414,852 = $297,964,852. Had GAAG sold stocks and then converted the proceeds to bonds, the value would have been

    Stocks: $150,000,000(1 − 0.03) = $145,500,000
    Bonds: $150,000,000(1.0125)   = $151,875,000
    Total: $297,375,000

This total is a slight difference of about 0.2 percent relative to the market value of the portfolio using derivatives.

We noted in Exhibit 7 that the manager wants to convert a portion of the portfolio to cash to increase liquidity. By selling the futures contracts, the manager maintains the securities in long-term bonds but reduces the volatility of those bonds to the equivalent of that of a short-term instrument. We might, however, question whether liquidity has actually been improved. If cash is needed, the fund would have to sell the long-term bonds and buy back the futures. The latter would not present a liquidity problem, but the sale of the long-term bonds could be a problem. Reducing the duration to replicate a short-term instrument does not remove the problem that long-term instruments, which are still held, may have to be liquidated. What it does is convert the volatility of the instrument to that of a short-term instrument. This conversion in no way handles the liquidity problem.

EXHIBIT 7	Adjusting the Allocation between One Bond Class and Another

Scenario (15 October)

Fixed Income Money Advisors (FIMA) manages bond portfolios for wealthy individual investors. It uses various tactical strategies to alter its mix between long- and short-term bonds to adjust its portfolio to a composition appropriate for its outlook for interest rates. Currently, it would like to alter a $30 million segment of its portfolio that has a modified duration of 6.5. To increase liquidity, it would like to move $10 million into cash but adjust the duration on the remaining $20 million to 7.5. These changes will take place on 15 October and will likely be reversed on 12 December.

Action

The bond futures contract that FIMA will use is priced at $87,500 and has an implied modified duration of 6.85. To convert $10 million of bonds at a duration of 6.5 into cash requires adjusting the duration to that of a cash equivalent. A cash equivalent is a short-term instrument with a duration of less than 1.0. The equivalent instruments that FIMA would use if it did the transactions in cash would be six-month instruments. The average duration of a six-month instrument is three months or 0.25. The interest rate that drives the long-term bond market is assumed to have a yield beta of 1.0 with respect to the interest rate that drives the futures market.

FIMA could solve this problem in either of two ways. It could lower the duration on $10 million of bonds from 6.5 to 0.25. Then it could raise the duration on $20 million from 6.5 to 7.5. If FIMA converts $10 million to a duration of 0.25 and $20 million to a duration of 7.5, the overall duration would be $(10/30)0.25 + (20/30)7.50 = 5.08$. As an alternative, FIMA could just aim for lowering the overall duration to 5.08, but we shall illustrate the approach of adjusting the duration in two steps.

Thus, FIMA needs to lower the duration on $10 million from 6.5 to 0.25. Accordingly, the appropriate number of futures contracts is

$$N_f = \left(\frac{MDUR_T - MDUR_B}{MDUR_f}\right)\left(\frac{B}{f}\right) = \left(\frac{0.25 - 6.50}{6.85}\right)\left(\frac{\$10{,}000{,}000}{\$87{,}500}\right) = -104.28$$

So, FIMA should sell 104 contracts.

To increase the duration on $20 million from 6.5 to 7.5, the appropriate number of futures contracts is

$$N_f = \left(\frac{MDUR_T - MDUR_B}{MDUR_f}\right)\left(\frac{B}{f}\right) = \left(\frac{7.5 - 6.5}{6.85}\right)\left(\frac{\$20{,}000{,}000}{\$87{,}500}\right) = 33.37$$

Thus, FIMA should buy 33 futures contracts.

Because these transactions involve the same futures contract, the net effect is that FIMA should sell 71 contracts. Therefore, FIMA does just one transaction to sell 71 contracts.

Scenario (12 December)

During this period, interest rates rose by 2 percent and the bonds decreased in value by 13 percent (6.5 duration times 2 percent). The futures price fell to

(Exhibit continued on next page . . .)

EXHIBIT 7	(continued)

$75,250. Thus, the $30 million bond portfolio fell by $30,000,000(0.13) = $3,900,000.

Outcome and Analysis

The profit on the futures contracts is $-71(\$75,250 - \$87,500) = \$869,750$. So the overall loss is $3,900,000 - $869,750 = $3,030,250. The change in the portfolio value of 13 percent was based on an assumed yield change of 2 percent (6.5 duration times $0.02 = 0.13$). A portfolio with a modified duration of 5.08 would, therefore, change by approximately $5.08(0.02) = 0.1016$, or 10.16 percent. The portfolio thus would decrease by $30,000,000(0.1016) = $3,048,000.

    The difference in this result and what was actually obtained is $17,750, or about 0.06 percent of the initial $30 million value of the portfolio. Some of this difference is due to rounding and some is due to the fact that bonds do not respond in the precise manner predicted by duration.

It simply means that given an interest rate change, the position will have the sensitivity of a short-term instrument.

    In Exhibit 8, we illustrate a similar situation involving a pension fund that would like to shift the allocation of its portfolio from large-cap stock to mid-cap stock. With futures contracts available on indices of both the large-cap and mid-cap sectors, the fund can do this by selling futures on the large-cap index and buying futures on the mid-cap index. The results come very close to replicating what would happen if it undertook transactions in the actual stocks. The futures transactions, however, take place in a market with much greater liquidity and lower transaction costs.

EXHIBIT 8	Adjusting the Allocation between One Equity Class and Another

Scenario (30 April)

The pension fund of US Integrated Technology (USIT) holds $50 million of large-cap domestic equity. It would like to move $20 million from large-cap stocks to mid-cap stocks. The large-cap stocks have an average beta of 1.03. The desired beta of mid-cap stocks is 1.20. A futures contract on large-cap stocks has a price of $263,750 and a beta of 0.98. A futures contract on mid-cap stocks has a price of $216,500 and a beta of 1.14. The transaction will be initiated on 30 April and terminated on 29 May.

    To distinguish the futures contracts, we use N_{Lf} and N_{Mf} as the number of large-cap and mid-cap futures contracts, f_L and f_M as the prices of large-cap and mid-cap futures contracts ($263,750 and $216,500, respectively), β_L and β_M as the betas of large-cap and mid-cap stocks (1.03 and 1.20, respectively), and β_{Lf} and β_{Mf} as the betas of the large-cap and mid-cap futures (0.98 and 1.14, respectively).

Action

USIT first wants to convert $20 million of stock to cash and then convert $20 million of cash into mid-cap stock. It can use large-cap futures to convert the beta from 1.03 to zero and then use mid-cap futures to convert the beta from 0 to 1.20.

(Exhibit continued on next page . . .)

EXHIBIT 8   **(continued)**

To convert the large-cap stock to cash will require

$$N_{Lf} = \left(\frac{\beta_T - \beta_S}{\beta_f}\right)\left(\frac{S}{f}\right) = \left(\frac{0.0 - 1.03}{0.98}\right)\left(\frac{\$20,000,000}{\$263,750}\right) = -79.70$$

So USIT sells 80 large-cap futures contracts. At this point, it has changed the beta to zero. Now it uses mid-cap futures to convert the beta from 0.0 to 1.20:

$$N_{Mf} = \left(\frac{\beta_T - \beta_B}{\beta_f}\right)\left(\frac{B}{f}\right) = \left(\frac{1.20 - 0.0}{1.14}\right)\left(\frac{\$20,000,000}{\$216,500}\right) = 97.24$$

So USIT buys 97 mid-cap futures contracts.

Scenario (29 May)

Large-cap stocks increase by 2.47 percent, and the large-cap futures price increases to $269,948. Mid-cap stocks increase by 2.88 percent, and the mid-cap futures price increases to $222,432. The $50 million large-cap portfolio is now worth $50,000,000(1.0247) = $51,235,000.

Outcome and Analysis

The profit on the large-cap futures contracts is $-80(\$269,948 - \$263,750) = -\$495,840$. The profit on the mid-cap futures contracts is $97(\$222,432 - \$216,500) = \$575,404$. The total value of the fund is, therefore, $51,235,000 - \$495,840 + \$575,404 = \$51,314,564$.

Had the transactions been executed by selling $20 million of large-cap stock and buying $20 million of mid-cap stock, the value of the large-cap stock would be $30,000,000(1.0247) = $30,741,000, and the value of the mid-cap stock would be $20,000,000(1.0288) = $20,576,000, for a total value of $30,741,000 + $20,576,000 = $51,317,000.

This amount produces a difference of $2,436 compared with making the allocation synthetically, an insignificant percentage of the original portfolio value. The difference comes from the fact that stocks do not always respond in the exact manner predicted by their betas and also that the number of futures contracts is rounded off.

EXAMPLE 6

Q-Tech Advisors manages a portfolio consisting of $100 million, allocated 70 percent to stock at a beta of 1.05 and 30 percent to bonds at a modified duration of 5.5. As a tactical strategy, it would like to temporarily adjust the allocation to 60 percent stock and 40 percent bonds. Also, it would like to change the beta on the stock position from 1.05 to 1.00 and the modified duration from 5.5 to 5.0. It will use a stock index futures contract, which is priced at $280,000 and has a beta of 0.98, and a bond futures contract, which is priced at $125,000 and has an implied modified duration of 6.50.

A. Determine how many stock index and bond futures contracts it should use and whether to go long or short.

B. At the horizon date, the stock portfolio has fallen by 3 percent and the bonds have risen by 1 percent. The stock index futures price is $272,160, and the bond futures price is $126,500. Determine the market value of the portfolio assuming the transactions specified in Part A are done, and compare it to the market value of the portfolio had the transactions been done in the securities themselves.

Solution to A: To reduce the allocation from 70 percent stock ($70 million) and 30 percent bonds ($30 million) to 60 percent stock ($60 million) and 40 percent bonds ($40 million), Q-Tech must synthetically sell $10 million of stock and buy $10 million of bonds. First, assume that Q-Tech will sell $10 million of stock and leave the proceeds in cash. Doing so will require

$$N_{sf} = \left(\frac{0 - 1.05}{0.98}\right)\left(\frac{\$10,000,000}{\$280,000}\right) = -38.27$$

futures contracts. It should sell 38 contracts, which creates synthetic cash of $10 million. To buy $10 million of bonds, Q-Tech should buy

$$N_{bf} = \left(\frac{5.50 - 0.0}{6.50}\right)\left(\frac{\$10,000,000}{\$125,000}\right) = 67.69$$

futures contracts, which rounds to 68. This transaction allows Q-Tech to synthetically borrow $10 million (selling a stock futures contract is equivalent to borrowing cash) and buy $10 million of bonds. Because we have created synthetic cash and a synthetic loan, these amounts offset. Thus, at this point, having sold 38 stock index futures and bought 65 bond futures, Q-Tech has effectively sold $10 million of stock and bought $10 million of bonds. It has produced a synthetically re-allocated portfolio of $60 million of stock and $40 million of bonds.

Now it now needs to adjust the beta on the $60 million of stock to its target of 1.00. The number of futures contracts would, therefore, be

$$N_{sf} = \left(\frac{1.00 - 1.05}{0.98}\right)\left(\frac{\$60,000,000}{\$280,000}\right) = -10.93$$

So it should sell an additional 11 contracts. In total, it should sell 38 + 11 = 49 contracts.

To adjust the modified duration from 5.50 to its target of 5.00 on the $40 million of bonds, the number of futures contracts is

$$N_{bf} = \left(\frac{5 - 5.50}{6.50}\right)\left(\frac{\$40,000,000}{\$125,000}\right) = -24.62$$

So it should sell 25 contracts. In total, therefore, it should buy 68 − 25 = 43 contracts.

Solution to B: The value of the stock will be $70,000,000(1 - 0.03) = $67,900,000.

The profit on the stock index futures will be $-49(\$272,160 - \$280,000) = \$384,160$.

The total value of the stock position is therefore $67,900,000 + $384,160 = $68,284,160.

The value of the bonds will be $30,000,000(1.01) = $30,300,000.

The profit on the bond futures will be $43(\$126,500 - \$125,000) = \$64,500$.

The total value of the bond position is, therefore, $30,300,000 + $64,500 = $30,364,500.

Therefore, the overall position is worth $68,284,160 + $30,364,500 = $98,648,660.

Had the transactions be done in the securities themselves, the stock would be worth $60,000,000(1 - 0.03) = $58,200,000. The bonds would be worth $40,000,000(1.01) = $40,400,000. The overall value of the portfolio would be $58,200,000 + $40,400,000 = $98,600,000, which is a difference of only $48,660 or 0.05 percent of the original value of the portfolio.

So far, we have looked only at allocating funds among different asset classes. In the next section, we place ourselves in the position that funds are not available to invest in any asset classes, but market opportunities are attractive. Futures contracts enable an investor to place itself in the market without yet having the actual cash in place.

4.2 Pre-Investing in an Asset Class

In all the examples so far, the investor is already in the market and wants to either alter the position to a different asset allocation or get out of the market altogether. Now consider that the investor might not be in the market but wants to get into the market. The investor might not have the cash to invest at a time when opportunities are attractive. Futures contracts do not require a cash outlay but can be used to add exposure. We call this approach pre-investing.

An advisor to a mutual fund would like to pre-invest $10 million in cash that it will receive in three months. It would like to allocate this money to a position of 60 percent stock and 40 percent bonds. It can do this by taking long positions in stock index futures and bond futures. The trick is to establish the position at the appropriate beta and duration. This strategy is illustrated in Exhibit 9. We see that the result using futures is very close to what it would have been if the fund had actually had the money and invested it in stocks and bonds.

In a transaction like the one just described, the fund is effectively borrowing against the cash it will receive in the future by pre-investing. Recall that

Long underlying + Short futures = Long risk-free bond

which means that

Long underlying = Long risk-free bond + Long futures

EXHIBIT 9	Pre-Investing in Asset Classes

Scenario (28 February)

Quantitative Mutual Funds Advisors (QMFA) uses modern analytical techniques to manage money for a number of mutual funds. QMFA is not necessarily an aggressive investor, but it does not like to be out of the market. QMFA has learned that it will receive an additional $10 million to invest. Although QMFA would like to receive the money now, the money is not available for three months. If it had the money now, QMFA would invest $6 million in stocks at an average beta of 1.08 and $4 million in bonds at a modified duration of 5.25. It believes the market outlook over the next three months is highly attractive. Therefore, QMFA would like to invest now, which it can do by trading stock and bond futures. An appropriate stock index futures contract is selling at $210,500 and has a beta of 0.97. An appropriate bond futures contract is selling for $115,750 and has an implied modified duration of 6.05. The current date is 28 February, and the money will be available on 31 May. The number of stock index futures contracts will be denoted as N_{sf}, and the number of bond futures contracts will be denoted as N_{bf}.

Action

QMFA wants to take a position in $6 million of stock index futures at a beta of 1.08. It currently has no position; hence, its beta is zero. The required number of stock index futures contracts to obtain this position is

$$N_{sf} = \left(\frac{\beta_T - \beta_S}{\beta_f}\right)\left(\frac{S}{f}\right) = \left(\frac{1.08 - 0.0}{0.97}\right)\left(\frac{\$6,000,000}{\$210,500}\right) = 31.74$$

So QMFA buys 32 stock index futures contracts.

To gain exposure at a duration of 5.25 on $4 million of bonds, the number of bond futures contracts is

$$N_{bf} = \left(\frac{MDUR_T - MDUR_B}{MDUR_f}\right)\left(\frac{B}{f}\right) = \left(\frac{5.25 - 0.0}{6.05}\right)\left(\frac{\$4,000,000}{\$115,750}\right) = 29.99$$

Thus, QMFA buys 30 bond futures contracts.

Scenario (31 May)

During this period, the stock increased by 2.2 percent and the bonds increased by 0.75 percent. The stock index futures price increased to $214,500, and the bond futures price increased to $116,734.

Outcome and Analysis

The profit on the stock index futures contracts is 32($214,500 − $210,500) = $128,000. The profit on the bond futures contracts is 30($116,734 − $115,750) = $29,520. The total profit is, therefore, $128,000 + $29,520 = $157,520.

Had QMFA actually invested the money, the stock would have increased in value by $6,000,000(0.022) = $132,000, and the bonds would have increased in value by $4,000,000(0.0075) = $30,000, for a total increase in value of $132,000 + $30,000 = $162,000, which is relatively close to the futures gain of $157,520. The difference of $4,480 between this approach and the synthetic one is about 0.04 percent of the $10 million invested. This difference is due to the fact that stocks and bonds do not always respond in the manner predicted by their betas and durations and also that the number of futures contracts is rounded off.

In this example, however, the investor does not have the long position in the risk-free bond. That would require cash. We can remove the long risk-free bond in the equation above by off-setting it with a loan in which we borrow the cash. Hence, adding a loan to both sides gives[31]

Long underlying + Loan = Long futures

An outright long position in futures is like a fully leveraged position in the underlying. So in this example, we have effectively borrowed against the cash we will receive in the future and invested in the underlying.

EXAMPLE 7

Total Asset Strategies (TAST) specializes in a variety of risk management strategies, one of which is to enable investors to take positions in markets in anticipation of future transactions in securities. One of its popular strategies is to have the client invest when it does not have the money but will be receiving it later. One client interested in this strategy will receive $6 million at a later date but wants to proceed and take a position of $3 million in stock and $3 million in bonds. The desired stock beta is 1.0, and the desired bond duration is 6.2. A stock index futures contract is priced at $195,000 and has a beta of 0.97. A bond futures contract is priced at $110,000 and has an implied modified duration of 6.0.

A. Find the number of stock and bond futures contracts TAST should trade and whether it should go long or short.

B. At expiration, the stock has gone down by 5 percent, and the stock index futures price is down to $185,737.50. The bonds are up 2 percent, and the bond futures price is up to $112,090. Determine the value of the portfolio and compare it with what it would have been had the transactions been made in the actual securities.

Solution to A: The approximate number of stock index futures is

$$\left(\frac{1.00 - 0.0}{0.97}\right)\left(\frac{\$3,000,000}{\$195,000}\right) = 15.86$$

So TAST should buy 16 contracts. The number of bond futures is

$$\left(\frac{6.2 - 0.0}{6.0}\right)\left(\frac{\$3,000,000}{\$110,000}\right) = 28.18$$

So it should buy 28 contracts.

---

[31] The right-hand side is long a risk-free bond and a loan of the same amount, which offset each other.

> **Solution to B:** The profit on the stock index futures is 16($185,737.50 − $195,000) = −$148,200.
>
> The profit on the bond futures is 28($112,090 − $110,000) = $58,520. The total profit is −$148,200 + $58,520 = $89,680, a loss of $89,680. Suppose TAST had invested directly. The stock would have been worth $3,000,000(1 − 0.05) = $2,850,000, and the bonds would have been worth $3,000,000(1.02) = $3,060,000, for a total value of $2,850,000 + $3,060,000 = $5,910,000, or a loss of $90,000, which is about the same as the loss using only the futures.

When the cash is eventually received, the investor will close out the futures position and invest the cash. This transaction is equivalent to paying off this implicit loan. The investor will then be long the underlying.

We should remember that this position is certainly a speculative one. By taking a leveraged long position in the market, the investor is speculating that the market will perform well enough to cover the cost of borrowing. If this does not happen, the losses could be significant. But such is the nature of leveraged speculation with a specific horizon.

So far, all of the strategies we have examined have involved domestic transactions. We now take a look at how foreign currency derivatives can be used to handle common transactions faced in global commerce.

5 STRATEGIES AND APPLICATIONS FOR MANAGING FOREIGN CURRENCY RISK

The risk associated with changes in exchange rates between currencies directly affects many companies. Any company that engages in business with companies or customers in other countries is exposed to this risk. The volatility of exchange rates results in considerable uncertainty for companies that sell products in other countries as well as for those companies that buy products in other countries. Companies are affected not only by the exchange rate uncertainty itself but also by its effects on their ability to plan for the future. For example, consider a company with a foreign subsidiary. This subsidiary generates sales in the foreign currency that will eventually be converted back into its domestic currency. To implement a business plan that enables the company to establish a realistic target income, the company must not only predict its foreign sales, but it must also predict the exchange rate at which it will convert its foreign cash flows into domestic cash flows. The company may be an expert on whatever product it makes or service it provides and thus be in a good position to make reasonable forecasts of sales. But predicting foreign exchange rates with much confidence is extremely difficult, even for experts in the foreign exchange business. A company engaged in some other line of work can hardly expect to be able to predict foreign exchange rates very well. Hence, many such business choose to manage this kind of risk by locking in the exchange rate on future cash flows with the use of derivatives. This type of exchange rate risk is called **transaction exposure**.

In addition to the risk associated with foreign cash flows, exchange rate volatility also affects a company's accounting statements. When a company combines the balance sheets of foreign subsidiaries into a consolidated balance sheet for the entire company, the numbers from the balance sheets of foreign subsidiaries must be converted into its domestic currency at an appropriate exchange rate. Hence, exchange rate risk manifests itself in this arena as well. This type of exchange rate risk is called **translation exposure**.

Finally, we should note that exchange rate uncertainty can also affect a company by making its products or services either more or less competitive with those of comparable foreign companies. This type of risk can affect any type of company, even if it does not sell its goods or services in foreign markets. For example, suppose the U.S. dollar is exceptionally strong. This condition makes U.S. products and services more expensive to non-U.S. residents and will lead to a reduction in travel to the United States. Hence, the owner of a hotel in the Disney World area, even though her cash flow is entirely denominated in dollars, will suffer a loss of sales when the dollar is strong because fewer non-U.S. residents will travel to the United States, visit Disney World, and stay in her hotel. Likewise, foreign travel will be cheaper for U.S. citizens, and more of them will visit foreign countries instead of Disney World.[32] This type of risk is called **economic exposure**.

In this reading, we shall focus on managing the risk of transaction exposure. The management of translation exposure requires a greater focus on accounting than we can provide here. Managing economic exposure requires the forecasting of demand in light of competitive products and exchange rates, and we shall not address this risk.

The management of a single cash flow that will have to be converted from one currency to another is generally done using forward contracts. Futures contracts tend to be too standardized to meet the needs of most companies. Futures are primarily used by dealers to manage their foreign exchange portfolios.[33] Therefore, in the two examples here, we use forward contracts to manage the risk of a single foreign cash flow.

5.1 Managing the Risk of a Foreign Currency Receipt

When due to receive cash flows denominated in a foreign currency, companies can be viewed as being long the currency. They will convert the currency to their domestic currency and, hence, will be selling the foreign currency to obtain the domestic currency. If the domestic currency increases in value while the company is waiting to receive the cash flow, the domestic currency will be more expensive, and the company will receive fewer units of the domestic currency for the given amount of foreign currency. Thus, being long the foreign currency, the company should consider selling the currency in the forward market by going short a currency forward contract.

Exhibit 10 illustrates the case of a company that anticipates the receipt of a future cash flow denominated in euros. By selling a forward contract on the amount of euros it expects to receive, the company locks in the exchange rate at which it will convert the euros. We assume the contract calls for actual delivery of the euros, as opposed to a **cash settlement**, so the company simply transfers the euros to the dealer, which sends the domestic currency to the company. If the transaction were structured to be settled in cash, the company would sell the euros on the market for the exchange rate at that time, S_T, and the forward

---

[32] Even U.S. citizens who would never travel abroad would not increase their trips to Disney World because of the more favorable exchange rate.

[33] In some cases, single cash flows are managed using currency options, which we cover in Reading 39. A series of foreign cash flows is usually managed using currency swaps, which we cover in Reading 40.

contract would be cash settled for a payment of $-(S_T - F)$, where F is the rate agreed on at the start of the forward contract—in other words, the forward exchange rate. The net effect is that the company receives F, the forward rate for the euros.

EXHIBIT 10	Managing the Risk of a Foreign Currency Receipt

Scenario (15 August)

H-Tech Hardware, a U.S. company, sells its products in many countries. It recently received an order for some computer hardware from a major European government. The sale is denominated in euros and is in the amount of €50 million. H-Tech will be paid in euros; hence, it bears exchange rate risk. The current date is 15 August, and the euros will be received on 3 December.

Action

On 15 August, H-Tech decides to lock in the 3 December exchange rate by entering into a forward contract that obligates it to deliver €50 million and receive a rate of $0.877. H-Tech is effectively long the euro in its computer hardware sale, so a short position in the forward market is appropriate.

Scenario (3 December)

The exchange rate on this day is S_T, but as we shall see, this value is irrelevant for H-Tech because it is hedged.

Outcome and Analysis

The company receives its €50 million, delivers it to the dealer, and is paid $0.877 per euro for a total payment of €50,000,000($0.877) = $43,850,000. H-Tech thus pays the €50 million and receives $43.85 million, based on the rate locked in on 15 August.

5.2 Managing the Risk of a Foreign Currency Payment

In Exhibit 11, we see the opposite type of problem. A U.S. company is obligated to purchase a foreign currency at a later date. Because an increase in the exchange rate will hurt it, the U.S. company is effectively short the currency. Hence, to lock in the rate now, it needs to go long the forward contract. Regardless of the exchange rate at expiration, the company purchases the designated amount of currency at the forward rate agreed to in the contract now.

In Exhibit 10, a company agreed to accept a fixed amount of the foreign currency for the sale of its computer hardware. In Exhibit 11, a company agreed to pay a fixed amount of the foreign currency to acquire the steel. You may be wondering why in both cases the transaction was denominated in the foreign currency. In some cases, a company might be able to lock in the amount of currency in domestic units. It all depends on the relative bargaining power of the buyer and the seller and on how badly each wants to make the sale. Companies with the expertise to manage foreign exchange risk can use that expertise to offer contracts denominated in either currency to their counterparts on the other side of the

EXHIBIT 11	Managing the Risk of a Foreign Currency Payment

Scenario (2 March)

American Manufacturing Catalyst (AMC) is a U.S. company that occasionally makes steel and copper purchases from non-U.S. companies to meet unexpected demand that cannot be filled through its domestic suppliers. On 2 March, AMC determines that it will need to buy a large quantity of steel from a Japanese company on 1 April. It has entered into a contract with the Japanese company to pay ¥900 million for the steel. At a current exchange rate of $0.0083 per yen, the purchase will currently cost ¥900,000,000($0.0083) = $7,470,000. AMC faces the risk of the yen strengthening.

Action

In its future steel purchase, AMC is effectively short yen, because it will need to purchase yen at a later date. Thus, a long forward contract is appropriate. AMC decides to lock in the exchange rate for 1 April by entering into a long forward contract on ¥900 million with a dealer. The forward rate is $0.008309. AMC will be obligated to purchase ¥900 million on 1 April and pay a rate of $0.008309.

Scenario (1 April)

The exchange rate for yen is S_T. As we shall see, this value is irrelevant for AMC, because it is hedged.

Outcome and Analysis

The company purchases ¥900 million from the dealer and pays $0.008309, for a total payment of ¥900,000,000($0.008309) = $7,478,100. This amount was known on 2 March. AMC gets the yen it needs and uses it to purchase the steel.

---

transaction. For example, in the second case, suppose the Japanese company was willing to lock in the exchange rate using a forward contract with one of its derivatives dealers. Then the Japanese company could offer the U.S. company the contract in U.S. dollars. The ability to manage exchange rate risk and offer customers a price in either currency can be an attractive feature for a seller.

EXAMPLE 8

Royal Tech Ltd. is a U.K. technology company that has recently acquired a U.S. subsidiary. The subsidiary has an underfunded pension fund, and Royal Tech has absorbed the subsidiary's employees into its own pension fund, bringing the U.S. subsidiary's defined benefit plan up to an adequate level of funding. Soon Royal Tech will be making its first payments to retired employees in the United States. Royal Tech is obligated to pay about $1.5 million to these retirees. It can easily set aside in risk-free bonds the amount of pounds it will need to make the payment, but it is concerned about the foreign currency risk in making the U.S. dollar payment. To manage this risk, Royal Tech is considering using a forward contract that has a contract rate of £0.60 per dollar.

A. Determine how Royal Tech would eliminate this risk by identifying an appropriate forward transaction. Be sure to specify the notional principal and state whether to go long or short. What domestic transaction should it undertake?

B. At expiration of the forward contract, the spot exchange rate is S_T. Explain what happens.

Solution to A: Royal Tech will need to come up with $1,500,000 and is obligated to buy dollars at a later date. It is thus short dollars. To have $1,500,000 secured at the forward contract expiration, Royal Tech would need to go long a forward contract on the dollar. With the forward rate equal to £0.60, the contract will need a notional principal of £900,000. So Royal Tech must set aside funds so that it will have £900,000 available when the forward contract expires. When it delivers the £900,000, it will receive £900,000(1/£0.60) = $1,500,000, where 1/£0.60 ≈ $1.67 is the dollar-per-pound forward rate.

Solution to B: At expiration, it will not matter what the spot exchange rate is. Royal Tech will deliver £900,000 and receive $1,500,000.

5.3 Managing the Risk of a Foreign-Market Asset Portfolio

One of the dominant themes in the world of investments in the last 20 years has been the importance of diversifying internationally. The increasing globalization of commerce has created a greater willingness on the part of investors to think beyond domestic borders and add foreign securities to a portfolio.[34] Thus, more asset managers are holding or considering holding foreign stocks and bonds. An important consideration in making such a decision is the foreign currency risk. Should a manager accept this risk, hedge the foreign market risk and the foreign currency risk, or hedge only the foreign currency risk?

It is tempting to believe that the manager should accept the foreign market risk, using it to further diversify the portfolio, and hedge the foreign currency risk. In fact, many asset managers claim to do so. A closer look, however, reveals that it is virtually impossible to actually do this.

Consider a U.S. asset management firm that owns a portfolio currently invested in euro-denominated stock worth S_0, where S_0 is the current stock price in euros. The exchange rate is FX_0 dollars per euro. Therefore, the portfolio is currently worth $S_0(FX_0)$ in dollars. At a future time, t, the portfolio is worth S_t in euros and the exchange rate is FX_t. So the portfolio would then be worth $S_t(FX_t)$. The firm is long both the stock and the euro.

A forward contract on the euro would require the firm to deliver a certain number of euros and receive the forward rate, F. The number of euros to be delivered, however, would need to be specified in the contract. In this situation,

---

[34] Ironically, the increasing globalization of commerce has increased the correlation among the securities markets of various countries. With this higher correlation, the benefits of international diversification are much smaller.

the firm would end up delivering S_t euros. This amount is unknown at the time the forward contract is initiated. Thus, it would not be possible to know how many euros the firm would need to deliver.

Some companies manage this problem by estimating an expected future value of the portfolio. They enter into a hedge based on that expectation and adjust the hedge to accommodate any changes in expectations. Other companies hedge a minimum portfolio value. They estimate that it is unlikely the portfolio value will fall below a certain level and then sell a forward contract for a size based on this minimum value.[35] This approach leaves the companies hedged for a minimum value, but any increase in the value of the portfolio beyond the minimum would not be hedged. Therefore, any such gains could be wiped out by losses in the value of the currency.

So, with the exception of one special and complex case we discuss below, it is not possible to leave the local equity market return exposed and hedge the currency risk.[36] If the local market return is hedged, then it would be possible to hedge the currency risk. The hedge of the local market return would lock in the amount of the foreign currency that would be converted at the hedge **termination date**. Of course, the company can hedge the local market return and leave the currency risk unhedged. Or it can hedge neither.[37]

In Exhibit 12, we examine the two possibilities that can be executed: hedging the local market risk and hedging both the local market risk *and* the foreign currency risk. We first use futures on the foreign equity portfolio as though no currency risk existed. This transaction attempts to lock in the future value of the portfolio. This locked-in return should be close to the foreign risk-free rate. If we also choose to hedge the currency risk, we then know that the future value of the portfolio will tell us the number of units of the foreign currency that we shall have available to convert to domestic currency at the hedge termination date. Then we would know the amount of notional principal to use in a forward contract to hedge the exchange rate risk.

EXHIBIT 12	Managing the Risk of a Foreign-Currency-Denominated Asset Portfolio

Scenario (31 December)

AZ Asset Management is a U.S. firm that invests money for wealthy individual investors. Concerned that it does not know how to manage foreign currency risk, so far AZ has invested only in U.S. markets. Recently, it began learning about managing currency risk and would like to begin investing in foreign markets with a small position worth €10 million. The proposed portfolio has a beta of 1.10. AZ is considering either hedging the European equity market return and leaving the currency risk unhedged, or hedging the currency risk as well as the European equity market return. If it purchases the €10 million portfolio, it will put this hedge in place on 31 December and plans to leave the position open until 31 December of the following year.

(Exhibit continued on next page . . .)

[35] One way to assure a minimum value would be use a put option. We shall take up this strategy in Reading 39.

[36] The foreign equity market return is often referred to as the local market return, a term we shall use henceforth.

[37] In fact, some compelling arguments exist for hedging neither. The currency risk can be unrelated to the domestic market risk, thereby offering some further diversifying risk-reduction possibilities.

> **EXHIBIT 12**   (continued)

For hedging the European equity market risk, it will use a stock index futures contract on a euro-denominated stock index. This contract is priced at €120,000 and has a beta of 0.95. If it hedges the currency risk, it will use a dollar-denominated forward contract on the euro. That contract has a price of $0.815 and can have any notional principal that the parties agree on at the start. The current spot exchange rate is $0.80. The foreign risk-free rate is 4 percent, which is stated as an annually compounded rate. The domestic risk-free rate is 6 percent.

Action

Hedging the equity market risk only: To eliminate the risk on the portfolio of stock that has a beta of 1.10 would require

$$N_f = \left(\frac{0 - 1.10}{0.95}\right)\left(\frac{10,000,000}{120,000}\right) = -96.49$$

contracts. This amount would be rounded to 96, so AZ would sell 96 contracts.

Hedging the equity market risk and the currency risk: Again, AZ would sell 96 stock index futures contracts. It would enter into a forward contract to lock in the exchange rate on a certain amount of euros on 31 December. The question is, how many euros will it have? If the futures contract hedges the stock portfolio, it should earn the foreign risk-free rate. Thus, the portfolio should be worth €10,000,000(1.04) = €10,400,000. So, AZ expects to have €10,400,000 on the following 31 December and will convert this amount back to dollars. So the notional principal on the forward contract should be €10.4 million. Note that the starting portfolio value in dollars is €10,000,000($0.80) = $8,000,000.

Scenario (31 December of the Following Year)

During the year, the European stock market went down 4.55 percent. Given the portfolio beta of 1.10, it declines by 4.55(1.10) = 5 percent. The portfolio is now worth €10,000,000(1 − 0.05) = €9,500,000. The exchange rate fell to $0.785, and the futures price fell to €110,600.

Outcome and Analysis

If nothing is hedged: The portfolio is converted to dollars at $0.785 and is worth €9,500,000(0.785) = $7,457,500. This amount represents a loss of 6.8 percent over the initial value of $8,000,000.

If only the European stock market is hedged: The profit on the futures would be −96(€110,600 − €120,000) = €902,400. Adding this amount to the value of the portfolio gives a value of €9,500,000 + €902,400 = €10,402,400, which is an increase in value of 4.02 percent, or approximately the foreign risk-free rate, as it should be. This amount is converted to dollars to obtain €10,402,400($0.785) = $8,165,884, a gain of 2.07 percent.

If the European stock market and the currency risk are both hedged: AZ sold €10.4 million of euros in the forward market at $0.815. The contract will settle in cash and show a profit of €10,400,000($0.785 − $0.815) = $312,000. This leaves the overall portfolio value at $8,165,884 + $312,000 = $8,477,884, a gain of 5.97 percent, or approximately the domestic risk-free rate.

(Exhibit continued on next page . . .)

| EXHIBIT 12 | (continued) |

In this case, the foreign stock market went down *and* the foreign currency went down. Without the hedge, the loss was almost 7 percent. With the foreign stock market hedge, the loss turns into a gain of 2 percent. With the currency hedge added, the loss becomes a gain of almost 6 percent. Of course, different outcomes could occur. Gains from a stronger foreign stock market and a stronger currency would be lost if the company had made these same hedges.

Note, however, that once AZ hedges the foreign market return, it can expect to earn only the foreign risk-free rate. If it hedges the foreign market return and the exchange rate, it can expect to earn only its domestic risk-free rate. Therefore, neither strategy makes much sense for the long run. In the short run, however, this strategy can be a good tactic for investors who are already in foreign markets and who wish to temporarily take a more defensive position without liquidating the portfolio and converting it to cash.

EXAMPLE 9

FCA Managers (FCAM) is a U.S. asset management firm. Among its asset classes is a portfolio of Swiss stocks worth SF10 million, which has a beta of 1.00. The spot exchange rate is $0.75, the Swiss interest rate is 5 percent, and the U.S. interest rate is 6 percent. Both of these interest rates are compounded in the LIBOR manner: Rate × (Days/360). These rates are consistent with a six-month forward rate of $0.7537. FCAM is considering hedging the local market return on the portfolio and possibly hedging the exchange rate risk for a six-month period. A futures contract on the Swiss market is priced at SF300,000 and has a beta of 0.90.

A. What futures position should FCAM take to hedge the Swiss market return? What return could it expect?

B. Assuming that it hedges the Swiss market return, how could it hedge the exchange rate risk as well, and what return could it expect?

Solution to A: To hedge the Swiss local market return, the number of futures contracts is

$$N_f = \left(\frac{0 - 1.00}{0.90}\right)\left(\frac{SF10,000,000}{SF300,000}\right) = -37.04$$

So FCAM should sell 37 contracts. Because the portfolio is perfectly hedged, its return should be the Swiss risk-free rate of 5 percent.

Solution to B: If hedged, the Swiss portfolio should grow to a value of SF10,000,000[1 + 0.05(180/360)] = SF10,250,000.

FCAM could hedge this amount with a forward contract with this much notional principal. If the portfolio is hedged, it will convert to a value of SF10,250,000($0.7537) = $7,725,425.

In dollars, the portfolio was originally worth SF10,000,000($0.75) = 7,500,000. Thus, the return is $\frac{\$7,725,425}{\$7,500,000} - 1 \approx 0.03$, which is the U.S. risk-free rate for six months.

We see that if only the foreign stock market return is hedged, the portfolio return is the foreign risk-free rate before converting to the domestic currency. If both the foreign stock market and the exchange rate risk are hedged, the return equals the domestic risk-free rate.

As a temporary and tactical strategy, hedging one or both risks can make sense. There are certainly periods when one might be particularly concerned about these risks and might wish to eliminate them. Executing this sort of strategy can be much easier than selling all of the foreign stocks and possibly converting the proceeds into domestic currency. But in the long run, a strategy of investing in foreign markets, hedging that risk, and hedging the exchange rate risk hardly makes much sense.

6   FUTURES OR FORWARDS?

As we have seen, numerous opportunities and strategies exist for managing risk using futures and forwards. We have largely ignored the issue of which instrument—futures or forwards—is better. Some types of hedges are almost always executed using futures, and some are almost always executed using forwards. Why the preference for one over the other? First, let us recall the primary differences between the two:

▶ Futures contracts are standardized, with all terms except for the price set by the futures exchange. Forward contracts are customized. The two parties set the terms according to their needs.

▶ Futures contracts are guaranteed by the clearinghouse against default. Forward contracts subject each party to the possibility of default by the other party.

▶ Futures contracts require margin deposits and the **daily settlement** of gains and losses. Forward contracts pay off the full value of the contract at expiration. Some participants in forward contracts agree prior to expiration to use margin deposits and occasional settlements to reduce the default risk.

▶ Futures contracts are regulated by federal authorities. Forward contracts are essentially unregulated.

▶ Futures contracts are conducted in a public arena, the futures exchange, and are reported to the exchanges and the regulatory authority. Forward contracts are conducted privately, and individual transactions are not generally reported to the public or regulators.

Risks that are associated with very specific dates, such as when interest rates are reset on a loan, usually require forward contracts. Thus, we used an FRA to lock in the rate on a loan. That rate is set on a specific day. A futures contract has specific expirations that may not correspond to the day on which the rate is reset. Although it is possible to use sophisticated models and software to compensate for this problem, typical borrowers do not usually possess the expertise to do so. It is much easier for them to use an FRA.

Oddly enough, however, the risk of most bond portfolios is managed using Treasury bond futures. Those portfolios have horizon dates for which the company is attempting to lock in values. But usually rates are not being reset on that date, and the hedge does not need to be perfect. Often there is flexibility with respect to the horizon date. Treasury bond futures work reasonably well for these investors. Likewise, the risk of equity portfolios tends to be managed with stock index futures. Even though the offsetting of risks is not precise, that is not a necessity. Equity and debt portfolio managers usually need only satisfactory protection against market declines. Nonetheless, in some cases equity and debt portfolio managers use over-the-counter instruments such as forward contracts. In fact, sometimes a portfolio manager will ask a derivatives dealer to write a forward contract on a specific portfolio. This approach is more costly than using futures and provides a better hedge, but, as noted, a perfect hedge is usually not needed. In practice, portfolio managers have traded off the costs of customized hedges with the costs of using standardized futures contracts and have found the latter to be preferable.[38]

Forward contracts are the preferred vehicle for the risk management of foreign currency. This preference partly reflects the deep liquidity in the forward market, which has been around longer than the futures market. Moreover, much of this trading is undertaken by corporations managing the risk of either the issuance of a bond or the inflows and outcomes of specific currency transactions, in which case the precision provided by customized transactions is preferred.

Nevertheless, one might wonder why certain contracts do not die out. Recall that most corporations do not use the Eurodollar futures market to hedge their floating-rate loans. Yet the Eurodollar futures contract is one of the most active of all futures contracts in the world. Where does this volume come from? It is from the dealers in swaps, options, and FRAs. When they enter into transactions with end users in which the underlying rate is LIBOR, they must manage the risk they have assumed, and they must do so very quickly. They cannot afford to leave their positions exposed for long. It is rarely possible for them to simply pick up the phone and find another customer to take the opposite side of the transaction. A corporate client with the exact opposite needs at the exact same time as some other end user would be rare. Therefore, dealers need to execute offsetting transactions very quickly. There is no better place to do this than in the Eurodollar futures markets, with its extremely deep liquidity. These dealer companies have sophisticated analysts and software and are able to manage the risk caused by such problems as the futures contract expiring on one day and the payoffs on the FRAs being set on another day. Thus, these risks can be more effectively measured and managed by dealers than by end users.

As we have emphasized, futures contracts require margin deposits and the daily settling of gains and losses. This process causes some administrative problems because money must be deposited into a futures account and cash flows must be managed on a daily basis. When futures brokers call for more money to cover losses, companies using futures contracts must send cash or very liquid securities. Although the brokers may be generating value on the other side of a hedge transaction, that value may not produce actual cash.[39] On the other hand, forward transactions, while not necessarily requiring margin deposits, generate concerns over whether the counterparty will be able to pay at expiration. Of course, those concerns lead some counterparties to require margins and periodic settlements.

Although forward contracts are essentially unregulated while futures contracts are heavily regulated, this factor is not usually a major consideration in deciding which type of contract to use. In some cases, however, regulation prevents use of a specific contract. For example, a country might prohibit foreign futures exchanges

---

[38] Portfolio managers do use swaps on occasion, as we cover in Reading 40.

[39] Consider, for example, a company that sells futures contracts to hedge the value of a bond portfolio. Suppose interest rates fall, the bond portfolio rises, and the futures price also rises. Losses will be incurred on the futures contracts and additional margin deposits will be required. The bond portfolio has increased in value, but it may not be practical to liquidate the portfolio to generate the necessary cash.

from offering their products in its markets. There would probably be no such prohibition on forward contracts.[40] In some cases, regulation prevents or delays usage of certain futures products, making it possible for innovative companies that can create forward products to offer them ahead of the comparable products of futures exchanges. The futures exchanges claim this is unfair by making it more difficult for them to compete with forward markets in providing risk management products.

We also noted that futures contracts are public transactions, whereas forward contracts are private transactions. This privacy characteristic can cause a company to prefer a forward transaction if it does not want others, such as traders on the futures exchange, to know its views.

7   FINAL COMMENTS

A few points are worth repeating. Because they can be somewhat unstable, betas and durations are difficult to measure, even under the best of circumstances. Even when no derivatives transactions are undertaken, the values believed to be the betas and durations may not truly turn out to reflect the sensitivities of stocks and bonds to the underlying sources of risk. Therefore, if derivatives transactions do not work out to provide the exact hedging results expected, users should not necessarily blame derivatives. If, however, speculative long (short) positions are added to an otherwise long position, risk should increase (decrease), although the exact amount of the increase (decrease) cannot be known for sure in advance.[41] Derivatives should not be maligned for their speculative use when there are valuable hedging uses.

We have mentioned that transaction costs are a major consideration in the use of derivatives, and this is clearly the case with futures and forwards. By some reports, transactions costs for stock index derivatives are approximately 95 percent lower than for stock indices.[42] Indeed, one of the major reasons that derivatives exist is that they provide a means of trading at lower transaction costs. To survive as risk management products, derivatives need to be much less expensive than the value of the underlying instruments. There are almost no situations in which transacting in the underlying securities would be preferable to using derivatives on a transaction-cost basis, when taking a position for a specified short horizon.

Transacting in futures and forwards also has a major advantage of being less disruptive to the portfolio and its managers. For example, the asset classes of many portfolios are managed by different persons or firms. If the manager of the overall portfolio wants to change the risk of certain asset classes or alter the allocations between asset classes, he can do so using derivatives. Instead of telling one manager that she must sell securities and another manager that he must buy securities, the portfolio manager can use derivatives to reduce the

---

[40] In some less developed but highly regulated countries, private financial transactions such as forward contracts can be prohibited.

[41] We use the expression "should increase (decrease)" to reflect the fact that some other factors could cause perverse results. We previously mentioned call features and credit risk of such assets as corporate and municipal bonds that could result in a bond price not moving in the same direction as a move in the general level of bond prices. A poorly diversified stock portfolio could move opposite to the market, thereby suggesting a negative beta that is really only diversifiable risk. We assume that these situations are rare or that their likelihood and consequences have been properly assessed by risk managers.

[42] These statements are based on trading all individual stocks that make up an index. Trading through exchange-traded funds would reduce some of these stock trading costs.

allocation to one class and increase the allocation to the other. The asset class managers need not even know that the overall asset allocation has been changed. They can concentrate on doing the best they can within their respective areas of responsibility.

In the matter of liquidity, however, futures and forwards do not always offer the advantages often attributed to them. They require less capital to trade than the underlying securities, but they are not immune to liquidity problems. Nowhere is this concern more evident than in using a futures contract that expires a long time from the present. The greatest liquidity in the futures markets is in the shortest expirations. Although there may be futures contracts available with long-term expirations, their liquidity is much lower. Many forward markets are very liquid, but others may not be. High liquidity should not automatically be assumed of all derivatives, although in general, derivatives are more liquid than the underlying securities.

Many organizations are not permitted to use futures or forwards. Futures and forwards are fully leveraged positions, because they essentially require no equity. Some companies might have a policy against fully leveraged positions but might permit options, which are not fully leveraged. Loss potential is much greater on purchased or sold futures or forwards, whereas losses are capped on purchased options. Some organizations, however, permit futures and forwards but prohibit options. Other organizations might prohibit credit-risky instruments, such as forwards and over-the-counter options, but permit credit-risk-free instruments, such as futures and exchange-listed options. These restrictions, although sometimes misguided, are realistic constraints that must be considered when deciding how to manage risk.

In conclusion, futures and forward contracts are both alike and different. On some occasions, one is preferred over the other. Both types of contracts have their niches. The most important point they have in common is that they have zero value at the start and offer linear payoffs, meaning that no one "invests" any money in either type of contract at the start, but the cost is paid for by the willingness to give up gains and incur losses resulting from movements in the underlying. Options, which require a cash investment at the start, allow a party to capture favorable movements in the underlying while avoiding unfavorable movements. This type of payoff is nonlinear. In some cases, options will be preferred to other types of derivatives.

SUMMARY

► A borrower can lock in the rate that will be set at a future date on a **single-payment loan** by entering into a long position in an FRA. The FRA obligates the borrower to make a fixed interest payment and receive a floating interest payment, thereby protecting the borrower if the loan rate is higher than the fixed rate in the FRA but also eliminating gains if the loan rate is lower than the fixed rate in the FRA.

► The duration of a bond futures contract is determined as the duration of the bond underlying the futures contract as of the futures expiration, based on the yield of the bond underlying the futures contract. The modified duration is obtained by dividing the duration by 1 plus the yield. The duration of a futures contract is implied by these factors and is called the implied (modified) duration.

► The implied yield of a futures contract is the yield implied by the futures price on the bond underlying the futures contract as of the futures expiration.

► The yield beta is the sensitivity of the yield on a bond portfolio relative to the implied yield on the futures contract.

► The number of bond futures contracts required to change the duration of a bond portfolio is based on the ratio of the market value of the bonds to the futures price multiplied by the difference between the target or desired modified duration and the actual modified duration, divided by the implied modified duration of the futures.

► The actual adjusted duration of a bond portfolio may not equal the desired duration for a number of reasons, including that the yield beta may be inaccurate or unstable or the bonds could contain call features or default risk. In addition, duration is a measure of instantaneous risk and may not accurately capture the risk over a long horizon without frequent portfolio adjustments.

► The number of equity futures contracts required to change the beta of an equity portfolio is based on the ratio of the market value of the stock to the futures price times the difference between the target or desired beta and the actual beta, divided by the beta of the futures.

► A long position in stock is equivalent to a long position in futures and a long position in a risk-free bond; therefore, it is possible to synthetically create a long position in stock by buying futures on stock and a risk-free bond. This process is called equitizing cash and can be used to create a synthetic stock index fund.

► A long position in cash is equivalent to a long position in stock and a short position in stock futures. Therefore, it is possible to synthetically create a long position in cash by buying stock and selling futures.

► The allocation of a portfolio between equity and debt can be adjusted using stock index and bond futures. Buy futures to increase the allocation to an asset class, and sell futures to decrease the allocation to an asset class.

► The allocation of a bond portfolio between cash and high-duration bonds can be adjusted by using bond futures. Sell futures to increase the allocation to cash, and buy futures to increase the allocation to long-term bonds.

► The allocation of an equity portfolio among different equity sectors can be adjusted by using stock index futures. Sell futures on an index representing one sector to decrease the allocation to that sector, and buy futures on an index representing another sector to increase the allocation to that sector.

▶ A portfolio manager can buy bond or stock index futures to take a position in an asset class without having cash to actually invest in the asset class. This type of strategy is sometimes used in anticipation of the receipt of a sum of cash at a later date, which will then be invested in the asset class and the futures position will be closed.

▶ Transaction exposure is the risk associated with a foreign exchange rate on a specific business transaction such as a purchase or sale. Translation exposure is the risk associated with the conversion of foreign financial statements into domestic currency. Economic exposure is the risk associated with changes in the relative attractiveness of products and services offered for sale, arising out of the competitive effects of changes in exchange rates.

▶ The risk of a future foreign currency receipt can be eliminated by selling a forward contract on the currency. This transaction locks in the rate at which the foreign currency will be converted to the domestic currency.

▶ The risk of a future foreign currency payment can be eliminated by buying a forward contract on the currency. This transaction locks in the rate at which the domestic currency will be converted to the foreign currency.

▶ It is not possible to invest in a foreign equity market and precisely hedge the currency risk only. To hedge the currency risk, one must know the exact amount of foreign currency that will be available at a future date. Without locking in the equity return, it is not possible to know how much foreign currency will be available.

▶ It is possible to hedge the foreign equity market return and accept the exchange rate risk or hedge the foreign equity market return *and* hedge the exchange rate risk. By hedging the equity market return, one would know the proper amount of currency that would be available at a later date and could use a futures or forward contract to hedge the currency risk. The equity return, however, would equal the risk-free rate.

▶ Forward contracts are usually preferred over futures contracts when the risk is related to an event on a specific date, such as an interest rate reset. Forward contracts on foreign currency are usually preferred over futures contracts, primarily because of the liquidity of the market. Futures contracts require margins and daily settlements but are guaranteed against credit losses and may be preferred when credit concerns are an issue. Either contract may be preferred or required if there are restrictions on the use of the other. Dealers use both instruments in managing their risk, occasionally preferring one instrument and sometimes preferring the other. Forward contracts are preferred if privacy is important.

▶ Futures and forwards, as well as virtually all derivatives, have an advantage over transactions in the actual instruments by virtue of their significantly lower transaction costs. They also allow a portfolio manager to make changes in the risk of certain asset classes or the allocation among asset classes without disturbing the asset class or classes themselves. This feature allows the asset class managers to concentrate on their respective asset classes without being concerned about buying and selling to execute risk-altering changes or asset allocation changes.

▶ Although futures and forwards tend to be more liquid than their underlying assets, they are not always highly liquid. Therefore, it cannot always be assumed that futures and forwards can solve liquidity problems.

PRACTICE PROBLEMS FOR READING 38

1. An investment management firm wishes to increase the beta for one of its portfolios under management from 0.95 to 1.20 for a three-month period. The portfolio has a market value of $175,000,000. The investment firm plans to use a futures contract priced at $105,790 in order to adjust the portfolio beta. The futures contract has a beta of 0.98.

   A. Calculate the number of futures contracts that should be bought or sold to achieve an increase in the portfolio beta.

   B. At the end of three months, the overall equity market is up 5.5 percent. The stock portfolio under management is up 5.1 percent. The futures contract is priced at $111,500. Calculate the value of the overall position and the effective beta of the portfolio.

2. Consider an asset manager who wishes to create a fund with exposure to the Russell 2000 stock index. The initial amount to be invested is $300,000,000. The fund will be constructed using the Russell 2000 Index futures contract, priced at 498.30 with a $500 multiplier. The contract expires in three months. The underlying index has a dividend yield of 0.75 percent, and the risk-free rate is 2.35 percent per year.

   A. Indicate how the money manager would go about constructing this synthetic index using futures.

   B. Assume that at expiration, the Russell 2000 is at 594.65. Show how the synthetic position produces the same result as investment in the actual stock index.

3. An investment management firm has a client who would like to temporarily reduce his exposure to equities by converting a $25 million equity position to cash for a period of four months. The client would like this reduction to take place without liquidating his equity position. The investment management firm plans to create a synthetic cash position using an equity futures contract. This futures contract is priced at 1170.10, has a multiplier of $250, and expires in four months. The dividend yield on the underlying index is 1.25 percent, and the risk-free rate is 2.75 percent.

   A. Calculate the number of futures contracts required to create synthetic cash.

   B. Determine the effective amount of money committed to this risk-free transaction and the effective number of units of the stock index that are converted to cash.

   C. Assume that the stock index is at 1031 when the futures contract expires. Show how this strategy is equivalent to investing the risk-free asset, cash.

4. Consider a portfolio with a 65 percent allocation to stocks and 35 percent to bonds. The portfolio has a market value of $200 million. The beta of the stock position is 1.15, and the modified duration of the bond position is 6.75. The portfolio manager wishes to increase the stock allocation to 85 percent and reduce the bond allocation to 15 percent for a period of six months. In addition to altering asset allocations, the manager would also like to increase the beta on the stock position to 1.20 and increase the modified duration of the bonds to 8.25. A stock index futures contract that expires in six months is priced at $157,500 and has a beta of 0.95. A bond futures contract that expires in six months is priced at $109,000 and has an implied modified duration of 5.25. The stock futures contract has a multiplier of one.

   A. Show how the portfolio manager can achieve his goals by using stock index and bond futures. Indicate the number of contracts and whether the manager should go long or short.

   B. After six months, the stock portfolio is up 5 percent and bonds are up 1.35 percent. The stock futures price is $164,005 and the bond futures price is $110,145. Compare the market value of the portfolio in which the allocation is adjusted using futures to the market value of the portfolio in which the allocation is adjusted by directly trading stocks and bonds.

5. A pension fund manager expects to receive a cash inflow of $50,000,000 in three months and wants to use futures contracts to take a $17,500,000 synthetic position in stocks and $32,500,000 in bonds today. The stock would have a beta of 1.15 and the bonds a modified duration of 7.65. A stock index futures contract with a beta of 0.93 is priced at $175,210. A bond futures contract with a modified duration of 5.65 is priced at $95,750.

   A. Calculate the number of stock and bond futures contracts the fund manager would have to trade in order to synthetically take the desired position in stock and bonds today. Indicate whether the futures positions are long or short.

   B. When the futures contracts expire in three months, stocks have declined by 5.4 percent and bonds have declined by 3.06 percent. Stock index futures are priced at $167,559, and bond futures are priced at $93,586. Show that profits on the futures positions are essentially the same as the change in the value of stocks and bonds during the three-month period.

6. A. Consider a U.S. company, GateCorp, that exports products to the United Kingdom. GateCorp has just closed a sale worth £200,000,000. The amount will be received in two months. Because it will be paid in pounds, the U.S. company bears the exchange risk. In order to hedge this risk, GateCorp intends to use a forward contract that is priced at $1.4272 per pound. Indicate how the company would go about constructing the hedge. Explain what happens when the forward contract expires in two months.

   B. ABCorp is a U.S.-based company that frequently imports raw materials from Australia. It has just entered into a contract to purchase A$175,000,000 worth of raw wool, to be paid in one month. ABCorp fears that the Australian dollar will strengthen, thereby raising the U.S. dollar cost. A forward contract is available and is priced at $0.5249 per Australian dollar. Indicate how ABCorp would go about constructing a hedge. Explain what happens when the forward contract expires in one month.

4⅝ 4¹¹⁄₁₆ 3⅜
5½ **5½** − ⅜
5½ **5½** − ¼
20⅝ 21¹³⁄₁₆ − ⅞
17⅜ **18⅛** + ⅞
18½ 6½ **6½** − ½
7¼ 6½ **6½** − ⅛
15⁄₁₆ 31⁄₃₂ − ⅛
9⁄₁₆ %₆
¹⁄₃₂ 7¹³⁄₁₆ 7¹⁵⁄₁₆
7¹⁵⁄₁₆ 2⅝ 2¹¹⁄₃₂ 2½ +
23¾ 2¼ 2¼
6⅛ 12¹⁄₁₆ 11⅜ 11¼ +
87 33¾ 33 33¼ −
802 25⅝ 24⁹⁄₁₆ 25⅝ +
833 12 11⅝ 11⅛ +
16 10½ 10½ 10½ −
78 15⅝ 15¹³⁄₁₆ 15⅞
608 9¹⁄₁₆ 8¼ 8⅞ +
430 11¼ 10⅛

RISK MANAGEMENT APPLICATIONS OF OPTION STRATEGIES

by Don M. Chance

READING 39

LEARNING OUTCOMES

The candidate should be able to:

a. determine and interpret the value at expiration, profit, maximum profit, maximum loss, breakeven underlying price at expiration, and general shape of the graph for the major option strategies (bull spread, bear spread, butterfly spread, collar, straddle, box spread);

b. determine the effective annual rate for a given interest rate outcome when a borrower (lender) manages the risk of an anticipated loan using an interest rate call (put) option;

c. determine the payoffs for a series of interest rate outcomes when a floating rate loan is combined with (1) an interest rate cap, (2) an interest rate floor, or (3) an interest rate collar;

d. explain why and how a dealer delta hedges an option portfolio, why the portfolio delta changes, and how the dealer adjusts the position to maintain the hedge;

e. identify the conditions in which a delta-hedged portfolio is affected by the second-order gamma effect.

INTRODUCTION 1

OPTIONAL SEGMENT BEGINS

In Reading 38, we examined strategies that employ forward and futures contracts. Recall that forward and futures contracts have linear payoffs and do not require an initial outlay. Options, on the other hand, have nonlinear payoffs and require the payment of cash up front. By having nonlinear payoffs, options permit their users to benefit from movements in the underlying in one direction and to not be harmed by movements in the other direction. In many respects, they offer the best of all worlds, a chance to profit if expectations are realized with minimal harm if expectations turn out to be wrong. The price for this opportunity

Analysis of Derivatives for the CFA® Program, by Don M. Chance. Copyright © 2003 by AIMR. Reprinted with permission.

is the cash outlay required to establish the position. From the standpoint of the holder of the short position, options can lead to extremely large losses. Hence, sellers of options must be well compensated in the form of an adequate up-front premium and must skillfully manage the risk they assume.

In this reading we examine the most widely used option strategies. The reading is divided into three parts. In the first part, we look at option strategies that are typically used in equity investing, which include standard strategies involving single options and strategies that combine options with the underlying. In the second part, we look at the specific strategies that are commonly used in managing interest rate risk. In the third part, we examine option strategies that are used primarily by dealers and sophisticated traders to manage the risk of option positions.

Let us begin by reviewing the necessary notation. First recall that time 0 is the time at which the strategy is initiated and time T is the time the option expires, stated as a fraction of a year. Accordingly, the amount of time until expiration is simply $T - 0 = T$, which is (Days to expiration)/365. The other symbols are

c_0, c_T = price of the call option at time 0 and time T
p_0, p_T = price of the put option at time 0 and time T[1]
X = exercise price
S_0, S_T = price of the underlying at time 0 and time T
V_0, V_T = value of the position at time 0 and time T
Π = profit from the transaction: $V_T - V_0$
r = risk-free rate

Some additional notation will be introduced when necessary.

Note that we are going to measure the profit from an option transaction, which is simply the final value of the transaction minus the initial value of the transaction. Profit does not take into account the time value of money or the risk. Although a focus on profit is not completely satisfactory from a theoretical point of view, it is nonetheless instructive, simple, and a common approach to examining options. Our primary objective here is to obtain a general picture of the manner in which option strategies perform. With that in mind, discussing profit offers probably the best trade-off in terms of gaining the necessary knowledge with a minimum of complexity.

In this reading, we assume that the option user has a view regarding potential movements of the underlying. In most cases that view is a prediction of the direction of the underlying, but in some cases it is a prediction of the volatility of

---

[1] Lower case indicates European options, and upper case indicates American options. In this reading, all options are European.

the underlying. In all cases, we assume this view is specified over a horizon that corresponds to the option's life or that the option expiration can be tailored to the horizon date. Hence, for the most part, these options should be considered customized, over-the-counter options.[2] Every interest rate option is a customized option.

Because the option expiration corresponds to the horizon date for which a particular view is held, there is no reason to use **American options**. Accordingly, all options in this reading are European options. Moreover, we shall not consider terminating the strategy early. Putting an option in place and closing the position prior to expiration is certainly a legitimate strategy. It could reflect the arrival of new information over the holding period, but it requires an understanding of more complex issues, such as valuation of the option and the rate at which the option loses its time value. Thus, we shall examine the outcome of a particular strategy over a range of possible values of the underlying only on the expiration day.

Section 2 of this reading focuses on option strategies that relate to equity investments. Section 3 concentrates on strategies using interest rate options. In Section 4, we focus on managing an option portfolio.

OPTION STRATEGIES FOR EQUITY PORTFOLIOS

Many typical illustrations of option strategies use individual stocks, but we shall use options on a stock index, the Nasdaq 100, referred to simply as the Nasdaq. We shall assume that in addition to buying and selling options on the Nasdaq, we can also buy the index, either through construction of the portfolio itself, through an index mutual fund, or an exchange-traded fund.[3] We shall simply refer to this instrument as a stock. We are given the following numerical data:

$S_0 = 2000$, value of the Nasdaq 100 when the strategy is initiated
$T = 0.0833$, the time to expiration (one month = 1/12)

The options available will be the following:[4]

Exercise Price	Call Price	Put Price
1950	108.43	56.01
2000	81.75	79.25
2050	59.98	107.39

---

[2] If the options discussed were exchange-listed options, it would not significantly alter the material in this reading.

[3] Exchange-traded shares on the Nasdaq 100 are called Nasdaq 100 Trust Shares and QQQs, for their ticker symbol. They are commonly referred to as Qubes, trade on the Amex, and are the most active exchange-traded fund and often the most actively traded of all securities. Options on the Nasdaq 100 are among the most actively traded as well.

[4] These values were obtained using the Black–Scholes–Merton model. By using this model, we know we are working with reasonable values that do not permit arbitrage opportunities.

Let us start by examining an initial strategy that is the simplest of all: to buy or sell short the underlying. Panel A of Exhibit 1 illustrates the profit from the transaction of buying a share of stock. We see the obvious result that if you buy the stock and it goes up, you make a profit; if it goes down, you incur a loss. Panel B shows the case of selling short the stock. Recall that this strategy involves borrowing the shares from a broker, selling them at the current price,

| EXHIBIT 1 | Simple Stock Strategies |

A. Buy Stock

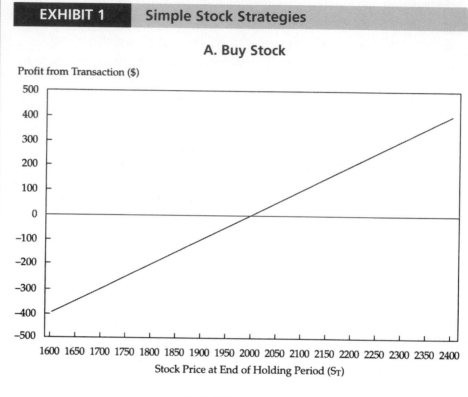

B. Sell Short Stock

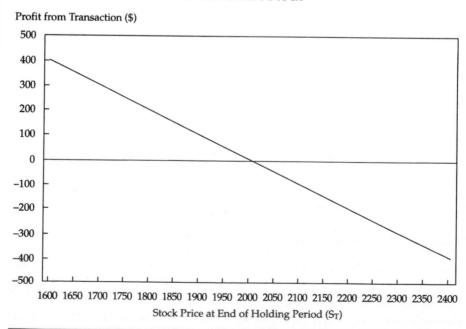

and then buying them back at a later date. In this case, if you sell short the stock and it goes down, you make a profit. Conversely, if it goes up, you incur a loss. Now we shall move on to strategies involving options, but we shall use the stock strategies again when we combine options with stock.

In this section we examine option strategies in the context of their use in equity portfolios. Although these strategies are perfectly applicable for fixed-income portfolios, corporate borrowing scenarios, or even commodity risk management situations, they are generally more easily explained and understood in the context of investing in equities or equity indices.

To analyze an equity option strategy, we first assume that we establish the position at the current price. We then determine the value of the option at expiration for a specific value of the index at expiration. We calculate the profit as the value at expiration minus the current price. We then generate a graph to illustrate the value at expiration and profit for a range of index values at expiration. Although the underlying is a stock index, we shall just refer to it as the underlying to keep things as general as possible. We begin by examining the most fundamental option transactions, long and short positions in calls and puts.

2.1 Standard Long and Short Positions

2.1.1 Calls

Consider the purchase of a call option at the price c_0. The value at expiration, c_T, is $c_T = \max(0, S_T - X)$. Broken down into parts,

$$c_T = 0 \qquad \text{if } S_T \leq X$$
$$c_T = S_T - X \quad \text{if } S_T > X$$

The profit is obtained by subtracting the option premium, which is paid to purchase the option, from the option value at expiration, $\Pi = c_T - c_0$. Broken down into parts,

$$\Pi = -c_0 \qquad \text{if } S_T \leq X$$
$$\Pi = S_T - X - c_0 \quad \text{if } S_T > X$$

Now consider this example. We buy the call with the exercise price of 2000 for 81.75. Consider values of the index at expiration of 1900 and 2100. For $S_T = 1900$,

$$c_T = \max(0, 1900 - 2000) = 0$$
$$\Pi = 0 - 81.75 = -81.75$$

For $S_T = 2100$,

$$c_T = \max(0, 2100 - 2000) = 100$$
$$\Pi = 100 - 81.75 = 18.25$$

Exhibit 2 illustrates the value at expiration and profit when S_T, the underlying price at expiration, ranges from 1600 to 2400. We see that buying a call results in a limited loss of the premium, 81.75. For an index value at expiration greater than the exercise price of 2000, the value and profit move up one-for-one with the index value, and there is no upper limit.

It is important to identify the breakeven index value at expiration. Recall that the formula for the profit is $\Pi = \max(0, S_T - X) - c_0$. We would like to know the value of S_T for which $\Pi = 0$. We shall call that value S_T^*. It would be nice to be able

EXHIBIT 2   **Buy Call**

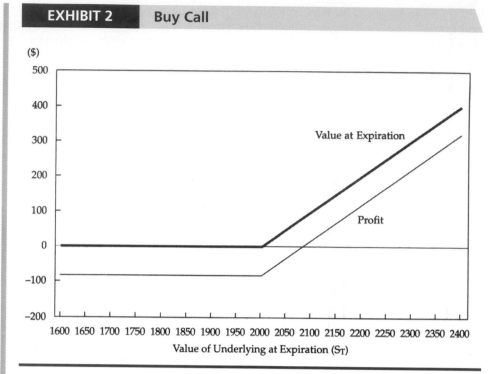

to solve $\Pi = \max(0, S_T^* - X) - c_0 = 0$ for S_T^*, but that is not directly possible. Instead, we observe that there are two ranges of outcomes, one in which $\Pi = S_T^* - X - c_0$ for $S_T^* > X$, the case of the option expiring in-the-money, and the other in which $\Pi = -c_0$ for $S_T \leq X$, the case of the option expiring out-of-the-money. It is obvious from the equation and by observing Exhibit 2 that in the latter case, there is no possibility of breaking even. In the former case, we see that we can solve for S_T^*. Setting $\Pi = S_T^* - X - c_0 = 0$, we obtain $S_T^* = X + c_0$.

Thus, the breakeven is the exercise price plus the option premium. This result should be intuitive: The value of the underlying at expiration must exceed the exercise price by the amount of the premium to recover the cost of the premium. In this problem, the breakeven is $S_T^* = 2000 + 81.75 = 2081.75$. Observe in Exhibit 2 that the profit line crosses the axis at this value.

In summarizing the strategy, we have the following results for the option buyer:

$c_T = \max(0, S_T - X)$
Value at expiration $= c_T$
Profit: $\Pi = c_T - c_0$
Maximum profit $= \infty$
Maximum loss $= c_0$
Breakeven: $S_T^* = X + c_0$

Call options entice naive speculators, but it is important to consider the *likely* gains and losses more than the *potential* gains and losses. For example, in this case, the underlying must go up by about 4.1 percent in one month to cover the cost of the call. This increase equates to an annual rate of almost 50 percent and is an unreasonable expectation by almost any standard. If the underlying does not move at all, the loss is 100 percent of the premium.

For the seller of the call, the results are just the opposite. The sum of the positions of the seller and buyer is zero. Hence, we can take the value and profit

EXHIBIT 3   Sell Call

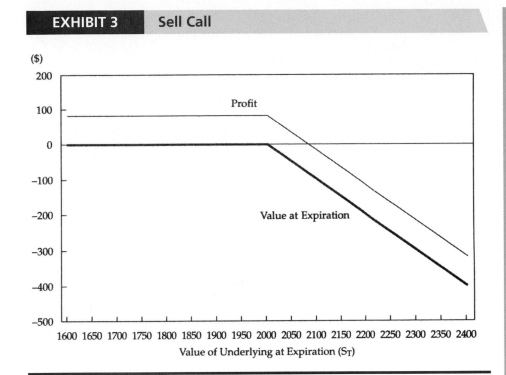

Value of Underlying at Expiration (S_T)

results for the buyer and change the signs. The results for the maximum profit and maximum loss are changed accordingly, and the breakeven is the same. Hence, for the option seller,

$c_T = \max(0, S_T - X)$
Value at expiration $= -c_T$
Profit: $\Pi = -c_T + c_0$
Maximum profit $= c_0$
Maximum loss $= \infty$
Breakeven: $S_T^* = X + c_0$

Exhibit 3 shows the results for the seller of the call. Note that the value and profit have a fixed maximum. The worst case is an infinite loss. Just as there is no upper limit to the buyer's potential gain, there is no upper limit to how much the seller can lose.

Call options are purchased by investors who are bullish. We now turn to put options, which are purchased by investors who are bearish.

EXAMPLE 1

Consider a call option selling for $7 in which the exercise price is $100 and the price of the underlying is $98.

A. Determine the value at expiration and the profit for a buyer under the following outcomes:

i. The price of the underlying at expiration is $102.
ii. The price of the underlying at expiration is $94.

B. Determine the value at expiration and the profit for a seller under the following outcomes:

    i. The price of the underlying at expiration is \$91.

    ii. The price of the underlying at expiration is \$101.

C. Determine the following:

    i. the maximum profit to the buyer (maximum loss to the seller)

    ii. the maximum loss to the buyer (maximum profit to the seller)

D. Determine the breakeven price of the underlying at expiration.

Solutions:

A. Call buyer

    i. Value at expiration $= c_T = \max(0, S_T - X)$

$$= \max(0, 102 - 100) = 2$$
$$\Pi = c_T - c_0 = 2 - 7 = -5$$

    ii. Value at expiration $= c_T = \max(0, S_T - X)$

$$= \max(0, 94 - 100) = 0$$
$$\Pi = c_T - c_0 = 0 - 7 = -7$$

B. Call seller

    i. Value at expiration $= -c_T = -\max(0, S_T - X)$

$$= -\max(0, 91 - 100) = 0$$
$$\Pi = -c_T + c_0 = -0 + 7 = 7$$

    ii. Value at expiration $= -c_T = -\max(0, S_T - X)$

$$= -\max(0, 101 - 100) = -1$$
$$\Pi = -c_T + c_0 = -1 + 7 = 6$$

C. Maximum and minimum

    i. Maximum profit to buyer (loss to seller) $= \infty$

    ii. Maximum loss to buyer (profit to seller) $= c_0 = 7$

D. $S_T{}^* = X + c_0 = 100 + 7 = 107$

2.1.2 Puts

The value of a put at expiration is $p_T = \max(0, X - S_T)$. Broken down into parts,

$$p_T = X - S_T \quad \text{if } S_T < X$$
$$p_T = 0 \qquad\quad \text{if } S_T \geq X$$

The profit is obtained by subtracting the premium on the put from the value at expiration:

$$\Pi = p_T - p_0$$

Broken down into parts,

$$\Pi = X - S_T - p_0 \quad \text{if } S_T < X$$
$$\Pi = -p_0 \qquad\qquad \text{if } S_T \geq X$$

For our example and outcomes of $S_T = 1900$ and 2100, the results are as follows:

$S_T = 1900$:

$$p_T = \max(0, 2000 - 1900) = 100$$
$$\Pi = 100 - 79.25 = 20.75$$

$S_T = 2100$:

$$p_T = \max(0, 2000 - 2100) = 0$$
$$\Pi = 0 - 79.25 = -79.25$$

| EXHIBIT 4 | Buy Put |

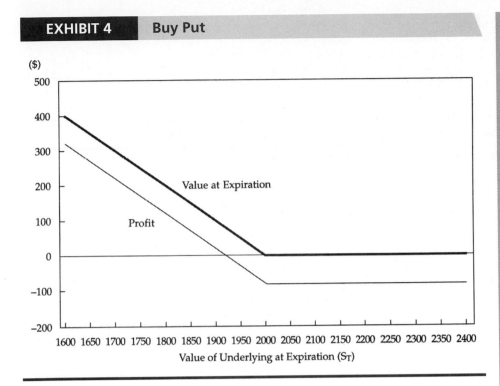

These results are shown in Exhibit 4. We see that the put has a maximum value and profit and a limited loss, the latter of which is the premium. The maximum value is obtained when the underlying goes to zero.[5] In that case, $p_T = X$. So the maximum profit is $X - p_0$. Here that will be $2000 - 79.25 = 1920.75$.

The breakeven is found by breaking up the profit equation into its parts, $\Pi = X - S_T - p_0$ for $S_T < X$ and $\Pi = -p_0$ for $S_T \geq X$. In the latter case, there is no possibility of breaking even. It refers to the range over which the entire premium is lost. In the former case, we denote the breakeven index value as S_T^*, set the equation to zero, and solve for S_T^* to obtain $S_T^* = X - p_0$. In our example, the breakeven is $S_T^* = 2000 - 79.25 = 1920.75$.

In summary, for the strategy of buying a put we have

$p_T = \max(0, X - S_T)$
Value at expiration $= p_T$
Profit: $\Pi = p_T - p_0$
Maximum profit $= X - p_0$
Maximum loss $= p_0$
Breakeven: $S_T^* = X - p_0$

Now consider the *likely* outcomes for the holder of the put. In this case, the underlying must move down by almost 4 percent in one month to cover the premium. One would hardly ever expect the underlying to move down at an annual rate of almost 50 percent. Moreover, if the underlying does not move downward at all (a likely outcome given the positive expected return on most assets), the loss is 100 percent of the premium.

---

[5] The maximum value and profit are not visible on the graph because we do not show S_T all the way down to zero.

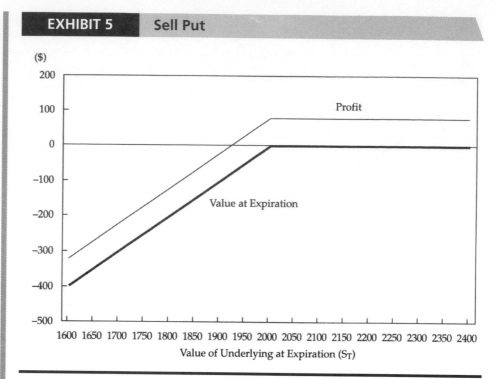

EXHIBIT 5   **Sell Put**

For the sale of a put, we simply change the sign on the value at expiration and profit. The maximum profit for the buyer becomes the maximum loss for the seller and the maximum loss for the buyer becomes the maximum profit for the seller. The breakeven for the seller is the same as for the buyer. So, for the seller,

$$p_T = \max(0, X - S_T)$$
Value at expiration $= -p_T$
Profit: $\Pi = -p_T + p_0$
Maximum profit $= p_0$
Maximum loss $= X - p_0$
Breakeven: $S_T^* = X - p_0$

Exhibit 5 graphs the value at expiration and the profit for this transaction.

EXAMPLE 2

Consider a put option selling for $4 in which the exercise price is $60 and the price of the underlying is $62.

A. Determine the value at expiration and the profit for a buyer under the following outcomes:
   i. The price of the underlying at expiration is $62.
   ii. The price of the underlying at expiration is $55.

B. Determine the value at expiration and the profit for a seller under the following outcomes:
   i. The price of the underlying at expiration is $51.
   ii. The price of the underlying at expiration is $68.

C. Determine the following:
   i. the maximum profit to the buyer (maximum loss to the seller)
   ii. the maximum loss to the buyer (maximum profit to the seller)

D. Determine the breakeven price of the underlying at expiration.

Solutions:

A. Put buyer
   i. Value at expiration $= p_T = \max(0, X - S_T)$
   $$= \max(0, 60 - 62) = 0$$
   $$\Pi = p_T - p_0 = 0 - 4 = -4$$
   ii. Value at expiration $= p_T = \max(0, X - S_T)$
   $$= \max(0, 60 - 55) = 5$$
   $$\Pi = p_T - p_0 = 5 - 4 = 1$$

B. Put seller
   i. Value at expiration $= -p_T = -\max(0, X - S_T)$
   $$= -\max(0, 60 - 51) = -9$$
   $$\Pi = -p_T + p_0 = -9 + 4 = -5$$
   ii. Value at expiration $= -p_T = -\max(0, X - S_T)$
   $$= -\max(0, 60 - 68) = 0$$
   $$\Pi = -p_T + p_0 = 0 + 4 = 4$$

C. Maximum and minimum
   i. Maximum profit to buyer (loss to seller) $= X - p_0 = 60 - 4 = 56$
   ii. Maximum loss to buyer (profit to seller) $= p_0 = 4$

D. $S_T^* = X - p_0 = 60 - 4 = 56$

It may be surprising to find that we have now covered all of the information we need to examine all of the other option strategies. We need to learn only a few basic facts. We must know the formula for the value at expiration of a call and a put. Then we need to know how to calculate the profit for the purchase of a call and a put, but that calculation is simple: the value at expiration minus the initial value. If we know these results, we can calculate the value at expiration of the option and the profit for any value of the underlying at expiration. If we can do that, we can graph the results for a range of possible values of the underlying at expiration. Because graphing can take a long time, however, it is probably helpful to learn the basic shapes of the value and profit graphs for calls and puts. Knowing the profit equation and the shapes of the graphs, it is easy to determine the maximum profit and maximum loss. The breakeven can be determined by setting the profit equation to zero for the case in which the profit equation contains S_T. Once we have these results for the long call and put, it is an easy matter to turn them around and obtain the results for the short call and put. Therefore, little if any memorization is required. From there, we can go on to strategies that combine an option with another option and combine options with the underlying.

2.2 Risk Management Strategies with Options and the Underlying

In this section, we examine two of the most widely used option strategies, particularly for holders of the underlying. One way to reduce exposure without selling the underlying is to sell a call on the underlying; the other way is to buy a put.

2.2.1 Covered Calls

A **covered call** is a relatively conservative strategy, but it is also one of the most misunderstood strategies. A covered call is a position in which you own the underlying and sell a call. The value of the position at expiration is easily found as the value of the underlying plus the value of the short call:

$$V_T = S_T - \max(0, S_T - X)$$

Therefore,

$$V_T = S_T \qquad\qquad\qquad \text{if } S_T \leq X$$
$$V_T = S_T - (S_T - X) = X \quad \text{if } S_T > X$$

We obtain the profit for the covered call by computing the change in the value of the position, $V_T - V_0$. First recognize that V_0, the value of the position at the start of the contract, is the initial value of the underlying minus the call premium. We are long the underlying and short the call, so we must subtract the call premium that was received from the sale of the call. The initial investment in the position is what we pay for the underlying less what we receive for the call. Hence, $V_0 = S_0 - c_0$. The profit is thus

$$\Pi = S_T - \max(0, S_T - X) - (S_0 - c_0)$$
$$= S_T - S_0 - \max(0, S_T - X) + c_0$$

With the equation written in this manner, we see that the profit for the covered call is simply the profit from buying the underlying, $S_T - S_0$, plus the profit from selling the call, $-\max(0, S_T - X) + c_0$. Breaking it down into ranges,

$$\Pi = S_T - S_0 + c_0 \qquad\qquad\qquad\qquad \text{if } S_T \leq X$$
$$\Pi = S_T - S_0 - (S_T - X) + c_0 = X - S_0 + c_0 \quad \text{if } S_T > X$$

In our example, $S_0 = 2000$. In this section we shall use a call option with the exercise price of 2050. Thus $X = 2050$, and the premium, c_0, is 59.98. Let us now examine two outcomes: $S_T = 2100$ and $S_T = 1900$. The value at expiration when $S_T = 2100$ is $V_T = 2100 - (2100 - 2050) = 2050$, and when $S_T = 1900$, the value of the position is $V_T = 1900$.

In the first case, we hold the underlying worth 2100 but are short a call worth 50. Thus, the net value is 2050. In the second case, we hold the underlying worth 1900 and the option expires out-of-the-money.

In the first case, $S_T = 2100$, the profit is $\Pi = 2050 - 2000 + 59.98 = 109.98$. In the second case, $S_T = 1900$, the profit is $\Pi = 1900 - 2000 + 59.98 = -40.02$. These results are graphed for a range of values of S_T in Exhibit 6. Note that for all values of S_T greater than 2050, the value and profit are maximized. Thus, 2050 is the maximum value and 109.98 is the maximum profit.[6]

As evident in Exhibit 6 and the profit equations, the maximum loss would occur when S_T is zero. Hence, the profit would be $S_T - S_0 + c_0$. The profit is $-S_0 + c_0$ when $S_T = 0$. This means that the maximum loss is $S_0 - c_0$. In this

---

[6] Note in Exhibit 6 that there is large gap between the value at expiration and profit, especially compared with the graphs of buying and selling calls and puts. This difference occurs because a covered call is mostly a position in the underlying asset. The initial value of the asset, S_0, accounts for most of the difference in the two lines. Note also that because of the put–call parity relationship, a covered call looks very similar to a short put.

| EXHIBIT 6 | Covered Call (Buy Underlying, Sell Call) |

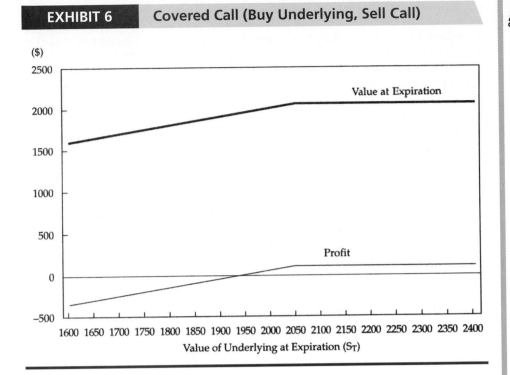

example, $-S_0 + c_0$ is $-2000 + 59.98 = -1940.02$. Intuitively, this would mean that you purchased the underlying for 2000 and sold the call for 59.98. The underlying value went to zero, resulting in a loss of 2000, but the call expired with no value, so the gain from the option is the option premium. The total loss is 1940.02.

The breakeven underlying price is found by examining the profit equations and focusing on the equation that contains S_T. In equation form, $\Pi = S_T - S_0 + c_0$ when $S_T \leq X$. We let S_T^* denote the breakeven value of S_T, set the equation to zero, and solve for S_T^* to obtain $S_T^* = S_0 - c_0$. The breakeven and the maximum loss are identical. In this example, the breakeven is $S_T^* = 2000 - 59.98 = 1940.02$, which is seen in Exhibit 6.

To summarize the covered call, we have the following:

Value at expiration: $V_T = S_T - \max(0, S_T - X)$
Profit: $\Pi = V_T - S_0 + c_0$
Maximum profit $= X - S_0 + c_0$
Maximum loss $= S_0 - c_0$
Breakeven: $S_T^* = S_0 - c_0$

Because of the importance and widespread use of covered calls, it is worthwhile to discuss this strategy briefly to dispel some misunderstandings. First of all, some investors who do not believe in using options fail to see that selling a call on a position in the underlying reduces the risk of that position. Options do not automatically increase risk. The option part of this strategy alone, viewed in isolation, seems an extremely risky strategy. We noted in Section 2.1.1 that selling a call without owning the stock exposes the investor to unlimited loss potential. But selling a covered call—adding a short call to a long position in a stock—reduces the overall risk. Thus, any investor who holds a stock cannot say he is too conservative to use options.

Following on that theme, however, one should also view selling a covered call as a strategy that reduces not only the risk but also the expected return compared with simply holding the underlying. Hence, one should not expect to make a lot of money writing calls on the underlying. It should be apparent that in fact the covered call writer could miss out on significant gains in a strong bull market. The compensation for this willingness to give up potential upside gains, however, is that in a bear market the losses on the underlying will be cushioned by the option premium.

It may be disconcerting to some investors to look at the profit profile of a covered call. The immediate response is to think that no one in their right mind would invest in a strategy that has significant downside risk but a limited upside. Just owning the underlying has significant downside risk, but at least there is an upside. But it is important to note that the visual depiction of the strategy, as in Exhibit 6, does not tell the whole story. It says nothing about the likelihood of certain outcomes occurring.

For example, consider the covered call example we looked at here. The underlying starts off at 2000. The maximum profit occurs when the option expires with the underlying at 2050 or above, an increase of 2.5 percent over the life of the option. We noted that this option has a one-month life. Thus, the underlying would have to increase at an approximate annual rate of at least $2.5\%(12) = 30\%$ for the covered call writer to forgo all of the upside gain. There are not many stocks, indices, or other assets in which an investor would expect the equivalent of an annual move of at least 30 percent. Such movements obviously do occur from time to time, but they are not common. Thus, covered call writers do not often give up large gains.

But suppose the underlying did move to 2050 or higher. As we previously showed, the value of the position would be 2050. Because the initial value of the position is $2000 - 59.98 = 1940.02$, the rate of return would be 5.7 percent for one month. Hence, the maximum return is still outstanding by almost anyone's standards.[7]

Many investors believe that the initial value of a covered call should not include the value of the underlying if the underlying had been previously purchased. Suppose, for example, that this asset, currently worth 2000, had been bought several months ago at 1900. It is tempting to ignore the current value of the underlying; there is no current outlay. This view, however, misses the notion of opportunity cost. If an investor currently holding an asset chooses to write a call on it, she has made a conscious decision not to sell the asset. Hence, the current value of the asset should be viewed as an opportunity cost that is just as real as the cost to an investor buying the underlying at this time.

Sellers of covered calls must make a decision about the chosen exercise price. For example, one could sell the call with an exercise price of 1950 for 108.43, or sell the call with exercise price of 2000 for 81.75, or sell the call with exercise price of 2050 for 59.98. The higher the exercise price, the less one receives for the call but the more room for gain on the upside. There is no clear-cut solution to deciding which call is best; the choice depends on the risk preferences of the investor.

Finally, we should note that anecdotal evidence suggests that writers of call options make small amounts of money, but make it often. The reason for this phenomenon is generally thought to be that buyers of calls tend to be overly

---

[7] Of course, we are not saying that the performance reflects a positive alpha. We are saying only that the upside performance given up reflects improbably high returns, and therefore the limits on the upside potential are not too restrictive.

optimistic, but that argument is fallacious. The real reason is that the expected profits come from rare but large payoffs. For example, consider the call with exercise price of 2000 and a premium of 81.75. As we learned in Section 2.1, the breakeven underlying price is 2081.75—a gain of about 4.1 percent in a one-month period, which would be an exceptional return for almost any asset. These prices were obtained using the Black–Scholes–Merton model, so they are fair prices. Yet the required underlying price movement to profit on the call is exceptional. Obviously someone buys calls, and naturally, someone must be on the other side of the transaction. Sellers of calls tend to be holders of the underlying or other calls, which reduces the enormous risk they would assume if they sold calls without any other position.[8] Hence, it is reasonable to expect that sellers of calls would make money often, because large underlying price movements occur only rarely. Following this line of reasoning, however, it would appear that sellers of calls can consistently take advantage of buyers of calls. That cannot possibly be the case. What happens is that buyers of calls make money less often than sellers, but when they do make money, the leverage inherent in call options amplifies their returns. Therefore, when call writers lose money, they tend to lose big, but most call writers own the underlying or are long other calls to offset the risk.

EXAMPLE 3

Consider a bond selling for $98 per $100 face value. A call option selling for $8 has an exercise price of $105. Answer the following questions about a covered call.

A. Determine the value of the position at expiration and the profit under the following outcomes:
  i. The price of the bond at expiration is $110.
  ii. The price of the bond at expiration is $88.

B. Determine the following:
  i. The maximum profit
  ii. The maximum loss

C. Determine the breakeven bond price at expiration.

Solutions:

A. i. $V_T = S_T - \max(0, S_T - X) = 110 - \max(0, 110 - 105)$
        $= 110 - 110 + 105 = 105$
   $\Pi = V_T - V_0 = 105 - (S_0 - c_0) = 105 - (98 - 8) = 15$
  ii. $V_T = S_T - \max(0, S_T - X) = 88 - \max(0, 88 - 105)$
        $= 88 - 0 = 88$
   $\Pi = V_T - V_0 = 88 - (S_0 - c_0) = 88 - (98 - 8) = -2$

B. i. Maximum profit $= X - S_0 + c_0 = 105 - 98 + 8 = 15$
  ii. Maximum loss $= S_0 - c_0 = 98 - 8 = 90$

C. $S_T^* = S_0 - c_0 = 98 - 8 = 90$

---

[8] Sellers of calls who hold other calls are engaged in transactions called spreads. We discuss several types of spreads in Section 2.3.

Covered calls represent one widely used way to protect a position in the underlying. Another popular means of providing protection is to buy a put.

2.2.2 Protective Puts

Because selling a call provides some protection to the holder of the underlying against a fall in the price of the underlying, buying a put should also provide protection. A put, after all, is designed to pay off when the price of the underlying moves down. In some ways, buying a put to add to a long stock position is much better than selling a call. As we shall see here, it provides downside protection while retaining the upside potential, but it does so at the expense of requiring the payment of cash up front. In contrast, a covered call generates cash up front but removes some of the upside potential.

Holding an asset and a put on the asset is a strategy known as a **protective put.** The value at expiration and the profit of this strategy are found by combining the value and profit of the two strategies of buying the asset and buying the put. The value is $V_T = S_T + \max(0, X - S_T)$. Thus, the results can be expressed as

$$V_T = S_T + (X - S_T) = X \quad \text{if } S_T \leq X$$
$$V_T = S_T \qquad\qquad\qquad\quad \text{if } S_T > X$$

When the underlying price at expiration exceeds the exercise price, the put expires with no value. The position is then worth only the value of the underlying. When the underlying price at expiration is less than the exercise price, the put expires in-the-money and is worth $X - S_T$, while the underlying is worth S_T. The combined value of the two instruments is X. When the underlying is worth less than the exercise price at expiration, the put can be used to sell the underlying for the exercise price.

The initial value of the position is the initial price of the underlying, S_0, plus the premium on the put, p_0. Hence, the profit is $\Pi = S_T + \max(0, X - S_T) - (S_0 + p_0)$. The profit can be broken down as follows:

$$\Pi = X - (S_0 + p_0) \quad \text{if } S_T \leq X$$
$$\Pi = S_T - (S_0 + p_0) \quad \text{if } S_T > X$$

In this example, we are going to use the put with an exercise price of 1950. Its premium is 56.01. Recalling that the initial price of the underlying is 2000, the value at expiration and profit for the case of $S_T = 2100$ are

$$V_T = 2100$$
$$\Pi = 2100 - (2000 + 56.01) = 43.99$$

For the case of $S_T = 1900$, the value at expiration and profit are

$$V_T = 1950$$
$$\Pi = 1950 - (2000 + 56.01) = -106.01$$

The results for a range of outcomes are shown in Exhibit 7. Note how the protective put provides a limit on the downside with no limit on the upside.[9] Therefore, we can say that the upper limit is infinite. The lower limit is a loss of

---

[9] Note that the graph for a protective put looks like the graph for a call. This result is due to put–call parity.

| EXHIBIT 7 | Protective Put (Buy Underlying, Buy Put) |

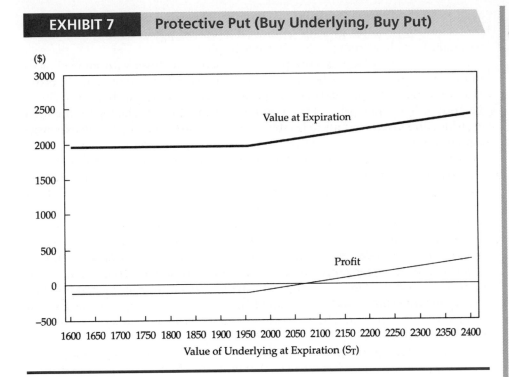

106.01. In the worst possible case, we can sell the underlying for the exercise price, but the up-front cost of the underlying and put are 2056.01, for a maximum loss of 106.01.

Now let us find the breakeven price of the underlying at expiration. Note that the two profit equations are $\Pi = S_T - (S_0 + p_0)$ if $S_T > X$ and $\Pi = X - (S_0 + p_0)$ if $S_T \leq X$. In the latter case, there is no value of the underlying that will allow us to break even. In the former case, $S_T > X$, we change the notation on S_T to S_T^* to denote the breakeven value, set this expression equal to zero, and solve for S_T^*:

$$S_T^* = S_0 + p_0$$

To break even, the underlying must be at least as high as the amount expended up front to establish the position. In this problem, this amount is $2000 + 56.01 = 2056.01$.

To summarize the protective put, we have the following:

Value at expiration: $V_T = S_T + max(0, X - S_T)$
Profit: $\Pi = V_T - S_0 - p_0$
Maximum profit $= \infty$
Maximum loss $= S_0 + p_0 - X$
Breakeven: $S_T^* = S_0 + p_0$

A protective put can appear to be a great transaction with no drawbacks. It provides downside protection with upside potential, but let us take a closer look. First recall that this is a one-month transaction and keep in mind that the option has been priced by the Black–Scholes–Merton model and is, therefore, a fair price. The maximum loss of 106.01 is a loss of $106.01/2056.01 = 5.2\%$. The breakeven of 2056.01 requires an upward move of 2.8 percent, which is an annual rate of about 34 percent. From this angle, the protective put strategy does not look quite as good, but in fact, these figures simply confirm that protection against downside loss is expensive. When the protective put is fairly priced, the protection buyer must give up considerable upside potential that may not be particularly evident from just looking at a graph.

The purchase of a protective put also presents the buyer with some choices. In this example, the buyer bought the put with exercise price of 1950 for 56.01. Had he bought the put with exercise price of 2000, he would have paid 79.25. The put with exercise price of 2050 would have cost 107.39. The higher the price for which the investor wants to be able to sell the underlying, the more expensive the put will be.

The protective put is often viewed as a classic example of insurance. The investor holds a risky asset and wants protection against a loss in value. He then buys insurance in the form of the put, paying a premium to the seller of the insurance, the put writer. The exercise price of the put is like the insurance deductible because the magnitude of the exercise price reflects the risk assumed by the party holding the underlying. The higher the exercise price, the less risk assumed by the holder of the underlying and the more risk assumed by the put seller. The lower the exercise price, the more risk assumed by the holder of the underlying and the less risk assumed by the put seller. In insurance, the higher the deductible, the more risk assumed by the insured party and the less risk assumed by the insurer. Thus, a higher exercise price is analogous to a lower insurance deductible.

Like traditional insurance, this form of insurance provides coverage for a period of time. At the end of the period of time, the insurance expires and either pays off or not. The buyer of the insurance may or may not choose to renew the insurance by buying another put.

EXAMPLE 4

Consider a currency selling for $0.875. A put option selling for $0.075 has an exercise price of $0.90. Answer the following questions about a protective put.

A. Determine the value at expiration and the profit under the following outcomes:
  i. The price of the currency at expiration is $0.96.
  ii. The price of the currency at expiration is $0.75.

B. Determine the following:
  i. the maximum profit
  ii. the maximum loss

C. Determine the breakeven price of the currency at expiration.

Solutions:

A. **i.** $V_T = S_T + \max(0, X - S_T) = 0.96 + \max(0, 0.90 - 0.96) = 0.96$
     $\Pi = V_T - V_0 = 0.96 - (S_0 + p_0) = 0.96 - (0.875 + 0.075) = 0.01$
   ii. $V_T = S_T + \max(0, X - S_T) = 0.75 + \max(0, 0.90 - 0.75) = 0.90$
       $\Pi = V_T - V_0 = 0.90 - (S_0 + p_0) = 0.90 - (0.875 + 0.075) = -0.05$

B. **i.** Maximum profit $= \infty$
   ii. Maximum loss $= S_0 + p_0 - X = 0.875 + 0.075 - 0.90 = 0.05$

C. $S_T^* = S_0 + p_0 = 0.875 + 0.075 = 0.95$

Finally, we note that a protective put can be modified in a number of ways. One in particular is to sell a call to generate premium income to pay for the purchase of the put. This strategy is known as a collar. We shall cover collars in detail in Section 2.4.1 when we look at combining puts and calls. For now, however, let us proceed with strategies that combine calls with calls and puts with puts. These strategies are called spreads.

2.3 Money Spreads

A spread is a strategy in which you buy one option and sell another option that is identical to the first in all respects except either exercise price or time to expiration. If the options differ by time to expiration, the spread is called a time spread. Time spreads are strategies designed to exploit differences in perceptions of volatility of the underlying. They are among the more specialized strategies, and we do not cover them here. Our focus is on money spreads, which are spreads in which the two options differ only by exercise price. The investor buys an option with a given expiration and exercise price and sells an option with the same expiration but a different exercise price. Of course, the options are on the same underlying asset. The term *spread* is used here because the payoff is based on the difference, or spread, between option exercise prices.

2.3.1 Bull Spreads

A **bull spread** is designed to make money when the market goes up. In this strategy we combine a long position in a call with one exercise price and a short position in a call with a higher exercise price. Let us use X_1 as the lower of the two exercise prices and X_2 as the higher. The European call prices would normally be denoted as $c(X_1)$ and $c(X_2)$, but we shall simplify this notation somewhat in this reading by using the symbols c_1 and c_2, respectively. The value of a call at expiration is $c_T = \max(0, S_T - X)$. So, the value of the spread at expiration is

$$V_T = \max(0, S_T - X_1) - \max(0, S_T - X_2)$$

Therefore,

$$
\begin{aligned}
V_T &= 0 - 0 = 0 & &\text{if } S_T \leq X_1 \\
V_T &= S_T - X_1 - 0 = S_T - X_1 & &\text{if } X_1 < S_T < X_2 \\
V_T &= S_T - X_1 - (S_T - X_2) = X_2 - X_1 & &\text{if } S_T \geq X_2
\end{aligned}
$$

The profit is obtained by subtracting the initial outlay for the spread from the above value of the spread at expiration. To determine the initial outlay, recall that a call option with a lower exercise price will be more expensive than a call option with a higher exercise price. Because we are buying the call with the lower exercise price and selling the call with the higher exercise price, the call we buy will cost more than the call we sell. Hence, the spread will require a net outlay of funds. This net outlay is the initial value of the position of $V_0 = c_1 - c_2$, which we call the net premium. The profit is $V_T - V_0$. Therefore,

$$\Pi = \max(0, S_T - X_1) - \max(0, S_T - X_2) - (c_1 - c_2)$$

In this manner, we see that the profit is the profit from the long call, $\max(0, S_T - X_1) - c_1$, plus the profit from the short call, $-\max(0, S_T - X_2) + c_2$. Broken down into ranges, the profit is

$$
\begin{aligned}
\Pi &= -c_1 + c_2 & &\text{if } S_T \leq X_1 \\
\Pi &= S_T - X_1 - c_1 + c_2 & &\text{if } X_1 < S_T < X_2 \\
\Pi &= X_2 - X_1 - c_1 + c_2 & &\text{if } S_T \geq X_2
\end{aligned}
$$

If S_T is below X_1, the strategy will lose a limited amount of money. The profit on the upside, if S_T is at least X_2, is also limited. When both options expire out-of-the-money, the investor loses the net premium, $c_1 - c_2$.

In this example, we use exercise prices of 1950 and 2050. Thus $X_1 = 1950$, $c_1 = 108.43$, $X_2 = 2050$, and $c_2 = 59.98$. Let us examine the outcomes in which the asset price at expiration is 2100, 2000, and 1900. In one outcome, the underlying is above the upper exercise price at expiration, and in one, the underlying is below the lower exercise price at expiration. Let us also examine one case between the exercise prices with S_T equal to 2000.

> When $S_T = 2100$, the value at expiration is $V_T = 2050 - 1950 = 100$
> When $S_T = 2000$, the value at expiration is $V_T = 2000 - 1950 = 50$
> When $S_T = 1900$, the value at expiration is $V_T = 0$

To calculate the profit, we simply subtract the initial value for the call with exercise price X_1 and add the initial value for the call with exercise price X_2.

> When $S_T = 2100$, the profit is $\Pi = 100 - 108.43 + 59.98 = 51.55$
> When $S_T = 2000$, the profit is $\Pi = 50 - 108.43 + 59.98 = 1.55$
> When $S_T = 1900$, the profit is $\Pi = -108.43 + 59.98 = -48.45$

When S_T is greater than 2100, we would obtain the same outcome as when S_T equals 2100. When S_T is less than 1900, we would obtain the same outcome as when S_T equals 1900.

Exhibit 8 depicts these results graphically. Note how the bull spread provides a limited gain as well as a limited loss. Of course, just purchasing a call provides a limited loss. But when selling the call in addition to buying the call, the investor gives up the upside in order to reduce the downside. In the bull spread, the investor sells gains from the call beyond the higher exercise price. Thus, a bull spread has some similarities to the covered call. With a covered call, the long

EXHIBIT 8	**Bull Spread (Buy Call with Exercise Price X_1, Sell Call with Exercise Price X_2)**

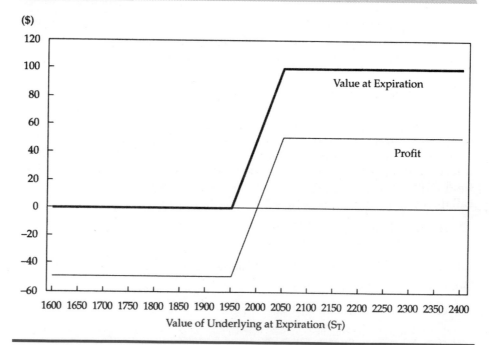

position in the underlying "covers" the short position in the call. In a bull spread, the long position in the call with the lower exercise price "covers" the short position in the call with the higher exercise price. For both strategies, the short call can be viewed as giving up the gains beyond its exercise price. The upside gain can also be viewed as paying a premium of $c_1 - c_2$ to buy the underlying for X_1 and sell it for X_2. Accordingly, the maximum gain is $X_2 - X_1 - c_1 + c_2 = 2050 - 1950 - 108.43 + 59.98 = 51.55$, as computed above. This amount represents a maximum return of about 106 percent.[10] The maximum loss is the net premium, 48.45, which is a 100 percent loss.

As can be seen from the graph and the profit equations, there is a breakeven asset price at expiration that falls between the two exercise prices. We let S_T^* be the breakeven asset price at expiration and set the profit for the case of $X_1 < S_T < X_2$ to zero:

$$S_T^* = X_1 + c_1 - c_2$$

To achieve a profit of zero or more, the asset price at expiration must exceed the lower exercise price by at least the net premium paid for the options. The long option must expire in-the-money by enough to cover the net premium. In our example,

$$S_T^* = 1950 + 108.43 - 59.98 = 1{,}998.45$$

What this result means is that the underlying must not move down by more than 0.08 percent.

To summarize the bull spread, we have

Value at expiration: $V_T = \max(0, S_T - X_1) - \max(0, S_T - X_2)$
Profit: $\Pi = V_T - c_1 + c_2$
Maximum profit $= X_2 - X_1 - c_1 + c_2$
Maximum loss $= c_1 - c_2$
Breakeven: $S_T^* = X_1 + c_1 - c_2$

EXAMPLE 5

Consider two call options on a stock selling for $72. One call has an exercise price of $65 and is selling for $9. The other call has an exercise price of $75 and is selling for $4. Both calls expire at the same time. Answer the following questions about a bull spread:

A. Determine the value at expiration and the profit under the following outcomes:
  i. The price of the stock at expiration is $78.
  ii. The price of the stock at expiration is $69.
  iii. The price of the stock at expiration is $62.
B. Determine the following:
  i. the maximum profit
  ii. the maximum loss
C. Determine the breakeven stock price at expiration.

---

[10] This calculation is based on the fact that the initial value of the position is $108.43 - 59.98 = 48.45$ and the maximum value is 100, which is a gain of 106.4 percent.

Solutions:

A. **i.** $V_T = \max(0, S_T - X_1) - \max(0, S_T - X_2)$
$= \max(0, 78 - 65) - \max(0, 78 - 75) = 13 - 3 = 10$
$\Pi = V_T - V_o = V_T - (c_1 - c_2) = 10 - (9 - 4) = 5$

  ii. $V_T = \max(0, S_T - X_1) - \max(0, S_T - X_2)$
$= \max(0, 69 - 65) - \max(0, 69 - 75) = 4 - 0 = 4$
$\Pi = V_T - V_0 = V_T - (c_1 - c_2) = 4 - (9 - 4) = -1$

  iii. $V_T = \max(0, S_T - X_1) - \max(0, S_T - X_2)$
$= \max(0, 62 - 65) - \max(0, 62 - 75) = 0 - 0 = 0$
$\Pi = V_T - V_0 = 0 - (c_1 - c_2) = 0 - (9 - 4) = -5$

B. **i.** Maximum profit $= X_2 - X_1 - (c_1 - c_2) = 75 - 65 - (9 - 4) = 5$

  ii. Maximum loss $= c_1 - c_2 = 9 - 4 = 5$

C. $S_T{}^* = X_1 + c_1 - c_2 = 65 + 9 - 4 = 70$

Bull spreads are used by investors who think the underlying price is going up. There are also bear spreads, which are used by investors who think the underlying price is going down.

2.3.2 Bear Spreads

If one uses the opposite strategy, selling a call with the lower exercise price and buying a call with the higher exercise price, the opposite results occur. The graph is completely reversed: The gain is on the downside and the loss is on the upside. This strategy is called a **bear spread.** The more intuitive way of executing a bear spread, however, is to use puts. Specifically, we would buy the put with the higher exercise price and sell the put with the lower exercise price.

The value of this position at expiration would be $V_T = \max(0, X_2 - S_T) - \max(0, X_1 - S_T)$. Broken down into ranges, we have the following relations:

$$
\begin{array}{ll}
V_T = X_2 - S_T - (X_1 - S_T) = X_2 - X_1 & \text{if } S_T \leq X_1 \\
V_T = X_2 - S_T - 0 = X_2 - S_T & \text{if } X_1 < S_T < X_2 \\
V_T = 0 - 0 = 0 & \text{if } S_T \geq X_2
\end{array}
$$

To obtain the profit, we subtract the initial outlay. Because we are buying the put with the higher exercise price and selling the put with the lower exercise price, the put we are buying is more expensive than the put we are selling. The initial value of the bear spread is $V_0 = p_2 - p_1$. The profit is, therefore, $V_T - V_0$, which is

$$\Pi = \max(0, X_2 - S_T) - \max(0, X_1 - S_T) - p_2 + p_1$$

We see that the profit is the profit from the long put, $\max(0, X_2 - S_T) - p_2$, plus the profit from the short put, $-\max(0, X_1 - S_T) + p_1$. Broken down into ranges, the profit is

$$
\begin{array}{ll}
\Pi = X_2 - X_1 - p_2 + p_1 & \text{if } S_T \leq X_1 \\
\Pi = X_2 - S_T - p_2 + p_1 & \text{if } X_1 < S_T < X_2 \\
\Pi = -p_2 + p_1 & \text{if } S_T \geq X_2
\end{array}
$$

In contrast to the profit in a bull spread, the bear spread profit occurs on the downside; the maximum profit occurs when $S_T \leq X_1$. This profit reflects the purchase of the underlying at X_1, which occurs when the short put is exercised, and the sale of the underlying at X_2, which occurs when the long put is exercised. The worst outcome occurs when $S_T > X_2$, in which case both puts expire out-of-the-money and the net premium is lost.

In the example, we again use options with exercise prices of 1950 and 2050. Their premiums are $p_1 = 56.01$ and $p_2 = 107.39$. We examine the three outcomes we did with the bull spread: S_T is 1900, 2000, or 2100.

With $S_T = 1900$, the value at expiration is $V_T = 2050 - 1950 = 100$
With $S_T = 2000$, the value at expiration is $V_T = 2050 - 2000 = 50$
With $S_T = 2100$, the value at expiration is $V_T = 0$

The profit is obtained by taking the value at expiration, subtracting the premium of the put with the higher exercise price, and adding the premium of the put with the lower exercise price:

When $S_T = 1900$, the profit is $\Pi = 100 - 107.39 + 56.01 = 48.62$
When $S_T = 2000$, the profit is $\Pi = 50 - 107.39 + 56.01 = -1.38$
When $S_T = 2100$, the profit is $\Pi = -107.39 + 56.01 = -51.38$

When S_T is less than 1900, the outcome is the same as when S_T equals 1900. When S_T is greater than 2100, the outcome is the same as when S_T equals 2100.

The results are graphed in Exhibit 9. Note how this strategy is similar to a bull spread but with opposite outcomes. The gains are on the downside underlying moves and the losses are on the upside underlying. The maximum profit

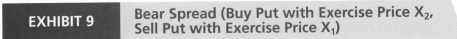

| EXHIBIT 9 | Bear Spread (Buy Put with Exercise Price X_2, Sell Put with Exercise Price X_1) |

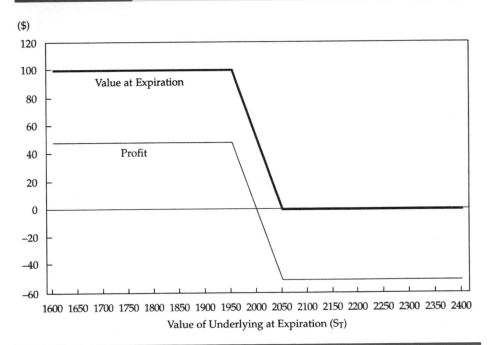

occurs when both puts expire in-the-money. You end up using the short put to buy the asset and the long put to sell the asset. The maximum profit is $X_2 - X_1 - p_2 + p_1$, which in this example is $100 - 107.39 + 56.01 = 48.62$, a return of 94 percent.[11] The maximum loss of $p_2 - p_1$ occurs when both puts expire out-of-the-money, and in this case is $107.39 - 56.01 = 51.38$, a loss of 100 percent.

The breakeven asset price occurs between the two exercise prices. Let S_T^* be the breakeven asset price at expiration, set the profit equation for the middle case to zero, and solve for S_T^* to obtain $S_T^* = X_2 - p_2 + p_1$. In this case, the breakeven is $S_T^* = 2050 - 107.39 + 56.01 = 1,998.62$. The underlying need move down only as little as 0.07 percent to make a profit.

To summarize the bear spread, we have

Value at expiration: $V_T = \max(0, X_2 - S_T) - \max(0, X_1 - S_T)$
Profit: $\Pi = V_T - p_2 + p_1$
Maximum profit $= X_2 - X_1 - p_2 + p_1$
Maximum loss $= p_2 - p_1$
Breakeven: $S_T^* = X_2 - p_2 + p_1$

EXAMPLE 6

Consider two put options on a bond selling for $92 per $100 par. One put has an exercise price of $85 and is selling for $3. The other put has an exercise price of $95 and is selling for $11. Both puts expire at the same time. Answer the following questions about a bear spread:

A. Determine the value at expiration and the profit under the following outcomes:
  i. The price of the bond at expiration is $98.
  ii. The price of the bond at expiration is $91.
  iii. The price of the bond at expiration is $82.

B. Determine the following:
  i. the maximum profit
  ii. the maximum loss

C. Determine the breakeven bond price at expiration.

Solutions:

A. **i.** $V_T = \max(0, X_2 - S_T) - \max(0, X_1 - S_T)$
          $= \max(0, 95 - 98) - \max(0, 85 - 98) = 0 - 0 = 0$
      $\Pi = V_T - V_0 = V_T - (p_2 - p_1) = 0 - (11 - 3) = -8$
  ii. $V_T = \max(0, X_2 - S_T) - \max(0, X_1 - S_T)$
          $= \max(0, 95 - 91) - \max(0, 85 - 91) = 4 - 0 = 4$
      $\Pi = V_T - V_0 = V_T - (p_2 - p_1) = 4 - (11 - 3) = -4$
  iii. $V_T = \max(0, X_2 - S_T) - \max(0, X_1 - S_T)$
          $= \max(0, 95 - 82) - \max(0, 85 - 82) = 13 - 3 = 10$
      $\Pi = V_T - V_0 = 10 - (p_2 - p_1) = 10 - (11 - 3) = 2$

---

[11] The net premium is $107.39 - 56.01 = 51.38$, so the maximum value of 100 is a return of about 94 percent.

B. **i.** Maximum profit $= X_2 - X_1 - (p_2 - p_1) = 95 - 85 - (11 - 3) = 2$

  ii. Maximum loss $= p_2 - p_1 = 11 - 3 = 8$

C. $S_T^* = X_2 - p_2 + p_1 = 95 - 11 + 3 = 87$

The bear spread with calls involves selling the call with the lower exercise price and buying the one with the higher exercise price. Because the call with the lower exercise price will be more expensive, there will be a cash inflow at initiation of the position and hence a profit if the calls expire worthless.

Bull and bear spreads are but two types of spread strategies. We now take a look at another strategy, which combines bull and bear spreads.

2.3.3 Butterfly Spreads

In both the bull and bear spread, we used options with two different exercise prices. There is no limit to how many different options one can use in a strategy. As an example, the **butterfly spread** combines a bull and bear spread. Consider three different exercise prices, X_1, X_2, and X_3. Suppose we first construct a bull spread, buying the call with exercise price of X_1 and selling the call with exercise price of X_2. Recall that we could construct a bear spread using calls instead of puts. In that case, we would buy the call with the higher exercise price and sell the call with the lower exercise price. This bear spread is identical to the sale of a bull spread.

Suppose we sell a bull spread by buying the call with exercise price X_3 and selling the call with exercise price X_2. We have now combined a long bull spread and a short bull spread (or a bear spread). We own the calls with exercise price X_1 and X_3 and have sold two calls with exercise price X_2. Combining these results, we obtain a value at expiration of

$$V_T = \max(0, S_T - X_1) - 2\max(0, S_T - X_2) + \max(0, S_T - X_3)$$

This can be broken down into ranges of

$$V_T = 0 - 2(0) + 0 = 0 \qquad\qquad \text{if } S_T \leq X_1$$
$$V_T = S_T - X_1 - 2(0) + 0 = S_T - X_1 \qquad \text{if } X_1 < S_T < X_2$$
$$V_T = S_T - X_1 - 2(S_T - X_2) + 0 = -S_T + 2X_2 - X_1 \qquad \text{if } X_2 \leq S_T < X_3$$
$$V_T = S_T - X_1 - 2(S_T - X_2) + S_T - X_3 = 2X_2 - X_1 - X_3 \quad \text{if } S_T \geq X_3$$

If the exercise prices are equally spaced, $2X_2 - X_1 - X_3$ would equal zero.[12] In virtually all cases in practice, the exercise prices are indeed equally spaced, and we shall make that assumption. Therefore,

$$V_T = 2X_2 - X_1 - X_3 = 0 \quad \text{if } S_T \geq X_3$$

To obtain the profit, we must subtract the initial value of the position, which is $V_0 = c_1 - 2c_2 + c_3$. Is this value positive or negative? It turns out that it will always be positive. The bull spread we buy is more expensive than the bull spread

---

[12] For example, suppose the exercise prices are equally spaced with $X_1 = 30$, $X_2 = 40$, and $X_3 = 50$. Then $2X_2 - X_3 - X_1 = 2(40) - 50 - 30 = 0$.

we sell, because the lower exercise price on the bull spread we buy (X_1) is lower than the lower exercise price on the bull spread we sell (X_2). Because the underlying is more likely to move higher than X_1 than to move higher than X_2, the bull spread we buy is more expensive than the bull spread we sell.

The profit is thus $V_T - V_0$, which is

$$\Pi = \max(0, S_T - X_1) - 2\max(0, S_T - X_2) + \max(0, S_T - X_3) - c_1 + 2c_2 - c_3$$

Broken down into ranges,

$$\Pi = -c_1 + 2c_2 - c_3 \qquad \text{if } S_T \leq X_1$$
$$\Pi = S_T - X_1 - c_1 + 2c_2 - c_3 \qquad \text{if } X_1 < S_T < X_2$$
$$\Pi = -S_T + 2X_2 - X_1 - c_1 + 2c_2 - c_3 \quad \text{if } X_2 \leq S_T < X_3$$
$$\Pi = -c_1 + 2c_2 - c_3 \qquad \text{if } S_T \geq X_3$$

Note that in the lowest and highest ranges, the profit is negative; a loss. It is not immediately obvious what happens in the middle two ranges. Let us look at our example. In this example, we buy the calls with exercise prices of 1950 and 2050 and sell two calls with exercise price of 2000. So, $X_1 = 1950$, $X_2 = 2000$, and $X_3 = 2050$. Their premiums are $c_1 = 108.43$, $c_2 = 81.75$, and $c_3 = 59.98$. Let us examine the outcomes in which $S_T = 1900$, 1975, 2025, and 2100. These outcomes fit into each of the four relevant ranges.

When $S_T = 1900$, the value at expiration is $V_T = 0 - 2(0) + 0 = 0$
When $S_T = 1975$, the value at expiration is $V_T = 1975 - 1950 = 25$
When $S_T = 2025$, the value at expiration is V_T
$$= -2025 + 2(2000) - 1950 = 25$$
When $S_T = 2100$, the value at expiration is $V_T = 0$

Now, turning to the profit,

When $S_T = 1900$, the profit will be Π
$$= 0 - 108.43 + 2(81.75) - 59.98 = -4.91$$
When $S_T = 1975$, the profit will be Π
$$= 25 - 108.43 + 2(81.75) - 59.98 = 20.09$$
When $S_T = 2025$, the profit will be Π
$$= 25 - 108.43 + 2(81.75) - 59.98 = 20.09$$
When $S_T = 2100$, the profit will be Π
$$= 0 - 108.43 + 2(81.75) - 59.98 = -4.91$$

Exhibit 10 depicts these results graphically. Note that the strategy is based on the expectation that the volatility of the underlying will be relatively low. The expectation must be that the underlying will trade near the middle exercise price. The maximum loss of 4.91 occurs if the underlying ends up below the lower strike, 1950, or above the upper strike, 2050. The maximum profit occurs if the underlying ends up precisely at the middle exercise price. This maximum profit is found by examining either of the middle two ranges with S_T set equal to X_2:

$$\Pi \text{ (maximum)} = S_T - X_1 - c_1 + 2c_2 - c_3$$
$$= X_2 - X_1 - c_1 + 2c_2 - c_3 \qquad \text{if } S_T = X_2$$
$$\Pi \text{ (maximum)} = -S_T + 2X_2 - X_1 - c_1 + 2c_2 - c_3$$
$$= X_2 - X_1 - c_1 + 2c_2 - c_3 \qquad \text{if } S_T = X_2$$

EXHIBIT 10	Butterfly Spread (Buy Calls with Exercise Price X_1 and X_3, Sell Two Calls with Exercise Price X_2)

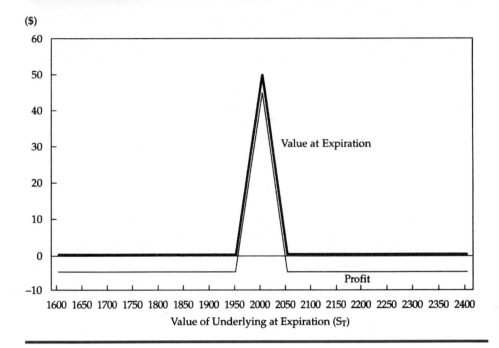

In this case, the maximum profit is Π (maximum) $= 2000 - 1950 - 108.43 + 2(81.75) - 59.98 = 45.09$, which is a return of 918 percent.[13]

There are two breakeven prices, and they lie within the two middle profit ranges. We find them as follows:

For $X_1 < S_T < X_2$:
$$\Pi = S_T{}^* - X_1 - c_1 + 2c_2 - c_3 = 0$$
$$S_T{}^* = X_1 + c_1 - 2c_2 + c_3$$
For $X_2 \leq S_T < X_3$:
$$\Pi = -S_T{}^* + 2X_2 - X_1 - c_1 + 2c_2 - c_3 = 0$$
$$S_T{}^* = 2X_2 - X_1 - c_1 + 2c_2 - c_3$$

In this example, therefore, the breakeven prices are

$$S_T{}^* = X_1 + c_1 - 2c_2 + c_3$$
$$= 1950 + 108.43 - 2(81.75) + 59.98 = 1954.91$$
$$S_T{}^* = 2X_2 - X_1 - c_1 + 2c_2 - c_3$$
$$= 2(2000) - 1950 - 108.43 + 2(81.75) - 59.98 = 2045.09$$

These movements represent a range of roughly ± 2.3 percent from the starting value of 2000. Therefore, if the underlying stays within this range, the strategy will be profitable.

---

[13] This return is based on a maximum value of $2000 - 1950 = 50$ versus the initial value of 4.91, a return of 918 percent.

In summary, for the butterfly spread

Value at expiration: $V_T = \max(0, S_T - X_1) - 2\max(0, S_T - X_2)$
$$+ \max(0, S_T - X_3)$$
Profit: $\Pi = V_T - c_1 + 2c_2 - c_3$
Maximum profit $= X_2 - X_1 - c_1 + 2c_2 - c_3$
Maximum loss $= c_1 - 2c_2 + c_3$
Breakeven: $S_T{}^* = X_1 + c_1 - 2c_2 + c_3$ and $S_T{}^* = 2X_2 - X_1 - c_1 + 2c_2 - c_3$

As we noted, a butterfly spread is a strategy based on the expectation of low volatility in the underlying. Of course, for a butterfly spread to be an appropriate strategy, the user must believe that the underlying will be less volatile than the market expects. If the investor buys into the strategy and the market is more volatile than expected, the strategy is likely to result in a loss. If the investor expects the market to be more volatile than he believes the market expects, the appropriate strategy could be to sell the butterfly spread. Doing so would involve selling the calls with exercise prices of X_1 and X_3 and buying two calls with exercise prices of X_2.[14]

Alternatively, a butterfly spread can be executed using puts. Note that the initial value of the spread using calls is $V_0 = c_1 - 2c_2 + c_3$. Recall that from put–call parity, $c = p + S - X/(1 + r)^T$. If we use the appropriate subscripts and substitute $p_i + S - X_i/(1 + r)^T$ for c_i where $i = 1, 2,$ and 3, we obtain $V_0 = p_1 - 2p_2 + p_3$. The positive signs on p_1 and p_3 and the negative sign on $2p_2$ mean that we could buy the puts with exercise prices X_1 and X_3 and sell two puts with exercise price of X_2 to obtain the same result. We would, in effect, be buying a bear spread with puts consisting of buying the put with exercise price of X_3 and selling the put with exercise price of X_2, and also selling a bear spread by selling the put with exercise price of X_2 and buying the put with exercise price of X_1. If the options are priced correctly, it does not really matter whether we use puts or calls.[15]

EXAMPLE 7

Consider three put options on a currency that is currently selling for $1.45. The exercise prices are $1.30, $1.40, and $1.50. The put prices are $0.08, $0.125, and $0.18, respectively. The puts all expire at the same time. Answer the following questions about a butterfly spread.

A. Determine the value at expiration and the profit under the following outcomes:
   i. The price of the currency at expiration is $1.26.
   ii. The price of the currency at expiration is $1.35.
   iii. The price of the currency at expiration is $1.47.
   iv. The price of the currency at expiration is $1.59.

---

[14] A short butterfly spread is sometimes called a **sandwich spread**.

[15] If puts were underpriced, it would be better to buy the butterfly spread using puts. If calls were underpriced, it would be better to buy the butterfly spread using calls. Of course, other strategies could also be used to take advantage of any mispricing.

B. Determine the following:
    i. the maximum profit
    ii. the maximum loss

C. Determine the breakeven currency price at expiration.

Solutions:

A. **i.** $V_T = \max(0, X_1 - S_T) - 2\max(0, X_2 - S_T) + \max(0, X_3 - S_T)$
      $= \max(0, 1.30 - 1.26) - 2\max(0, 1.40 - 1.26)$
      $+ \max(0, 1.50 - 1.26) = 0.04 - 2(0.14) + 0.24 = 0.0$
      $\Pi = V_T - V_0 = V_T - (p_1 - 2p_2 + p_3) = 0.0 - [0.08 - 2(0.125)$
      $+ 0.18] = -0.01$

  ii. $V_T = \max(0, X_1 - S_T) - 2\max(0, X_2 - S_T) + \max(0, X_3 - S_T)$
      $= \max(0, 1.30 - 1.35) - 2\max(0, 1.40 - 1.35)$
      $+ \max(0, 1.50 - 1.35) = 0.0 - 2(0.05) + 0.15 = 0.05$
      $\Pi = V_T - V_0 = V_T - (p_1 - 2p_2 + p_3) = 0.05$
      $- [0.08 - 2(0.125) + 0.18] = 0.04$

  iii. $V_T = \max(0, X_1 - S_T) - 2\max(0, X_2 - S_T) + \max(0, X_3 - S_T)$
      $= \max(0, 1.30 - 1.47) - 2\max(0, 1.40 - 1.47)$
      $+ \max(0, 1.50 - 1.47) = 0.0 - 2(0) + 0.03 = 0.03$
      $\Pi = V_T - V_0 = V_T - (p_1 - 2p_2 + p_3) = 0.03$
      $- [0.08 - 2(0.125) + 0.18] = 0.02$

  iv. $V_T = \max(0, X_1 - S_T) - 2\max(0, X_2 - S_T) + \max(0, X_3 - S_T)$
      $= \max(0, 1.30 - 1.59) - 2\max(0, 1.40 - 1.59)$
      $+ \max(0, 1.50 - 1.59) = 0.0 - 2(0) + 0.0 = 0.0$
      $\Pi = V_T - V_0 = V_T - (p_1 - 2p_2 + p_3) = 0.0 - [0.08 - 2(0.125)$
      $+ 0.18] = -0.01$

B. **i.** Maximum profit $= X_2 - X_1 - (p_1 - 2p_2 + p_3) = 1.40 - 1.30$
      $- [0.08 - 2(0.125) + 0.18] = 0.09$

  ii. Maximum loss $= p_1 - 2p_2 + p_3 = 0.08 - 2(0.125)$
      $+ 0.18 = 0.01$

C. $S_T^* = X_1 + p_1 - 2p_2 + p_3 = 1.30 + 0.08 - 2(0.125) + 0.18 = 1.31$
    $S_T^* = 2X_2 - X_1 - p_1 + 2p_2 - p_3 = 2(1.40) - 1.30 - 0.08$
    $+ 2(0.125) - 0.18 = 1.49$

So far, we have restricted ourselves to the use of either calls or puts, but not both. We now look at strategies that involve positions in calls *and* puts.

2.4 Combinations of Calls and Puts

2.4.1 Collars

Recall that in Section 2.2 we examined the protective put. In that strategy, the holder of the underlying asset buys a put to provide protection against downside loss. Purchasing the put requires the payment of the put premium. One way to get around paying the put premium is to sell another option with a premium equal to the put premium, which can be done by selling a call with an exercise price above the current price of the underlying.

Although it is not necessary that the call premium offset the put premium, and the call premium can even be more than the put premium, the typical collar has the call and put premiums offset. When this offsetting occurs, no net premium is required up front. In effect, the holder of the asset gains protection below a certain level, the exercise price of the put, and pays for it by giving up gains above a certain level, the exercise price of the call. This strategy is called a **collar.** When the premiums offset, it is sometimes called a **zero-cost collar.** This term is a little misleading, however, as it suggests that there is no "cost" to this transaction. The cost takes the form of forgoing upside gains. The term "zero-cost" refers only to the fact that no cash is paid up front.

A collar is a modified version of a protective put and a covered call and requires different exercise prices for each. Let the put exercise price be X_1 and the call exercise price be X_2. With X_1 given, it is important to see that X_2 is not arbitrary. If we want the call premium to offset the put premium, the exercise price on the call must be set such that the price of the call equals the price of the put. We thus can select any exercise price of the put. Then the call exercise price is selected by determining which exercise price will produce a call premium equal to the put premium. Although the put can have any exercise price, typically the put exercise price is lower than the current value of the underlying. The call exercise price then must be above the current value of the underlying.[16]

So let X_1 be set. The put with this exercise price has a premium of p_1. We now need to set X_2 such that the premium on the call, c_2, equals the premium on the put, p_1. To do so, we need to use an option valuation model, such as Black–Scholes–Merton, to find the exercise price of the call that will make $c_2 = p_1$. Recall that the Black–Scholes–Merton formula is

$$c = S_0 N(d_1) - X e^{-r^c T} N(d_2)$$

where

$$d_1 = \frac{\ln(S_0/X) + (r^c + \sigma^2/2)T}{\sigma\sqrt{T}}$$

$$d_2 = d_1 - \sigma\sqrt{T}$$

and where r^c is the continuously compounded risk-free rate and $N(d_1)$ and $N(d_2)$ are normal probabilities associated with the values d_1 and d_2. Ideally we would turn the equation around and solve for X in terms of c, but the equation is too complex to be able to isolate X on one side. So, we must solve for X by trial and error. We substitute in values of X until the option price equals c, where c is the call premium that we want to equal the put premium.

Consider the Nasdaq example. Suppose we use the put with exercise price of 1950. Its premium is 56.01. So now we need a call with a premium of 56.01. The call with exercise price of 2000 is worth 81.75. So to get a lower call premium, we need a call with an exercise price higher than 2000. By trial and error, we insert higher and higher exercise prices until the call premium falls to 56.01, which occurs at an exercise price of about 2060.[17] So now we have it. We buy the put

---

[16] It can be proven in general that the call exercise price would have to be above the current value of the underlying. Intuitively, it can be shown through put–call parity that if the call and put exercise prices were equal to the current value of the underlying, the call would be worth more than the put. If we lower the put exercise price below the price of the underlying, the put price would decrease. Then the gap between the call and put prices would widen further. We would then need to raise the call exercise price above the current price of the underlying to make its premium come down.

[17] The other necessary information to obtain the exercise price of the call are that the volatility is 0.35, the risk-free rate is 0.02, and the dividend yield is 0.005. The actual call price at a stock price of 2060 is 56.18. At 2061, the call price is 55.82. Thus, the correct exercise price lies between 2060 and 2061; we simply round to 2060.

with an exercise price of 1950 for 56.01 and sell the call with exercise price of 2060 for 56.01. This transaction requires no cash up front.

The value of the position at expiration is the sum of the value of the underlying asset, the value of the put, and the value of the short call:

$$V_T = S_T + \max(0, X_1 - S_T) - \max(0, S_T - X_2)$$

Broken down into ranges, we have

$$
\begin{aligned}
V_T &= S_T + X_1 - S_T - 0 = X_1 &&\text{if } S_T \le X_1 \\
V_T &= S_T + 0 - 0 = S_T &&\text{if } X_1 < S_T < X_2 \\
V_T &= S_T + 0 - (S_T - X_2) = X_2 &&\text{if } S_T \ge X_2
\end{aligned}
$$

The initial value of the position is simply the value of the underlying asset, S_0. The profit is $V_T - V_0$:

$$\Pi = S_T + \max(0, X_1 - S_T) - \max(0, S_T - X_2) - S_0$$

Broken down into ranges, we have

$$
\begin{aligned}
\Pi &= X_1 - S_0 &&\text{if } S_T \le X_1 \\
\Pi &= S_T - S_0 &&\text{if } X_1 < S_T < X_2 \\
\Pi &= X_2 - S_0 &&\text{if } S_T \ge X_2
\end{aligned}
$$

Using our example where $X_1 = 1950$, $p_1 = 56.01$, $X_2 = 2060$, $c_2 = 56.01$, and $S_0 = 2000$, we obtain the following values at expiration:

$$
\begin{aligned}
&\text{If } S_T = 1900, V_T = 1950 \\
&\text{If } S_T = 2000, V_T = 2000 \\
&\text{If } S_T = 2100, V_T = 2060
\end{aligned}
$$

The profit for $S_T = 1900$ is $\Pi = 1950 - 2000 = -50$.

$$
\begin{aligned}
&\text{If } S_T = 2000, \Pi = 2000 - 2000 = 0 \\
&\text{If } S_T = 2100, \Pi = 2060 - 2000 = 60
\end{aligned}
$$

A graph of this strategy is shown in Exhibit 11. Note that the lines are flat over the range of S_T up to the put exercise price of 1950 and in the range beyond the call exercise price of 2060. Below 1950, the put provides protection against loss. Above 2060, the short call forces a relinquishment of the gains, which are earned by the buyer of the call. In between these ranges, neither the put nor the call has value. The profit is strictly determined by the underlying and moves directly with the value of the underlying. The maximum profit is $X_2 - S_0$, which here is $2060 - 2000 = 60$, a return of 3 percent. The maximum loss is $S_0 - X_1$, which here is $2000 - 1950 = 50$, a loss of 2.5 percent. Keep in mind that these options have lives of one month, so those numbers represent one-month returns. The breakeven is simply the original underlying price of 2000.

In summary, for the collar

Value at expiration: $V_T = S_T + \max(0, X_1 - S_T) - \max(0, S_T - X_2)$
Profit: $\Pi = V_T - S_0$
Maximum profit $= X_2 - S_0$
Maximum loss $= S_0 - X_1$
Breakeven: $S_T^* = S_0$

EXHIBIT 11	Zero-Cost Collar (Buy Put with Exercise Price X_1, Sell Call with Exercise Price X_2, Put and Call Premiums Offset)

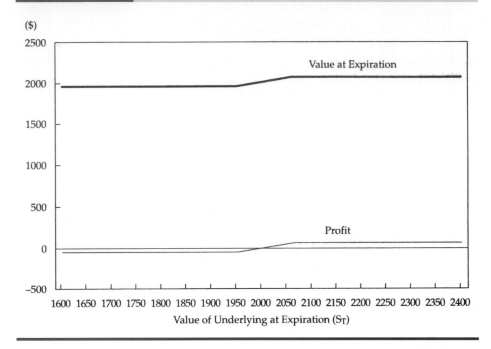

Collars are also known as range forwards and risk reversals.[18] Asset managers often use them to guard against losses without having to pay cash up front for the protection. Clearly, however, they are virtually the same as bull spreads. The latter has a cap on the gain and a floor on the loss but does not involve actually holding the underlying. In Section 3 we shall encounter this strategy again in the form of an interest rate collar, which protects floating-rate borrowers against high interest rates.

EXAMPLE 8

The holder of a stock worth $42 is considering placing a collar on it. A put with an exercise price of $40 costs $5.32. A call with the same premium would require an exercise price of $50.59.

A. Determine the value at expiration and the profit under the following outcomes:
  i. The price of the stock at expiration is $55.
  ii. The price of the stock at expiration is $48.
  iii. The price of the stock at expiration is $35.

---

[18] It is not clear why a collar is sometimes called a risk reversal. It is clear, however, why a collar is sometimes called a range forward. Like a forward contract, it requires no initial outlay other than for the underlying. Unlike a forward contract, which has a strictly linear payoff profile, the collar payoff breaks at the two exercise prices, thus creating a range.

B. Determine the following:
  i. the maximum profit
  ii. the maximum loss
C. Determine the breakeven stock price at expiration.

Solutions:

A. **i.** $V_T = S_T + \max(0, X_1 - S_T) - \max(0, S_T - X_2) = 55$
$+ \max(0, 40 - 55) - \max(0, 55 - 50.59) = 55 + 0$
$- (55 - 50.59) = 50.59$
$\Pi = V_T - S_0 = 50.59 - 42 = 8.59$

ii. $V_T = S_T + \max(0, X_1 - S_T) - \max(0, S_T - X_2) = 48$
$+ \max(0, 40 - 48) - \max(0, 48 - 50.59) = 48 + 0 - 0 = 48$
$\Pi = V_T - S_0 = 48 - 42 = 6$

iii. $V_T = S_T + \max(0, X_1 - S_T) - \max(0, S_T - X_2) = 35$
$+ \max(0, 40 - 35) - \max(0, 35 - 50.59) = 35 + 5 - 0 = 40$
$\Pi = V_T - S_0 = 40 - 42 = -2$

B. **i.** Maximum profit $= X_2 - S_0 = 50.59 - 42 = 8.59$
  ii. Maximum loss $= S_0 - X_1 = 42 - 40 = 2$

C. $S_T^* = S_0 = 42$

Collars are one of the many directional strategies, meaning that they perform based on the direction of the movement in the underlying. Of course, butterfly spreads perform based on the volatility of the underlying. Another strategy in which performance is based on the volatility of the underlying is the straddle.

2.4.2 Straddle

To justify the purchase of a call, an investor must be bullish. To justify the purchase of a put, an investor must be bearish. What should an investor do if he believes the market will be volatile but does not feel particularly strongly about the direction? We discussed earlier that a short butterfly spread is one strategy. It benefits from extreme movements, but its gains are limited. There are other, more complex strategies, such as time spreads, that can benefit from high volatility; however, one simple strategy, the **straddle,** also benefits from high volatility.

Suppose the investor buys both a call and a put with the same exercise price on the same underlying with the same expiration. This strategy enables the investor to profit from upside or downside moves. Its cost, however, can be quite heavy. In fact, a straddle is a wager on a large movement in the underlying.

The value of a straddle at expiration is the value of the call and the value of the put: $V_T = \max(0, S_T - X) + \max(0, X - S_T)$. Broken down into ranges,

$$V_T = X - S_T \quad \text{if } S_T < X$$
$$V_T = S_T - X \quad \text{if } S_T \geq X$$

The initial value of the straddle is simply $V_0 = c_0 + p_0$. The profit is $V_T - V_0$ or $\Pi = \max(0, S_T - X) + \max(0, X - S_T) - c_0 - p_0$. Broken down into ranges,

$$\Pi = X - S_T - c_0 - p_0 \quad \text{if } S_T < X$$
$$\Pi = S_T - X - c_0 - p_0 \quad \text{if } S_T \geq X$$

In our example, let X = 2000. Then $c_0 = 81.75$ and $p_0 = 79.25$.

If $S_T = 2100$, the value of the position at expiration is
$$V_T = 2100 - 2000 = 100$$
If $S_T = 1900$, the value of the position at expiration is
$$V_T = 2000 - 1900 = 100$$
If $S_T = 2100$, the profit is $\Pi = 100 - 81.75 - 79.25 = -61$
If $S_T = 1900$, the profit is $\Pi = 100 - 81.75 - 79.25 = -61$

Note the symmetry, whereby a move of 100 in either direction results in a change in value of 61. The put and call payoffs are obviously symmetric. It is also apparent that these outcomes are below breakeven.

Observe the results in Exhibit 12. Note that the value and profit are V-shaped, thereby benefiting from large moves in the underlying in either direction. Like the call option the straddle contains, the gain on the upside is unlimited. Like the put, the downside gain is not unlimited, but it is quite large. The underlying can go down no further than zero. Hence, on the downside the maximum profit is $X - c_0 - p_0$, which in this case is $2000 - 81.75 - 79.25 = 1839$. The maximum loss occurs if the underlying ends up precisely at the exercise price. In that case, neither the call nor the put expires with value and the premiums are lost on both. Therefore, the maximum loss is $c_0 + p_0$, which is $81.75 + 79.25 = 161$.

There are two breakevens. Using S_T^* to denote the breakevens, we set each profit equation to zero and solve for S_T^*:

If $S_T \geq X$,
$$\Pi = S_T^* - X - c_0 - p_0 = 0$$
$$S_T^* = X + c_0 + p_0$$
If $S_T < X$,
$$\Pi = X - S_T^* - c_0 - p_0 = 0$$
$$S_T^* = X - c_0 - p_0$$

EXHIBIT 12	Straddle (Buy Call and Put with Exercise Price X)

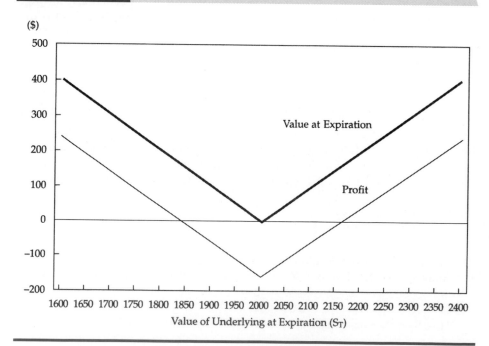

The breakevens thus equal the exercise price plus or minus the premiums. So in this case, the breakevens are $2000 \pm 161 = 2161$ and 1839. A move of 161 is a percentage move of 8.1 percent over a one-month period. Hence, in this example, the purchase of a straddle is a bet that the underlying will move at nearly a 100 percent annual rate over a one-month period, quite a risky bet. An investor would make such a bet only when he felt that the underlying would be exceptionally volatile. An obvious time to use a straddle would be around major events such as earnings announcements. But because earnings announcements are known and anticipated events, the greater uncertainty surrounding them should already be reflected in the options' prices. Recall that the greater the volatility, the higher the prices of both puts and calls. Therefore, using a straddle in anticipation of an event that everyone knows is coming is not necessarily a good idea. Only when the investor believes the market will be more volatile than everyone else believes would a straddle be advised.

In summary, for a straddle

Value at expiration: $V_T = \max(0,S_T - X) + \max(0,X - S_T)$
Profit: $\Pi = V_T - (c_0 + p_0)$
Maximum profit $= \infty$
Maximum loss $= c_0 + p_0$
Breakeven: $S_T^* = X \pm (c_0 + p_0)$

As we have noted, a straddle would tend to be used by an investor who is expecting the market to be volatile but does not have strong feelings one way or the other on the direction. An investor who leans one way or the other might consider adding a call or a put to the straddle. Adding a call to a straddle is a strategy called a **strap**, and adding a put to a straddle is called a **strip**. It is even more difficult to make a gain from these strategies than it is for a straddle, but if the hoped-for move does occur, the gains are leveraged. Another variation of the straddle is a **strangle**, in which the put and call have different exercise prices. This strategy creates a graph similar to a straddle but with a flat section instead of a point on the bottom.

EXAMPLE 9

Consider a stock worth $49. A call with an exercise price of $50 costs $6.25 and a put with an exercise price of $50 costs $5.875. An investor buys a straddle.

A. Determine the value at expiration and the profit under the following outcomes:
  i. The price of the stock at expiration is $61.
  ii. The price of the stock at expiration is $37.
B. Determine the following:
  i. the maximum profit
  ii. the maximum loss
C. Determine the breakeven stock price at expiration.

Solutions:

A.   **i.** $V_T = \max(0, S_T - X) + \max(0, X - S_T) = \max(0, 61 - 50) + \max(0, 50 - 61) = 11 - 0 = 11$
$\Pi = V_T - (c_0 + p_0) = 11 - (6.25 + 5.875) = -1.125$

      ii. $V_T = \max(0, S_T - X) + \max(0, X - S_T) = \max(0, 37 - 50) + \max(0, 50 - 37) = 0 + 13 = 13$
$\Pi = V_T - S_0 = 13 - (6.25 + 5.875) = 0.875$

B.   **i.** Maximum profit $= \infty$

      ii. Maximum loss $= c_0 + p_0 = 6.25 + 5.875 = 12.125$

C. $S_T^* = X \pm (c_0 + p_0) = 50 \pm (6.25 + 5.875) = 62.125, 37.875$

Now we turn to a strategy that combines more than one call and more than one put. It should not be surprising that we shall recognize this strategy as just a combination of something we have already learned.

2.4.3 Box Spreads

We can exploit an arbitrage opportunity with a neutral position many alternative ways: using put–call parity, using the binomial model, or using the Black–Scholes–Merton model. Exploiting put-call parity requires a position in the underlying. Using the binomial or Black–Scholes–Merton model requires that the model holds in the market. In addition, both models require a position in the underlying and an estimate of the volatility.

A **box spread** can also be used to exploit an arbitrage opportunity but it requires that neither the binomial nor Black–Scholes–Merton model holds, it needs no estimate of the volatility, and all of the transactions can be executed within the options market, making implementation of the strategy simpler, faster, and with lower transaction costs.

In basic terms, a box spread is a combination of a bull spread and a bear spread. Suppose we buy the call with exercise price X_1 and sell the call with exercise price X_2. This set of transactions is a bull spread. Then we buy the put with exercise price X_2 and sell the put with exercise price X_1. This is a bear spread. Intuitively, it should sound like a combination of a bull spread and a bear spread would leave the investor with a fairly neutral position, and indeed, that is the case.

The value of the box spread at expiration is

$$V_T = \max(0, S_T - X_1) - \max(0, S_T - X_2) + \max(0, X_2 - S_T) - \max(0, X_1 - S_T)$$

Broken down into ranges, we have

$$V_T = 0 - 0 + X_2 - S_T - (X_1 - S_T) = X_2 - X_1 \quad \text{if } S_T \leq X_1$$
$$V_T = S_T - X_1 - 0 + X_2 - S_T - 0 = X_2 - X_1 \quad \text{if } X_1 < S_T < X_2$$
$$V_T = S_T - X_1 - (S_T - X_2) + 0 - 0 = X_2 - X_1 \quad \text{if } S_T \geq X_2$$

These outcomes are all the same. In each case, two of the four options expire in-the-money, and the other two expire out-of-the-money. In each case, the holder of the box spread ends up buying the underlying with one option, using either the long call at X_1 or the short put at X_1, and selling the underlying with another option, using either the long put at X_2 or the short call at X_2. The box spread thus results in buying the underlying at X_1 and selling it at X_2. This outcome is known at the start.

The initial value of the transaction is the value of the long call, short call, long put, and short put, $V_0 = c_1 - c_2 + p_2 - p_1$. The profit is, therefore, $\Pi = X_2 - X_1 - c_1 + c_2 - p_2 + p_1$.

In contrast to all of the other strategies, the outcome is simple. In all cases, we end up with the same result. Using the options with exercise prices of 1950 and 2050, which have premiums of $c_1 = 108.43$, $c_2 = 59.98$, $p_1 = 56.01$, and $p_2 = 107.39$, the value at expiration is always $2050 - 1950 = 100$ and the profit is always $\Pi = 100 - 108.43 + 59.98 - 107.39 + 56.01 = 0.17$. This value may seem remarkably low. We shall see why momentarily.

The initial value of the box spread is $c_1 - c_2 + p_2 - p_1$. The payoff at expiration is $X_2 - X_1$. Because the transaction is risk free, the present value of the payoff, discounted using the risk-free rate, should equal the initial outlay. Hence, we should have

$$(X_2 - X_1)/(1 + r)^T = c_1 - c_2 + p_2 - p_1$$

If the present value of the payoff exceeds the initial value, the box spread is underpriced and should be purchased.

In this example, the initial outlay is $V_0 = 108.43 - 59.98 + 107.39 - 56.01 = 99.83$. To obtain the present value of the payoff, we need an interest rate and time to expiration. The prices of these options were obtained using a time to expiration of one month and a risk-free rate of 2.02 percent. The present value of the payoff is

$$(X_2 - X_1)/(1 + r)^r = (2050 - 1950)/(1.0202)^{1/12} = 99.83$$

In other words, this box spread is correctly priced. This result should not be surprising, because we noted that we used the Black–Scholes–Merton model to price these options. The model should not allow arbitrage opportunities of any form.

Recall that the profit from this transaction is 0.17, a very low value. This profit reflects the fact that the box spread is purchased at 99.83 and matures to a value of 100, a profit of 0.17, which is a return of the risk-free rate for one month.[19] The reason the profit seems so low is that it is just the risk-free rate.

Let us assume that one of the long options, say the put with exercise price of 2050, is underpriced. Let its premium be 105 instead of 107.39. Then the net premium would be $108.43 - 59.98 + 105 - 56.01 = 97.44$. Again, the present value of the payoff is 99.83. Hence, the box spread would generate a gain in value clearly in excess of the risk-free rate. If some combination of the options was such that the net premium is more than the present value of the payoff, then the box spread would be overpriced. Then we should sell the X_1 call and X_2 put and buy the X_2 call and X_1 put. Doing so would generate an outlay at expiration with a present value less than the initial value.

So to summarize the box spread, we say that

Value at expiration: $V_T = X_2 - X_1$
Profit: $\Pi = X_2 - X_1 - (c_1 - c_2 + p_2 - p_1)$
Maximum profit = (same as profit)
Maximum loss = (no loss is possible, given fair option prices)
Breakeven: no breakeven; the transaction always earns the risk-free rate, given fair option prices.

---

[19] That is, $99.83(1.0202)^{1/12} \approx 100$. Hence, the profit of 0.17 is about 2.02 percent, for one month.

EXAMPLE 10

Consider a box spread consisting of options with exercise prices of 75 and 85. The call prices are 16.02 and 12.28 for exercise prices of 75 and 85, respectively. The put prices are 9.72 and 15.18 for exercise prices of 75 and 85, respectively. The options expire in six months and the discrete risk-free rate is 5.13 percent.

A. Determine the value of the box spread and the profit for any value of the underlying at expiration.

B. Show that this box spread is priced such that an attractive opportunity is available.

Solution to A: The box spread always has a value at expiration of $X_2 - X_1$
$$= 85 - 75 = 10$$
$$\Pi = V_T - (c_1 - c_2 + p_2 - p_1) = 10 - (16.02 - 12.28 + 15.18 - 9.72) = 0.80$$

Solution to B: The box spread should be worth $(X_2 - X_1)/(1 + r)^T$, or

$$(85 - 75)/(1.0513)^{0.5} = 9.75$$

The cost of the box spread is $16.02 - 12.28 + 15.18 - 9.72 = 9.20$. The box spread is thus underpriced. At least one of the long options is priced too low or at least one of the short options is priced too high; we cannot tell which. Nonetheless, we can execute this box spread, buying the call with exercise price $X_1 = 75$ and put with exercise price $X_2 = 85$ and selling the call with exercise price $X_2 = 85$ and put with exercise price $X_1 = 75$. This would cost 9.20. The present value of the payoff is 9.75. Therefore, the box spread would generate an immediate increase in value of 0.55.

We have now completed our discussion of equity option strategies. Although the strategies are applicable, with minor changes, to fixed-income securities, we shall not explore that area here. We shall, however, look at interest rate option strategies, which require some significant differences in presentation and understanding compared with equity option strategies.

3   INTEREST RATE OPTION STRATEGIES

Consider a group of options in which the underlying is an interest rate and the exercise price is expressed in terms of a rate. Recall that this group of options consists of calls, which pay off if the option expires with the underlying interest rate above the exercise rate, and puts, which pay off if the option expires with the underlying interest rate below the exercise rate. **Interest rate call** and put options are usually purchased to protect against changes in interest rates. For dollar-based interest rate derivatives, the underlying is usually LIBOR but is always a specific rate, such as the rate on a 90- or 180-day underlying instrument. An interest rate option is based on a specific notional principal, which determines the payoff when the option is exercised. Traditionally, the payoff does not occur immediately upon exercise but is delayed by a period corresponding to the life of the underlying instrument from which the interest rate is taken, an issue we review below.

The payoff of an interest rate call option is

$$(\text{Notional principal}) \max\left(0, \text{Underlying rate at expiration} - \text{Exercise rate}\right)\left(\frac{\text{Days in underlying rate}}{360}\right)$$

where "days in underlying" refers to the maturity of the instrument from which the underlying rate is taken. In some cases, "days in underlying" may be the exact day count during a period. For example, if an interest rate option is used to hedge the interest paid over an m-day period, then "days in underlying" would be m. Even though LIBOR of 30, 60, 90, 180 days, etc., whichever is closest to m, might be used as the underlying rate, the actual day count would be m, the exact number of days. In such cases, the payment date is usually set at 30, 60, 90, 180, etc. days after the option expiration date. So, for example, 180-day LIBOR might be used as the underlying rate, and "days in underlying" could be 180 or perhaps 182, 183, etc. The most important point, however, is that the rate is determined on one day, the option expiration, and payment is made m days later. This practice is standard in **floating-rate loans** and thus is used with interest rate options, which are designed to manage the risk of floating-rate loans.

Likewise, the payoff of an interest rate put is

$$(\text{Notional principal}) \max\left(0, \text{Exercise rate} - \text{Underlying rate at expiration}\right)\left(\frac{\text{Days in underlying rate}}{360}\right)$$

Now let us take a look at some applications of interest rate options.

3.1 Using Interest Rate Calls with Borrowing

Let us examine an application of an interest rate call to establish a maximum interest rate for a loan to be taken out in the future. In brief, a company can buy an interest rate call that pays off from increases in the underlying interest rate beyond a chosen level. The call pay-off then compensates for the higher interest rate the company has to pay on the loan.

Consider the case of a company called Global Computer Technology (GCT), which occasionally takes out short-term loans in U.S. dollars with the rate tied to LIBOR. Anticipating that it will take out a loan at a later date, GCT recognizes the potential for an interest rate increase by that time. In this example, today is 14 April, and GCT expects to borrow $40 million on 20 August at LIBOR plus 200 basis points. The loan will involve the receipt of the money on 20 August with full repayment of principal and interest 180 days later on 16 February. GCT would like protection against higher interest rates, so it purchases an interest rate call on 180-day LIBOR to expire on 20 August. GCT chooses an exercise rate of 5 percent. This option gives it the right to receive an interest payment of the difference between the 20 August LIBOR and 5 percent. If GCT exercises the option on 20 August, the payment will occur 180 days later on 16 February when the loan is paid off. The cost of the call is $100,000, which is paid on 14 April. LIBOR on 14 April is 5.5 percent.

The transaction is designed such that if LIBOR is above 5 percent on 20 August, GCT will benefit and be protected against increases in interest rates. To determine how the transaction works, we need to know the effective rate on the loan. Note that the sequence of events is as follows:

14 April ——————→ 20 August ——————→ 16 February
GCT buys call   Call expires; loan starts   Loan repaid and
                                                          call payoff made

So cash is paid for the call on 14 April. Cash proceeds from the loan are received on 20 August. On 16 February, the loan is repaid and the call payoff (if any) is made.

To evaluate the effectiveness of the overall transaction, we need to determine how the call affects the loan. Therefore, we need to incorporate the payment of the call premium on 14 April into the cash flow on the loan. So, it would be appropriate to compound the call premium from 14 April to 20 August. In effect, we need to know what the call, purchased on 14 April, effectively costs on 20 August. We compound its premium for the 128 days from 14 April to 20 August at the rate at which GCT would have to borrow on 14 April. This rate would be LIBOR on 14 April plus 200 basis points, or 7.5 percent. The call premium thus effectively costs

$$\$100,000 \left[1 + 0.075\left(\frac{128}{360}\right) \right] = \$102,667$$

on 20 August.[20] On that date, GCT takes out the loan, thereby receiving \$40 million. We should, however, reduce this amount by \$102,667, because GCT effectively receives less money because it must buy the call. So, the loan proceeds are effectively \$40,000,000 − \$102,667 = \$39,897,333.

Next we must calculate the amount of interest paid on the loan and the amount of any call payoff. Let us assume that LIBOR on 20 August is 8 percent. In that case, the loan rate will be 10 percent. The interest on the loan will be

$$\$40,000,000(0.10)\left(\frac{180}{360}\right) = \$2,000,000$$

This amount, plus \$40 million principal, is repaid on 16 February. With LIBOR assumed to be 8 percent on 20 August, the option payoff is

$$\$40,000,000 \max(0,0.08 - 0.05)\left(\frac{180}{360}\right) = \$40,000,000(0.03)\left(\frac{180}{360}\right) = \$600,000$$

This amount is paid on 16 February. The effective interest paid on 16 February is thus \$2,000,000 − \$600,000 = \$1,400,000. So, GCT effectively receives \$39,897,333 on 20 August and pays back \$40,000,000 plus \$1,400,000 or \$41,400,000 on 16 February. The effective annual rate is

$$\left(\frac{\$41,400,000}{\$39,897,333}\right)^{365/180} - 1 = 0.0779$$

---

[20] The interpretation of this calculation is that GCT's cost of funds is 7.5 percent, making the option premium effectively \$102,667 by the time the loan is taken out.

Exhibit 13 presents a complete description of the transaction and the results for a range of possible LIBORs on 20 August. Exhibit 14 illustrates the effective loan rate compared with LIBOR on 20 August. We see that the strategy places an effective ceiling on the rate on the loan of about 7.79 percent while enabling GCT to benefit from decreases in LIBOR. Of course, a part of this maximum rate is the 200 basis point spread over LIBOR that GCT must pay.[21] In effect, the company's maximum rate without the spread is 5.79 percent. This reflects the exercise rate of 5.5 percent plus the effect of the option premium.

EXHIBIT 13	Outcomes for an Anticipated Loan Protected with an Interest Rate Call

Scenario (14 April)

Global Computer Technology (GCT) is a U.S. corporation that occasionally undertakes short-term borrowings in U.S. dollars with the rate tied to LIBOR. To facilitate its cash flow planning, it buys an interest rate call to put a ceiling on the rate it pays while enabling it to benefit if rates fall. A call gives GCT the right to receive the difference between LIBOR on the expiration date and the exercise rate it chooses when it purchases the option. The payoff of the call is determined on the expiration date, but the payment is not received until a certain number of days later, corresponding to the maturity of the underlying LIBOR. This feature matches the timing of the interest payment on the loan.

Action

GCT determines that it will borrow $40 million at LIBOR plus 200 basis points on 20 August. The loan will be repaid with a single payment of principal and interest 180 days later on 16 February.

To protect against increases in LIBOR between 14 April and 20 August, GCT buys a call option on LIBOR with an exercise rate of 5 percent to expire on 20 August with the underlying being 180-day LIBOR. The call premium is $100,000. We summarize the information as follows:

Loan amount	$40,000,000
Underlying	180-day LIBOR
Spread	200 basis points over LIBOR
Current LIBOR	5.5 percent
Expiration	20 August (128 days later)
Exercise rate	5 percent
Call premium	$100,000

Scenario (20 August)

LIBOR on 20 August is 8 percent.

(Exhibit continued on next page . . .)

---

[21] It should be noted that the effective annual rate is actually more than 200 basis points. For example, if someone borrows $100 at 2 percent for 180 days, the amount repaid would be $100[1 + 0.02(180/360)] = 101. The effective annual rate would be $(\$101/\$100)^{365/180} - 1 = 0.0204$.

| EXHIBIT 13 | (continued) |

Outcome and Analysis

For any LIBOR, the call payoff at expiration is given below and will be received 180 days later:

$$\$40,000,000 \max(0, \text{LIBOR} - 0.05)\left(\frac{180}{360}\right)$$

For LIBOR of 8 percent, the payoff is

$$\$40,000,000 \max(0, 0.08 - 0.05)\left(\frac{180}{360}\right) = \$600,000$$

The premium compounded from 14 April to 20 August at the original LIBOR of 5.5 percent plus 200 basis points is

$$\$100,000\left[1 + (0.055 + 0.02)\left(\frac{128}{360}\right)\right] - \$102,667$$

So the call costs $100,000 on 14 April, which is equivalent to $102,667 on 20 August. The effective loan proceeds are $40,000,000 − $102,667 = $39,897,333. The loan interest is

$$\$40,000,000(\text{LIBOR on 20 August} + 200 \text{ basis points})\left(\frac{180}{360}\right)$$

For LIBOR of 8 percent, the loan interest is

$$\$40,000,000(0.08 + 0.02)\left(\frac{180}{360}\right) = \$2,000,000$$

The call payoff was given above. The loan interest minus the call payoff is the effective interest. The effective rate on the loan is

$$\left(\frac{\$40,000,000 \text{ plus effective interest}}{\$39,897,333}\right)^{365/180} - 1$$

$$= \left(\frac{\$40,000,000 + \$2,000,000 - \$600,000}{\$39,897,333}\right)^{365/180} - 1 = 0.0779$$

or 7.79 percent.

The results are shown below for a range of LIBORs on 20 August.

LIBOR on 20 August	Loan Rate	Loan Interest Paid on 16 February	Call Payoff	Effective Interest	Effective Loan Rate
0.010	0.030	$600,000	$0	$600,000	0.0360
0.015	0.035	700,000	0	700,000	0.0412
0.020	0.040	800,000	0	800,000	0.0464

(Exhibit continued on next page . . .)

EXHIBIT 13	(continued)

LIBOR on 20 August	Loan Rate	Loan Interest Paid on 16 February	Call Payoff	Effective Interest	Effective Loan Rate
0.025	0.045	900,000	0	900,000	0.0516
0.030	0.050	1,000,000	0	1,000,000	0.0568
0.035	0.055	1,100,000	0	1,100,000	0.0621
0.040	0.060	1,200,000	0	1,200,000	0.0673
0.045	0.065	1,300,000	0	1,300,000	0.0726
0.050	0.070	1,400,000	0	1,400,000	0.0779
0.055	0.075	1,500,000	100,000	1,400,000	0.0779
0.060	0.080	1,600,000	200,000	1,400,000	0.0779
0.065	0.085	1,700,000	300,000	1,400,000	0.0779
0.070	0.090	1,800,000	400,000	1,400,000	0.0779
0.075	0.095	1,900,000	500,000	1,400,000	0.0779
0.080	0.100	2,000,000	600,000	1,400,000	0.0779
0.085	0.105	2,100,000	700,000	1,400,000	0.0779
0.090	0.110	2,200,000	800,000	1,400,000	0.0779

EXHIBIT 14	The Effective Rate on an Anticipated Future Loan Protected with an Interest Rate Call Option

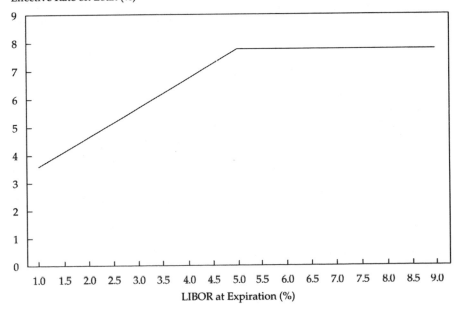

Effective Rate on Loan (%)

LIBOR at Expiration (%)

EXAMPLE 11

On 10 January, ResTex Ltd. determines that it will need to borrow $5 million on 15 February at 90-day LIBOR plus 300 basis points. The loan will be an **add-on interest** loan in which ResTex will receive $5 million and pay it back plus interest on 16 May. To manage the risk associated with the interest rate on 15 February, ResTex buys an interest rate call that expires on 15 February and pays off on 16 May. The exercise rate is 5 percent, and the option premium is $10,000. The current 90-day LIBOR is 5.25 percent. Assume that this rate, plus 300 basis points, is the rate it would borrow at for any period of up to 90 days if the loan were taken out today. Interest is computed on the exact number of days divided by 360.

Determine the effective annual rate on the loan for each of the following outcomes:

1. 90-day LIBOR on 15 February is 6 percent.

2. 90-day LIBOR on 15 February is 4 percent.

Solutions: First we need to compound the premium from 10 January to 15 February, which is 36 days. This calculation tells us the effective cost of the call as of the time the loan is taken out:

$$\$10,000\left[1 + (0.0525 + 0.03)\left(\frac{36}{360}\right)\right] = \$10,083$$

The loan proceeds will therefore be $5,000,000 − $10,083 = $4,989,917.

1. LIBOR is 6 percent. The loan rate will be 9 percent.

The interest on the loan will be $5,000,000(0.06 + 0.03)(90/360) = $112,500.

The option payoff will be $5,000,000 max(0,0.06 − 0.05)(90/360) = $12,500.

Therefore, the effective interest will be $112,500 − $12,500 = $100,000.

The effective rate on the loan will be

$$\left(\frac{\$5,000,000 + \$100,000}{\$4,989,917}\right)^{365/90} - 1 = 0.0925$$

Of course, a little more than 300 basis points of this amount is the spread.

2. LIBOR is 4 percent. The loan rate will be 7 percent.

The interest on the loan will be $5,000,000(0.04 + 0.03)(90/360) = $87,500.

The option payoff will be $5,000,000 max(0,0.04 − 0.05)(90/360) = $0.00.

The effective interest will, therefore, be $87,500.

The effective rate on the loan will be

$$\left(\frac{\$5,000,000 + \$87,500}{\$4,989,917}\right)^{365/90} - 1 = 0.0817$$

Of course, a little more than 300 basis points of this amount is the spread.

Whereas interest rate call options are appropriate for borrowers, lenders also face the risk of interest rates changing. As you may have guessed, they make use of interest rate puts.

3.2 Using Interest Rate Puts with Lending

Now consider an application of an interest rate put to establish a minimum interest rate for a commitment to give a loan in the future. A lender can buy a put that pays off if the interest rate falls below a chosen level. The put payoff then compensates the bank for the lower interest rate on the loan.

For example, consider Arbitrage Bank Inc. (ABInc) which makes loan commitments to corporations. It stands ready to make a loan at LIBOR at a future date. To protect itself against decreases in interest rates between the time of the commitment and the time the loan is taken out, it buys **interest rate puts**. These options pay off if LIBOR is below the exercise rate at expiration. If LIBOR is above the exercise rate at expiration, the option expires unexercised and the lender benefits from the higher rate on the loan.

In this example, ABInc makes a commitment on 15 March to lend $50 million at 90-day LIBOR plus 2.5 percent on 1 May, which is 47 days later. Current LIBOR is 7.25 percent. It buys a put with an exercise rate of 7 percent for $62,500. Assume that the opportunity cost of lending in the LIBOR market is LIBOR plus a spread of 2.5 percent. Therefore, the effective cost of the premium compounded to the option's expiration is[22]

$$\$62,500\left[1 + (0.0725 + 0.025)\left(\frac{47}{360}\right)\right] = \$63,296$$

When it lends $50 million on 1 May, it effectively has an outlay of $50,000,000 + $63,296 = $50,063,296. The loan rate is set on 1 May and the interest, paid 90 days later on 30 July, is

$$\$50,000,000\left[\text{LIBOR on 1 May plus 250 basis points}\left(\frac{90}{360}\right)\right]$$

The put payoff is

$$\$50,000,000 \max(0, 0.07 - \text{LIBOR on 1 May})\left(\frac{90}{360}\right)$$

The loan interest plus the put payoff make up the effective interest. The effective rate on the loan is

$$\left(\frac{\text{Principal plus effective interest}}{\$50,063,296}\right)^{365/90} - 1$$

Suppose LIBOR on 1 May is 6 percent. In that case, the loan rate will be 8.5 percent, and the interest on the loan will be

$$\$50,000,000\left[(0.06 + 0.025)\left(\frac{90}{360}\right)\right] = \$1,062,500$$

---

[22] The interpretation of this calculation is that the bank could have otherwise made a loan of $62,500, which would have paid back $63,296 on 1 May.

The put payoff is

$$\$50,000,000 \max(0, 0.07 - 0.06)\left(\frac{90}{360}\right) = \$125,000$$

This amount is paid on 30 July. The put cost of $62,500 on 15 March is equivalent to paying $63,296 on 1 May. Thus, on 1 May the bank effectively commits $50,000,000 + $63,296 = $50,063,296. The effective interest it receives is the loan interest of $1,062,500 plus the put payoff of $125,000, or $1,187,500. The effective annual rate is

$$\left(\frac{\$50,000,000 + \$1,187,500}{\$50,063,296}\right)^{365/90} - 1 = 0.0942$$

Exhibit 15 presents the results for a range of possible LIBORs at expiration, and Exhibit 16 graphs the effective loan rate against LIBOR on 1 May. Note how there is a minimum effective loan rate of 9.42 percent. Of this rate, 250 basis points is automatically built in as the loan spread.[23] The remaining amount reflects the exercise rate on the put of 7 percent minus the cost of the put premium.

EXHIBIT 15	Outcomes for an Anticipated Loan Protected with an Interest Rate Put

Scenario (15 March)

Arbitrage Bank Inc. (ABInc) is a U.S. bank that makes loan commitments to corporations. When ABInc makes these commitments, it recognizes the risk that LIBOR will fall by the date the loan is taken out. ABInc protects itself against interest rate decreases by purchasing interest rate puts, which give it the right to receive the difference between the exercise rate it chooses and LIBOR at expiration. LIBOR is currently 7.25 percent.

Action

ABInc commits to lending $50 million to a company at 90-day LIBOR plus 250 basis points. The loan will be a **single-payment loan**, meaning that it will be made on 1 May and the principal and interest will be repaid 90 days later on 30 July.

To protect against decreases in LIBOR between 15 March and 1 May, ABInc buys a put option with an exercise rate of 7 percent to expire on 1 May with the underlying being 90-day LIBOR. The put premium is $62,500. We summarize the information as follows:

Loan amount	$50,000,000
Underlying	90-day LIBOR
Spread	250 basis points over LIBOR
Current LIBOR	7.25 percent
Expiration	1 May
Exercise rate	7 percent
Put premium	$62,500

(Exhibit continued on next page . . .)

---

[23] As in the case of the borrower, the spread is effectively more than 250 basis points when the effective annual rate is determined. For this 90-day loan, this effectively amounts to 256 basis points.

| **EXHIBIT 15** | **(continued)** |

Scenario (1 May)

LIBOR is now 6 percent.

Outcome and Analysis

For any LIBOR, the payoff at expiration is given below and will be received 90 days later:

$$\$50,000,000 \max(0, 0.07 - \text{LIBOR})\left(\frac{90}{360}\right)$$

For LIBOR of 6 percent, the payoff is

$$\$50,000,000 \max(0, 0.07 - 0.060)\left(\frac{90}{360}\right) = \$125,000$$

The premium compounded from 15 March to 1 May at current LIBOR plus 250 basis points is

$$\$62,500\left[1 + (0.0725 + 0.025)\left(\frac{47}{360}\right)\right] = \$63,296$$

So the put costs $62,500 on 15 March, which is equivalent to $63,296 on 1 May. The effective amount loaned is $50,000,000 + $63,296 = $50,063,296. For any LIBOR, the loan interest is

$$\$50,000,000\left[\text{LIBOR on 1 May plus 250 basis points}\left(\frac{90}{360}\right)\right]$$

With LIBOR at 6 percent, the interest is

$$\$50,000,000\left[(0.06 + 0.025)\left(\frac{90}{360}\right)\right] = \$1,062,500$$

The loan interest plus the put payoff is the effective interest on the loan. The effective rate on the loan is

$$\left(\frac{\text{Principal plus effective interest}}{\$50,063,296}\right)^{365/90} - 1$$

$$= \left(\frac{\$50,000,000 + \$1,062,500 + \$125,000}{\$50,063,296}\right)^{365/90} - 1 = 0.0942$$

or 9.42 percent. The results are shown below for a range of LIBORs on 1 May.

(Exhibit continued on next page . . .)

EXHIBIT 15		(continued)			

LIBOR on 1 May	Loan Rate	Loan Interest Paid on 30 July	Put Payoff	Effective Interest	Effective Loan Rate
0.030	0.055	$687,500	$500,000	$1,187,500	0.0942
0.035	0.060	750,000	437,500	1,187,500	0.0942
0.040	0.065	812,500	375,000	1,187,500	0.0942
0.045	0.070	875,000	312,500	1,187,500	0.0942
0.050	0.075	937,500	250,000	1,187,500	0.0942
0.055	0.080	1,000,000	187,500	1,187,500	0.0942
0.060	0.085	1,062,500	125,000	1,187,500	0.0942
0.065	0.090	1,125,000	62,500	1,187,500	0.0942
0.070	0.095	1,187,500	0	1,187,500	0.0942
0.075	0.100	1,250,000	0	1,250,000	0.0997
0.080	0.105	1,312,500	0	1,312,500	0.1051
0.085	0.110	1,375,000	0	1,375,000	0.1106
0.090	0.115	1,437,500	0	1,437,500	0.1161
0.095	0.120	1,500,000	0	1,500,000	0.1216
0.100	0.125	1,562,500	0	1,562,500	0.1271
0.105	0.130	1,625,000	0	1,625,000	0.1327
0.110	0.135	1,687,500	0	1,687,500	0.1382

EXHIBIT 16	The Effective Rate on an Anticipated Loan with an Interest Rate Put Option

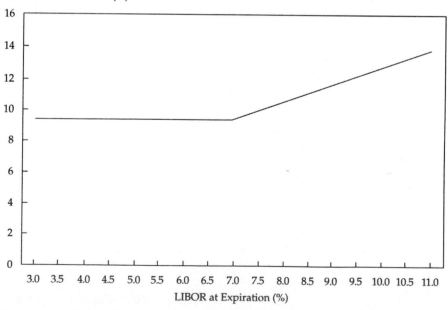

Effective Rate on Loan (%)

LIBOR at Expiration (%)

EXAMPLE 12

State Bank and Trust (SBT) is a lender in the floating-rate instrument market, but it has been hurt by recent interest rate decreases. SBT often makes loan commitments for its customers and then accepts the rate in effect on the day the loan is taken out. SBT has avoided floating-rate financing in the past. It takes out a certain amount of fixed-rate financing in advance to cover its loan commitments. One particularly large upcoming loan has it worried. This is a $100 million loan to be made in 65 days at 180-day LIBOR plus 100 basis points. The loan will be paid back 182 days after being taken out, and interest will be based on an exact day count and 360 days in a year. Current LIBOR is 7.125 percent, which is the rate it could borrow at now for any period less than 180 days. SBT considers the purchase of an interest rate put to protect it against an interest rate decrease over the next 65 days. The put will have an exercise price of 7 percent and a premium of $475,000.

Determine the effective annual rate on the loan for the following outcomes:

1. 180-day LIBOR at the option expiration is 9 percent.

2. 180-day LIBOR at the option expiration is 5 percent.

Solutions:

First we need to compound the premium for 65 days. This calculation tells us the effective cost of the put as of the time the loan is made:

$$\$475,000\left[1 + (0.07125 + 0.01)\left(\frac{65}{360}\right)\right] = \$481,968$$

The outlay will effectively be $100,000,000 + $481,968 = $100,481,968.

1. LIBOR is 9 percent. The loan rate will be 10 percent.

The interest on the loan will be
$100,000,000 (0.09 + 0.01)(182/360) = $5,055,556.

The option payoff will be
$100,000,000 max (0,0.07 − 0.09)(182/360) = $0.0.

Because there is no option payoff, the effective interest will be $5,055,556. The effective rate on the loan will be

$$\left(\frac{\$100,000,000 + \$5,055,556}{\$100,481,968}\right)^{365/182} - 1 = 0.0934$$

Of course, a little more than 100 basis points of this amount is the spread.

2. LIBOR is 5 percent. The loan will be 6 percent.

The interest on the loan will be $100,000,000 (0.05 + 0.01)(182/360) = $3,033,333.

The option payoff will be $100,000,000 max(0,0.07 − 0.05)(182/360) = $1,011,111.

The effective interest will, therefore, be $3,033,333 + $1,011,111 = $4,044,444.

The effective rate on the loan will be

$$\left(\frac{\$100,000,000 + \$4,044,444}{\$100,481,968} \right)^{365/182} - 1 = 0.0724$$

Of course, a little more than 100 basis points of this amount is the spread.

Interest rate calls and puts can be combined into packages of multiple options, which are widely used to manage the risk of floating-rate loans.

3.3 Using an Interest Rate Cap with a Floating-Rate Loan

Many corporate loans are floating-rate loans. They require periodic interest payments in which the rate is reset on a regularly scheduled basis. Because there is more than one interest payment, there is effectively more than one distinct risk. If a borrower wanted to use an interest rate call to place a ceiling on the effective borrowing rate, it would require more than one call. In effect, it would require a distinct call option expiring on each interest rate reset date. A combination of interest rate call options designed to align with the rates on a loan is called a **cap**. The component options are called **caplets**. Each caplet is distinct in having its own expiration date, but typically the exercise rate on each caplet is the same.

To illustrate the use of a cap, consider a company called Measure Technology (MesTech), which borrows in the floating-rate loan market. It usually takes out a loan for several years at a spread over LIBOR, paying the interest semiannually and the full principal at the end. On 15 April, MesTech takes out a $10 million three-year loan at 100 basis points over 180-day LIBOR from a bank called SenBank. Current 180-day LIBOR is 9 percent, which sets the rate for the first six-month period at 10 percent. Interest payments will be on the 15th of October and April for three years. This means that the day counts for the six payments will be 183, 182, 183, 182, 183, and 182.

To protect against increases in interest rates, MesTech purchases an **interest rate cap** with an exercise rate of 8 percent. The component caplets expire on 15 October, the following 15 April, and so forth until the last caplet expires on a subsequent 15 October. The loan has six interest payments, but because the first rate is already set, there are only five risky payments so the cap will contain five caplets. The payoff of each caplet will be determined on its expiration date, but the caplet payoff, if any, will actually be made on the next payment date. This enables the caplet payoff to line up with the date on which the loan interest is paid. The cap premium, paid up front on 15 April, is $75,000.

In the example of a single interest rate call, we looked at a range of outcomes several hundred basis points around the exercise rate. In a cap, however, many more outcomes are possible. Ideally we would examine a range of outcomes for each caplet. In the example of a single cap, we looked at the exercise rate and 8 rates above and below for a total of 17 rates. For five distinct rate resets, this same procedure would require 5^{17} or more than 762 billion different possibilities. So, we shall just look at one possible combination of rates.

We shall examine a set of outcomes in which LIBOR is

8.50 percent on 15 October
7.25 percent on 15 April the following year
7.00 percent on the following 15 October
6.90 percent on the following 15 April
8.75 percent on the following 15 October

The loan interest is computed as

$$\$10,000,000(\text{LIBOR on previous reset date} + 100 \text{ basis points}) \times \left(\frac{\text{Days in settlement period}}{360}\right)$$

Thus, the first interest payment is

$$\$10,000,000(0.10)\left(\frac{183}{360}\right) = \$508,333$$

which is based on 183 days between 15 April and 15 October. This amount is certain, because the first interest rate has already been set. The remaining interest payments are based on the assumption we made above about the course of LIBOR over the life of the loan.

The results for these assumed rates are shown in the table at the end of Exhibit 17. Note several things about the effective interest, displayed in the last column. First, the initial interest payment is much higher than the other interest payments because the initial rate is somewhat higher than the remaining rates that prevailed over the life of the loan. Also, recall that the initial rate is already set, and it would make no sense to add a caplet to cover the initial rate, because the caplet would have to expire immediately in order to pay off on the first 15 October. If the caplet expired immediately, the amount MesTech would have to pay for it would be the amount of the caplet payoff, discounted for the deferral of the payoff. In other words, it would make no sense to have an option, or any derivative for that matter, that is purchased and expires immediately. Note also the variation in the effective interest payments, which occurs for two reasons. One is that, in contrast to previous examples, interest is computed over the exact number of days in the period. Thus, even if the rate were the same, the interest could vary by the effect of one or two days of interest. The other reason is that in some cases the caplets do expire with value, thereby reducing the effective interest paid.

| **EXHIBIT 17** | **Interest Rate Cap** |

Scenario (15 April)

Measure Technology (MesTech) is a corporation that borrows in the floating-rate instrument market. It typically takes out a loan for several years at a spread over LIBOR. MesTech pays the interest semiannually and the full principal at the end.

To protect against rising interest rates over the life of the loan, MesTech usually buys an interest rate cap in which the component caplets expire on the dates on which the loan rate is reset. The cap seller is a derivatives dealer.

(Exhibit continued on next page . . .)

EXHIBIT 17	(continued)

Action

MesTech takes out a $10 million three-year loan at 100 basis points over LIBOR. The payments will be made semiannually. The lender is SenBank. Current LIBOR is 9 percent, which means that the first rate will be at 10 percent. Interest will be based on 1/360 of the exact number of days in the six-month period. MesTech selects an exercise rate of 8 percent. The caplets will expire on 15 October, 15 April of the following year, and so on for three years, but the caplet payoffs will occur on the next payment date to correspond with the interest payment based on LIBOR that determines the cap payoff. The cap premium is $75,000. We thus have the following information:

Loan amount	$10,000,000
Underlying	180-day LIBOR
Spread	100 basis points over LIBOR
Current LIBOR	9 percent
Interest based on	actual days/360
Component caplets	five caplets expiring 15 October, 15 April, etc.
Exercise rate	8 percent
Cap premium	$75,000

Scenario (Various Dates throughout the Loan)

Shown below is one particular set of outcomes for LIBOR:

8.50 percent on 15 October

7.25 percent on 15 April the following year

7.00 percent on the following 15 October

6.90 percent on the following 15 April

8.75 percent on the following 15 October

Outcome and Analysis

The loan interest due is computed as

$$\$10,000,000(\text{LIBOR on previous reset date} + 100 \text{ basis points}) \times \left(\frac{\text{Days in settlement period}}{360}\right)$$

The caplet payoff is

$$\$10,000,000 \max(0, \text{LIBOR on previous reset date} - 0.08) \times \left(\frac{\text{Days in settlement period}}{360}\right)$$

(Exhibit continued on next page . . .)

EXHIBIT 17	(continued)

The previous reset date is the expiration date of the caplet. The effective interest is the interest due minus the caplet payoff.

The first caplet expires on the first 15 October and pays off the following April, because LIBOR on 15 October was 8.5 percent. The payoff is computed as

$$\$10,000,000 \max\left(0, 0.085 - 0.08\right)\left(\frac{182}{360}\right)$$

$$= \$10,000,000(0.005)\left(\frac{182}{360}\right) = \$25,278$$

which is based on 182 days between 15 October and 15 April. The following table shows the payments on the loan and cap:

Date	LIBOR	Loan Rate	Days in Period	Interest Due	Caplet Payoffs	Effective Interest
15 April	0.0900	0.1000				
15 October	0.0850	0.0950	183	$508,333		$508,333
15 April	0.0725	0.0825	182	480,278	$25,278	455,000
15 October	0.0700	0.0800	183	419,375	0	419,375
15 April	0.0690	0.0790	182	404,444	0	404,444
15 October	0.0875	0.0975	183	401,583	0	401,583
15 April			182	492,917	37,917	455,000

Note that on the following three dates, the caplets are out-of-the-money, because the LIBORs are all lower than 8 percent. On the final 15 October, however, LIBOR is 8.75 percent, which leads to a final caplet payoff of $37,917 on the following 15 April, at which time the loan principal is repaid.

We do not show the effective rate on the loan. Because the loan has multiple payments, the effective rate would be analogous to the internal rate of return on a capital investment project or the yield-to-maturity on a bond. This rate would have to be found with a financial calculator or spreadsheet, and we would have to account for the principal received up front and paid back at maturity, as well as the cap premium. It is sufficient for us to see that the cap protects the borrower any time the rate rises above the exercise rate and allows the borrower to benefit from rates lower that the exercise rate.

Finally, there is one circumstance under which this cap might contain a sixth caplet, one expiring on the date on which the loan is taken out. If the borrower purchased the cap in advance of taking out the loan, the first loan rate would not be set until the day the loan is actually taken out. The borrower would thus have an incentive to include a caplet that would protect the first rate setting.

EXAMPLE 13

Healthy Biosystems (HBIO) is a typical floating-rate borrower, taking out loans at LIBOR plus a spread. On 15 January 2002, it takes out a loan of $25 million for one year with quarterly payments on 12 April, 14 July,

16 October, and the following 14 January. The underlying rate is 90-day LIBOR, and HBIO will pay a spread of 250 basis points. Interest is based on the exact number of days in the period. Current 90-day LIBOR is 6.5 percent. HBIO purchases an interest rate cap for $20,000 that has an exercise rate of 7 percent and has caplets expiring on the rate reset dates.

Determine the effective interest payments if LIBOR on the following dates is as given:

12 April	7.250 percent
14 July	6.875 percent
16 October	7.125 percent

Solution: The interest due for each period is computed as $25,000,000(LIBOR on previous reset date + 0.0250)(Days in period/360). For example, the first interest payment is calculated as $25,000,000(0.065 + 0.025)(87/360) = $543,750, based on the fact that there are 87 days between 15 January and 12 April. Each caplet payoff is computed as $25,000,000 max(0,LIBOR on previous reset date − 0.07)(Days in period/360), where the "previous reset date" is the caplet expiration. Payment is deferred until the date on which the interest is paid at the given LIBOR. For example, the caplet expiring on 12 April is worth $25,000,000 max(0,0.0725 − 0.07)(93/360) = $16,145, which is paid on 14 July and is based on the fact that there are 93 days between 12 April and 14 July.

The effective interest is the actual interest minus the caplet payoff. The payments are shown in the table below:

Date	LIBOR	Loan Rate	Days in Period	Interest Due	Caplet Payoff	Effective Interest
15 January	0.065	0.09				
12 April	0.0725	0.0975	87	$543,750		$543,750
14 July	0.06875	0.09375	93	629,688	$16,146	613,542
16 October	0.07125	0.09625	94	611,979	0	611,979
14 January			90	601,563	7,813	593,750

Lenders who use floating-rate loans face the same risk as borrowers. As such they can make use of combinations of interest rate puts.

3.4 Using an Interest Rate Floor with a Floating-Rate Loan

Let us now consider the same problem from the point of view of the lender, which is SenBank in this example. It would be concerned about falling interest rates. It could, therefore, buy a combination of interest rate put options that expire on the various interest rate reset dates. This combination of puts is called a **floor**, and the component options are called **floorlets**. Specifically, let SenBank buy a floor with floorlets expiring on the interest rate reset dates and with an exercise rate of

8 percent. The premium is $72,500.[24] Exhibit 18 illustrates the results using the same outcomes we looked at when examining the interest rate cap. Note that the floorlet expires in-the-money on three dates when LIBOR is less than 8 percent, and out-of-the-money on two dates when LIBOR is greater than 8 percent. In those cases in which the floorlet expires in-the-money, the actual payoff does not occur until the next **settlement period**. This structure aligns the floorlet payoffs with the interest payments they are designed to protect. We see that the floor protects the lender against falling interest rates. Any time the rate is below 8 percent, the floor compensates the bank for any difference between the rate and 8 percent. When the rate is above 8 percent, the floorlets simply expire unused.

EXHIBIT 18	Interest Rate Floor

Scenario (15 April)

SenBank lends in the floating-rate instrument market. Often it uses floating-rate financing, thereby protecting itself against decreases in the floating rates on its loans. Sometimes, however, it finds it can get a better rate with fixed-rate financing, but it then leaves itself exposed to interest rate decreases on its floating-rate loans. Its loans are typically for several years at a spread over LIBOR with interest paid semiannually and the full principal paid at the end.

To protect against falling interest rates over the life of the loan, SenBank buys an **interest rate floor** in which the component floorlets expire on the dates on which the loan rate is reset. The floor seller is a derivatives dealer.

Action

SenBank makes a $10 million three-year loan at 100 basis points over LIBOR to MesTech (see cap example). The payments will be made semiannually. Current LIBOR is 9 percent, which means that the first interest payment will be at 10 percent. Interest will be based on the exact number of days in the six-month period divided by 360. SenBank selects an exercise rate of 8 percent. The floorlets will expire on 15 October, 15 April of the following year, and so on for three years, but the floorlet payoffs will occur on the next payment date so as to correspond with the interest payment based on LIBOR that determines the floorlet payoff. The floor premium is $72,500. We thus have the following information:

Loan amount	$10,000,000
Underlying	180-day LIBOR
Spread	100 basis points over LIBOR
Current LIBOR	9 percent
Interest based on	actual days/360
Component floorlets	five floorlets expiring 15 October, 15 April, etc.
Exercise rate	8 percent
Floor premium	$72,500

(Exhibit continued on next page . . .)

---

[24] Note that the premiums for the cap and floor are not the same. This difference occurs because the premiums for a call and a put with the same exercise price are not the same, as can be seen by examining put–call parity.

| EXHIBIT 18 | (continued) |

Outcomes (Various Dates throughout the Loan)

Shown below is one particular set of outcomes for LIBOR:

8.50 percent on 15 October

7.25 percent on 15 April the following year

7.00 percent on the following 15 October

6.90 percent on the following 15 April

8.75 percent on the following 15 October

Outcome and Analysis

The loan interest is computed as

$$\$10,000,000(\text{LIBOR on previous reset date} + 100 \text{ basis points}) \times \left(\frac{\text{Days in settlement period}}{360}\right)$$

The floorlet payoff is

$$\$10,000,000 \max(0, 0.08 - \text{LIBOR on previous reset date}) \times \left(\frac{\text{Days in settlement period}}{360}\right)$$

The effective interest is the interest due plus the floorlet payoff. The following table shows the payments on the loan and floor:

Date	LIBOR	Loan Rate	Days in Period	Interest Due	Floorlet Payoffs	Effective Interest
15 April	0.0900	0.1000				
15 October	0.0850	0.0950	183	$508,333		$508,333
15 April	0.0725	0.0825	182	480,278	$0	480,278
15 October	0.0700	0.0800	183	419,375	38,125	457,500
15 April	0.0690	0.0790	182	404,444	50,556	455,000
15 October	0.0875	0.0975	183	401,583	55,917	457,500
15 April			182	492,917	0	492,917

| EXAMPLE 14 |

Capitalized Bank (CAPBANK) is a lender in the floating-rate loan market. It uses fixed-rate financing on its floating-rate loans and buys floors to hedge the rate. On 1 May 2002, it makes a loan of $40 million at 180-day

LIBOR plus 150 basis points. Interest will be paid on 1 November, the following 5 May, the following 1 November, and the following 2 May, at which time the principal will be repaid. The exercise rate is 4.5 percent, the floorlets expire on the rate reset dates, and the premium will be $120,000. Interest will be calculated based on the actual number of days in the period over 360. The current 180-day LIBOR is 5 percent.

Determine the effective interest payments CAPBANK will receive if LIBOR on the following dates is as given:

1 November	4.875 percent
5 May	4.25 percent
1 November	5.125 percent

Solution: The interest due for each period is computed as $40,000,000(LIBOR on previous reset date + 0.0150)(Days in period/360). For example, the first interest payment is $40,000,000(0.05 + 0.0150)(184/360) = $1,328,889, based on the fact that there are 184 days between 1 May and 1 November. Each floorlet payoff is computed as $40,000,000 max(0,0.045 − LIBOR on previous reset date)(Days in period/360), where the "previous reset date" is the floorlet expiration. Payment is deferred until the date on which the interest is paid at the given LIBOR. For example, the floorlet expiring on 5 May is worth $40,000,000 max(0,0.045 − 0.0425)(180/360) = $50,000, which is paid on 1 November and is based on the fact that there are 180 days between 5 May and 1 November.

The effective interest is the actual interest plus the floorlet payoff. The payments are shown in the table below:

Date	LIBOR	Loan Rate	Days in Period	Interest Due	Caplet Payoff	Effective Interest
1 May	0.05	0.065				
1 November	0.04875	0.06375	184	$1,328,889		$1,328,889
5 May	0.0425	0.0575	185	1,310,417	$0	1,310,417
1 November	0.05125	0.06625	180	1,150,000	50,000	1,200,000
2 May			182	1,339,722	0	1,339,722

When studying equity option strategies, we combined puts and calls into a single transaction called a collar. In a similar manner, we now combine caps and floors into a single transaction, also called a collar.

3.5 Using an Interest Rate Collar with a Floating-Rate Loan

As we showed above, borrowers are attracted to caps because they protect against rising interest rates. They do so, however, at the cost of having to pay a premium in cash up front. A collar combines a long position in a cap with a short position in a floor. The sale of the floor generates a premium that can be used to offset the premium on the cap. Although it is not necessary that the floor premium completely offset the cap premium, this arrangement is common.[25] The exercise rate on the floor is selected such that the floor premium is precisely the cap premium. As with **equity options**, this type of strategy is called a zero-cost collar. Recall, however, that this term is a bit misleading because it suggests that this transaction has no true "cost." The cost is simply not up front in cash. The sale of the floor results in the borrower giving up any gains from interest rates below the exercise rate on the floor. Therefore, the borrower pays for the cap by giving away some of the gains from the possibility of falling rates.

Recall that for equity investors, the collar typically entails ownership of the underlying asset and the purchase of a put, which is financed with the sale of a call. In contrast, an interest rate collar is more commonly seen from the borrower's point of view: a position as a borrower and the purchase of a cap, which is financed by the sale of a floor. It is quite possible, however, that a lender would want a collar. The lender is holding an asset, the loan, and wants protection against falling interest rates, which can be obtained by buying a floor, which itself can be financed by selling a cap. Most interest rate collars, however, are initiated by borrowers.

In the example we used previously, MesTech borrows $10 million at LIBOR plus 100 basis points. The cap exercise rate is 8 percent, and the premium is $75,000. We now change the numbers a little and let MesTech set the exercise rate at 8.625 percent. To sell a floor that will generate the same premium as the cap, the exercise rate is set at 7.5 percent. It is not necessary for us to know the amounts of the cap and floor premiums; it is sufficient to know that they offset.

Exhibit 19 shows the collar results for the same set of interest rate outcomes we have been previously using. Note that on the first 15 October, LIBOR is between the cap and floor exercise rates, so neither the caplet nor the floorlet expires in-the-money. On the following 15 April, 15 October, and the next 15 April, the rate is below the floor exercise rate, so MesTech has to pay up on the expiring floorlets. On the final 15 October, LIBOR is above the cap exercise rate, so MesTech gets paid on its cap.

EXHIBIT 19	**Interest Rate Collar**

Scenario (15 April)

Consider the Measure Technology (MesTech) scenario described in the cap and floor example in Exhibits 17 and 18. MesTech is a corporation that borrows in the floating-rate instrument market. It typically takes out a loan for several years at a spread over LIBOR. MesTech pays the interest semiannually and the full principal at the end.

To protect against rising interest rates over the life of the loan, MesTech usually buys an interest rate cap in which the component caplets expire on the dates on which the loan rate is reset. To pay for the cost of the interest rate cap, MesTech can sell a floor at an exercise rate lower than the cap exercise rate.

Action

Consider the $10 million three-year loan at 100 basis points over LIBOR. The payments are made semiannually. Current LIBOR is 9 percent, which means that

(Exhibit continued on next page . . .)

---

[25] It is even possible for the floor premium to be greater than the cap premium, thereby *generating cash* up front.

EXHIBIT 19   (continued)

the first rate will be at 10 percent. Interest is based on the exact number of days in the six-month period divided by 360. MesTech selects an exercise rate of 8.625 percent for the cap. Generating a floor premium sufficient to offset the cap premium requires a floor exercise rate of 7.5 percent. The caplets and floorlets will expire on 15 October, 15 April of the following year, and so on for three years, but the payoffs will occur on the following payment date to correspond with the interest payment based on LIBOR that determines the caplet and floorlet payoffs. Thus, we have the following information:

Loan amount	$10,000,000
Underlying	180-day LIBOR
Spread	100 basis points over LIBOR
Current LIBOR	9 percent
Interest based on	actual days/360
Component options	five caplets and floorlets expiring 15 October, 15 April, etc.
Exercise rate	8.625 percent on cap, 7.5 percent on floor
Premium	no net premium

Scenario (Various Dates throughout the Loan)

Shown below is one particular set of outcomes for LIBOR:

8.50 percent on 15 October

7.25 percent on 15 April the following year

7.00 percent on the following 15 October

6.90 percent on the following 15 April

8.75 percent on the following 15 October

Outcome and Analysis

The loan interest is computed as

$$\$10,000,000(\text{LIBOR on previous reset date} + 100 \text{ basis points}) \times \left(\frac{\text{Days in settlement period}}{360}\right)$$

The caplet payoff is

$$\$10,000,000 \max(0, \text{LIBOR on previous reset date} - 0.08625) \times \left(\frac{\text{Days in settlement period}}{360}\right)$$

(Exhibit continued on next page . . .)

| **EXHIBIT 19** | **(continued)** |

The floorlet payoff is

$$(\$10{,}000{,}000 \max(0, 0.075 - \text{LIBOR on previous reset date}) \times$$
$$\left(\frac{\text{Days in settlement period}}{360}\right)$$

The effective interest is the interest due minus the caplet payoff minus the floorlet payoff. Note that because the floorlet was sold, the floorlet payoff is either negative (so we would subtract a negative number, thereby adding an amount to obtain the total interest due) or zero.

The following table shows the payments on the loan and collar:

Date	LIBOR	Loan Rate	Days in Period	Interest Due	Caplet Payoffs	Floorlet Payoffs	Effective Interest
15 April	0.0900	0.1000					
15 October	0.0850	0.0950	183	$508,333			$508,333
15 April	0.0725	0.0825	182	480,278	$0	$0	480,278
15 October	0.0700	0.0800	183	419,375	0	−12,708	432,083
15 April	0.0690	0.0790	182	404,444	0	−25,278	429,722
15 October	0.0875	0.0975	183	401,583	0	−30,500	432,083
15 April			182	492,917	6,319	0	486,598

A collar establishes a range, the cap exercise rate minus the floor exercise rate, within which there is interest rate risk. The borrower will benefit from falling rates and be hurt by rising rates within that range. Any rate increases above the cap exercise rate will have no net effect, and any rate decreases below the floor exercise rate will have no net effect. The net cost of this position is zero, provided that the floor exercise rate is set such that the floor premium offsets the cap premium.[26] It is probably easy to see that collars are popular among borrowers.

| **EXAMPLE 15** |

Exegesis Systems (EXSYS) is a floating-rate borrower that manages its interest rate risk with collars, purchasing a cap and selling a floor in which the cost of the cap and floor are equivalent. EXSYS takes out a $35 million one-year loan at 90-day LIBOR plus 200 basis points. It establishes a collar with a cap exercise rate of 7 percent and a floor exercise rate of 6 percent. Current 90-day LIBOR is 6.5 percent. The interest

---

[26] It is certainly possible that the floor exercise rate would be set first, and the cap exercise rate would then be set to have the cap premium offset the floor premium. This would likely be the case if a lender were doing the collar. We assume, however, the case of a borrower who wants protection above a certain level and then decides to give up gains below a particular level necessary to offset the cost of the protection.

payments will be based on the exact day count over 360. The caplets and floorlets expire on the rate reset dates. The rates will be set on the current date (5 March), 4 June, 5 September, and 3 December, and the loan will be paid off on the following 3 March.

Determine the effective interest payments if LIBOR on the following dates is as given:

4 June	7.25 percent
5 September	6.5 percent
3 December	5.875 percent

Solution: The interest due for each period is computed as $35,000,000(LIBOR on previous reset date $+$ 0.02)(Days in period/360). For example, the first interest payment is $35,000,000(0.065 + 0.02)(91/360) = $752,014, based on the fact that there are 91 days between 5 March and 4 June. Each caplet payoff is computed as $35,000,000 max(0,LIBOR on previous reset date $-$ 0.07)(Days in period/360), where the "previous reset date" is the caplet expiration. Payment is deferred until the date on which the interest is paid at the given LIBOR. For example, the caplet expiring on 4 June is worth $35,000,000 max(0,0.0725 $-$ 0.07)(93/360) = $22,604, which is paid on 5 September and is based on the fact that there are 93 days between 4 June and 5 September. Each floorlet payoff is computed as $35,000,000 max(0,0.06 $-$ LIBOR on previous reset date)(Days in period/360). For example, the floorlet expiring on 3 December is worth $35,000,000 max(0,0.06 $-$ 0.05875)(90/360) = $10,938, based on the fact that there are 90 days between 3 December and 3 March. The effective interest is the actual interest minus the caplet payoff plus the floorlet payoff. The payments are shown in the table below:

Date	LIBOR	Loan Rate	Days in Period	Interest Due	Caplet Payoff	Floorlet Payoff	Effective Interest
5 March	0.065	0.085					
4 June	0.0725	0.0925	91	$752,014			$752,014
5 September	0.065	0.085	93	836,354	$22,604	$0	813,750
3 December	0.05875	0.07875	89	735,486	0	0	735,486
3 March			90	689,063	0	−10,938	700,001

Of course, caps, floors, and collars are not the only forms of protection against interest rate risk. We have previously covered FRAs and interest rate futures. The most widely used protection, however, is the interest rate swap. We cover swap strategies in Reading 40.

In the final section of this reading, we examine the strategies used to manage the risk of an option portfolio.

4   OPTION PORTFOLIO RISK MANAGEMENT STRATEGIES

So far we have looked at examples of how companies and investors use options. As we have described previously, many options are traded by dealers who make markets in these options, providing liquidity by first taking on risk and then hedging their positions in order to earn the bid–ask spread without taking the risk. In this section, we shall take a look at the strategies dealers use to hedge their positions.[27]

Let us assume that a customer contacts a dealer with an interest in purchasing a call option. The dealer, ready to take either side of the transaction, quotes an acceptable **ask price** and the customer buys the option. Recall from earlier in this reading that a short position in a call option is a very dangerous strategy, because the potential loss on an upside underlying move is open ended. The dealer would not want to hold a short call position for long. The ideal way to lay off the risk is to find someone else who would take the exact opposite position, but in most cases, the dealer will not be so lucky.[28] Another ideal posibility is for the dealer to lay off the risk using put–call parity. Recall that put–call parity says that $c = p + S - X/(1 + r)^T$. The dealer that has sold a call needs to buy a call to hedge the position. The put–call parity equation means that a long call is equivalent to a long put, a long position in the asset, and issuing a zero-coupon bond with a face value equal to the option exercise price and maturing on the option expiration date. Therefore, if the dealer could buy a put with the same exercise price and expiration, buy the asset, and sell a bond or take out a loan with face value equal to the exercise price and maturity equal to that of the option's expiration, it would have the position hedged. Other than buying an identical call, as described above, this hedge would be the best because it is static: No change to the position is required as time passes.

Unfortunately, neither of these transactions can be commonly employed. The necessary options may not be available or may not be favorably priced. As the next best alternative, dealers **delta hedge** their positions using an available and attractively priced instrument. The dealer is short the call and will need an offsetting position in another instrument. An obvious offsetting instrument would be a long position of a certain number of units of the underlying. The size of that long position will be related to the option's delta. Let us briefly review delta here. By definition,

$$\text{Delta} = \frac{\text{Change in option price}}{\text{Change in underlying price}}$$

Delta expresses how the option price changes relative to the price of the underlying. Technically, we should use an approximation sign ($\approx$) in the above equation, but for now we shall assume the approximation is exact. Let ΔS be the change in the underlying price and Δc be the change in the option price. Then

---

[27] For over-the-counter options, these dealers are usually the financial institutions that make markets in these options. For exchange-traded options, these dealers are the traders at the options exchanges, who may trade for their own accounts or could represent firms.

[28] Even luckier would be the dealer's original customer who might stumble across a party who wanted to sell the call option. The two parties could then bypass the dealer and negotiate a transaction directly between each other, which would save each party half of the bid–ask spread.

Delta = $\Delta c/\Delta S$. The delta usually lies between 0.0 and 1.0.[29] Delta will be 1.0 only at expiration and only if the option expires in-the-money. Delta will be 0.0 only at expiration and only if the option expires out-of-the-money. So most of the time, the delta will be between 0.0 and 1.0. Hence, 0.5 is often given as an "average" delta, but one must be careful because even before expiration the delta will tend to be higher than 0.5 if the option is in-the-money.

Now, let us assume that we construct a portfolio consisting of N_S units of the underlying and N_c call options. The value of the portfolio is, therefore,

$$V = N_S S + N_c c$$

The change in the value of the portfolio is

$$\Delta V = N_S \Delta S + N_c \Delta c$$

If we want to hedge the portfolio, then we want the change in V, given a change in S, to be zero. Dividing by ΔS, we obtain

$$\frac{\Delta V}{\Delta S} = N_S \frac{\Delta S}{\Delta S} + N_c \frac{\Delta c}{\Delta S}$$

$$= N_S + N_c \frac{\Delta c}{\Delta S}$$

Setting this result equal to zero and solving for N_c/N_S, we obtain

$$\frac{N_c}{N_S} = -\frac{1}{\Delta c/\Delta S}$$

The ratio of calls to shares has to be the negative of 1 over the delta. Thus, if the dealer sells a given number of calls, say 100, it will need to own 100(Delta) shares.

How does delta hedging work? Let us say that we sell call options on 200 shares (this quantity is 2 standardized call contracts on an options exchange) and the delta is 0.5. We would, therefore, need to hold 200(0.5) = 100 shares. Say the underlying falls by \$1. Then we lose \$100 on our position in the underlying. If the delta is accurate, the option should decline by \$0.50. By having 200 options, the loss in value of the options collectively is \$100. Because we are short the options, the loss in value of the options is actually a gain. Hence, the loss on the underlying is offset by the gain on the options. If the dealer were long the option, it would need to sell short the shares.

This illustration may make delta hedging sound simple: Buy (sell) delta shares for each option short (long). But there are three complicating issues. One is that delta is only an approximation of the change in the call price for a change in the underlying. A second issue is that the delta changes if anything else changes. Two factors that change are the price of the underlying and time. When the price of the underlying changes, delta changes, which affects the number of

---

[29] In the following text, we always make reference to the delta lying between 0.0 and 1.0, which is true for calls. For puts, the delta is between -1.0 and 0.0. It is common, however, to refer to a put delta of -1.0 as just 1.0, in effect using its absolute value and ignoring the negative. In all discussions in this reading, we shall refer to delta as ranging between 1.0 and 0.0, recalling that a put delta would range from -1.0 to 0.0.

options required to hedge the underlying. Delta also changes as time changes; because time changes continuously, delta also changes continuously. Although a dealer can establish a delta-hedged position, as soon as anything happens—the underlying price changes or time elapses—the position is no longer delta hedged. In some cases, the position may not be terribly out of line with a delta hedge, but the more the underlying changes, the further the position moves away from being delta hedged. The third issue is that the number of units of the underlying per option must be rounded off, which leads to a small amount of imprecision in the balancing of the two opposing positions.

In the following section, we examine how a dealer delta hedges an option position, carrying the analysis through several days with the additional feature that excess cash will be invested in bonds and any additional cash needed will be borrowed.

4.1 Delta Hedging an Option over Time

In the previous section, we showed how to set up a delta hedge. As we noted, a delta-hedged position will not remain delta hedged over time. The delta will change as the underlying changes and as time elapses. The dealer must account for these effects.

Let us first examine how actual option prices are sensitive to the underlying and what the delta tells us about that sensitivity. Consider a call option in which the underlying is worth 1210, the exercise price is 1200, the continuously compounded risk-free rate is 2.75 percent, the volatility of the underlying is 20 percent, and the expiration is 120 days. There are no dividends or cash flows on the underlying. Substituting these inputs into the Black–Scholes–Merton model, the option is worth 65.88. Recall from our study of the Black–Scholes–Merton model that delta is the term "$N(d_1)$" in the formula and represents a normal probability associated with the value d_1, which is provided as part of the Black–Scholes–Merton formula. In this example, the delta is 0.5826.[30]

Suppose that the underlying price instantaneously changes to 1200, a decline of 10. Using the delta, we would estimate that the option price would be

$$65.88 + (1200 - 1210)(0.5826) = 60.05$$

If, however, we plugged into the Black–Scholes–Merton model the same parameters but with a price of the underlying of 1200, we would obtain a new option price of 60.19—not much different from the previous result. But observe in Exhibit 20 what we obtain for various other values of the underlying. Two patterns become apparent: (1) The further away we move from the current price, the worse the delta-based approximation, and (2) the effects are asymmetric. A given move in one direction does not have the same effect on the option as the same move in the other direction. Specifically, for calls, the delta underestimates the effects of increases in the underlying and overestimates the effects of decreases in the underlying.[31] Because of this characteristic, the delta hedge will not be perfect. The larger the move in the underlying, the worse the hedge. Moreover, whenever the underlying price changes, the delta changes, which requires a rehedging or adjustment to the position.

---

[30] All calculations were done on a computer for best precision.

[31] For puts, delta underestimates the effects of price decreases and overestimates the effects of price increases.

EXHIBIT 20	Delta and Option Price Sensitivity

$S = 1210$

$X = 1200$

$r^c = 0.0275$ (continuously compounded)

$\sigma = 0.20$

$T = 0.328767$ (based on 120 days/365)

No dividends

$c = 65.88$ (from the Black–Scholes–Merton model)

New Price of Underlying	Delta-Estimated Call Price[a]	Actual Call Price[b]	Difference (Actual − Estimated)	New Delta
1180	48.40	49.69	1.29	0.4959
1190	54.22	54.79	0.57	0.5252
1200	60.05	60.19	0.14	0.5542
1210	65.88	65.88	0.00	0.5826
1220	71.70	71.84	0.14	0.6104
1230	77.53	78.08	0.55	0.6374
1240	83.35	84.59	1.24	0.6635

[a] Delta-estimated call price = Original call price + (New price of underlying − Original price of underlying)Delta.

[b] Actual call price obtained from Black–Scholes–Merton model using new price of underlying; all other inputs are the same.

Observe in the last column of the table in Exhibit 20 we have recomputed the delta using the new price of the underlying. A dealer must adjust the position according to this new delta.

Now let us consider the effect of time on the delta. Exhibit 21 shows the delta and the number of units of underlying required to hedge 1,000 short options when the option has 120 days, 119, etc. on down to 108. A critical assumption is that we are holding the underlying price constant. Of course, this constancy would not occur in practice, but to focus on understanding the effect of time on the delta, we must hold the underlying price constant. Observe that the delta changes slowly and the number of units of the underlying required changes gradually over this 12-day period. Another not-so-obvious effect is also present: When we round up, we have more units of the underlying than needed, which has a negative effect that hurts when the underlying goes down. When we round down, we have fewer units of the underlying than needed, which hurts when the underlying goes up.

The combined effects of the underlying price changing and the time to expiration changing interact to present great challenges for delta hedgers. Let us set up a delta hedge and work through a few days of it. Recall that for the option we have been working with, the underlying price is $1,200, the option price is $65.88, and the delta is 0.5826. Suppose a customer comes to us and asks to buy calls on 1,000 shares. We need to buy a sufficient number of shares to offset the

| EXHIBIT 21 | The Effect of Time on the Delta |

S = 1210

X = 1200

r^c = 0.0275 (continuously compounded)

σ = 0.20

T = 0.328767 (based on 120 days/365)

No dividends

c = 65.88 (from the Black–Scholes–Merton model)

Delta = 0.5826

Delta hedge 1,000 short options by holding 1,000(0.5826) = 582.6 units of the underlying.

Time to Expiration (Days)	Delta	Number of Units of Underlying Required
120	0.5826	582.6
119	0.5825	582.5
118	0.5824	582.4
117	0.5823	582.3
116	0.5822	582.2
115	0.5821	582.1
114	0.5820	582.0
113	0.5819	581.9
112	0.5818	581.8
111	0.5817	581.7
110	0.5816	581.6
109	0.5815	581.5
108	0.5814	581.4

sale of the 1,000 calls. Because we are short 1,000 calls, and this number is fixed, we need 0.5826 shares per call or about 583 shares. So we buy 583 shares to balance the 1,000 short calls. The value of this portfolio is

$$583(\$1{,}210) - 1{,}000(\$65.88) = \$639{,}550$$

So, to initiate this delta hedge, we would need to invest $639,550. To determine if this hedge is effective, we should see this value grow at the risk-free rate. Because the Black–Scholes–Merton model uses continuously compounded interest, the formula for compounding a value at the risk-free rate for one day is $\exp(r^c/365)$, where r^c is the continuously compounded risk-free rate. One day later, this value should be $639,550 $\exp(0.0275/365)$ = $639,598. This value becomes our benchmark.

Now, let us move forward one day and have the underlying go to $1,215. We need a new value of the call option, which now has one less day until expiration and is based on an underlying with a price of $1,215. The market would tell us the option price, but we do not have the luxury here of asking the market for the price. Instead, we have to appeal to a model that would tell us an appropriate price. Naturally, we turn to the Black–Scholes–Merton model. We recalculate the value of the call option using Black–Scholes–Merton, with the price of the underlying at $1,215 and the time to expiration at $119/365 = 0.3260$. The option value is $68.55, and the new delta is 0.5966. The portfolio is now worth

$$583(\$1,215) - 1,000(\$68.55) = \$639,795$$

This value differs from the benchmark by a small amount: $639,795 − $639,598 = $197. Although the hedge is not perfect, it is off by only about 0.03 percent.

Now, to move forward and still be delta hedged, we need to revise the position. The new delta is 0.5966. So now we need $1,000(0.5966) = 597$ units of the underlying and must buy 14 units of the underlying. This purchase will cost $14(\$1,215) = \$17,010$. We obtain this money by borrowing it at the risk-free rate. So we issue bonds in the amount of $17,010. Now our position is 597 units of the underlying, 1,000 short calls, and a loan of $17,010. The value of this position is still

$$597(\$1,215) - 1,000(\$68.55) - \$17,010 = \$639,795$$

Of course, this is the same value we had before adjusting the position. We could not expect to generate or lose money just by rearranging our position. As we move forward to the next day, we should see this value grow by one day's interest to $639,795 \exp(0.0275/365) = \$639,843$. This amount is the benchmark for the next day.

Suppose the next day the underlying goes to $1,198, the option goes to 58.54, and its delta goes to 0.5479. Our loan of $17,010 will grow to $17,010 \exp(0.0275/365) = \$17,011$. The new value of the portfolio is

$$597(\$1,198) - 1,000(\$58.54) - \$17,011 = \$639,655$$

This amount differs from the benchmark by $639,655 − $639,843 = −$188, an error of about 0.03 percent.

With the new delta at 0.5479, we now need 548 shares. Because we have 597 shares, we now must sell $597 − 548 = 49$ shares. Doing so would generate $49(\$1,198) = \$58,702$. Because the value of our debt was $17,011 and we now have $58,702 in cash, we can pay back the loan, leaving $58,702 − $17,011 = $41,691 to be invested at the risk-free rate. So now we have 548 units of the underlying, 1,000 short calls, and bonds of $41,691. The value of this position is

$$548(\$1,198) - 1,000(\$58.54) + \$41,691 = \$639,655$$

Of course, this is the same value we had before buying the underlying. Indeed, we cannot create or destroy any wealth by just rearranging the position.

Exhibit 22 illustrates the delta hedge, carrying it through one more day. After the third day, the value of the position should be $639,655 \exp(0.0275/365) = \$639,703$. The actual value is $639,870, a difference of $639,870 − $639,703 = $167.

As we can see, the delta hedge is not perfect, but it is pretty good. After three days, we are off by $167, only about 0.03 percent of the benchmark.

In our example and the discussions here, we have noted that the dealer would typically hold a position in the underlying to delta-hedge a position in

EXHIBIT 22	Delta Hedge of a Short Options Position

S = $1,210

X = $1,200

r^c = 0.0275 (continuously compounded)

σ = 0.20

T = 0.328767 (based on 120 days/365)

No dividends

c = $65.88 (from the Black–Scholes–Merton model)

Delta = 0.5826

Units of option constant at 1,000

Units of underlying required = 1000 × Delta

Units of underlying purchased = (Units of underlying required one day) − (Units of underlying required previous day)

Bonds purchased = −S(Units of underlying purchased)

Bond balance = (Previous balance) $\exp(r^c/365)$ + Bonds purchased

Value of portfolio = (Units of underlying)S + (Units of options)c + Bond balance

Day	S	c	Delta	Options Sold	Units of Underlying Required	Units of Underlying Purchased	Value of Bonds Purchased	Bond Balance	Value of Portfolio
0	$1,210	$65.88	0.5826	1,000	583	583	$0	$0	$639,550
1	1,215	68.55	0.5965	1,000	597	14	−17,010	−17,010	639,795
2	1,198	58.54	0.5479	1,000	548	−49	58,702	41,691	639,655
3	1,192	55.04	0.5300	1,000	530	−18	21,456	63,150	639,870

the option. Trading in the underlying would not, however, always be the preferred hedge vehicle. In fact, we have stated quite strongly that trading in derivatives is often easier and more cost effective than trading in the underlying. As noted previously, ideally a short position in a particular option would be hedged by holding a long position in that same option, but such a hedge requires that the dealer find another customer or dealer who wants to sell that same option. It is possible, however, that the dealer might be able to more easily buy a different option on the same underlying and use that option as the hedging instrument.

For example, suppose one option has a delta of Δ_1 and the other has a delta of Δ_2. These two options are on the same underlying but are not identical. They differ by exercise price, expiration, or both. Using c_1 and c_2 to represent their prices and N_1 and N_2 to represent the quantity of each option in a portfolio that hedges the value of one of the options, the value of the position is

$$V = N_1 c_1 + N_2 c_2$$

Dividing by ΔS, we obtain

$$\frac{\Delta V}{\Delta S} = N_1 \frac{\Delta c_1}{\Delta S} + N_2 \frac{\Delta c_2}{\Delta S}$$

To delta hedge, we set this amount to zero and solve for N_1/N_2 to obtain

$$\frac{N_1}{N_2} = -\frac{\Delta c_2}{\Delta c_1}$$

The negative sign simply means that a long position in one option will require a short position in the other. The desired quantity of Option 1 relative to the quantity of Option 2 is the ratio of the delta of Option 2 to the delta of Option 1. As in the standard delta-hedge example, however, these deltas will change and will require monitoring and modification of the position.[32]

EXAMPLE 16

DynaTrade is an options trading company that makes markets in a variety of derivative instruments. DynaTrade has just sold 500 call options on a stock currently priced at $125.75. Suppose the trade date is 18 November. The call has an exercise price of $125, 60 days until expiration, a price of $10.89, and a delta of 0.5649. DynaTrade will delta-hedge this transaction by purchasing an appropriate number of shares. Any additional transactions required to adjust the delta hedge will be executed by borrowing or lending at the continuously compounded risk-free rate of 4 percent.

DynaTrade has begun delta hedging the option. Two days later, 20 November, the following information applies:

Stock price	$122.75
Option price	$9.09
Delta	0.5176
Number of options	500
Number of shares	328
Bond balance	−$6,072
Market value	$29,645

A. At the end of 19 November, the delta was 0.6564. Based on this number, show how 328 shares of stock is used to delta hedge 500 call options.

B. Show the allocation of the $29,645 market value of DynaTrade's total position among stock, options, and bonds on 20 November.

C. Show what transactions must be done to adjust the portfolio to be delta hedged for the following day (21 November).

D. On 21 November, the stock is worth $120.50 and the call is worth $7.88. Calculate the market value of the delta-hedged portfolio and compare it with a benchmark, based on the market value on 20 November.

Solutions:

A. If the stock moves up (down) $1, the 328 shares should change by $328. The 500 calls should change by $500(0.6564) = 328.20,

---

[32] Because the position is long one option and short another, whenever the options differ by exercise price, expiration, or both, the position has the characteristics of a spread. In fact, it is commonly called a ratio spread.

rounded off to $328. The calls are short, so any change in the value of the stock position is an opposite change in the value of the options.

B. Stock worth 328($122.75) = $40,262
Options worth −500($9.09) = −$4,545
Bonds worth −$6,072
  Total of $29,645

C. The new required number of shares is 500(0.5176) = 258.80. Round this number to 259. So we need to have 259 shares instead of 328 shares and must sell 69 shares, generating 69($122.75) = $8,470. We invest this amount in risk-free bonds. We had a bond balance of −$6,072, so the proceeds from the sale will pay off all of this debt, leaving a balance of $8,470 −$6,072 = $2,398 going into the next day. The composition of the portfolio would then be as follows:

Shares worth 259($122.75) = $31,792
Options worth −500($9.09) = −$4,545
Bonds worth $2,398
  Total of $29,645

D. The benchmark is $29,645 exp(0.04/365) = $29,648. Also, the value of the bond one day later will be $2,398 exp(0.04/365) = $2,398. (This is less than a half-dollar's interest, so it essentially leaves the balance unchanged.) Now we have

Shares worth 259($120.50) = $31,210
Options worth −500($7.88) = −$3,940
Bonds worth $2,398
  Total of $29,668

This is about $20 more than the benchmark.

As previously noted, the delta is a fairly good approximation of the change in the option price for a very small and rapid change in the price of the underlying. But the underlying does not always change in such a convenient manner, and this possibility introduces a risk into the process of delta hedging.

Note Exhibit 23, a graph of the actual option price and the delta-estimated option price from the perspective of day 0 in Exhibit 20. At the underlying price of $1,210, the option price is $65.88. The curved line shows the exact option price, calculated with the Black–Scholes–Merton model, for a range of underlying prices. The heavy line shows the option price estimated using the delta as we did in Exhibit 20. In that exhibit, we did not stray too far from the current underlying price. In Exhibit 23, we let the underlying move a little further. Note that the further we move from the current price of the underlying of $1,210, the further the heavy line deviates from the solid line. As noted earlier, the actual call price moves up more than the delta approximation and moves down less than the delta approximation. This effect occurs because the option price is convex with respect to the underlying price. This convexity, which is quite

EXHIBIT 23	Actual Option Price (—) and Delta-Estimated Option Price (—)

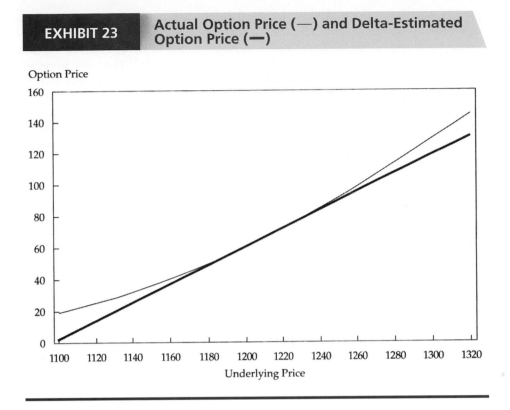

Option Price

similar to the convexity of a bond price with respect to its yield, means that a first-order price sensitivity measure like delta, or its duration analog for bonds, is accurate only if the underlying moves by a small amount. With duration, a second-order measure called convexity reflects the extent of the deviation of the actual pricing curve from the approximation curve. With options, the second-order measure is called **gamma**.

4.2 Gamma and the Risk of Delta

A gamma is a measure of several effects. It reflects the deviation of the exact option price change from the price change as approximated by the delta. It also measures the sensitivity of delta to a change in the underlying. In effect, it is the delta of the delta. Specifically,

$$\text{Gamma} = \frac{\text{Change in delta}}{\text{Change in underlying price}}$$

Like delta, gamma is actually an approximation, but we shall treat it as exact. Although a formula exists for gamma, we need to understand only the concept.

If a delta-hedged position were risk free, its gamma would be zero. The larger the gamma, the more the delta-hedged position deviates from being risk free. Because gamma reflects movements in the delta, let us first think about how delta moves. Focusing on call options, recall that the delta is between 0.0 and 1.0. At expiration, the delta is 1.0 if the option expires in-the-money and 0.0 if it expires out-of-the-money. During its life, the delta will tend to be above 0.5 if the option is in-the-money and below 0.5 if the option is out-of-the-money. As expiration approaches, the deltas of in-the-money options will move toward 1.0 and the deltas of out-of-the-money options will move toward 0.0.[33] They will, however, move slowly in their respective directions. The largest moves occur near expiration, when the deltas of at-the-money options move quickly toward 1.0 or 0.0. These rapid movements are the ones that cause the most problems for delta hedgers. Options that are deep in-the-money or deep out-of-the-money tend to have their deltas move closer to 1.0 or 0.0 well before expiration. Their movements are slow and pose fewer problems for delta hedgers. Thus, it is the rapid movements in delta that concern delta hedgers. These rapid movements are more likely to occur on options that are at-the-money and/or near expiration. Under these conditions, the gammas tend to be largest and delta hedges are hardest to maintain.

When gammas are large, some delta hedgers choose to also gamma hedge. This somewhat advanced strategy requires adding a position in another option, combining the underlying and the two options in such a manner that the delta is zero and the gamma is zero. Because it is a somewhat advanced and specialized topic, we do not cover the details of how this is done.

The delta is not the only important factor that changes in the course of managing an option position. The volatility of the underlying can also change.

4.3 Vega and Volatility Risk

The sensitivity of the option price to the volatility is called the **vega** and is defined as

$$\text{Vega} = \frac{\text{Change in option price}}{\text{Change in volatility}}$$

As with delta and gamma, the relationship above is an approximation, but we shall treat it as exact. An option price is very sensitive to the volatility of the underlying. Moreover, the volatility is the only unobservable variable required to value an option. Hence, volatility is the most critical variable. When we examined option-pricing models, we studied the Black–Scholes–Merton and binomial models. In neither of these models is the volatility allowed to change. Yet no one believes that volatility is constant; on some days the stock market is clearly more volatile than on other days. This risk of changing volatility can greatly affect a dealer's position in options. A delta-hedged position with a zero or insignificant gamma can greatly change in value if the volatility changes. If, for example, the dealer holds the underlying and sells options to delta hedge, an increase in volatility will raise the value of the options, generating a potentially large loss for the dealer.

Measuring the sensitivity of the option price to the volatility is difficult. The vega from the Black–Scholes–Merton or binomial models is a somewhat artificial construction. It represents how much the model price changes if one changes the volatility by a small amount. But in fact, the model itself is based on the assumption that volatility does not change. Forcing the volatility to change in a model that does not acknowledge that volatility can change has unclear implica-

---

[33] The deltas of options that are very slightly in-the-money will temporarily move down as expiration approaches. Exhibit 21 illustrates this effect. But they will eventually move up toward 1.0.

tions.[34] It is clear, however, that an option price is more sensitive to the volatility when it is at-the-money.

Dealers try to measure the vega, monitor it, and in some cases hedge it by taking on a position in another option, using that option's vega to offset the vega on the original option. Managing vega risk, however, cannot be done independently of managing delta and gamma risk. Thus, the dealer is required to jointly monitor and manage the risk associated with the delta, gamma, and vega. We should be aware of the concepts behind managing these risks.

FINAL COMMENTS   5

In Reading 38, we examined forward and futures strategies. These types of contracts provide gains from movements of the underlying in one direction but result in losses from movements of the underlying in the other direction. The advantage of a willingness to incur losses is that no cash is paid at the start. Options offer the advantage of having one-directional effects: The buyer of an option gains from a movement in one direction and loses only the premium from movements in the other direction. The cost of this advantage is that options require the payment of cash at the start. Some market participants choose forwards and futures because they do not have to pay cash at the start. They can justify taking positions without having to come up with the cash to do so. Others, however, prefer the flexibility to benefit when their predictions are right and suffer only a limited loss when wrong. The trade-off between the willingness to pay cash at the start versus incurring losses, given one's risk preferences, is the deciding factor in whether to use options or forwards/futures.

All option strategies are essentially rooted in the transactions of buying a call or a put. Understanding a short position in either type of option means understanding the corresponding long position in the option. All remaining strategies are just combinations of options, the underlying, and risk-free bonds. We looked at a number of option strategies associated with equities, which can apply about equally to index options or options on individual stocks. The applicability of these strategies to bonds is also fairly straightforward. The options must expire before the bonds mature, but the general concepts associated with equity option strategies apply similarly to bond option strategies.

Likewise, strategies that apply to equity options apply in nearly the same manner to interest rate options. Nonetheless, significant differences exist between interest rate options and equity or bond options. If nothing else, the notion of bullishness is quite opposite. Bullish (bearish) equity investors buy calls (puts). In interest rate markets, bullish (bearish) investors buy puts (calls) on interest rates, because being bullish (bearish) on interest rates means that one thinks rates are going down (up). Interest rate options pay off as though they were interest payments. Equity or bond options pay off as though the holder were selling or buying stocks or bonds. Finally, interest rate options are very often combined into portfolios in the form of caps and floors for the purpose of

---

[34] If this point seems confusing, consider this analogy. In the famous Einstein equation $E = mc^2$, E is energy, m is mass, and c is the constant representing the speed of light. For a given mass, we could change c, which would change E. The equation allows this change, but in fact the speed of light is constant at 186,000 miles per second. So far as scientists know, it is a universal constant and can never change. In the case of option valuation, the model assumes that volatility of a given stock is like a universal constant. We can change it, however, and the equation would give us a new option price. But are we allowed to do so? Unlike the speed of light, volatility does indeed change, even though our model says that it does not. What happens when we change volatility in our model? We do not know.

hedging floating-rate loans. Standard option strategies such as straddles and spreads are just as applicable to interest rate options.

Despite some subtle differences between the option strategies examined in this reading and comparable strategies using options on futures, the differences are relatively minor and do not warrant separate coverage here. If you have a good grasp of the basics of the option strategies presented in this reading, you can easily adapt those strategies to ones in which the underlying is a futures contract.

In Reading 40, we take up strategies using swaps. As we have so often mentioned, interest rate swaps are the most widely used financial derivative. They are less widely used with currencies and equities than are forwards, futures, and options. Nonetheless, there are many applications of swaps to currencies and equities, and we shall certainly look at them. To examine swaps, however, we must return to the types of instruments with two-directional payoffs and no cash payments at the start. Indeed, swaps are a lot like forward contracts, which themselves are a lot like futures.

SUMMARY

▶ The profit from buying a call is the value at expiration, $\max(0, S_T - X)$, minus c_0, the option premium. The maximum profit is infinite, and the maximum loss is the option premium. The breakeven underlying price at expiration is the exercise price plus the option premium. When one sells a call, these results are reversed.

▶ The profit from buying a put is the value at expiration, $\max(0, X - S_T)$, minus p_0, the option premium. The maximum profit is the exercise price minus the option premium, and the maximum loss is the option premium. The breakeven underlying price at expiration is the exercise price minus the option premium. When one sells a put, these results are reversed.

▶ The profit from a covered call—the purchase of the underlying and sale of a call—is the value at expiration, $S_T - \max(0, S_T - X)$, minus $S_0 - c_0$, the cost of the underlying minus the option premium. The maximum profit is the exercise price minus the original underlying price plus the option premium, and the maximum loss is the cost of the underlying less the option premium. The breakeven underlying price at expiration is the original price of the underlying minus the option premium.

▶ The profit from a protective put—the purchase of the underlying and a put—is the value at expiration, $S_T + \max(0, X - S_T)$, minus the cost of the underlying plus the option premium, $S_0 + p_0$. The maximum profit is infinite, and the maximum loss is the cost of the underlying plus the option premium minus the exercise price. The breakeven underlying price at expiration is the original price of the underlying plus the option premium.

▶ The profit from a bull spread—the purchase of a call at one exercise price and the sale of a call with the same expiration but a higher exercise price—is the value at expiration, $\max(0, S_T - X_1) - \max(0, S_T - X_2)$, minus the net premium, $c_1 - c_2$, which is the premium of the long option minus the premium of the short option. The maximum profit is $X_2 - X_1$ minus the net premium, and the maximum loss is the net premium. The breakeven underlying price at expiration is the lower exercise price plus the net premium.

▶ The profit from a bear spread—the purchase of a put at one exercise price and the sale of a put with the same expiration but a lower exercise price—is the value at expiration, $\max(0, X_2 - S_T) - \max(0, X_1 - S_T)$, minus the net premium, $p_2 - p_1$, which is the premium of the long option minus the premium of the short option. The maximum profit is $X_2 - X_1$ minus the net premium, and the maximum loss is the net premium. The breakeven underlying price at expiration is the higher exercise price minus the net premium.

▶ The profit from a butterfly spread—the purchase of a call at one exercise price, X_1, sale of two calls at a higher exercise price, X_2, and the purchase of a call at a higher exercise price, X_3—is the value at expiration, $\max(0, S_T - X_1) - 2\max(0, S_T - X_2), + \max(0, S_T - X_3)$, minus the net premium, $c_1 - 2c_2 + c_3$. The maximum profit is $X_2 - X_1$ minus the net premium, and the maximum loss is the net premium. The breakeven underlying prices at expiration are $2X_2 - X_1$ minus the net premium and X_1 plus the net premium. A butterfly spread can also be constructed by trading the corresponding put options.

▶ The profit from a collar—the holding of the underlying, the purchase of a put at one exercise price, X_1, and the sale of a call with the same expiration and a higher exercise price, X_2, and in which the premium on the put equals the premium on the call—is the value at expiration, $S_T + \max(0,X_1 - S_T) - \max(0,S_T - X_2)$, minus S_0, the original price of the underlying. The maximum profit is $X_2 - S_0$, and the maximum loss is $S_0 - X_1$. The breakeven underlying price at expiration is the initial price of the underlying.

▶ The profit from a straddle—a long position in a call and a put with the same exercise price and expiration—is the value at expiration, $\max(0,S_T - X) + \max(0,X - S_T)$, minus the premiums on the call and put, $c_0 + p_0$. The maximum profit is infinite, and the maximum loss is the sum of the premiums on the call and put, $c_0 + p_0$. The breakeven prices at expiration are the exercise price plus and minus the premiums on the call and put.

▶ A box spread is a combination of a bull spread using calls and a bear spread using puts, with one call and put at an exercise price of X_1 and another call and put at an exercise price of X_2. The profit is the value at expiration, $X_2 - X_1$, minus the net premiums, $c_1 - c_2 + p_2 - p_1$. The transaction is risk free, and the net premium paid should be the present value of this risk-free payoff.

▶ A long position in an interest rate call can be used to place a ceiling on the rate on an anticipated loan from the perspective of the borrower. The call provides a payoff if the interest rate at expiration exceeds the exercise rate, thereby compensating the borrower when the rate is higher than the exercise rate. The effective interest paid on the loan is the actual interest paid minus the call payoff. The call premium must be taken into account by compounding it to the date on which the loan is taken out and deducting it from the initial proceeds received from the loan.

▶ A long position in an interest rate put can be used to lock in the rate on an anticipated loan from the perspective of the lender. The put provides a payoff if the interest rate at expiration is less than the exercise rate, thereby compensating the lender when the rate is lower than the exercise rate. The effective interest paid on the loan is the actual interest received plus the put payoff. The put premium must be taken into account by compounding it to the date on which the loan is taken out and adding it to initial proceeds paid out on the loan.

▶ An interest rate cap can be used to place an upper limit on the interest paid on a floating-rate loan from the perspective of the borrower. A cap is a series of interest rate calls, each of which is referred to as a caplet. Each caplet provides a payoff if the interest rate on the loan reset date exceeds the exercise rate, thereby compensating the borrower when the rate is higher than the exercise rate. The effective interest paid is the actual interest paid minus the caplet payoff. The premium is paid at the start and is the sum of the premiums on the component caplets.

▶ An interest rate floor can be used to place a lower limit on the interest received on a floating-rate loan from the perspective of the lender. A floor is a series of interest rate puts, each of which is called a floorlet. Each floorlet provides a payoff if the interest rate at the loan reset date is less than the exercise rate, thereby compensating the lender when the rate is lower than the exercise rate. The effective interest received is the actual interest plus the floorlet payoff. The premium is paid at the start and is the sum of the premiums on the component floorlets.

▶ An interest rate collar, which consists of a long interest rate cap at one exercise rate and a short interest rate floor at a lower exercise rate, can be used to place an upper limit on the interest paid on a floating–rate loan. The floor, however, places a lower limit on the interest paid on the floating-rate loan. Typically the floor exercise rate is set such that the premium on the floor equals the premium on the cap, so that no cash outlay is required to initiate the transaction. The effective interest is the actual interest paid minus any payoff from the long caplet plus any payoff from the short floorlet.

▶ Dealers offer to take positions in options and typically hedge their positions by establishing delta-neutral combinations of options and the underlying or other options. These positions require that the sensitivity of the option position with respect to the underlying be offset by a quantity of the underlying or another option. The delta will change, moving toward 1.0 for in-the-money calls (-1.0 for puts) and 0.0 for out-of-the-money options as expiration approaches. Any change in the underlying price will also change the delta. These changes in the delta necessitate buying and selling options or the underlying to maintain the delta-hedged position. Any additional funds required to buy the underlying or other options are obtained by issuing risk-free bonds. Any additional funds released from selling the underlying or other options are invested in risk-free bonds.

▶ The delta of an option changes as the underlying changes and as time elapses. The delta will change more rapidly with large movements in the underlying and when the option is approximately at-the-money and near expiration. These large changes in the delta will prevent a delta-hedged position from being truly risk free. Dealers usually monitor their gammas and in some cases hedge their gammas by adding other options to their positions such that the gammas offset.

▶ The sensitivity of an option to volatility is called the vega. An option's volatility can change, resulting in a potentially large change in the value of the option. Dealers monitor and sometimes hedge their vegas so that this risk does not impact a delta-hedged portfolio.

PRACTICE PROBLEMS FOR READING 39

1. You are bullish about an underlying that is currently trading at a price of $80. You choose to go long one call option on the underlying with an exercise price of $75 and selling at $10, and go short one call option on the underlying with an exercise price of $85 and selling at $2. Both the calls expire in three months.

   A. What is the term commonly used for the position that you have taken?

   B. Determine the value at expiration and the profit for your strategy under the following outcomes:

      i. The price of the underlying at expiration is $89.

      ii. The price of the underlying at expiration is $78.

      iii. The price of the underlying at expiration is $70.

   C. Determine the following:

      i. the maximum profit

      ii. the maximum loss

   D. Determine the breakeven underlying price at expiration of the call options.

   E. Verify that your answer to Part D above is correct.

2. You expect a currency to depreciate with respect to the U.S. dollar. The currency is currently trading at a price of $0.75. You decide to go long one put option on the currency with an exercise price of $0.85 and selling at $0.15, and go short one put option on the currency with an exercise price of $0.70 and selling at $0.03. Both the puts expire in three months.

   A. What is the term commonly used for the position that you have taken?

   B. Determine the value at expiration and the profit for your strategy under the following outcomes:

      i. The price of the currency at expiration is $0.87.

      ii. The price of the currency at expiration is $0.78.

      iii. The price of the currency at expiration is $0.68.

   C. Determine the following:

      i. the maximum profit

      ii. the maximum loss

   D. Determine the breakeven underlying price at the expiration of the put options.

   E. Verify that your answer to Part D above is correct.

3. A stock is currently trading at a price of $114. You construct a butterfly spread using calls of three different strike prices on this stock, with the calls expiring at the same time. You go long one call with an exercise price of $110 and selling at $8, go short two calls with an exercise price of $115 and selling at $5, and go long one call with an exercise price of $120 and selling at $3.

  A. Determine the value at expiration and the profit for your strategy under the following outcomes:

   i. The price of the stock at the expiration of the calls is $106.

   ii. The price of the stock at the expiration of the calls is $110.

   iii. The price of the stock at the expiration of the calls is $115.

   iv. The price of the stock at the expiration of the calls is $120.

   v. The price of the stock at the expiration of the calls is $123.

  B. Determine the following:

   i. the maximum profit

   ii. the maximum loss

   iii. the stock price at which you would realize the maximum profit

   iv. the stock price at which you would incur the maximum loss

  C. Determine the breakeven underlying price at expiration of the call options.

4. A stock is currently trading at a price of $114. You construct a butterfly spread using puts of three different strike prices on this stock, with the puts expiring at the same time. You go long one put with an exercise price of $110 and selling at $3.50, go short two puts with an exercise price of $115 and selling at $6, and go long one put with an exercise price of $120 and selling at $9.

  A. Determine the value at expiration and the profit for your strategy under the following outcomes:

   i. The price of the stock at the expiration of the puts is $106.

   ii. The price of the stock at the expiration of the puts is $110.

   iii. The price of the stock at the expiration of the puts is $115.

   iv. The price of the stock at the expiration of the puts is $120.

   v. The price of the stock at the expiration of the puts is $123.

  B. Determine the following:

   i. the maximum profit

   ii. the maximum loss

   iii. the stock price at which you would realize the maximum profit

   iv. the stock price at which you would incur the maximum loss

  C. Determine the breakeven underlying price at expiration of the put options.

  D. Verify that your answer to Part C above is correct.

5. A stock is currently trading at a price of $80. You decide to place a collar on this stock. You purchase a put option on the stock, with an exercise price of $75 and a premium of $3.50. You simultaneously sell a call option on the stock with the same maturity and the same premium as the put option. This call option has an exercise price of $90.

   A. Determine the value at expiration and the profit for your strategy under the following outcomes:

      i. The price of the stock at expiration of the options is $92.

      ii. The price of the stock at expiration of the options is $90.

      iii. The price of the stock at expiration of the options is $82.

      iv. The price of the stock at expiration of the options is $75.

      v. The price of the stock at expiration of the options is $70.

   B. Determine the following:

      i. the maximum profit

      ii. the maximum loss

      iii. the stock price at which you would realize the maximum profit

      iv. the stock price at which you would incur the maximum loss

   C. Determine the breakeven underlying price at expiration of the put options.

6. You believe that the market will be volatile in the near future, but you do not feel particularly strongly about the direction of the movement. With this expectation, you decide to buy both a call and a put with the same exercise price and the same expiration on the same underlying stock trading at $28. You buy one call option and one put option on this stock, both with an exercise price of $25. The premium on the call is $4 and the premium on the put is $1.

   A. What is the term commonly used for the position that you have taken?

   B. Determine the value at expiration and the profit for your strategy under the following outcomes:

      i. The price of the stock at expiration is $35.

      ii. The price of the stock at expiration is $29.

      iii. The price of the stock at expiration is $25.

      iv. The price of the stock at expiration is $20.

      v. The price of the stock at expiration is $15.

   C. Determine the following:

      i. the maximum profit

      ii. the maximum loss

   D. Determine the breakeven stock price at expiration of the options.

RISK MANAGEMENT APPLICATIONS OF SWAP STRATEGIES

by Don M. Chance

LEARNING OUTCOMES

The candidate should be able to:

a. demonstrate how an interest rate swap can be used to convert a floating-rate (fixed-rate) loan to a fixed-rate (floating-rate) loan;

b. calculate and interpret the duration of an interest rate swap;

c. explain the impact to cash flow risk and market value risk when a borrower converts a fixed-rate loan to a floating-rate loan;

d. determine the notional principal value needed on an interest rate swap to achieve a desired level of duration in a fixed-income portfolio;

e. explain how a company can generate savings by issuing a loan or bond in its own currency and using a currency swap to convert the obligation into another currency;

f. demonstrate how a firm can use a currency swap to convert a series of foreign cash receipts into domestic cash receipts;

g. explain how equity swaps can be used to diversify a concentrated equity portfolio, provide international diversification to a domestic portfolio, and alter portfolio allocations to stocks and bonds;

h. demonstrate the use of an interest rate swaption (1) to change the payment pattern of an anticipated future loan and (2) to terminate a swap.

INTRODUCTION   1

This reading is the final in a series of three in which we examine strategies and applications of various derivative instruments. Reading 38 covered forwards and futures, and Reading 39 covered options. We now turn to swaps. Recall that a swap is a transaction in which two parties agree to exchange a series of cash flows over a specific period of time. At least one set of cash flows must be

Analysis of Derivatives for the CFA® Program, by Don M. Chance. Copyright © 2003 by AIMR. Reprinted with permission.

219

variable—that is, not known at the beginning of the transaction and determined over the life of the swap by the course of an underlying source of uncertainty. The other set of cash flows can be fixed or variable. Typically, no net exchange of money occurs between the two parties at the start of the contract.[1]

Because at least one set of swap payments is random, it must be driven by an underlying source of uncertainty. This observation provides a means for classifying swaps. The four types of swaps are interest rate, currency, equity, and commodity swaps. Interest rate swaps typically involve one side paying at a floating interest rate and the other paying at a fixed interest rate. In some cases both sides pay at a floating rate, but the floating rates are different. Currency swaps are essentially interest rate swaps in which one set of payments is in one currency and the other is in another currency. The payments are in the form of interest payments; either set of payments can be fixed or floating, or both can be fixed or floating. With currency swaps, a source of uncertainty is the exchange rate so the payments can be fixed and still have uncertain value. In equity swaps, at least one set of payments is determined by the course of a stock price or stock index. In commodity swaps at least one set of payments is determined by the course of a commodity price, such as the price of oil or gold. In this reading we focus exclusively on financial derivatives and, hence, do not cover commodity swaps.

Swaps can be viewed as combinations of forward contracts. A forward contract is an agreement between two parties in which one party agrees to buy from another an underlying asset at a future date at a price agreed on at the start. This agreed-upon price is a fixed payment, but the value received for the asset at the future date is a variable payment because it is subject to risk. A swap extends this notion of an exchange of variable and fixed payments to more than one payment. Hence, a swap is like a series of forward contracts.[2] We also saw that a swap is like a combination of options. We showed that pricing a swap involves determining the terms that the two parties agree to at the start, which usually involves the amount of any fixed payment. Because no net flow of money changes hands at the start, a swap is a transaction that starts off with zero market value. Pricing the swap is done by finding the terms that result in equivalence of the present values of the two streams of payments.

After a swap begins, market conditions change and the present values of the two streams of payments are no longer equivalent. The swap then has a nonzero

---

[1] Currency swaps can be structured to have an exchange of the notional principals in the two currencies at the start, but because these amounts are equivalent after adjusting for the exchange rate, no *net* exchange of money takes place. At expiration of the swap, the two parties reverse the original exchange, which does result in a net flow of money if the exchange rate has changed, as will probably be the case. A few swaps, called *off-market swaps*, involve an exchange of money at the start, but they are the exception, not the rule.

[2] There are some technical distinctions between a series of forward contracts and a swap, but the essential elements of equivalence are there.

market value. To one party, the swap has a positive market value; to the other, its market value is negative. The process of valuation involves determining this market value. For the most part, valuation and pricing is a process that requires only the determination of present values using current interest rates and, as necessary, stock prices or exchange rates.

We also examined the swaption, an instrument that combines swaps and options. Specifically, a swaption is an option to enter into a swap. There are two kinds of swaptions: those to make a fixed payment, called payer swaptions, and those to receive a fixed payment, called receiver swaptions. Like options, swaptions require the payment of a premium at the start and grant the right, but not the obligation, to enter into a swap.[3]

In this reading, we shall examine ways in which swaps can be used to achieve risk management objectives. We already examined certain risk management strategies when we discussed swaps in Reading 39. Here, we go into more detail on these strategies and, of course, introduce quite a few more. We shall also discuss how swaptions are used to achieve risk management objectives.

STRATEGIES AND APPLICATIONS FOR MANAGING INTEREST RATE RISK

2

In previous readings, we examined the use of forwards, futures, and options to manage interest rate risk. The interest rate swap, however, is unquestionably the most widely used instrument to manage interest rate risk.[4] In Readings 38 and 39, we examined two primary forms of interest rate risk. One is the risk associated with borrowing and lending in short-term markets. This risk itself has two dimensions: the risk of rates changing from the time a loan is anticipated until it is actually taken out, and the risk associated with changes in interest rates once the loan is taken out. Swaps are not normally used to manage the risk of an anticipated loan; rather, they are designed to manage the risk on a series of cash flows on loans already taken out or in the process of being taken out.[5]

The other form of interest rate risk that concerns us is the risk associated with managing a portfolio of bonds. As we saw in Reading 38, managing this risk generally involves controlling the portfolio duration. Although futures are commonly used to make duration changes, swaps can also be used, and we shall see how in this reading.

In this section, we look at one more situation in which swaps can be used to manage interest rate risk. This situation involves the use of a relatively new

---

[3] Forward swaps, on the other hand, are obligations to enter into a swap.

[4] The Bank for International Settlements, in its June 2002 survey of derivative positions of global banks published on 8 November 2002, indicates that swaps make up more than 75 percent of the total notional principal of all interest rate derivative contracts (see www.bis.org).

[5] It is technically possible to use a swap to manage the risk faced in anticipation of taking out a loan, but it would not be easy and would require a great deal of analytical skill to match the volatility of the swap to the volatility of the gain or loss in value associated with changes in interest rates prior to the date on which a loan is taken out. Other instruments are better suited for managing this type of risk.

financial instrument called a **structured note**, which is a variation of a floating-rate note that has some type of unusual characteristic. We cover structured notes in Section 2.3.

2.1 Using Interest Rate Swaps to Convert a Floating-Rate Loan to a Fixed-Rate Loan (and Vice Versa)

Because much of the funding banks receive is at a floating rate, most banks prefer to make floating-rate loans. By lending at a floating rate, banks pass on the interest rate risk to borrowers. Borrowers can use forwards, futures, and options to manage their exposure to rising interest rates, but swaps are the preferred instrument for managing this risk.[6] A typical situation involves a corporation agreeing to borrow at a floating rate even though it would prefer to borrow at a fixed rate. The corporation will use a swap to convert its floating-rate loan to a fixed-rate loan.

Internet Book Publishers (IBP) is a corporation that typically borrows at a floating rate from a lender called Prime Lending Bank (PLB). In this case, it takes out a one-year $25 million loan at 90-day LIBOR plus 300 basis points. The payments will be made at specific dates about 91 days apart. The rate is initially set today, the day the loan is taken out, and is reset on each payment date: On the first payment date, the rate is reset for the second interest period. With four loan payments, the first rate is already set, but IBP is exposed to risk on the other three reset dates. Interest is calculated based on the actual day count since the last payment date, divided by 360. The loan begins on 2 March and the interest payment dates are 2 June, 2 September, 1 December, and the following 1 March.

IBP manages this interest rate risk by using a swap. It contacts a swap dealer, Swaps Provider Inc. (SPI), which is the derivatives subsidiary of a major investment banking firm. Under the terms of the swap, SPI will make payment to IBP at a rate of LIBOR, and IBP will pay SPI a fixed rate of 6.27 percent, with payments to be made on the dates on which the loan interest payments are made.

The dealer prices the fixed rate on a swap into the swap such that the present values of the two payment streams are equal. The floating rates on the swap will be set today and on the first, second, and third loan interest payment dates, thereby corresponding to the dates on which the loan interest rate is reset. The notional principal on the swap is $25 million, the face value of the loan. The swap interest payments are structured so that the actual day count is used, as is done on the loan.

So, IBP borrows $25 million at a floating rate and arranges for the swap, which involves no cash flows at the origination date. The flow of money on each loan/swap payment date is illustrated in Exhibit 1. We see that IBP makes its loan payments at LIBOR plus 0.03.[7] The actual calculation of the loan interest is as follows:

$$(\$25 \text{ million})(\text{LIBOR} + 0.03)(\text{Days}/360)$$

---

[6] It is not clear why swaps are preferred over other instruments to manage the exposure to rising interest rates, but one possible reason is that when swaps were first invented, they were marketed as equivalent to a pair of loans. By being long one loan and short another, a corporation could alter its exposure without having to respond to claims that it was using such instruments as futures or options, which might be against corporate policy. In other words, while swaps are derivatives, their equivalence to a pair of loans meant that no policy existed to prevent their use. Moreover, because of the netting of payments and no exchange of notional principal, interest rate swaps were loans with considerably less credit risk than ordinary loans. Hence, the corporate world easily and widely embraced them.

[7] Remember that when we refer to the payment at a rate of LIBOR, that rate was established at the previous settlement date or at the beginning of the swap if this is the first settlement period.

| EXHIBIT 1 | Converting a Floating-Rate Loan to a Fixed-Rate Loan Using an Interest Rate Swap |

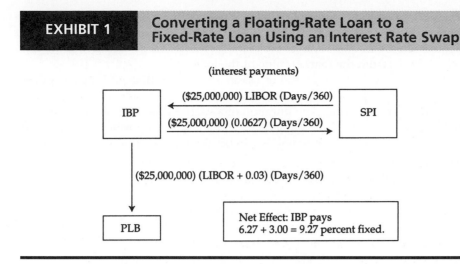

(interest payments)

($25,000,000) LIBOR (Days/360)

IBP ← SPI

($25,000,000) (0.0627) (Days/360) →

($25,000,000) (LIBOR + 0.03) (Days/360)

PLB

Net Effect: IBP pays
6.27 + 3.00 = 9.27 percent fixed.

The swap payments are calculated in the same way but are based on either LIBOR or the fixed rate of 6.27 percent. The interest owed on the loan based on LIBOR is thus offset by the interest received on the swap payment based on LIBOR.[8] Consequently, IBP does not *appear to be exposed* to the uncertainty of changing LIBOR, but we shall see that it is indeed exposed. The net effect is that IBP pays interest at the swap fixed rate of 6.27 percent plus the 3 percent spread on the loan for a total of 9.27 percent.

IBP's swap transaction appears to remove its exposure to LIBOR. Indeed, having done this transaction, most corporations would consider themselves hedged against rising interest rates, which is usually the justification corporations give for doing swap transactions. It is important to note, however, that IBP is also speculating on rising interest rates. If rates fall, IBP will not be able to take advantage, as it is locked in to a synthetic fixed-rate loan at 9.27 percent. There can be a substantial opportunity cost to taking this position and being wrong. To understand this point, let us reintroduce the concept of duration.

We need to measure the sensitivity of the market value of the overall position compared to what it would have been had the loan been left in place as a floating-rate loan. For that we turn to duration, a measure of sensitivity to interest rates. If a default-free bond is a floating-rate bond, its duration is nearly zero because interest sensitivity reflects how much the market value of an asset changes for a given change in interest rates. A floating-rate bond is designed with the idea that its market value will not drift far from par. Because the coupon will catch up with the market rate periodically, only during the period between interest payment dates can the market value stray from par value. Moreover, during this period, it would take a substantial interest rate change to have much effect on the market value of the floating-rate bond. Without showing the details, we shall simply state the result that a floating-rate bond's duration is approximately the amount of time remaining until the next coupon payment. For a bond with quarterly payments, the maximum duration is 0.25 years and the minimum duration is zero. Consequently, the average duration is about 0.125 years. From the perspective of the *issuer* rather than the holder, the duration of the position is −0.125.

The duration of IBP's floating-rate loan position in this example is an average of −0.125, which is fairly low compared with most financial instruments.

---

[8] Of course in practice, the swap payments are netted and only a single payment flows from one party to the other. Netting reduces the credit risk but does not prevent the LIBOR component of the net swap payment from offsetting the floating loan interest payment, which is the objective of the swap.

Therefore, the market value of the loan is not very interest-rate sensitive. If interest rates fall, the loan rate will fall in three months, and IBP will not have much of a loss from the market value of the loan. If interest rates rise, IBP will not have much of a gain from the market value of the loan.

Now let us discuss the duration of a swap. Remember that entering a pay-fixed, receive-floating swap is similar to issuing a fixed-rate bond and using the proceeds to buy a floating-rate bond. The duration of a swap is thus equivalent to the duration of a long position in a floating-rate bond and a short position in a fixed-rate bond. The duration of the long position in the floating-rate bond would, again, be about 0.125. What would be the duration of the short position in the fixed-rate bond? A one-year fixed-rate bond with quarterly payments would probably have a duration of between 0.6 and 1.0. Let us assume this duration is about 0.75 (nine months) or 75 percent of the maturity, an assumption we shall make from here out. So the duration of the swap would be roughly $0.125 - 0.75 = -0.625$.

Combining the swap with the loan means that the duration of IBP's overall position will be $-0.125 - 0.625 = -0.75$. The swap was designed to convert the floating-rate loan to a fixed-rate loan. Hence, the position should be equivalent to that of taking out a fixed-rate loan. As we assumed for a one-year fixed-rate bond with quarterly payments, the duration would be 0.75. The duration of a borrower's position in a fixed-rate loan would be -0.75, the same as the duration of borrowing with the floating-rate loan and engaging in the swap. The negative duration means that a fixed-rate borrower will be helped by rising rates and a falling market value.[9]

Although the duration of the one-year fixed-rate loan is not large, at least relative to that of bonds and longer-term loans, it is nonetheless six times that of the floating-rate loan. Consequently, the sensitivity of the market value of the overall position is six times what it would have been had the loan been left in place as a floating-rate loan. From this angle, it is hard to see how such a transaction could be called a hedge because declining rates and increasing market values will hurt the fixed-rate borrower. The actual risk increases sixfold with this transaction![10]

So, can this transaction be viewed as a hedge? If not, why is it so widely used? From a cash flow perspective, the transaction does indeed function as a hedge. IBP knows that its interest payments will all be $25,000,000(0.0927)(Days/360)$. Except for the slight variation in days per quarter, this amount is fixed and can be easily built into plans and budgets. So from a planning and accounting perspective, the transaction serves well as a hedge. From a market value perspective, however, it is tremendously speculative. But does market value matter? Indeed it does. From the perspective of finance theory, maximizing the market value of shareholders' equity is the objective of a corporation. Moreover, under recently enacted accounting rules, companies must mark derivative and asset positions to market values, which has improved transparency.

So, in summary, using a swap to convert a floating-rate loan to a fixed-rate loan is a common transaction, one ostensibly structured as a hedge. Such a transaction, despite stabilizing a company's cash outflows, however, increases the risk of the company's market value. Whether this issue is of concern to most companies is not clear. This situation remains one of the most widely encountered scenarios and the one for which interest rate swaps are most commonly employed.

---

[9] Remember from Reading 38 that the percentage change in the market value of an asset or portfolio is -1 times the duration times the change in yield over 1 plus the yield. So, if the duration is negative, the double minus results in the position benefiting from rising interest rates.

[10] In the example here, the company is a corporation. A bank might have assets that would be interest sensitive and could be used to balance the duration. A corporation's primary assets have varying, inconsistent, and difficult-to-measure degrees of interest sensitivity.

EXAMPLE 1

Consider a bank that holds a $5 million loan at a fixed rate of 6 percent for three years, with quarterly payments. The bank had originally funded this loan at a fixed rate, but because of changing interest rate expectations, it has now decided to fund it at a floating rate. Although it cannot change the terms of the loan to the borrower, it can effectively convert the loan to a floating-rate loan by using a swap. The fixed rate on three-year swaps with quarterly payments at LIBOR is 7 percent. We assume the number of days in each quarter to be 90 and the number of days in a year to be 360.

A. Explain how the bank could convert the fixed-rate loan to a floating-rate loan using a swap.

B. Explain why the effective floating rate on the loan will be less than LIBOR.

Solution to A: The interest payments it will receive on the loan are $5,000,000(0.06)(90/360) = $75,000. The bank could do a swap to pay a fixed rate of 7 percent and receive a floating rate of LIBOR. Its fixed payment would be $5,000,000(0.07)(90/360) = $87,500. The floating payment it would receive is $5,000,000L(90/360), where L is LIBOR established at the previous reset date. The overall cash flow is thus $5,000,000(L − 0.01)(90/360), LIBOR minus 100 basis points.

Solution to B: The bank will effectively receive less than LIBOR because when the loan was initiated, the rate was 6 percent. Then when the swap was executed, the rate was 7 percent. This increase in interest rates hurts the fixed-rate lender. The bank cannot implicitly change the loan from fixed rate to floating rate without paying the price of this increase in interest rates. It pays this price by accepting a lower rate than LIBOR when the loan is effectively converted to floating. Another factor that could contribute to this rate being lower than LIBOR is that the borrower's credit risk at the time the loan was established is different from the bank's credit risk as reflected in the swap fixed rate, established in the LIBOR market when the swap is initiated.

Equipped with our introductory treatment of the duration of a swap, we are now in a position to move on to understanding how to use swaps to manage the risk of a longer-term position that is also exposed to interest rate risk.

2.2 Using Swaps to Adjust the Duration of a Fixed-Income Portfolio

We saw in the previous section that the duration of a swap is the net of the durations of the equivalent positions in fixed- and floating-rate bonds. Thus, the position of the pay-fixed party in a pay-fixed, receive-floating swap has the duration of a floating-rate bond minus the duration of a fixed-rate bond, where the floating-

and fixed-rate bonds have cash flows equivalent to the corresponding cash flows of the swap.[11] The pay-fixed, receive-floating swap has a negative duration, because the duration of a fixed-rate bond is positive and larger than the duration of a floating-rate bond, which is near zero. Moreover, the negative duration of this position makes sense in that the position would be expected to benefit from rising interest rates.

Consider the following transaction. Quality Asset Management (QAM) controls a $500 million fixed-income portfolio that has a duration of 6.75. It is considering reducing the portfolio duration to 3.50 by using interest rate swaps. QAM has determined that the interest sensitivity of the bond portfolio is adequately captured by its relationship with LIBOR; hence, a swap using LIBOR as the underlying rate would be appropriate. But first there are several questions to ask:

▶ Should the swap involve paying fixed, receiving floating or paying floating, receiving fixed?

▶ What should be the terms of the swap (maturity, payment frequency)?

▶ What should be the notional principal?

As for whether the swap should involve paying fixed or receiving fixed, the value of the bond portfolio is inversely related to interest rates. To reduce the duration, it would be necessary to hold a position that moves directly with interest rates. To do this we must add a negative-duration position. Hence, the swap should be a pay-fixed swap to receive floating.

The terms of the swap will affect the need to renew it as well as its duration and the notional principal required. It would probably be best for the swap to have a maturity at least as long as the period during which the duration adjustment applies. Otherwise, the swap would expire before the bond matures, and QAM would have to initiate another swap. The maturity and payment frequency of the swap affect the duration. Continuing with the assumption (for convenience) that the duration of the fixed-rate bond is approximated as 75 percent of its maturity, we find, for example, that a one-year swap with semi-annual payments would have a duration of $0.25 - 0.75 = -0.50$. A one-year swap with quarterly payments would have a duration of $0.125 - 0.75 = -0.625$. A two-year swap with semiannual payments would have a duration of $0.25 - 1.50 = -1.25$. A two-year swap with quarterly payments would have a duration of $0.125 - 1.50 = -1.375$.

These different durations affect the notional principal required, which leads us to the third question. Prior to the duration adjustment, the portfolio consists of $500 million at a duration of 6.75. QAM then adds a position in a swap with a notional principal of NP and a modified duration of $MDUR_S$. The swap will have zero market value.[12] The bonds and the swap will then combine to make up a portfolio with a market value of $500 million and a duration of 3.50. This relationship can be expressed as follows:

$$\$500,000,000(6.75) + NP(MDUR_S) = \$500,000,000(3.50)$$

---

[11] Recall, however, that an interest rate swap does not involve a notional principal payment up front or at expiration. But because a swap is equivalent to being long a fixed- (or floating-) rate bond and short a floating- (or fixed-) rate bond, the principals on the bonds offset, leaving their cash flows identical to that of a swap.

[12] Recall that the market value of a swap is zero at the start. This market value can obviously vary over time from zero, and such deviations should be taken into account, but to start, the market value will be zero.

The solution for NP is

$$NP = \$500,000,000 \left(\frac{3.50 - 6.75}{\text{MDUR}_S} \right)$$

The duration of the swap is determined once QAM decides which swap to use. Suppose it uses a one-year swap with semiannual payments. Then, as shown above, the duration would be -0.50. The amount of notional principal required would, therefore, be

$$NP = \$500,000,000 \left(\frac{3.50 - 6.75}{-0.50} \right) = \$3,250,000,000$$

In other words, this portfolio adjustment would require a swap with a notional principal of more than $3 billion! This would be a very large swap, probably too large to execute. Consider the use of a five-year swap with semiannual payments. Its duration would be $0.25 - 3.75 = -3.50$. Then the notional principal would be

$$NP = \$500,000,000 \left(\frac{3.50 - 6.75}{-3.50} \right) = \$464,290,000$$

With this longer duration, the notional principal would be about $464 million, a much more reasonable amount, although still a fairly large swap.

So, in general, the notional principal of a swap necessary to change the duration of a bond portfolio worth B from MDUR_B to a target duration, MDUR_T, is

$$NP = B \left(\frac{\text{MDUR}_T - \text{MDUR}_B}{\text{MDUR}_S} \right)$$

EXAMPLE 2

A $250 million bond portfolio has a duration of 5.50. The portfolio manager wants to reduce the duration to 4.50 by using a swap. Consider the possibility of using a one-year swap with monthly payments or a two-year swap with semiannual payments.

A. Determine the durations of the two swaps under the assumption of paying fixed and receiving floating. Assume that the duration of a fixed-rate bond is 75 percent of its maturity.

B. Choose the swap with the longer absolute duration and determine the notional principal of the swap necessary to change the duration as desired. Explain your results.

Solution to A: The duration of a one-year pay-fixed, receive-floating swap with monthly payments is the duration of a one-year floating-rate bond with monthly payments minus the duration of a one-year fixed-rate bond with monthly payments. The duration of the former is about one-half of the length of the payment interval. That is 1/24 of a year, or 0.042. Because the duration of the one-year fixed-rate bond is 0.75 (75 percent of one year), the duration of the swap is $0.042 - 0.75 = -0.708$.

The duration of a two-year swap with semiannual payments is the duration of a two-year floating-rate bond with semiannual payments minus the duration of a two-year fixed-rate bond. The duration of the former is about one-quarter of a year, or 0.25. The duration of the latter is 1.50 (75 percent of two years). The duration of the swap is thus $0.25 - 1.50 = -1.25$.

Solution to B: The longer (more negative) duration swap is the two-year swap with semiannual payments. The current duration of the $250 million portfolio is 5.50 and the target duration is 4.50. Thus, the required notional principal is

$$NP = B \left(\frac{MDUR_T - MDUR_B}{MDUR_S} \right)$$

$$= \$250,000,000 \left(\frac{4.50 - 5.50}{-1.25} \right) = \$200,000,000$$

So, to lower the duration requires the addition of an instrument with a duration lower than that of the portfolio. The duration of a receive-floating, pay-fixed swap is negative and, therefore, lower than that of the existing portfolio.

2.3 Using Swaps to Create and Manage the Risk of Structured Notes

Structured notes are short- or intermediate-term floating-rate securities that have some type of unusual feature that distinguishes them from ordinary floating-rate notes. This unusual feature can be in the form of leverage, which results in the interest rate on the note moving at a multiple of market rates, or can be an inverse feature, meaning that the interest rate on the note moves opposite to market rates. Structured notes are designed to be sold to specific investors, who are often motivated by constraints that restrict their ability to hold derivatives or use leverage. For example, many insurance companies and pension funds are attracted to structured notes, because the instruments qualify as fixed-income securities but have features that are similar to options, swaps, and margin transactions. Issuers typically create the notes, sell them to these investors, and then manage the risk, earning a profit by replicating the opposite position at a cost lower than what they could sell the notes for.

In this section, we shall use the notation FP as the principal/face value of the note, ci as the fixed interest rate on a bond, and FS as the fixed interest rate on the swap.

2.3.1 Using Swaps to Create and Manage the Risk of Leveraged Floating-Rate Notes

Kappa Alpha Traders (KAT) engages in a variety of arbitrage-related transactions designed to make small risk-free or low-risk profits. One such transaction involves the issuance of structured notes, which it sells to insurance companies. KAT plans to issue a leveraged structured note with a principal of FP that pays an interest rate of 1.5 times LIBOR. This type of instrument is usually called a **leveraged floating-rate note**, or **leveraged floater**. The reference to *leverage* is to the fact that the coupon is a multiple of a specific market rate of interest such as LIBOR. The note will be purchased by an insurance company called LifeCo. KAT will use the proceeds to buy a fixed-rate bond that pays an interest rate of ci. It will then combine the position with a **plain vanilla swap** with dealer Omega Swaps. Exhibit 2 illustrates how this works.

KAT issues the leveraged floater, selling it to LifeCo Insurance with the intent of financing it with a fixed-rate bond and swapping the fixed rate for a floating rate to match the leveraged floater. The periodic interest payment on the leveraged floater will be 1.5L, where L is LIBOR, times FP.[13] It then takes the proceeds and buys a fixed-rate bond issued by a company called American Factories Inc. This bond will have face value of 1.5(FP) and pay a coupon of ci. KAT is then in a position of receiving a fixed coupon of ci on principal of 1.5(FP) and paying a floating coupon of 1.5L on a principal of FP. It then enters into a swap with dealer Omega Swaps on notional principal of 1.5FP. KAT will pay a fixed rate of FS and receive a floating rate of LIBOR (L). Note the net effect: KAT's obligation on the leveraged floater of 1.5L(FP) is matched by its receipt on the swap. KAT receives 1.5(ci)(FP) on the fixed-rate bond and pays out 1.5(FS)(FP) on the swap, netting 1.5(FP)(ci − FS). Is this amount an inflow or outflow? It depends. If the interest rate on American Factories' debt reflects greater credit risk than that implied by the fixed rate on the swap, then KAT receives a net payment. Generally that would be the case. Thus, KAT identifies an attractively priced fixed-rate note and captures its return over the swap rate, offsetting the floating rate on the swap with the structured note. Of course, KAT is assuming some credit risk, the risk of default by American Factories, as well as the risk of default by Omega Swaps. On the other hand, KAT put up no capital to engage in this transaction. The cost of the American Factories bond was financed by issuing the structured note.

EXHIBIT 2	Proceeds from a Leveraged Floater Used to Buy a Fixed-Rate Bond, with Risk Managed with a Plain Vanilla Swap

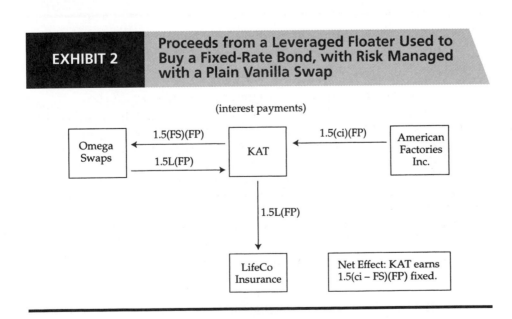

---

[13] These payments could be made semiannually, in which case they would be half of 1.5L(FP).

EXAMPLE 3

A company issues a floating-rate note that pays a rate of twice LIBOR on notional principal FP. It uses the proceeds to buy a bond paying a rate of ci. It also enters into a swap with a fixed rate of FS to manage the risk of the LIBOR payment on the leveraged floater.

A. Demonstrate how the company can engage in these transactions, leaving it with a net cash flow of 2(FP)(ci − FS).

B. Explain under what condition the amount (ci − FS) is positive.

Solution to A: The company has issued a leveraged floater at a rate of 2L on notional principal FP. Then it should purchase a bond with face value of 2(FP) and coupon ci. It enters into a swap to pay a fixed rate of FS and receive a floating rate of L on notional principal 2(FP). The net cash flows are as follows:

From leveraged floater	−2L(FP)
From bond	+(ci)2(FP)
Floating side of swap	+(L)2(FP)
Fixed side of swap	−(FS)2(FP)
Total	2FP(ci − FS)

Solution to B: The difference between the bond coupon rate, ci, and the swap fixed rate, FS, will be positive if the bond has greater credit risk than is implied by the fixed rate in the swap, which is based on the LIBOR term structure and reflects the borrowing rate of London banks. Thus, the gain of 2(ci − FS)(FP) is likely to reflect a credit risk premium.

2.3.2 Using Swaps to Create and Manage the Risk of Inverse Floaters

Another type of structured note is the **inverse floater**. Consider a company called Vega Analytics that, like KAT, engages in a variety of arbitrage trades using structured notes. Vega wants to issue an inverse floater paying a rate of b minus LIBOR, b − L, on notional principal FP. Vega sets the value of b in negotiation with the buyer of the note, taking into account a number of factors. The rate on the note moves inversely with LIBOR, but if LIBOR is at the level b, the rate on the note goes to zero. If LIBOR rises above b, the rate on the note is negative! We shall address this point later in this section.

The pattern will be the same as the pattern used for the leveraged floater: Finance the structured note by a fixed-rate note and then swap the fixed rate for a floating rate to match the structured note. Exhibit 3 shows how Vega issues the note to a company called Metrics Finance and uses the proceeds to purchase a fixed-rate note issued by a company called Telltale Systems, Inc., which pays a rate of (ci)(FP). Vega then enters into an interest rate swap with notional principal FP with a counterparty called Denman Dealer Holdings. In this swap, Vega receives a fixed rate of FS and pays L. Observe that the net effect is that Vega's overall cash flow is FP[−(b − L) + ci + FS − L] = FP(FS + ci − b).

EXHIBIT 3	Proceeds from an Inverse Floater Used to Buy a Fixed-Rate Bond, with Risk Managed with a Plain Vanilla Swap

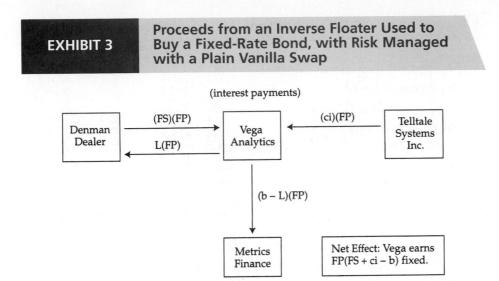

Clearly if b is set below FS + ci, then the overall cash flow is positive. Vega can potentially do this because of the credit risk it assumes. Vega sets b but cannot set FS, and ci is based on both the level of market interest rates and the credit risk of Telltale. The lower Vega sets b, the larger its cash flow from the overall transactions. But one major consideration forces Vega to limit how low it sets b: The lower it sets b, the less attractive the note will be to potential investors.

Remember that the inverse floater pays b − L. When L reaches the level of b, the interest rate on the inverse floater is zero. If L rises above b, then the interest rate on the inverse floater becomes negative. A negative interest rate would imply that the lender (Metrics) pays interest to the borrower (Vega). Most lenders would find this result unacceptable, but the lower b is set, the more likely this outcome will occur. Thus, Vega will want to set b at a reasonably high level but below FS + ci.

Regardless of where Vega sets b, the possibility remains that L will exceed b. Metrics may have Vega guarantee that the interest rate on the floater will go no lower than 0 percent. To manage the risk associated with this guarantee, Vega will buy an interest rate cap. Let us see how all of this works with a numerical example.

Suppose the swap fixed rate, FS, is 6 percent, and ci, the rate on Telltale's note, is 7 percent. Vega sets b at 12 percent and guarantees to Metrics that the interest rate will go no lower than zero. Then the inverse floater pays 12 percent − L. As long as LIBOR is below 12 percent, Vega's cash flow is 6 + 7 − 12 = 1 percent. Suppose L is 14 percent. Then Vega's cash flows are

+7 percent from the Telltale note

0 percent to Metrics

+6 percent from Denman

14 percent to Denman

Net: outflow of 1 percent

Vega's net cash flow is negative. To avoid this problem, Vega would buy an interest rate cap in which the underlying is LIBOR and the exercise rate is b. The cap would have a notional principal of FP and consist of individual caplets expiring on the dates on which the inverse floater rates are set. Thus, on a payment date, when L exceeds b, the inverse floater does not pay interest, but the caplet expires in-the-money and pays L − b. Then the cash flows would be

+7 percent from the Telltale note

0 percent to Metrics

+6 percent from Denman

14 percent to Denman

(14% − 12%) = 2 percent from the caplet

Net: inflow of 1 percent

Thus, Vega has restored its guaranteed cash inflow of 1 percent.

Of course, the premium on the cap would be an additional cost that Vega would pass on in the form of a lower rate paid to Metrics on the inverse floater. In other words, for Metrics to not have to worry about ever having a negative interest rate, it would have to accept a lower overall rate. Thus, b would be set a little lower.

EXAMPLE 4

A company issues an inverse floating-rate note with a face value of $30 million and a coupon rate of 14 percent minus LIBOR. It uses the proceeds to buy a bond with a coupon rate of 8 percent.

A. Explain how the company would manage the risk of this position using a swap with a fixed rate of 7 percent, and calculate the overall cash flow given that LIBOR is less than 14 percent.

B. Explain what would happen if LIBOR exceeds 14 percent. What could the company do to offset this problem?

Solution to A: The company would enter into a swap in which it pays LIBOR and receives a fixed rate of 7 percent on notional principal of $30 million. The overall cash flows are as follows:

From the inverse floater	−(0.14 − L)$30,000,000
From the bond it buys	+(0.08)$30,000,000
From the swap	
Fixed payment	+(0.07)$30,000,000
Floating payment	−(L)$30,000,000
Overall total	+(0.01)$30,000,000

Solution to B: If LIBOR is more than 14 percent, then the inverse floater payment of (0.14 − L) would be negative. The lender would then have to pay interest to the borrower. For this reason, in most cases, an inverse floater has a floor at zero. In such a case, the total cash flow to this company would be (0 + 0.08 + 0.07 − L)$30,000,000. There would be zero total cash flow at L = 15 percent. But at an L higher than 15 percent, the otherwise positive cash flow to the lender becomes negative.

> To offset this effect, the lender would typically buy an interest rate cap with an exercise rate of 14 percent. The cap would have caplets that expire on the interest rate reset dates of the swap/loan and have a notional principal of $30 million. Then when $L > 0.14$, the caplet would pay off $L - 0.14$ times the $30 million. This payoff would make up the difference. The price paid for the cap would be an additional cost.

Interest rate swaps are special cases of currency swaps—cases in which the payments are made in different currencies. We now take a look at ways in which currency swaps are used.

STRATEGIES AND APPLICATIONS FOR MANAGING EXCHANGE RATE RISK

3

Currency swaps are designed for the purpose of managing exchange rate risk. They also play a role in managing interest rate risk, but only in cases in which exchange rate risk is present. In this section, we look at three situations in which exchange rate risk can be managed using currency swaps.

3.1 Converting a Loan in One Currency into a Loan in Another Currency

Royal Technology Ltd. (ROTECH) is a British high-tech company that is currently planning an expansion of about £30 million into Europe. To implement this expansion, it requires funding in euros. The current exchange rate is €1.62/£, so the expansion will cost €48.6 million. ROTECH could issue a euro-denominated bond, but it is not as well known in the euro market as it is in the United Kingdom where, although not a top credit, its debt is rated investment grade. As an alternative, ROTECH could issue a pound-denominated bond and convert it to a euro-denominated bond using a currency swap. Exhibit 4 illustrates how it could do this.

The transaction begins on 1 June. ROTECH will borrow for three years. It issues a bond for £30 million, receiving the proceeds from its bondholders. The bond carries an interest rate of 5 percent and will require annual interest payments each 1 June. ROTECH then enters into a currency swap with a dealer called Starling Bank (SB). It pays SB £30 million and receives from SB €48.6 million. The terms of the swap call for ROTECH to pay interest to SB at a rate of 3.25 percent in euros and receive interest from SB at a rate of 4.5 percent in pounds. With the exchange of principals up front, ROTECH then has the euros it needs to proceed with its expansion. Panel A of Exhibit 4 illustrates the flow of funds at the start of the transaction.

The interest payments and swap payments, illustrated in Panel B, occur each year on 1 June. The interest payments on the pound-denominated bond will be £30,000,000(0.05) = £1,500,000. The interest due to ROTECH from SB is £30,000,000(0.045) = £1,350,000. The interest ROTECH owes SB is €48,600,000(0.0325) = €1,579,500. The net effect is that ROTECH pays interest

EXHIBIT 4	Issuing a Pound-Denominated Bond and Using a Currency Swap to Convert to a Euro-Denominated Bond

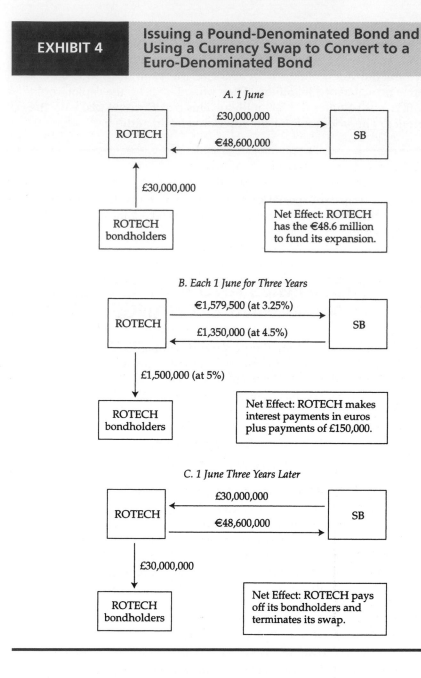

A. 1 June

ROTECH → £30,000,000 → SB
ROTECH ← €48,600,000 ← SB

£30,000,000 ↑

ROTECH bondholders

Net Effect: ROTECH has the €48.6 million to fund its expansion.

B. Each 1 June for Three Years

ROTECH → €1,579,500 (at 3.25%) → SB
ROTECH ← £1,350,000 (at 4.5%) ← SB

£1,500,000 (at 5%) ↓

ROTECH bondholders

Net Effect: ROTECH makes interest payments in euros plus payments of £150,000.

C. 1 June Three Years Later

ROTECH ← £30,000,000 ← SB
ROTECH → €48,600,000 → SB

£30,000,000 ↓

ROTECH bondholders

Net Effect: ROTECH pays off its bondholders and terminates its swap.

in euros. The interest received from the dealer, however, does not completely offset the interest it owes on its bond. ROTECH cannot borrow in pounds at the swap market fixed rate, because its credit rating is not as good as the rating implied in the LIBOR market term structure.[14] The net effect is that ROTECH will pay additional interest of $(0.05 - 0.045)£30,000,000 = £150,000$.

Panel C of Exhibit 4 shows the cash flows that occur at the end of the life of the swap and the maturity date of the bond. ROTECH receives the principal of £30 million from SB and pays it to its bondholders, discharging its liability. It then pays €48.6 million to SB to make the final principal payment on the swap.

---

[14] Remember that swap fixed rates are determined in the LIBOR market. This market consists of high-quality London banks, which borrow at an excellent rate. Hence, it is unlikely that ROTECH can borrow at as favorable a rate as these London banks.

This type of transaction is an extremely common use of currency swaps. The advantage of borrowing this way rather than directly in another currency lies in the fact that the borrower can issue a bond or loan in the currency in which it is better known as a creditor. Then, by engaging in a swap with a bank with which it is familiar and probably already doing business, it can borrow in the foreign currency indirectly. For example, in this case, SB is probably a large multinational bank and is well known in foreign markets. But SB also has a longstanding banking relationship with ROTECH. Consequently, SB can operate in foreign exchange markets, using its advantage, and pass that advantage on to ROTECH.[15]

Another reason this transaction is attractive for borrowers like ROTECH is that the company can lower its borrowing cost by assuming some credit risk. If ROTECH had issued debt in euros directly, it would face no credit risk.[16] By engaging in the swap, however, ROTECH assumes the credit risk that SB will default on its swap payments. If SB defaults, ROTECH would still have to make its interest and principal payments to its bondholders. In exchange for accepting this risk, it is likely that ROTECH would get a better overall deal. Of course, the desired result would not be achieved if SB defaults. But ROTECH would not engage in the transaction if it thought there was much chance of default. Therefore, ROTECH acknowledges and accepts some credit risk in return for expecting a better overall rate than if it issues euro-denominated debt.

Because it cannot borrow at the same rate as the fixed rate on the swap, ROTECH must pay £150,000 more in interest annually. Recall that the fixed rate on the swap is the rate that would be paid if a London bank issued a par bond. ROTECH, like most companies, would not be able to borrow at a rate that attractive. The £150,000 in interest that ROTECH pays can be viewed as a credit risk premium, which it would have to pay regardless of whether it borrowed directly in the euro market or indirectly through a swap.

In this transaction, the interest payments were made at a fixed rate. As we previously learned, a currency swap can be structured to have both sides pay fixed, both pay floating, or one pay fixed and the other floating. If ROTECH wanted to issue debt in euros at a floating rate, it could issue the bond at a fixed rate and structure the swap so that the dealer pays it pounds at a fixed rate and it pays the dealer euros at a floating rate. Alternatively, it could issue the pound-denominated bond at a floating rate and structure the swap so that the dealer pays it pounds at a floating rate and ROTECH pays euros at a floating rate.[17] A currency swap party's choice to pay a fixed or floating rate depends on its views about the direction of interest rate movements. Companies typically choose floating rates when they think interest rates are likely to fall. They choose fixed rates when they think interest rates are likely to rise.

It should also be noted that companies often choose a particular type of financing (fixed or floating) and then change their minds later by executing another swap. For example, suppose ROTECH proceeds with this transaction as we illustrated it: paying a fixed rate on its pound-denominated bonds, receiving a fixed rate on the pound payments on its swap, and paying a fixed rate on its euro payments on the swap. Suppose that part of the way through the life of the swap, ROTECH thinks that euro interest rates are going down. If it wants to take action based on this view, it could enter into a plain vanilla interest rate swap in

---

[15] SB accepts the foreign exchange in the swap from ROTECH and almost surely passes on that risk by hedging its position with some other type of foreign exchange transaction.

[16] Of course, ROTECH's bondholders would face the credit risk that ROTECH could default.

[17] It would not matter how ROTECH structured the payments on the pound-denominated bond. Either type of payment would be passed through with the currency swap, which would be structured to match that type of payment.

EXHIBIT 5	Reversing a Prior Swap to Change from a Fixed-Rate to an Overall Floating-Rate Status

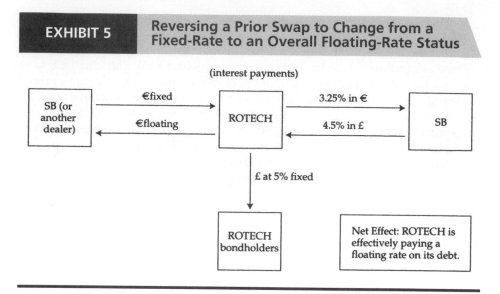

euros with SB or some other dealer. It would promise to pay the counterparty interest in euros at a floating rate and receive interest in euros at a fixed rate. This transaction would shift the euro interest obligation to floating.

Exhibit 5 illustrates this example. Of course, this transaction is speculative, based as it is on a perception of likely interest rate movements. Moreover, the fixed payments would not offset due to different interest rates.

One important way in which currency swaps differ from interest rate swaps is that currency swaps involve the payment of notional principal. However, not all currency swaps involve the payment of notional principal. In transactions such as the ROTECH swap with SB described here, the payment of notional principal is important. The notional principal payment is required, because it offsets the principal on the bond that ROTECH issued in pounds. In the next section, we look at a currency swap in which the notional principal is not paid.

EXAMPLE 5

A Japanese company issues a bond with face value of ¥1.2 billion and a coupon rate of 5.25 percent. It decides to use a swap to convert this bond into a euro-denominated bond. The current exchange rate is ¥120/€. The fixed rate on euro-denominated swaps is 6 percent, and the fixed rate on yen-denominated swaps is 5 percent. All payments will be made annually, so there is no adjustment such as Days/360.

A. Describe the terms of the swap and identify the cash flows at the start.

B. Identify all interest cash flows at each interest payment date.

C. Identify all principal cash flows at the maturity of the bond.

Solution to A: The company will enter into a swap with notional principal of ¥1,200,000,000/(¥120/€1) = €10,000,000. The swap will involve an exchange of notional principals at the beginning and end. The annual cash flows will involve paying euros and receiving yen. The following cash flows occur at the start:

From issuance of yen bond	+ ¥1,200,000,000
From swap	−¥1,200,000,000
	+ €10,000,000
Net	+ €10,000,000

Solution to B: The following cash flows occur at the annual interest payment dates:

Interest payments on bond	$(¥1,200,000,000)(0.0525) = -¥63,000,000$
Swap payments	
Yen	$+ (¥1,200,000,000)(0.05) = +¥60,000,000$
Euro	$-(€10,000,000)(0.06) = -€600,000$
Net	$-¥3,000,000 - €600,000$

Solution to C: The following cash flows occur at the end of the life of the swap:

Principal repayment on bond	− ¥1,200,000,000
Swap principal payments	
Yen	+ ¥1,200,000,000
Euro	− €10,000,000
Net	− €10,000,000

3.2 Converting Foreign Cash Receipts into Domestic Currency

Companies with foreign subsidiaries regularly generate cash in foreign currencies. Some companies repatriate that cash back into their domestic currency on a regular basis. If these cash flows are predictable in quantity, the rate at which they are converted can be locked in using a currency swap.

Colorama Software (COLS) is a U.S. company that writes software for digital imaging. So far it has expanded internationally only into the Japanese market, where it generates a net cash flow of about ¥1.2 billion a year. It converts this cash flow into U.S. dollars four times a year, with conversions taking place on the last day of March, June, September, and December. The amounts converted are equal to ¥300 million at each conversion.

COLS would like to lock in its conversion rate for several years, but it does not feel confident in predicting the amount it will convert beyond one year. Thus, it feels it can commit to only a one-year transaction to lock in the conversion rate. It engages in a currency swap with a dealer bank called U.S. Multinational Bank (USMULT) in which COLS will make fixed payments in Japanese yen and receive fixed payments in U.S. dollars. The current spot exchange rate is ¥132/$, which is $0.00757576/¥, or $0.757576 per 100 yen.

The fixed rate on plain vanilla swaps in Japan is 6 percent, and the fixed rate on plain vanilla swaps in the United States is 6.8 percent. To create a swap that will involve the exchange of ¥300 million per quarter into U.S. dollars would require a Japanese notional principal of ¥300,000,000/(0.06/4) = ¥20,000,000,000, which is

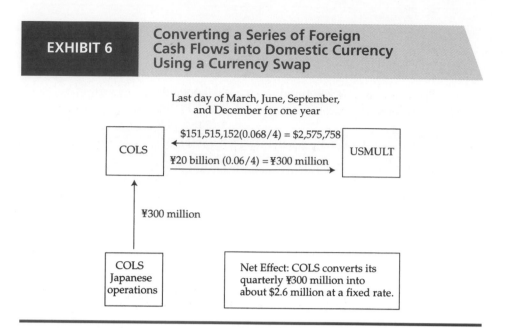

| EXHIBIT 6 | Converting a Series of Foreign Cash Flows into Domestic Currency Using a Currency Swap |

Last day of March, June, September, and December for one year

COLS ← $151,515,152(0.068/4) = $2,575,758 — USMULT

COLS → ¥20 billion (0.06/4) = ¥300 million → USMULT

¥300 million

COLS Japanese operations

Net Effect: COLS converts its quarterly ¥300 million into about $2.6 million at a fixed rate.

equivalent to a U.S. dollar notional principal of ¥20,000,000,000/¥132 = $151,515,152.[18]

Thus, COLS engages in a swap for ¥20 billion in which it will pay 6 percent on a quarterly basis, or 1.5 percent per quarter in Japanese yen, and receive 6.8 percent on a quarterly basis, or 1.7 percent on $151,515,152. There is no initial or final exchange of notional principals. The cash flows in the swap are illustrated in Exhibit 6.

COLS pays USMULT ¥20,000,000,000(0.06/4) = ¥300,000,000 quarterly on the swap. This amount corresponds to the cash flow it generates on its Japanese operations. It then receives 6.8 percent on a dollar notional principal of $151,515,152 for a total of $151,515,152(0.068/4) = $2,575,758. So the swap effectively locks in the conversion of its quarterly yen cash flows for one year.

COLS does face some risk in this transaction. Besides the credit risk of the swap counterparty defaulting, COLS faces the risk that its operations will not generate at least ¥300 million. Of course, COLS' operations could generate more than ¥300 million, but that would mean only that some of its cash flows would not convert at a locked-in rate. If its operations do not generate at least ¥300 million, COLS still must pay ¥300 million to the swap counterparty.

Currency swaps can be used for purposes other than managing conversion risks. These swaps are also used by dealers to create synthetic strategies that allow them to offer new instruments or hedge existing instruments. In the next section, we look at how currency swaps can be used to synthesize an instrument called a dual-currency bond.

EXAMPLE 6

A Canadian corporation with a French subsidiary generates cash flows of €10 million a year. It wants to use a currency swap to lock in the rate at which it converts to Canadian dollars. The current exchange rate is

---

[18] A currency swap at 6 percent with quarterly payments and a notional principal of ¥20 billion would require payments of (¥20,000,000,000)(0.06/4) = ¥300,000,000 per quarter.

C\$0.825/€. The fixed rate on a currency swap in euros is 4 percent, and the fixed rate on a currency swap in Canadian dollars is 5 percent.

A. Determine the notional principals in euros and Canadian dollars for a swap with annual payments that will achieve the corporation's objective.

B. Determine the overall periodic cash flow from the subsidiary operations and the swap.

Solution to A: With the euro fixed rate at 4 percent, the euro notional principal should be

$$\frac{€10,000,000}{0.04} = €250,000,000$$

The equivalent Canadian dollar notional principal would be €250,000,000 × C\$0.825 = C\$206,250,000.

Solution to B: The cash flows will be as follows:

From subsidiary operations	€10,000,000
Swap euro payment	−0.04(€250,000,000) = −€10,000,000
Swap Canadian dollar payment	0.05(C\$206,250,000) = C\$10,312,500

The net effect is that the €10 million converts to C\$10,312,500.

3.3 Using Currency Swaps to Create and Manage the Risk of a Dual-Currency Bond

A financial innovation in recent years is the dual-currency bond, on which the interest is paid in one currency and the principal is paid in another. Such a bond can be useful to a multinational company that might generate sufficient cash in a foreign currency to pay interest but not enough to pay the principal, which it thus might want to pay in its home currency. Dual-currency bonds can be shown to be equivalent to issuing an ordinary bond in one currency and combining it with a currency swap that has no principal payments. Consider the following transactions:

▶ Issue a bond in dollars.

▶ Engage in a currency swap with no principal payments. The swap will require the company to pay interest in the foreign currency and receive interest in dollars.

Because the company issued the bond in dollars, it will make interest payments in dollars. The currency swap, however, will result in the company receiving interest in dollars to offset the interest paid on the dollar-denominated bond and making interest payments on the currency swap in the foreign currency.[19]

---

[19] It does not matter if the dollar bond has fixed- or floating-rate interest. The currency swap would be structured to have the same type of interest to offset.

Effectively, the company will make interest payments in the foreign currency. At the maturity date of the bond and swap, the company will pay off the dollar-denominated bond, and there will be no payments on the swap.

Of course, this example illustrates the synthetic creation of a dual-currency bond. Alternatively, a company can create the dual-currency bond directly by issuing a bond in which it promises to pay the principal in one currency and the interest in another. Then, it might consider offsetting the dual-currency bond by synthetically creating the opposite position. The company is short a dual-currency bond. A synthetic dual-currency bond can be created through the purchase of a domestic bond and a currency swap. If the synthetic dual-currency bond is cheaper than the actual dual-currency bond, the company can profit by offsetting the short position in the actual bond by a long position in the synthetic bond. Let us see how this strategy can be implemented using a trading firm that finds an opportunity to earn an arbitrage profit doing so.

Trans Mutual Arbitrage (TMARB) is such a firm. It has a major client, Omega Construction (OGCONS), that would like to purchase a five-year dual-currency bond. The bond will have a face value of $10 million and an equivalent face value in euros of €12.5 million.[20] The bond will pay interest in euros at a rate of 4.5 percent. TMARB sees an opportunity to issue the bond, take the proceeds, and buy a 5.25 percent (coupon rate) U.S. dollar-denominated bond issued by an insurance company called Kappa Insurance Co. (KINSCO). TMARB will also engage in a currency swap with dealer American Trading Bank (ATB) in which TMARB will receive interest payments in euros at a rate of 4.5 percent on notional principal of €12.5 million and pay interest at a rate of 5.0 percent on notional principal of $10 million.[21] The swap does not involve the payment of notional principals. The swap and bond begin on 15 May and involve annual payments every 15 May for five years.

Exhibit 7 illustrates the structure of this swap. In Panel A, we see the initial cash flows. TMARB receives $10 million from OGCONS for the issuance of the dual-currency bond. It then takes the $10 million and buys a $10 million dollar-denominated bond issued by KINSCO. There are no initial cash flows on the currency swap.

Panel B shows the annual cash flows, which occur on 15 May for five years. TMARB pays interest of €12,500,000(0.045) = €562,500 to OGCONS on the dual-currency bond. It receives interest of an equivalent amount from ATB on the currency swap. It pays interest of $10,000,000(0.5) = $500,000 on the currency swap and receives interest of $10,000,000 × 0.0525 = $525,000 from KINSCO on the dollar-denominated bond. TMARB's euro interest payments are fully covered, and it nets a gain from its dollar interest payments. This opportunity resulted because TMARB found a synthetic way to issue a bond at 5.00 percent and buy one paying 5.25 percent. Of course, TMARB will be accepting some credit risk, from both the swap dealer and KINSCO, and its gain may reflect only this credit risk.

Panel C provides the final payments. TMARB pays off OGCONS its $10 million obligation on the dual-currency bond and receives $10 million from KINSCO on the dollar-denominated bond. There are no payments on the swap.

The end result is that TMARB issued a dual-currency bond and offset it with an ordinary dollar-denominated bond and a currency swap with no principal payments. TMARB earned a profit, which may be compensation for the credit risk taken.

---

[20] The current exchange rate must, therefore, be $0.80/€.

[21] We have made the fixed rate on the bond the same as the euro fixed rate on the swap for convenience. In practice, there probably would be a spread between the two rates, but the size of the spread would be fixed.

EXHIBIT 7	Issuing a Dual-Currency Bond and Managing the Risk with an Ordinary Bond and a Currency Swap

A. 15 May

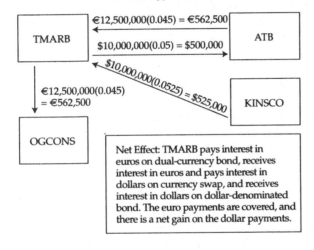

TMARB — $0 (no cash flow) → **ATB (swap dealer)**

TMARB ← $0 (no cash flow) — **ATB (swap dealer)**

$10,000,000 → **KINSCO (issuer of dollar-denominated bond)**

OGCONS (holder of dual-currency bond) — $10,000,000 → **TMARB**

Net Effect: TMARB issues dual-currency bond in dollars, uses funds to buy dollar-denominated bond, and enters into currency swap with no notional principal payments.

B. Each 15 May for Five Years

TMARB ← €12,500,000(0.045) = €562,500 — **ATB**

TMARB — $10,000,000(0.05) = $500,000 → **ATB**

$10,000,000(0.0525) = $525,000 ← **KINSCO**

TMARB — €12,500,000(0.045) = €562,500 → **OGCONS**

Net Effect: TMARB pays interest in euros on dual-currency bond, receives interest in euros and pays interest in dollars on currency swap, and receives interest in dollars on dollar-denominated bond. The euro payments are covered, and there is a net gain on the dollar payments.

C. 15 May Five Years Later

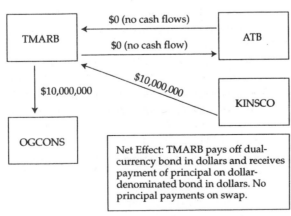

TMARB ← $0 (no cash flows) — **ATB**

TMARB — $0 (no cash flow) → **ATB**

$10,000,000 ← **KINSCO**

TMARB — $10,000,000 → **OGCONS**

Net Effect: TMARB pays off dual-currency bond in dollars and receives payment of principal on dollar-denominated bond in dollars. No principal payments on swap.

> **EXAMPLE 7**
>
> From the perspective of the issuer, construct a synthetic dual-currency bond in which the principal is paid in U.S. dollars and the interest is paid in Swiss francs. The face value will be $20 million, and the interest rate will be 5 percent in Swiss francs. The exchange rate is $0.80/SF. Assume that the appropriate interest rate for a $20 million bond in dollars is 5.5 percent. The appropriate fixed rates on a currency swap are 5.5 percent in dollars and 5.0 percent in Swiss francs.
>
> **Solution:** Issue a $20 million bond in dollars, paying interest at 5.5 percent. Enter into a currency swap on $20 million, equivalent to SF25 million. The currency swap will involve the receipt of dollar interest at 5.5 percent and payment of Swiss franc interest at 5.0 percent. You will receive $20 million at the start and pay back $20 million at maturity. The annual cash flows will be as follows:
>
> | | |
> |---|---|
> | On dollar bond issued: | $-0.055(\$20,000,000) = -\$1,100,000$ |
> | On swap: | |
> | Dollars | $+0.055(\$20,000,000) = +\$1,100,000$ |
> | Swiss francs | $-0.05(\text{SF25},000,000) = -\text{SF1},250,000$ |
> | Net | $-\text{SF1},250,000$ |

In the next section, we look at swap strategies in the management of equity market risk.

4 STRATEGIES AND APPLICATIONS FOR MANAGING EQUITY MARKET RISK

Equity portfolio managers often want to realign the risk of their portfolios. Swaps can be used for this purpose. In Reading 38, we covered equity swaps, which are swaps in which at least one set of payments is tied to the price of a stock or stock index. Equity swaps are ideal for use by equity managers to make changes to portfolios by synthetically buying and selling stock without making any trades in the actual stock. Of course, equity swaps have a defined expiration date and thus achieve their results only temporarily. To continue managing equity market risk, a swap would need to be renewed periodically and would be subject to whatever new conditions exist in the market on the renewal date.

4.1 Diversifying a Concentrated Portfolio

Diversification is one of the most important principles of sound investing. Some portfolios, however, are not very diversified. A failure to diversify can be due to investor ignorance or inattention, or it can arise through no fault of the investor. For example, a single large donation to a charitable organization can result in a high degree of concentration of an endowment portfolio. The recipient could be constrained or at least feel constrained from selling the stock. Equity swaps can be used to achieve diversification without selling the stock, as we shall see in the following example.

Commonwealth Foundation (CWF) is a charitable organization with an endowment of $50 million invested in diversified stock. Recently, Samuel Zykes, a wealthy member of the community, died and left CWF a large donation of stock in a company he founded called Zykes Technology (ZYKT). The stock is currently worth $30 million. The overall endowment value is now at $80 million, but the portfolio is highly undiversified, with more than a third of its value concentrated in one stock. CWF has considered selling the stock, but its development director believes that the Zykes family will possibly give more money to the foundation at a later date. If CWF sells the stock, the Zykes family may get the impression that the foundation does not want or appreciate the gift. Therefore, the foundation has concluded that it must hold onto the stock. The prospects for very limited growth in the portfolio through other sources, combined with the desire to attract further donations from the Zykes family, lead CWF to conclude that it cannot diversify the portfolio by traditional means anytime soon.

CWF's bank suggests that it consult with a swap dealer called Capital Swaps (CAPS). CAPS recommends an equity swap in which CWF would pay CAPS the return on the $30 million of ZYKT stock, while CAPS would pay CWF the return on $30 million of the S&P 500 Index, considered by all parties to be an acceptable proxy for a diversified portfolio. The payments will be made quarterly. CAPS mentions that technically the transaction would need an ending date. Anticipating the possibility of another transaction of this sort pending further donations by the Zykes family in about five years, the parties agree to set the maturity date of the swap at five years. The transaction entails no exchange of notional principal at the start or at the end of the life of the swap. Thus, CWF will maintain possession of the stock, including the voting rights. Exhibit 8 illustrates the structure of the transaction.

So, CWF passes through the return on $30 million of ZYKT stock and receives the return on the S&P 500. Both parties, however, must keep in mind a number of considerations. One is that a cash flow problem could arise for CWF, which must make cash payments each quarter equal to the return on the ZYKT stock. Though CWF will receive cash payments equal to the return on the S&P 500, CWF will have a net cash outflow if ZYKT outperforms the S&P 500. In fact, it is quite possible that in some quarters, ZYKT will have a positive total return,

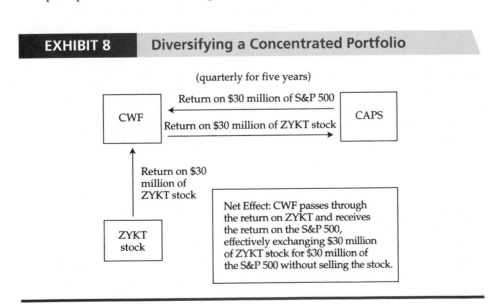

EXHIBIT 8 | **Diversifying a Concentrated Portfolio**

necessitating a cash obligation, and the S&P 500 will have a negative total return. In that case, the cash payment that CAPS would ordinarily make to CWF for the S&P 500 return would actually be reversed: CWF would owe CAPS for the S&P 500. In short, CWF would owe on both legs of the swap. This possibility could pose a significant cash flow problem and might necessitate the actual sale of some ZYKT stock. The position would then be imbalanced because CWF would own less than $30 million of ZYKT stock but still owe payments on $30 million of ZYKT stock. Cash flow management can be a major difficulty in equity swaps.

EXAMPLE 8

The manager of a charitable foundation's $50 million stock portfolio is concerned about the portfolio's heavy concentration in one stock, Noble Petroleum (NBP). Specifically, the fund has $20 million of this stock as a result of a recent donation to the fund. She is considering using an equity swap to reduce the exposure to NBP and allow the fund to invest indirectly in the Wilshire 5000 Index. The stock is currently selling for $20 a share, and the fund owns 1 million shares. The manager is not quite ready to reduce all of the fund's exposure to NBP, so she decides to synthetically sell off one-quarter of the position. Explain how she would do this and identify some problems she might encounter.

Solution: To reduce her exposure on one quarter of her NBP holdings, the manager would have the fund enter into a swap to sell the total return on $5 million of NBP stock, which is 250,000 shares. The fund will receive from the swap dealer the return on $5 million invested in the Wilshire 5000.

The swap may result in cash flow problems, however, because the fund must pay out the return on 250,000 shares of NBP stock but does not want to sell that stock. If the return received on $5 million invested in the Wilshire 5000 is significantly less than the return the fund pays, or if the return on the Wilshire is negative, the fund could have insufficient cash to make its payment. Then it might be forced to sell the stock, something it was trying to avoid in the first place.

Continuing with the example of ZYKT stock, what is the position of the dealer CAPS? It agrees to accept the return on ZYKT stock and pay the return on the S&P 500. This means it is long ZYKT and short the S&P 500. It is likely to hedge its position by buying the equivalent of the S&P 500 through either an index fund or an exchange-traded fund, and selling short ZYKT stock.[22] In fact, its short sale of the ZYKT stock is analogous to CWF selling the stock. CAPS effectively sells the stock for CWF. Also, CAPS is not likely to be able to sell all of the ZYKT stock at one time so it will probably do so over a period of a few days. CAPS may also have a cash flow problem on occasion. If it owes more on the S&P 500 payment than is due it on the ZYKT payment, CAPS may have to liquidate some S&P 500 stock.[23]

---

[22] Instead of buying or selling short stock, it could use any of a variety of derivative strategies in which it would benefit from a decrease in the price of ZYKT relative to the S&P 500.

[23] To make matters worse, if the S&P goes up and ZYKT goes down, it will owe both sets of payments.

In addition, to make a profit CAPS would probably either not pay quite the full return on the S&P 500 stock or require that CWF pay slightly more than the full return on the ZYKT stock.

We see that equity swaps can be used to diversify a concentrated portfolio. Next we turn to a situation in which equity swaps can be used to achieve diversification on an international scale.

4.2 Achieving International Diversification

The benefits of international diversification are well documented. The correlations between foreign markets and domestic markets generally lead to greater diversification and more efficient investing. Nonetheless, many investors have not taken the step of diversifying their portfolios across international boundaries. Here we shall take a look at a situation in which equity swaps can facilitate the transition from domestic to global diversification.

In this example, Underscore Retirement Management (USRM) is responsible for a $500 million fund of retirement accounts in the United States. It has never diversified internationally, investing all of its funds in U.S. stock. Representing U.S. large-, medium- and small-cap stocks, the Russell 3000 Index is the portfolio's benchmark. USRM has decided that it needs to add non-U.S. stocks to its portfolio. It would like to start by selling 10 percent of its U.S. stock and putting the funds in non-U.S. stock. Its advisor, American Global Bank (AGB), has suggested that an equity swap would be a better way to do this than to transact in the stock directly. AGB often deals in non-U.S. stock and has subsidiaries and correspondent relationships in many countries to facilitate the transactions. It is capable of transacting in all stock at lower costs than its clients, and can pass on those savings through derivative transactions.

AGB suggests an equity swap with quarterly payments in which USRM would pay it the return on $50 million of the Russell 3000 Index. USRM would presumably generate this return from the portfolio it holds. AGB would, in turn, pay USRM the return on $50 million invested in the Morgan Stanley Capital International (MSCI) EAFE Index, which provides broad coverage of equity markets in Europe, Australasia, and the Far East. This transaction would result in USRM giving up some diversified domestic stock performance and receiving diversified international stock performance. Exhibit 9 illustrates the structure of the transaction.

EXHIBIT 9	Achieving International Diversification

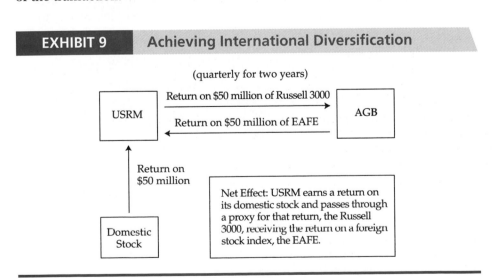

(quarterly for two years)

USRM → Return on $50 million of Russell 3000 → AGB

AGB → Return on $50 million of EAFE → USRM

Return on $50 million → USRM

Domestic Stock

Net Effect: USRM earns a return on its domestic stock and passes through a proxy for that return, the Russell 3000, receiving the return on a foreign stock index, the EAFE.

USRM must also consider a number of additional factors. The points made in Section 4.1 regarding the possibility of negative cash flow are highly relevant here as well, and we shall not repeat them. In addition, USRM's domestic stock holding generates a return that will not match perfectly the return on the Russell 3000. This difference in returns, in which the performance of an index does not match the performance of a portfolio that is similar to the index, is called the **tracking error**. In an extreme case, the domestic stock may go down while the Russell index goes up, which could pose a serious cash flow problem for USRM. USRM may be able to quantify this problem and find that it can effectively manage it. Otherwise, this concern could be an important one for USRM to weigh against the benefits of doing this transaction, which are primarily the savings in transaction costs on the domestic side and on the foreign side. In addition, AGB has currency risk and market risk and passes on to USRM its costs of hedging that risk.

EXAMPLE 9

A Canadian trust fund holds a portfolio of C$300 million of Canadian domestic stock. The manager would like to sell off C$100 million and invest the funds in a pan-European portfolio. The manager arranges to do so using an equity swap in which the domestic stock is represented by the Toronto 300 Composite and the European portfolio is represented by the Dow Jones Euro STOXX 50, an index of leading stocks in the eurozone. Explain how to structure such a swap, and describe how tracking error could potentially interfere with the success of the transaction.

Solution: The swap would specify the following transactions on a periodic basis for a specific number of years:

▶ receive return on DJ Euro STOXX 50
▶ pay return on Toronto 300

Tracking error here is the failure of the derivative cash flow to match precisely the cash flow from the underlying portfolio. In this case, tracking error means that the return actually earned on the domestic portfolio is not likely to perfectly match the Toronto 300 return. These returns are supposed to offset, but they are not likely to do so, certainly not with perfection. The return received on the DJ Euro STOXX 50 does not give rise to tracking error concerns. The index will simply represent the return on the investment in European stocks. If an actual investment in European stocks were made, it would likely differ from this return.

We see in this example that a company can use an equity swap to change its asset allocation. Indeed, an asset allocation change is the major use of equity swaps. In the next section, we shall see a company use equity swaps, combined with a similar swap based on a fixed-income instrument, to implement an asset allocation change. This fixed-income swap will be a slightly new and different instrument from what we have already seen.

4.3 Changing an Asset Allocation between Stocks and Bonds

Consider an investment management firm called Tactical Money Management (TMM). It is interested in changing the asset allocation on a $200 million segment of its portfolio. This money is invested 75 percent in domestic stock and 25 percent in U.S. government and corporate bonds. Within the stock sector, the funds are invested 60 percent in large cap, 30 percent in mid cap, and 10 percent in small cap. Within the bond sector, the funds are invested 80 percent in U.S. government and 20 percent in investment-grade corporate bonds. TMM would like to change the overall allocation to 90 percent stock and 10 percent bonds. Within each class, TMM would also like to make some changes. Specifically, TMM would like to change the stock allocation to 65 percent large cap and 25 percent mid cap, leaving the small-cap allocation at 10 percent. It would like to change the bond allocation to 75 percent U.S. government and 25 percent investment-grade corporate. TMM knows that these changes would entail a considerable amount of trading in stocks and bonds. Below we show the current position, the desired new position, and the necessary transactions to get from the current position to the new position:

Stock	Current ($150 million, 75%)	New ($180 million, 90%)	Transaction
Large cap	$90 million (60%)	$117 million (65%)	Buy $27 million
Mid cap	$45 million (30%)	$45 million (25%)	None
Small cap	$15 million (10%)	$18 million (10%)	Buy $3 million

Bonds	Current ($50 million, 25%)	New ($20 million, 10%)	Transaction
Government	$40 million (80%)	$15 million (75%)	Sell $25 million
Corporate	$10 million (20%)	$5 million (25%)	Sell $5 million

TMM decides it can execute a series of swaps that would enable it to change its position temporarily, but more easily and less expensively than by executing the transactions in stock and bonds. It engages a dealer, Dynamic Derivatives Inc. (DYDINC), to perform the swaps. The return on the large-cap sector is represented by the return on $27 million invested in the S&P 500 (SP500) Index. Note that the mid-cap exposure of $45 million does not change, so we do not need to incorporate a mid-cap index into the swap. The return on the small-cap sector is represented by the return on $3 million invested in the S&P Small Cap 600 Index (SPSC). The return on the government bond sector is represented by the return on $25 million invested in the Lehman Long Treasury Bond index (LLTB), and the return on the corporate bond sector is represented by the return on $5 million invested in the Merrill Lynch Corporate Bond index (MLCB). Note that for the overall fixed-income sector, TMM will be reducing its exposure.

TMM must decide the frequency of payments and the length of the swap. Equity swap payments tend to be set at quarterly intervals. Fixed-income payments in the form of coupon interest tend to occur semiannually. TMM could arrange for quarterly equity swap payments and semiannual fixed-income swap payments. It decides, however, to structure the swap to have all payments occur on the same dates six months apart. The length of the swap should correspond to the period during which the firm wants this new allocation to hold. TMM decides on one year. Should it wish to extend this period, TMM would need to renegotiate the swap at expiration. Likewise, TMM could decide to unwind the position prior to one year, which it could do by executing a new swap with opposite payments for the remainder of the life of the original swap.

The equity swaps in this example involve receiving payments tied to the SP500 and the SPSC and making either fixed payments or floating payments tied to LIBOR. Let us start by assuming that the equity swap payments will be paired with LIBOR-based floating payments. For the fixed-income payments, however, TMM needs a slightly different type of swap—specifically, a fixed-income swap. This instrument is exactly like an equity swap, but instead of the payment being tied to a stock or stock index, it is tied to a bond or bond index. This type of swap is not the same as an interest rate swap, which involves payments tied to a floating rate such as LIBOR. Fixed-income swaps, like equity swaps, require the payment of the total return on a bond or bond index against some other index, such as LIBOR. They are very similar to equity swaps in many respects: The total return is not known until the end of the settlement period, and because the capital gain can be negative, it is possible for the overall payment to be negative. In contrast to equity swaps, however, fixed-income swaps are more dominated by the fixed payment of interest. For equities, the dividends are small, not fixed, and do not tend to dominate capital gains. Other than the amounts paid, however, fixed-income swaps are conceptually the same as equity swaps.[24]

The swaps are initially structured as follows:

Equity swaps
   Receive return on SP500 on $27 million
      Pay LIBOR on $27 million
   Receive return on SPSC on $3 million
      Pay LIBOR on $3 million
Fixed-income swaps
   Receive LIBOR on $25 million
      Pay return on LLTB on $25 million
   Receive LIBOR on $5 million
      Pay return on MLCB on $5 million

Note that the overall position involves no LIBOR payments. TMM pays LIBOR on $27 million and on $3 million from its equity swaps, and it receives LIBOR on $25 million and on $5 million from the fixed-income swaps. Therefore, the LIBOR payments can be eliminated. Furthermore, the equity and fixed-income swaps can be combined into a single swap with the following payments:

   Receive return on SP500 on $27 million
   Receive return on SPSC on $3 million
      Pay return on LLTB on $25 million
      Pay return on MLCB on $5 million

This combined equity/fixed-income swap is a single transaction that accomplishes TMM's objective. Exhibit 10 illustrates the overall transaction.

Of course, this transaction will not completely achieve TMM's goals. The performance of the various sectors of its equity and fixed-income portfolios are not likely to match perfectly the indices on which the swap payments are based.

---

[24] Fixed-income swaps, when referred to as total return swaps, are a form of a credit derivative.

EXHIBIT 10   Changing an Asset Allocation

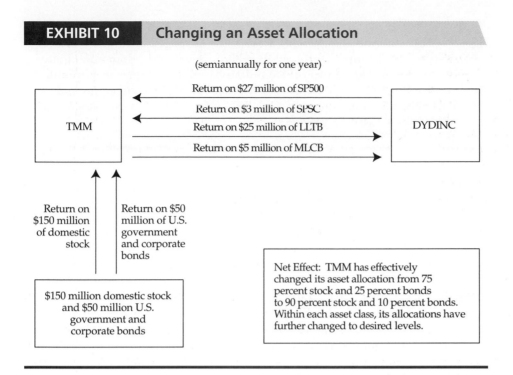

(semiannually for one year)

Return on $27 million of SP500

Return on $3 million of SPSC

Return on $25 million of LLTB

Return on $5 million of MLCB

TMM

DYDINC

Return on $150 million of domestic stock

Return on $50 million of U.S. government and corporate bonds

$150 million domestic stock and $50 million U.S. government and corporate bonds

Net Effect: TMM has effectively changed its asset allocation from 75 percent stock and 25 percent bonds to 90 percent stock and 10 percent bonds. Within each asset class, its allocations have further changed to desired levels.

This problem is what we referred to previously as tracking error. In addition, TMM could encounter a cash flow problem if its fixed-income payments exceed its equity receipts and its portfolio does not generate enough cash to fund its net obligation. The actual stock and bond portfolio will generate cash only from dividends and interest. The capital gains on the stock and bond portfolio will not be received in cash unless a portion of the portfolio is liquidated. But avoiding liquidation of the portfolio is the very reason that TMM wants to use swaps.[25]

EXAMPLE 10

A $30 million investment account of a bank trust fund is allocated one-third to stocks and two-thirds to bonds. The portfolio manager wants to change the overall allocation to 50 percent stock and 50 percent bonds, and the allocation within the stock fund from 70 percent domestic stock and 30 percent foreign stock to 60 percent domestic and 40 percent foreign. The bond allocation will remain entirely invested in domestic corporate issues. Explain how an equity swap could be used to implement this adjustment. You do not need to refer to specific stock indices.

Solution: Currently the allocation is $10 million stock and $20 million bonds. Within the stock category, the current allocation is $7 million domestic and $3 million foreign. The desired allocation is $15 million stock and $15 million bonds. Thus, the allocation must change by moving $5 million into stock and out of bonds. The desired stock allocation is $9 million domestic and $6 million foreign. The desired bond allocation is $15 million, all domestic corporate.

---

[25] Even worse would be if its fixed-income payments were positive and its equity receipts were negative.

> To make the change with a swap, the manager must enter into a swap to receive the return on $5 million based on a domestic equity index and pay the return on $5 million based on a domestic corporate bond index. The $5 million return based on a domestic equity index should be allocated such that $2 million is based on domestic stock and $3 million is based on foreign stock.

So far we have seen that an equity swap can be used to reduce or increase exposure to a stock or stock index. One type of investor that is highly exposed to the performance of a single stock is a corporate insider. In the following section, we examine a swap strategy that has been increasingly used in recent years to reduce such exposure.

4.4 Reducing Insider Exposure

Michael Spelling is the founder and sole owner of a U.S.-based company called Spelling Software and Technology (SPST). After founding the company about 10 years ago, Spelling took it public 2 years ago and retains significant ownership in the form of 10,200,000 shares, currently valued at $35 a share, for a total value of $357 million, which represents about 10 percent of the company. Spelling wants to retain this degree of control of the company, so he does not wish to sell any of his shares. He is concerned, however, that his personal wealth is nearly 100 percent exposed to the fortunes of a single company.

A swap dealer called Swap Solutions Inc. (SSI) approaches Spelling about a strategy that it has been using lately with much success. This transaction involves an equity swap whereby Spelling would pay the dealer the return on some of his shares in SPST and receive a diversified portfolio return. Spelling finds the idea intriguing and begins thinking about how he would like to structure the arrangement. He decides to initially base the transaction on 500,000 shares of stock, about 4.9 percent of his ownership. If he is satisfied with how the strategy works, he may later increase his commitment to the swap. At $35 a share, this transaction has an exposure of $17.5 million. Specifically, Spelling will pay the total return on 500,000 shares of SPST stock and receive a diversified portfolio return on $17.5 million. He decides to split the diversified return into 80 percent stock and 20 percent bonds. The former will be represented by the return on $14.0 million invested in the Russell 3000, and the latter will be represented by the return on $3.5 million invested in the Lehman Brothers Government Bond Index (LGB). The payments will occur quarterly for two years, at which time Spelling will re-evaluate his position and may choose to extend the swap, terminate it, or change the allocation or other terms.

Exhibit 11 illustrates the structure of the swap. Spelling achieves his objectives, but he must consider some important issues in addition to the cash flow problem we have already mentioned. One is that under U.S. law, this transaction is considered an insider sale and must be reported to the regulatory authorities Thus, there is some additional paperwork. Shareholders and potential investors may consider the sale a signal of bad prospects for the company. U.S. tax laws also require that the synthetic sale of securities through equity swaps forces a termination of the holding period on the stock. Hence, this transaction has no tax advantages. Spelling will also want to consider the fact that he has sold off some of his exposure but retains control. Shareholders will surely resent the fact that

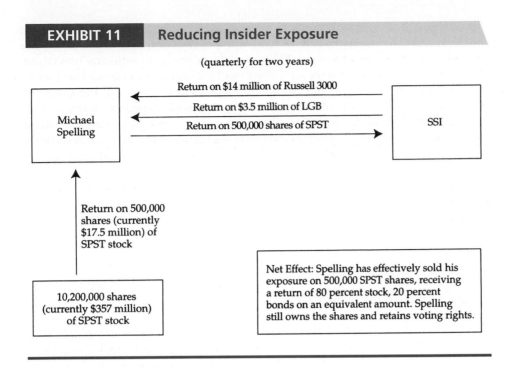

| EXHIBIT 11 | Reducing Insider Exposure |

(quarterly for two years)

Return on $14 million of Russell 3000

Return on $3.5 million of LGB

Return on 500,000 shares of SPST

Michael Spelling

SSI

Return on 500,000 shares (currently $17.5 million) of SPST stock

10,200,000 shares (currently $357 million) of SPST stock

Net Effect: Spelling has effectively sold his exposure on 500,000 SPST shares, receiving a return of 80 percent stock, 20 percent bonds on an equivalent amount. Spelling still owns the shares and retains voting rights.

Spelling controls 500,000 votes but does not have any exposure to this stock.[26] Of course, he still retains exposure to 9.7 million shares.

EXAMPLE 11

The CEO of a corporation owns 100 million shares of his company's stock, which is currently priced at €30 a share. Given the tremendous exposure of his personal wealth to this one company, he has decided to sell 10 percent of his position and invest the funds in a floating interest rate instrument. A derivatives dealer suggests that he do so using an equity swap. Explain how to structure such a swap.

Solution: The swap is structured so that the executive pays the return on 10 million shares, which is 10 percent of his holdings, of the company's stock and receives the return based on a floating interest rate, such as LIBOR, on a notional principal of €300 million.

Equity swaps of this sort can be a significant concern for financial analysts. Their possible use makes it difficult to determine if executives have the full exposure represented by the number of shares they own.

Equity swaps involving executives can also have significant agency cost implications. A company incurs agency costs when an executive does not act on behalf of shareholders. Consider the extreme case of an executive who owns more than

---

[26] An interesting question in this regard is whether the shareholders would actually know that the executive had done such a transaction. Careful research is required to identify that executives have made these transactions.

50 percent of a company but who reduces her equity exposure to zero with equity swaps. The executive retains full control of the company, although she has eliminated her equity exposure. This action could entail significant costs to outside shareholders, as the executive does not bear any of the costs of actions or expenditures that increase her personal welfare at the expense of the company. Of course, executives are unlikely to sell off all of their exposure, but the elimination of any exposure on shares still retained for control purposes raises significant questions about whether an executive would act in the best interests of the shareholders. The executive's incentive to perform well would certainly be reduced.

In Sections 2, 3, and 4, we examined the use of interest rate swaps, currency swaps, and equity swaps for managing risk. In the following section, we examine strategies involving the use of swaptions to manage risk.

5   STRATEGIES AND APPLICATIONS USING SWAPTIONS

A swaption is an option to enter into a swap. Although there are swaptions to enter into equity, currency, and **commodity swaps**, we will focus exclusively on swaptions to enter into interest rate swaps, which is by far the largest swaptions market. Let us briefly review swaptions.

First, recall that there are two types of swaptions, payer swaptions and receiver swaptions, which are analogous to puts and calls. A payer swaption is an option that allows the holder to enter into a swap as the fixed-rate payer, floating-rate receiver. A receiver swaption is an option that allows the holder to enter into a swap as the fixed-rate receiver, floating-rate payer. In both cases, the fixed rate is specified when the option starts. The buyer of a swaption pays a premium at the start of the contract and receives the right to enter into a swap. The counterparty is the seller of the swaption. The seller receives the premium at the start and grants the right to enter into the swap at the specified fixed rate to the buyer of the swaption. A swaption can be European style or American style, meaning that it can be exercised only at expiration (European) or at any time prior to expiration (American). We shall illustrate applications of both.

A swaption is based on an underlying swap. The underlying swap has a specific set of terms: the notional principal, the underlying interest rate, the time it expires, the specific dates on which the payments will be made, and how the interest is calculated. *All* of the terms of the underlying swap must be specified. Although an ordinary option on an asset has an exercise *price,* a swaption is more like an interest rate option in that it has an exercise *rate.* The exercise rate is the fixed rate at which the holder can enter into the swap as either a fixed-rate payer or fixed-rate receiver. When a swaption expires, the holder decides whether to exercise it based on the relationship of the then-current market rate on the underlying swap to the exercise rate on the swaption. A swaption can be exercised either by actually entering into the swap or by having the seller pay the buyer an equivalent amount of cash. The method used is determined by the parties when the contract is created.

For example, suppose the underlying swap is a three-year swap with semiannual payments with LIBOR as the underlying floating rate. Consider a payer swaption, which allows entry into this swap as the fixed-rate payer, with an exercise rate of 7 percent. At expiration, let us say that three-year, semiannual-pay LIBOR swaps have a fixed rate of 7.25 percent. If the holder exercises the swaption, it enters a swap, agreeing to pay a fixed rate of 7 percent and receive a floating rate of LIBOR. If the holder has another position for which it might want to maintain the swap, it might simply hold the swap in place. If the holder does not want to maintain the swap, it can enter into a swap in the market, specifying the opposite set of payments—it can pay LIBOR and receive the market fixed rate of 7.25 percent. If this swap is done with a different counterparty than the swaption seller, then the two sets of LIBOR payments are made but are equivalent in amount. Then the payer swaption holder finds itself with a stream of cash flows consisting of 7 percent payments and 7.25 percent receipts, for a net overall position of an annuity of 0.25 percent, split into 0.125 percent twice a year, for three years. If this swap at the market rate of 7.25 percent is done with the swaption seller, the two parties are likely to agree to offset the LIBOR payments and have the swaption seller pay the holder the stream of payments of 0.125 percent twice a year. If the parties settle the contract in cash, the swaption seller pays the swaption holder the present value of a series of six semiannual payments of 0.125 percent.

A swaption can also be viewed as an option on a coupon bond. Specifically, a payer swaption with exercise rate x in which the underlying is a swap with notional principal P and maturity of N years at the swaption expiration is equivalent to an at-the-money put option in which the underlying is an N-year bond at expiration with a coupon of x percent. Likewise, a receiver swaption is analogous to an at-the-money call option on a bond. These identities will be useful in understanding swaption strategies.

5.1 Using an Interest Rate Swaption in Anticipation of a Future Borrowing

We have illustrated extensively the use of swaps to convert fixed-rate loans to floating-rate loans and vice versa. We now consider a situation in which a company anticipates taking out a loan at a future date. The company expects that the bank will require the loan to be at a floating rate, but the company would prefer a fixed rate. It will use a swap to convert the payment pattern of the loan. A swaption will give it the flexibility to enter into the swap at an attractive rate.

In this section, we will use the notation FS(1,3) for the fixed rate on a swap established at time 1 and ending at time 3.

Benelux Chemicals (BCHEM) is a Brussels-based industrial company that often takes out floating-rate loans. In the course of planning, BCHEM finds that it must borrow €10 million in one year at the floating rate of Euribor, the rate on euros in Frankfurt, from the Antwerp National Bank (ANB). The loan will require semiannual payments for two years. BCHEM knows that it will swap the loan into a fixed-rate loan, using the going rate for two-year Euribor-based swaps at the time the loan is taken out. BCHEM is concerned that interest rates will rise before it takes out the loan. DTD, a Rotterdam derivatives dealer, approaches BCHEM with the idea of doing a European-style swaption. Specifically, for a cash payment up front of €127,500, BCHEM can obtain the right to enter into the swap in one year as a fixed-rate payer at a rate of 7 percent. BCHEM decides to go ahead with the deal; that is, it buys a 7 percent payer swaption.

Exhibit 12 illustrates this transaction. In Panel A, BCHEM pays DTD €127,500 in cash and receives the payer swaption. In Panel B, we examine what happens starting when the swaption expires one year later. Note first that regardless of the outcome of the swaption, BCHEM will make floating interest payments of Euribor(180/360)€10 million on its loan.[27] In Part (i) of Panel B, we

---

[27] Again, recall that being a floating rate, Euribor is set at the beginning of the settlement period, and the payment is made at the end of that period.

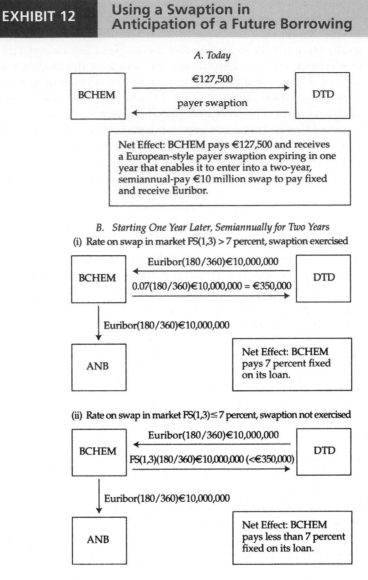

EXHIBIT 12   Using a Swaption in Anticipation of a Future Borrowing

A. Today

BCHEM — €127,500 → DTD

BCHEM ← payer swaption — DTD

Net Effect: BCHEM pays €127,500 and receives a European-style payer swaption expiring in one year that enables it to enter into a two-year, semiannual-pay €10 million swap to pay fixed and receive Euribor.

B. Starting One Year Later, Semiannually for Two Years

(i) Rate on swap in market FS(1,3) > 7 percent, swaption exercised

BCHEM ← Euribor(180/360)€10,000,000 — DTD

BCHEM — 0.07(180/360)€10,000,000 = €350,000 → DTD

BCHEM — Euribor(180/360)€10,000,000 → ANB

Net Effect: BCHEM pays 7 percent fixed on its loan.

(ii) Rate on swap in market FS(1,3)≤ 7 percent, swaption not exercised

BCHEM ← Euribor(180/360)€10,000,000 — DTD

BCHEM — FS(1,3)(180/360)€10,000,000 (<€350,000) → DTD

BCHEM — Euribor(180/360)€10,000,000 → ANB

Net Effect: BCHEM pays less than 7 percent fixed on its loan.

assume that at expiration of the swaption, the rate in the market on the underlying swap, FS(1,3), is greater than the swaption exercise rate of 7 percent. In this case, the swaption is worth exercising.[28] BCHEM enters into the swap with DTD, thereby making payments of 0.07(180/360)€10 million and receiving payments of Euribor(180/360)€10 million.[29] Both streams of floating payments at Euribor are made, but the payment from DTD exactly offsets the payment to ANB. BCHEM is left paying 7 percent fixed.

In Part (ii) of Panel B, at expiration of the swaption, the rate in the market on the underlying swap, FS(1,3), is less than or equal to the swaption exercise

---

[28] To review, remember that at the swaption expiration in one year, which we denote as time 1, the underlying swap is a two-year swap. If the fixed rate on a two-year swap is higher than the rate at which the swaption holder can pay to enter a two-year swap, the swaption is in-the-money. As we showed in Section 5 of this reading, its value at that point is the present value of a stream of payments equal to the difference between the market fixed rate and the exercise rate on the swaption.

[29] The swap payments would, of course, be netted, but that fact does not affect the point we are making here.

rate of 7 percent. The swaption, therefore, expires out-of-the-money. BCHEM still enters into a swap with DTD but does so at the market rate of FS(1,3), which is less than 7 percent and the payments are less than €350,000. Of course, both sets of Euribor payments must be made on the loan.

Thus, BCHEM obtained the advantage of flexibility, the right to pay a fixed rate of 7 percent or less. Of course, this right does not come without a cost. BCHEM had to pay a premium of €127,500 for that right. Therefore, when the loan was taken out one year after the swaption was purchased, the €10 million received was effectively reduced by the €127,500 paid one year earlier plus one year's interest. Whether this premium would be worth paying depends on whether the swaption is correctly priced.[30] Whether this premium was worth it after the fact depends on how far the market rate ended above 7 percent at the time the loan was taken out.

EXAMPLE 12

A company plans to take out a $10 million floating-rate loan in two years. The loan will be for five years with annual payments at the rate of LIBOR. The company anticipates using a swap to convert the loan into a fixed-rate loan. It would like to purchase a swaption to give it the flexibility to enter into the swap at an attractive rate. The company can use a payer or a receiver swaption. Assume that the exercise rate would be 6.5 percent.

A. Identify what type of swaption would achieve this goal and whether the company should buy or sell the swaption.

B. Calculate the company's annual cash flows beginning two years from now for two cases: The fixed rate on a swap two years from now to terminate five years later, FS(2,7), is 1) greater or 2) not greater than the exercise rate. Assume the company takes out the $10 million floating-rate loan as planned.

C. Suppose that when the company takes out the loan, it has changed its mind and prefers a floating-rate loan. Now assume that the swaption expires in-the-money. What would the company do, given that it now no longer wants to convert to a fixed-rate loan?

Solution to A: The company wants the option to enter into the swap as a fixed-rate payer, so the company would buy a payer swaption.

Solution to B: The outcomes based on the swap rate at swaption expiration, denoted as FS(2,7), are as follows:

> FS(2,7) > 6.5 percent
> Exercise the swaption, entering into a swap. The annual cash flows will be as follows:
> > Pay 0.065($10 million) = $650,000 on swap
> > Receive L($10 million) on swap
> > Pay L($10 million) on loan
> > Net, pay $650,000

---

[30] The basic idea behind swaption pricing is that a model would be used to obtain a fair price for the swaption, to which the market price of €127,500 would be compared.

FS(2,7) ≤ 6.5 percent
Do not exercise swaption; enter into swap at market rate. The annual cash flows will be as follows:
    Pay FS(2,7)($10 million) on swap
    Receive L($10 million) on swap
    Pay L($10 million) on loan
    Net, pay FS(2,7)($10 million)
    (Note: This is less than $650,000)

Solution to C: In this situation, the company has changed its mind about converting the floating-rate loan to a fixed-rate loan. If the swaption expires out-of-the-money, the company will simply take out the floating-rate loan. If the swaption expires in-the-money, it has value and the company should not fail to exercise it. But exercising the swaption will initiate a swap to pay fixed and receive floating, which would leave the company in the net position of paying a fixed rate of 6.5 percent when it wants a floating-rate loan. The company would exercise the swaption and then enter into the opposite swap in the market, receiving a fixed rate of FS(2,7) and paying L. The net effect is that the company will pay 6.5 percent, receive FS(2,7), which is more than 6.5 percent, and pay L. So in effect it will pay a floating-rate loan of less than LIBOR.

In this example, we showed how a swaption is used to create a swap. Similarly, a swaption can be used to terminate a swap.

5.2 Using an Interest Rate Swaption to Terminate a Swap

When a company enters a swap, it knows it may need to terminate the swap before the expiration day. It can do so by either entering an offsetting swap or buying a swaption.

As with any over-the-counter option, the holder of a swap can terminate the swap by entering into an identical swap from the opposite perspective at whatever rate exists in the market. Consider, for example, a Japanese company that enters into a five-year ¥800 million notional principal swap in which it pays a fixed rate and receives a floating rate; that is, it enters a pay-fixed swap. Two years later, the company wants to terminate the swap. It can do so by entering into a new swap with a notional principal of ¥800 million, a remaining life of three years, and with the company paying the floating rate and receiving the fixed rate. If it engages in this swap with a different counterparty than the counterparty of the original swap, then both swaps would remain in place, but the floating payments would be equivalent. The net effect would be that the company would make a stream of fixed payments at one rate and receive a stream of fixed payments at another rate. The rate that is greater depends on the course of interest rates since the time the original swap was put into place. If the new swap is done with the same counterparty as in the original swap, the two parties would likely agree to offset and eliminate both swaps. Then one party would be paying the other a lump sum of the present value of the difference between the two streams of fixed payments. If the company offsets the swap with a new swap in this manner, it must accept the conditions in the market at the time it offsets the swap.

The second way of terminating a swap is for a company to buy a swaption before it wants to offset the swap. Suppose that when this Japanese company enters into a pay-fixed, receive-floating swap, it also purchases a receiver swaption that allows it to enter into an ¥800 million swap to receive fixed and pay floating with the same terms as the original swap. The swaption exercise rate is 8 percent. The company must pay cash up front for the swaption, but it then has the right to enter into a new swap to receive a fixed rate of 8 percent and pay the floating rate. We assume for maximum flexibility that the swaption is structured as an American-style option, allowing the company to exercise it at any time. We also assume that the swaption counterparty is the counterparty to the swap, so that if the swaption is exercised, the payments can be canceled and replaced by a lump sum payment.

Consider this example. Internet Marketing Solutions (IMS) takes out a $20 million one-year loan with quarterly floating payments at LIBOR from a lender called Financial Solutions (FINSOLS). Fearing an increase in interest rates, IMS engages in a pay-fixed, receive-floating swap that converts the loan into a fixed-rate loan at 8 percent. IMS believes, however, that the interest rate outlook could change, and it would like the flexibility to terminate the swap, thereby returning to the status of a floating-rate payer. To give it this flexibility, IMS purchases an American-style receiver swaption for $515,000. The swaption allows it to enter into a receive-fixed, pay-floating swap at a fixed rate of 8 percent at the swaption expiration. The swap and swaption counterparty is Wheatstone Dealer (WHD).

Exhibit 13 illustrates this transaction. In Panel A, IMS takes out the loan from FINSOLS, receiving $20 million. It engages in the swap with WHD, thereby committing to pay fixed and receive LIBOR. There are no cash flows at the start of the swap contract, but IMS pays WHD $515,000 for the swaption. Now let us move to the expiration of the swaption, at which time we shall assume that IMS is no longer concerned about rising interest rates and would like to return to the status of a floating-rate borrower. In Panel B(i), at the expiration of the swaption, the market swap rate is greater than or equal to 8 percent. This panel shows the cash flows if the loan plus swap (note that the loan is floating rate) is converted to a fixed rate using the market fixed rate because the swaption is out-of-the-money. IMS makes interest payments of LIBOR(90/360)$20 million to FINSOLS. IMS makes a swap payment of 8 percent, which is $400,000, to WHD, which pays LIBOR.[31] Thus, to offset the effect of the pay-fixed swap, IMS is better off entering a new swap rather than exercising its swaption. IMS then enters into a swap to receive the market fixed rate, FS, which is greater than or equal to 8 percent, and pay LIBOR. IMS is, in effect, paying a floating rate less than LIBOR (or equal to LIBOR if the market swap rate is exactly 8 percent).[32]

In Panel B(ii), the market swap rate is less than 8 percent and the loan is converted back to a floating-rate loan by exercising the swaption. IMS makes loan interest payments at LIBOR to FINSOLS and swap payment of 8 percent or $400,000 to WHD, which pays LIBOR. Exercise of the swaption results in IMS entering into a swap to receive a fixed rate of 8 percent and pay a floating rate of LIBOR. The swap and swaption would probably be structured to offset and terminate both swaps. At the end of the transaction, the loan is paid off and there are no payments on the swap or swaption. If IMS wants to continue as a fixed-rate payer, the swaption would still be exercised if it is in-the-money but not if it is out-of-the-money.

---

[31] In practice, the two parties would net the difference and have one party pay the other.

[32] In practice, IMS might choose to not enter into the swap at the market fixed rate and just carry the old swap to reduce the cost of the loan.

EXHIBIT 13	Using an American-Style Swaption to Terminate a Swap

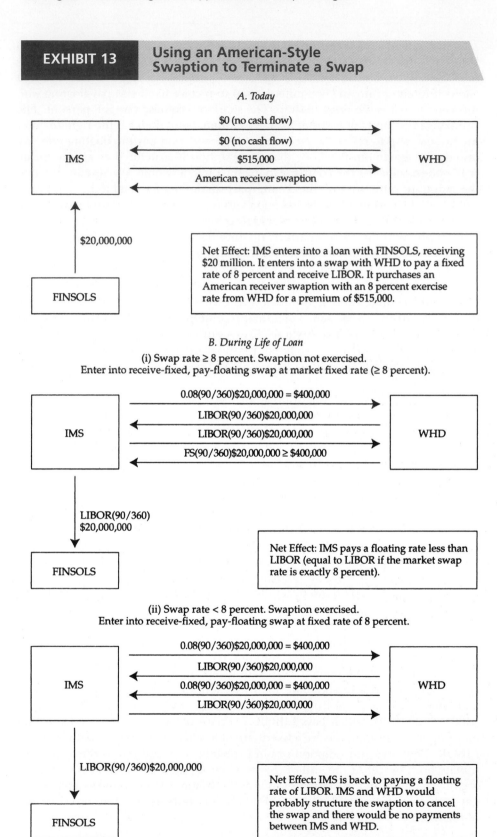

A. Today

$0 (no cash flow)

$0 (no cash flow)

$515,000

American receiver swaption

IMS

WHD

$20,000,000

FINSOLS

Net Effect: IMS enters into a loan with FINSOLS, receiving $20 million. It enters into a swap with WHD to pay a fixed rate of 8 percent and receive LIBOR. It purchases an American receiver swaption with an 8 percent exercise rate from WHD for a premium of $515,000.

B. During Life of Loan

(i) Swap rate ≥ 8 percent. Swaption not exercised.
Enter into receive-fixed, pay-floating swap at market fixed rate (≥ 8 percent).

0.08(90/360)$20,000,000 = $400,000

LIBOR(90/360)$20,000,000

LIBOR(90/360)$20,000,000

FS(90/360)$20,000,000 ≥ $400,000

IMS

WHD

LIBOR(90/360)
$20,000,000

FINSOLS

Net Effect: IMS pays a floating rate less than LIBOR (equal to LIBOR if the market swap rate is exactly 8 percent).

(ii) Swap rate < 8 percent. Swaption exercised.
Enter into receive-fixed, pay-floating swap at fixed rate of 8 percent.

0.08(90/360)$20,000,000 = $400,000

LIBOR(90/360)$20,000,000

0.08(90/360)$20,000,000 = $400,000

LIBOR(90/360)$20,000,000

IMS

WHD

LIBOR(90/360)$20,000,000

FINSOLS

Net Effect: IMS is back to paying a floating rate of LIBOR. IMS and WHD would probably structure the swaption to cancel the swap and there would be no payments between IMS and WHD.

We see that the swaption offers the holder the opportunity to terminate the swap at the exercise rate or better. Because the swaption is American style, a variety of complex issues are involved in the exercise decision, but let us focus on the **moneyness** and the holder's view of market conditions. If a borrower feels that rates will fall, it would then want to convert its pay-fixed position to a pay-floating position. If the market rate is more than the exercise rate, the borrower can do so by entering into a swap at the market rate. It can then receive more than the exercise rate, which more than offsets the rate it pays on the swap. The borrower would then effectively be paying less than LIBOR. If the rate in the market is less than the exercise rate, the borrower can exercise the swaption, thereby receiving the exercise rate to offset the rate it pays on the swap. Alternatively, it can choose to continue paying a floating rate but can still exercise the swaption if doing so is optimal.

As we previously described, swaptions are equivalent to options on bonds. A payer swaption is equivalent to a put option on a bond, and a receiver swaption is equivalent to a call option on a bond. The interest rate swaptions market is a very liquid one, and many companies use swaptions as substitutes for options on bonds. Any strategy that one might apply with options on bonds can be applied with swaptions. We shall not go over the myriad of such strategies, as they have been covered extensively in other literature. We shall, however, look at a particular one, in which a swaption can be used to substitute for a callable bond.

EXAMPLE 13

A company is engaged in a two-year swap with quarterly payments. It is paying 6 percent fixed and receiving LIBOR. It would like the flexibility to terminate the swap at any time prior to the end of the two-year period.

A. Identify the type of swaption that would achieve this objective.

B. Consider a time t during this two-year life of the swaption in which it is being considered for exercise. Use a 7 percent exercise rate. The fixed rate in the market on a swap that would offset the existing swap is denoted as FS(t,2). Examine the payoffs of the swaption based on whether FS(t,2) is 1) equal to or above 7 percent or 2) below 7 percent.

Solution to A: Because the company is paying a fixed rate and receiving a floating rate, it should enter into a swap to receive a fixed rate and pay a floating rate. It thus would want a receiver swaption. For maximum flexibility, it should structure the transaction as an American-style swaption.

Solution to B: FS(t,2) ≥ 7 percent

The swaption is out-of-the-money and is not exercised. To terminate the existing swap, one would enter into a swap at the market rate. This swap would involve receiving the market rate FS(t,2), which is at least 7 percent, and paying LIBOR. The LIBOR payments offset, and the net effect is a net positive cash flow of FS(t,2) − 6 percent.

FS(t,2) < 7 percent

Exercise the swaption, entering into a swap to receive 7 percent and pay LIBOR. The other swap involves paying 6 percent and receiving LIBOR. The LIBORs offset, leaving a net positive cash flow of 7 − 6 = 1 percent.

Note: It is not necessary that the net cash flow be positive. The positive net cash flow here is a result of choosing a 7 percent exercise rate, but a lower exercise rate could be chosen. The higher the exercise rate, the more expensive the receiver swaption.

5.3 Synthetically Removing (Adding) a Call Feature in Callable (Noncallable) Debt

A callable bond is a bond in which the issuer has the right to retire it early. The issuer has considerable flexibility to take advantage of declining interest rates. This feature is like a call option on the bond. As interest rates fall, bond prices rise. By calling the bond, the issuer essentially buys back the bond at predetermined terms, making it equivalent to exercising a call option to buy the bond. The issuer pays for this right by paying a higher coupon rate on the bond.

In some cases, the issuer of a callable bond may find that it no longer expects interest rates to fall sufficiently over the remaining life of the bond to justify calling the bond. Then it would feel that it is not likely to use the call feature, but it is still paying the higher coupon rate for the call feature. A swaption can be used to effectively sell the embedded call. This strategy involves synthetically removing the call from callable debt by selling a receiver swaption.[33] A receiver swaption (receive fixed) becomes more valuable as rates decline, thus balancing the short call. In effect, the call feature is sold for cash. Recall that a receiver swaption is like a call option on a bond. Because the issuer of the callable bond holds a call on the bond, it would need to sell a call to offset the call embedded in the debt. It can effectively do so by selling a receiver swaption. This swaption will not cancel the bond's call feature. Both options will be in force, but both options should behave identically. If the call feature is worth exercising, so should the swaption. Let us see how this strategy works.

5.3.1 Synthetically Removing the Call from Callable Debt

Several years ago, Chemical Industries (CHEMIND) issued a callable $20 million face value bond that pays a fixed rate of 8 percent interest semiannually. The bond now has five years until maturity. CHEMIND does not believe it is likely to call the bond for the next two years and would like to effectively eliminate the call feature during that time. To simplify the problem somewhat, we shall assume that the bond would be called only in exactly two years and not any time sooner. Thus, CHEMIND can manage this problem by selling a European swaption that would expire in two years.[34] Because the bond would have a three-year life when it is called, the swap underlying the swaption would be a three-year swap. It would also be a swap to receive fixed and pay floating, with payment dates aligned with the interest payment dates on the bond.

---

[33] This strategy is sometimes referred to as *monetizing* a call.

[34] CHEMIND might prefer an American swaption to give it the flexibility to exercise at any time, but we simplify the problem a little and use a European swaption.

Let us suppose that the 8 percent rate CHEMIND is paying on the bond includes a credit spread of 2.5 percent, which should be viewed as a credit premium paid over the LIBOR par rate. CHEMIND is paying 2.5 percent for the credit risk it poses for the holder of the bond. On the receiver swaption it wants to sell, CHEMIND must set the exercise rate at $8 - 2.5 = 5.5$ percent. Note that the credit spread is not part of the exercise rate. The swaption can be used to manage only the risk of interest rate changes driven by the term structure and not credit. We are assuming no change in CHEMIND's credit risk. Hence, it will continue to pay the credit spread in the rate on the new bond that it issues if it calls the old bond.

The swaption dealer, Top Swaps (TSWAPS), prices the swaption at $425,000. The strategy is illustrated in Exhibit 14.

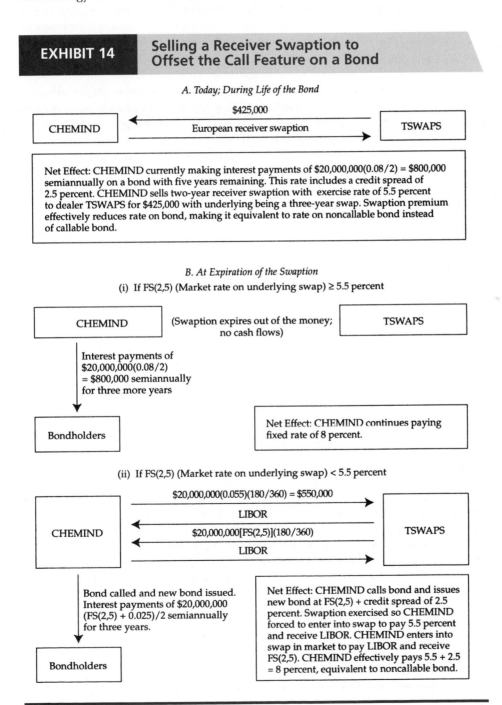

EXHIBIT 14 **Selling a Receiver Swaption to Offset the Call Feature on a Bond**

A. Today; During Life of the Bond

$425,000

CHEMIND ← European receiver swaption → TSWAPS

Net Effect: CHEMIND currently making interest payments of $20,000,000(0.08/2) = $800,000 semiannually on a bond with five years remaining. This rate includes a credit spread of 2.5 percent. CHEMIND sells two-year receiver swaption with exercise rate of 5.5 percent to dealer TSWAPS for $425,000 with underlying being a three-year swap. Swaption premium effectively reduces rate on bond, making it equivalent to rate on noncallable bond instead of callable bond.

B. At Expiration of the Swaption

(i) If FS(2,5) (Market rate on underlying swap) ≥ 5.5 percent

CHEMIND   (Swaption expires out of the money; no cash flows)   TSWAPS

Interest payments of $20,000,000(0.08/2) = $800,000 semiannually for three more years

↓

Bondholders

Net Effect: CHEMIND continues paying fixed rate of 8 percent.

(ii) If FS(2,5) (Market rate on underlying swap) < 5.5 percent

$20,000,000(0.055)(180/360) = $550,000

LIBOR

$20,000,000[FS(2,5)](180/360)

LIBOR

CHEMIND   TSWAPS

Bond called and new bond issued. Interest payments of $20,000,000 (FS(2,5) + 0.025)/2 semiannually for three years.

↓

Bondholders

Net Effect: CHEMIND calls bond and issues new bond at FS(2,5) + credit spread of 2.5 percent. Swaption exercised so CHEMIND forced to enter into swap to pay 5.5 percent and receive LIBOR. CHEMIND enters into swap in market to pay LIBOR and receive FS(2,5). CHEMIND effectively pays 5.5 + 2.5 = 8 percent, equivalent to noncallable bond.

Panel A shows that CHEMIND receives $425,000 from selling the receiver swaption to dealer TSWAPS. This cash effectively reduces its remaining interest payments on the bond. In Panel B, we see what happens at the swaption expiration in two years. Remember that the swaption is identical to a call option on the bond, so if the swaption is exercised, the call on the bond will be exercised at the same time. Let FS(2,5) be the fixed rate at the swaption expiration on a three-year swap. We first assume that FS(2,5) is greater than or equal to the exercise rate on the swaption of 5.5 percent. Because interest rates have not fallen below 5.5 percent, it is unprofitable to exercise the swaption or call the bond. CHEMIND continues making interest payments of 8 percent on $20 million, which is $800,000 semiannually for three more years. Panel B(i) illustrates this outcome.

In Panel B(ii), we let FS(2,5) be less than 5.5 percent. Then the swaption will be exercised and the bond will be called. To fund the bond call, a new bond will be issued at a rate of FS(2,5) plus the credit spread of 2.5 percent, which we assume has not changed. The swaption is exercised, so CHEMIND is obligated to enter into a swap to pay 5.5 percent and receive LIBOR. Now, however, CHEMIND is receiving LIBOR and making fixed payments to its bondholders and to TSWAPS. It can reverse the LIBOR flow by entering into a swap at the market rate of FS(2,5). In other words, it enters into a new swap to receive FS(2,5) and pay LIBOR. Note from the figure that it receives LIBOR and pays LIBOR. These two flows would likely be canceled. CHEMIND makes fixed swap payments at a rate of 5.5 percent and receives fixed swap payments at a rate of FS(2,5), which is 250 basis points (the credit spread) less than the rate on the new fixed rate bond it has issued. These payments at the rate FS(2,5) offset all but the credit spread portion of the interest payments on its loan. CHEMIND then effectively pays a fixed rate of 5.5 percent, the swaption exercise rate, plus 2.5 percent, the credit spread. So, CHEMIND ends up paying 8 percent, the same as the rate on the original debt. The swaption has effectively converted the callable bond into a noncallable bond by removing the call feature from the bond. It hopes that this outcome, in which the bond is called and the swaption is exercised, does not occur, or it will regret having removed the call feature. Nonetheless, it received cash up front for the swaption and is paying a lower effective interest rate as it would had the bond been noncallable in the first place, so it must accept this risk.

5.3.2 Synthetically Adding a Call to Noncallable Debt

If a swaption can undo a call feature, it can also add a call feature. Market Solutions, Inc. (MSI) has a $40 million noncallable bond outstanding at a rate of 9 percent paid semiannually with three more years remaining. Anticipating the possibility of declining interest rates in about one year, MSI wishes this bond were callable. It can synthetically add the call feature by purchasing a receiver swaption. A receiver swaption is equivalent to a call option on a bond because the option to receive a fixed rate increases in value as rates decline. By purchasing the receiver swaption, it has in effect purchased an option on the bond.

To structure the receiver swaption properly, MSI notes that the interest rate it is paying on the bond includes a credit spread of 3 percent over the par bond rate from the LIBOR term structure. It should set the exercise rate on the swaption at $9 - 3 = 6$ percent. The swaption will be on a two-year swap with payment dates coinciding with the interest payment dates on the bond. The notional principal will be the $40 million face value on the bond. To simplify the problem, we assume a European swaption, meaning that the only time MSI will consider exercising the swaption or calling the bond will be in exactly one year, with the bond having two years to maturity at that time. The swaption will cost $625,000, and the counterparty dealer will be Swap Shop (SWSHP). Exhibit 15 illustrates the transaction.

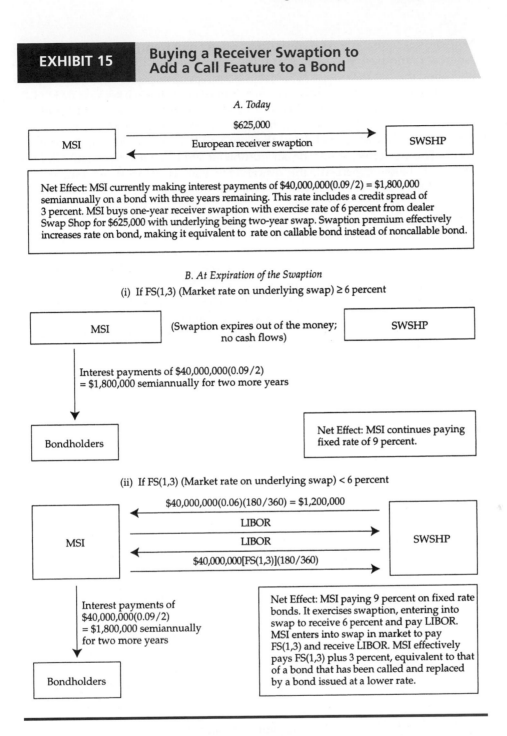

EXHIBIT 15 Buying a Receiver Swaption to Add a Call Feature to a Bond

A. Today

$625,000

MSI → European receiver swaption → SWSHP

Net Effect: MSI currently making interest payments of $40,000,000(0.09/2) = $1,800,000 semiannually on a bond with three years remaining. This rate includes a credit spread of 3 percent. MSI buys one-year receiver swaption with exercise rate of 6 percent from dealer Swap Shop for $625,000 with underlying being two-year swap. Swaption premium effectively increases rate on bond, making it equivalent to rate on callable bond instead of noncallable bond.

B. At Expiration of the Swaption

(i) If FS(1,3) (Market rate on underlying swap) ≥ 6 percent

MSI — (Swaption expires out of the money; no cash flows) — SWSHP

Interest payments of $40,000,000(0.09/2) = $1,800,000 semiannually for two more years

→ Bondholders

Net Effect: MSI continues paying fixed rate of 9 percent.

(ii) If FS(1,3) (Market rate on underlying swap) < 6 percent

$40,000,000(0.06)(180/360) = $1,200,000
LIBOR
LIBOR
$40,000,000[FS(1,3)](180/360)

MSI ↔ SWSHP

Interest payments of $40,000,000(0.09/2) = $1,800,000 semiannually for two more years

→ Bondholders

Net Effect: MSI paying 9 percent on fixed rate bonds. It exercises swaption, entering into swap to receive 6 percent and pay LIBOR. MSI enters into swap in market to pay FS(1,3) and receive LIBOR. MSI effectively pays FS(1,3) plus 3 percent, equivalent to that of a bond that has been called and replaced by a bond issued at a lower rate.

In Panel A, we see MSI paying $625,000 for the swaption. This cost effectively raises the interest rate MSI pays on the bond to that of a callable bond. Panel B(i) illustrates the case in which the fixed rate on the underlying swap, FS(1,3), is greater than or equal to the exercise rate on the swaption at the swaption expiration. Remember that if market conditions are such that the swaption would be exercised, then the bond would be called. In this case, however, interest rates are not low enough to justify exercise of the swaption or calling of the bond. MSI will continue making its 9 percent interest payments on the bond.

In Panel B(ii), we let FS(1,3) be less than 6 percent. Then MSI will exercise the swaption, thereby entering into a swap to pay LIBOR and receive 6 percent.

Note, however, that it is receiving a fixed rate of 6 percent, paying a fixed rate of 9 percent, and paying LIBOR. Here, this transaction is not equivalent to it having called the bond, because MSI makes floating payments. To offset the floating payments, it enters into a new swap in the market at the market rate of FS(1,3). Specifically, it pays FS(1,3) and receives LIBOR. The two streams of LIBOR payments would offset and would probably be canceled, leaving an inflow of 6 percent and an outflow of FS(1,3) on the swaps and an outflow of 9 percent on the bond. The net effect would be an outflow of FS(1,3) plus 3 percent. Because FS(1,3) is below 6 percent, the overall rate paid is below 9 percent, thereby making this position similar to that of a bond that has been called, with a new bond issued in its place at a lower rate.

So we see that a swaption can be used to replicate the call feature on a callable bond. A swaption can synthetically add a call feature when it does not exist or offset a call feature that does exist. The cash paid or received from the swaption occurs all at once, but if allocated appropriately over time, it would be equivalent to the additional amount of interest that a borrower pays for the call feature. Of course, there are some tricky elements to making this strategy work. We have ignored taxes and transaction costs, which can affect exercise and call decisions. Also, when the swaption is held by another party, there is no guarantee that exercise will occur at the optimal time.

EXAMPLE 14

A German company issues a five-year noncallable bond with a face value of €40 million. The bond pays a coupon annually of 10 percent, of which 3 percent is estimated to be a credit premium.

A. The company would like to make the bond callable in exactly two years. Design a strategy using a European swaption that will achieve this goal. When the swaption expires, the fixed rate on the underlying swap will be denoted as FS(2,5). Evaluate what happens when this rate is at least the exercise rate and also when it is less than the exercise rate.

B. Reconsider the bond described above and assume it was actually issued as a callable bond with a 10 percent coupon. Construct a swaption strategy that will synthetically remove the call feature. As in Part A, let the swaption expire in two years and evaluate the outcomes.

Solution to A: To synthetically add the call feature to this bond, the company should purchase a receiver swaption. The exercise rate should be the coupon rate on the bond minus the credit premium: $10 - 3 = 7$ percent. At the swaption expiration, we have the following outcomes:

FS(2,5) ≥ 7 percent

The swaption will not be exercised, and the bond will not be called. The company continues to pay 10 percent on its bond.

FS(2,5) < 7 percent
 The swaption is exercised.
  Enter into swap
  Receive 7 percent
  Pay LIBOR
 Enter into a new swap at the market rate.
  Receive LIBOR
  Pay FS(2,5)
  Company continues to pay 10 percent on its bond
 Net effect: Pay FS(2,5) + 10% − 7% = Pay FS(2,5) + 3% < 10%

The company has thus effectively issued a new bond at a lower rate. The option premium, however, effectively raised the coupon rate on the old bond to that of a callable bond.

Solution to B: To synthetically remove the call feature on this bond, the company should sell a receiver swaption. The exercise rate should be the coupon rate on the bond minus the credit premium: 10 − 3 = 7 percent. At the swaption expiration, we have the following outcomes:

FS(2,5) ≥ 7 percent
 The swaption will not be exercised. The company continues to pay 10 percent on its bond.

FS(2,5) < 7 percent
 The swaption is exercised.
  Enter into swap
  Receive LIBOR
  Pay 7 percent
 Enter into a new swap at the market rate.
  Receive FS(2,5)
  Pay LIBOR
  Bond called. Issue new bond at FS(2,5) + 3%
 Net effect: Pay FS(2,5) + 3% + 7% − FS(2,5) = 10%

Therefore, if the company sells the receiver swaption, the bond's call option is offset and effectively removed. The option premium, received up front, effectively reduces the coupon rate on the outstanding bond to make it equivalent to that of a noncallable bond.

Finally, you may be wondering why a receiver swaption was used in these strategies. Why not a payer swaption? Remember that a call feature on a bond is a call option. To add or offset a call feature, we need to use an instrument equivalent to a call option. A receiver swaption is equivalent to a call option. A payer swaption is equivalent to a put option. Payer swaptions would be useful in situations involving put features. Putable bonds do exist but are not particularly common. A putable bond allows the bondholder to sell the bond back, usually at par, to the issuer. Therefore, the option, which is a put, is held by the bondholder and sold by the bond issuer. If a bond is putable, the coupon rate on the bond would be lower. If the issuer of the bond wanted to synthetically add a put to an otherwise nonputable bond, it would sell a payer swaption. The premium received would effectively lower the coupon rate on the bond. If the issuer of a putable bond wanted to eliminate the put, it would buy a payer swaption. This would give it the right to exercise the swaption, which is a put on the bond, at the same time as the put feature would be exercised by the holder of the bond. Again, we note that put features are not common, and we shall not pursue this strategy here.

5.4 A Note on Forward Swaps

There are also forward contracts on swaps. Called **forward swaps**, these instruments are commitments to enter into swaps. They do not require a cash payment at the start but force the parties to enter into a swap at a later date at terms, including the fixed rate, set at the start. Although we shall not examine forward swap strategies, note that the same strategies examined in this section can all be used with forward swaps.

6　CONCLUSIONS

In Readings 38, 39, and 40 we saw how to use forwards, futures, options, and swaps in strategies. These instruments are designed to manage risk. Managing risk involves the buying and selling of risk, perhaps to increase the overall level of one's risk or perhaps to offset an existing risk. As we have seen, these instruments are highly leveraged. As you can imagine, proper use of derivatives requires a significant amount of expertise. More importantly, however, monitoring and control are essential ingredients for the proper use of derivatives. Managing risk is the primary justification for the use of derivatives.

SUMMARY

▶ A floating-rate loan can be converted to a fixed-rate loan by entering into an interest rate swap to pay a fixed rate and receive a floating rate. The floating cash flows offset, leaving the borrower with a net fixed payment. Likewise, a fixed-rate loan can be converted to a floating-rate loan by entering into an interest rate swap to pay a floating rate and receive a fixed rate. The fixed cash flows offset, leaving the party paying a floating rate.

▶ To obtain the duration of an interest rate swap, consider the difference between the duration of a fixed-rate bond and the duration of a floating-rate bond. The latter is close to zero, leaving the duration of an interest rate swap close to that of a fixed-rate bond. If the party pays a fixed rate and receives a floating rate, the duration of the position is that of the equivalent floating-rate bond minus that of the equivalent fixed-rate bond.

▶ When a floating-rate loan is converted to a fixed-rate loan, the resulting duration is that of a fixed-rate loan. The duration of a fixed-rate loan is normally much higher than that of a floating-rate loan, which has a duration relatively close to zero. Compared with a floating-rate loan, however, a fixed-rate loan has stable cash flows, which reduce cash flow risk, but has a much greater duration, which increases market value risk.

▶ The notional principal on an interest rate swap added to a position to adjust its overall duration is determined by the existing duration of the portfolio, the duration of the swap, the desired duration, and the market value of the portfolio. A swap can be used to change the duration of the position without changing the market value.

▶ An interest rate swap can be used to manage the risk related to a structured note with a coupon at a multiple of a floating rate by adjusting the notional principal on the swap to reflect the coupon multiple for the structured note. The swap should be a receive-floating, pay-fixed swap.

▶ An interest rate swap can be used to manage the risk of the issuance of an inverse floating-rate note by paying the floating rate to the swap dealer. When interest rates rise (fall), the inverse floater payments decrease (increase), and this effect is passed on to the dealer, which in turn pays a fixed rate.

▶ A loan in one currency can be converted into a loan in another currency by entering into a currency swap in which it pays interest in one currency and receives interest in the currency in which it makes its loan interest payments. This strategy leaves the borrower paying interest in a different currency than the one in which the loan interest is paid. To offset the principal payment, the currency swap should provide for payment of the notional principal as well.

▶ Converting a loan in one currency into a loan in another using a currency swap can offer savings because a borrower can normally issue debt at a more attractive rate in its own currency. By entering into a swap with a dealer that can operate more efficiently in global markets, the borrower can effectively convert its domestic debt into foreign debt. In addition, by engaging in the currency swap rather than borrowing in the desired currency in the first place, the borrower takes on a small amount of credit risk that can generate savings if no default takes place.

▶ The party to a currency swap would make the payments be fixed or floating depending on whether a loan paired with the currency swap is made at a fixed or floating rate and whether the party wants to make payments at a fixed or floating rate. This decision is usually made based on the expected direction of interest rates.

► A series of foreign cash receipts can be combined with a currency swap with no notional principal payments to convert the receipts into domestic currency cash flows. The foreign interest payments on the currency swap must equal the amounts of the foreign cash flows.

► In a dual-currency bond, the interest is paid in one currency and the principal is paid in another. A borrower issuing a dual-currency bond can use the proceeds to buy a bond denominated in the currency of the principal repayment on the dual-currency bond. It can then enter into a currency swap with no notional principal payment, enabling it to fund the interest payments from the dual-currency bond in one currency and make interest payments in another currency.

► An equity swap can be used to provide diversification to a concentrated portfolio by having the party pay the return on the stock that makes up too large a portion of the portfolio and receive the return on a diversified market proxy.

► An equity swap can add international diversification to a domestic portfolio by having the party pay the return on a domestic market benchmark and receive the return on an international market benchmark.

► An equity swap can be used to change the allocation between stock and bond asset classes by having the party pay the return on the asset class in which it wants to reduce its exposure and receive the return on the asset class in which it wants to increase its exposure.

► A corporate insider can use an equity swap to reduce exposure to his company by paying the return on the company's stock and receiving the return on a diversified portfolio benchmark or a fixed- or floating-rate interest payment.

► There can be important implications if corporate insiders use equity swaps. Insiders can reduce their exposure without giving up their voting rights, which can lead to significant agency costs. Although it is clearly necessary for investors and analysts to gauge the exposure of corporate insiders, equity swaps can make this task more difficult.

► Equity swaps pose some difficulties not faced in interest rate and currency swaps. In particular, equity swaps can generate significant cash flow problems, resulting from the fact that equity returns can be negative, meaning that one party can be required to make both sides of payments. In addition, equity swaps can involve tracking error, in which the swap returns, which are pegged to an index, do not match the returns on the actual equity portfolio that is combined with the swap.

► A party would use an interest rate swaption if it anticipates taking out a loan at a future date and entering into a swap to convert the loan from floating rate to fixed rate or vice versa. The swaption gives the party the right to enter into the swap at a specific fixed rate or better. The cost of this flexibility is the swaption premium paid up front.

► An interest rate swaption can be used to provide a means of terminating a swap at a favorable rate. A party engaged in a swap can use a swap with the opposite cash flows to effectively terminate the position. By purchasing a swaption, the party can enter into this swap at a specific rate, established in advance, or take a better rate as given in the market.

▶ An interest rate receiver swaption is equivalent to a call option on a bond. A party that has issued a callable bond and believes it will not call the bond can sell an interest rate receiver swaption to offset the call feature. The swaption premium received at the start offsets the higher coupon paid for the call feature on the bond. If interest rates fall enough to trigger the bond being called, the swaption will also be exercised. The party must enter into the underlying swap and can enter into an opposite swap at the market rate. The net effect is that the party ends up paying the same rate it would have paid if it had not called the bond.

▶ A party that has issued a noncallable bond can synthetically add a call feature by purchasing an interest rate receiver swaption. The premium paid for the swaption effectively raises the coupon rate on the bond. If rates fall sufficiently, the receiver swaption is exercised and the party enters into the underlying swap. The party then enters into a swap in the market at the market rate. The net effect is that the party pays a lower fixed rate, as though the bond had been called.

PRACTICE PROBLEMS FOR READING 40

1. A company has issued floating-rate notes with a maturity of one year, an interest rate of LIBOR plus 125 basis points, and total face value of $50 million. The company now believes that interest rates will rise and wishes to protect itself by entering into an interest rate swap. A dealer provides a quote on a swap in which the company will pay a fixed rate 6.5 percent and receive LIBOR. Interest is paid quarterly, and the current LIBOR is 5 percent. Indicate how the company can use a swap to convert the debt to a fixed rate. Calculate the overall net payment (including the loan) by the company. Assume that all payments will be made on the basis of 90/360.

2. Assume that you manage a $100 million bond portfolio with a duration of 1.5 years. You wish to increase the duration of the bond portfolio to 3.5 years by using a swap. Assume the duration of a fixed-rate bond is 75 percent of its maturity.

   A. Discuss whether the swap you enter into should involve paying fixed, receiving floating or paying floating, receiving fixed.

   B. Would you prefer a four-year swap with quarterly payments or a three-year swap with semiannual payments?

   C. Determine the notional principal of the swap you would prefer.

3. A company issues a leveraged floating-rate note with a face value of $5,000,000 that pays a coupon of 2.5 times LIBOR. The company plans to generate a profit by selling the notes, using the proceeds to purchase a bond with a fixed coupon rate of 7 percent a year, and hedging the risk by entering into an appropriate swap. A swap dealer provides a quote with a fixed rate of 6 percent and a floating rate of LIBOR. Discuss whether the company should enter into a swap involving paying fixed, receiving floating or paying floating, receiving fixed. Calculate the amount of the arbitrage profit the company can earn by entering into the appropriate swap. In your answer, indicate the cash flows generated at each step. Also explain what additional risk the company is taking on by doing the swap.

4. A U.S. company needs to raise €100,000,000. It plans to raise this money by issuing dollar-denominated bonds and using a currency swap to convert the dollars to euros. The company expects interest rates in both the United States and the eurozone to fall.

   A. Should the swap be structured with interest paid at a fixed or a floating rate?

   B. Should the swap be structured with interest received at a fixed or a floating rate?

5. A company based in the United Kingdom has a German subsidiary. The subsidiary generates €15,000,000 a year, received in equivalent semiannual installments of €7,500,000. The British company wishes to convert the euro cash flows to pounds twice a year. It plans to engage in a currency swap in order to lock in the exchange rate at which it can convert the euros to pounds. The current exchange rate is €1.5/£. The fixed rate on a plain vanilla currency swap in pounds is 7.5 percent per year, and the fixed rate on a plain vanilla currency swap in euros is 6.5 percent per year.

   A. Determine the notional principals in euros and pounds for a swap with semiannual payments that will help achieve the objective.

   B. Determine the semiannual cash flows from this swap.

6. A portfolio has a total market value of $105,000,000. The portfolio is allocated as follows: $65,000,000 is invested in a broadly diversified portfolio of domestic stocks, and $40,000,000 is invested in the stock of the JK Corporation. The portfolio manager wishes to reduce exposure to JK stock by $30,000,000. The manager plans to achieve this objective by entering into a three-year equity swap using the S&P 500. Assume that settlement is made at the end of each year. Also assume that after one year the return on JK stock is 4 percent and the return on the S&P 500 market index is −3 percent.

A. Explain the structure of the equity swap.

B. Calculate the net cash flow for the swap at the end of one year.

7. The LKS Company is a U.S.-based mutual fund company that manages a global portfolio 80 percent invested in domestic stocks and 20 percent invested in international stocks. The international component mimics the MSCI EAFE index. The total market value of the portfolio is $750,000,000. The fund manager wishes to reduce the allocation to domestic stocks to 70 percent and increase the international allocation to 30 percent. The manager plans to achieve this objective by entering into a two-year equity swap using the Russell 3000 and the EAFE index. Assume that settlement is made at the end of the first year. Also assume that after one year, the return on the Russell 3000 market index is 5 percent and the return on the EAFE index is 6 percent.

A. Explain the structure of the equity swap.

B. Calculate the net cash flow for the swap at the end of one year.

8. A diversified portfolio with a market value of $800,000,000 currently has the following allocations:

Equity	80 percent	$640,000,000
Bonds	20 percent	$160,000,000

The equity portion of the portfolio is allocated as follows:

U.S. large-cap stocks	70 percent	$448,000,000
International stocks	30 percent	$192,000,000

The bond portion of the portfolio is allocated as follows:

U.S. government bonds	80 percent	$128,000,000
U.S corporate bonds	20 percent	$32,000,000

The portfolio manager wishes to change the overall allocation of the portfolio to 75 percent equity and 25 percent bonds. Within the equity category, the new allocation is to be 75 percent U.S. large cap and 25 percent international stocks. In the bond category, the new allocation is to be 75 percent U.S. government bonds and 25 percent U.S. corporate bonds. The manager wants to use four-year swaps to achieve the desired allocations, with settlements at the end of each year. Assume that the counterparty payments or receipts are tied to LIBOR. Use generic stock or bond indices where appropriate. Indicate how the manager can use swaps to achieve the desired allocations. Construct the most efficient overall swap, in which all equivalent but opposite LIBOR payments are consolidated.

9. A company plans to borrow $20,000,000 in two years. The loan will be for three years and pay a floating interest rate of **LIBOR** with interest payments made every quarter. The company expects interest rates to rise in future years and thus is certain to swap the loan into a fixed-rate loan. In order to ensure that it can lock in an attractive rate, the company plans to purchase a payer swaption expiring in two years, with an exercise rate of 5 percent a year. The cost of the swaption is $250,000, and the settlement dates coincide with the interest payment dates for the original loan. Assume **LIBOR** at the beginning of the settlement period is 6.5 percent a year.

   A. Calculate the net cash flows on the first settlement date if FS(2,5) is above the exercise rate.

   B. Calculate the net cash flows on the first settlement date if FS(2,5) is below the exercise rate.

Questions 10–15 relate to Catherine Gide

All rely on Readings 38, 39, and 40, excepting Question 12, which relies on Reading 46.

Catherine Gide is the risk management director of the Millau Corporation, a large, diversified, French multinational corporation with subsidiaries in Japan, the United States, and Switzerland. One of Gide's primary responsibilities is to manage Millau's currency exposure. She has the flexibility to take tactical positions in foreign exchange markets if these positions are justified by her research. Gide and her assistant, Albert Darc, are meeting to discuss how best to deal with Millau's currency exposure over the next 12 months.

Specifically, Gide is concerned about the following:

1. Millau has just sold a Japanese subsidiary for 65 billion yen (JPY65,000,000,000). Because of an impending tax law change, Gide wishes to wait six months before repatriating these funds. Gide plans to invest the sale proceeds in six-month Japanese government securities and hedge the currency risk by using forward contracts. Gide's research indicates that the yen will depreciate against the euro (EUR) over the next six months. Darc has gathered the exchange rate and interest rate information given in Exhibit 1. The day-count convention is 30/360.

2. Millau has a contract to deliver computerized machine tools to a U.S. buyer in three months. A payment of 50 million U.S. dollars (USD50,000,000) is due from the buyer at that time. Gide is concerned about the dollar weakening relative to the euro. She plans to use options to hedge this currency exposure. Specifically, Gide expects the U.S. dollar to weaken to 1.2250USD/EUR in the next three months. Euro options quotations are given in Exhibit 2. All options are European-style and expire in three months.

3. Darc says to Gide:

   "I believe the volatility of the USD/EUR exchange rate will soon increase by more than the market expects. We may be able to profit from this volatility increase by buying an equal number of at-the-money call and put options on the euro at the same strike price and expiration date."

4. Millau needs 100 million Swiss francs (CHF100,000,000) for a period of one year. Millau can issue at par a 2.8 percent one-year euro-denominated note with semiannual coupons and swap the proceeds into Swiss francs. The euro swap fixed rate is 2.3 percent and the Swiss franc swap fixed rate is 0.8 percent.

Darc tells Gide that he expects interest rates in both the euro currency zone and Switzerland to rise in the near future. Exchange rate and interest rate information is given in Exhibit 1.

| EXHIBIT 1 | Exchange Rate and Interest Rate Information | | | |

Currency Exchange Rates	Spot	3-Month Forward	6-Month Forward	1-Year Forward
U.S. dollars per euro (USD/EUR)	1.1930	1.1970	1.2030	1.2140
Japanese yen per euro (JPY/EUR)	133.83	133.14	132.46	131.13
Swiss francs per euro (CHF/EUR)	1.5540	1.5490	1.5440	1.5340

Annualized Risk-free Interest Rates (%)	1 Month	3 Month	6 Month	1 Year
Euro area	2.110	2.120	2.130	2.150
United States	3.340	3.560	3.770	3.990
Japan	0.040	0.056	0.066	0.090
Switzerland	0.730	0.750	0.760	0.780

| EXHIBIT 2 | Euro Options Quotations (Options Expire in Three Months) | |

Strike (USD/EUR)	Calls on Euro (USD/EUR)	Puts on Euro (USD/EUR)
1.1800	0.0275	0.0125
1.1900	0.0216	0.0161
1.2000	0.0169	0.0211
1.2100	0.0127	0.0278

10. If Gide uses a six-month forward currency contract to convert the yen received from the sale of the Japanese subsidiary into euros, the total amount Millau will receive is *closest* to:

A. EUR490,714,000.

B. EUR490,876,000.

C. EUR490,935,000.

D. EUR491,038,000.

11. If Gide uses a six-month forward currency contract to convert the yen received from the sale of the Japanese subsidiary into euros, the annualized return in euros that Millau will realize is *closest* to:

A. 0.066%.

B. 2.064%.

C. 2.130%.

D. 2.196%.

12. Based on Gide's expectation for the USD/EUR rate in concern #2, Gide's *most* appropriate action with regard to the USD50,000,000 due in three months is to:

   A. remain unhedged.

   B. buy euro puts with a strike price of 1.2100USD/EUR.

   C. buy euro calls with a strike price of 1.1800USD/EUR.

   D. buy euro puts with a strike price of 1.2100USD/EUR and sell euro calls with a strike price of 1.1800USD/EUR.

13. Darc's statement to Gide (in concern #3) about the option strategy to use in order to profit from a volatility increase of the euro/U.S. dollar exchange rate is:

   A. correct.

   B. incorrect, because he is describing a strategy that benefits only from a weakening euro.

   C. incorrect, because he is describing a strategy that benefits only from a strengthening euro.

   D. incorrect, because he is describing a strategy that benefits from low volatility in the exchange rate.

14. If Millau issues euro-denominated debt and enters into a fixed-rate currency swap (in concern #4), which of the following *best* describes transactions between Millau and the swap counterparty in six months? Millau pays the swap counterparty:

   A. EUR740,026 and receives CHF400,000.

   B. EUR900,901 and receives CHF800,000.

   C. CHF400,000 and receives EUR740,026.

   D. CHF800,000 and receives EUR900,901.

15. Based on Darc's interest rate expectations for the euro currency zone and Switzerland, Gide's *best* choice is to structure the currency swap so that Millau pays interest at a:

   A. fixed rate and receives it at a fixed rate.

   B. fixed rate and receives it at a floating rate.

   C. floating rate and receives it at a fixed rate.

   D. floating rate and receives it at a floating rate.

Questions 16–21 relate to Hadley Elbridge

All rely on Readings 38, 39, and 40.

Hadley Elbridge, managing director for Humber Wealth Managers, LLC, is concerned about the risk level of a client's equity portfolio. The client, Pat Cassidy, has 60 percent of this portfolio invested in two equity positions: Hop Industries and Sure Securities. Cassidy refuses to sell his shares in either company, but has agreed to use option strategies to manage these concentrated equity positions. Elbridge recommends either a collar strategy or a protective put strategy on the Hop position, and a covered call strategy on the Sure position. The options available to construct the positions are shown in Exhibit 1.

EXHIBIT 1	Equity Positions and Options Available			
Stock	**Shares**	**Stock Price**	**Options**	**Option Price**
Hop	375,000	$26.20	September 25.00 put	$0.80
			September 27.50 call	$0.65
Sure	300,000	$34.00	September 32.50 put	$0.85
			September 35.00 call	$1.20

Cassidy makes the following comments:

1. "The Hop protective put position provides a maximum per share loss of $2.00 and a breakeven underlying price at expiration of $27.00."

2. "The Sure covered call position provides a maximum per share gain of $2.20 and a breakeven underlying price at expiration of $32.80."

3. "The general shape of a profit-and-loss graph for the protective put closely resembles the general shape of the graph for another common option position."

Elbridge also investigates whether a privately negotiated equity swap could be used to reduce the risk of the Hop and Sure holdings. A swap dealer offers Elbridge the following:

▶ The dealer will receive the return on 250,000 shares of Hop and 200,000 shares of Sure from Cassidy.

▶ The dealer will pay Cassidy the return on an equivalent dollar amount on the Russell 3000 index.

The dealer demonstrates the quarterly cash flows of this transaction under the assumptions that Hop is up 2 percent, Sure is up 4 percent, and the Russell 3000 is up 5 percent for the quarter.

The remaining 40 percent of Cassidy's equity portfolio is invested in a diversified portfolio of equities valued at $13,350,000. Elbridge believes this portfolio is too risky, so he recommends lowering the beta of this portfolio from its current level of 1.20 to a target beta of 0.80. To accomplish this, he will use a two-month futures contract with a price (including multiplier) of $275,000 and a beta of 0.97.

16. Disregarding the initial cost of the Hop collar strategy, the value per share of the strategy at expiration with the stock at $26.90 is:

    A. $26.05.

    B. $26.20.

    C. $26.75.

    D. $26.90.

17. Cassidy's comments #1 and #2 about the Hop protective put and Sure covered call positions, respectively, are:

	Protective Put	Covered Call
A.	Correct	Correct
B.	Correct	Incorrect
C.	Incorrect	Correct
D.	Incorrect	Incorrect

18. The general shape of the profit-and-loss graph in Cassidy's comment #3 is *most* similar to the general shape of the profit-and-loss graph for:

    A. buying a call.

    B. selling a call.

    C. buying a put.

    D. selling a put.

19. If an options dealer takes the other side of the Sure option position, the dealer's initial option delta and hedging transaction, respectively, will be:

	Dealer's Initial Option Delta	Dealer's Hedging Transaction
A.	Negative	Buy the underlying
B.	Negative	Sell the underlying
C.	Positive	Buy the underlying
D.	Positive	Sell the underlying

20. What is the payoff to Cassidy in the equity swap example?

    A. −$269,500.

    B. −$264,500.

    C. $264,500.

    D. $269,500.

2006 exam

21. To achieve the target beta on Cassidy's diversified stock portfolio, Elbridge would sell the following number of futures contracts (rounded to the nearest whole contract):

A. 6.

B. 13.

C. 20.

D. 27.

STUDY SESSION 14
EXECUTION OF PORTFOLIO DECISIONS

Because the investment process is not complete until securities are bought or sold, the quality of trade execution is an important determinant of investment results. The methods by which managers and traders interact with markets, choose appropriate trading strategies and tactics, and measure success in execution are key topics in Reading 41.

READING ASSIGNMENT

Reading 41 Execution of Portfolio Decisions

LEARNING OUTCOMES

Reading 41: Execution of Portfolio Decisions

The candidate should be able to:

a. compare and contrast market orders to limit orders, including the price and execution uncertainty of each;

b. calculate and interpret the effective spread of a market order and contrast it to the quoted bid-ask spread as a measure of trading cost;

c. compare and contrast alternative market structures and their relative advantages;

d. compare and contrast the roles of brokers and dealers;

e. explain the criteria of market quality and evaluate the quality of a market when given a description of its characteristics;

f. review the components of execution costs, including explicit and implicit costs, and evaluate a trade in terms of these costs;

g. calculate, interpret, and explain the importance of implementation shortfall as a measure of transaction costs;

h. contrast volume weighted average price (VWAP) and implementation shortfall as measures of transaction costs;

i. explain the use of econometric methods in pre-trade analysis to estimate implicit transaction costs;

j. discuss the major types of traders, based on their motivation to trade, time versus price preferences, and preferred order types;

279

k. describe the suitable uses of major trading tactics, evaluate their relative costs, advantages, and weaknesses, and recommend a trading tactic when given a description of the investor's motivation to trade, the size of the trade, and key market characteristics;

l. explain the motivation for algorithmic trading and discuss the basic classes of algorithmic trading strategies;

m. discuss and justify the factors that typically determine the selection of a specific algorithmic trading strategy, including order size, average daily trading volume, bid-ask spread, and the urgency of the order;

n. explain the meaning and criteria of best execution;

o. evaluate a firm's investment and trading procedures, including processes, disclosures, and record keeping, with respect to best execution;

p. discuss the role of ethics in trading.

EXECUTION OF PORTFOLIO DECISIONS

by Ananth Madhavan, Jack L. Treynor, and Wayne H. Wagner

LEARNING OUTCOMES

The candidate should be able to:

a. compare and contrast market orders to limit orders, including the price and execution uncertainty of each;

b. calculate and interpret the effective spread of a market order and contrast it to the quoted bid-ask spread as a measure of trading cost;

c. compare and contrast alternative market structures and their relative advantages;

d. compare and contrast the roles of brokers and dealers;

e. explain the criteria of market quality and evaluate the quality of a market when given a description of its characteristics;

f. review the components of execution costs, including explicit and implicit costs, and evaluate a trade in terms of these costs;

g. calculate, interpret, and explain the importance of implementation shortfall as a measure of transaction costs;

h. contrast volume weighted average price (VWAP) and implementation shortfall as measures of transaction costs;

i. explain the use of econometric methods in pre-trade analysis to estimate implicit transaction costs;

j. discuss the major types of traders, based on their motivation to trade, time versus price preferences, and preferred order types;

k. describe the suitable uses of major trading tactics, evaluate their relative costs, advantages, and weaknesses, and recommend a trading tactic when given a description of the investor's motivation to trade, the size of the trade, and key market characteristics;

l. explain the motivation for algorithmic trading and discuss the basic classes of algorithmic trading strategies;

m. discuss and justify the factors that typically determine the selection of a specific algorithmic trading strategy, including order size, average daily trading volume, bid-ask spread, and the urgency of the order;

n. explain the meaning and criteria of best execution;

Managing Investment Portfolios: A Dynamic Process, Third Edition, John L. Maginn, Donald L. Tuttle, Jerald E. Pinto, and Dennis W. McLeavey, editors. Copyright © 2007 by CFA Institute. Reprinted with permission.

> **o.** evaluate a firm's investment and trading procedures, including processes, disclosures, and record keeping, with respect to best execution;
>
> **p.** discuss the role of ethics in trading.

1 INTRODUCTION

The investment process has been described as a three-legged stool supported equally by securities research, portfolio management, and securities trading. Of the three, trading is often the least understood and least appreciated function. As we will show, a deeper appreciation for the trading function can be a powerful help in achieving investment success.

In this reading, we will build the knowledge and explain the concepts needed to understand how managers and traders interact with markets, choose trading strategies and tactics, and measure their success in trading. Our perspective is chiefly that of a portfolio manager (or investment advisor) whose objective is to execute portfolio decisions in the best interests of the client. The portfolio manager's agents in doing so are the firm's traders. These **buy-side traders** are the professional traders employed by investment managers or institutional investors who place the trades that execute the decisions of portfolio managers. The job of such traders is to execute the desired trades quickly, without error, and at favorable prices. Execution is the final, critical step in the interlinked investment process: *The portfolio decision is not complete until securities are bought or sold.*

A portfolio manager is not a professional trader. However, a portfolio manager does need to:

▶ communicate effectively with professional traders;

▶ evaluate the quality of the execution services being provided for the firm's clients; and

▶ take responsibility for achieving best execution on behalf of clients in his or her role as a fiduciary.

To accomplish those goals, the portfolio manager needs a grounding in:

▶ the market institutions within which traders work, including the different types of trading venues to which traders may direct orders;

▶ the measurement of trading costs; and

▶ the tactics and strategies available to the firm's traders and the counterparties with whom they deal, including important innovations in trading technology.

The reading is organized as follows. Section 2 presents essential information for the portfolio manager on the types of orders, the variety of market venues where orders are executed, the roles of dealers and brokers, and the evaluation of market quality. Section 3 addresses the costs of trading. The next two sections discuss topics relevant to trading strategy: the types of traders and their preferred order types (Section 4) and trade execution decisions and tactics (Section 5). Section 6 discusses serving the client's interests in trading and is followed by concluding remarks (Section 7) and a summary of major points.

THE CONTEXT OF TRADING: MARKET MICROSTRUCTURE

2

The portfolio manager needs to be familiar with **market microstructure**: the market structures and processes that affect how the manager's interest in buying or selling an asset is translated into executed trades (represented by trade prices and volumes).

Knowledge of market microstructure helps a portfolio manager understand how orders will be handled and executed. The formulation of trading strategies depends on accurate microstructure information. Such information can also help the practitioner understand the frictions that can cause asset prices to diverge from full-information expectations of value, possibly suggesting opportunities and pitfalls in trading.

The portfolio manager also needs to understand the characteristics of the major order types as he or she communicates with the trading desk on such matters as the emphasis to put on speed of execution versus price of execution. The next section presents some essential information on order types.

2.1 Order Types

Market orders and limit orders are the two major types of orders that traders use and that portfolio managers need to understand.

1. A **market order** is an instruction to execute an order promptly in the public markets at the best price available.

    For example, an order to buy 10,000 shares of BP p.l.c. directed to the London Stock Exchange (LSE) would execute at the best price available when the order reached that market. Suppose that when the order reaches the LSE, the lowest price at which a seller is ready to sell BP shares is 642p (pence) in quantity up to 8,000 shares (for a buyer, the lower the price, the better). The second-lowest price is 643p in quantity up to 6,000 shares. Thus, 8,000 shares of the market order would be filled (executed) at 642p and the balance of $10,000 - 8,000 = 2,000$ shares would fill at 643p.

    A market order emphasizes immediacy of execution. However, a market order usually bears some degree of **price uncertainty** (uncertainty about the price at which the order will execute). In today's markets, most market orders are effectively automated from the point of origin straight through to reporting and clearing.

2. A **limit order** is an instruction to trade at the best price available but only if the price is at least as good as the limit price specified in the order. For buy orders, the trade price must not exceed the limit price, while for sell orders, the trade price must be at least as high as the limit price. An instruction always accompanies a limit order specifying when it will expire.

Suppose that instead of the market order above, the trader places an order to buy 10,000 shares of BP p.l.c. at 641p limit (which means at a price of 641p or lower), good for one day (the order expires at the end of trading that day). Suppose that this buy order's price is higher than that of any other limit buy order for BP shares at the time. If that is the case, then 641p becomes the best available bid, or **market bid**, for BP shares. If a market sell order for 6,000 shares of BP arrives the instant after the trader's buy limit order for 10,000 shares, it will execute against that limit order. The trader will get a fill (execution) for 6,000 shares at 641p, leaving 4,000 shares of the order unfilled. At that point, favorable news on BP might reach the market. If so, the price of BP could move up sharply and not trade at or below 641p for the remainder of the day. If that is the case, at the end of the day, the trader will have 4,000 shares of his or her order unfilled and the order, which was good for one day, will expire.

By specifying the least favorable price at which an order can execute, *a limit order emphasizes price.* However, limit orders can execute only when the market price reaches the limit price specified by the limit order. The timing of the execution, or even whether the execution happens at all, is determined by the ebb and flow of the market. Limit orders thus have **execution uncertainty**.

Each trading venue specifies the types of orders permitted and other trading protocols. The professional trader needs to know the range of order types permitted. The list of all possible kinds of orders is long, but most order types represent variations on the elemental market and limit orders.[1] Some of these order types may serve to enlist the experience, presence, and knowledge of the trader's agent (broker) in executing a trade. Others may serve to conceal the quantity of a security that the trader wants to buy or sell, or serve some other purpose. A few additional important order types are as follows:

▶ **Market-not-held order.** This type of order is relevant for trades placed on certain **exchanges** (regulated trading venues) where an order may be handled by an agent of the trader in executing trades (a **broker**). This variation of the market order is designed to give the agent greater discretion than a simple market order would allow. "Not held" means that the broker is not required to trade at any specific price or in any specific time interval, as would be required with a simple market order. Discretion is placed in the hands of a representative of the broker (such as a **floor broker**—an agent of the broker who, for certain exchanges, physically represents the trade on the exchange). The broker may choose not to participate in the flow of orders on the exchange if the broker believes he or she will be able to get a better price in subsequent trading.

▶ **Participate (do not initiate) order.** This is a variant of the market-not-held order. The broker is to be deliberately low-key and wait for and respond to initiatives of more active traders. Buy-side traders who use this type of order

---

[1] See Harris (2003) for an in-depth treatment of order types.

hope to capture a better price in exchange for letting the other side determine the timing of the trade.

▶ **Best efforts order.** This type of order gives the trader's agent even more discretion to work the order only when the agent judges market conditions to be favorable. Some degree of immediacy is implied, but not immediacy at any price.

▶ **Undisclosed limit order**, also known as a **reserve, hidden,** or **iceberg order.** This is a limit order that includes an instruction not to show more than some maximum quantity of the unfilled order. For example, a trader might want to buy 200,000 shares of an issue traded on Euronext Amsterdam. The order size would represent a substantial fraction of average daily volume in the issue, and the trader is concerned that share price might move up if the full extent of his or her interest were known. The trader places an undisclosed limit order to buy the 200,000 shares, specifying that no more than 20,000 shares of the unfilled order be shown to the public at a time.

▶ **Market on open order.** This is a market order to be executed at the opening of the market. Similarly, a **market on close order** is a market order to be executed at the market close. These are examples of orders with an instruction for execution at a specific time. The rationale for using these two types of orders is that the opening and close in many markets provide good liquidity.

The above types of orders describe how an order to buy or sell will be presented to the market. The following describe special types of trades:

▶ **Principal trade.** A principal trade is a trade with a broker in which the broker commits capital to facilitate the prompt execution of the trader's order to buy or sell. Principal trades are used most frequently when the order is larger and/or more urgent than can be accommodated within the normal ebb and flow of exchange trading. A price concession provides an incentive for the broker acting as a principal in the trade.

▶ **Portfolio trade** (or **program trade** or **basket trade**). A portfolio trade involves an order that requires the execution of purchases (or sales) in a specified **basket** (list) of securities at as close to the same time as possible. For example, an S&P 500 index fund manager with new cash to invest could execute a portfolio trade to buy the S&P 500 (the shares in the S&P 500 in their index weights). Portfolio trades are often relatively low cost because the diversification implied by multiple security issues reduces the risk to the other side of the trade.

With some essential information on order types in hand, we can discuss market structures for trading.

2.2 Types of Markets

Markets are organized to provide **liquidity** (the ability to trade without delay at relatively low cost and in relatively large quantities), **transparency** (availability of timely and accurate market and trade information), and **assurity of completion** (trades settle without problems under all market conditions—**trade settlement** involves the buyer's payment for the asset purchased and the transfer of formal ownership of that asset).

In what follows, we describe the chief ways trading is organized:

▶ Quote-driven (or dealer) markets, in which members of the public trade with dealers rather than directly with one another.

▶ Order-driven markets, in which members of the public trade with one another without the intermediation of dealers.

▶ Brokered markets, in which the trader relies on a broker to find the other side of a desired trade.

These distinctions are valuable in understanding the dynamics of trading and price formation, although, as we discuss later, the lines between the categories are often blurry. Furthermore, markets evolve, and the portfolio manager needs to keep abreast of important new developments.

Fixed-income and equity markets have evolved very rapidly over the 1990s and early 2000s. There are many more choices as to where to trade such bonds and equities than was the case historically—a phenomenon that has been called **market fragmentation**. Another trend is the increasing amount of trading that is partly or fully automated, in the sense that the execution of a trader's order after entry requires minimal or no human intervention or trader-to-trader communication. Reflecting the concern to minimize settlement errors and costs in security markets, the settlement of the trade after execution may also be automated within a given trading system or venue (**straight through processing**, or STP).

Forward and futures markets are also in transition. For example, at the Chicago Board of Trade (a U.S. commodities exchange), an automated trading system (e-cbot) operates alongside a type of market dating back centuries (an **open outcry auction market**). In an open outcry auction market, representatives of buyers and sellers meet at a specified location on the floor of an exchange, with voices raised ("open outcry") so they can be heard, to conduct auctions to fill customers' orders.

Alternative investment markets have also been affected by changes. For example, hedge funds (loosely regulated pooled investment vehicles) have been aggressive in exploiting advances in trading technology.

All the above developments are better understood when the structures by which trading is organized are grasped. The first type of market that we will discuss is called a quote-driven or dealer market.

2.2.1 Quote-Driven (Dealer) Markets

Quote-driven markets rely on dealers to establish firm prices at which securities can be bought and sold. These markets are therefore also called **dealer markets**, as trades are executed with a dealer. A **dealer** (sometimes referred to as a market maker) is a business entity that is ready to buy an asset for inventory or sell an asset from inventory to provide the other side of an order to buy or sell the asset.

In the traditional view, market makers or dealers passively provide immediacy or bridge liquidity, the price of which is the **bid–ask spread** (the ask price minus the bid price). A dealer's (or any trader's) **bid price** (or **bid**) is the price at which he or she will buy a specified quantity of a security. A dealer's (or any trader's) **ask price** (or **ask**, or **offer price**, or **offer**) is the price at which he or she will sell a specified quantity of a security. On the principle of buying low and selling high, a dealer's ask price is greater than his bid price. The quantity associated with the bid price is often referred to the **bid size**; the quantity associated with the ask price is known as the **ask size**. From the perspective of a trader executing an order to *buy* a security from a dealer, a *lower ask* from the dealer is favorable to the trader. If the trader is executing an order to *sell* a security to a dealer, a *higher bid* from the dealer is favorable to the trader.

Suppose that a portfolio manager gives the firm's trading desk an order to buy 1,000 shares of Economical Chemical Systems, Inc. (ECSI), which is traded in a dealer market, and that three dealers (coded A, B, and C) make a market in those shares. At the time the trader views the market in ECSI on his computer screen, 10:22 a.m., the three dealers have put in the following quotes:

▶ Dealer A: *bid*: 98.85 for 600 shares; *ask*: 100.51 for 1,000 shares

▶ Dealer B: *bid*: 98.84 for 500 shares; *ask*: 100.55 for 500 shares

▶ Dealer C: *bid*: 98.82 for 700 shares; *ask*: 100.49 for 800 shares

Thus, the bid–ask spreads of Dealers A, B, and C are, respectively,

▶ 100.51 − 98.85 = 1.66

▶ 100.55 − 98.84 = 1.71

▶ 100.49 − 98.82 = 1.67

The trader might see the quote information organized on his screen as shown in Exhibit 1. In Exhibit 1, the bids and asks are ordered from best to worst and time-stamped. These are actually limit orders because the prices at which the dealers are ready to trade are specified. Because Exhibit 1 lists limit orders, it is called a **limit order** book. The **inside bid**, or **market bid**, which is the highest and best bid, is 98.85 from Dealer A. However, Dealer C is quoting the **inside ask**, or **market ask**, which is the lowest ask, at 100.49. The **inside quote**, or **market quote**, is therefore 98.85 bid, 100.49 ask. The **inside bid–ask spread**, or **market bid–ask spread** (or **inside spread** or **market spread** for short), is 100.49 − 98.85 = 1.64, which in this case is lower than any individual dealer's spread. (Prevailing is also used for *inside* or *market* in all these expressions.) The trader also notes that the **midquote** (halfway between the market bid and ask prices) is (100.49 + 98.85)/2 = 99.67.

EXHIBIT 1	The Limit Order Book for Economical Chemical Systems, Inc.						
	Bid				**Ask**		
Dealer	**Time Entered**	**Price**	**Size**	**Dealer**	**Time Entered**	**Price**	**Size**
A	10:21 a.m.	98.85	600	C	10:21 a.m.	100.49	800
B	10:21 a.m.	98.84	500	A	10:21 a.m.	100.51	1,000
C	10:19 a.m.	98.82	700	B	10:19 a.m.	100.55	500

Note: The bids are ordered from highest to lowest, while the asks are ordered from lowest to highest. These orderings are from best bid or ask to worst bid or ask.

If the trader executes a market buy order for 1,000 shares, the trader would purchase 800 shares from Dealer C at 100.49 per share and 200 shares from Dealer A at 100.51 per share. However, in some markets, it is also possible for the trader to direct the buy order to a specific dealer—for example, Dealer A. The trader may do so for a variety of reasons. For example, the trader may believe that Dealer A is reliable in standing behind quotes but that Dealer C is not. As one example, currency markets are dealer markets, and institutions active in those markets may screen counterparties on credit criteria.

In some dealer markets, a public trader might not have real-time access to all quotes in the security as in our example; that is, the limit order book is not "open," meaning visible in real time to the public. In such **closed-book markets**, the trader would rely on a broker to locate the best ask price, paying the broker a commission. Another notable point concerns limit orders. Historically, in dealer markets, rules would restrict a limit order from a public trader from competing with dealers' bids and asks for other public trades. In a "pure" dealer market, a dealer is a counterparty to every trade. However, in some quote-driven markets, such as the U.S. NASDAQ market for equities, public traders' limit orders are displayed and compete with dealers' bids and asks.[2]

If the portfolio manager communicated that he or she had a focus on price rather than immediacy, the trader might consider placing a limit order within the market spread—for example, an order to buy 1,000 shares at 100 limit. The trader's limit order in a market such as NASDAQ would establish a new market bid at 100, and the revised market quote would be 100 bid, 100.49 ask. If nothing else had changed, an incoming market order to sell ECSI shares would "hit" the trader's bid of 100. The trader might also hope that one of the dealers would revise the ask downward and fill part or all of the trader's order. On the other hand, it is also possible that the trader's limit order would expire unfilled.

Dealers have played important roles in bond and equity markets because *dealers can help markets operate continuously.* Bond markets, in particular, are overwhelmingly dealer markets. The explanation lies in a lack of natural liquidity for many bonds. (**Natural liquidity** is an extensive pool of investors who are aware of and have a potential interest in buying and/or selling a security.) Many bonds are extremely infrequently traded. If an investor wanted to buy such a bond, the investor might have a very long wait before the other side of the trade (an interest to sell) appeared from the public. Dealers help markets in such securities operate more nearly continuously by being ready to take the opposite side of a trade.

A study of U.S. corporate bond markets highlights the issue of lack of natural liquidity. In 2003, approximately 70,000 U.S. corporate bond issues potentially tradable in dealer markets were outstanding.[3] However, only 22,453 issues, about 23 percent of the total, traded at least *once* in 2003. Of the bonds that did trade at least once, the "active" bond issues, the median number of trades per day was less than one. Only 1 percent of active bonds traded on average more than about 22 times per day.[4] Even in the relatively frequently traded issues, an opportunity is thus created for an entity—the dealer—to "make" the market (i.e., create liquidity when no natural liquidity exists). A market is made when the dealer stands ready to provide bridge liquidity by buying stock offered by a seller and holding it until a buyer arrives, in return for earning a spread.

Similar considerations often operate in equities. For example, the London Stock Exchange has a quote-driven, competing dealer market called SEAQ for infrequently traded shares. Dealers also play important roles in markets requiring negotiation of the terms of the instrument, such as forward markets and swap markets, where otherwise finding a counterparty to the instrument would often not be feasible.

---

[2] The display of public limit orders on NASDAQ followed a U.S. reform in 1997 that was triggered by a controversy about dealer collusion in setting quotes.

[3] See Edwards, Harris, and Piwowar (2004). The estimate comes from the number of U.S. corporate bonds whose trades must be reported to the TRACE (Trade Reporting and Compliance Engine) bond price reporting system, which has been operative since 1 July 2002.

[4] See Edwards et al., Table 2.

The size of the *quoted* bid–ask spread (reflecting the market quote), particularly as a proportion of the quote midpoint, is one measure of trading costs. However, the quoted bid–ask spread may be different from the spread at which a trader actually transacts. The trader's focus is therefore often on the *effective* spread.

The **effective spread** is two times the deviation of the actual execution price from the midpoint of the market quote at the time an order is entered. (If parts of the order execute at different prices, the weighted-average execution price is used in computing the deviation from the midpoint.) The quoted spread is the simplest measure of round-trip transaction costs for an average-size order. The effective spread is a better representation of the true cost of a round-trip transaction because it captures both **price improvement** (i.e., execution within the quoted spread at a price such that the trader is benefited) and the tendency for larger orders to move prices (**market impact**).[5] Exhibit 2 gives the market bid–ask in a hypothetical common equity issue that we can use to illustrate the difference between these two kinds of spreads.

EXHIBIT 2	A Market Bid–Ask at 10:03:14 (Order Entry)		
Bid Price	**Bid Size**	**Ask Price**	**Ask Size**
$19.97	400	$20.03	1,000

With the information in Exhibit 2 before him, a trader with instructions to buy 500 shares with minimal delay enters a market order for 500 shares. As the order is received in the system at 10:03:18, a dealer in the issue enters a quote of $19.96 bid (bid size: 100 shares) and $20.01 ask (ask size: 500 shares) to improve on ("step in front of") the prior best ask price of $20.03 and take the incoming market order. This can happen because the dealer quickly decides that the profit from the trade is satisfactory. Exhibit 3 shows the market bid–ask at 10:03:18, when the order executes.

EXHIBIT 3	A Market Bid–Ask at 10:03:18 (Order Execution)		
Bid Price	**Bid Size**	**Ask Price**	**Ask Size**
$19.97	400	$20.01	500

Thus, 500 shares of the trader's market order execute at $20.01, which represents a price improvement of $0.02 relative to the market ask of $20.03 that the trader saw when the order was entered. (The lower purchase price represents a price improvement for the buyer.)

From Exhibit 2 we see that the quoted bid–ask spread is $20.03 − $19.97 = $0.06. The midquote is ($20.03 + $19.97)/2 = $20.00. The effective spread is 2 × ($20.01 − $20.00) = 2 × $0.01 = $0.02, which is $0.06 − $0.02 = $0.04 less than the quoted spread. *The price improvement has resulted in an effective spread that is lower than the quoted spread.*

---

[5] Price improvement happens when a trader improves on (or "steps in front of") the best current bid or ask price to take the other side of an incoming market order.

The **average effective spread** is the mean effective spread (sometimes dollar weighted) over all transactions in the stock in the period under study. The average effective spread attempts to measure the liquidity of a security's market.

EXAMPLE 1

The Effective Spread of an Illiquid Stock

Charles McClung, portfolio manager of a Canadian small-cap equity mutual fund, is reviewing with his firm's chief trader the execution of a ticket to sell 1,000 shares of Alpha Company. The ticket was split into three trades executed in a single day as follows:

A. A market order to sell 200 shares was executed at a price of C$10.15. The quote that was in effect at that time was as follows:

Ask Price	Ask Size	Bid Price	Bid Size
C$10.24	200	C$10.12	300

B. A market order to sell 300 shares was executed at a price of C$10.11. The quote that was in effect at that time was as follows:

Ask Price	Ask Size	Bid Price	Bid Size
C$10.22	200	C$10.11	300

C. A market order to sell 500 shares was executed at an average price of C$10.01. The quote that was in effect at that time was as follows:

Ask Price	Ask Size	Bid Price	Bid Size
C$10.19	200	C$10.05	300

This order exceeded the quoted bid size and "walked down" the limit order book (i.e., after the market bid was used, the order made use of limit order(s) to buy at lower prices than the market bid).

1. For each of the above market orders, compute the quoted spread. Also, compute the average quoted spread for the stock for the day.

2. For each of the above, compute the effective spread. Also, compute the average effective spread and the share-volume-weighted effective spread for the stock for the day.

3. Discuss the relative magnitudes of quoted and effective spreads for each of the three orders.

Solution to 1: The quoted spread is the difference between the ask and bid prices. So, for the first order, the quoted spread is C$10.24 − C$10.12 = C$0.12. Similarly, the quoted spreads for the second and third orders are C$0.11 and C$0.14, respectively. The average quoted spread is (C$0.12 + C$0.11 + C$0.14)/3 = C$0.1233.

Solution to 2: Effective spread for a sell order = 2 × (Midpoint of the market at the time an order is entered − Actual execution price).

For the first order, the midpoint of the market at the time the order is entered = (C$10.12 + C$10.24)/2 = C$10.18. So, the effective spread = 2 × (C$10.18 − C$10.15) = C$0.06.

The effective spread for the second order = 2 × [(C$10.11 + C$10.22)/2 − C$10.11] = C$0.11.

The effective spread for the third order = 2 × [(C\$10.05 + C\$10.19)/2 − C\$10.01] = C\$0.22.

The average effective spread = (C\$0.06 + C\$0.11 + C\$0.22)/3 = C\$0.13. The share-volume-weighted effective spread = [(200 × C\$0.06) + (300 × C\$0.11) + (500 × C\$0.22)]/(200 + 300 + 500) = (C\$12.00 + C\$33.00 + C\$110.00)/1,000 = C\$155.00/1,000 = C\$0.155.

Solution to 3: In the first trade, there was a price improvement because the shares were sold at a price above the bid price. Therefore, the effective spread is less than the quoted spread. In the second trade, there was no price improvement because the shares were sold at the bid price. Also, there was no impact on the execution price because the entire order was fulfilled at the quoted bid. Accordingly, the effective and quoted spreads are equal. In the third trade, the effective spread is greater than the quoted spread because the order size was greater than the bid size and the order had to walk down the limit order book, resulting in a lower average price for the sale and therefore a higher effective spread.

Empirical research confirms that effective bid–ask spreads are lower in higher-volume securities because dealers can achieve faster turnaround in inventory, which reduces their risk. Spreads are wider for riskier and less liquid securities. Later research provided a deeper understanding of trading costs by explaining variation in bid–ask spreads as part of intraday price dynamics. This research showed that market makers are not simply passive providers of immediacy but must also take an active role in price setting to rapidly turn over inventory without accumulating significant positions on one side of the market.

Price may depart from expectations of value if the dealer is long or short relative to desired (target) inventory, giving rise to transitory price movements during the day—and possibly over longer periods. This intuition drives the models of inventory control developed by, among others, Madhavan and Smidt (1993).

2.2.2 Order-Driven Markets

Order-driven markets are markets in which transaction prices are established by public limit orders to buy or sell a security at specified prices. Such markets feature trades between public investors, *usually without intermediation by designated dealers* (market makers). The limit order book shown in Exhibit 1 for the hypothetical Economical Chemical Systems, Inc., would also be a possible limit order book for the company if it were traded in an order-driven market, but typically with public traders replacing dealers (dealers may trade in order-driven markets but do so alongside other traders). There might be more competition for orders, because a trader does not have to transact with a dealer (as in a "pure" dealer market). But it is also possible that a trader might be delayed in executing a trade or be unable to execute it because a dealer with an inventory of the security is not present. Orders from the public "drive," or determine, liquidity, explaining the term *order-driven markets*. In order-driven markets, a trader cannot choose with whom he or she trades because a prespecified set of rules (based on factors such as price and time of order entry) mechanically governs the execution of orders submitted to the market.

Examples of order-driven markets include the Toronto Stock Exchange for equities, the International Securities Exchange for options, and Hotspot FX for foreign exchange. For equity markets, a worldwide trend has favored order-driven markets at the expense of quote-driven markets. Various types of order-driven markets are distinguished:

Electronic Crossing Networks   Electronic crossing networks are markets in which buy and sell orders are batched (accumulated) and crossed at a specific point in time, usually in an anonymous fashion. Electronic crossing networks execute trades at prices taken from other markets. An example of a crossing network is the POSIT trading system, which matches buyers and sellers at the average of prevailing bid and ask prices at fixed points in the day. Crossing networks serve mainly institutional investors.[6]

In using crossing networks, both buyer and seller avoid the costs of dealer services (the bid–ask spread), the effects a large order can have on execution prices, and information leakage. Commissions are paid to the crossing network but are typically low. However, crossing participants cannot be guaranteed that their trades will find an opposing match: The volume in a crossing system is determined by the smallest quantity submitted.

To illustrate how trades on a crossing network are executed, we will suppose that an investment manager, coded A in Exhibit 4, wishes to buy 10,000 shares of a stock. At the same time, two different mutual fund traders, coded B and C, wish to sell 3,000 and 4,000 shares, respectively. The crossing of orders occurs at 12:00 p.m. on each business day. The market bid and ask prices of the stock are €30.10 and €30.16, respectively.

In this example, total volume is 7,000 shares and the execution price is at the **midquote** (halfway between the prevailing bid and ask prices) of €30.13 = (€30.10 + €30.16)/2. Both sellers have their orders executed in full, but buyer A receives a **partial fill** of 7,000 shares. The buyer has the option of sending the remaining 3,000 shares back to the crossing system for another attempt at execution at the next scheduled crossing or trying to trade this remainder in the open market. None of the participants observes the identities or original submission sizes of the others in the match pool.

Crossing networks provide no price discovery. **Price discovery** means that transaction prices adjust to equilibrate supply and demand. Because the crossing network did not provide price discovery, price could not adjust upward to uncover additional selling interest and fully satisfy trader A's demand to buy.

EXHIBIT 4	Electronic Crossing Network: Crossing of Orders at 12:00 p.m. (Numerical Entries Are Numbers of Shares)	
Trader Identity	**Buy Orders**	**Sell Orders**
A	10,000	
B		3,000
C		4,000

[6] In discussions of U.S. equity markets in particular, a term that is occasionally used for direct trading of securities between institutional investors is the **fourth market**; the fourth market would include trading on electronic crossing networks.

Auction Markets   Many order-driven markets are auction markets—that is, markets in which the orders of multiple buyers compete for execution. Auction markets can be further categorized into **periodic** or **batch auction markets** (where multilateral trading occurs at a single price at a prespecified point in time) and **continuous auction markets** (where orders can be executed at any time during the trading day). Examples of batch auction markets are the open and close of some stock exchanges and the reopening of the Tokyo Stock Exchange after the midday lunch break; at these times, orders are aggregated for execution at a single price. In contrast to electronic crossing markets, auction markets provide price discovery, lessening the problem of partial fills that we illustrated above for crossing networks.

Automated Auctions (Electronic Limit-Order Markets)   These are computer-based auctions that operate continuously within the day using a specified set of rules to execute orders. **Electronic communications networks** (**ECNs**), such as Island and Archipelago Exchange in the United States and the Paris **Bourse** in France, are examples of automated auctions for equities. Like crossing networks, ECNs provide anonymity and are computer-based. In contrast to crossing networks, ECNs operate continuously and, as auction markets, provide price discovery. (Following usual practice, the acronym "ECN" is reserved to refer to electronic communications networks.)

Automated auctions have been among the fastest-growing segments in equity trading. ECNs in particular have blurred the traditional difference between order-driven markets and quote-driven dealer markets. In an ECN, it can be difficult to distinguish between participants who are regulated, professional dealers and other participants who, in effect, are also attempting to earn spread profits by providing liquidity. Hedge funds or day traders, for example, might actively supply liquidity to the market to capture the dealer-like spread profits. From the perspective of an investor, the result is added liquidity and tighter spreads.[7]

2.2.3 Brokered Markets

A broker is an agent of the buy-side trader who collects a commission for skillful representation of the trade. The broker may represent the trade to dealers in the security or to the market order flow. However, the term **brokered markets** refers specifically to markets in which transactions are largely effected through a search-brokerage mechanism away from public markets.[8] Typically, these markets are important in countries where the underlying public markets (e.g., stock exchanges) are relatively small or where it is difficult to find liquidity in size. Consequently, brokered markets are mostly used for block transactions.

Brokers can help locate natural counterparties to a difficult order—for example, a block order. A **block order** is an order to sell or buy in a quantity that is large relative to the liquidity ordinarily available from dealers in the security or in other markets. The trader might use the services of a broker to carefully try to uncover the other side of the trade in return for a commission; the broker might occasionally position a portion of the block. (To **position a trade** is to take the other side of it, acting as a principal with capital at risk.) Brokers can also provide

---

[7] For further reading on this subject, see Wagner (2004).

[8] In the United States, brokered equity markets were traditionally referred to as upstairs markets. The reference is to trades executed not on the floor of an exchange ("downstairs") but via communications "upstairs" in brokerage firms' offices.

a reputational screen to protect uninformed or liquidity-motivated traders. For example, the broker might "shop the block" only to those potential counterparties that the broker believes are unlikely to **front-run** the trade (trade ahead of the initiator, exploiting privileged information about the initiator's trading intentions). These attributes of brokerage markets facilitate trading and hence add value for all parties to the transaction.

EXAMPLE 2

Market Classifications Are Simplifications

Although it is convenient to equate the dealer function with the activities of professional market makers, many parties can and do perform parts of the dealer function. As discussed, brokerage firms' "upstairs" trading desks may commit capital to support clients' trading desires. Thus, these firms are often called broker/dealers, recognizing that they function as both brokers and dealers. Equally important, investors can compete with dealers. Buy-side traders can reduce their trading costs by providing accommodative, dealer-like services to other market participants—for example, by submitting limit orders that other participants may "hit" to fulfill liquidity needs.

2.2.4 Hybrid Markets

Hybrid markets are combinations of the previously described market types. A good example is the New York Stock Exchange (NYSE), which offers elements of batch auction markets (e.g., the opening) and continuous auction markets (intraday trading), as well as quote-driven markets (the important role of NYSE dealers, who are known as specialists).

2.3 The Roles of Brokers and Dealers

Having discussed the types of markets, we now discuss the roles of brokers and dealers, because it is essential that portfolio managers and traders understand their different roles.[9]

A broker is an agent of the investor. As such, in return for a commission, the broker provides various execution services, including the following:

▶ **Representing the order**. The broker's primary task is to represent the order to the market. The market will accommodate, usually for a price, someone who feels he or she must trade immediately.

▶ **Finding the opposite side of a trade**. If interest in taking the opposite side of a trade is not currently evident in the market, it usually falls to the broker to try to locate the seller for the desired buy, or the buyer for the desired sale. Often this service requires that the broker act as a dealer and actively buy or sell shares for the broker's own account. The broker/dealer does

---

[9] Many sell-side firms are both brokers and dealers. A given firm may deal in a security at the same time that it collects an agency commission for representing an order in it.

not bear risk without compensation. Depending on the dealer's inventory position, this service may come at a high cost.

▶ **Supplying market information**. Market information includes the identity of buyers and sellers, the strength of buying and selling interest, and other information that is relevant to assessing the costs and risks of trading. This market intelligence, which can be provided by the broker, is very valuable to buy-side traders as they consider their trading tactics.

▶ **Providing discretion and secrecy**. Buy-side traders place great value on preserving the anonymity of their trading intentions. Notice, however, that such secrecy does not extend to the selected broker, whose stock in trade is the knowledge of supply and demand. That an investor is willing to trade is a very valuable piece of information the broker gains as result of his or her relationship with the trader.

▶ **Providing other supporting investment services**. A broker may provide a range of other services, including providing the client with financing for the use of leverage, record keeping, cash management, and safekeeping of securities. A particularly rich set of supporting services, often including introduction to potential clients, is provided in relationships that have come to be known as **prime brokerage**.

▶ **Supporting the market mechanism**. Brokerage commissions indirectly assure the continuance of the needed market facilities.

In contrast to the agency relationship of the broker with the trader, the relationship between the trader and a dealer is essentially adversarial. Like any other merchant, the dealer wants to sell merchandise at a higher price (the ask) than the purchase price (the bid). Holding trade volume constant, a dealer gains by wider bid–ask spreads while the trader gains by narrower bid–ask spreads. The dealer is wary of trading with a better-informed counterparty. Consider a portfolio manager who has concluded through new and original analysis that a bond issue currently in the portfolio has more credit risk than the rest of the market perceives. The dealer who makes a market in the company's bonds has set a bid price unaware of the fact that the bond's credit rating may be too high. The dealer's bid is too high relative to the true credit risk of the bond. The portfolio manager's trader liquidates the portfolio position in the bond issue at the dealer's bid price. The dealer's inventory in the bond issue increases, and subsequently the bond's price trends down as the rest of the market becomes aware of the bond's actual credit risk. The dealer has just experienced **adverse selection risk** (the risk of trading with a more informed trader). Dealers want to know who is active in the market, how informed traders are, and how urgent their interest in transacting with the dealer is, in order to manage profits and adverse selection risk. The tension occurs because the informed or urgent trader does not want the dealer to know those facts.

Buy-side traders are often strongly influenced by sell-side traders such as dealers (the **sell side** consists of institutions that sell services to firms such as investment managers and institutional investors). The buy-side trader may have more interaction with dealers than with other units of the trader's own firm (which might simply communicate computer files of orders). In contrast, the sell-side trader, who possesses information vital to the buy-side trader's success, is a constant verbal window on the world. Over the years, the buy-side trader may build a reservoir of trust, friendship, comfort, and goodwill with his or her sell-side counterparts. It is often necessary to rely on the sell side's reputation for integrity and its long-term desire to maintain relationships. The trader should manage the relationships with dealers, remembering that the buy-side trader's first allegiance must always be to the firm's clients, for whom the trader acts in a fiduciary capacity.

We now have an overview of how markets function and have discussed in some detail the differences between the roles of brokers and dealers. But how *well* does a market function? Does a particular trading venue deserve order flow? The next section provides some ways to think about these questions.

2.4 Evaluating Market Quality

Markets are organized to provide liquidity, transparency, and assurity of completion, so they may be judged by the degree to which they have these qualities in practice. In detail, a liquid market is one that has the following characteristics:[10]

▶ **The market has relatively low bid–ask spreads**. Such a market is often called tight. Quoted spreads and effective spreads are low. The costs of trading small amounts of an asset are themselves small. As a result, investors can trade positions without excessive loss of value. If bid–ask spreads are high, investors cannot profitably trade on information except when the information is of great value.

▶ **The market is deep**. Depth means that big trades tend not to cause large price movements. As a result, the costs of trading large amounts of an asset are relatively small. Deep markets have high **quoted depth,** which is the number of shares available for purchase or sale at the quoted bid and ask prices.

▶ **The market is resilient**. A market is resilient (in the sense used here) if any discrepancies between market price and intrinsic value tend to be small and corrected quickly.

The great advantage of market liquidity is that traders and investors can trade rapidly without a major impact on price. This, in turn, makes it easy for those with relevant information to bring their insights and opinions into the price of securities. Corporations can then attract capital because investors can see that prices efficiently reflect the opportunities for profit and that they can buy and sell securities at will at relatively low cost. Liquidity adds value to the companies whose securities trade on the exchange. Investors will pay a premium for securities that possess the valuable trait of liquidity. Higher security prices enhance corporate value and lower the cost of capital.

Many factors contribute to making a market liquid:

▶ **Many buyers and sellers**. The presence of many buyers and sellers increases the chance of promptly locating the opposite side of a trade at a competitive price. Success breeds success in that the liquidity resulting from many buyers and sellers attracts additional participants to the market. Investors are more willing to hold shares that they can dispose of whenever they choose to do so.

▶ **Diversity of opinion, information**, **and investment needs among market participants**. If the investors in a given market are highly alike, they are likely to want to take similar investment actions and make similar trades. Diversity in the factors described above increases the chance that a buyer of a security, who might have a positive opinion about it, can find a seller, who

---

[10] This list follows a well-known analysis and definition of liquidity by Kyle (1985).

might have a negative opinion about it or a need for cash. In general, a large pool of investors enhances diversity of opinion.

▶ **Convenience**. A readily accessible physical location or an easily mastered and well-thought-out electronic platform attracts investors.

▶ **Market integrity**. Investors who receive fair and honest treatment in the trading process will trade again. The ethical tone set by professional market operatives plays a major role in establishing this trust, as does effective regulation. For example, audits of the financial condition and regulatory compliance of brokers and dealers operating in a market increase public confidence in the market's integrity, as do procedures for the disinterested investigation of complaints about the execution of trades.

Transparency means that individuals interested in or transacting in the market can quickly, easily, and inexpensively obtain accurate information about quotes and trades (**pretrade transparency**), and that details on completed trades are quickly and accurately reported to the public (**post-trade transparency**). Without transparency, the chance that the integrity of the trading process can be compromised increases. Assurity of completion depends on **assurity of the contract** (the parties to trades are held to fulfilling their obligations). To ensure the certainty of trade completion, participating brokers or clearing entities may guarantee the trade to both buyer and seller and be subject to standards of financial strength to ensure that the guarantee has "bite."

EXAMPLE 3

Assessing Market Quality after a Market Structure Change

U.S. equity markets switched from price increments in sixteenths of a dollar to one-cent price increments in the first half of 2001. This decimalization of the U.S. markets has received a lot of attention. Several studies have examined the changes that have taken place on the NYSE and NASDAQ (the major dealer market for U.S. equities) as a consequence of decimalization, and some of their findings regarding the changes are as follows.[11]

A. Quoted spreads have declined from the predecimalization period to the postdecimalization period.

B. Effective spreads have declined.

C. Quoted depths have declined.

For each of the above changes, state whether it suggests an improvement or deterioration in market quality after decimalization, and justify your assertion.

Solution to A: This change suggests an improvement in market quality. Lower quoted spreads are consistent with lower trading costs, which suggest greater liquidity and an improvement in market quality.

---

[11] See Bacidore, Battalio, Jennings, and Farkas (2001), Bessembinder (2003), Chakravarty, Wood, and Van Ness (2004), and Oppenheimer and Sabherwal (2003).

Solution to B: This change also suggests an improvement in market quality. Lower effective spreads are consistent with lower trading costs, which suggest greater liquidity and an improvement in market quality. Effective spreads are a more accurate measure of trading costs than quoted spreads. One would need to examine changes in commission costs (if any) subsequent to decimalization to get a more complete picture of the changes in trading costs that resulted from decimalization.

Solution to C: Reduced quoted depths imply that large investors placing large orders are forced to split their orders more often after decimalization. Though small investors who place small orders are not likely to be affected by reduced depths, the trading costs for institutional investors could increase due to reduced depths. By itself, a decline in quoted depths after decimalization implies reduced liquidity supply and deterioration in market quality.

EXAMPLE 4

The Market Quality of Electronic Crossing Networks

Electronic crossing networks offer participants anonymity and low cost through the avoidance of dealer costs and the effect of large orders on execution price. For example, a large sell order in an auction market may be interpreted as conveying negative information and cause bid prices to be revised downward, lowering execution prices. These qualities of crossing networks are particularly valuable for the large trades institutional investors often need to make. As a result of these market quality positives, electronic crossing networks have won significant market share.

Understanding and judging the available alternatives in trading is the new challenge to the buy-side trader. One of the key elements in assessing these alternatives is their costs. Effectively measuring the trading experience over time provides another valuable piece of information to the portfolio manager: On average, how much information advantage do I need to recover the hurdle-rate costs of implementing my decisions? The costs of trading are the subject of the next section.

3   THE COSTS OF TRADING

The view of investment managers on the importance of measuring and managing trading costs has evolved over time. Into the 1970s, trading was viewed as inexpensive and unimportant when contrasted to the hoped-for benefits of securities research. In those early days, portfolio managers were highly dependent on sell-side firms for investment intelligence and ideas. The traditional way to reward the broker for investment ideas was to channel the resultant trading activity to the broker.

In the early 1970s, several important trends converged to change buy-side trading forever. As pension fund assets grew, the prevailing use of fixed commission schedules for trades on exchanges created an unjustifiable bonanza for the exchange community. Buy-side investors exerted pressure to bring commission charges more in line with the cost of providing trading services. The result was a move to fully negotiated commissions, beginning in 1975 in the United States and continuing worldwide.[12] As a result, different levels of execution services could be bought for different commission charges, presenting the buy-side trader with new choices.

In addition, the first practical applications of the efficient market hypothesis (EMH) came to life in the form of index funds. Index fund managers strongly disagreed with the then-traditional view of trading as being "just a cost of doing business." Since index fund managers have no expectation of recovering trading costs through security selection, reducing these costs is a paramount goal for them. Traders are often the most "active" part of the passive management team.

As the 1980s progressed, trading processes were subjected to analytical thinking. The theory of trading costs measurement received attention. Investors continued to be concerned that trading costs were too high and exacted too great a penalty on investment performance. This concern encouraged a view that trading tactics need to be carefully designed and tailored to the investment decision with due attention paid to managing trading costs.

Today, the prevalent view is that all costs of trading are negative performance. The lower the transaction costs, the more portfolio management ideas that can be executed to add value to the portfolio. The management of transaction costs is today a leading concern of investors and many other market participants. Fund sponsors track transaction costs as part of their responsibility to conserve assets. Investment managers do so both to document their performance in managing costs and to gain information for improving the trading function. Brokers, exchanges, and regulators are also concerned with measuring and evaluating trading costs. Transaction cost measurement not only provides feedback on the success of the trading function; today, its concepts are used in setting trading strategy. An overview of the topic is one building block for our later discussion of trading strategy.

3.1 Transaction Cost Components

Trading costs can be thought of as having two major components: explicit costs and implicit costs. **Explicit costs** are the direct costs of trading, such as broker commission costs, taxes, stamp duties, and fees paid to exchanges. They are costs for which a trader could be given a receipt. **Implicit costs**, by contrast, represent indirect trading costs. No receipt could be given for implicit costs; they are real nonetheless. Implicit costs include the following:[13]

► The **bid–ask spread**.

► **Market impact** (or **price impact**) is the effect of the trade on transaction prices. For example, suppose a trader splits a purchase of 400 bonds into two equal market orders when the quote for a bond is 100.297 to 100.477. The first order executes at the ask price of 100.477, after which the market

---

[12] Some adoption dates for negotiated commissions were 1983 in Canada, 1986 in the United Kingdom, and 1999 in Japan.

[13] Not every trade will incur each of these costs.

quotation becomes 100.300 to 100.516. The second order is placed and executes at 100.516. The trader moved the price obtained in the second order up by $100.516 - 100.477 = 0.039$, or \$0.39 per thousand dollars of face value.

▶ **Missed trade opportunity costs** (or unrealized profit/loss) arise from the failure to execute a trade in a timely manner. For example, suppose a futures trader places a limit order to buy 10 contracts at a price of 99.00 (or better), good for one day, when the market quote is 99.01 to 99.04. The order does not execute, and the contract closes at 99.80. The difference $(99.80 - 99.04 = \$0.76)$ reflects the missed trade opportunity cost per contract.[14] By trading more aggressively, the trader might have avoided these costs. Missed trade opportunity costs are difficult to measure. In the example, the time frame (one day) was arbitrary, and the estimate could be quite sensitive to the time frame chosen for measurement.

▶ **Delay costs** (also called **slippage**) arise from the inability to complete the desired trade immediately due to its size and the liquidity of markets. Delay costs are often measured on the portion of the order carried over from one day to the next. One reason delay can be costly is that while a trade is being stretched out over time, information is leaking into the market.

Most traders measure implicit costs (i.e., costs excluding commissions) with reference to some price benchmark or reference point. We have already mentioned one price benchmark: the time-of-trade midquote (quotation midpoint), which is used to calculate the effective spread. When such precise information is lacking, the price benchmark is sometimes taken to be the **volume-weighted average price (VWAP)**. The VWAP of a security is the average price at which the security traded during the day, where each trade price is weighted by the fraction of the day's volume associated with the trade. The VWAP is an appealing price benchmark because it allows the fund sponsor to identify when it transacted at a higher or lower price than the security's average trade price during the day. For example, if a buy order for 500 shares was executed at €157.25 and the VWAP for the stock for the day was €156.00, the estimated implicit cost of the order would be $500 \times (€157.25 - €156.00) = €625$.[15] If explicit costs were €25, the total estimated cost would be €650. Alternative price benchmarks include the opening and closing prices for a security, which use less information about prices and are less satisfactory. Although VWAP involves a data-intensive calculation, a number of vendors supply it.[16]

VWAP is less informative for trades that represent a large fraction of volume. In the extreme, if a single trading desk were responsible for all the buys in a security during a day, that desk's average price would equal VWAP and thus appear to be good, however high the prices paid. Another limitation of VWAP (and of the effective spread) is that a broker with sufficient discretion can try to "game" this measure. (To *game* a cost measure is to take advantage of a weakness in the measure, so that the value of the measure may be misleading.) Furthermore, VWAP is partly determined at any point in the day; by using weights based on volume to that point in the day, a trader can estimate the final value of VWAP.

---

[14] The comparison to closing price is for illustrative purposes and only one alternative. For example, the Plexus Group calculates the missed trade opportunity costs with respect to the price of the instrument 30 days after the decision to trade was made.

[15] Were this a sell order, in the calculation, we would subtract the trade price from the benchmark price; in this example, we would calculate $500 \times (€156.00 - €157.25) = -€625$. Executing a sell order at a price above the VWAP is good.

[16] For example, Bloomberg terminals report VWAPs.

The accuracy of such an estimate would tend to increase as the close of trading approaches. By comparing the current price to that estimate, the trader can judge the chances of doing better than VWAP.

EXAMPLE 5

Taking Advantage of Weaknesses in Cost Measures

Reginald Smith is consulting to Apex Wealth Management on the use of transaction cost measures. Smith correctly explains to Apex's CIO:

> A broker who has flexibility on how aggressively to fill an order can try to game the effective spread measure by waiting for the trade to come to him—that is, by offering liquidity. The broker with a buy order can wait until an order to sell hits his bid; with a sell order, he can wait until an order to buy hits his ask. By executing buys at the bid and sells at the ask, the broker will always show negative estimated transaction costs if performance is measured by the effective spread. However, the delay costs of this approach to the client may be high. A broker with discretion on timing can also try to improve performance relative to a VWAP benchmark, because VWAP is partly determined at any point into the day. For example, if a buy order is received near the end of the day and the stock's ask price exceeds the VWAP up to that point, the broker might try to move the order into the next day, when he will be benchmarked against a fresh VWAP.

The CIO asserts: "I see your point. Nevertheless, using the opening price as a benchmark might be much more vulnerable to gaming than using VWAP." Critique the CIO's statement.

Solution: The CIO's statement is correct. In contrast to the VWAP, which is partly determined as the trading day progresses, the opening price is known with certainty at any point into the trading day, making it easier to game.

To address the possibility of gaming VWAP, VWAP could be measured over multiple days (spanning the time frame over which the order is executed), because traders would often be expected to try to execute trades within a day. However, the cost of measuring VWAP over a longer time frame is less precision in estimating trading costs.

Probably the most exact approach to cost measurement—and one not vulnerable to gaming—is the implementation shortfall approach. This approach is also attractive because it views trading from an investment management perspective: What does it cost to actuate investment decisions? This view was first articulated by Andre Perold of the Harvard Business School,[17] following ideas first put forward by Jack Treynor.[18] The approach involves a

---

[17] Perold (1988).

[18] See Treynor (1987).

comparison of the actual portfolio with a paper portfolio, using a price benchmark that represents the price when the decision to trade is made (when the trade list is cut).

Implementation shortfall is defined as the difference between the money return on a notional or paper portfolio in which positions are established at the prevailing price when the decision to trade is made (known as the **decision price**, the **arrival price**, or the **strike price**) and the actual portfolio's return. The implementation shortfall method correctly captures all elements of transaction costs. The method takes into account not only explicit trading costs, but also the implicit costs, which are often significant for large orders.[19]

Implementation shortfall can be analyzed into four components:

1. *Explicit costs*, including commissions, taxes, and fees.

2. *Realized profit/loss*, reflecting the price movement from the decision price (usually taken to be the previous day's close)[20] to the execution price for the part of the trade executed on the day it is placed.

3. *Delay costs* (*slippage*), reflecting the change in price (close-to-close price movement) over the day an order is placed when the order is not executed that day; the calculation is based on the amount of the order actually filled subsequently.

4. *Missed trade opportunity cost* (unrealized profit/loss), reflecting the price difference between the trade cancellation price and the original benchmark price based on the amount of the order that was not filled.

Market movement is a component of the last three of these costs. However, market movement is a random element for which the trader should not bear responsibility. It is now common to adjust implementation shortfall for market movements. An illustration of the calculation of implementation shortfall might be helpful. Consider the following facts:

▶ On Monday, the shares of Impulse Robotics close at £10.00 per share.

▶ On Tuesday, before trading begins, a portfolio manager decides to buy Impulse Robotics. An order goes to the trading desk to buy 1,000 shares of Impulse Robotics at £9.98 per share or better, good for one day. The benchmark price is Monday's close at £10.00 per share. No part of the limit order is filled on Tuesday, and the order expires. The closing price on Tuesday rises to £10.05.

▶ On Wednesday, the trading desk again tries to buy Impulse Robotics by entering a new limit order to buy 1,000 shares at £10.07 per share or better, good for one day. That day, 700 shares are bought at £10.07 per share. Commissions and fees for this trade are £14. Shares for Impulse Robotics close at £10.08 per share on Wednesday.

▶ No further attempt to buy Impulse Robotics is made, and the remaining 300 shares of the 1,000 shares the portfolio manager initially specified are never bought.

---

[19] The Plexus Group estimates that average implementation shortfall costs in 2004 for institutional traders in Asia, excluding Japan, were 153 bps, with just 22 bps from commissions. Of the implicit costs, market impact costs were 18 bps, delay costs were 84 bps, and opportunity costs from missed trades were 29 bps.

[20] The midquote at the time the decision is made is another possible benchmark price.

The paper portfolio traded 1,000 shares on Tuesday at £10.00 per share. The return on this portfolio when the order is canceled after the close on Wednesday is the value of the 1,000 shares, now worth £10,080, less the cost of £10,000, for a net gain of £80. The real portfolio contains 700 shares (now worth 700 × £10.08 = £7,056), and the cost of this portfolio is 700 × £10.07 = £7,049, plus £14 in commissions and fees, for a total cost of £7,063. Thus, the total net gain on this portfolio is −£7. The implementation shortfall is the return on the paper portfolio minus the return on the actual portfolio, or £80 − (−£7) = £87. More commonly, the shortfall is expressed as a fraction of the total cost of the paper portfolio trade, or £87/£10,000 = 87 basis points.

We can break this implementation shortfall down further:

▶ Commissions and fees are calculated naturally as £14/£10,000 = 0.14%.

▶ Realized profit/loss reflects the difference between the execution price and the relevant decision price (here, the closing price of the previous day). The calculation is based on the amount of the order actually filled:

$$\frac{700}{1,000}\left(\frac{10.07 - 10.05}{10.00}\right) = 0.14\%$$

▶ Delay costs reflect the price difference due to delay in filling the order. The calculation is based on the amount of the order actually filled:

$$\frac{700}{1,000}\left(\frac{10.05 - 10.00}{10.00}\right) = 0.35\%$$

▶ Missed trade opportunity cost reflects the difference between the cancellation price and the original benchmark price. The calculation is based on the amount of the order that was not filled:

$$\frac{300}{1,000}\left(\frac{10.08 - 10.00}{10.00}\right) = 0.24\%$$

▶ Implementation cost as a percent is 0.14% + 0.14% + 0.35% + 0.24% = 0.87%, or 87 bps.

The shortfall computation is simply reversed for sells (for sells, the return on the paper portfolio is subtracted from the return on the actual portfolio).

In this example, shortfall was positive, but this will not always be the case, especially if the effect of the return on the market is removed. To illustrate the adjustment for market return using the market model, suppose that the market had risen 100 basis points (1 percent) over the period of trading and the beta of Impulse Robotics is 1.0. The **market model** is $\hat{R}_i = \alpha_i + \beta_i R_M$, where $\hat{R}_i$ is the predicted return on asset i, R_M is the return on the market portfolio, α_i is the average return on asset i unrelated to the market return, and β_i is the sensitivity of the return on asset i to the return on the market portfolio. In practice, with daily returns, α_i will be often very close to 0, and $\hat{R}_i \approx \beta_i R_M$. With a beta of 1.0, the predicted return on the shares would be 1.0 × 1% = 1%, and the **market-adjusted implementation shortfall** would be 0.87% − 1.0% = −0.13%. Here, the shortfall is actually negative. By contrast, pretrade cost estimates are always

EXHIBIT 5	Facts on Implementation Shortfall Costs	
	Total Implementation Shortfall Costs	
Market Sector	**4th Quarter 2000**	**4th Quarter 2003**
U.S. NYSE	0.88%	0.55%
U.S. NASDAQ	1.38	0.83
Europe	1.11	0.63
Emerging Markets	2.20	1.25
All Markets	1.66	0.74

Source: Plexus Group.

positive. Exhibit 5 lists implementation shortfall costs for various global equity market sectors.[21]

Changes in the U.S. market structure between 2000 and 2003, especially decimalization and changes in order handling rules, brought a sharp decline in the cost of trading in U.S. equity markets. However, the reduction in the costs of equity trading was widespread beyond the United States: European equity trading costs dropped from 111 bps to 63 bps, a 43 percent decrease. Emerging markets also dropped 43 percent, from 220 bps to 125 bps. The costs of implementing investment ideas were down significantly across all equity markets.

As a complement to implementation shortfall, some investment management firms measure shortfall with respect not to the above paper portfolio, but with respect to a portfolio in which all trades are transacted in expected markets and the component costs are at expected levels. This approach accounts for the anticipated cost of the trades.[22]

The application of the implementation shortfall approach is hampered when an asset trades infrequently because the decision price is then hard to determine. If the market closing price of a security is "stale"—in the sense of reflecting a trade that happened much earlier—it is not valid. The application of a benchmark price based on trading cost measures, including implementation shortfall, VWAP, and effective spread, is also compromised when a market lacks transparency (accurate price and/or quote information).

Having illustrated trade cost measurement using VWAP and implementation shortfall, we now compare these two major approaches to trade cost measurement in Exhibit 6. VWAP has theoretical disadvantages compared to implementation shortfall but is readily obtained and interpreted and is a useful measure of quality of execution for smaller trades in nontrending markets in particular. The portfolio manager should be familiar with both measures.

---

[21] Note that these transaction cost totals, particularly in the earlier period, are large enough to explain the 0.50 percent to 0.75 percent one-way transaction costs inferred from the difference between active and passive management.

[22] See Cheng (2003).

EXHIBIT 6	Comparison of VWAP and Implementation Shortfall	
	Volume Weighted Average Price	**Implementation Shortfall**
Advantages	► Easy to compute. ► Easy to understand. ► Can be computed quickly to assist traders during the execution. ► Works best for comparing smaller trades in nontrending markets.	► Links trading to portfolio manager activity; can relate cost to the value of investment ideas. ► Recognizes the tradeoff between immediacy and price. ► Allows attribution of costs. ► Can be built into portfolio optimizers to reduce turnover and increase realized performance. ► Cannot be gamed.
Disadvantages	► Does not account for costs of trades delayed or canceled. ► Becomes misleading when trade is a substantial proportion of trading volume. ► Not sensitive to trade size or market conditions. ► Can be gamed by delaying trades.	► Requires extensive data collection and interpretation. ► Imposes an unfamiliar evaluation framework on traders.

EXAMPLE 6

Commissions: The Most Visible Part of Transaction Costs (1)

Implementation shortfall totals can be divided into categories that define the nature of trading costs. Each component cost is as real as the other costs. Nevertheless, brokerage commissions are the most visible portion of trading costs. The dealer spreads and responses to market pressures are more difficult to gauge. The commissions, however, are printed on every ticket. For better or worse, efforts to reduce transaction costs focus first on commissions.

A good deal of attention has focused on the use of commissions to buy services other than execution services—that is, a practice known as **soft dollars** (or **soft dollar arrangements**, or **soft commissions**). Many investment managers have traditionally allocated a client's brokerage business to buy research services that aid portfolio management. In those cases, commissions pay for research received and execution, with clerical personnel assigned to the trade desk managing the commission budget. However, the practice of soft dollars makes accounting for transaction costs less exact and can be abused. CFA Institute in 1998 issued *Soft Dollar Standards* to provide disclosure standards and other guidance related to soft dollar arrangements.[23] Furthermore, individuals who are CFA Institute members or candidates have an overriding responsibility to adhere to the Code of Ethics and Standards of Professional Conduct. Standard III: Duties to Clients, (A) Loyalty, Prudence, and Care, specifies that CFA Institute members using soft dollars should develop policies and procedures with respect to the use of client brokerage, including soft dollars, and that those policies and procedures should reflect that members and candidates must seek best execution for their clients, among other duties.[24]

EXAMPLE 7

Commissions: The Most Visible Part of Transaction Costs (2)

Transaction costs can be thought of as an iceberg, with the commission being the tip visible above the water's surface. The major parts of transaction costs are unobservable. They do not appear in accounting statements, and they appear only indirectly in manager evaluations. Extensive data collection and analysis are required to gauge the size and relative importance of transaction cost components. Exhibit 7 illustrates the concept with numbers based on the Plexus Client Universe covering U.S. equity market transactions in 2005, with the corresponding data for 2001 given for comparison.

The exhibit shows that total U.S. equity transaction costs have decreased by 91 bps from 142 bps in 2001 to 51 bps in 2005, representing a steep 64 percent decline. The most visible part of equity transaction costs—commissions—was by far the least important cost component in 2001, having already experienced long-term downward pressure. With relatively little more available to be taken out of commissions, the implicit costs of transacting came under the greatest pressure between 2001 and 2005, with missed trade opportunity costs reaching the level of commission costs. In 2005, as in 2001, implicit costs ranked from largest to smallest were delay costs, market impact, and missed trade opportunity costs. The trade that is never completed is often the most expensive trade.

Although the very long-term trend is down, the costs of equity trading can be expected to vary over time. When trading is frenzied, as it was in the internet market of the late 1990s, costs will rise as investors become less sensitive to costs in their eagerness to participate in exciting companies and situations.

---

[23] See www.cfainstitute.org for any updates. As of early 2006, no substantive revisions had been made to the 1998 release.

[24] See the *Standards of Practice Handbook*, 9th ed. (Charlottesville, VA: CFA Institute, 2005). See www.cfainstitute.org for any updates.

EXHIBIT 7   **The Iceberg of Transaction Costs**

Commissions
2005: 9 bps | 2001: 12 bps

Market Impact
2005: 12 bps | 2001: 35 bps

Delay Costs
2005: 21 bps | 2001: 76 bps

Missed Trade Opportunity Costs
2005: 9 bps | 2001: 20 bps

2005: 51 bps, 2001: 142 bps

Note: The 2001 components do not sum to exactly 142 bps due to rounding.
Source: Plexus Group, Inc.

3.2 Pretrade Analysis: Econometric Models for Costs

Given post-trade shortfall estimates, we can build reliable pretrade estimates using econometric models. The theory of market microstructure suggests that trading costs are systematically related to certain factors, including the following:[25]

▶ stock liquidity characteristics (e.g., market capitalization, price level, trading frequency, volume, index membership, bid–ask spread)

▶ risk (e.g., the volatility of the stock's returns)

▶ trade size relative to available liquidity (e.g., order size divided by average daily volume)

▶ momentum (e.g., it is more costly to buy in an up market than in a down market)

▶ trading style (e.g., more aggressive styles using market orders should be associated with higher costs than more passive styles using limit orders)

Given these factors, we can estimate the relation between costs and these variables using regression analysis. Since theory suggests a nonlinear relationship, we

---

[25] See Madhavan (2000, 2002).

can use nonlinear methods to estimate the relationship. The key point to note is that the estimated cost function can be used in two ways:

▶ to form a pretrade estimate of the cost of trading that can then be juxtaposed against the actual realized cost once trading is completed to assess execution quality; and

▶ to help the portfolio manager gauge the right trade size to order in the first place.

For example, a portfolio manager may want to invest in a stock with an expected excess return target of 5 percent relative to the manager's benchmark over the intended holding period. Initially, a trade of 200,000 shares is proposed with a price currently at $10 per share. However, based on pretrade cost estimates, the cost of a 200,000-share position is 2.5 percent, so that expected round-trip transaction costs are $2 \times 2.5\% = 5\%$, which would fully erode the excess return. The optimal trade size will be much smaller than the 200,000 shares initially proposed.

Quantitative managers will balance three factors—return, risk, and cost—in selecting the optimal trade size. But even nonquantitative managers need to make the right choices in terms of balancing expected return against expected entry and exit costs.

EXAMPLE 8

An Econometric Model for Transaction Costs

Several Canadian companies' stocks are listed not only on the Toronto Stock Exchange (TSE), but also on the New York Stock Exchange (NYSE). There are no legal restrictions on cross-border ownership and trading of these stocks. Some of the clients of an American brokerage firm have occasionally asked the brokerage firm for execution of trades in some of the Canadian stocks cross-listed in the United States. These trades can be executed on either the NYSE or TSE, and the American brokerage firm has entered into an alliance with a TSE member firm to facilitate execution of trades on the TSE if desired. John Reynolds is an economist at the brokerage firm. Reynolds has identified 55 of the cross-listed Canadian companies as those in which the firm's clients typically execute trades. Reynolds observes that the implicit transaction costs for some trades in these stocks are lower on the NYSE than on the TSE, or vice versa. Reynolds has built an econometric model that can be used for pretrade assessment of the difference in the implicit costs of transacting on the two exchanges, so that traders can direct trades to the lower-cost venue. Using historic data on trade and firm characteristics and transaction costs, Reynolds developed the following model:

$$\text{Pred. } \Delta\text{Cost} = 0.25 + 1.31 \ln(\text{Mkt Cap}) - 14.91 \text{ (U.S. Share)}$$
$$+ 1.64 \ln(\text{Order Size}) - 1.40 \text{ (High Tech)}$$

where
Pred. ΔCost = Predicted difference between the implicit transaction costs on the NYSE and TSE in basis points
Mkt Cap   = Market capitalization of the company in millions of U.S. dollars

U.S. Share = Proportion (stated as a decimal) of total trading in the stock in the United States and Canada that occurs in the United States

Order Size = Number of shares ordered

High Tech is an industry dummy with a value of 1 if the company is a high-tech company and 0 otherwise.

Reynolds has also concluded that the *explicit* transaction costs for the stocks he has analyzed are lower on the NYSE than on the TSE by about 12 bps.

1. Consider an order to sell 50,000 shares of a non-high-tech company that was included in the companies analyzed by Reynolds. The company has a market capitalization of US$100 million, and the U.S. share of overall trading volume in the company is 0.30. Based on the model estimated above and the assessment of the explicit transaction costs, recommend where the order should be placed.

2. Consider an order to sell 1,000 shares of a high-tech company that was included in the companies analyzed by Reynolds. The company has a market capitalization of US$100 million, and the U.S. share of overall trading volume in the company is 0.50. Based on the model estimated above and the assessment of the explicit transaction costs, recommend where the order should be placed.

Solution to 1: Pred. ΔCost = 0.25 + 1.31 ln(Mkt Cap) − 14.91 (US Share) + 1.64 ln(Order Size) − 1.40 (High Tech) = 0.25 + 1.31 ln(100) − 14.91 (0.30) + 1.64 ln(50,000) − 1.40 (0) = 19.6 bps. The econometric model suggests that the implicit cost of executing this trade is greater on the NYSE than on the TSE by almost 20 bps. Thus, since the explicit transaction costs are lower on the NYSE by about 12 bps, the total cost of executing the trade on the TSE is expected to be less than the cost on the NYSE by almost 8 bps. The recommendation would be to direct the order to the TSE.

Solution to 2: Pred. ΔCost = 0.25 + 1.31 ln(Mkt Cap) − 14.91 (US Share) + 1.64 ln(Order Size) − 1.40 (High Tech) = 0.25 + 1.31 ln(100) − 14.91 (0.50) + 1.64 ln(1,000) − 1.40 (1) = 8.8 bps. The econometric model suggests that the implicit cost of executing this trade is greater on the NYSE than on the TSE by about 9 bps. However, since the explicit transaction costs are lower on the NYSE by about 12 bps, the total cost of executing the trade on the NYSE is expected to be less than the cost on the TSE by about 3 bps. The recommendation would be to direct the order to the NYSE.

TYPES OF TRADERS AND THEIR PREFERRED ORDER TYPES

4

Beginning with this section and continuing with Section 5, we discuss traders, trading objectives, strategies, and tactics. We first need to understand how investment style affects trading objectives. Implementation strategy and cost are direct consequences of investment management style. Some investment strategies are inherently inexpensive to implement—for example, contrarian, passive, and other "slow idea" strategies. Other strategies, particularly those based on stock price momentum or widely disseminated "news," are inherently more expensive to implement.

The success of the investment strategy depends on whether the information content of the decision process is sufficient relative to the costs of executing the strategy, including trading costs. Thus, the keystone of the buy-side trader's choice of trading strategy is the **urgency of the trade** (the importance of certainty of execution). Is the decision based on slow changes in fundamental value, valuable new information, or the need to increase cash balances? Will the value of completing the trade disappear or dissipate if it is not completed quickly?

From the portfolio manager's perspective, the key to effective trading is to realize that the portfolio decision is not complete until securities are bought or sold. Because execution is so important, market information is critical. When a trade is first seriously contemplated, the trader needs to ask: How sensitive is the security to buying or selling pressure? How much volume can be accumulated without having the price move out of the desirable range? Are there any special considerations (e.g., news, rumors, competing buyers, or anxious sellers) that make this a particularly good or particularly poor time to deal in this stock? In other words, how resilient is the market? Is the price being driven to a level at which a dealer wants to reduce or increase inventory (i.e., the dealer's layoff or buy-in position, respectively)? Armed with this tactical information, the portfolio manager fine-tunes his interest in the security.

The trader can use the answers to these questions to increase his or her awareness of market conditions and security trading behavior. The crucial function of the trading desk is to achieve the best price–time trade-off for the impending transaction given current market circumstances. This trade-off may change rapidly because of market conditions, dealer inventories, news, and changes in the portfolio manager's desires.

The above considerations regarding investment style and the urgency of the trade in particular lead to the following classification of traders according to their motivation in trading.

4.1 The Types of Traders

Traders can be classified by their motivation to trade, as follows.

Information-motivated traders trade on information that has limited value if not quickly acted upon. Accordingly, they often stress liquidity and speed of execution over securing a better price. They are likely to use market orders and rely on market makers to accommodate their desire to trade quickly. They must execute their orders before the information on which they are buying or selling becomes valueless.

Information traders often trade in large blocks. Their information frequently concerns the prospects of one stock, and they seek to maximize the value of the information. Successful information-motivated traders are wary of acquiring a public reputation for astute trading, because if they did, who would wish to trade against them? Accordingly, information traders often use deceptive actions to hide their intentions.

Value-motivated traders act on value judgments based on careful, sometimes painstaking research. They trade only when the price moves into their value range. As explained earlier, they trade infrequently and are motivated only by price and value. They tend to accumulate and distribute large positions quietly over lengthy trading horizons. Value-motivated traders are ready to be patient to secure a better price.

Liquidity-motivated traders do not transact to reap profit from an information advantage of the securities involved. Rather, liquidity-motivated transactions are more a means than an end; such transactions may, for example, release cash proceeds to facilitate the purchase of another security, adjust market exposure, or fund cash needs. Lacking the information sensitivity of the information and value traders, liquidity-motivated traders tend to be natural trading counterparties to more knowledgeable traders. Thus, they need to be aware of the value their liquidity brings to knowledgeable traders.

Passive traders, acting on behalf of passive or index fund portfolio managers, similarly seek liquidity in their rebalancing transactions, but they are much more concerned with the cost of trading. They tend to use time-insensitive techniques in the hope of exchanging a lack of urgency for lower-cost execution. Passive traders have the flexibility to use lower-cost trading techniques. Because of the types of orders and markets they use, these traders resemble dealers in the sense that they allow the opposing party to determine the timing of the trade in exchange for determining the acceptable trade price.

Other types of traders do not fit exactly into the above categories. Dealers, whose profits depend on earning bid–ask spreads, have short trading time horizons like information-motivated traders. Given that a transaction is profitable, however, they have no specific emphasis on time versus price. Arbitrageurs are sensitive to both price of execution and speed of execution as they attempt to exploit small price discrepancies between closely related assets trading in different markets. **Day traders** rapidly buy and sell stocks in the hope that the stocks will continue to rise or fall in value for the seconds or minutes they are ready to hold a position. Like dealers, they often seek to profitably accommodate the trading demands of others.

Exhibit 8 summarizes the attitudes toward trading displayed by the various traders in the market. In the exhibit, the final column gives the trader's emphasis on price or time (i.e., avoiding delay in execution).

EXHIBIT 8	Summary of Trading Motivations, Time Horizons, and Time versus Price Preferences		
Trader	**Motivation**	**Trading Time Horizon**	**Time versus Price Preference**
Information-motivated	New information	Minutes to hours	Time
Value-motivated	Perceived valuation errors	Days to weeks	Price
Liquidity-motivated	Invest cash or divest securities	Minutes to hours	Time
Passive	Rebalancing, investing/divesting cash	Days to weeks	Price
Dealers and day traders	Accommodation	Minutes to hours	Passive, indifferent

This classification of traders is relevant to both equity markets and fixed-income markets.

Alternative investments tend to be characterized by infrequent trading and illiquidity; day traders are not relevant as a trader type in such markets, in general. However, the thematic differences among the major types of traders (information-motivated, value-motivated, liquidity-motivated, and passive) still have recognizable counterparts in many alternative investment markets, although the relevant time horizons are longer. For example, in real estate, information concerning planned future construction, perceived valuation errors, and the need for liquidity can motivate transactions, and some investors may seek long-term, broad, diversified exposure, corresponding roughly to the passive trader type.

4.2 Traders' Selection of Order Types

All of the orders discussed in earlier sections above, as well as others discussed in advanced treatments, are used tactically by buy-side traders as warranted by market conditions and the motivations of the portfolio manager.

4.2.1 Information-Motivated Traders

Information traders believe that they need to trade immediately and often trade large quantities in specific names. Demands for high liquidity on short notice may overwhelm the ready supply of stock in the market, triggering adverse price movements as the effect of these demands reverberates through the market. Information traders may use fast action principal trades. By transacting with a dealer, the buy-side trader quickly secures execution at a guaranteed price. The major cost of these trades arises because the dealer demands a price concession to cover the inventory risks undertaken. Furthermore, information-motivated traders fear that the price may move quickly to embed the information, devaluing their information edge. They are aware that their trading often moves the market, but they believe their information justifies the increased trading cost. Accordingly, information-motivated traders may wish to disguise their anxious trading need. Where possible, they use less obvious orders, such as market orders, to disguise their trading intentions. This behavior has led information traders to be called "wolves in sheep's clothing."

4.2.2 Value-Motivated Traders

The value-motivated trader develops an independent assessment of value and waits for market prices to move into the range of that assessment. Thus, the market comes with excess inventory to the trader and presents him with attractive opportunities.

The typical value-motivated trader uses limit orders or their computerized institutional market equivalent. An attractive price is more important than timely activity. Thus, price is controlled but timing is not. Even though value-motivated traders may act quickly, they are still accommodative and pay none of the penalties of more anxious traders. As Treynor (1987) pointed out, value traders can sometimes operate as "the dealer's dealer," buying stock when dealers most want to sell stock.

4.2.3 Liquidity-Motivated Traders

The commitment or release of cash is the primary objective of liquidity-motivated traders. The types of orders used include market, market-not-held, best efforts, participate, principal trades, portfolio trades, and orders on ECNs and crossing networks. Low commissions and small impact are desirable, and liquidity traders can often tolerate somewhat more uncertainty about timely trade completion than can information-motivated traders.

Many liquidity-motivated traders believe that displaying their true liquidity-seeking nature works in their favor. When trading with a liquidity-motivated trader, dealers and other market participants can relax some of the protective measures that they use to prevent losses to informed traders.

4.2.4 Passive Traders

Low-cost trading is a strong motivation of passive traders, even though they are liquidity-motivated in their portfolio-rebalancing operations. As a result, these traders tend to favor limit orders, portfolio trades, and crossing networks. The advantages, in addition to certainty of price, are low commissions, low impact, and the possible reduction or elimination of bid–ask spread costs. The major weakness is the uncertainty of whether trades will be completed within a reasonable time frame. These orders and markets are best suited to trading that is neither large nor heavily concentrated.

TRADE EXECUTION DECISIONS AND TACTICS 5

The diversity of markets, order types, and characteristics of the particular securities that must be traded means that the task of selecting a trading strategy and promptly executing it is quite complex. In the following, we first discuss decisions related to the handling of a trade. Then, we address objectives in trading and trading tactics, including automated trading.

5.1 Decisions Related to the Handling of a Trade

Trading costs are controllable, necessitating thoughtful approaches to trading strategies. Poor trading involving inattentive or inappropriate trading tactics leads to higher transaction costs. Conversely, good trading lowers transaction costs and improves investment performance.

A head trader thinking about how to organize his or her team needs to develop a daily strategy which balances the trading needs of the portfolio manager(s) and the condition of the market. The head trader, of course, controls neither but has to devise a strategy for trading the daily blotter. Considerations that come into play include the following:

▶ Small, liquidity-oriented trades can be packaged up and executed via direct market access and algorithmic trading. **Direct market access** (DMA) refers to platforms sponsored by brokers that permit buy-side traders to directly access equities, fixed income, futures, and foreign exchange markets, clearing via the broker.[26] Algorithmic trading, a type of automated electronic trading, will be discussed later. Larger trades can receive custom handling. Why waste the talent of senior traders and the most competent brokers on trades in which it is not possible to make an economically significant difference?

---

[26] As of 2004, estimates were that about a third of buy-side equity orders were executed via DMA (www.wstonline.com) in the United States.

► Large, information-laden trades demand immediate skilled attention. Senior traders are needed to manage the tradeoff between impact and delay costs by releasing the minimum amount of information into the market that is required to get the trade done.

► In addition to best execution, the trader must be cognizant of client trading restrictions, cash balances, and brokerage allocations, if any.

Once the strategy is determined and traders are handed their assignments, the problem of best execution practice becomes tactical. Of course, trading tactics change in response to the market conditions encountered. Each trader, while working orders, should be asking the following questions:

1. What is the right trading tactic for this particular trade at this point in time?
2. Is the trade suitable for DMA or algorithmic trading, or is manual handling of the trade appropriate?
3. If a broker is used, by my experience and measurement, which broker is best suited to handle this order?
4. What is the expected versus experienced cost for this type of trading tactic?
5. Where is the lowest-cost liquidity likely to be found?
6. If the low-cost alternatives fail, where should I go to increase the aggressiveness of the trading?
7. Is the market responding as I would expect, or are there messages that should be conveyed to portfolio management?
8. How can I find out as much as possible about the market situation while revealing as little as possible of my own unfulfilled intentions?
9. What can be done to minimize any negative tax consequences of the trade (such as earmarking specifically the lot of securities being sold so as to control their cost basis)?

The process starts with an order-by-order understanding of the urgency and size constraints. These constraints determine the appropriate processes that the desk can use. Order tactics, in turn, determine the market venues that represent the best alternative. At that point, specific order handling depends on the desk's commitments, activity by brokers currently trafficking in the name, and the desk's comfort with the specific broker or electronic venue.

In summary, the key function of trade desk organization is to prioritize trading. Good desks quickly identify the dangerous trades and assign the priority. They know how their managers think, in general and in relation to the specific individual trade. They attune the mix of brokers to their trading needs, often concentrating trading to increase their clout. Finally, they are constantly innovating and experimenting, trying new trade routes and refining desk processes.

5.2 Objectives in Trading and Trading Tactics

How does a trader decide which type of order to use? Earlier in this reading, the strategic decision of the trade was identified as one of buying or selling time (deciding how much urgency to attach to trade completion). Perhaps the most common trader errors are selling time too cheaply when executing value-motivated transactions and buying time too expensively when executing information-motivated transactions. A third error, and the most serious error for a liquidity trader, is to act in a manner that evokes protective or exploitative responses from dealers and other market participants who sense an information motivation or other time-sensitive motivation.

One tactical decision faced by buy-side traders is the type of order to be used. Few portfolio managers base their investment decisions solely on value, information, or liquidity. Most managers mix strategic goals in response to client agreements, manager perceptions, and market cycles. For example, clients may require full investment in equities at all times, regardless of whether superior investment alternatives are available. Accordingly, trading tactics may at times appear inconsistent with the stated long-term strategic investment objectives. Thus, all buy-side traders need to understand, and occasionally use, the full range of trading techniques. The subsections that follow discuss a categorization of similarities and differences among various trading techniques.

5.2.1 Liquidity-at-Any-Cost Trading Focus

Information traders who believe they need to trade in institutional block size with immediacy use these trading techniques. The problem, of course, is that everyone is wary of trading with an informed trader. On the other hand, dealers are mightily interested in finding out whether these anxious traders have any valuable information. Thus, these traders can usually attract brokers willing to represent their order, but often at a high commission rate or price concession.

These trades demand high liquidity on short notice. They may overwhelm the available liquidity in the market and cause prices to move when their presence is detected. Traders who use these techniques usually recognize that these methods are expensive but pay the price in order to achieve timely execution.

On occasion, urgency will place a normally nonaggressive trader into this category. A mutual fund with unusual end-of-day sales, for example, may need to liquidate security positions whatever the cost.

5.2.2 Costs-Are-Not-Important Trading Focus

Market orders and the variations on this type (such as market on close) are examples of orders resulting from a costs-are-not-important focus. Some investors seldom consider using anything other than market orders when trading securities. Market orders work acceptably well for most mixes of investment strategies, in which it is difficult to assign pure information, value, or liquidity motivation. They also serve to mask trading intention, since all market orders look alike.

Traders who use market orders trust the competitive market to generate a fair price. For many orders, fair market price is a reasonable assumption. Exchanges encourage market orders and set up elaborate procedures to assure that these orders receive fair "best execution" prices. Active control of the order is not required.

Market orders work best for smaller trades and more liquid stocks. They are sometimes called "no-brainers" because they require little trading skill on the part of the buy-side trader or the broker. Because they require little effort or risk taking by market makers, they are inexpensive for a broker to execute and have been used to produce "soft dollar" commissions in exchange for broker-supplied services.

Traders who use these orders pay ordinary spreads and commissions to have their orders executed rapidly. Trade costs are accepted without question; indeed, they are seldom even considered.

The weakness of market orders is that all trader discretion is surrendered. The trader has no control over the trade, and the broker exercises only the most rudimentary cautions. The marketplace processes are viewed as sufficient to assure fair treatment. To retain discretion, such a trader may also consider using an aggressive limit order—for example, a limit buy order that improves on the best bid or a limit sell order that improves on the best ask price.

5.2.3 Need-Trustworthy-Agent Trading Focus

Buy-side traders often need to execute larger orders than the exchange can accommodate at any given moment, particularly when dealing with thinly traded issues. They recognize that their orders may create adverse impact if they are not handled carefully. Accordingly, these traders engage the services of a carefully selected floor broker to skillfully "work" such orders by placing a best efforts, market-not-held, or participate order. The advantage of these trades is that they match trading desires to interest in taking the other side of the trade as such interest is uncovered or arrives in the market. Orders are usually completed through a series of partial trades. Obviously, immediate execution is not of primary importance, so such orders are less useful for information-motivated traders.

These orders are the epitome of the agency relationship. The trader passes control of the order to the broker, who then controls when and at what price the orders execute. The trader frequently does not know how much of an order was cleared until after the market closes.

The agent, however, may serve multiple masters, including other clients and even the agent's own brokerage firm. The valuable information that a buyer or seller exists is revealed to the broker. It is difficult for the trader to know whether that information is used exclusively in the trader's best interests.

5.2.4 Advertise-to-Draw-Liquidity Trading Focus

Advertising is an explicit liquidity-enhancing technique used with initial public offerings (IPOs), secondary offerings, and **sunshine trades**, which publicly display the trading interest in advance of the actual order. If publicity attracts enough traders taking the opposite side, the trade may execute with little or no market impact.

Implied in agency orders is an authorization to do some low-level advertising on the exchange floor. Advertising lets the market know that a willing buyer or seller is around. That presence may draw out the other side of the trade. However, such an order may also bear the risk of trading in front of the order. For example, if a large block purchase order is announced, traders may take long positions in the security in the hope of realizing a profit by selling the stock at a higher price.

5.2.5 Low-Cost-Whatever-the-Liquidity Trading Focus

Limit orders are the chief example of this type of order, particularly limit orders that specify prices that are "behind the market": either a limit buy order at a price below the best bid, or a limit sell order at a price above the best ask price. The objective is to improve on the market bid or the market ask, respectively. Minimizing trading costs is the primary interest of buy-side traders who use this type of order. There may not be a counterparty to the trader's order who is willing to trade on the terms suggested. This order type is best suited to passive and value-motivated trading situations.

The advantages of such orders are low commissions, low impact, and possibly the elimination of the market maker spread. One major weakness, of course, is execution uncertainty (the uncertainty of whether any trades will be made at all). Traders could end up "chasing the market" if the market moves away from the limit price. Furthermore, if the limit price becomes "stale" because significant new information on the security reaches the public, the trader could find that a trade has been executed before he or she has been able to revise the limit price. For example, a limit buy order specifying a price that is well below the most recent transaction price runs the risk of being executed only if major negative news relating to the security reaches the public. If that happens, the security could trade down to even lower levels.

5.2.6 Trading Technique Summary

Exhibit 9 summarizes the uses, costs, advantages, and weaknesses of these trading techniques.

EXHIBIT 9	Objectives in Trading			
Focus	**Uses**	**Costs**	**Advantages**	**Weaknesses**
Liquidity at any cost (I must trade)	Immediate execution in institutional block size	High cost due to tipping supply/demand balance	Guarantees execution	High potential for market impact and information leakage
Need trustworthy agent (Possible hazardous trading situation)	Large-scale trades; low-level advertising	Higher commission; possible leakage of information	Hopes to trade time for improvement in price	Loses direct control of trade
Costs are not important	Certainty of execution	Pays the spread; may create impact	Competitive, market-determined price	Cedes direct control of trade; may ignore tactics with potential for lower cost
Advertise to draw liquidity	Large trades with lower information advantage	High operational and organizational costs	Market-determined price for large trades	More difficult to administer; possible leakage to front-runners
Low cost whatever the liquidity	Non-informational trading; indifferent to timing	Higher search and monitoring costs	Low commission; opportunity to trade at favorable price	Uncertainty of trading; may fail to execute and create a need to complete at a later, less desirable price

5.3 Automated Trading

Trading strategy will vary according to the specifics of the trade and the markets in which the trade might be executed. For example, traders attempting to trade very large orders relative to typical trading volume may involve brokers to avail themselves of the brokers' network of contacts and market knowledge in locating counterparties. By contrast, traders in quote-driven markets will typically try to negotiate trades with dealers, attempting to find the best possible quotes for their trades. As noted earlier, the rapid evolution of market structure worldwide toward order-driven systems, and electronic automated auctions in particular, has important implications for the trading process. Indeed, one of the more important implications of the growth of automated venues is the rapid expansion in algorithmic trading.

Algorithmic trading refers to automated electronic trading subject to quantitative rules and user-specified benchmarks and constraints. Related, but distinct, trading strategies include using portfolio trades, in which the trader simultaneously executes a set of trades in a basket of stocks, and smart routing, whereby algorithms are used to intelligently route an order to the most liquid venue. The term **automated trading** is the most generic, referring to any form of trading that is not manual, including trading based on algorithms.

Estimates of automated trading usage vary widely, and some estimates put it as high as 25 percent of average share volume. Informed commentators all agree that this share is increasing, with some projecting algorithmic volume growing at a 30–35 percent rate per annum over the next few years.[27] This revolution raises natural questions: How do algorithmic systems work? What goes inside the "black box" of algorithmic trading? Will algorithmic systems displace human traders, or can savvy human traders infer the logic of the algorithm and profit by gaming the computer? Do algorithms always work as advertised, or do traders put too much trust in them? Are algorithms really effective in controlling transaction costs and hence adding alpha? What is the future of algorithmic trading? The following discussion sheds light on these issues and focuses on an in-depth analysis of the anatomy of algorithmic trading.

5.3.1 The Algorithmic Revolution

The rapid growth of algorithmic trading by institutional traders reflects complex regulatory and technological factors. In the United States, decimalization (the use of a minimum price increment of 0.01, for U.S. currency $0.01) has led to a dramatic reduction in spreads in U.S. equities but has also reduced quoted depths. Average trade size in many U.S. markets, including the New York Stock Exchange and NASDAQ, which constitute a substantial fraction of world equity market value, has fallen dramatically.[28] For institutions with large orders, these changes greatly complicate the task of trading. Institutional orders are typically large relative to normal trading volume. *The underlying logic behind algorithmic trading is to exploit market patterns of trading volume so as to execute orders with controlled risk and costs.* This approach typically involves breaking large orders up into smaller orders that blend into the normal flow of trades in a sensible way to moderate price impact. For active equity trading desks, algorithmic or automated trading is the only recourse for efficiently handling increased volumes given increasingly smaller average trade size.

EXAMPLE 9

The Changing Roles of Traders

Algorithmic trading involves programming a computer to "slice and dice" a large order in a liquid security into small pieces, then meters the pieces into an automated exchange using FIX communications technology (FIX is a messaging protocol in equity markets that facilitates electronic trading).

---

[27] As of 2005, one estimate is that 15–20 percent of U.S. investment firms have adopted algorithmic trading. See Schmerken (2005).

[28] According to the *NYSE Fact Book* (various editions), the average number of shares per trade peaked at 2,568 in June 1988 and then began to decline. The number of shares per trade remained in the low 1,000s for most of the late 1990s, falling below 1,000 shares in March of 2001, the year of decimalization, and steadily declining since. In December 2003, the average reached 433 shares per trade. Decimalization, adopted by the United States and Canada during the early 2000s, has long been the international standard in equity marketplaces.

Trading in 400-share nibbles may sound inefficient, but it is not. Due to the speed of the analytics and the connectivity, trading engines can execute many trades per minute, all without human intervention or human error. Algorithmic trading has changed the role of the trader. Today's traders have become strategists and tacticians, whereas in the past, the primary task of a trader was managing broker relationships.

Of course, the role of the broker also changes when the buy-side institution takes active control of the order. Brokers have in many cases been eliminated from trades they would have formerly been given responsibility for executing. Rather than serving as agents or dealers, brokers increasingly compete on the basis of the quality of their analytic engine.

EXAMPLE 10

Order Fragmentation: The Meat-Grinder Effect[29]

Plexus Group has documented a trade in Oracle Corporation (NAS-DAQ: ORCL) that occurred on 21 November 2002 that illustrates well both order fragmentation and electronic trading.

Before the market opening, a momentum manager sent a 1,745,640-share buy order to his trading desk, and the process unfolded as follows. The desk fed the order to Bloomberg B-Trade, one of several ECNs available to the trade desk. Trading in the issue began at 9:53 a.m. The order was small, in the sense that it was slightly less than 3 percent of Oracle's trading volume that day, and was completed in just 51 minutes in 1,014 separate executions. At times, there were up to 153 executions per minute—more than any human could handle. Average trade size was about 1,700 shares, roughly a 1,000:1 fragmentation ratio (i.e., the ratio of the size of the order to average trade size). The largest execution was roughly 64,000 shares and occurred in a cluster of rapid trading when almost 190,000 shares were executed in less than one minute. The smallest execution was for 13 shares. Seventeen percent of the executions were for 100 shares or less, and 44 percent were for less than 1,000 shares. Implementation shortfall was $0.15 per share, including $0.14 from market impact and delay and $0.01 per share commissions.

The aggressive trading strategy paid off: ORCL rose at the close to yield a trading profit for the day of 4.1 percent, or $785,538. In order for the 1,700,000-odd-share order to be executed, it had to be forced through a constriction 1,700 shares wide on average. This is the meat-grinder effect: In order for a large equity order to get done, it must often be broken up into many smaller orders.

Ever-faster trade message speed and increased volumes in automated trading systems or electronic limit order books, such as the International Securities Exchange for options and Hotspot FX for foreign exchange, have spurred the

---

[29] This example is based on Wagner (2003).

development of algorithmic systems. It is expected that the merger between the NYSE and the Archipelago Exchange will also stimulate greater use of algorithmic systems.

Automated trading requires constant monitoring to avoid taking unintentional risk. For example, if the process executes the easiest trades first, the portfolio manager might wind up later in the day with an unbalanced portfolio or unintended exposure to certain sectors or industries. Algorithmic execution systems that skillfully participate in order flow over time are well adapted to control such portfolio risks.

5.3.2 Classification of Algorithmic Execution Systems

Algorithmic trading has gained considerable popularity among more sophisticated institutional traders looking for a technological solution to a complex, fast-moving, and fragmented market environment. These strategies are typically offered through algorithmic execution systems from institutional brokers, although some institutions and hedge funds have developed their own internal algorithms.

Algorithmic trading has its roots in the simple portfolio trades of the 1980s, in which large baskets of stocks were bought and sold (often as part of an index arbitrage strategy) with the push of a button. In the 1990s, automated systems such as ITG's QuantEX™ allowed for so-called rules-based trading. One example of rules-based trading is "pairs trading," in which the trading engine will automatically enter into (or exit from) a long and short position in a predesignated pair of stocks if certain conditions are met. The user can, for instance, specify a rule that calls for buying XYZ and simultaneously selling ABC if the price ratio of the two stocks crosses a certain threshold. The success of rules-based trading gave rise in the late 1990s to algorithmic trading, in which decisions regarding trading horizon, style, and even venue are automatically generated by a computer using specified algorithms based on specified inputs and then executed electronically. Before we delve into the details of how algorithms actually work, it is useful to develop a classification of algorithmic strategies.

EXHIBIT 10	Algorithmic Trading Classification		
Logical Participation Strategies		Opportunistic Strategies	Specialized Strategies
Simple Logical Participation Strategies	Implementation Shortfall Strategies		

The most common class of algorithms in use is **logical participation strategies**, protocols for breaking up an order for execution over time.

Simple Logical Participation Strategies Institutional traders use the following simple logical participation strategies to participate in overall market volumes without being unduly visible.

▶ One of the most popular logical participation strategies involves breaking up an order over time according to a prespecified volume profile. The objective of this **volume-weighted average price (VWAP) strategy** is to match or improve upon the VWAP for the day.

In a VWAP strategy, the trader attempts to match the expected volume pattern in the stock, typically over the whole day. Forecasts of the volume pattern are generally based on historical data (e.g., 21-day stock-specific or industry averages); increasingly, these forecasts are based on forward-looking volume predictors. Since the actual volume for the day is unknown before the end of the day, however, dynamic predictors are quite volatile.

▶ The **time-weighted average price (TWAP) strategy** is a particularly simple variant that assumes a flat volume profile and trades in proportion to time.

The TWAP strategy breaks up the order over the day in proportion to time, which is useful in thinly traded assets whose volume patterns might be erratic. The objective here is normally to match or beat a time-weighted or equal-weighted average price. The participation strategy trades at a constant fraction of volume (usually 5–20 percent), attempting to blend in with market volumes. This strategy can be reactive if based on past trades or proactive if based on a dynamic forecast of incoming volume.

▶ Another common participation strategy is a **percentage-of-volume strategy**, in which trading takes place in proportion to overall market volume (typically at a rate of 5–20 percent) until the order is completed.

Implementation Shortfall Strategies   Recently, a newer logical participation strategy, the so-called **implementation shortfall strategy** (or **arrival price strategy**), has gained popularity. Unlike simple logical participation strategies, implementation shortfall strategies solve for the optimal trading strategy that minimizes trading costs as measured by the implementation shortfall method.

As discussed earlier, implementation shortfall is defined as the difference between the return on a notional or paper portfolio, in which positions are executed at a price representing the prevailing price when the decision to trade is made, and the actual portfolio's return.

Implementation shortfall strategies seek to minimize implementation shortfall or overall execution costs, usually represented by a weighted average of market impact and opportunity costs. Opportunity costs are related to the risk of adverse price movements, which increases with trading horizon. Consequently, implementation shortfall strategies are typically "front-loaded" in the sense of attempting to exploit market liquidity early in the trading day. Implementation shortfall strategies are especially valuable for portfolio trades, in which controlling the risk of not executing the trade list is critical. They are also useful in transition management (handing over a portfolio to a new portfolio manager), where multiperiod trading is common and there is a need for formal risk controls.

Interest in implementation shortfall strategies is also driven by an increased awareness of the limitations of traditional simple logical participation strategies using VWAP as an objective or benchmark. In addition, the objective of implementation shortfall strategies is consistent with the mean–variance framework used by many quantitative managers, a point we expand upon below. As of the date of this writing, roughly 90 percent of the value of orders traded algorithmically is executed using simple logical participation and implementation shortfall strategies. Exhibit 11 shows the hypothetical trade schedule for an implementation shortfall algorithmic order. Notice that the order is traded aggressively to minimize a weighted average of market impact costs and trade risk. The black line shows the cumulative fraction of the order that is complete, with the order fully complete by noon EST.

| EXHIBIT 11 | Trade Schedule for an Implementation Shortfall Strategy |

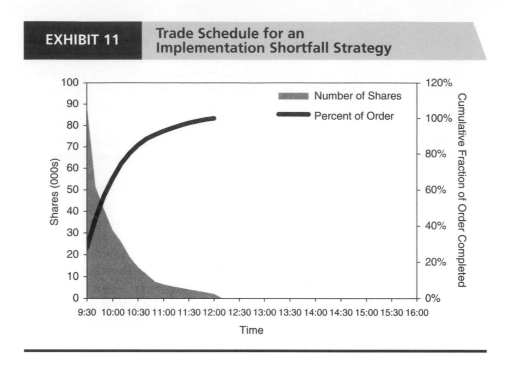

The remaining major types of algorithmic trading are opportunistic participation strategies and specialized strategies.

Opportunistic Participation Strategies   Opportunistic participation strategies also involve trading over time. The opportunistic trading strategy involves passive trading combined with the opportunistic seizing of liquidity. The most common examples are pegging and discretion strategies, in which the trader who wishes to buy posts a bid, hoping others will sell to him or her, yielding negative implicit trading costs. If the bid–offer spread is sufficiently small, however, the trader might buy at the ask. This strategy typically involves using reserve or hidden orders and crossing (internally or externally) to provide additional sources of liquidity at low cost. Because trading is opportunistic, the liquidity strategy is not a true participation strategy.

Specialized Strategies   Other strategies include passive order strategies, which do not necessarily guarantee execution; "hunter" strategies, which opportunistically seek liquidity when it is offered; and more specialized strategies that target particular benchmarks. Market-on-close algorithms that target the closing price are an example of this last category. Smart routing, in which algorithms are used to intelligently route an order to the most liquid venue, can be viewed as a specialized form of algorithmic trading.

The next section gives further insight into the reasoning behind the main type of algorithmic trading, logical participation strategies.

5.3.3 The Reasoning behind Logical Participation Algorithmic Strategies

To take simple logical participation strategies first, underlying such strategies is the implicit assumption that participating in proportion to the actual trading volume can minimize trading costs. A large body of empirical evidence suggests that the price impact of equity trades is an increasing function of order size. Breaking up the order into smaller sub-blocks may therefore yield a lower average market or price impact. This approach is intuitive, as the cost of an immediate demand for a large amount of liquidity is likely to be quite high, whereas if the same order were spread out in time, more liquidity providers could supply the needed opposite party, lessening the adverse price effects. Under certain assumptions (e.g., if prices are linearly related to the order size), breaking up the order in proportion to expected market liquidity yields lower market impact cost.

An implementation shortfall strategy involves minimizing a weighted average of market impact costs and missed trade opportunity costs. Missed trade opportunity cost refers to the risk of not executing a trade because of adverse price movements. A common proxy for such costs is the volatility of trade value or trade cost, which increases with trading horizon. Intuitively, the sooner an order is made available to the market, the greater the opportunity it usually has to find the opposing side of the trade. Consequently, implementation shortfall strategies are typically front-loaded, in the sense that they can involve trading significant fractions of market volume in the early periods of trading, in contrast to simple logical participation strategies.[30]

The logic for implementation shortfall strategies differs from that of the more traditional participation strategy. Recall that breaking up an order yields the lowest market impact cost. However, there is a cost to extending trade duration by breaking the order very finely, namely, risk. The implementation shortfall strategy—after the user specifies a weight on market impact cost and opportunity cost or risk—solves for the optimal trading strategy.[31] The intuition is straightforward. If the trader is very risk averse, then the strategy will trade aggressively in early periods to complete the order quickly to avoid undue risk. The more formal problem solved by the implementation shortfall algorithm can be expressed mathematically as

$$\text{Min}\{S_1, S_2, \ldots, S_T\} \text{ Expected cost}(S_1, S_2, \ldots, S_T) + \lambda \text{Var}[\text{Cost}(S_1, S_2, \ldots, S_T)]$$

where T is the horizon (some algorithms actually solve for this), S_t represents the shares to be traded in trading interval (or bucket) t, λ is the weight placed on risk (aversion parameter), and Var[Cost] represents the variance of the cost of trading. The expression given is an **objective function** (a quantitative expression of the objective or goal of a process). In words, the objective function states that an implementation shortfall algorithm selects the set of trades that minimizes a quantity equal to the expected total cost of the trades and a penalty term that increases with the variance of the possible cost outcomes for the set of trades. The penalty term reflects the trader's desire for certainty as to costs.

Observe the close correspondence between this problem and the classic mean–variance portfolio optimization problem. Indeed, for a quantitative manager using a mean–variance optimization approach, it is logical to use an implementation shortfall algorithm. Implementation shortfall costs directly reduce the portfolio's return and hence are part of the expected return component in the portfolio optimization problem. Transaction costs are an integral element of portfolio performance because the variance of cost is ultimately manifested in the variance of portfolio returns, and expected costs directly reduce alpha.

---

[30] The exception might occur when there is significant volume expected at the end of the day that the strategy takes into consideration.

[31] See, for example, Almgren and Chriss (2000/2001).

Although many managers do not recognize this dependence, it is quantitatively important. For example, a small-capitalization fund rebalancing daily might easily incur costs of trading of, say, 80 bps, with a standard deviation of 150–200 bps. On an annualized basis, these figures are large relative to the expected returns and risks of the portfolio. The implementation shortfall algorithm is thus consistent with the ultimate portfolio optimization problem.

Choosing among algorithms and setting the right parameters are difficult tasks. A simple illustration can help us understand the types of considerations that enter into selecting tactics. Exhibit 12 shows summary output from a trader's order management system (OMS) or trade blotter indicating trade size (in shares), various market attributes, and an urgency level from the portfolio manager. (A **trade blotter** is a device for entering and tracking orders to trade and trade executions.)

EXHIBIT 12		Order Management System				
Symbol	Side	Size (shares)	Avg. Daily Volume	Price	Spread (%)	Urgency
ABC	B	100,000	2,000,000	55.23	0.05	Low
DEF	S	30,000	60,000	10.11	0.55	Low
GHIJ	B	25,000	250,000	23.45	0.04	High

What tactics are appropriate for each order? Although the first order in ABC is the largest in shares and value, it is actually the smallest as a percentage of average daily volume, and given the low spreads and low urgency level, it is ideally suited for algorithmic execution, probably with a VWAP algorithm using the entire day's liquidity. Similarly, the order in GHIJ is just 10 percent of average daily volume, but given the high urgency, an implementation shortfall algorithm might be preferred with a high urgency setting to aggressively execute the purchase. By contrast, the order in DEF is large relative to average daily volume and would likely be traded using a broker or crossing system to mitigate the large spreads.

EXAMPLE 11

A Trading Strategy

Charles Lee is discussing execution strategy with Rachel Katz, the head of equity trading at his investment management firm. Lee has decided to increase the position in Curzon Enterprises for growth-oriented equity accounts. Katz shows Lee Exhibit 13, which depicts the execution of a buy order in Curzon Enterprises that established the initial position in it. In Exhibit 13, the black line shows the cumulative fraction of the order that is complete as the trading day progresses, with the order fully complete by the close at 4:00 p.m. EST. The shaded area represents trading volume over half-hour intervals.

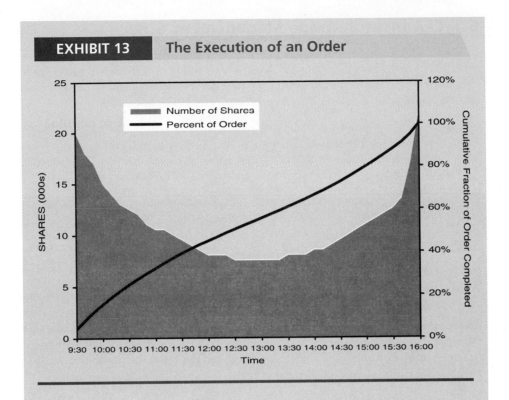

EXHIBIT 13   The Execution of an Order

Using the information in Exhibit 13, address the following:

1. Interpret the pattern of intraday trading in Curzon Enterprises.
2. Identify and evaluate the execution strategy depicted in Exhibit 13.

Solution to 1: Trading in Curzon Enterprises follows a U shape, with highest volume at the opening and close and lowest volume at midday.

Solution to 2: The exhibit depicts a VWAP algorithmic order. The execution strategy split the order up into pieces to be executed throughout the day. The curve indicating the cumulative fraction executed has a steeper slope earlier and later in the day than in midsession, indicating that the volume of orders the algorithm sent to the market was highest near the opening and the close, following the lead of the U-shaped trading volume, which indicates greatest volume at those times.

SERVING THE CLIENT'S INTERESTS

6

For the portfolio manager and buy-side trader, the effectiveness with which portfolio decisions are executed has an impact on the investment performance delivered to the client. The following sections discuss important issues related to protecting the client's interests.

6.1 CFA Institute Trade Management Guidelines

In 2002, CFA Institute published the Trade Management Guidelines[32] to offer investment managers "a framework from which to make consistently good trade-execution suggestions that, together, form a systematic, repeatable, and demonstrable approach to seeking Best Execution." The Guidelines state:

> The concept of "Best Execution" is similar to that of "prudence" in intent and practice. Although prudence and Best Execution may be difficult to define or quantify, a general determination can be made as to whether they have been met. . . . Prudence addresses the appropriateness of holding certain securities, while Best Execution addresses the appropriateness of the methods by which securities are acquired or disposed. Security selection seeks to add value to client portfolios by evaluating future prospects; Best Execution seeks to add value by reducing frictional trading costs. These two activities go hand in hand in achieving better investment performance and in meeting standards of prudent fiduciary behavior.

The Guidelines define best execution as "*the trading process Firms apply that seeks to maximize the value of a client's portfolio within the client's stated investment objectives and constraints.*" (Emphasis added; "Firms" refers to investment management firms.) The definition goes on to identify the four characteristics shown in the left-hand column of Exhibit 14. In the right-hand column, the authors amplify the thinking behind the guidelines.

EXHIBIT 14	Best Execution
Characteristic	**Explanation**
Best execution is intrinsically tied to portfolio-decision value and cannot be evaluated independently.	The purpose of trading is to capture the value of investment decisions. Thus, the definition has strong symmetry to the definition of prudent expert that guides fiduciary decisions.
Best execution is a prospective, statistical, and qualitative concept that cannot be known with certainty *ex ante*.	Trading is a negotiation, with each side of the trade having equal standing. Both buyer and seller—or their appointed agents—jointly determine what "best execution" is for every trade.
Best execution has aspects that may be measured and analyzed over time on an *ex post* basis, even though such measurement on a trade-by-trade basis may not be meaningful in isolation.	Trading occurs in a volatile environment subject to high statistical variability. One would not evaluate a card player on an individual hand; one would need to observe a sequence of hands to determine skill; similarly for traders. Despite the variability, overall trades contain some information useful in evaluating the process. By compiling trade data, one can deduce useful information about the quality of the process.
Best execution is interwoven into complicated, repetitive, and continuing practices and relationships.	Trading is a process, not an outcome. The standards are behavioral.

---

[32] See www.cfainstitute.org for any updates.

The Trade Management Guidelines are divided into three areas: processes, disclosures, and record keeping:

1. *Processes.* Firms should establish formal policies and procedures that have the ultimate goal of maximizing the asset value of client portfolios through best execution. A firm's policies and procedures should provide guidance to measure and manage effectively the quality of trade decisions.

2. *Disclosures.* Firms should disclose to clients and prospects (1) their general information regarding trading techniques, venues, and agents and (2) any actual or potential trading-related conflicts of interest. Such disclosure provides clients with the necessary information to help them assess a firm's ability to deliver best execution.

3. *Record keeping.* Firms should maintain proper documentation that supports (1) compliance with the firm's policies and procedures and (2) the disclosures provided to clients. In addition to aiding in the determination of best execution, the records may support a firm's broker selection practices when examined by applicable regulatory organizations.

At the time these guidelines were written, the state of the art in transaction cost measurement was such that it was not possible to specify specific methodologies for transaction cost measurement. Rather, the guidelines are a compilation of recommended practices and not standards.

In the end, best execution is primarily an exercise in serving the needs of the investment management clients. Adherence to standards of documentation and disclosure, as important as these are to ensuring best practices, is simply a means to achieving this overriding objective.[33]

6.2 The Importance of an Ethical Focus

"My word is my honor." The code of both buy-side and sell-side traders is that verbal agreements will be honored. The code is self-enforcing: Any trader who does not adhere to it quickly finds that no one is willing to deal with him.

Nonetheless, valuable information is the stock-in-trade of market participants, and the temptations are great. One of the side effects of the explosion of trading techniques and trading alternatives is that it is difficult to trace the uses to which information is being put. It is often necessary to rely on the strength of a trader's reputation and his or her avid desire to maintain and build long-term relationships.

Trading can be looked at as a "zero-sum game" in which one trader's losses are another trader's gains. The near disappearance of the brokerage commission has caused more trading costs to be implicit rather than explicit. Markets are thus becoming more adversarial and less agency-oriented, making it more difficult to align investor or buy-side interests with broker/dealer or sell-side interests.

In every case, the ethical focus for the portfolio manager and the buy-side trader must be the interests of the client. As previously mentioned, the buy-side trader acts in a fiduciary capacity, with access to the client's assets. Loyalties to the trader's own firm and relationships with sell-side traders must be consistent with the trader's fiduciary responsibilities.

---

[33] For further background on the subject, see Wagner and Edwards (1993), Wagner (2003), and Schwartz and Wood (2003).

7   CONCLUDING REMARKS

The ability of the sell-side system of brokers and exchanges to adapt and create solutions to investment requirements is impressive. In general, and increasingly, traders get the trading services they demand. Different order types and different venues serve investors with different motives and trading needs. In return, the broker/dealers and exchanges earn a competitive price for providing the services.

Technological advances continue to play a major role in reducing transaction costs. Faster dissemination of information, improved public access, more sophisticated analysis, and eventually the replacement of exchange floor trading by electronic trading can be expected. These efficiencies will reduce the cost of running the exchange system, but they will not necessarily reduce the cost of dealer services provided. Nor will the pressure to reduce costs and improve portfolio performance diminish.

Because of the intensity of competition and the readiness to adapt and innovate, costs continue to fall. Buy-side traders who demand the facilities and conveniences provided by the exchange community must expect to pay the costs. To reduce trading costs, an ever-evolving understanding of the trading process and its implied costs is essential. Sponsors and investment advisors may face make-or-buy decisions concerning future trading and trading-subsidized services. High-speed connectivity and algorithmic trading are clear examples of how costs can be effectively reduced by removing extraneous middlemen from the trading process.

Investors and traders are accustomed to a market that handles the duties, costs, and risks of trading. In addition, the sell side delivers an array of valuable but sometimes dimly related services without additional charge. Such services do not come free, however. In the future, pension plan sponsors and other clients will demand that portfolio managers and traders make more informed choices that reconcile trade costs with benefits received. Sponsors and other clients pay the costs of trading and are entitled to—and are increasingly demanding—a clear accounting of benefits derived.

SUMMARY

The portfolio decision is not complete until securities are bought or sold. How well that last step is accomplished is a key factor affecting investment results. This reading has made the following points.

▶ Market microstructure refers to the particular trading protocols that govern how a trader's latent demands are translated into executed trades. Knowledge of market microstructure helps investors understand how their trades will be executed and how market frictions may give rise to discrepancies between price and full-information expectations of value.

▶ Order-driven markets are those in which prices are established by public limit orders and include auction markets and electronic crossing networks (where trading occurs at prespecified points in time), as well as automated auctions (where trading takes place continuously). Quote-driven markets rely on market makers or dealers to establish prices at which securities can be bought and sold. Brokered markets are markets in which transactions are largely effected by brokers through a search mechanism. Hybrid markets are those, such as the NYSE, that incorporate features of more than one type of market.

▶ Execution services secured through a broker include the following: representing the order, finding the buyer, market information for the investor, discretion and secrecy, escrow, and support of the market mechanism. A trader's broker stands in an agency relationship to the trader, in contrast to dealers. Dealers provide bridge liquidity to buyers and sellers in that they take the other side of the trade when no other liquidity is present.

▶ The effective spread is two times the deviation of the price received or paid from the midpoint of the market at the time an order is entered to the actual execution price. The bid–ask spread is the difference between the bid and the ask prices. The effective spread is a better representation of the true cost of trading than the bid–ask spread because it captures both price improvement and price impact.

▶ Market quality is judged by the following criteria, which are positives for a market's liquidity: many buyers and sellers; diversity of opinion, information, and investment needs; a readily accessible location; continuous operation during convenient market hours; a reasonable cost of transacting; market integrity, in effect the honesty of market participants; assurity of the contract's integrity.

▶ Transaction costs include explicit costs and implicit costs. Explicit costs are the direct costs of trading and include broker commission costs, taxes, stamp duties, and fees. Implicit costs include indirect costs such as the impact of the trade on the price received.

▶ Implementation shortfall is an estimate of transaction costs that amounts to subtracting the all-in transaction costs from the market price at the time the decision was made to buy or sell the security.

▶ Econometric models for costs are useful for obtaining pretrade estimates of the costs of a trade. These models may use variables such as stock liquidity, risk, trade size relative to available liquidity, momentum, and trading style.

▶ The major types of traders are information-motivated traders (who trade on information with limited time value), value-motivated traders (who trade on valuation judgments), liquidity-motivated traders (who trade based on liquidity needs), and passive traders (who trade for indexed portfolios). Information-motivated and liquidity-motivated traders have very short trading time horizons and are more sensitive to time than price in execution. By contrast, value-motivated and passive traders have longer trading time horizons and are more sensitive to price than time in execution.

► The two major order types are market orders (for prompt execution in public markets at the best price available) and limit orders (specifying a price at which the order becomes executable). Market orders are among the order types preferred by information-motivated and liquidity-motivated traders because of their time preference. Limit orders are among the order types preferred by value-motivated and passive traders because they are sensitive to price.

► Major focuses influencing the choice of trading strategy include the following: liquidity needed at any cost, need trustworthy agent for possibly hazardous trading situation, costs are not important, advertise to draw liquidity, and low cost whatever the liquidity.

► Algorithmic trading refers to automated electronic trading subject to quantitative rules and user-specified benchmarks and constraints. Three broad categories of algorithmic trading strategies are logical participation strategies (which involve protocols for breaking up an order for execution over time), opportunistic strategies (which involve passive trading combined with the opportunistic seizing of liquidity), and specialized strategies (which cover a range of strategies that serve special purposes).

PRACTICE PROBLEMS FOR READING 41

1. An analyst is estimating various measures of spread for Airnet Systems, Inc. (NYSE: ANS). The following is a sample of quotes in ANS on the New York Stock Exchange on 10 March 2004 between 10:49:00 and 10:57:00.

Time	Bid Price ($)	Ask Price ($)
10:49:44	4.69	4.74
10:50:06	4.69	4.75
10:50:11	4.69	4.76
10:50:14	4.70	4.76
10:54:57	4.70	4.75
10:56:32	4.70	4.75

Source: Trade and Quote (TAQ) database, NYSE.

A buyer-initiated trade in ANS was entered at 10:50:06 and was executed at 10:50:07 at a price of $4.74. For this trade, answer the following:

A. What is the quoted spread?

B. What is the effective spread?

C. When would the effective and quoted spreads be equal?

2. In a report dated 15 December 2004, the Office of Economic Analysis of the U.S. Securities and Exchange Commission (SEC) compared trade execution quality on the NYSE and NASDAQ using a matched sample of 113 pairs of firms. The comparison is based on six months of data from January–June 2004. The results regarding which market has the better execution quality (NYSE or NASDAQ) vary across order size, firm size, and order type. The results below are for small market orders (100–499 shares) in shares of large market capitalization firms.

Spread (cents)	NASDAQ	NYSE
Quoted spread	2.737	2.791
Effective spread	2.650	2.490

Source: Office of Economic Analysis, SEC, 15 December 2004.

On the basis of the above results, address the following:

A. Determine whether dealers in NASDAQ shares and dealers ("specialists") in NYSE shares in the particular market being discussed provided price improvements.

B. Contrast the relative performance of dealers in the two markets with regard to any price improvements.

3. E-Crossnet is an electronic crossing network that operates in Europe. It runs a total of 14 crosses every day at half-hour intervals. After a cross is run, there are some stocks for which there are unmatched buy quantities and some stocks with unmatched sell quantities. Discuss whether E-Crossnet should disclose these unmatched quantities after a cross is run.

4. For each of the following, discuss which of the two orders in shares of Sunny Corporation will have a greater market impact. Assume that all other factors are the same.

   A. **i.** An order to buy 5,000 shares placed by a trader on the NYSE.
      ii. An order to buy 50,000 shares placed by the same trader on the NYSE.

   B. **i.** An order to buy 25,000 shares placed by a trader on the NYSE.
      ii. An order to buy 25,000 shares placed on the NYSE by another trader who is believed to represent informed investors in the stock.

   C. **i.** An order to sell 20,000 shares placed by a trader on the NYSE.
      ii. An order to sell 20,000 shares placed by the same trader on POSIT, an electronic crossing network.

5. An investment manager placed a limit order to buy 500,000 shares of Alpha Corporation at $21.35 limit at the opening of trading on 8 February. The closing market price of Alpha Corporation on 7 February was also $21.35. The limit order filled 40,000 shares, and the remaining 460,000 shares were never filled. Some good news came out about Alpha Corporation on 8 February, and its price increased to $23.60 by the end of that day. However, by the close of trading on 14 February, the price had declined to $21.74. The investment manager is analyzing the missed trade opportunity cost using the closing price on 7 February as the benchmark price.

   A. What is the estimate of the missed trade opportunity cost if it is measured at a one-day interval after the decision to trade?

   B. What is the estimate of the missed trade opportunity cost if it is measured at a one-week interval after the decision to trade?

   C. What are some of the problems in estimating the missed trade opportunity cost?

6. A portfolio manager would like to buy 5,000 shares of a very recent IPO stock. However, he was not able to get any shares at the IPO price of £30. The portfolio manager would still like to have 5,000 shares, but not at a price above £45 per share. Should he place a market order or a limit order? What would be the advantage and disadvantage of each type of order, given his purposes?

7. An asset management firm wants to purchase 500,000 shares of a company. It decides to shop the order to various broker/dealer firms to see which firm can offer the best service and lowest cost. Discuss the potential negatives of shopping the order.

8. Able Energy, Inc., is a company listed on NASDAQ (symbol: ABLE). A trader sold 100 shares of this company on 10 May 2004 at 15:52:59 at a price of $2.66 per share. All the trades that occurred in Able Energy on that day are listed below.

Time	Trade Price ($)	Shares Traded
10:00:39	2.71	200
10:00:39	2.72	200
10:00:43	2.76	100
13:09:07	2.77	100
14:13:11	2.70	1100
15:52:59	2.66	100
15:53:01	2.65	100

Source: Trade and Quote (TAQ) database, NYSE.

The trader is analyzing the implicit costs of the trade, focusing on the bid–ask spread and market impact using specified price benchmarks.

A. What would be the estimated implicit transaction costs using each of the following as the price benchmark?

   i. opening price

   ii. closing price

   iii. volume-weighted average price (VWAP)

B. Evaluate the effect on estimated implicit transaction costs of the choice of benchmark price.

9. A client of a broker evaluates the broker's performance by measuring transaction costs with a specified price benchmark. The broker has discretion over the timing of his trades for the client. Discuss what the broker could do to make his performance look good to the client (even though the broker's execution decisions may not be in the best interests of the client) if the price benchmark used by the client for evaluation is the:

A. opening price.

B. closing price.

C. volume-weighted average price (VWAP).

10. A trader decided to sell 30,000 shares of a company. At the time of this decision, the quoted price was €53.20 to €53.30. Because of the large size of the order, the trader decided to execute the sale in three equal orders of 10,000 shares spread over the course of the day. When she placed the first order, the quoted price was €53.20 to €53.30, and she sold the shares at €53.22. The trade had a market impact, and the quoted price had fallen to €53.05 to €53.15 when she placed the next order. Those shares were sold at €53.06. The quoted price had fallen to €52.87 to €52.98 when she placed the last order. Those shares were sold at €52.87. Suppose this was the market closing price of the shares that day. Answer the following questions. Ignore commissions.

A. Estimate the total transaction cost of the sale of 30,000 shares if the closing price is used as the price benchmark.

B. What is the implementation shortfall estimate of the total cost of executing the sale?

C. Discuss and compare the answers to A and B above. Which of the two approaches is appropriate for the situation in this problem?

11. Suppose 1,000 shares of Acme Co. stock are ordered to be bought on Monday with a benchmark price of $10.00. On Monday, 600 shares are purchased at $10.02 per share. Commissions and fees are $20. On Tuesday, the benchmark price has fallen to $9.99 per share. On Tuesday, 100 more shares are purchased at $10.08 per share. Commissions and fees are $12. Shares for Acme close on Tuesday at $10.01 per share. The remaining shares are not purchased, and the order is canceled on Wednesday just as the market closes at $10.05 per share.

A. Calculate the implementation shortfall for this trade.

B. Calculate the components of the implementation shortfall for this trade.

12. Jane Smith manages an equity fund. She has decided to undertake a major portfolio restructuring by increasing the exposure of the fund to the telecommunications sector. The implementation of her decision would involve investing more than $2 million in the stocks of about 20 telecommunications companies. Contrast the use of a portfolio trade to the use of purchase orders for these stocks placed individually (stock by stock) in terms of the probable market impact of the two approaches.

13. Famed Investments has a C$25 million portfolio. It follows an active approach to investment management and, on average, turns the portfolio over twice a year. That is, it expects to trade 200 percent of the value of the portfolio over the next year. Every time Famed Investments buys or sells securities, it incurs execution costs of 75 basis points, on average. It expects an annual return before execution costs of 8 percent. What is the expected return net of execution costs?

14. Several British stocks trade on both the London Stock Exchange and the New York Stock Exchange. Due to the time difference between London and New York, these stocks trade for six hours every day in London only, followed by the opening of the NYSE and a two-hour period when both markets are open before London closes. Werner and Kleidon (1996) found that the volatility of prices in London is much higher during the two-hour period when both markets are open than during the preceding six-hour period when only London is open. What could be an information-motivated reason for this finding? Assume that U.S. traders do not trade in London.

15. An employee retirement fund manager believes he has special information about a particular company. Based on this information, he believes the company is currently undervalued and decides to purchase 50,000 shares of the company. The manager decides that he will not place a large single order for 50,000 shares but will instead place several medium-sized orders of 2,500–5,000 shares spread over a period of time. Why do you think the manager chooses to follow this strategy?

16. Consider some stocks that trade in two markets, with a trader being able to trade in these stocks in either market. Suppose that the two markets are identical in all respects except that bid–ask spreads are lower and depths (the number of shares being offered at the bid and ask prices) are greater in one of the two markets. State in which market liquidity-motivated and information-motivated traders would prefer to transact. Justify your answer.

17. A trader has been given two trades to execute with the following characteristics. What tactics do you recommend?

Trade	Size (shares)	Average Daily Volume (ADV)	Price	Spread (%)	Urgency
A	200,000	6,000,000	10.00	0.03	High
B	150,000	200,000	10.00	0.60	High

18. A trader must rebalance a pension plan's actively managed $500 million U.S. small-cap equity portfolio to an S&P 500 indexed portfolio in order to effect a change in the plan's strategic asset allocation. He is told that his primary goal is to minimize explicit costs in this rebalance. What should his trading strategy be?

STUDY SESSION 15
MONITORING AND REBALANCING

Ongoing monitoring and rebalancing of the investment portfolio are integral parts of the portfolio management process. Portfolio managers must understand the reasons for monitoring portfolios and be able to formulate appropriate portfolio rebalancing policies.

READING ASSIGNMENT

Reading 42   Monitoring and Rebalancing

335

$4\frac{5}{8}$ $4\frac{11}{16}$ — $\frac{3}{8}$
$5\frac{1}{2}$ $5\frac{1}{2}$ — $\frac{3}{8}$
$5\frac{1}{2}$ $2\frac{13}{16}$ — $\frac{1}{16}$
$20\frac{5}{8}$ $21\frac{3}{16}$ — $\frac{1}{16}$
$17\frac{3}{8}$ $18\frac{1}{8}$ + $\frac{7}{8}$
$19\frac{1}{2}$ $6\frac{1}{2}$ $6\frac{1}{2}$ — $\frac{1}{2}$
$7\frac{1}{4}$ $3\frac{1}{32}$ — $\frac{1}{8}$
$15\frac{1}{16}$
$9\frac{1}{16}$ $\frac{9}{16}$
$\frac{19}{32}$ $9\frac{1}{16}$
$7\frac{15}{16}$ $7\frac{13}{16}$ $7\frac{15}{16}$
$2\frac{5}{8}$ $2\frac{11}{32}$ $2\frac{1}{2}$ +
$2\frac{3}{4}$ $2\frac{1}{4}$ $2\frac{1}{4}$
$12\frac{1}{16}$ $11\frac{3}{8}$ $11\frac{3}{4}$ +
87 $33\frac{3}{4}$ 33 $33\frac{1}{16}$ —
802 $25\frac{5}{8}$ $24\frac{9}{16}$ $25\frac{3}{8}$ +
833 12 $11\frac{5}{8}$ $11\frac{7}{8}$ +
16 $10\frac{1}{2}$ $10\frac{1}{2}$ $10\frac{1}{2}$ —
78 $15\frac{7}{8}$ $15\frac{13}{16}$ $15\frac{7}{8}$ —
608 $9\frac{1}{16}$ $8\frac{1}{4}$ $8\frac{1}{4}$
430 $11\frac{1}{4}$ $10\frac{1}{4}$

MONITORING AND REBALANCING

by Robert D. Arnott, Terence E. Burns, Lisa Plaxco, and Philip Moore

LEARNING OUTCOMES

The candidate should be able to:

a. explain and justify a fiduciary's responsibilities in monitoring an investment portfolio;

b. describe and justify the monitoring of investor circumstances, market/economic conditions, and portfolio holdings and explain the effects that changes in each of these areas can have on the investor's portfolio;

c. recommend and justify revisions to an investor's investment policy statement and strategic asset allocation, given a change in investor circumstances;

d. discuss the benefits and costs of rebalancing a portfolio to the investor's strategic asset allocation;

e. contrast calendar rebalancing to percentage-of-portfolio rebalancing;

f. discuss the key determinants of the optimal corridor width of an asset class in a percentage-of-portfolio rebalancing program, including transaction costs, risk tolerance, correlation, asset class volatility, and the volatility of the remainder of the portfolio, and evaluate the effects of a change in any of these factors;

g. compare and contrast the benefits of rebalancing an asset class to its target portfolio weight versus rebalancing the asset class to stay within its allowed range;

h. explain the performance consequences, in up, down, and nontrending markets, of (1) rebalancing to a constant mix of equities and bills, (2) buying and holding equities, and (3) constant-proportion portfolio insurance (CPPI);

i. distinguish among linear, concave, and convex rebalancing strategies;

j. judge the appropriateness of constant mix, buy-and-hold, and CPPI rebalancing strategies, when given an investor's risk tolerance and asset return expectations.

Managing Investment Portfolios: A Dynamic Process, Third Edition, John L. Maginn, Donald L. Tuttle, Jerald E. Pinto, and Dennis W. McLeavey, editors. Copyright © 2007 by CFA Institute. Reprinted with permission.

1

INTRODUCTION

After a portfolio manager has worked closely with a client to document investment objectives and constraints in an investment policy statement (IPS), agreed on the strategic asset allocation that best positions the client to achieve stated objectives, and executed the strategic asset allocation through appropriate investment strategies for each asset class segment, the manager must constantly monitor and rebalance the portfolio. The need arises for several reasons.

First, clients' needs and circumstances change, and portfolio managers must respond to these changes to ensure that the portfolio reflects those changes. Life-cycle changes are expected for individual investors, so the portfolio manager must plan for these changes and respond to them when they occur. Institutional investors face changing circumstances just as commonly. A pension fund may receive a mandate from its trustees to assume less volatility. A university endowment may need to react to higher-than-anticipated inflation in faculty salaries.

Second, capital market conditions change. Portfolio managers must monitor such changes, adjust their capital market expectations appropriately, and reflect changed expectations in how the portfolio is invested. For example, if a client's return requirement is 8 percent but the strategic asset allocation promises to return on average 6.5 percent in the current climate, what changes should a portfolio manager recommend in light of the anticipated 150 bp shortfall?

Third, fluctuations in the market values of assets create differences between a portfolio's current asset allocation and its strategic asset allocation. These differences may be trivial on a daily basis; over longer periods of time, however, they can result in a significant divergence between the intended and actual allocations. When and how a portfolio manager rebalances the portfolio to the strategic asset allocation is one of the primary focuses of this reading.

For a portfolio manager, designing and building a portfolio is only the beginning of the dynamic and interactive process that lasts for as long as she is the client's trusted advisor. As markets evolve, maintaining the alignment between a client's portfolio and his investment objectives requires constant vigilance. Therefore, monitoring and rebalancing the portfolio is one of the most important elements of the dynamic process of portfolio management.

We divide this reading into two major sections, the first covering monitoring and the second covering rebalancing.

MONITORING   **2**

To monitor something means to systematically keep watch over it to collect information that is relevant to one's purpose. In investments, the purpose is to achieve investment goals. And a reality of investing is that what you don't know *can* hurt you. An overlooked fact may mean not reaching a goal. A portfolio manager should track everything affecting the client's portfolio. We can categorize most items that need to be monitored in one of three ways:

▶ investor circumstances, including wealth and constraints;

▶ market and economic changes; and

▶ the portfolio itself.

Monitoring investor-related factors sometimes results in changes to a client's investment policy statement, strategic asset allocation, or individual portfolio holdings. Monitoring market and economic changes sometimes results in changes to the strategic asset allocation (when they relate to long-term capital market expectations), tactical asset allocation adjustments (when they relate to shorter-term capital market expectations), changes in style and sector exposures, or adjustments in individual holdings. Monitoring the portfolio can lead to additions or deletions to holdings or to rebalancing the strategic asset allocation.

Fiduciaries need to pay particular attention to adequate monitoring in fulfilling their ethical and legal responsibilities to clients. Investment managers for individual and/or institutional separate accounts; managers of pooled funds (including mutual funds and unit trusts); and trustees of private trusts, pension plans, and charitable organizations are all fiduciaries because of their positions of trust with respect to the management of assets owned by or benefiting others. Fiduciaries have a range of ethical, reporting, auditing, disclosure, and other responsibilities to clients. But germane to this discussion, when taking investment actions, fiduciaries must consider the appropriateness and suitability of the portfolio relative to (1) the client's needs and circumstances, (2) the investment's basic characteristics, or (3) the basic characteristics of the total portfolio. These factors change over time. Only by systematic monitoring can a fiduciary secure an informed view of the appropriateness and suitability of a portfolio for a client.

The following sections provide a fuller explanation of monitoring.

2.1 Monitoring Changes in Investor Circumstances and Constraints

Each client has needs and circumstances that will most likely change over time. A successful portfolio manager makes every effort to remain sensitive to client needs and to anticipate events that might alter those needs. Periodic client meetings are an ideal time to ask whether needs, circumstances, or objectives have changed. If they have, the manager may need to revise the IPS and bring the portfolio into line with the revisions. In many cases, minor changes are needed that do not require revising the IPS. In the field of private wealth management, reviews are usually semiannual or quarterly. In institutional investing, the asset allocation review is a natural time for reviewing the range of changes in circumstance. Such reviews are often held annually. In all contacts with any type of client, however, the advisor should be alert to new client circumstances.

When a review is undertaken, what areas should be covered? Changes in investor circumstances and wealth, liquidity requirements, time horizons, legal and regulatory factors, and unique circumstances all need to be monitored.

2.1.1 Changes in Investor Circumstances and Wealth

Changes in circumstances and wealth often affect a client's investment plans. For private wealth clients, events such as changes in employment, marital status, and the birth of children may affect income, expenditures, risk exposures, and risk preferences. Each such change may affect the client's income, expected retirement income, and perhaps risk preferences. The responsibilities of marriage or children have repercussions for nearly all aspects of a client's financial situation. Such events often mark occasions to review the client's investment policy statement and overall financial plan. For institutional clients, operating performance, constituent pressures (such as demands for increased support from the beneficiaries of endowments), and changes in governance practices are among the factors that may affect income, expenditures, risk exposures, and risk preferences. A portfolio manager should communicate regularly with the client to become aware of such changes.

Wealth or net worth is one client factor that is central to investment plans. Wealth, when evaluated in the context of an investor's other circumstances, is both a measure of achieved financial success and an influence on future investment planning. Changes in wealth result from saving or spending, investment performance, and events such as gifts, donations, and inheritances. The investor's return requirements may change as a result, as financial goals recede or move closer to achievement, and risk tolerance may change too. Utility theory suggests that increases in wealth allow investors to increase their level of risk tolerance, accepting more systematic risk with its attendant expected reward. In reality, however, portfolio managers should consider only substantial and permanent changes in wealth in establishing the client's risk tolerance, even though client risk perceptions can vary quite substantially with recently experienced market performance. The portfolio manager's appraisal of a client's risk tolerance should be largely unaffected by transient changes in wealth. The investment manager thus has a difficult role to moderate some investors' desire to dramatically change asset allocations in response to market volatility. In contrast, more-conservative investors may be unprepared to increase their risk tolerance even when a substantial increase in wealth suggests an increased capacity for bearing risk. Such a client's goal may become merely preserving gains that they never expected to have despite the opportunity costs. The portfolio manager should try to understand this mindset and, working within the client's comfort level, seek to restrain its excesses.

2.1.2 Changing Liquidity Requirements

When a client needs money to spend, the portfolio manager should strive to provide it. A liquidity requirement is a need for cash in excess of new contributions or savings as a consequence of some event, either anticipated or unanticipated.

Individual clients experience changes in liquidity requirements as a result of a variety of events, including unemployment, illness, court judgments, retirement, divorce, the death of a spouse, or the building or purchase of a home. Changes in liquidity requirements occur for a variety of reasons for institutional clients, such as the payment of claims by insurers or of retirement benefits by defined-benefit pension plans, or the funding of a capital project by a foundation or endowment.

The possibility of major withdrawals may constrain a portfolio manager's commitments to illiquid investments because of the costs in exiting those investments quickly. Managers who do not face major withdrawals are better positioned to earn the return premium such investments supply. Managers who do face major withdrawals near term may need to hold some part of their portfolio in liquid and low-price-risk assets such as money market instruments.

2.1.3 Changing Time Horizons

Individuals age and pension funds mature. Reducing investment risk is generally advisable as an individual moves through the life cycle and his time horizon shortens; bonds become increasingly suitable investments as this process occurs. Today's life-cycle mutual funds reflect that principle in their asset allocations. In contrast to individuals, some entities such as endowment funds have the hope of perpetual life; the passage of time in and of itself does not change their time horizon, risk budgets, or appropriate asset allocation.

Many private wealth clients have multistage time horizons. For example, a working person typically faces an accumulation stage up to retirement in which she builds wealth through saving and investment, followed by a retirement stage in which she spends wealth and ultimately bequeaths it to heirs. Accumulating funds for a child's higher education can create one or more stages before retirement. Changes in investment policy are usually needed as one time horizon (for example, reaching retirement or selling a closely-held family business) is reached and another begins.

Although some changes in time horizon are forecastable, time horizons can also shift abruptly. For instance, when the last income beneficiary of a trust dies and the **residue** (remaining funds) passes to the **remaindermen** (beneficiaries with a claim on the trust's residue), investment policy, as well as the portfolio, should be adjusted promptly. Annuitizing the benefits for older participants in a pension plan can result in an abrupt change in the plan's remaining liability stream. That should lead to an overhaul of the asset structure and rebalancing to a portfolio structure that more closely fits the new needs. The untimely death of an income-earning spouse requires immediate attention. Portfolio managers need to think about how they will respond to these changes and events and must monitor the client's circumstances for changes in time horizon. Example 1 addresses a change in investment horizon for an individual investor.

EXAMPLE 1

Monitoring a Change in Investment Horizon

William and Mary deVegh, both 32 years old, met and married when they were university students. They each embarked on promising and highly demanding executive careers after leaving college. They are hoping to retire at age 55 to travel and otherwise enjoy the fruits of their hard work. Now well established at their companies, they also want to start a family and are expecting the birth of their first child in two months. They hope the child will follow their tracks and obtain a four-year private university education. The deVeghs anticipate supporting their child through college. Assume that the deVeghs will each live to age 85.

1. Compare and contrast the deVeghs' investment time horizons prior to and immediately subsequent to the birth of their first child.

2. Interpret the challenges the birth will present to their retirement objectives and discuss approaches to meeting those challenges, including investing more aggressively.

Solution to 1: Prior to the birth of their child, the deVeghs have a two-stage time horizon. The first horizon extends from age 32 up to age 55. This first time horizon could be described as an accumulation period in which the deVeghs save and invest for early retirement. The second time horizon is their retirement and is expected to extend from age 55 to age 85. After the birth of their child, they will have a three-stage time horizon. The first stage extends from age 32 through age 50, when they expect their child to enter university at age 18. During this period, the deVeghs must accumulate funds both for retirement and their child's university education. The second stage extends from age 51 up to age 55. In this period the deVeghs must anticipate disbursing substantial funds for tuition, room and board, and other expenses associated with a private university education. The third stage is retirement, expected to extend from age 55 to age 85 as before.

Solution to 2: The birth of the child creates a four-year period of heavy expenses immediately prior to the deVeghs' intended retirement date. Those expenses could put their intended retirement date at risk. The most direct way to mitigate this risk is to increase the amount of money saved and to invest savings for the child's education in a tax-efficient way (tax-advantaged education saving vehicles are available in certain tax jurisdictions). Can the deVeghs mitigate their risk by increasing their risk tolerance? The need for a larger future sum of money does not in itself increase an investor's ability to take risk, although it may affect the investor's willingness to do so. There is no indication that the child's birth will be accompanied by a salary raise or other event increasing the ability to take risk. If the deVeghs' stated risk tolerance prior to the child's birth accurately reflects their ability to bear risk, investing more aggressively after the child's birth will not help them meet the challenges the event poses to their retirement objective.

2.1.4 Tax Circumstances

Taxes are certain; the form they will take and their amount in the future are uncertain. Taxable investors should make all decisions on an after-tax basis. Managers for taxable investors must construct portfolios that deal with each client's current tax situation and take future possible tax circumstances into account. For taxable investors, holding period length and portfolio turnover rates are important because of their effect on after-tax returns. In evaluating investment strategies to meet a taxable investor's changed objective, a portfolio manager will take into account each strategy's **tax efficiency** (the proportion of the expected pretax total return that will be retained after taxes). Monitoring a client's tax situation may suggest the following actions, for example:

▶ Deferring the realization of income from a higher-tax year to an anticipated lower-tax year.

▶ Accelerating expenses to a high-tax year.

▶ Realizing short-term losses at year-end to offset realized short-term gains in the same year.

▶ Deploying assets with high unrealized gains so as to use a step-up in tax basis from original cost to market value (a break allowed investors for certain transactions in some tax jurisdictions). For example, if the client intends to make a charitable donation, making the contribution in appreciated securities may be tax advantageous in some tax jurisdictions.

▶ Reducing or increasing commitments to tax-exempt securities, where available.

2.1.5 Changes in Laws and Regulations

Laws and regulations create the environment in which the investor can lawfully operate, and the portfolio manager must monitor them to ensure compliance and understand how they affect the scope of the advisor's responsibility and discretion in managing client portfolios. For example, in the United States in recent years, corporate trustees have reevaluated how they manage investment portfolios for trust clients in light of the adoption of the Uniform Prudent Investor Rule (versus the traditional prudent man rule) and the Uniform Principal and Income Act.

Besides that necessity, portfolio managers should seek to grasp the implication of such legal and regulatory changes for current portfolio holdings and investment opportunities. Portfolio managers for both taxable and tax-exempt investors should monitor changes in tax regulations because such changes typically affect not only taxes but the equilibrium relationships among assets.

2.1.6 Unique Circumstances

A unique circumstance is an internal factor (other than a liquidity requirement, time horizon, or tax concern) that may constrain portfolio choice. The client may present the portfolio manager with a variety of challenges in this respect. For example, some clients direct portfolio managers to retain concentrated stock positions because of an emotional attachment to the particular holding, because the client must maintain the stock position to demonstrate his or her commitment as an officer of the company, or because the concentrated position effectively has an extremely large unrealized capital gain. Is it feasible and appropriate to hedge or monetize the position through one of several special strategies? If not, given the volatility and concentrated risk of this single holding, how should the portfolio manager allocate the balance of the client's portfolio? As a portfolio manager, what investment actions will you recommend or implement when the emotional attachment is gone, when the client is no longer an officer of the company, or when the client's heirs receive the position?

Institutional clients may have a range of special concerns. For example, a client may adopt principles of socially responsible investing (often referred to by its acronym, SRI). Endowments and public employee pension plans often have been particularly active in SRI. As an example, a fund may decide to reduce or eliminate holdings in "sin" stocks, such as gaming, alcohol, and tobacco. SRI constraints have tended to tilt a portfolio away from large companies, which introduces non-market-related risks and causes a small-capitalization stock bias. In the mid-1980s, when small-cap stocks were demonstrating a return advantage over large-cap stocks, SRI seemed a costless (even profitable) strategy. However, the client should be aware of the potential costs in adopting an SRI policy.

Institutional clients are focusing significant attention on evaluating and fostering improvements in corporate governance, believing that those efforts will in the long run enhance return and/or reduce portfolio risk. Indeed, European fund managers themselves have demanded better integration of extrafinancial issues such as corporate governance, human capital management, value creation or destruction during mergers and acquisitions, and global environment challenges in sell-side analysis.[1] Portfolio managers must respect such client concerns in evaluating the appropriateness of investments.

In Example 2, an investment advisor determines an appropriate investment recommendation for an inheritance and later, a new investment advisor makes changes to the client's IPS in light of dramatically changed needs. This example shows the detailed analysis and judgment that enters into revising an IPS.

EXAMPLE 2

Monitoring Changes in an Investor's Circumstances and Wealth[2]

John Stern, 55 years old and single, is a dentist. Stern has accumulated a $2.0 million investment portfolio with a large concentration in small-capitalization U.S. equities. Over the last five years, the portfolio has averaged 20 percent annual total return on investment. Stern does not expect to retire before age 70. His current income is more than sufficient to meet his expenses. Upon retirement, he plans to sell his dentistry practice and use the proceeds to purchase an annuity to cover his retirement cash flow needs. He has no additional long-term goals or needs.

In consultation with Stern, his investment advisor, Caroline Roppa, has drawn up an investment policy statement with the following elements. (Roppa's notes justifying each item are included.)

Elements of Stern's Investment Policy Statement

Risk tolerance: Stern has above-average risk tolerance. *Roppa's notes:*

▶ Stern's present investment portfolio and his desire for large returns indicate a high *willingness* to take risk.

▶ His financial situation (large current asset base, ample income to cover expenses, lack of need for liquidity or cash flow, and long time horizon) indicates a high *ability* to assume risk.

---

[1] In 2004, four major European fund managers representing €330 billion under management announced an Enhanced Analytics Initiative in which 5 percent of brokerage commissions would be awarded on the basis of the integration of these concerns in brokerage house analysis.

[2] Adapted from the 2001 Level III CFA examination.

Return objective: The return objective is an average total return of 10 percent or more with a focus on long-term capital appreciation. *Roppa's notes:* Stern's circumstances warrant an above-average return objective that emphasizes capital appreciation for the following reasons:

▶ Stern has a sizable asset base and ample income to cover his current spending; therefore, the focus should be on growing the portfolio.

▶ Stern's low liquidity needs and long time horizon support an emphasis on a long-term capital appreciation approach.

▶ Stern does not rely on the portfolio to meet living expenses.

The numerical objective of 10 percent represents an estimate of a target Stern can aim for rather than a minimum return required to meet a specific financial goal.

Liquidity: Stern's liquidity needs are low. *Roppa's notes:*

▶ Stern has no regular cash flow needs from the portfolio because the income from his dentistry practice meets all current spending needs.

▶ No large, one-time cash needs are stated. However, it could be considered appropriate to keep a small cash reserve for emergencies.

Time horizon: Stern's time horizon is long term and consists of two stages:

▶ The first stage consists of the time until his retirement, which he expects to be 15 years.

▶ The second consists of his lifetime following retirement, which could range from 10 to 20 years.

Roppa has also summarized Stern's current portfolio in Exhibit 1.

EXHIBIT 1	Summary of Stern's Current Portfolio			
	Value	Percent of Total	Expected Annual Return	Expected Annual Standard Deviation
Short-term bonds	$200,000	10%	4.6%	1.6%
Domestic large-cap equities	600,000	30	12.4	19.5
Domestic small-cap equities	1,200,000	60	16.0	29.9
Total portfolio	$2,000,000	100%	13.8%	23.1%

Stern expects to soon receive an inheritance of $2.0 million. Stern and Roppa sit down to discuss its investment in one of four index funds. Given Stern's already above-average risk tolerance and level of portfolio risk, Roppa and Stern have concluded that the risk tolerance description in the current IPS remains valid; they do not want to contemplate a further increase in portfolio risk. On the other hand, they do not wish to reduce expected return. Roppa is evaluating the four index funds shown in Exhibit 2 for their ability to produce a portfolio that will meet the following two criteria relative to the current portfolio:

▶ maintain or enhance expected return

▶ maintain or reduce volatility

Each fund is invested in an asset class that is not substantially represented in the current portfolio as shown in Exhibit 1. Exhibit 2 presents statistics on those index funds.

EXHIBIT 2	Index Fund Characteristics		
Index Fund	Expected Annual Return	Expected Annual Standard Deviation	Correlation of Returns with Current Portfolio's Returns
Fund A	15%	25%	+0.80
Fund B	11	22	+0.60
Fund C	16	25	+0.90
Fund D	14	22	+0.65

1. Recommend the most appropriate index fund to add to Stern's portfolio. Justify your recommendation by describing how your chosen fund *best* meets both of the stated criteria. No calculations are required.

Twenty years later, Stern is meeting with his new financial advisor, Jennifer Holmstrom. Holmstrom is evaluating whether Stern's investment policy remains appropriate for his new circumstances.

▶ Stern is now 75 years old and retired. His spending requirements are expected to increase with the rate of general inflation, which is expected to average 3.0 percent annually.

▶ Stern estimates his current living expenses at $150,000 annually. An annuity, purchased with the proceeds from the sale of his dentistry practice, provides $20,000 of this amount. The annuity is adjusted for inflation annually using a national price index.

▶ Because of poor investment performance and a high level of spending, Stern's asset base has declined to $1,200,000 exclusive of the value of the annuity.

▶ Stern sold all of his small-cap investments last year and invested the proceeds in domestic bonds.

▶ Because his past international equity investments have performed poorly, Stern has become markedly uncomfortable with holding international equities.

▶ Stern plans to donate $50,000 to a charity in three months.

2. Discuss how *each* of the following components of Stern's investment policy statement should now reflect the changes in his circumstances.

  i. risk tolerance

  ii. return requirement

  iii. liquidity needs

  iv. time horizon

Note: Your discussion should focus on, but not be limited to, the *direction* and *magnitude of change* in each component rather than on a specific numeric change.

Stern's investment portfolio at age 75 is summarized in Exhibit 3.

EXHIBIT 3	Stern's Investment Portfolio at Age 75		
	Current Allocation	**Expected Return**	**Expected Standard Deviation**
Cash equivalents	2%	5%	3%
Fixed income	75	7	8
Domestic equities	10	10	16
International equities	3	12	22
Domestic real estate	10	10	17

3. Given Stern's changed circumstances, state whether the current allocation to *each* asset class should be lower, the same, or higher. Justify your response with *one* reason for *each* asset class. No calculations are required.

  i. cash equivalents

  ii. fixed income

  iii. domestic equities

  iv. international equities

  v. domestic real estate

Note: Your response should be based only on Stern's changed circumstances and the information in Exhibit 3.

4. Explain one way in which Stern might seek to reduce the tension between his current return requirement and his current risk tolerance.

Solution to 1: Fund D represents the single *best* addition to complement Stern's current portfolio, given the selection criteria. Fund D's expected return (14.0 percent) has the potential to increase the portfolio's return somewhat. Second, Fund D's relatively low correlation coefficient with his current portfolio (+0.65) indicates that it will provide larger diversification benefits than any of the other alternatives except Fund B. The result of adding Fund D should be a portfolio with about the same expected return and somewhat lower volatility compared to the original portfolio.

The other three funds have shortcomings in either expected return enhancement or volatility reduction through diversification:

► Fund A offers the potential for increasing the portfolio's return but is too highly correlated with other holdings to provide substantial volatility reduction through diversification.

► Fund B provides substantial volatility reduction through diversification but is expected to generate a return well below the current portfolio's return.

► Fund C has the greatest potential to increase the portfolio's return but is too highly correlated with other holdings to provide substantial volatility reduction through diversification.

Solution to 2:

i. *Risk tolerance.* Stern's risk tolerance has declined as a result of investment losses and the material erosion of his asset base. His *willingness* to accept risk as reflected in his portfolio holdings and aversion to international equities has declined. Also, Stern's return requirement has risen sharply at the same time that assets available to generate that return are lower. Thus, Stern's *ability* to accept risk has also declined. Investments should emphasize less volatile securities.

ii. *Return requirement.* Stern now has a return requirement that represents an increase in both dollar and percentage terms from his return objective of 20 years earlier. In contrast to his prior situation, Stern now must use investments to meet normal living expenses.

Stern's annual expenses not covered by annuity payments total $130,000 (10.8 percent of his now reduced assets). His expenses are increasing at a rate at least as high as the 3 percent general inflation rate. To stay ahead of inflation without eroding the principal value of his portfolio, Stern needs to earn 13.8 percent. This percentage will increase to 14.3 percent after the $50,000 charitable donation occurs, because this distribution will further diminish Stern's asset base.

iii. *Liquidity needs.* Stern will require $50,000 (4.2 percent of assets) in three months for a charitable donation. In addition, Stern's need to fund a large part of his living expenses from his portfolio has created a substantial ongoing liquidity need. Investments should emphasize liquid securities in part to meet any unplanned near-term expenses without incurring substantial transaction costs.

iv. *Time horizon.* Stern is now 20 years older than when his initial investment policy was written. Assuming his life expectancy is normal, Stern's time horizon remains long term (i.e., in excess of 10 years) but shorter than when the initial policy was drafted.

Solution to 3:

i. Cash equivalents should have a substantially higher weight than 2 percent. Stern requires $50,000 (4.2 percent of assets) in three months for the charitable donation. Compared with his position 20 years ago, his willingness and ability to accept volatility have decreased, his liquidity needs have increased, and his time horizon is now shorter. Stern needs a larger portion of his portfolio in low-risk, highly liquid assets.

ii. Fixed income should have a lower weight than 75 percent. Bonds are expected to provide a greater return than cash equivalents, which would help to meet Stern's return requirement. To meet additional liquidity needs and provide higher returns for expenses and inflation, however, a lower allocation is warranted.

iii. Domestic equities should have a higher weight than 10 percent. Stern requires fairly high returns and protection from inflation. Domestic equity investments would help meet those needs, but his lower ability and willingness to assume risk suggest only a moderate allocation to this somewhat volatile asset class, although higher than the current allocation.

iv. International equities should be eliminated. Although international equities may provide higher returns and diversification benefits, Stern is uncomfortable with holding international equities because of his experience with them. In the interests of respecting client wishes, Holmstrom should thus eliminate this asset class from the portfolio.

v. Domestic real estate should have a lower weight than 10 percent because of Stern's substantial liquidity requirements and reduced risk tolerance. Domestic equities have the same expected return as real estate with lower expected standard deviation and generally greater liquidity; therefore, domestic equities would be favored over domestic real estate among the higher expected return asset classes. Nevertheless, a smaller (i.e., less than 10 percent) real estate allocation could be maintained to obtain diversification benefits, to possibly generate income, and as a potential hedge against inflation.

Solution to 4: Based on his current expenses of $150,000 annually, Stern has a very high return requirement in relation to his current risk tolerance. The most direct way to reduce this tension would be to decrease annual expenses, although that might involve a change in living arrangements or lifestyle. For example, if annual expenses were cut by one-third to $100,000, only $80,000 would need to be supplied by investments after annuity payments. That would represent $80,000/$1,200,000 = 6.7% of assets, resulting in a return requirement of 9.7% prior to the charitable contribution. All else equal, the higher the return requirement relative to actual returns earned, the greater the need to spend principal and the greater longevity risk (the risk that one will outlive one's funds). Reducing expenses would mitigate that risk.

High-net-worth individuals often face the issue of concentrated stock holdings, which may be complicated by the issue of high unrealized capital gains. In Example 3, a change in client circumstances leads an investment advisor to search for the appropriate means to address the problem.

EXAMPLE 3

An Investor with a Concentrated Stock Position

Jonathan Wiese, CFA, serves as investment counsel for the Lane family. Franklin Lane, 62 years old, has a 2,000,000 share position in Walton Energy, Inc. (WEI), an actively traded mid-cap energy company, accumulated through five years' service on its board of directors and earlier service as chief operating officer. At current market prices, the position is worth $24,000,000, representing 40 percent of Lane's total portfolio of $60,000,000. Another 20 percent of his portfolio is invested in other common equities, with the balance of 40 percent invested in Treasury inflation-protected and government agency securities. The cost basis of the WEI position is $2,400,000, and the sale of the position would trigger a tax liability exceeding $3.2 million. In the past Lane has insisted on maintaining his position in WEI shares to show his commitment to the company, but with Lane's recent retirement from WEI's board Wiese has suggested that a portfolio review is appropriate. WEI shares are part of a mid-cap stock index, and Lane's position is substantial compared to average daily trading volume of WEI. Techniques to deal with concentrated stock positions fall under the rubric of hedging and monetization strategies. Wiese has organized several of these strategies in Exhibit 4, one or more of which may be appropriate to deal with Lane's concentrated position.

EXHIBIT 4   Hedging and Monetization Strategies

Strategy and Description	Advantages	Drawbacks
Zero-premium collar. Simultaneous purchase of puts and sale of call options on the stock. The puts are struck below and the calls are struck above the underlying's market price. The call premiums fund the cost of the puts.	▶ Locks in a band of values for the stock position. ▶ Defers capital gains until stock is actually sold.	▶ Hedge lasts only the duration of the option's life. ▶ Involves commissions. ▶ Provides downside protection but gives away most of upside.
Variable prepaid forward. In effect, combines a collar with a loan against the value of the shares. When the loan comes due (often in two to four years), shares are sold to pay off the loan and part of any appreciation is shared with the lender.	▶ Converts 70 to 90 percent of the value of the position to cash. ▶ Defers capital gains until stock is actually sold.	▶ Involves commissions and interest expenses. ▶ Surrenders part of any appreciation in the stock.
Exchange fund. Fund into which several investors place their different share holdings in exchange for shares in the diversified fund itself. At the end of a period of time (often seven years), the fund distributes assets to shareholders pro rata.	▶ Diversifies holdings without triggering tax consequences.	▶ Expense ratio often 2 percent and other fees usually apply. ▶ Diversification may be incomplete.

(Exhibit continued on next page . . .)

EXHIBIT 4	(continued)	

Strategy and Description	Advantages	Drawbacks
Private exchange. Shares that are a component of an index are exchanged for shares of an index mutual fund in a privately arranged transaction with the fund.	▶ Exchange is tax free. ▶ Low continuing expenses. ▶ Greatly increases diversification.	▶ Shares usually must be part of an index so not generally applicable. ▶ Share position must be very substantial. ▶ Concession to market value of shares exchanged may need to be offered. ▶ May not be possible to arrange because fund interest may be lacking.

Note: Zero-premium collars and variable prepaid forwards may involve a tax liability; the taxation of these strategies varies across tax jurisdictions.

Lane faces no liquidity requirements, at least in the short term. At the review, Wiese and Lane agree that a 60/40 stock/bond mix remains appropriate for Lane.

1. Identify and evaluate Lane's primary investment need and the primary constraint on addressing that need.

2. Determine and justify the two strategies that most directly address the need identified in Part 1.

Solution to 1: Lane's primary need is for diversification of his concentrated stock position. Having ended his last ties to WEI, Lane should be in a position to satisfy that need. The tax liability that would result from a sale of WEI stock, however, acts as a constraint on addressing that need: Selling the WEI position and investing the proceeds in a diversified stock portfolio would incur a tax liability of about $3.2 million.

Solution to 2: The exchange fund and private exchange options most directly address Lane's diversification need. The zero-premium collar would hedge the value of WEI position but would not diversify Lane's equity position. Also, the zero-premium collar would essentially convert the WEI holding into a position with volatility not dissimilar to short-term bonds, over the collar's duration, changing the effective asset allocation. The variable prepaid forward would convert a large fraction of the value of the position to cash, which could then be invested in a diversified equity position; so that instrument could be used to address the diversification need. Because of the huge built-in tax liability, however, Lane would need to roll over the forward indefinitely with the attendant expenses. The exchange fund is a costly option because of its fee structure, but it does address Lane's needs more directly and on a longer-term basis. The same can be said of the private exchange option, which appears to be more cost effective than the exchange fund while achieving a similar purpose.

2.2 Monitoring Market and Economic Changes

In addition to changes in individual client circumstances, the economic and financial markets contexts of investments also require monitoring. Those contexts are not static. The economy moves through phases of expansion and contraction, each with some unique characteristics. Financial markets, which are linked to the economy and expectations of its future course, reflect the resulting changing relationships among asset classes and individual securities.[3] A portfolio manager's monitoring of market and economic conditions should be broad and inclusive. Changes in asset risk attributes, market cycles, central bank policy, and the yield curve and inflation are among the factors that need to be monitored.

2.2.1 Changes in Asset Risk Attributes

The historical record reflects that underlying mean return, volatility, and correlations of asset classes sometimes meaningfully change. An asset allocation that once promised to satisfy an investor's investment objectives may no longer do so after such a shift. If that is the case, investors will need either to adjust their asset allocations or to reconsider their investment objectives. Monitoring changes in asset risk attributes is thus essential. Fiduciaries also owe their clients a duty to understand the risk factors in individual investments as such factors evolve.

Changes in asset risk attributes also present investment opportunities. Market prices for all assets reflect consensus perceptions of risk and reward. Changes in those perceptions produce immediate gains or losses. Successful active managers assess differences between actual risk and perceived risk of an investment and embrace that investment when the consensus view is unduly pessimistic.

Investment theoreticians and practitioners have long recognized the risk–reward trade-off. Long-run incremental rewards are generally unattainable without incurring incremental risk. Conversely, an investor must sacrifice some return when seeking to minimize risk. Systematic risk, which diversification cannot eliminate, is the most likely type of risk to promise reward according to asset pricing theory. Although a link exists between systematic risk and return, it is less consistent than pure theory suggests. For active managers, the key to exploiting inconsistencies lies in determining when risk is already priced into an asset and when perceptions of risk deviate enough from quantifiable risk so that a courageous investor can profit from favorable mispricings and avoid the others. In equity markets historically, increasing volatility has signaled opportunity more often than not, providing buying opportunities when fear prompts others to sell.

2.2.2 Market Cycles

Investors monitor market cycles and valuation levels to form a view on the short-term risks and rewards that financial markets offer. Based on these opinions, investors may make tactical adjustments to asset allocations or adjust individual securities holdings.

Tactically, the markets' major swings present unusual opportunities to be either very right or very wrong. When things are going well, securities eventually perform too well; during economic weakness, stock prices often decline excessively. Weakness engenders an environment that may foreshadow extraordinary profits, while ebullient markets provide unusual opportunities to sell, reinvesting elsewhere. Although this point is easily illustrated by looking over our shoulders at

---

[3] See Reading 23, on capital market expectations, for more information.

the U.S. stock market in 1999 and 2000, it should be remembered that it was only the extremeness of the 1999–2000 market peak that is notable; these cycles recur nearly every decade or so. Market veterans may recall the environment of late 1974 as one of extraordinary opportunity. At one point the earnings yield of the U.S. stock market was 600 bps higher than bond yields, a difference not seen since the early 1950s. Conversely, in 1980 and 1981 and again in 1999 and 2000, bond yields exceeded earnings yields by a wide margin. That cyclical top presented another historic tactical opportunity as well as a shining example of the power and speed of mean reversion of asset-class returns. Reducing exposure to outperforming asset classes and increasing exposure to underperforming asset classes at the asset-class level—selling the stocks that had proven so comfortable and buying the bonds that the investment world seemed then to abhor—would have had a profound positive influence on total portfolio risk and return during those times.

Individual securities routinely show similar excesses. There are always securities whose issuers have either received such laudatory notices or suffered such unremitting adversity that their prices depart from reality. It is difficult to isolate those securities and then to act; only those investors suitably prepared and armed with courage will accept the challenge.

2.2.3 Central Bank Policy

Central banks wield power in the capital markets through the influence of their monetary and interest rate decisions on liquidity and interest rates. Their influence is felt in both bond and stock markets.

In bond markets, the most immediate impact of monetary policy is on money market yields rather than long-term bond yields. A central bank's influence on bond market *volatility*, however, is profound.

An example of this influence occurred in 1979, when the board of the U.S. Federal Reserve Bank under Paul Volcker changed its focus from controlling interest rates to controlling monetary growth. Previously the board had adjusted the discount rate in response to movements in the money supply, while simultaneously trying to manage that supply. Interest rates took a back seat in the board's deliberations, and T-bill rates rose from 9 percent to 14 percent in an eight-month period. The effect was dramatic. Volatility in the bond market exploded between late 1979 and mid-1982 (at which time policy was quietly reversed to combat recession). High-yielding bonds provided a compelling alternative to stocks, putting downward pressure on stock prices until the summer of 1982, when rallying bond prices and declining bond yields finally eased the pressure, making stocks again more attractive.

Turning to the stock market, "Do not fight the Fed" has been a longstanding warning from Martin Zweig—a warning that it can be problematic to invest in the market when the Fed is tightening the money supply. Jensen, Johnson, and Mercer (2000) and Conover, Jensen, Johnson, and Mercer (2005) have documented that in the United States, stock returns are on average higher during periods of expansionary monetary policy than in periods of restrictive monetary policy, as indicated by decreases and increases in the discount rate, respectively.[4]

These lessons bear repetition. Fed policy does matter and should not be ignored: Restricted credit and higher interest rates usually hurt stock returns; eased credit and lower interest rates usually enhance stock returns.

---

[4] The discount rate is the rate a Federal Reserve member bank pays for borrowing reserves from the Federal Reserve system. Along with open market operations (the purchase and sale of government securities by the Fed) and changes in reserve requirement, discount rate policy is one of the three tools of U.S. monetary policy.

2.2.4 The Yield Curve and Inflation

The default-risk-free yield curve reflects investors' required return at various maturities. It incorporates not only individuals' time preferences for current versus future real consumption but also expected inflation and the maturity premium demanded. Yield curve changes reflect changes in bond values, and bond value changes affect equity values through the competition that bonds supply to equities. Thus investors closely monitor the yield curve.

The premium on long-term bonds over short-term bonds tends to be countercyclical (i.e., high during recessions and low at the top of expansions) because investors demand greater rewards for bearing risk during bad times. By contrast, short-term yields tend to be procyclical because central banks tend to lower short rates in an attempt to stimulate economic activity during recessions. Yield curves thus tend to become steeply upward-sloping during recessions, to flatten in the course of expansions, and to be downward sloping (inverted) before an impending recession. In the United States, for example, nearly every recession after the mid-1960s was predicted by an inverted yield curve within six quarters of the recession; only one inverted yield curve was not followed by a recession during this period.[5] Thus the evidence suggests that the yield curve contains information about future GDP growth. Theory also suggests that the yield curve reflects expectations about future inflation.

Investors monitor a number of variables to gauge opportunities in bond markets. If relative yields of lower-quality issues exceed historical norms, the prospect of higher returns by investing in bonds of lower quality is enhanced. Even a measure as simple as the slope of the bond market yield curve is an indicator of bond performance relative to (short-term) cash equivalents.

Looking back at the late 1970s and early 1980s and focusing on yield curve slope rather than height, the spread between bond yields and cash yields steepened, starting with a flat to mildly inverted yield curve from late 1978 through mid-1981 and increasing to a 4 percent bond risk premium by July 1982. This increased bond risk premium preceded the bond rally of August–October 1982, during which 30-year Treasuries rallied 29 percent in three months. Although it is the rise in interest rates that catalyzes subsequent stock bear markets, it is the spread between long-term and short-term rates that presages bond rallies. If the yield curve is unusually steep (i.e., if bond yields are high relative to cash equivalent yields), the outlook tends to be good for bonds. This relationship is significant when either cash yield or the inflation rate is used as a proxy for the underlying risk-free rate.[6]

This interpretation of steep yield curves is unconventional. The usual fear is that the forward curve[7] foreshadows rising yields and falling bond prices. Empirical evidence tends to refute any basis for that apprehension.

Inflation has a pervasive influence on investors' ability to achieve their financial and investment objectives. On the one hand, it affects the nominal amount of money required to purchase a given basket of goods and services. On the other hand, inflation influences returns and risk in capital markets. When inflation rises

---

[5] See Ang, Piazzesi, and Wei (2006).

[6] T-bills and other cash instruments are not truly risk free, as they have both nonzero durations and nonzero standard deviations. Although they are generally an excellent reflection of the theoretical risk-free rate, the inflation rate can sometimes be preferable as a proxy for the risk-free rate, because it is not directly subject to manipulation by a central bank.

[7] A "forward curve" shows the incremental yield earned by going one step further out on the yield curve. Suppose a one-year bond yields 2 percent and an equivalent-credit two-year bond yields 4 percent. The two-year bond must have a one-year forward yield of approximately 6 percent during its second year in order for its two-year average yield to be 4 percent. A steep yield curve implies an expectation of rising future bond yields.

beyond expectations, bond investors face a cut in *real yield*. As nominal yields rise in turn to counteract this loss, bond prices fall. Unexpected changes in the inflation rate are highly significant to stock market returns as well.

2.3 Monitoring the Portfolio

Monitoring a portfolio is a continuous process that requires the manager to evaluate (1) events and trends affecting the prospects of individual holdings and asset classes and their suitability for attaining client objectives and (2) changes in asset values that create unintended divergences from the client's strategic asset allocation. The former tend to lead to changes in investment policy or to substitutions of individual holdings; the latter lead directly to rebalancing to the existing strategic asset allocation.

In a perfect-markets world, we could hold portfolio managers to a demanding standard: If a portfolio manager were to begin building a portfolio afresh today, would it mirror the existing portfolio? If not, he should consider changing the existing portfolio. Of course, taxes and transaction costs, discussed later, mean managers do not continuously revise portfolios. After even one day no portfolio is exactly optimal; however, the costs of adjustment may well outweigh any expected benefits from eliminating small differences between the current portfolio and the best possible one.

New information on economic and market conditions or on individual companies may lead a portfolio manager to take a variety of investment actions in an effort to add value for the client. The following examples offer some perspectives for the practitioner to consider as he or she translates monitoring into investment action.

EXAMPLE 4

How Active Managers May Use New Analysis and Information

As portfolio managers gather and analyze information that leads to capital market expectation revisions, they may attempt to add value through at least three types of portfolio actions:

▶ **Tactical asset allocation.** The portfolio manager may, in the short term, adjust the target asset mix within the parameters of the investment policy statement by selling perceived overpriced asset classes and reinvesting the proceeds in perceived underpriced asset classes in an attempt to profit from perceived disequilibria. When an investor's long-term capital market expectations change, however, the manager must revisit the strategic asset allocation.

▶ **Style and sector exposures.** Portfolio managers may alter investment emphasis within asset classes because of changes in capital market expectations. For example, a portfolio manager may lengthen the duration in the fixed-income allocation based on expectations of a sustained period of declining interest rates or adjust the style of the equity portfolio based on expectations that an economy is entering a period of sustained economic growth. Portfolio managers also may adjust the exposure to certain sectors back to or closer to historical weightings to reduce sector exposure relative to the index. For example, consider the impact on portfolio risk and return of reducing the exposure to the technology sector (within the large-cap U.S. equity allocation) in January 2000, when technology represented more than 31 percent of the S&P 500 Index relative to the historical average of about 17 percent.

▶ **Individual security exposures.** A portfolio manager may trade an individual issue for one that seems to offer better value or reduce the exposure of a specific security as the returns of a single security begin to contribute a greater proportion of the total return than the manager believes to be appropriate.

EXAMPLE 5

The Characteristics of Successful Active Investors

Ironic gaps exist between the theory of revising portfolios and its practice. Some managers persist in constantly juggling the asset mix and churning portfolios in response to their basic emotions, clouded thinking, classic behavioral finance errors, and the desire to maximize fee revenue—often shrouding their "illusion of action" with marketing glitz. Clients tend to hire managers after recent success and fire them after recent disappointment. This chasing of investment performance, which reflects human nature, infrequently benefits investment results. What then are the elements of investment success?

Successful active investors stray from established roles. Nature conditions us to feel that what has been working will continue to work and that failure heralds failure. In investments, experience belies this notion. Consider investment managers who scramble to find a fix when their style is out of fashion. Often they (and their clients) change their approach during a period of disappointment, just before results rebound. We see the same pattern in customers' decisions to hire and fire managers. These costly errors stem from a quest for comfort that capital markets rarely reward and a lack of discipline to remain committed to long-term strategy as defined in the investment policy statement. Investors crave the solace that companionship affords. In the investment business, when one has too much company, success is improbable.

Successful active investors are not swayed by the crowd. The cultures of successful corporations and winning investors are profoundly different. Corporations, which are cooperative enterprises, prize teamwork and reward triumph while dismissing failure. The exceptional investor pursues an opposite course, staying far from the crowd and seeking opportunities in overlooked areas while avoiding excesses of the crowd. Investing in areas that are not popular while refusing to join in trends sets the successful investor apart.

Successful active investors are disciplined. There is a subtle pattern in the trading of successful investors and a key ingredient of investment success—discipline. Successful investors make disciplined changes even when they are performing well, and they often are willing to endure disappointment patiently.

Opportunistic investors must steel themselves against discomfort. Only knowledge and discipline can give them the confidence needed to transact. Indeed, even then, consideration for clients (or fears of their reactions) may inhibit the profitable move. Many investors fear the consequences of acting contrary to recent market experience. Disciplined investment decision processes add value by providing an *objective* basis for having confidence in an uncomfortable investment action.

As we shall discuss in more detail later, disciplined rebalancing to the strategic asset allocation reinforces the strategy of selling high and buying low or reducing exposure to outperforming asset classes and increasing exposure to underperforming asset classes. That behavior and discipline unfortunately is at odds with human nature. When investments have performed poorly, less successful investors and portfolio managers tend to address the problem by making changes for the sake of change or by abandoning a strategy altogether! If investments are doing well, the tendency is to coast with the winning strategy. These common patterns can often make underperformance problems significantly worse (i.e., selling near the bottom) or result in forgoing some portion of handsome market gains (i.e., not selling near the top).

EXAMPLE 6

The Nonfinancial Costs of Portfolio Revision

When a portfolio manager revises a portfolio, he obviously incurs financial costs as detailed later in Section 3.1.2. Financial costs will indeed be a focus of the section on rebalancing. But the costs of transacting can also take nonfinancial forms. If a client grows uncomfortable with portfolio turnover she considers excessive, the portfolio manager may lose credibility and the client may limit future trading. Even if trading is timely and likely to be profitable, it may impose subjective costs that are all too real. Finance theory recognizes these costs by directing managers to focus on optimizing client satisfaction rather than maximizing return. Even the most profitable strategy or investment process is useless if the client abandons it.

REBALANCING THE PORTFOLIO   3

Monitoring and rebalancing a portfolio is similar to flying an airplane: The pilot monitors and adjusts, if necessary, the plane's altitude, speed, and direction to make sure that the plane ultimately arrives at the predetermined destination. Just as a pilot makes in-flight adjustments, so does the portfolio manager. An important question in this regard is how far off course can the plane get before the pilot must make an adjustment? In the following sections we address that issue, but we first must be clear on the scope of what we will discuss under the rubric of rebalancing.

The term "rebalancing" has been used in the literature of investing to cover a range of distinct actions including (1) adjusting the actual portfolio to the current strategic asset allocation because of price changes in portfolio holdings; (2) revisions to the investor's target asset class weights because of changes in the investor's investment objectives or constraints, or because of changes in his capital market expectations; and (3) tactical asset allocation (TAA). For pedagogical reasons and because subjects such as TAA are covered in other readings, in this section we use "rebalancing" to refer only to the first type of action: rebalancing to the strategic asset allocation in reaction to price changes. Both individual and institutional investors need to set policy with respect to this type of action.

3.1 The Benefits and Costs of Rebalancing

Portfolio rebalancing involves a simple trade-off: the cost of rebalancing versus the cost of not rebalancing.

3.1.1 Rebalancing Benefits

Clients and their investment managers work hard to have their normal asset policy mix reflect an educated judgment of their appetite for reward and their aversion to risk. That having been done, however, the mix often drifts with the tides of day-to-day market fluctuations. If we assume that an investor's strategic asset allocation is optimal, then any divergence in the investor's portfolio from this strategic asset allocation is undesired and represents an expected utility loss to the investor. Rebalancing benefits the investor by reducing the present value of expected losses from not tracking the optimum. In theory, the basic cost of not rebalancing is this present value of expected utility losses.[8] Equivalently, the cost of not rebalancing is the present value of expected utility losses from straying from the optimum.

There are also several practical risk management benefits to rebalancing. First, if higher-risk assets earn higher returns on average and we let the asset mix drift, higher-risk assets will tend to represent ever-larger proportions of the portfolio over time. Thus the level of portfolio risk will tend to drift upward.[9] Portfolio risk will tend to be greater than that established for the client in the investment policy statement. Rebalancing controls drift in the overall level of portfolio risk. Second, as asset mix drifts, the *types* of risk exposures drift. Rebalancing maintains the client's desired systematic risk exposures. Finally, not rebalancing may mean holding assets that have become overpriced, offering inferior future rewards. A commitment to rebalance to the strategic asset allocation offers an effective way to dissuade clients from abandoning policy at inauspicious moments. Once signed on to the concept, clients are more likely to stay the course.

Example 7 illustrates the benefits of disciplined rebalancing judged against the do-nothing alternative of letting asset mix drift.

---

[8] See Leland (2000).

[9] This type of drift will be more acute for portfolios with asset classes with dissimilar volatility and/or with low correlations.

EXAMPLE 7

An Illustration of the Benefits of Disciplined Rebalancing

Although portfolios can be rebalanced using a variety of methods that we shall soon discuss, it is important to recognize that, in comparison to letting an asset mix drift, any disciplined approach to rebalancing tends to add value over a long-term investment horizon either by enhancing portfolio returns and/or reducing portfolio risk.

For example, assume an institutional client wishes to maintain the stated policy mix of 60 percent stocks and 40 percent bonds and requires monthly rebalancing to the equilibrium 60/40 mix. That asset mix is not uncommon for North American pension funds and provides a reasonable baseline from which to quantify the likely benefits from disciplined rebalancing. Transaction costs of 10 bps on each side of a trade are assumed to be attainable using futures.

In the three decades (1973–2003) summarized in Exhibits 5 and 6, simple monthly rebalancing produced an average annual return of 10.22 percent versus 9.95 percent for a drifting mix, a 27 bp enhancement. Furthermore, the incremental return involved significantly less risk. That is, the rebalanced portfolio's standard deviation during that time period was 11.38 percent versus 13.39 percent—200 bps less than that of the drifting mix!

Despite a six-year losing streak in the 1990s, annual rebalancing to the 60/40 mix outperformed a drifting mix for the January 1988 through July 2003 period, much of which constituted the largest equity bull market in U.S. history. As Exhibit 7 indicates, annual rebalancing produced an average incremental return of 27 bps with a standard deviation of returns that is 1.16 bps smaller than that of the drifting mix. Because rebalancing avoids the passive increases in risk that result from drifting during trending periods, it manages to reduce risk by more than 100 bps, while accumulating a modest 27 bps of additional return. As with the 1973–2003 time period, this translates to a reward-to-risk ratio for the rebalanced portfolio that much improves on that of the drifting mix.

EXHIBIT 5	Full-Period Rebalancing Results January 1973–July 2003		
	Rebalancing Return	Drifting Mix Return	Difference
Average	10.22%	9.95%	0.27%
Maximum	35.25	35.75	
Minimum	−15.71	−13.57	
Median	12.97	11.96	
Standard deviation	11.38	13.39	
Reward/risk ratio (Average/Std dev)	0.90	0.74	

EXHIBIT 6	Annual Rebalancing Results		
Calendar Year	Rebalancing Return	Drifting Mix Return	Difference
1973	−10.22%	−10.19%	−0.03%
1974	−15.71	−13.57	−2.14
1975	24.87	21.66	3.21
1976	20.80	20.15	0.65
1977	−5.10	−4.62	−0.48
1978	3.28	2.51	0.77
1979	8.00	7.15	0.85
1980	16.09	15.46	0.63
1981	−1.51	−1.99	0.48
1982	29.40	28.90	0.50
1983	13.14	13.39	−0.25
1984	9.91	9.38	0.53
1985	32.41	32.29	0.12
1986	20.43	19.99	0.44
1987	2.73	1.30	1.43
1988	13.27	13.45	−0.18
1989	26.54	26.93	−0.39
1990	1.36	0.78	0.58
1991	26.26	26.74	−0.48
1992	7.64	7.55	0.09
1993	12.97	12.49	0.48
1994	−1.90	−1.36	−0.54
1995	35.25	35.75	−0.50
1996	13.58	16.23	−2.65
1997	26.38	29.00	−2.62
1998	24.45	26.60	−2.15
1999	9.12	15.72	−6.60
2000	−0.29	−6.98	6.69
2001	−5.17	−8.47	3.30
2002	−7.83	−12.88	5.05
2003 (Jan–Jul)	7.23	8.45	−1.22

EXHIBIT 7	Recent Rebalancing Results January 1988–July 2003		
	Rebalancing Return	Drifting Mix Return	Difference
Average	11.29%	11.02%	0.27%
Maximum	35.25	35.75	
Minimum	−7.83	−12.88	
Median	12.97	14.78	
Standard deviation	10.01	11.17	
Reward/risk ratio	1.13	0.99	

Example 7 makes the point that disciplined rebalancing has tended to reduce risk while incrementally adding to returns. "Tended" means just that: It does not work in every year or even in every market cycle, but it should work over long-term investment horizons. For the two periods examined in Example 7 and making the assumptions therein, the incremental return was earned with turnover of just 0.9 percent per month in both periods. Historically, the benefit justifies this minimal activity. Studies such as Arnott and Lovell (1993), Plaxco and Arnott (2002), and Buetow et al. (2002) have supported this conclusion using both historical and simulated data. Rebalancing to a fixed asset mix, because it involves both selling appreciated assets and buying depreciated assets, can be viewed as a contrarian investment discipline that can be expected to earn a positive return for supplying liquidity.

3.1.2 Rebalancing Costs

Despite its benefits, rebalancing exacts financial costs. These costs are of two types—transaction costs and, for taxable investors, tax costs.

Transaction Costs   Transaction costs can never be recovered, and their cumulative erosion of value can significantly deteriorate portfolio performance. Transaction costs offset the benefits of rebalancing. Yet the true trade-off is not easy to gauge because transaction costs are difficult to measure.

Relatively illiquid investments such as private equity and real estate have become increasingly important in the portfolios of investors such as endowments and pension funds. These investments pose special challenges to rebalancing because the costs of rebalancing these investments represent a high hurdle. At the same time, the valuations given such assets often underestimate their true volatility because the valuations may be based on appraisals. If rebalancing requires reducing the value of illiquid holdings, this reduction may sometimes be accomplished through reinvestment of cash flows from them.[10] At the same time, portfolio managers cannot increase the allocations of these assets as quickly as in liquid asset markets.

---

[10] See Horvitz (2002).

Focusing on more liquid markets such as public equities, we can estimate transaction costs but only with error. There is in fact no exact answer to the question of what the transaction costs of a trade are. Transaction costs consist of more than just explicit costs such as commissions. They include implicit costs, such as those related to the bid–ask spread and market impact. Market impact is the difference between realized price and the price that *would have prevailed in the absence of the order.* That cost is inherently unobservable. In an analogy to the Heisenberg principle in physics, the process of executing a trade masks what would exist without the trade taking place. Furthermore, the trades one seeks but fails to execute impose yet another tariff—an opportunity cost. This missed trade opportunity cost may be more onerous than the others, and it is equally unobservable. Trading costs take on the character of an iceberg: Commissions rise above the surface, visible to all, while the submerged leviathan encompasses the market impact of trades and the imponderable cost of the trades that never happened.

A useful analogy can be drawn from the bond market. Most bond portfolios are priced from matrix prices, which may better represent "fair value" than actual transaction prices.[11] Bond transaction prices can be too dependent on the idiosyncratic meeting of one buyer and one seller. The same curious conclusion can be drawn for equities. Actual prices are set by the marginal seller and buyer who represent not a consensus but the strongest motivation to transact at a particular point in time.[12]

Because unaffected prices are unobservable, market impact costs can never be more than indirectly estimated. Still, this is not a fatal flaw: Total transaction costs can be estimated to a useful degree of accuracy, relative to the imprecision of other financial measurements (e.g., beta, value or future internal rate of return).

Tax Costs   In rebalancing, a portfolio manager sells appreciated asset classes and buys depreciated asset classes to bring the asset mix in line with target proportions. In most jurisdictions the sale of appreciated assets triggers a tax liability for taxable investors and is a cost of rebalancing for such investors.[13] The U.S. tax code distinguishes between long- and short-term capital gains based on the length of the holding period (as of 2004, holding periods greater than 12 months qualify as long-term). As of 2004 the maximum tax rates applicable to short- and long-term capital gains in the United States, 35 percent and 15 percent respectively, differed significantly. For a U.S. taxable investor, therefore, a rebalancing trade that realizes a short-term rather than long-term capital gain can be very costly. However, an appreciated asset class may contain assets with not only unrealized short- and long-term capital gains but also short- and long-term capital losses. Realizing short-term losses, long-term capital losses, long-term capital gains, and lastly short-term gains, in that order, would usually be the tax-efficient priority in selling. In contrast to the difference between long- and short-term capital gains, the value of the deferral of a long-term capital gain is generally much less in magnitude.[14]

---

[11] **Matrix prices** are prices determined by comparisons to other securities of similar credit risk and maturity.

[12] The need to outbid competitive traders suggests that market impact can even be negative. Prices would always be the same or lower without the most motivated buyer's willingness to buy. Prices similarly would always be the same or higher without the most motivated seller's willingness to sell.

[13] Some tax jurisdictions such as Jamaica, Hong Kong, and Singapore do not impose taxes on capital gains. See Ernst & Young (2005).

[14] See Horvitz (2002). The value of tax deferral of X years is the tax bill if the sale is today (call this Y) minus the present value of Y to be paid in X years, using a default-risk-free tax-exempt rate.

3.2 Rebalancing Disciplines

A rebalancing discipline is a strategy for rebalancing. In practice, portfolio managers have most commonly adopted either calendar rebalancing or percentage-of-portfolio rebalancing.

3.2.1 Calendar Rebalancing

Calendar rebalancing involves rebalancing a portfolio to target weights on a periodic basis, for example, monthly, quarterly, semiannually, or annually. Quarterly rebalancing is one popular choice; the choice of rebalancing frequency is sometimes linked to the schedule of portfolio reviews.[15]

If an investor's policy portfolio has three asset classes with target proportions of 45/15/40, and his investment policy specifies rebalancing at the beginning of each month, at each rebalancing date asset proportions would be brought back to 45/15/40. Calendar rebalancing is the simplest rebalancing discipline. It does not involve continuously monitoring portfolio values within the rebalancing period. If the rebalancing frequency is adequate given the portfolio's volatility, calendar rebalancing can suffice in ensuring that the actual portfolio does not drift far away from target for long periods of time. A drawback of calendar rebalancing: It is unrelated to market behavior. On any given rebalancing date, the portfolio could be very close to or far away from optimal proportions. In the former case, the portfolio would be nearly optimal and the costs in rebalancing might swamp the benefits. In the latter case, an investor might incur unnecessarily high costs in terms of market impact by rebalancing.

3.2.2 Percentage-of-Portfolio Rebalancing

Percentage-of-portfolio rebalancing (also called percent-range or interval rebalancing) offers an alternative to calendar rebalancing. Percentage-of-portfolio rebalancing involves setting rebalancing thresholds or trigger points stated as a percentage of the portfolio's value. For example, if the target proportion for an asset class is 40 percent of portfolio value, trigger points could be at 35 percent and 45 percent of portfolio value. We would say that 35 percent to 45 percent (or 40% ± 5%) is the corridor or tolerance band for the value of that asset class. The portfolio is rebalanced when an asset class's weight first passes through one of its rebalancing thresholds, or equivalently, outside the corridor.

For example, consider a three-asset class portfolio of domestic equities, international equities, and domestic bonds. The target asset proportions are 45/15/40 with respective corridors 45% ± 4.5%, 15% ± 1.5%, and 40% ± 4%. Suppose the portfolio manager observes the actual allocation to be 50/14/36; the upper threshold (49.5%) for domestic equities has been breached. The asset mix would be rebalanced to 45/15/40.

Rebalancing trades can occur on any calendar date for percentage-of-portfolio rebalancing, in contrast to calendar rebalancing. Compared with calendar rebalancing (particularly at lower frequencies such as semiannual or annual), percentage-of-portfolio rebalancing can exercise tighter control on divergences from target proportions because it is directly related to market performance.

[15] In practice, some portfolio managers will rebalance a portfolio just before a scheduled client meeting so the portfolio manager appears to be fulfilling his or her responsibility, although that practice may reflect more the concerns of the portfolio manager than the concerns of the client. By contrast, other portfolio managers may rebalance a portfolio just after the client meeting so the client or investment committee has the opportunity to approve the manager's actions.

Percentage-of-portfolio rebalancing requires monitoring of portfolio values at an agreed-upon frequency in order to identify instances in which a trigger point is breached. To be implemented with greatest precision, monitoring should occur daily. Daily monitoring obviously requires having an efficient custodian, one who can accurately monitor and quickly process and communicate portfolio and asset class valuations.

An obvious and important question is: How are the corridors for asset classes determined?

Investors sometimes set ad hoc corridors. We have already illustrated example of one well-known yet ad hoc approach, based on a hypothetical portfolio of domestic equities, international equities, and domestic bonds. The corridors were set according to a formula based on a percentage of the target allocation, target $\pm$ (target allocation $\times$ $P\%$), where $P\%$ was 10% (but could be another percentage such as 5%). Following that formula, a corridor of 45% $\pm$ (45% $\times$ 10%) = 45% $\pm$ 4.5% applied to domestic stocks, 15% $\pm$ 1.5% applied to international equities, and 40% $\pm$ 4% applied to domestic bonds. However, *ad hoc* approaches such this one are open to several criticisms. The approach illustrated does not account for differences in transaction costs in rebalancing these three asset classes, for example.

The literature suggests that at least five factors should play a role in setting the corridor for an asset class:

► transaction costs
► risk tolerance concerning tracking risk versus the strategic asset allocation
► correlation with other asset classes
► volatility
► volatilities of other asset classes

The more expensive it is to trade an asset class (or the lower its liquidity), the wider its corridor should be, because the marginal benefit in rebalancing must at least equal its marginal cost. The higher the risk tolerance (i.e., the lower the investor's sensitivity to straying from target proportions), the wider corridors can be.

Correlations also should be expected to play a role. In a two asset-class case, a higher correlation should lead to wider tolerance bands. Suppose one asset class has moved above its target allocation (so the other asset class is below its target weight). A further increase in value has an expected smaller effect on asset weights if the assets classes' returns are more highly positively correlated because the denominator in computing the asset class's weight is the sum of the values of the two asset classes. That denominator's value is likely to be higher for a given up-move of the asset class of concern if the two asset classes' returns are positively correlated. In a multi-asset-class case, all pairwise asset class correlations would need to be considered, making the interpretation of correlations complex. To expand the application of the two-asset case's intuition, one simplification involves considering the balance of a portfolio to be a single hypothetical asset and computing an asset class's correlation with it.[16]

A higher volatility should lead to a narrower corridor, all else equal. It hurts more to be a given percent off target for a more highly volatile asset class because it has a greater chance of a further large move away from target. In a two-asset case the more volatile the second asset, the more risk there is in being a given percent off target for the first asset class, all else equal. All asset classes' volatili-

---

[16] As in Masters (2003).

EXHIBIT 8	Factors Affecting Optimal Corridor Width	
Factor	Effect on Optimal Width of Corridor (all else equal)	Intuition
Factors Positively Related to Optimal Corridor Width		
Transaction costs	The higher the transaction costs, the wider the optimal corridor.	High transaction costs set a high hurdle for rebalancing benefits to overcome.
Risk tolerance	The higher the risk tolerance, the wider the optimal corridor.	Higher risk tolerance means less sensitivity to divergences from target.
Correlation with rest of portfolio	The higher the correlation, the wider the optimal corridor.	When asset classes move in synch, further divergence from targets is less likely.
Factors Inversely Related to Optimal Corridor Width		
Asset class volatility	The higher the volatility of a given asset class, the narrower the optimal corridor.	A given move away from target is potentially more costly for a high-volatility asset class, as a further divergence becomes more likely.
Volatility of rest of portfolio	The higher this volatility, the narrower the optimal corridor.	Makes large divergences from strategic asset allocation more likely.

ties would affect the optimal corridor in the multi-asset-class case. Again, a simplification is to treat the balance of the portfolio as one asset. Exhibit 8 summarizes the discussion. (It applies to the two-asset-class case, or to the multi-asset-class case with the simplification of treating all other asset classes—the balance of the portfolio—as one asset class.)

EXAMPLE 8

Tolerance Bands for an Asset Allocation

An investment committee is reviewing the following strategic asset allocation:

Domestic equities	50% ± 5%
International equities	15% ± 1.5%
Domestic bonds	35% ± 3.5%

The committee views the above corridors as appropriate if each asset class has identical risk and transaction-cost characteristics. It now wants to account for differences among the asset classes in setting the corridors.

Evaluate the implications of the following sets of facts on the stated tolerance band (set off by italics), given an all-else-equal assumption in each case:

1. Domestic bond volatility is much lower than that of domestic or international equities, which are equal. *Tolerance band for domestic bonds.*

2. Transaction costs in international equities are 10 percent higher than those for domestic equities. *Tolerance band for international equities.*

3. Transaction costs in international equities are 10 percent higher than those for domestic equities, and international equities have a much lower correlation with domestic bonds than do domestic equities. *Tolerance band for international equities.*

4. The correlation of domestic bonds with domestic equities is higher than their correlation with international equities. *Tolerance band for domestic equities.*

5. The volatility of domestic bonds has increased. *Tolerance band for international equities.*

Solution to 1: The tolerance band for domestic bonds should be wider than 35% ± 3.5%.

Solution to 2: The tolerance band for international equities should be wider than 15% ± 1.5%.

Solution to 3: Transaction costs point to widening the tolerance band for international equities, but correlations to narrowing it. The overall effect is indeterminate.

Solution to 4: The tolerance band for domestic equities should be wider than 50% ± 5%.

Solution to 5: The tolerance band for international equities should be narrower than 15% ± 1.5%.

3.2.3 Other Rebalancing Strategies

The investment literature includes rebalancing disciplines other than those discussed above. Calendar rebalancing can be combined with percentage-of-portfolio rebalancing (as described in Buetow et al.). In this approach (which may be called **calendar-and-percentage-of-portfolio rebalancing**), the manager monitors the portfolio at regular frequencies, such as quarterly. The manager then decides to rebalance based on a percentage-of-portfolio principle (has a trigger point been exceeded?). This approach mitigates the problem of incurring rebalancing costs when near the optimum that can occur in the calendar rebalancing.

McCalla (1997) describes an **equal probability rebalancing** discipline. In this discipline, the manager specifies a corridor for each asset class as a common multiple of the standard deviation of the asset class's returns. Rebalancing to the target proportions occurs when any asset class weight moves outside its corridor. In this discipline each asset class is equally likely to trigger rebalancing if the normal distribution describes asset class returns. However, equal probability rebalancing does not account for differences in transaction costs or asset correlations.

Goodsall and Plaxco (1996) and Plaxco and Arnott (2002) discuss as **tactical rebalancing** a variation of calendar rebalancing that specifies less frequent rebalancing when markets appear to be trending and more frequent rebalancing when they are characterized by reversals. This approach seeks to add value by tying rebalancing frequency to expected market conditions that most favor rebalancing to a constant mix.

3.2.4 Rebalancing to Target Weights versus Rebalancing to the Allowed Range

In the descriptions of rebalancing strategies, we have presented the standard paradigm in which a rebalancing involves adjusting asset class holdings to their target proportions. The alternative, applicable to rebalancing approaches that involve corridors, is to rebalance the asset allocation so that all asset class weights are within the allowed range but not necessarily at target weights. The rebalancing may follow a rule, such as adjusting weights halfway back to target (e.g., if an asset class's corridor is 50% ± 5% and the asset class's weight is 57 percent, reducing the weight to 52.5%), or to some judgmentally determined set of proportions. Compared with rebalancing to target weight, rebalancing to the allowed range results in less close alignment with target proportions but lower transaction costs; it also provides some room for tactical adjustments. For example, suppose that a U.S. investor's target allocation to non-U.S equities is 15 percent and that its weight moves above its corridor on the upside. During an expected transitory period of a depreciating U.S. dollar, the portfolio manager may want to rebalance the exposure only part way to the target proportion to take advantage of the apparent exchange rate tactical opportunity. The discipline of rebalancing to the allowed range also allows portfolio managers to better manage the weights of relatively illiquid assets.

A number of studies have contrasted rebalancing to target weights to rebalancing to the allowed range based on particular asset classes, time periods, and measures of the benefits of rebalancing. They have reached a variety of conclusions which do not permit one to state that one discipline is unqualifiedly superior to the other.

3.2.5 Setting Optimal Thresholds

The optimal portfolio rebalancing strategy should maximize the present value of the *net* benefit of rebalancing to the investor. Equivalently, the optimal strategy minimizes the present value of the sum of two costs: expected utility losses (from divergences from the optimum) and transaction costs (from rebalancing trades). Despite the apparent simplicity of the above formulations, finding the optimal strategy in a completely general context remains a complex challenge:

► If the costs of rebalancing are hard to measure, the benefits of rebalancing are even harder to quantify.

► The return characteristics of different asset classes differ from each other, and at the same time interrelationships (correlations) exist among the asset classes that a rebalancing strategy may need to reflect.

► The optimal rebalancing decisions at different points in time are linked; one decision affects another.

► Accurately reflecting transaction costs may be difficult; for example, transaction costs can be nonlinear in the size of a rebalancing trade.

► The optimal strategy is likely to change through time as prices evolve and new information becomes available.

► Rebalancing has tax implications for taxable investors.

Researchers are beginning to make headway in addressing optimal rebalancing in a general context.[17] At some future date, investors may be able to update optimal rebalancing thresholds in real time based on a lifetime utility of wealth formulation, including a transaction costs penalty component. Implementing such a system lies in the future rather than present of industry practice. If reasonable simplifying assumptions are permitted, some models are currently available to suggest specific values for optimal corridors, although no industry standard has been established yet.

3.3 The Perold–Sharpe Analysis of Rebalancing Strategies

Prior sections discussed rebalancing to a strategic asset allocation for a portfolio of many risky asset classes. That discipline of rebalancing, which can also be called a constant-mix strategy, is a bread-and-butter topic for investment practitioners. The following sections share the insights of Perold and Sharpe's (1988) analysis contrasting constant mix with other strategies. To make its points, the Perold–Sharpe analysis assumes a simple two-asset class setting in which just one asset class is risky. Nevertheless, the analysis throws light on the underlying features of the strategies and what market dynamics and investor attitudes to risk favor or disfavor each of them.

3.3.1 Buy-and-Hold Strategies

A buy-and-hold strategy is a passive strategy of buying an initial asset mix (e.g., 60/40 stocks/Treasury bills) and doing absolutely nothing subsequently. Whatever the market does, no adjustments are made to portfolio weights. It is a "do-nothing" strategy resulting in a drifting asset mix.

The investment in Treasury bills (bills, for short) is risk-free and for the sake of simplicity is assumed to earn a zero return; it is essentially cash. In a buy-and-hold strategy, the value of risk-free assets represents a floor for portfolio value. For instance, take €100 and invest it initially according to 60/40 stocks/cash asset allocation. If the value of the stock allocation were to fall to zero, we would still have the €40 invested in cash. Therefore, the following expression pertains:

Portfolio value = Investment in stocks + Floor value

For a 60/40 stock/cash allocation the equation is

Portfolio value = Investment in stocks + Floor value of €40

Portfolio value is a linear function of the investment in stocks (the risky asset). If the buy-and hold strategy has a floor, it is also true that there is no limit on

---

[17] See Leland (2000) and Donohue and Yip (2003).

upside potential so long as the portfolio is above the floor. The higher the initial allocation to stocks, the greater the increase (decrease) in value when stocks outperform (underperform) bills.

The amount by which portfolio value exceeds the investment in cash is the cushion (i.e., a buffer of value above the floor value). For a buy-and-hold strategy, the value of the investment in stocks moves 1:1 with the value of the cushion, as can be seen from rearranging the previous expression for portfolio value:

$$\text{Investment in stocks} = \text{Cushion} = \text{Portfolio value} - \text{Floor value} \quad \textbf{(42-1)}$$

In our one-risky-asset portfolio, the portfolio return (the percent change in portfolio value over a given holding period) equals the fraction of assets in stocks multiplied by the return on stocks (under the assumption of a zero return on bills).

$$\text{Portfolio return} = (\text{Percent in stocks}) \times (\text{Return on stocks})$$

For example, if stocks earn a 10 percent return, the value of stocks rises by 6 from 60 to 66; the value of the portfolio goes up by 6 from 100 to 106 (equal to 66 + 40). For the portfolio, that represents a 6 percent return as $6/100 = 6\%$. And $6\% = 0.6 \times 10\%$.

The investor's percent allocation to stocks is directly related to stock performance. For example if stocks earn a -100 percent return, the stock/bills allocation goes from 60/40 to 0/100 (the cushion is zero, the value of the portfolio is 40, which is the amount invested in bills). If stocks earn a $+100$ percent return, the asset allocation goes from 60/40 to 75/25 (the value of stocks goes from 60 to 120, increasing portfolio value from 100 to 160; $120/160 = 0.75$ or 75%, which becomes the new stock allocation). A higher allocation to stocks reflects a greater risk tolerance. Therefore, a buy-and-hold strategy would work well for an investor whose risk tolerance is positively related to wealth and stock market returns.

To summarize, for a buy-and-hold strategy the following holds:

▶ Upside is unlimited, but portfolio value can be no lower than the allocation to bills.

▶ Portfolio value is a linear function of the value of stocks, and portfolio return is a linear function of the return on stocks.

▶ The value of stocks reflects the cushion (above floor value) 1:1.

▶ The implication of using this strategy is that the investor's risk tolerance is positively related to wealth and stock market returns. Risk tolerance is zero if the value of stocks declines to zero.

3.3.2 Constant-Mix Strategies

What we have called rebalancing to the strategic asset allocation in prior sections is a constant-mix strategy in the terminology of Perold–Sharpe. Constant mix is a "do-something" (or "dynamic") strategy in that it reacts to market movements with trades. An investor decides, for example, that his portfolio will be 60 percent equities and 40 percent bills and rebalances to that proportion regardless of his level of wealth. In particular, the target investment in stocks in the constant-mix strategy is

$$\text{Target investment in stocks} = m \times \text{Portfolio value} \quad \textbf{(42-2)}$$

where m is a constant between 0 and 1 that represents the target proportion in stocks. If the equity market moves up, the actual stock proportion increases, but then it is adjusted down to m. If the equity market moves down, the actual stock proportion decreases, but then it is adjusted up to m.

Although a constant-mix strategy is "do-something," its effect is to maintain stable portfolio systematic risk characteristics over time, in contrast to a buy-and-hold strategy and the other "do-something" strategies that we will discuss shortly.

So far as returns alone are concerned, the adjustment policy of a constant-mix strategy will prove inferior to a buy-and-hold strategy if returns either move straight up, or move straight down. Strong bull and bear markets favor a buy-and-hold strategy. In the bull market case, the investor is cutting back on the shares of stock through rebalancing prior to further moves upwards. The buy-and-hold investor, by contrast, would profit by holding the number of shares constant (actually representing an increasing fraction of the portfolio invested in stocks). In the bear market case, the investor buys more shares prior to further moves down. The buy-and-hold investor does better by not changing his share holdings.

On the other hand, the constant-mix strategy tends to offer superior returns compared with buy-and hold strategies if the equities returns are characterized more by reversals than by trends. For example, suppose the corridor for equities is 60% ± 5%. The stock market drops and the equity allocation falls below 55 percent; the equity allocation is rebalanced to 60 percent by selling bills and purchasing shares. The stock market then appreciates to its initial level (i.e., a return reversal occurs). The shares purchased in rebalancing under a constant-mix strategy show a gain. On the other hand, if the stock market first goes up, triggering a sale of shares and purchase of bills, and then drops back to its initial level, the constant-mix strategy also realizes a gain. Either returns reversal pattern is neutral for the buy-and-hold strategy. The constant-mix strategy is contrarian and supplies liquidity. Buying shares as stock values fall and selling shares as stock values rise are actions that supply liquidity because the investor is taking the less popular side of trades.

A constant-mix strategy is consistent with a risk tolerance that varies proportionately with wealth.[18] An investor with such risk tolerance desires to hold stocks at all levels of wealth.

3.3.3 A Constant-Proportion Strategy: CPPI

A constant-proportion strategy is a dynamic strategy in which the target equity allocation is a function of the value of the portfolio less a floor value for the portfolio. The following equation is used to determine equity allocation:

$$\text{Target investment in stocks} = m \times (\text{Portfolio value} - \text{Floor value}) \quad \textbf{(42-3)}$$

where m is a fixed constant. Constant-proportion strategies are so called because stock holdings are held to a constant proportion of the cushion. A characteristic of constant-proportion strategies is that they are consistent with a zero tolerance for risk (and hence no holdings in stocks) when the cushion is zero. Comparing Equation 42-1 with Equation 42-3, we see that a buy-and-hold strategy is a special

---

[18] That is, with a constant-mix strategy, the amount of money invested in risky assets increases with increasing wealth, implying increasing risk tolerance. Because the amount of money held in risky assets increases to maintain a constant ratio of risky assets to wealth, risk tolerance increases proportionately with wealth (constant *relative* risk tolerance or constant *relative* risk aversion).

case of a constant-proportion strategy in which $m = 1$. (For a buy-and-hold strategy, there is no distinction between the actual and target investment in stocks. The desired investment is whatever the actual level is.) When m exceeds 1, the constant-proportion strategy is called constant-proportion portfolio insurance (CPPI).[19]

CPPI is consistent with a higher tolerance for risk than a buy-and-hold strategy (when the cushion is positive), because the investor is holding a larger multiple of the cushion in stocks. Whereas a buy-and-hold strategy is do-nothing, CPPI is dynamic, requiring a manager to sell shares as stock values decline and buy shares as stock values rise. The floor in a buy-and-hold strategy is established with a fixed investment in bills; by contrast, in a CPPI strategy it is established dynamically. When stock values are trending up, the investment in stocks increases more than 1:1 with the increase in the value of stocks. The holding of bills may be minimal. When stocks are trending down, the allocation to stocks decreases more than 1:1 with the decrease in the value of stocks. The holding in bills rapidly increases until it reaches the floor value.

To manage transaction costs, a CPPI strategy requires some rules to determine when rebalancing to the stated multiple of the cushion should take place. One approach transacts when the portfolio value changes by a given percentage. At this point, the portfolio incurs transaction costs to rebalance. Because taxes can be a material consideration for taxable investors, they create a need for a rebalancing rule.

We expect a CPPI strategy to earn high returns in strong bull markets because the share purchases as the cushion increases are profitable. In a severe bear market, the sale of shares also is profitable in avoiding losses on them. By contrast, CPPI performs poorly in markets characterized more by reversals than by trends. CPPI requires a manager to sell shares after weakness and buy shares after strength; those transactions are unprofitable if drops are followed by rebounds and increases are retraced. The CPPI strategy is just the opposite of the constant-mix strategy in using liquidity and being momentum oriented.

3.3.4 Linear, Concave, and Convex Investment Strategies

A buy-and-hold strategy has been called a linear investment strategy because portfolio returns are a linear function of stock returns. The share purchases and sales involved in constant-mix and CPPI strategies introduce nonlinearities in the relationship. For constant-mix strategies, the relationship between portfolio returns and stock returns is concave; that is, portfolio return increases at a decreasing rate with positive stock returns and decreases at an increasing rate with negative stock returns.[20] In contrast, a CPPI strategy is convex. Portfolio return increases at an increasing rate with positive stock returns, and it decreases at a decreasing rate with negative stock returns.[21] Concave and convex strategies graph as mirror images of each other on either side of a buy-and-hold strategy. Convex strategies represent the purchase of portfolio insurance, concave strategies the sale of portfolio insurance. That is, convex strategies dynamically establish a floor value while concave strategies provide or sell the liquidity to convex strategies.

---

[19] A value of m between 0 and 1 (and a floor value of zero) represents a constant-mix strategy.

[20] The graph of portfolio return against stock return would have an inverted saucer shape.

[21] The graph of portfolio return against stock return has a saucer shape.

EXHIBIT 9	Relative Return Performance of Different Strategies in Various Markets		
Market Condition	**Constant Mix**	**Buy and Hold**	**CPPI**
Up	Underperform	Outperform	Outperform
Flat (but oscillating)	Outperform	Neutral	Underperform
Down	Underperform	Outperform	Outperform
Investment Implications			
Payoff curve	Concave	Linear	Convex
Portfolio insurance	Selling insurance	None	Buying insurance
Multiplier	$0 < m < 1$	$m = 1$	$m > 1$

3.3.5 Summary of Strategies

Exhibit 9 summarizes the prior discussion of Perold–Sharpe analysis. The multiplier refers to Equation 42-3 which integrates all the models discussed.

It is important to recognize that we have focused the discussion of performance in Exhibit 9 and the text on return performance, not risk (except to mention the downside risk protection in the CPPI and stock/bills buy-and-hold strategies).

Finally, the appropriateness of buy-and-hold, constant-mix, and constant-proportion portfolio insurance strategies for an investor depends on the investor's risk tolerance, the types of risk with which she is concerned (e.g., floor values or downside risk), and asset-class return expectations, as Example 9 illustrates.

EXAMPLE 9

Strategies for Different Investors

For each of the following cases, suggest the appropriate strategy:

1. Jonathan Hansen, 25 years old, has a risk tolerance that increases by 20 percent for each 20 percent increase in wealth. He wants to remain invested in equities at all times.

2. Elaine Cash has a $1 million portfolio split between stocks and money market instruments in a ratio of 70/30. Her risk tolerance increases more than proportionately with changes in wealth, and she wants to speculate on a flat market or moderate bull market.

3. Jeanne Roger has a €2 million portfolio. She does not want portfolio value to drop below €1 million but also does not want to incur the drag on returns of holding a large part of her portfolio in cash equivalents.

Solution to 1: Given his proportional risk tolerance (constant relative risk tolerance) and desire to remain invested in equities at all times, a constant-mix strategy is appropriate for Hansen.

Solution to 2: Her risk tolerance is greater than that of a constant-mix investor, yet Cash's forecasts include the possibility of a flat market in which CPPI would do poorly. A buy-and-hold strategy is appropriate for Cash.

Solution to 3: The concern for downside risk suggests either a buy-and-hold strategy with €1 million in cash equivalents as a floor or dynamically providing the floor with a CPPI strategy. The buy-and-hold strategy would incur the greater cash drag, so the CPPI strategy is appropriate.

3.4 Execution Choices in Rebalancing

In our discussion of rebalancing we have skirted the important issue of transaction execution. The particulars of execution depend on the specific asset classes held, the availability of relevant derivative markets in addition to cash markets, and the tax consequences of different execution means for taxable investors. The major choices are to rebalance by selling and buying portfolio assets (cash market trades) or by overlaying derivative positions onto the portfolio (derivative trades).

3.4.1 Cash Market Trades

Cash market trades represent the most direct means of portfolio rebalancing. Such trades represent adjustment at the "retail" level of risk because they typically involve buying and selling individual security positions.[22] If the investor employs active managers, then such adjustments need to be executed with care to minimize the impact on active managers' strategies. Cash market trades generally are more costly, and slower to execute, than equivalent derivative trades. For taxable investors, however, tax considerations may favor cash market trades over derivative market trades. First, there may be no exact derivative market equivalent to a cash market trade on an after-tax basis. Second, in some tax jurisdictions such as the United States, derivative market trades may have unfavorable tax consequences relative to cash market trades.[23] In addition, even if differences in taxation are irrelevant (as in the case of tax-exempt investors), not all asset class exposures can be closely replicated using derivatives, and individual derivative markets may have liquidity limitations. To some extent, the level of granularity with which asset classes have been defined affects the availability of adequate derivative equivalents.

3.4.2 Derivative Trades

Portfolio managers can also often use derivative trades involving instruments such as futures contracts and total return swaps for rebalancing. Trades are carried out so that the total exposure to asset classes (portfolio and derivative positions) closely mimics the effect of rebalancing by buying and selling underlying assets.

---

[22] An exception would be rebalancing a passive exposure through an available exchange-traded fund (ETF) or basket trade.

[23] See Horvitz (2002) for some details.

Rebalancing through derivatives markets, for the portion of the portfolio that can be closely replicated through derivative markets, has a number of major advantages:

▶ lower transaction costs;

▶ more rapid implementation—in derivative trades one is buying and selling systematic risk exposures rather than individual security positions; and

▶ leaving active managers' strategies undisturbed—in contrast to cash market trades, which involve trading individual positions, derivative trades have minimal impact on active managers' strategies.[24]

Besides the possibility that an asset class exposure may not be closely replicable with available derivatives, individual derivatives markets may have liquidity limits. Many investors, including tax-exempt investors, find it appropriate to use both cash and derivative trades in rebalancing their portfolios.

4   CONCLUDING REMARKS

Managers must accord markets the respect they deserve. Implementation of portfolio strategies and tactics must be as rigorous as the investment decision process. A manager should understand his or her clients. Nothing is more important than a client's inherent tolerance for risk. Each client is unique; so should be the manager's understanding of the client's needs. When those needs change sufficiently, transaction costs assume a secondary role.

A portfolio manager must constantly monitor changes in investor circumstances, market and economic changes, and the portfolio itself, making sure that the IPS, asset allocation, and individual holdings continue to appropriately address the client's situation and investment objectives. The manager must serve as the client's champion in the investment realm, understand changes in the client's needs, and incorporate those changes into the dynamic management of the portfolio.

Legitimate chances to improve on diversified portfolios are rare. It pays to be wary of the multitude of vendors whose commercial interest argues otherwise.

A predetermined policy portfolio designed to be the continuing ideal and standard for an investor's combination of objectives, risk tolerance, and available asset classes, while hardly sacred, is the beacon one should generally steer toward.

---

[24] There may also be tactical advantages to using futures. For example, futures may trade cheaply in relation to the underlying cash market when the cash market is falling. See Kleidon and Whaley (1992).

SUMMARY

Even the most carefully constructed portfolios do not manage themselves. In this reading we have discussed two ingredients to ensuring an investment program's continuing relevancy: monitoring and rebalancing.

▶ Portfolio managers need to monitor everything that is relevant to positioning a portfolio to satisfy the client's objectives and constraints. Three areas that the portfolio manager must monitor are changes in investor circumstances and wealth, market and economic changes, and the portfolio itself.

▶ Fiduciaries have an ethical and legal responsibility for adequate monitoring. Only by systematic monitoring can the fiduciary secure an informed view of the appropriateness and suitability of a portfolio for a particular client.

▶ Rebalancing to an investor's strategic asset allocation has benefits and costs. If the target asset class proportions of an investor's strategic asset allocation represent his optimum, any divergence from the target proportions represents an expected utility loss to the investor. The benefit in rebalancing equals the reduction in the present value of expected utility losses from not tracking the optimum. Rebalancing is a risk-control discipline that helps ensure an appropriate level of portfolio risk.

▶ The costs of rebalancing include transaction costs and, for taxable investors, tax costs (tax liabilities that are triggered by rebalancing trades).

▶ Calendar rebalancing involves rebalancing the portfolio to target weights on a periodic basis such as monthly, quarterly, semiannually, or annually. Calendar rebalancing is the simplest rebalancing discipline; it has the drawback of being unrelated to market performance. Yet it can suffice in ensuring that the actual portfolio does not drift far away from target for long periods of time if the rebalancing frequency is adequate given the portfolio's volatility.

▶ Percentage-of-portfolio rebalancing involves setting rebalancing thresholds (trigger points) that define a corridor or tolerance band for the value of that asset class such as $50\% \pm 5\%$. Compared with calendar rebalancing (particularly at lower frequencies such as semiannually or annually), percentage-of-portfolio rebalancing can exercise tighter control on divergences from target proportions because it is directly related to market performance.

▶ In rebalancing, two disciplines are rebalancing to target weights and rebalancing to the allowed range. The former exercises tighter discipline on risk exposures, the latter allows for more control of costs and for tactical adjustment.

▶ Factors positively related to optimal corridor width for an asset class include transaction costs, risk tolerance, and correlation with the rest of the portfolio. The greater these factors, the wider the optimal corridor, in general.

▶ Factors negatively related to optimal corridor width for an asset class include the asset class's volatility and the volatility of the rest of the portfolio. The greater these factors, the narrower the optimal corridor, in general.

▶ Three contrasting strategies are buy and hold, constant mix (rebalancing to the strategic asset allocation), and constant proportion (which includes constant-proportion portfolio insurance).

▶ A buy-and-hold strategy is a passive strategy of buying an initial asset mix (e.g., 60/40 stocks/bills) and doing absolutely nothing subsequently. It is synonymous with a drifting asset mix. A constant-mix strategy involves rebalancing so that the investment in stocks is a constant fraction of portfolio value. A constant-proportion portfolio insurance strategy involves making trades so the investment in stocks represents a constant multiple of the cushion of portfolio value above a floor value.

▶ In strong bull markets, CPPI outperforms a buy-and-hold strategy, while a buy-and-hold strategy outperforms a constant-mix strategy, in general. In strong bear markets, the same priority of performance holds. In a market characterized more by reversals than by trends, a constant-mix strategy tends to do best, followed by buy-and-hold and then CPPI strategies.

PRACTICE PROBLEMS FOR READING 42

1. Evaluate the most likely effects of the following events on the investor's investment objectives, constraints, and financial plan.

   A. A childless working married couple in their late 20s adopts an infant for whom they hope to provide a college education.

   B. An individual decides to buy a house in one year. He estimates that he will need $102,000 at that time for the down payment and closing costs on the house. The portfolio from which those costs will be paid has a current value of $100,000 and no additions to it are anticipated.

   C. A foundation with a €150,000,000 portfolio invested 60 percent in equities, 25 percent in long-term bonds, and 15 percent in absolute return strategies has approved a grant totaling €15,000,000 for the construction of a radio telescope observatory. The foundation anticipates a new contribution from a director in the amount of €1,000,000 towards the funding of the grant.

2. **[Adapted from the 2001 Level III Examination]** Duane Rogers, as chief investment officer for the Summit PLC defined benefit pension scheme, has developed an economic forecast for presentation to the plan's board of trustees. Rogers projects that U.K. inflation will be substantially higher over the next three years than the board's current forecast.

   Rogers recommends that the board immediately take the following actions based on his forecast:

   A. Revise the pension scheme's investment policy statement to account for a change in the U.K. inflation forecast.

   B. Reallocate pension assets from domestic (U.K.) to international equities because he also expects inflation in the U.K. to be higher than in other countries.

   C. Initiate a program to protect the pension scheme's financial strength from the effects of U.K. inflation by indexing benefits paid by the scheme.

   State whether *each* recommended action is correct or incorrect. Justify *each* of your responses with *one* reason.

The following two interpretative monitoring problems (3–4) are presented as two-part narratives: initial client circumstances, which comprise the gist of a client's IPS and the detailed information going into its formulation, followed by the changed client circumstances.

3. **[Adapted from the 2002 CFA Level III Examination]**

   Initial Client Circumstances   Claire Wisman, a vice president for Spencer Design, is a 42-year-old widow who lives in the U.S. She has two children: a daughter, age 21, and a son, age 7. She has a $2,200,000 portfolio; half of the portfolio is invested in Spencer Design, a publicly traded common stock, which has a cost basis of $350,000. Despite a substantial drop in the value of her portfolio over the last two years, her long-term annual total returns have averaged 7 percent before tax. The recent drop in value has caused her great anxiety, and she believes that she can no longer tolerate an annual decline greater than 10 percent.

   Wisman intends to retire in 20 years and her goals for the next 20 years, in order of priority, are as follows. The present values given are gross of taxes.

   ► Funding the cost of her daughter's upcoming final year of college, which has a present value of $26,000, and her son's future college costs, which have a present value of $130,000.

   ► Increasing the portfolio to a level that will fund her retirement living expenses, which she estimates to be $257,000 for the first year of her retirement.

   ► Building her "dream house" in five years, the cost of which (including land) has a present value of $535,000.

   ► Giving, if possible, each of her children $1,000,000 when they reach age 40.

   After subtracting the present value (before tax) of her children's education costs and her homebuilding costs, the present value of her portfolio is $1,509,000. With returns from income and gains taxable at 30 percent and with continued annual growth of 7 percent before tax ($7\% \times (1 - 0.30) = 4.9\%$ after taxes), the portfolio's value will be approximately $3,928,000 net of taxes at the end of 20 years.

   Wisman's annual salary is $145,000, her annual living expenses are currently $100,000, and both are expected to increase at an inflation rate of 3 percent annually. Taxes on income and short-term capital gains (holding period one year or less) are substantially higher than taxes on long-term capital gains (holding period greater than one year). For planning purposes, however, Wisman wants to assume that her average tax rate on all income and gains is 30 percent. The inflation and tax rates are expected to remain constant. Currently, Wisman rents a townhouse, has no debt, and adamantly intends to remain debt-free. Spencer Design has no pension plan but provides company-paid medical insurance for executives for life and for their children to age 25. After taxes, Wisman's salary just covers her living expenses and thus does not allow her to make further meaningful capital contributions to her portfolio.

   Wisman's current investment policy statement has the following elements:

   Return requirement. A total return objective of 7 percent before tax is sufficient to meet Claire Wisman's educational, housing, and retirement goals. If the portfolio earns total return of 7 percent annually, the value at retirement ($3.93 million) should be adequate to meet ongoing spending needs then ($257,000/$3,928,000 = 6.5 percent spending rate) and fund all Wisman's extraordinary needs (college and homebuilding costs) in the meantime. The million-dollar gifts to her children are unrealistic goals that she should be encouraged to modify or drop.

Risk tolerance. Wisman has explicitly stated her limited (below average) willingness to take risk. Wisman appears to have an average ability to take risk. Her portfolio has some flexibility, because her expected return objective of 7 percent will meet her goals of funding her children's education, building her "dream house," and funding her retirement. Overall her risk tolerance is below average.

Time horizon. Her time horizon is multistage. The time horizon could be described as three-stage (the next 5 pre-retirement years defined by work/housing costs; the subsequent 15 pre-retirement years defined by work/college costs; and beyond 20 years postretirement).

Liquidity. Wisman has only a minor liquidity need ($26,000 in present value terms) to cover education expenses for her daughter next year. After that she has no liquidity need for the next five years. Only then ($535,000 in present value terms, for home construction) and in Years 11 through 14 ($130,000 in present value terms, for her son's education) will significant liquidity concerns exist.

Taxes. Taxes are a critical concern because Wisman needs to fund outlays with after-tax dollars.

Unique circumstances. A significant unique circumstance is the large concentration (50 percent of her assets) in Spencer Design stock. Another factor is her desire to build a new home in five years yet incur no debt. Also, she would "like" to give each child $1 million, but this goal is unrealistic and should not drive portfolio decisions.

Wisman indicates that Spencer Design has a leading and growing market share. The company has shown steady fundamental growth trends, and Wisman intends to hold her Spencer Design stock, which is expected to return at least 9 percent annually before tax with a standard deviation of returns of 20 percent.

Changed Client Circumstances　Claire Wisman, now 47 years old, has recently married a coworker at Spencer Design. Wisman and her husband are buying their dream house at a total cost of $700,000, and they have decided to make an immediate down payment of $430,000 and finance the remainder over 15 years. Wisman also indicates that her son has contracted a rare disease, requiring major surgery; the disease will prevent him from attending college. Although Wisman and her husband have medical insurance that will pay her son's ongoing medical expenses, her son's surgery will cost an additional $214,000 immediately. The cost of medical expenditures is expected to grow at a rate exceeding the general inflation rate for the foreseeable future. Wisman has decided to quit work to care for her son, whose remaining life expectancy is 40 years. She also insists on the need to provide care for her son when she and her husband are no longer capable of doing so. Wisman's parents died one year ago, and her daughter is now financially independent. Wisman's husband intends to retire in 25 years.

Given these circumstances, the investment portfolio held by Wisman and her husband will need to provide an amount equal to $1,713,000 (present value) to meet their living expenses until his retirement. They also want their portfolio to grow enough to cover their living expenses at retirement, which they estimate to be $100,000 annually. They believe they will need a before tax portfolio growth rate of approximately 8 to 10 percent annually to achieve this goal. Based on a retirement spending goal of $400,000, their corresponding effective postretirement spending rate will be approximately 6 to 7 percent annually before tax.

Wisman summarizes her new financial information in Exhibit P-1 below. She indicates that her portfolio and her husband's portfolio should be considered as one. She further states that her husband has taken well above-average risk in the past but he is now willing to leave the investment management decisions to her.

EXHIBIT P-1	New Financial Information			

	Claire Wisman	Husband	Combined	Current Allocation Percentage of Combined Portfolio
Salary	$0	$150,000	$150,000	—
Assets				
Money market	$61,000	$27,000	$88,000	2.4%
Diversified bond fund	$1,129,000	$0	$1,129,000	30.5%
Equities				
Large-capitalization equities	$385,000	$0	$385,000	10.4%
Emerging market equities	$0	$407,000	$407,000	11.0%
Spencer Design common stock	$1,325,000	$122,000	$1,447,000	39.1%
Undeveloped commercial land	$0	$244,000	$244,000	6.6%
Total portfolio	**$2,900,000**	**$800,000**	**$3,700,000**	**100.0%**

A. Indicate how *each* component of Wisman's investment policy statement should change as a result of Wisman's new circumstances. Justify *each* of your responses with *two* reasons based on Wisman's new circumstances.

B. Recommend whether the current allocation percentage (given in the exhibit) for *each* of the following assets should be decreased or increased as a result of Wisman's new circumstances. Justify *each* of your responses with *one* reason based on Wisman's new circumstances.

   i. Spencer Design common stock

   ii. money market

   iii. diversified bond fund

   iv. large-capitalization equities

   v. emerging market equities

   vi. undeveloped commercial land

4. [Adapted from the 2003 CFA Level III Examination]

Initial Client Circumstances   Both parents of 12-year-old Andrew Campbell recently died in an accident. The parents had been supporting Andrew and his grandmother, Lisa Javier, age 77. The parents' accumulated assets prior to their death were $640,000 in a diversified common stock (both domestic and international) portfolio and $360,000 in the common stock of Newman Enterprises, a publicly traded company founded by Javier's husband. The parents' assets will now be held in a single U.S.-based trust—the Javier–Campbell Trust (the Trust)—to benefit both Javier and Campbell. In addition to these assets, the Trust received life insurance proceeds of $2,000,000.

Newman Enterprises will continue to provide medical coverage for Javier until her death. Campbell has government-provided healthcare until he reaches age 22. Campbell will attend university for four years beginning at age 18. In addition to normal living expenses, initial annual university costs are projected to be $38,000, rising 8 percent annually.

According to the provisions of the Trust document:

▶ The Trust should provide for Javier's and Campbell's annual living expenses, currently estimated to total $78,000 per year (after tax). The Trust portfolio should earn a return sufficient to cover the living expenses of Javier and Campbell, taking taxes into consideration and allowing for inflation (expected to be 2 percent annually). Income and capital gains are taxed at 30 percent, and this tax treatment is not expected to change.

▶ The Trust should limit shortfall risk (defined as expected total return minus two standard deviations) to no lower than a −10 percent return in any one year.

▶ Campbell is entitled to receive distributions from the Trust until he reaches age 32. At that point, the Trust will continue making distributions for Javier's living expenses.

▶ Upon Javier's death, the Trust's assets will go to Campbell, provided he is at least 32 years old. If Campbell is not yet aged 32 when Javier dies, the Trust will then distribute income and principal to Campbell until he reaches age 32, at which point the Trust will terminate and the assets will be distributed to Campbell.

▶ The Newman Enterprises common stock cannot be sold without Javier's approval for as long as she is alive. Javier has stated her strong desire to retain the Newman stock indefinitely, to fulfill a promise she made to her husband.

▶ The Trust must hold in cash equivalents an amount equal to nine months of living expenses (on a pretax basis) for Javier and Campbell.

▶ In the unlikely event that Campbell dies before Javier, distributions will continue for Javier's benefit until she dies, at which point any remaining Trust assets will be distributed to several charities.

As a result of poor financial advice, Javier lost all of her inheritance from her husband's estate. Because her assets are nearly depleted, she wants to minimize any future losses in the Trust portfolio; in fact, she has expressed serious concerns about the Trust's ability to meet Campbell's and her needs during her lifetime.

The risk tolerance and return requirement elements of the Javier–Campbell Trust's IPS are as follows:

Risk Tolerance

Ability. The Trust has average ability to assume risk, largely because of its substantial asset base in relation to its spending needs. Because the portfolio is Javier's only source of support, the Trust's ability to assume risk is lower than it might otherwise be.

Willingness. The Trust has below-average willingness to assume risk. The Trust document requires that the account be invested so that shortfall risk (defined as expected total return minus two standard deviations) is limited to a −10 percent return in any one year. This limitation implies that the Trust will be unwilling to tolerate any substantial volatility in portfolio returns.

Overall risk tolerance. The Trust has below-average risk tolerance and will continue to have it for many years, especially while Javier is alive.

Return Requirement

The return requirement reflects two major factors: the need to cover living expenses and the need to protect the portfolio from the adverse effects of inflation. Specifically, the Trust must generate a total before-tax return of at least 6.57 percent on an annual basis to meet these return requirements.

The living expenses, estimated at \$78,000 per year, represent a \$78,000/\$3,000,000 = 2.6 percent spending rate in real, after-tax terms. However, because the Trust is taxed at 30 percent, it will need to earn a pretax return of $(2.6\% + 2\%)/(1 − 0.30) = 6.57$ percent to meet Javier and Campbell's living expenses.

Changed Client Circumstances   Ten years have now passed, and the Javier–Campbell Trust portfolio returns over the previous 10 years have failed to meet expectations. Lower returns, coupled with Lisa Javier's and Andrew Campbell's living expenses and Campbell's college costs, have combined to reduce the value of the Trust portfolio to \$2,000,000.

Javier, now 87, recently moved to an assisted-living care facility. With her health failing, doctors have determined she will live no longer than three years and will require full-time care for the remaining time until her death. Javier's medical expenses are covered by insurance, but her care and living expenses now require \$84,000 per year (after tax and adjusted for inflation) from the Trust. Inflation is expected to be 3 percent annually over the next several years. Javier has no other support and depends on the Trust to meet her financial needs. She has continued to express her concern that the Trust will not provide enough distributions to cover her expenses during her remaining lifetime. She still wishes to retain the Newman Enterprises common stock, which now constitutes 15 percent of the Trust portfolio and has an expected annual yield of 2 percent over the next several years. Legal constraints have not changed, and the Trust still requires nine months of living expenses (on a pretax basis) to be held in reserve.

Campbell, now 22, is a recent college graduate and has accepted a job with Elkhorn Consulting Partners. In the job offer, Elkhorn agreed to pay the cost of Campbell's M.B.A. degree. Campbell also has the opportunity to buy a partnership stake in the company by making equal annual payments of \$600,000 per year for five years. He will begin making those payments in ten years. Campbell's starting salary is sufficient to cover his living expenses.

Although Campbell is concerned about providing for Javier, he believes that with the appropriate asset allocation, the Trust assets should be sufficient to take care of her expenditures until she dies and to provide the growth he needs to meet his partnership obligations. Campbell views growth from the Trust to be essential in meeting his long-term goals. Assuming that Campbell lives longer than Javier, the individual assets in the Trust will be distributed to Campbell upon termination of the Trust; the Trust portfolio will become Campbell's portfolio.

The trustee believes that circumstances have changed enough to warrant revising certain components of the investment policy statements for Campbell and the Trust.

Formulate revised statements about the Javier–Campbell Trust's willingness to take risk that reflect the changed circumstances of both Javier and Campbell. Your response should include appropriate supporting justification.

5. A foundation holds an equally weighted portfolio of domestic equities, international equities, private equity, and inflation-protected bonds.

   A. Critique a percentage-of-portfolio discipline that involves establishing a corridor of target percentage allocation ± 5% for each asset class in the foundation's portfolio.

   B. Evaluate the implications of the following sets of facts on the stated corridor, given an all-else-equal assumption in each case:

   i. The Foundation's risk tolerance has decreased. *Corridor for international equities.*

   ii. Transaction costs in international equities are one-half those for private equity. *Corridor for inflation-protected bonds.*

   iii. The correlation of private equity with the rest of the portfolio is lower than the correlation of domestic equities with the rest of the portfolio. *Corridor for private equity.*

   iv. The volatility of domestic equities is higher than that of inflation-protected bonds. *Corridor for domestic equities.*

6. A. Recommend an appropriate rebalancing discipline for an investor who cannot monitor portfolio values on a daily basis yet holds an above-average risk portfolio and low risk tolerance.

   B. How would the investment results of the recommended rebalancing discipline be affected if markets were nontrending?

7. **[Adapted from the 2002 CFA Level III Examination]** Marvis University (MU) is a private, multiprogram U.S. university with a $2 billion endowment fund as of fiscal year-end May 31, 2002. With little government support, MU is heavily dependent on its endowment fund to support ongoing expenditures, especially because the university's enrollment growth and tuition revenue have not met expectations in recent years. The endowment fund must make a $126 million annual contribution, which is indexed to inflation, to MU's general operating budget. The U.S. Consumer Price Index is expected to rise 2.5 percent annually, and the U.S. higher education cost index is anticipated to rise 3 percent annually. The endowment has also budgeted $200 million due on January 31, 2003, representing the final payment for construction of a new main library.

In a recent capital campaign, MU met its fundraising goal only with the help of one very successful alumna, Valerie Bremner, who donated $400 million of Bertocchi Oil and Gas common stock at fiscal year-end May 31, 2002. Bertocchi Oil and Gas is a large-capitalization, publicly traded U.S.

company. Bremner donated the stock on the condition that no more than 25 percent of the initial number of shares may be sold in any fiscal year. No substantial additional donations are expected in the future.

Given the large contribution to and distributions from the endowment fund, the fund's Investment Committee has decided to revise its investment policy statement.

In the revised IPS, the endowment portfolio manager established that MU's return requirement is 10 percent. MU's average ability to take risk restrains its risk tolerance.

Five years have passed, and the Marvis University endowment fund's willingness and ability to assume risk have increased. The endowment fund's Investment Committee asks its consultant, James Chan, to discuss and recommend a rebalancing strategy to incorporate the new risk tolerance. Chan anticipates a bull market in growth assets over the next three to five years. He also believes that volatility will be below historical averages during that same time period. The Investment Committee directs Chan to incorporate his views into his recommendation. The Committee also does not want the market value of the portfolio to decline more than 15 percent below its current market value.

A. Describe the following *three* primary rebalancing strategies:

　　i. buy and hold

　　ii. constant mix

　　iii. constant-proportion portfolio insurance

B. Determine which *one* of the three rebalancing strategies in Part A Chan should recommend for the Marvis University endowment fund. Justify your response with two reasons based on the circumstances described above.

APPENDIX

Appendix A Solutions to End-of-Reading Problems

SOLUTIONS FOR READING 37

1. Centralized risk control systems bring all risk management activities under the responsibility of a single risk control unit. Under decentralized systems, each business unit is responsible for its own risk control. The advantages of a centralized system are that it brings risk control closer to the key decision makers in the organization and enables the organization to better manage its risk budget by recognizing the diversification embedded across business units. The decentralized approach has the advantage of placing risk control in nearer proximity to the source of risk taking. However, it has the disadvantage of not accounting for portfolio effects across units.

2. The following risk exposures should be reported as part of an Enterprise Risk Management System for Ford Motor Company:

   ▶ *Market risks*

      ▶ Currency risk, because expenditures and receipts denominated in non-domestic currencies create exposure to changes in exchange rates.

      ▶ Interest rate risk, because the values of securities that Ford has invested in are subject to changes in interest rates. Also, Ford has borrowings and loans, which could be affected by interest rate changes.

      ▶ Commodity risk, because Ford has exposure in various commodities and finished products.

   ▶ *Credit risk*, because of financing provided to customers who have purchased Ford's vehicles on credit.

   ▶ *Liquidity risk*, because of the possibility that Ford's funding sources may be reduced or become unavailable and Ford may then have to sell its securities at a short notice with a significant concession in price.

   ▶ *Settlement risk*, because of Ford's investments in fixed-income instruments and derivative contracts, some of which effect settlement through the execution of bilateral agreements and involve the possibility of default by the counterparty.

   ▶ *Political risk*, because Ford has operations in several countries. This exposes it to political risk. For example, the adoption of a restrictive policy by a non-U.S. government regarding payment of dividends by a subsidiary in that country to the parent company could adversely affect Ford.

3. Two types of risk that were inadequately managed were model risk and operational risk. Systematic errors in a major input of the options pricing model, implied volatility, resulted in mispricing options and trading losses. Thus model risk was inadequately managed. Furthermore, the systems and procedures at NatWest failed to prevent or detect and bring to the attention of senior management the trading losses. Thus operational risk also was not well managed.

4. Trader 1's statement is incorrect. Buyers are concerned about the transaction costs of trades as much as sellers, so a security's liquidity is highly relevant to buyers. In certain cases, such as a short position in a stock with limited float, the liquidity risk for the purchase side of a trade can be considerable.

   Trader 2's statement is incorrect. Derivatives usually do not help in managing liquidity risk because the lack of liquidity in the spot market typically passes right through to the derivatives market.

Trader 3's statement is correct. Businesses need to take risks in areas in which they have expertise and possibly a comparative advantage in order to earn profits. Risk management can entail taking risk as well as reducing risk.

5. A. Assuming that the desk pays its traders a percentage of the profits on their own trading books, the −€20 million loss generated by an individual trader implies that the rest of the desk made €30 million and that the bank will have to pay the other traders an incentive fee on this larger amount, even though it generated only €10 million in net revenues. By contrast, if every trader had made money and the revenues to the desk were €10 million, the incentive payouts to traders would have been much lower and the net profits to the bank much higher.

 B. In the scenario described above, the trader in question appears to have increased his risk exposure at year-end. The asymmetric nature of the incentive fee arrangement may induce risk taking because it is a call option on a percentage of profits and the value of a call option increases in the volatility of the underlying. In this sense, the interests of the bank and the trader diverged to the detriment of the bank.

 C. First and foremost, it is clear that senior management was out of touch with the risk dynamics of the desk because it should have known that the trader in question was over his limits at some points much earlier in the scenario. The fact that management discovered this violation only after the loss occurred reflects poor risk governance.

6. *Strengths:* The sensitivity analysis reported by Ford is useful in highlighting the possible adverse effect of a 1 percent decline in interest rates on Ford Credit's net income. It also is based on an objective measure of interest rate risk, duration.

 Weaknesses: The sensitivity analysis reported in the table assumes that interest rate changes are instantaneous, small, parallel shifts in the yield curve. From a risk management perspective, one would have a special interest in the effects of larger interest rate changes, including major discontinuities in interest rates. The inclusion of value at risk would help fill this gap in the analysis. Furthermore, changes in the yield curve other than parallel shifts should be examined, such as nonparallel shifts (twists) in the yield curve. The text mentions the recommendation of the Derivatives Policy Group to examine both parallel shifts and twists of the yield curve.

7. A. There is a 1 percent chance that the portfolio will lose at least £4.25 million in any given week.

 B. There is a 99 percent chance that the portfolio will lose no more than £4.25 million in one week.

8. Statement A, which is the definition of VAR, is clearly correct. Statement B is also correct, because it lists the important decisions involved in measuring VAR. Statement D is correct: The longer the time period, the larger the possible losses. Statement C, however, is incorrect. The VAR number would be larger for a 1 percent probability than for a 5 percent probability. Accordingly, the correct answer is C.

9. A. The probability is 0.005 that the portfolio will lose at least 50 percent in a year. The probability is 0.005 that the portfolio will lose between 40 percent and 50 percent in a year. Cumulating these two probabilities implies that the probability is 0.01 that the portfolio will lose at least 40 percent in a year. So, the 1 percent yearly VAR is 40 percent of the market value of $10 million, which is $4 million.

B. The probability is 0.005 that the portfolio will lose at least 50 percent in a year, 0.005 that it will lose between 40 and 50 percent, 0.010 that it will lose between 30 and 40 percent, 0.015 that it will lose between 20 and 30 percent, and 0.015 that it will lose between 10 and 20 percent. Cumulating these probabilities indicates that the probability is 0.05 that the portfolio will lose at least 10 percent in a year. So, the 5 percent yearly VAR is 10 percent of the market value of $10 million, which is $1 million.

10. First, we must calculate the monthly portfolio expected return and standard deviation. Using "1" to indicate the U.S. government bonds and "2" to indicate the U.K. government bonds, we have

$$\mu_P = w_1\mu_1 + w_2\mu_2 = 0.50(0.0085) + 0.50(0.0095) = 0.0090$$
$$\sigma_P^2 = w_1^2\sigma_1^2 + w_2^2\sigma_2^2 + 2w_1w_2\sigma_1\sigma_2\rho$$
$$= (0.50)^2(0.0320)^2 + (0.50)^2(0.0526)^2$$
$$+ 2(0.50)(0.50)(0.0320)(0.0526)(0.35)$$
$$= 0.001242$$
$$\sigma_P = \sqrt{0.001242} = 0.0352$$

A. For a 5 percent monthly VAR, we have $\mu_P - 1.65\sigma_P = 0.0090 - 1.65(0.0352) = -0.0491$. Then the VAR would be $100,000,000(0.0491) = $4.91 million.

B. For a 1 percent monthly VAR, we have $\mu_P - 2.33\sigma_P = 0.0090 - 2.33(0.0352) = -0.0730$. Then the VAR would be $100,000,000(0.0730) = $7.30 million.

C. There are 12 months or 52 weeks in a year. So, to convert the monthly return of 0.0090 to weekly return, we first multiply the monthly return by 12 to convert it to an annual return, and then we divide the annual return by 52 to convert it to a weekly return. So, the expected weekly return is $0.0090(12/52) = 0.0021$. Similarly, we adjust the standard deviation to $0.0352(\sqrt{12}/\sqrt{52}) = 0.01691$. The 5 percent weekly VAR would then be $\mu_P - 1.65\sigma_P = 0.0021 - 1.65(0.01691) = -0.0258$. Then the VAR in dollars would be $100,000,000(0.0258) = $2.58 million.

D. The 1 percent weekly VAR would be $\mu_P - 2.33\sigma_P = 0.0021 - 2.33(0.01691) = -0.0373$. Then the VAR would be $100,000,000(0.0373) = $3.73 million.

11. A. For the five-year period, there are 60 monthly returns. Of the 60 returns, the 5 percent worst are the 3 worst returns. Therefore, based on the historical method, the 5 percent VAR would be the third worst return. From the returns given, the third worst return is −0.2463. So, the VAR in dollars is 0.2463($25,000) = $6,157.50.

B. Of the 60 returns, the 1 percent worst are the 0.6 worst returns. Therefore, we would use the single worst return. From the returns given, the worst return is −0.3475. So, the VAR in dollars is 0.3475($25,000) = $8,687.50.

12. A. Of the 700 outcomes, the worst 5 percent are the 35 worst returns. Therefore, the 5 percent VAR would be the 35th-worst return. From the data given, the 35th worst return is −0.223. So, the 5 percent annual VAR in dollars is 0.223($10,000,000) = $2,230,000.

B. Of the 700 outcomes, the worst 1 percent are the 7 worst returns. Therefore, the 1 percent VAR would be the seventh-worst return. From the data given, the seventh worst return is −0.347. So, the 1 percent annual VAR in dollars is 0.347($10,000,000) = $3,470,000.

13. A. The analytical or variance–covariance method begins with the assumption that portfolio returns are normally distributed. A normal distribution has an unlimited upside and an unlimited downside. The assumption of a normal distribution is inappropriate when the portfolio contains options because the return distributions of options are far from normal. Call options have unlimited upside potential, as in a normal distribution, but the downside return is truncated at a loss of 100 percent. Similarly, put options have a limited upside and a large but limited downside. Likewise, covered calls and protective puts have limits in one direction or the other. Therefore, for the portfolio that has options, the assumption of a normal distribution to estimate VAR has a number of problems. In addition, it is very difficult to calculate a covariance between either two options or an option and a security with more linear characteristics—among other reasons because options have different dynamics at different points in their life cycle.

B. Portfolios with simple, linear characteristics, particularly those with a limited budget for computing resources and analytical personnel, might select the variance/covariance method. For more complex portfolios containing options and time-sensitive bonds, the historical method might be more appropriate. The Monte Carlo simulation method typically would not be a wise choice unless it were managed by an organization with a portfolio of complex derivatives that is willing to make and sustain a considerable investment in technology and human capital.

14. A. The observed outcomes are consistent with the VAR calculation's prediction on the frequency of losses exceeding the VAR. Therefore, the VAR calculation is accurate.

B. The VAR results indicate that under "normal" market conditions that would characterize 19 out of 20 days, the portfolio ought to lose less than €3 million. It provides no other information beyond this.

C. The portfolio certainly lends itself to scenario analysis. In this particular case, given the substantial short options position, it might be instructive to create a customized scenario under which the portfolio was analyzed in the wake of a large increase in option-implied volatility.

15. The fact that credit losses occur infrequently makes Statement A incorrect. Unlike a European-style option, which cannot be exercised prior to expiration and thus has no current credit risk, an American-style option does have the potential for current credit risk. Therefore, Statement C is incorrect. Statement B, however, is correct.

16. A. The decision not to hedge this risk was correct. Suppose the company had hedged this risk. If the price of oil were to increase, the favorable effect of the increase on income would be offset by the loss on the oil futures, but the home currency should appreciate against the U.S. dollar, leaving the company worse off. If the price of oil were to decrease, the unfavorable effect on income would be offset by the futures position and the home currency should depreciate, leaving the company better off. In short, the company would remain exposed to exchange rate risk associated with oil price movements.

B. The decision not to hedge this risk was correct. The company should remain exposed to market risk associated with exchange rate movements (i.e., currency risk). Hedging would remove currency risk but leave the company with market risk associated with oil price movements. If the home currency declined, the price of oil would likely decline because it is positively correlated with the U.S. dollar value of the home currency. That would be a negative for income. On the other hand, appreciation of the home currency is likely to be accompanied by an oil price increase, which would be positive for income.

   C. The risk management strategy adopted is logical because it exploits a natural hedge. A decline in the price of oil (a negative) is likely to be accompanied by a depreciation of the home currency relative to the U.S. dollar (a positive), and an increase in the price of oil (a positive) is likely to be accompanied by appreciation of the home currency (a negative). Hedging both currency and market risk would be an alternative risk management strategy to consider, but in comparison to the strategy adopted, it would incur transaction costs.

17. A. Because the option is a European-style option, it cannot be exercised prior to expiration. Therefore, there is no current credit risk.

   B. The current value of the potential credit risk is the current market value of the option, which is $6. Of course, at expiration, the option is likely to be worth a different amount and could even expire out of the money.

   C. Options have unilateral credit risk. The risk is borne by the buyer of the option, Tony Smith, because he will look to the seller for the payoff at expiration if the option expires in the money.

18. The Sharpe ratio uses standard deviation of portfolio return as the measure of risk. Standard deviation is a measure of total risk. RAROC uses capital at risk (defined in various ways) as the measure of risk. RoMAD uses maximum drawdown as a risk measure. Maximum drawdown is the difference between a portfolio's maximum point of return and the lowest point of return over a given time interval. The Sortino ratio measures risk using downside deviation, which computes volatility using only rate of return data points below a minimum acceptable return. In contrast to the Sharpe ratio, its focus is on downside risk.

19. D is correct. The monthly return is 9.6%/12 = 0.8%.

   The monthly standard deviation is $18.0\%/\sqrt{12} = 5.196\%$.

   The percent VAR is 0.8% − 1.65 (5.196%) = −7.7734%.

   The dollar VAR is 7.7734% (€50 million) = €3.8867 million, or €3.9 million.

20. C is correct. Stolz's statement #3 is the only incorrect statement because the VAR number will be larger for a 1 percent probability than for a 5 percent probability. The other statements are fine. Statement #1 is actually correct as a definition of VAR. Statement #2 actually correctly describes decisions involved in measuring VAR. Statement #4 is actually correct because the longer the time period, the larger the possible losses.

21. A is correct. Kreuzer is wrong on both. For the currency forward contract, the London securities house is bearing credit risk because the London house is the party who would be owed (or paid) at current prices. For option contracts, including puts, the option buyer is the only party with credit risk. So Kalton Corporation is bearing credit risk on its long put position.

22. A is correct. In a credit default swap, the protection seller would make payments to the protection buyer in the event of a specified credit event. Thus, the protection seller is assuming credit risk. The other positions would not give a desired increase in credit risk exposure in corporate bonds.

23. B is correct. A 5% VAR would be equal to the expected monthly portfolio return minus 1.65 × (monthly portfolio standard deviation), or $-\text{VAR} = \mu_p - 1.65\sigma_p$. The increase in expected return would result in a lower calculated VAR (smaller losses). An increase in the correlation would increase the portfolio standard deviation, which would result in a higher calculated VAR (larger losses). So the correct answers are, respectively, No and Yes.

24. B is correct. Kreuzer's statement about an advantage of VAR is wrong because the VAR for individual positions does not generally aggregate in a simple way into portfolio VAR. Kreuzer's statement about the Sharpe ratio is correct.

SOLUTIONS FOR READING 38

1. A. The number of futures contracts that must be bought is

$$N_f = \left(\frac{1.2 - 0.95}{0.98}\right)\left(\frac{\$175,000,000}{\$105,790}\right) = 421.99$$

Rounded off, this is 422 contracts.

B. The value of the stock portfolio is $\$175,000,000(1 + 0.051)$
$= \$183,925,000$.

The profit on the long futures position is $422(\$111,500 - \$105,790)$
$= \$2,409,620$.

The overall value of the position (stock plus long futures) is
$\$183,925,000 + \$2,409,620 = \$186,334,620$.

The overall rate of return is $\left(\frac{\$186,334,620}{\$175,000,000}\right) - 1 = 0.0648$.

The effective beta is $0.0648/0.055 = 1.18$, which is approximately equal to the target beta of 1.2.

2. A. The number of futures contracts that must be bought is

$$N_f = \frac{\$300,000,000(1.0235)^{0.25}}{\$500(498.30)} = 1,211.11$$

Rounded off, this is 1,211 contracts long.

Now invest the following amount in risk-free bonds, which pay 2.35 percent interest:

$$\frac{1,211(\$500)(498.30)}{(1.0235)^{0.25}} = \$299,973,626$$

This amount will grow to $\$299,973,626(1.0235)^{0.25} = \$301,720,650$. The number of synthetic units of stock is

$$\frac{1211(500)}{(1.0075)^{0.25}} = 604,369.98$$

which would grow to $604,369.98(1.0075)^{0.25} = 605,500$ with the reinvestment of dividends.

B. At expiration in three months, the payoff on the futures is
$1,211(\$500)(594.65 - 498.30) = 605,500(594.65) - \$301,720,650$. In order to settle the futures contract, the money manager will owe $\$301,720,650$. This amount can be paid off with the proceeds from the investment in risk-free bonds, leaving the money manager with 605,500 units of the stock index, each worth 594.65. This transaction achieves the desired exposure to the stock index.

3. A. In order to create a synthetic cash position, the number of futures contracts to be sold is

$$N_f = \frac{\$25,000,000(1.0275)^{4/12}}{\$250(1170.10)} = 86.24$$

Rounded off, this is 86 contracts short.

Analysis of Derivatives for the CFA® Program, by Don M. Chance. Copyright © 2003 by AIMR. Reprinted with permission.

B. The effective amount of stock committed to this transaction is actually

$$\frac{86(\$250)(1170.10)}{(1.0275)^{4/12}} = \$24{,}930{,}682$$

This amount invested at the risk-free rate should grow to $\$24{,}930{,}682(1.0275)^{4/12} = \$25{,}157{,}150$, resulting in the following number of shares:

$$\frac{86(\$250)}{(1.0125)^{4/12}} = 21{,}411.16$$

With reinvestment of dividends, this number would grow to $21{,}411.16(1.0125)^{4/12} = 21{,}500$ shares. The short position in futures is equivalent to selling $\$24{,}930{,}682$ of stock.

C. In four months when the futures contract expires, the stock index is at 1031. The payoff of the futures contract is $-86(\$250)(1031 - 1170.10) = -\$21{,}500(1031) + \$25{,}157{,}150 = \$2{,}990{,}650$.

  Netting the futures payoff against the stock position produces $\$25{,}157{,}150$, equivalent to investing $\$24{,}930{,}682$ at 2.75 percent for four months. The short futures position has thus effectively converted equity to cash.

4. A. The current allocation is as follows: stocks, $0.65(200{,}000{,}000) = \$130{,}000{,}000$; bonds, $0.35(\$200{,}000{,}000) = \$70{,}000{,}000$. The new allocation desired is as follows: stocks, $0.85(\$200{,}000{,}000) = \$170{,}000{,}000$; bonds, $0.15(\$200{,}000{,}000) = \$30{,}000{,}000$. So, to achieve the new allocation, the manager must buy stock futures on $\$170{,}000{,}000 - \$130{,}000{,}000 = \$40{,}000{,}000$. An equivalent amount of bond futures must be sold.

  To synthetically sell $40 million in bonds and convert into cash, the manager must sell futures:

$$N_{bf} = \left(\frac{0.0 - 6.75}{5.25}\right)\left(\frac{\$40{,}000{,}000}{\$109{,}000}\right) = -471.82$$

He should sell 454 contracts and create synthetic cash.

  To synthetically buy $40 million of stock with synthetic cash, the manager must buy futures:

$$N_{sf} = \left(\frac{1.15 - 0}{0.95}\right)\left(\frac{\$40{,}000{,}000}{\$157{,}500}\right) = 307.44$$

He should buy 307 contracts. Now the manager effectively has $170 million (85 percent) in stocks and $30 million (15 percent) in bonds.

  The next step is to increase the beta on the $170 million in stock to 1.20 by purchasing futures. The number of futures contracts would, therefore, be

$$N_{sf} = \left(\frac{1.20 - 1.15}{0.95}\right)\left(\frac{\$170{,}000{,}000}{\$157{,}500}\right) = 56.81$$

An additional 57 stock futures contracts should be purchased. In total, $307 + 57 = 364$ contracts are bought.

To increase the modified duration from 6.75 to 8.25 on the $30 million of bonds, the number of futures contracts is

$$N_{bf} = \left(\frac{8.25 - 6.75}{5.25}\right)\left(\frac{\$30,000,000}{\$109,000}\right) = 78.64$$

An additional 79 bond futures contracts should be purchased. In total, $472 - 79 = 393$ contracts are sold.

B. The value of the stock will be $130,000,000(1 + 0.05) = $136,500,000. The profit on the stock index futures will be $364(\$164,005 - \$157,500) = \$2,367,820$.
The value of the bonds will be $70,000,000(1 + 0.0135) = $70,945,000. The profit on the bond futures will be $-393(\$110,145 - \$109,000) = -\$449,985$.
The total value of the position, therefore, is $136,500,000 + $2,367,820 + $70,945,000 − $449,985 = $209,362,835.

If the reallocation were carried out by trading bonds and stocks:
The stock would be worth $170,000,000(1 + 0.05) = $178,500,000.
The bonds would be worth $30,000,000(1 + 0.0135) = $30,405,000.
The overall value of the portfolio would be $178,500,000 + $30,405,000 = $208,905,000.

The difference between the two approaches is $457,835, only 0.229 percent of the original value of the portfolio.

5. A. In order to gain effective exposure to stock and bonds today, the manager must use futures to synthetically buy $17,500,000 of stock and $32,500,000 of bonds.

To synthetically buy $17,500,000 in stock, the manager must buy futures:

$$N_{sf} = \left(\frac{1.15 - 0}{0.93}\right)\left(\frac{\$17,500,000}{\$175,210}\right) = 123.51$$

He should buy 124 contracts.
To synthetically buy $32,500,000 of bonds, the manager must buy futures:

$$N_{bf} = \left(\frac{7.65 - 0}{5.65}\right)\left(\frac{\$32,500,000}{\$95,750}\right) = 459.57$$

He should buy 460 contracts.
Now the manager effectively has invested $17,500,000 in stock and $32,500,000 in bonds.

B. The profit on the stock index futures will be $124(\$167,559 - \$175,210) = -\$948,724$.
The profit on the bond futures will be $460(\$93,586 - \$95,750) = -\$995,440$.
The total profit with futures $= -\$948,724 - \$995,440 = -\$1,944,164$.

If bonds and stocks were purchased today, in three months:
The change in value of stock would be $17,500,000(−0.054) = −$945,000.
The change in value of bonds would be $32,500,000(−0.0306) = −$994,500.

The overall change in value of the portfolio would be −$945,000 − $994,500 = −$1,939,500.

The difference between the two approaches is $4,664, only 0.009 percent of the total expected cash inflow.

6. A. GateCorp will receive £200,000,000 in two months. To hedge the risk that the pound may weaken during this period, the firm should enter into a forward contract to deliver pounds and receive dollars two months from now at a price fixed now. Because it is effectively long the pound, GateCorp will take a short position on the pound in the forward market. GateCorp will thus enter into a two-month short forward contract to deliver £200,000,000 at a rate of $1.4272 per pound.

When the forward contract expires in two months, irrespective of the spot exchange rate, GateCorp will deliver £200,000,000 and receive ($1.4272/£1)(£200,000,000) = $285,440,000.

B. ABCorp will have to pay A$175,000,000 in one month. To hedge the risk that the Australian dollar may strengthen against the U.S. dollar during this period, it should enter into a forward contract to purchase Australian dollars one month from now at a price fixed today. Because it is effectively short the Australian dollar, ABCorp takes a long position in the forward market. ABCorp thus enters into a one-month long forward contract to purchase A$175,000,000 at a rate of US$0.5249 per Australian dollar.

When the forward contract expires in one month, irrespective of the spot exchange rate, ABCorp will pay ($0.5249/A$)(A$175,000,000) = $91,857,500 to purchase A$175,000,000. This amount is used to purchase the raw material needed.

SOLUTIONS FOR READING 39

1. A. This position is commonly called a bull spread.

  B. Let X_1 be the lower of the two strike prices and X_2 be the higher of the two strike prices.

   i. $V_T = \max(0, S_T - X_1) - \max(0, S_T - X_2)$
        $= \max(0, 89 - 75) - \max(0, 89 - 85) = 14 - 4 = 10$
    $\Pi = V_T - V_0 = V_T - (c_1 - c_2) = 10 - (10 - 2) = 2$

   ii. $V_T = \max(0, S_T - X_1) - \max(0, S_T - X_2)$
         $= \max(0, 78 - 75) - \max(0, 70 - 85) = 3 - 0 = 3$
    $\Pi = V_T - V_0 = V_T - (c_1 - c_2) = 3 - (10 - 2) = -5$

   iii. $V_T = \max(0, S_T - X_1) - \max(0, S_T - X_2)$
          $= \max(0, 70 - 75) - \max(0, 70 - 85) = 0 - 0 = 0$
    $\Pi = V_T - V_0 = V_T - (c_1 - c_2) = 0 - (10 - 2) = -8$

  C. **i.** Maximum profit $= X_2 - X_1 - (c_1 - c_2) = 85 - 75 - (10 - 2) = 2$

   ii. Maximum loss $= c_1 - c_2 = 10 - 2 = 8$

  D. $S_T{}^* = X_1 + (c_1 - c_2) = 75 + (10 - 2) = 83$

  E. $V_T = \max(0, S_T - X_1) - \max(0, S_T - X_2)$
     $= \max(0, 83 - 75) - \max(0, 83 - 85) = 8 - 0 = 8$
   $\Pi = V_T - V_0 = V_T - (c_1 - c_2) = 8 - (10 - 2) = 0$

    Therefore, the profit or loss if the price of the underlying increases to 83 at expiration is indeed zero.

2. A. This position is commonly called a bear spread.

  B. Let X_1 be the lower of the two strike prices and X_2 be the higher of the two strike prices.

   i. $V_T = \max(0, X_2 - S_T) - \max(0, X_1 - S_T)$
        $= \max(0, 0.85 - 0.87) - \max(0, 0.70 - 0.87) = 0 - 0 = 0$
    $\Pi = V_T - V_0 = V_T - (p_2 - p_1) = 0 - (0.15 - 0.03) = -0.12$

   ii. $V_T = \max(0, X_2 - S_T) - \max(0, X_1 - S_T)$
         $= \max(0, 0.85 - 0.78) - \max(0, 0.70 - 0.78) = 0.07 - 0 = 0.07$
    $\Pi = V_T - V_0 = V_T - (p_2 - p_1) = 0.07 - (0.15 - 0.03) = -0.05$

   iii. $V_T = \max(0, X_2 - S_T) - \max(0, X_1 - S_T)$
          $= \max(0, 0.85 - 0.68) - \max(0, 0.70 - 0.68) = 0.17 - 0.02 = 0.15$
    $\Pi = V_T - V_0 = V_T - (p_2 - p_1) = 0.15 - (0.15 - 0.03) = 0.03$

  C. **i.** Maximum profit $= X_2 - X_1 - (p_2 - p_1) = 0.85 - 0.70$
                      $- (0.15 - 0.03) = 0.03$

   ii. Maximum loss $= p_2 - p_1 = 0.15 - 0.03 = 0.12$

  D. Breakeven point $= X_2 - (p_2 - p_1) = 0.85 - (0.15 - 0.03) = 0.73$

  E. $V_T = \max(0, X_2 - S_T) - \max(0, X_1 - S_T)$
     $= \max(0, 0.85 - 0.73) - \max(0, 0.70 - 0.73) = 0.12 - 0 = 0.12$
   $\Pi = V_T - V_0 = V_T - (p_2 - p_1) = 0.12 - (0.15 - 0.03) = 0$

    Therefore, the profit or loss if the price of the currency decreases to $0.73 at expiration of the puts is indeed zero.

3. A. Let X_1 be 110, X_2 be 115, and X_3 be 120.

$V_0 = c_1 - 2c_2 + c_3 = 8 - 2(5) + 3 = 1$

i. $V_T = \max(0, S_T - X_1) - 2\max(0, S_T - X_2) + \max(0, S_T - X_3)$

$V_T = \max(0, 106 - 110) - 2\max(0, 106 - 115)$
$\qquad + \max(0, 106 - 120) = 0$

$\Pi = V_T - V_0 = 0 - 1 = -1$

ii. $V_T = \max(0, S_T - X_1) - 2\max(0, S_T - X_2) + \max(0, S_T - X_3)$

$V_T = \max(0, 110 - 110) - 2\max(0, 110 - 115)$
$\qquad + \max(0, 110 - 120) = 0$

$\Pi = V_T - V_0 = 0 - 1 = -1$

iii. $V_T = \max(0, S_T - X_1) - 2\max(0, S_T - X_2) + \max(0, S_T - X_3)$

$V_T = \max(0, 115 - 110) - 2\max(0, 115 - 115)$
$\qquad + \max(0, 115 - 120) = 5$

$\Pi = V_T - V_0 = 5 - 1 = 4$

iv. $V_T = \max(0, S_T - X_1) - 2\max(0, S_T - X_2) + \max(0, S_T - X_3)$

$V_T = \max(0, 120 - 110) - 2\max(0, 120 - 115)$
$\qquad + \max(0, 120 - 120) = 10 - 10 + 0 = 0$

$\Pi = V_T - V_0 = 0 - 1 = -1$

v. $V_T = \max(0, S_T - X_1) - 2\max(0, S_T - X_2) + \max(0, S_T - X_3)$

$V_T = \max(0, 123 - 110) - 2\max(0, 123 - 115)$
$\qquad + \max(0, 123 - 120) = 13 - 16 + 3 = 0$

$\Pi = V_T - V_0 = 0 - 1 = -1$

B. **i.** Maximum profit $= X_2 - X_1 - (c_1 - 2c_2 + c_3) = 115 - 110 - 1 = 4$

ii. Maximum loss $= c_1 - 2c_2 + c_3 = 1$

iii. The maximum profit would be realized if the price of the stock at expiration of the options is at the exercise price of $115.

iv. The maximum loss would be incurred if the price of the stock is at or below the exercise price of $110, or if the price of the stock is at or above the exercise price of $120.

C. Breakeven: $S_T{}^* = X_1 + (c_1 - 2c_2 + c_3)$ and $S_T{}^* = 2X_2 - X_1 - (c_1 - 2c_2 + c_3)$. So, $S_T{}^* = 110 + 1 = 111$ and $S_T{}^* = 2(115) - 110 - 1 = 119$

4. A. Let X_1 be 110, X_2 be 115, and X_3 be 120.

$V_0 = p_1 - 2p_2 + p_3 = 3.50 - 2(6) + 9 = 0.50$

i. $V_T = \max(0, X_1 - S_T) - 2\max(0, X_2 - S_T) + \max(0, X_3 - S_T)$

$V_T = \max(0, 110 - 106) - 2\max(0, 115 - 106)$
$\qquad + \max(0, 120 - 106) = 4 - 2(9) + 14 = 0$

$\Pi = V_T - V_0 = 0 - 0.50 = -0.50$

ii. $V_T = \max(0, X_1 - S_T) - 2\max(0, X_2 - S_T) + \max(0, X_3 - S_T)$

$V_T = \max(0, 110 - 110) - 2\max(0, 115 - 110)$
$\qquad + \max(0, 120 - 110) = 0 - 2(5) + 10 = 0$

$\Pi = V_T - V_0 = 0 - 0.50 = -0.50$

iii. $V_T = \max(0, X_1 - S_T) - 2\max(0, X_2 - S_T) + \max(0, X_3 - S_T)$

$V_T = \max(0, 110 - 115) - 2\max(0, 115 - 115)$
$\qquad + \max(0, 120 - 115) = 0 - 2(0) + 5 = 5$

$\Pi = V_T - V_0 = 5 - 0.50 = 4.50$

iv. $V_T = \max(0, X_1 - S_T) - 2\max(0, X_2 - S_T) + \max(0, X_3 - S_T)$

$V_T = \max(0, 110 - 120) - 2\max(0, 115 - 120)$
$\qquad + \max(0, 120 - 120) = 0$

$\Pi = V_T - V_0 = 0 - 0.50 = -0.50$

v. $V_T = \max(0, X_1 - S_T) - 2\max(0, X_2 - S_T) + \max(0, X_3 - S_T)$
$V_T = \max(0, 110 - 123) - 2\max(0, 115 - 123)$
$\qquad + \max(0, 120 - 123) = 0$
$\Pi = V_T - V_0 = 0 - 0.50 = -0.50$

B. **i.** Maximum profit $= X_2 - X_1 - (p_1 - 2p_2 + p_3) = 115 - 110 - 0.50 = 4.50$

ii. Maximum loss $= p_1 - 2p_2 + p_3 = 0.50$

iii. The maximum profit would be realized if the expiration price of the stock is at the exercise price of $115.

iv. The maximum loss would be incurred if the expiration price of the stock is at or below the exercise price of $110, or if the expiration price of the stock is at or above the exercise price of $120.

C. Breakeven: $S_T^* = X_1 + (p_1 - 2p_2 + p_3)$ and $S_T^* = 2X_2 - X_1 - (p_1 - 2p_2 + p_3)$. So, $S_T^* = 110 + 0.50 = 110.50$ and $S_T^* = 2(115) - 110 - 0.50 = 119.50$

D. For $S_T = 110.50$:
$V_T = \max(0, X_1 - S_T) - 2\max(0, X_2 - S_T) + \max(0, X_3 - S_T)$
$V_T = \max(0, 110 - 110.50) - 2\max(0, 115 - 110.50)$
$\qquad + \max(0, 120 - 110.50) = -2(4.50) + 9.50 = 0.50$
$\Pi = V_T - V_0 = 0.50 - 0.50 = 0$
For $S_T = 119.50$:
$V_T = \max(0, X_1 - S_T) - 2\max(0, X_2 - S_T) + \max(0, X_3 - S_T)$
$V_T = \max(0, 110 - 119.50) - 2\max(0, 115 - 119.50)$
$\qquad + \max(0, 120 - 119.50) = 0.50$
$\Pi = V_T - V_0 = 0.50 - 0.50 = 0$

Therefore, we see that the profit or loss at the breakeven points computed in Part D above is indeed zero.

5. A. **i.** $V_T = S_T + \max(0, X_1 - S_T) - \max(0, S_T - X_2)$
$\qquad = 92 + \max(0, 75 - 92) - \max(0, 92 - 90) = 92 + 0 - 2 = 90$
$\Pi = V_T - S_0 = 90 - 80 = 10$

ii. $V_T = S_T + \max(0, X_1 - S_T) - \max(0, S_T - X_2)$
$\qquad = 90 + \max(0, 75 - 90) - \max(0, 90 - 90) = 90 + 0 - 0 = 90$
$\Pi = V_T - S_0 = 90 - 80 = 10$

iii. $V_T = S_T + \max(0, X_1 - S_T) - \max(0, S_T - X_2)$
$\qquad = 82 + \max(0, 75 - 82) - \max(0, 82 - 90) = 82 + 0 - 0 = 82$
$\Pi = V_T - S_0 = 82 - 80 = 2$

iv. $V_T = S_T + \max(0, X_1 - S_T) - \max(0, S_T - X_2)$
$\qquad = 75 + \max(0, 75 - 75) - \max(0, 75 - 90) = 75 + 0 - 0 = 75$
$\Pi = V_T - S_0 = 75 - 80 = -5$

v. $V_T = S_T + \max(0, X_1 - S_T) - \max(0, S_T - X_2)$
$\qquad = 70 + \max(0, 75 - 70) - \max(0, 70 - 90) = 70 + 5 - 0 = 75$
$\Pi = V_T - S_0 = 75 - 80 = -5$

B. **i.** Maximum profit $= X_2 - S_0 = 90 - 80 = 10$

ii. Maximum loss $= -(X_1 - S_0) = -(75 - 80) = 5$

iii. The maximum profit would be realized if the price of the stock at the expiration of options is at or above the exercise price of $90.

iv. The maximum loss would be incurred if the price of the stock at the expiration of options were at or below the exercise price of $75.

C. Breakeven: $S_T^* = S_0 = 80$

6. A. This position is commonly called a straddle.

    B. **i.** $V_T = \max(0, S_T - X) + \max(0, X - S_T)$
              $= \max(0, 35 - 25) + \max(0, 25 - 35) = 10 + 0 = 10$
         $\Pi = V_T - (c_0 + p_0) = 10 - (4 + 1) = 5$

        ii. $V_T = \max(0, S_T - X) + \max(0, X - S_T)$
              $= \max(0, 29 - 25) + \max(0, 25 - 29) = 4 + 0 = 4$
         $\Pi = V_T - (c_0 + p_0) = 4 - (4 + 1) = -1$

      iii. $V_T = \max(0, S_T - X) + \max(0, X - S_T)$
              $= \max(0, 25 - 25) + \max(0, 25 - 25) = 0 + 0 = 0$
         $\Pi = V_T - (c_0 + p_0) = 0 - (4 + 1) = -5$

      iv. $V_T = \max(0, S_T - X) + \max(0, X - S_T)$
              $= \max(0, 20 - 25) + \max(0, 25 - 20) = 0 + 5 = 5$
         $\Pi = V_T - (c_0 + p_0) = 5 - (4 + 1) = 0$

       v. $V_T = \max(0, S_T - X) + \max(0, X - S_T)$
              $= \max(0, 15 - 25) + \max(0, 25 - 15) = 0 + 10 = 10$
         $\Pi = V_T - (c_0 + p_0) = 10 - (4 + 1) = 5$

    C. **i.** Maximum profit $= \infty$

        ii. Maximum loss $= c_0 + p_0 = 4 + 1 = 5$

    D. $S_T{}^* = X \pm (c_0 + p_0) = 25 \pm (4 + 1) = 30, 20$

SOLUTIONS FOR READING 40

1. The company can enter into a swap to pay a fixed rate of 6.5 percent and receive a floating rate. The first floating payment will be at 5 percent.

> Interest payment on the floating rate note = $50,000,000(0.05 + 0.0125)(90/360) = $781,250
> Swap fixed payment = $50,000,000(0.065)(90/360) = $812,500
> Swap floating receipts = $50,000,000(0.05)(90/360) = $625,000

> The overall cash payment made by the company is $812,500 + $781,250 − $625,000 = $968,750.

2. **A.** The value of the bond portfolio is inversely related to interest rates. To increase the duration, it would be necessary to hold a position that moves inversely with the interest rates. Hence the swap should be pay floating, receive fixed.

   B. Duration of a four-year pay-floating, receive-fixed swap with quarterly payments = (0.75)(4) − 0.125 = 2.875

   Duration of a three-year pay-floating, receive-fixed swap with semiannual payments = (0.75)(3) − 0.25 = 2.0

   > Because the objective is to increase the duration of the bond portfolio, the four-year pay-floating, receive-fixed swap is the better choice.

   C. The notional principal is

   $$NP = B\left(\frac{MDUR_T - MDUR_B}{MDUR_S}\right)$$
   $$NP = \$100,000,000\left(\frac{3.5 - 1.5}{2.875}\right) = \$69,565,217$$

3. Because the company has a floating-rate obligation on the floating-rate note, it should enter into a swap involving receiving a floating rate. Accordingly, the appropriate swap to hedge the risk and earn a profit would be a pay-fixed, receive-floating swap. Let LIBOR be L. Cash flows generated at each step are as follows:

   A. Issue leveraged floating-rate notes and pay coupon
   = L(2.5)($5,000,000) = $12,500,000L

   B. Buy bonds with a face value = (2.5)($5,000,000) = $12,500,000
   Receive a coupon = (0.07)($12,500,000) = $875,000

   C. Enter into a pay-fixed, receive-floating swap:
   Pay = (0.06)(2.5)($5,000,000) = $750,000
   Receive = L(2.5)($5,000,000) = $12,500,000L

   D. Net cash flow = −$12,500,000L + $875,000 − $750,000 + $12,500,000L = $125,000

   > In addition to the risk of default by the bond issuer, the company is taking the credit risk of the dealer by entering into a swap. The profit of $125,000 may be compensation for taking on this additional risk.

Solutions to 1–9 taken from *Analysis of Derivatives for the CFA® Program*, by Don M. Chance. Copyright © 2003 by AIMR. Reprinted with permission. All other solutions copyright © CFA Institute.

4. A. The U.S. company would pay the interest rate in euros. Because it expects that the interest rate in the eurozone will fall in the future, it should choose a swap with a floating rate on the interest paid in euros to let the interest rate on its debt float down.

B. The U.S. company would receive the interest rate in dollars. Because it expects that the interest rate in the United States will fall in the future, it should choose a swap with a fixed rate on the interest received in dollars to prevent the interest rate it receives from going down.

5. A. The semiannual cash flow that must be converted into pounds is €15,000,000/2 = €7,500,000. In order to create a swap to convert €7,500,000, the equivalent notional principals are

- Euro notional principal = €7,500,000/(0.065/2) = €230,769,231
- Pound notional principal = €230,769,231/€1.5/£ = £153,846,154

B. The cash flows from the swap will now be

- Company makes swap payment = €230,769,231(0.065/2) = €7,500,000
- Company receives swap payment = £153,846,154(0.075/2) = £5,769,231

The company has effectively converted euro cash receipts to pounds.

6. A. The portfolio manager can reduce exposure to JK stock by entering into an equity swap in which the manager:

- pays or sells the return on $30,000,000 of JK stock.
- receives or buys the return on $30,000,000 worth of the S&P 500.

B. On the equity swap, at the end of each year, the manager will:

Pay (0.04)($30,000,000) = $1,200,000
Receive (−0.03)($30,000,000) = −$900,000
(Note: Receiving a negative value means paying.)

Net cash flow = −$1,200,000 − $900,000 = −$2,100,000

Notice here that because the return on the index is significantly lower than the return on the stock, the swap has created a large cash flow problem.

7. A. The manager needs to reduce the allocation to domestic stocks by 10 percent and increase the allocation to international stocks by 10 percent. So the manager needs to reduce the allocation to domestic stocks by (0.10)($750,000,000) = $75,000,000 and increase the allocation to international stocks by $75,000,000. This can be done by entering into an equity swap in which the manager:

- pays or sells the return on the Russell 3000 on notional principal of $75,000,000.
- receives or buys the return on the MSCI EAFE index on notional principal of $75,000,000.

B. On the equity swap, at the end of the first year, the manager will:

Pay (0.05)($75,000,000) = $3,750,000
Receive (0.06)($75,000,000) = $4,500,000

Net cash flow = −$3,750,000 + $4,500,000 = $750,000

8. The following are the current allocations, the desired new allocations, and the transactions needed to go from the current positions to the new positions.

Stock	Current ($640 million, 80%)	New ($600 million, 75%)	Transaction
Large cap	$448 million (70%)	$450 million (75%)	Buy $2 million
International	$192 million (30%)	$150 million (25%)	Sell $42 million

Bonds	Current ($160 million, 20%)	New ($200 million, 25%)	Transaction
Government	$128 million (80%)	$150 million (75%)	Buy $22 million
Corporate	$32 million (20%)	$50 million (25%)	Buy $18 million

The following swap transactions would achieve the desired allocations:

Equity Swaps
 Receive return on U.S. large-cap index on $2,000,000

 Pay LIBOR on $2,000,000

 Pay return on international stock index on $42,000,000

 Receive LIBOR on $42,000,000

Fixed-Income Swaps
 Receive return on U.S. government bond index on $22,000,000

 Pay LIBOR on $22,000,000

 Receive return on U.S. corporate bond index on $18,000,000

 Pay LIBOR on $18,000,000

The overall position involves no LIBOR payments or receipts. The portfolio receives LIBOR on $42 million on equity swaps. It pays LIBOR on $2 million on equity swaps, and $22 million and $18 million on fixed-income swaps, for a total payment of LIBOR on $42 million. Thus, overall, there are no LIBOR payments or receipts.

9. A. If FS(2,5) is above the exercise rate, it will be worth exercising the swaption to enter a three-year swap to pay a fixed rate of 5 percent and receive LIBOR of 6.5 percent.

 Swap payments on first quarterly settlement date:
  Pay $20,000,000(90/360)(0.05) = $250,000
  Receive $20,000,000(90/360)(0.065) = $325,000
  Loan payment = $20,000,000(90/360)(0.065) = $325,000
 Net cash flow = −$250,000

 B. If FS(2,5) is below the exercise rate, it will not be worth exercising the swaption. However, the company can enter a three-year swap to pay a fixed rate of 4 percent, for example, and receive LIBOR of 6.5 percent.

 Swap payments on first quarterly settlement date:
  Pay $20,000,000(90/360)(0.04) = $200,000
  Receive $20,000,000(90/360)(0.065) = $325,000
  Loan payment = $20,000,000(90/360)(0.065) = $325,000
 Net cash flow = $200,000

10. B is correct. Gide will invest the 65 billion yen for six months at 0.066% (refer to Exhibit 1). She will convert the yen to euros using the 6-month forward rate of 132.46. Solve 65,000,000,000 × (1 + 0.00066 × (180/360))/132.46 = 490,876,114.

11. C is correct. Assuming that interest parity holds, if Gide uses a six-month forward to convert the yen she should expect to earn the six-month euro rate of 2.13% as shown in Exhibit 1. As a check, you can convert 65 billion yen to euros at the spot exchange rate. Then, calculate the return associated with this number and the answer in question 40.1. To wit, solve 65,000,000,000/133.83 = 485,690,802. Next, solve 490,876,114/485,690,802 = 1.01067616. Annualizing this six-month HPR provides the answer of 2.13%.

12. C is correct. If Gide remains unhedged and her expectation of a future exchange rate of 1.225 USD/EUR comes true, the $50,000,000 will convert to €40,816,327. If she buys a call on the euro (the right to buy euros with dollars) with a strike of 1.18, her effective conversion rate will be 1.2075 (1.18 (the strike) + 0.0275 (the call premium)). Continuing, 50,000,000/1.2075 = 41,407,867. This exceeds the expected amount of euros under the unhedged option. Answers B and D do not provide a hedge against a weaker dollar.

13. A is correct. Darc's statement in comment #3 describes buying a straddle. A long straddle is one way to profit from an increase in volatility as the increase in volatility will, ceteris paribus, increase the values of both the put and the call.

14. C is correct. In order to raise 100 million Swiss francs, Millau needs to issue bonds totaling €64,350,064 (divide 100 by the spot rate of 1.554). To convert the euros into Swiss francs, Millau could enter into a currency swap. In a currency swap, notional amounts are exchanged at initiation. In this case, Millau will pay €64,350,064 and receive 100 million in Swiss francs. Subsequent payments do not net as they are denominated in different currencies. Remembering to adjust the given swap rates for semi-annual payments, in six months Millau will pay (0.008/2) × 100,000,000 = 400,000 Swiss francs and receive 64,350,064 × (0.023/2) = 740,026 euros.

15. B is correct. Darc expects interest rates in the eurozone and in Switzerland to increase. Given such an expectation, the best swap would be to pay fixed and receive floating. If the expected increases come about, the amount paid remains fixed while the amount received increases.

16. D is correct. If the stock price at expiration of the options is $26.90, the put will expire worthless, the call will expire worthless, and the value of the strategy will reflect solely the value of the stock.

17. A is correct. The protective put combines a long stock position with a long put position. The stock price of $26.20 plus the cost of the put, $0.80, provides the breakeven point for the combination, which is $27.00. If the stock price declines below $25.00, the value of the put at expiration will increase dollar-for-dollar with the stock decline. Thus, Cassidy effectively locks in a sales price of at least $25.00. At that $25.00 stock price, Cassidy loses $1.20 per share on his stock as well as the $0.80 put premium. Thus, his maximum loss is $2.00. Regarding the Sure covered call, if the Sure stock price increases above $35.00, the value of the call at expiration will increase dollar-for-dollar with increases in the share price. As Cassidy is short the call, this represents a dollar-for-dollar loss to him. Thus, the maximum gain of the covered call is the difference between today's stock price and the strike ($1.00) plus the premium received ($1.20) equals $2.20. If the stock price falls, the $1.20 premium offsets, in part, the loss. At $32.80, the $1.20 premium exactly offsets the loss on the stock. Thus, $32.80 is the breakeven point for the strategy.

18. A is correct. A protective put combines a long stock position with a long put. The put effectively "clips" the downside risk of the stock while allowing upside potential. A long call also exhibits a truncated downside and upside potential.

19. D is correct. Initially, the dealer will be long the call. Long calls have positive deltas. If stock prices fall, the value of the call will decrease, harming the dealer. To hedge the risk of a price decline, the dealer will sell the underlying.

20. C is correct. Multiply 250,000 shares times the price per share of Hop. 250,000 × $26.20 = $6,550,000. Multiply 200,000 shares times the price per share of Sure. 200,000 × $34.00 = $6,800,000. The total notional value of the swap is the sum of these two amounts. $6,550,000 + $6,800,000 = $13,350,000. If Hop is up 2%, Sure is up 4%, and the Russell 3000 is up 5%, the swap cash flows will be 0.02 × $6,550,000 plus 0.04 × $6,800,000 equals $403,000 from Eldridge to the dealer and 0.05 × $13,350,000 = $667,500 from the dealer to Eldridge. Only the net payment, $264,500 from the dealer to Cassidy, is actually paid.

21. C is correct. The target beta is 0.80 and the dollar value of the portfolio is $13,350,000. Multiply 0.80 × $13,350,000 = $10,680,000. This is the desired result. Currently, the beta of the portfolio is 1.20. Multiplying the current beta by the portfolio value generates a value of $16,020,000 (1.20 × $13,350,000). The short futures position must reduce the beta-times-dollar amount by $5,340,000 ($16,020,000 − $13,350,000). Given that the beta of the futures contract is 0.97, the dollar amount of futures contracts needed is $5,505,155 ($5,340,000/0.97). Divide this number by the per contract value of the futures contract to calculate the needed number of contracts; $5,505,155/$275,000 = 20.018 contracts. Round to 20 contracts.

SOLUTIONS FOR READING 41

1. A. Quoted spread is the difference between the ask and bid prices in the quote prevailing at the time the trade is entered. The prevailing quote is the one at 10:50:06, with a bid of $4.69 and an ask of $4.75. So, Quoted spread = Ask − Bid = $4.75 − $4.69 = $0.06.

   B. The time-of-trade quotation midpoint = ($4.69 + $4.75)/2 = $4.72. Effective spread = 2 × (Trade price − Time-of-trade quotation midpoint) = 2 × ($4.74 − $4.72) = 2 × $0.02 = $0.04.

   C. The effective and quoted spreads would be equal if a purchase took place at the ask price and a sale took place at the bid price.

2. A. The difference between quoted spreads and effective spreads reflects the price improvement provided by dealers. If the effective spreads are lower than the quoted spreads, dealers are providing price improvements. Since the effective spreads are lower than the quoted spreads on both the NYSE and NASDAQ, dealers in both markets provided price improvements in the period being examined.

   B. The difference between the quoted and effective spreads is much greater on the NYSE (0.301 cents) than on NASDAQ (0.087 cents). Therefore, the dealers on the NYSE provided greater price improvement than those on NASDAQ.

3. E-Crossnet should not disclose unmatched quantities. Crossing networks maintain complete confidentiality not only in regard to the size of the orders and the names of the investors placing the orders, but also in regard to the unmatched quantities. If E-Crossnet were to disclose the unmatched quantities, it would provide useful information to other parties that would affect the supply and demand of these stocks in which clients want to transact. As a result of the information leakage, transaction costs for its clients would likely rise.

4. A. The second order will have a greater market impact because it is bigger in size.

   B. The second order will have a greater market impact because the trader placing it has a reputation of representing informed investors in the stock. Thus, other traders may believe that the stock's intrinsic value differs from the current market price and adjust their quotations accordingly. In contrast to most other situations in which a reputation of being smart is beneficial, in stock trading, it is not to one's advantage.

   C. By definition, orders executed on crossing networks, such as POSIT, avoid market impact costs because the orders are crossed at the existing market price determined elsewhere, regardless of size. Therefore, the first order will have greater market impact. Note, however, that a part of a large order may go unfilled on the crossing network.

5. A. Missed trade opportunity cost is the unfilled size times the difference between the subsequent price and the benchmark price for buys (or times the difference between the benchmark price and the subsequent price for sells). So, using the closing price on 8 February as the subsequent price, the estimated missed trade opportunity cost is 460,000 × ($23.60 − $21.35) = $1,035,000.

B. Using the closing price on 14 February as the subsequent price, the estimated missed trade opportunity cost is 460,000 × ($21.74 − $21.35) = $179,400.

C. One of the problems in estimating missed trade opportunity cost is that the estimate depends upon when the cost is measured. As the solutions to Parts A and B of this problem indicate, the estimate could vary substantially when a different interval is used to measure the missed trade opportunity cost. Another problem in estimating the missed trade opportunity cost is that it does not consider the impact of order size on prices. For example, the estimates above assume that if the investment manager had bought the 500,000 shares on 8 February, he would have been able to sell these 500,000 shares at $23.60 each on 8 February (or at $21.74 each on 14 February). However, an order to sell 500,000 shares on 8 February (or on 14 February) would have likely led to a decline in price, and the entire order of 500,000 shares would not have been sold at $23.60 (or at $21.74). Thus, the missed trade opportunity costs above are likely to be overestimates.

6. Since the portfolio manager does not want to pay more than £45 per share, he should place a limit order to buy 5,000 shares at no more than £45 per share. An advantage of placing the limit order is that he avoids the risk of paying too high a price and then suffering substantial losses if the stock price subsequently declines. However, a disadvantage is that his order may not be filled because the market price may never touch his limit order price of £45, incurring a missed trade opportunity cost. For example, consider a situation in which the stock's ask price is £47 when the order to buy at £45 limit is placed and the stock trades up to £80. If the portfolio manager had placed a market order, he would have been able to purchase the stock at £47 and make a profit by selling the stock at the current price of £80. An advantage of a market order is certainty of execution. The disadvantage of a market order is uncertainty concerning the price at which the order will be executed. Because the portfolio manager's chief focus is on execution price, the limit order would be preferred.

7. One negative of shopping the order is that it could delay the execution of the order, and the stock price could increase in the meantime. Another important negative of shopping the order is that it leaks information to others about the buying intention of the asset management firm. This information leakage could result in an adverse price movement in the shares that the asset management firm wants to buy because the broker/dealers could revise their quotes or trade based on the information gained.

8. A. Estimated implicit costs = Trade size × (Trade price − Benchmark price) for a buy, or Trade size × (Benchmark price − Trade price) for a sale. In this problem, Trade size = 100 and Trade price = $2.66.

   i. Opening price = $2.71
   Estimated implicit costs = 100 × ($2.71 − $2.66) = $5

   ii. Closing price = $2.65
   Estimated implicit costs = 100 × ($2.65 − $2.66) = −$1

   iii. We need to first calculate the VWAP.
   VWAP = Dollar volume/Trade volume
   Dollar volume = (200 × $2.71) + (200 × $2.72) + (100 × $2.76) + (100 × $2.77) + (1100 × $2.70) + (100 × $2.66) + (100 × $2.65) = $5,140

Trade volume = 200 + 200 + 100 + 100 + 1100 + 100 + 100 = 1,900 shares

So, VWAP = $5,140/1,900 = $2.7053 per share.

Estimated implicit costs = 100 × ($2.7053 − $2.66) = $4.53

B. Using VWAP as a benchmark, implicit costs are $4.53, whereas implicit costs are −$1 if the closing price is used as a benchmark. Estimated implicit costs may be quite sensitive to the choice of benchmark.

9. A. If the order is received late in the day, the broker would act based on how the prices have changed during the day. If the order is a sell order and prices have increased since the opening, the broker would immediately fill the order so that the sale price is greater than the benchmark price. If prices have fallen during the day, the broker would wait until the next day to avoid recording a low-priced sale on a day when the market opened higher. The broker would do the opposite if the order is a buy order. If prices have increased since the opening, the broker would wait until the next day to avoid recording a high-priced buy on a day when the market opened lower. If the prices have fallen during the day, the broker would immediately fill the order so that the purchase price is lower than the benchmark price.

B. The broker would execute the order just before closing so that the transaction price is the same as the closing price.

C. The broker would split the order and spread its execution throughout the day so that the transaction price is close to the market VWAP.

10. A. For a sale, Estimated cost = Trade size × (Benchmark price − Trade price). Using €52.87 as the benchmark price, the transaction cost estimate of the first trade is 10,000 × (€52.87 − €53.22) = −€3,500. The transaction cost estimate of the second trade is 10,000 × (€52.87 − €53.06) = −€1,900. The transaction cost estimate of the third trade is 10,000 × (€52.87 − €52.87) = €0. The total transaction cost estimate = −€3,500 + (−€1,900) + €0 = −€5,400.

B. The quotation midpoint that prevailed at the time of the decision to trade was €53.25. This is the benchmark price, and the implementation shortfall estimate of the cost of executing the first order is 10,000 × (€53.25 − €53.22) = €300. The implementation shortfall estimate of the cost of executing the second order is 10,000 × (€53.25 − €53.06) = €1,900. The implementation shortfall estimate of the cost of executing the third order is 10,000 × (€53.25 − €52.87) = €3,800. So, the implementation shortfall estimate of the total cost of executing the three orders is €300 + €1,900 + €3,800 = €6,000.

C. The estimated transaction cost using the closing price as the benchmark is negative. This result makes it seem as if the trader had a trading profit. This conclusion is not reasonable because the trader did pay the bid–ask spread and her trades had a market impact, making prices less favorable in her subsequent trades. For example, in the first trade, the trader sold the shares close to the bid price and the trade resulted in a decline in prices. Overall, the use of closing price as the benchmark is not appropriate in this problem because the benchmark itself is significantly affected by the large size of the order.

In contrast, the implementation shortfall estimate uses a benchmark which is determined before the order has an impact on prices. The implementation shortfall approach, which results in a reasonable estimate of €6,000 as the total cost of executing the sale, is the appropriate approach in this problem.

11. A. The paper portfolio traded 1,000 shares on Monday for $10.00 per share. The value of the portfolio at the close on Wednesday is $10,050. The net value is $50.

The real portfolio contains only 700 shares and was traded over the course of two days. On Wednesday's close, it is worth $700 \times \$10.05 = \$7,035$.

The cost of the portfolio is $7,052:

Monday: $600 \times \$10.02 = \$6,012 + \$20$ commissions $= \$6,032$
Tuesday: $100 \times \$10.08 = \$1,008 + \$12$ commissions $= \$1,020$

The net value of the real portfolio is $\$7,035 - 7,052 = -\$17$.

Thus, the implementation shortfall is $\$50 - (-\$17) = \$67$, or 67 bps.

B. Implementation shortfall broken into components is as follows:

▶ Delay
Monday: $600/1,000 \times [(\$10.00 - \$10.00)/\$10.00] = 0.00\%$
Tuesday: $100/1,000 \times [(\$9.99 - \$10.00)/\$10.00] = -0.01\%$

▶ Realized profit and loss
Monday: $600/1,000 \times [(\$10.02 - \$10.00)/\$10.00] = 0.12\%$
Tuesday: $100/1,000 \times [(\$10.08 - \$9.99)/\$9.99] = 0.09\%$

▶ Missed trade opportunity cost
$300/1,000 \times [(\$10.05 - \$10.00)/\$10.00] = 0.15\%$

Commissions are $0.20\% + 0.12\% = 0.32\%$.
Total implementation shortfall is 0.67%, or 67 bps.

12. Portfolio trades involve the purchase or sale of a basket of stocks, with the buy or sell orders placed as a coordinated transaction. Jane Smith could ask a broker for a quote for the entire basket of telecommunications stocks that she wants to purchase. Because there are multiple stocks in the basket being purchased, it is clear to the counterparty that the purchase is not motivated by information about a particular stock and the market impact of the trade is likely to be less. As a consequence, the cost of trading the basket of stocks is expected to be lower than the total trading cost of buying each stock individually.

13. The average execution cost for a purchase of securities is 75 basis points, or 0.75 percent, and the average execution cost for a sale of securities is also 0.75 percent. So, the average execution for a round-trip trade is $2 \times 0.75\%$, or 1.5%. Since the portfolio is expected to be turned over twice, expected execution costs are $1.5\% \times 2 = 3\%$. Therefore, the expected return net of execution costs is $8\% - 3\% = 5\%$.

14. Just as some traders in London possess information about stocks that traders in New York may not, some New York–based traders possess information that London-based traders may not. When New York–based traders begin to trade with the opening of U.S. markets, their trades reveal new information. The new information is incorporated into prices not only in New York but also in London during the hours of overlap between the markets. This incorporation of additional information from New York in London results in higher volatility of prices in London after the opening of the U.S. markets.

15. One reason the manager may have chosen not to trade more aggressively is that he does not think there are other informed traders who have the same information he has about the company's stock. That is, he does not expect other traders to trade in the stock based on information, thus quickly eliminating his informational advantage. By trading in smaller sizes over a period of time, the manager attempts to reduce the chance that other traders will infer that the fund manager is trading based on special information. By spreading his trades over time, the manager is trying to reduce the price impact of trading by not revealing his full trading intentions.

16. Liquidity-motivated traders transact only to meet liquidity needs and desire low transaction costs. So, they would prefer the market with the lower bid–ask spreads. The information-motivated traders trade strategically to maximize the profits from their information. Some of their profits are made in trades in which liquidity-motivated traders are the counterparty. Since the liquidity-motivated traders trade in the market with the lower spreads, information-motivated traders will trade with them in that market. Also, information-motivated traders prefer to place larger orders to profit from any superior information they have. Such traders with large orders are particularly concerned about the market impact cost in the form of a price change for large trades. Since the quoted prices are firm for only a fixed depth, larger orders may move the bid (ask) price downward (upward). In a market with greater depth, the market impact cost is less. Thus, the market with greater depths would be preferred by information-motivated traders. Overall, between the two alternate trading venues, the one with lower spreads and greater depths would be preferred by both types of traders.

17. *Trade A:* In spite of the high urgency level, this trade represents 3 percent ADV. This trade is suitable for an implementation shortfall algorithm.

    Trade B: This trade represents 75 percent ADV and has high spreads. It is not suitable for an algorithmic trade and should be traded using a broker.

18. Although the goal is to minimize explicit transaction costs, the trader needs also to consider the opportunity cost of not being invested in the S&P 500 portfolio. The trader should use an implementation shortfall strategy to control the risk of this rebalance. In short, he should minimize explicit costs by waiting for trades to cross in an electronic crossing network, such as the POSIT trading system, but he should also submit names not likely to cross to a broker in order to minimize opportunity costs. Such a strategy would balance the costs of a delay in implementing a strategic asset allocation against the concern to minimize explicit transaction costs.

SOLUTIONS FOR READING 42

1. A. Accumulating funds for the child's education is a new investment goal. Prior to the adoption, the couple's time horizon was two-stage (preretirement and postretirement). In their late 40s, they will have a period in which they need to pay for the cost of the child's education; this will involve substantial costs for which they must plan. The couple's multistage time horizon now includes the period up to the child's entering college, the child's college years, the remaining period to retirement, and retirement.

B. Given the investor's circumstances, the decision to buy a house in one year's time makes the addition of a shortfall risk objective appropriate. He needs to earn at least 2 percent if he is to have sufficient funds to buy the house. An appropriate shortfall risk objective is to minimize the probability that the return on the portfolio falls below 2 percent over a one-year horizon. The decision also creates a liquidity requirement. The need for $102,000 in cash at the end of the investment period means that the investor cannot tie up his money in a way such that he does not have ready access to it in a year's time.

C. The approval of the grant has created a liquidity requirement of €15,000,000 − €1,000,000 = €14,000,000.

2. The first action ("Revise the investment policy statement of the pension scheme to take into account a change in the forecast for inflation in the U.K.") is incorrect. The Investment Policy Statement depends on the client's particular circumstances, including risk tolerance, time horizon, liquidity and legal constraints, and unique needs. Therefore, a change in economic forecast would not affect the Investment Policy Statement. The Investment Policy Statement also considers a client's return requirement. This return requirement may change over the long term if the inflation outlook has changed over the long term. A change in the inflation outlook over a short period, such as in this question, would not necessitate a change in the return portion or any other aspect of the Investment Policy Statement.

The second action ("Reallocate pension assets from domestic (U.K.) to international equities because he also expects inflation in the U.K. to be higher than in other countries") is correct. A change in economic forecast might necessitate a change in asset allocation and investment strategy. An expectation of increased inflation in the U.K. might lead to expectations that U.K. equity performance will slow and would likely result in both weaker U.K. equity returns and stronger returns from overseas markets. This would justify an increased allocation to international equities.

The third action ("Initiate a program to protect the financial strength of the pension scheme from the effects of U.K. inflation by indexing benefits paid by the scheme") is incorrect. The implementation of an inflation index adjustment program would protect the plan participants, not the plan itself, from the effects of higher U.K. inflation. With an inflation index adjustment program, Summit's costs of funding the defined benefit scheme would actually increase (thereby weakening the plan's financial position) as U.K. inflation increases.

Managing Investment Portfolios: A Dynamic Process, Third Edition, John L. Maginn, Donald L. Tuttle, Jerald E. Pinto, and Dennis W. McLeavey, editors. Copyright © 2007 by CFA Institute. Reprinted with permission.

3. A. The return requirement should be higher to:

- ► fund her additional living expenses; and
- ► meet her new retirement goals.

The following calculations are not required but provide basis for the statement that the return must be higher than the previous 7 percent to generate a retirement portfolio that will support the desired retirement spending level (at a reasonable retirement spending rate). The portfolio must now produce a return of approximately 9 percent, depending on the retirement spending rate assumption made.

Current portfolio (gross)	$3,700,000
Less surgery	$214,000
Less house down payment	$430,000
Less living expenses	$1,713,000
Current portfolio (net)	**$1,343,000**

After-tax return = Before-tax return $(1 - T) = 9.0\% \, (0.7) = 6.3\%$

Years = 25

Retirement portfolio	$6,185,967 = \$1,343,000(1.063)^{25}$
Retirement spending (after tax)	$280,000
Retirement spending (before tax)	$400,000
Spending rate (before tax)	$6.47\% = \$400,000/\$6,185,967$

Risk tolerance should be higher. Wisman's risk tolerance should be higher because:

- ► her husband's intention to work for another 25 years gives her the ability to assume more risk; and
- ► the increase in assets affords her the ability to assume more risk.

Her time horizon is still multistage, but the stages have changed. In the first stage expected to last 25 years, her husband will be working. The second stage is retirement.

The liquidity requirement should be higher. Wisman has a higher liquidity requirement because of the cost of the surgery for her son and the down payment for the house.

B. **i.** The allocation to Spencer Design Stock (currently 39.1 percent) should be decreased. Having a large percentage of her portfolio in one risky and potentially illiquid equity security exposes the portfolio to unnecessary and significant security-specific risk.

ii. The allocation to cash (currently 2.4 percent) should be increased. Wisman needs $430,000 for a house down payment, $214,000 for her son's surgery, and the current year's portion of the $1,713,000 present value of ongoing living expenses.

iii. The allocation to the diversified bond fund (currently 30.5 percent) should be increased. The couple's portfolio must support the $1,713,000 present value of ongoing living expenses and can sustain only moderate portfolio volatility. The regular income stream and diversification benefits offered by bonds are consistent with those needs.

    iv. The allocation to large-capitalization equities (currently 10.4 percent) should be increased. Wisman requires growth and inflation protection to meet her current and future spending needs. A diversified equity portfolio is likely to meet these requirements over time without imparting unacceptable volatility to principal values.

    v. The allocation to emerging market equities (currently 11 percent) should be decreased. Wisman requires high returns but cannot afford to sustain large losses. Having a large percentage of total assets in volatile emerging markets securities is too risky for Wisman.

    vi. The allocation to undeveloped commercial land (currently 6.6 percent) should be decreased. Wisman needs income and liquidity to meet ongoing portfolio disbursement requirements. Undeveloped land requires cash payments (taxes, etc.) and is often illiquid.

4. The Javier–Campbell Trust's willingness to take risk is now below average because of its need to have a high probability of covering Javier's living expenses during the remainder of her lifetime, which encompasses a short time horizon. Javier's below-average willingness to take risk (coupled with her short time horizon) dominates Campbell's above-average willingness (coupled with his long time horizon). Of course, once Javier is no longer living, the Trust can reflect Campbell's higher willingness to take risk.

5. A. The suggested approach has several disadvantages:

    ▶ A fixed ±5% corridor takes no account of differences in transaction costs among the asset classes. For example, private equity has much higher transaction costs than inflation-protected bonds and should have a wider corridor, all else equal.

    ▶ The corridors do not take account of differences in volatility. Rebalancing is most likely to be triggered by the highest volatility asset class.

    ▶ The corridors do not take account of asset class correlations.

  B. **i.** The corridor for international equities should be narrower than it was previously.

    ii. The corridor for inflation-protected bonds should be unaffected. The transaction costs should have an effect on the relative widths of the corridors for private equity and international equities.

    iii. The corridor for private equity should be narrower than that for domestic equities.

    iv. The corridor for domestic equities should be narrower than that for inflation-protected bonds.

6. A. Calendar rebalancing at a relatively high frequency such as weekly or monthly would be appropriate. In contrast to percentage-of-portfolio rebalancing, calendar rebalancing does not require continuous monitoring of portfolio values. The riskiness of the portfolio suggests frequent rebalancing to control drift.

  B. Such markets tend to be characterized by reversal and enhance the investment results from rebalancing to the strategic asset allocation, according to Perold–Sharpe analysis.

7. A. **i.** *Buy and hold.* The buy-and-hold strategy maintains an exposure to equities that is linearly related to the value of equities in general. The strategy involves buying, then holding, an initial mix (equities/bills). No matter what happens to relative values, no rebalancing is required; hence this is sometimes termed the "do nothing" strategy. The investor sets a floor below which he or she does not wish the portfolio's value to fall. An amount equal to the value of that floor is invested in some nonfluctuating asset (e.g., Treasury bills or money market funds). The payoff diagram for a buy-and-hold strategy is a straight line, so the portfolio's value rises (falls) as equity values rise (fall), with a slope equal to the equity proportion in the initial mix. The value of the portfolio will never fall below the specified floor, and the portfolio has unlimited upside potential. Increasing equity prices favor a buy-and-hold strategy; the greater the equity proportion in the initial mix, the better (worse) the strategy will perform when equities outperform (underperform) bills.

The strategy is particularly appropriate for an investor whose risk tolerance above the specified floor varies with wealth but drops to zero at or below that floor. After the initial portfolio transaction, transaction costs are not an issue. The strategy is tax efficient for taxable investors.

ii. *Constant mix.* The constant-mix strategy maintains an exposure to equities that is a constant percentage of total wealth. Periodic rebalancing to return to the desired mix requires the purchase (sale) of equities as they decline (rise) in value. This strategy, which generates a concave payoff diagram, offers relatively little downside protection and performs relatively poorly in up markets. The strategy performs best in relatively flat (but oscillating or volatile) markets and capitalizes on market reversals. The constant-mix strategy performs particularly well in a time period when equity values oscillate greatly but end close to their beginning levels; greater volatility around the beginning values accentuates the positive performance.

The constant-mix strategy is particularly appropriate for an investor whose risk tolerance varies proportionately with wealth; such an investor will hold equities at all levels of wealth. This strategy requires some rule to determine when rebalancing should take place; typical approaches avoid transaction costs until asset-class weights have changed by a given percentage. At this point, transaction costs are incurred to rebalance. Taxes can be material for taxable investors.

iii. *Constant-proportion portfolio insurance.* The constant-proportion portfolio insurance (CPPI) strategy maintains an exposure to equities that is a constant multiple greater than 1 of a "cushion" specified by the investor. The investor sets a floor below which he does not wish assets to fall, and the value of that floor is invested in some nonfluctuating asset (e.g., Treasury bills or money market funds). Under normal market conditions the value of the portfolio will not fall below this specified floor. As equity values rise (fall), the CPPI strategy requires the investor to purchase (sell) additional equities. Thus following this strategy keeps equities at a constant multiple of the cushion (assets − floor) and generates a convex payoff diagram. The CPPI strategy tends to give good downside protection and performs best in directional, especially up, markets; the strategy does poorly in flat but oscillating markets and is especially hurt by sharp market reversals.

The strategy is particularly appropriate for an investor who has zero tolerance for risk below the stated floor but whose risk tolerance increases quickly as equity values move above the stated floor. To control transaction costs, this strategy requires some rule to determine when rebalancing takes place. One approach avoids transaction costs until the value of the portfolio has changed by a given percentage. At this point, transaction costs are incurred to rebalance. Taxes can be a material consideration for taxable investors.

B. The CPPI strategy is the most appropriate rebalancing strategy for the MU endowment fund, taking into account the major circumstances described: the endowment's increased risk tolerance, the outlook for a bull market in growth assets over the next five years, the expectation of lower than normal volatility, and the endowment's desire to limit downside risk.

The CPPI strategy is consistent with higher risk tolerance, because the strategy calls for purchasing more equities as equities increase in value; higher risk tolerance is reflected in the resulting increased allocation to equities over time.

▶ The CPPI strategy will do well in an advancing equities market; because equities are purchased as their values rise, each marginal purchase has a high payoff.

▶ The CPPI strategy would do poorly in a higher-volatility environment for equities, because the strategy would sell on weakness but buy on strength, only to experience reversals; conversely, the strategy does much better in the face of lower volatility.

▶ The CPPI strategy provides good downside protection, because the strategy sells on weakness and reduces exposure to equities as a given floor is approached.

In summary, given that MU receives little other funding, the endowment fund must produce the maximum return for a specified level of risk. Given that the level of acceptable risk is generally higher, although with a very specific downside floor, the market outlook suggests that the constant-proportion strategy is the endowment fund's best rebalancing strategy.

Absolute return objective A return objective that is independent of a reference or benchmark level of return.

Absolute-return vehicles Investments that have no direct benchmark portfolios.

Accounting risk The risk associated with accounting standards that vary from country to country or with any uncertainty about how certain transactions should be recorded.

Accreting swap A swap where the notional amount increases over the life of the swap.

Accumulated benefit obligation (ABO) The present value of pension benefits, assuming the pension plan terminated immediately such that it had to provide retirement income to all beneficiaries for their years of service up to that date.

Accumulated service Years of service of a pension plan participant as of a specified date.

Active investment approach An approach to portfolio construction in which portfolio composition responds to changes in the portfolio manager's expectations concerning asset returns.

Active management An approach to investing in which the portfolio manager seeks to outperform a given benchmark portfolio.

Active return The portfolio's return in excess of the return on the portfolio's benchmark.

Active risk A synonym for tracking risk.

Active/immunization combination A portfolio with two component portfolios: an immunized portfolio which provides an assured return over the planning horizon and a second portfolio that uses an active high-return/high-risk strategy.

Active/passive combination Allocation of the core component of a portfolio to a passive strategy and the balance to an active component.

Active-lives The portion of a pension fund's liabilities associated with active workers.

Actual extreme events A type of scenario analysis used in stress testing. It involves evaluating how a portfolio would have performed given movements in interest rates, exchange rates, stock prices, or commodity prices at magnitudes such as occurred during past extreme market events (e.g., the stock market crash of October 1987).

Ad valorem fees Fees that are calculated by multiplying a percentage by the value of assets managed; also called assets under management (AUM) fees.

Add-on interest A procedure for determining the interest on a bond or loan in which the interest is added onto the face value of a contract.

Adverse selection risk The risk associated with information asymmetry; in the context of trading, the risk of trading with a more informed trader.

Algorithmic trading Automated electronic trading subject to quantitative rules and user-specified benchmarks and constraints.

Allocation/selection interaction return A measure of the joint effect of weights assigned to both sectors and individual securities; the difference between the weight of the portfolio in a given sector and the portfolio's benchmark for that sector, times the difference between the portfolio's and the benchmark's returns in that sector, summed across all sectors.

Alpha Excess risk-adjusted return.

Alpha and beta separation An approach to portfolio construction that views investing to earn alpha and investing to establish systematic risk exposures as tasks that can and should be pursued separately.

Alpha research Research related to capturing excess risk-adjusted returns by a particular strategy; a way investment research is organized in some investment management firms.

Alternative investments Groups of investments with risk and return characteristics that differ markedly from those of traditional stock and bond investments.

American Depositary Receipt (ADR) A certificate of ownership issued by a U.S. bank to promote local trading in a foreign stock. The U.S. bank holds the foreign shares and issues ADRs against them.

American option An option that can be exercised on any day through the expiration day. Also referred to as American-style exercise.

Amortizing and accreting swaps A swap in which the notional principal changes according to a formula related to changes in the underlying.

Anchoring trap The tendency of the mind to give disproportionate weight to the first information it receives on a topic.

Angel investor An accredited individual investing chiefly in seed and early-stage companies.

Appraisal data Valuation data based on appraised rather than market values.

Arbitrage The simultaneous purchase of an under-valued asset or portfolio and sale of an overvalued but equivalent asset or portfolio, in order to obtain a riskless profit on the price differential. Taking advantage of a market inefficiency in a risk-free manner.

Arrears swap A type of interest rate swap in which the floating payment is set at the end of the period and the interest is paid at that same time.

Ask price (or ask, offer price, offer) The price at which a dealer will sell a specified quantity of a security.

Ask size The quantity associated with the ask price.

Asset allocation Dividing of investment funds among several asset classes to achieve diversification.

Asset allocation reviews A periodic review of the appropriateness of a portfolio's asset allocation.

Asset covariance matrix The covariance matrix for the asset classes or markets under consideration.

Asset swap A swap, typically involving a bond, in which fixed bond payments are swapped for payments based on a floating rate.

Asset/liability management The management of financial risks created by the interaction of assets and liabilities.

Asset/liability management approach In the context of determining a strategic asset allocation, an asset/liability management approach involves explicitly modeling liabilities and adopting the allocation of assets that is optimal in relationship to funding liabilities.

Asset-only approach In the context of determining a strategic asset allocation, an approach that focuses on the characteristics of the assets without explicitly modeling the liabilities.

Assurity of completion In the context of trading, confidence that trades will settle without problems under all market conditions.

Assurity of the contract In the context of trading, confidence that the parties to trades will be held to fulfilling their obligations.

Asynchronism A discrepancy in the dating of observations that occurs because stale (out-of-date) data may be used in the absence of current data.

At the money An option in which the underlying value equals the exercise price.

AUM fee A fee based on assets under management; an ad valorem fee.

Automated trading Any form of trading that is not manual, including trading based on algorithms.

Average effective spread A measure of the liquidity of a security's market. The mean effective spread (sometimes dollar weighted) over all transactions in the stock in the period under study.

Back office Administrative functions at an investment firm such as those pertaining to transaction processing, record keeping, and regulatory compliance.

Backtesting A method for gaining information about a model using past data. As used in reference to VAR, it is the process of comparing the number of violations of VAR thresholds over a time period with the figure implied by the user-selected probability level.

Back-to-back transaction A transaction where a dealer enters into offsetting transactions with different parties, effectively serving as a go-between.

Backwardation A condition in the futures markets in which the benefits of holding an asset exceed the costs, leaving the futures price less than the spot price.

Balance of payments An accounting of all cash flows between residents and nonresidents of a country.

Bancassurance The sale of insurance by banks.

Barbell portfolio A portfolio made up of short and long maturities relative to the investment horizon date and interim coupon payments.

Basis The difference between the cash price and the futures price.

Basis point value (BPV) Also called present value of a basis point or price value of a basis point (PVBP), the change in the bond price for a 1 basis point change in yield.

Basis risk The risk that arises from fluctuation in the basis.

Basis swap A swap in which both parties pay a floating rate.

Bear spread An option strategy that involves selling a put with a lower exercise price and buying a put with a higher exercise price. It can also be executed with calls.

Behavioral finance An approach to finance based on the observation that psychological variables affect and often distort individuals' investment decision making.

Benchmark Something taken as a standard of comparison; a comparison portfolio; a collection of securities or risk factors and associated weights that represents the persistent and prominent investment characteristics of an asset category or manager's investment process.

Best efforts order A type of order that gives the trader's agent discretion to execute the order only when the agent judges market conditions to be favorable.

Beta A measure of the sensitivity of a given investment or portfolio to movements in the overall market.

Beta research Research related to systematic (market) risk and return; a way investment research is organized in some investment management firms.

Bid price (or bid) The price at which a dealer will buy a specified quantity of a security.

Bid size The quantity associated with the bid price.

Bid–ask spread The difference between the quoted ask and the bid prices.

Binary credit options Options that provide payoffs contingent on the occurrence of a specified negative credit event.

Binomial model A model for pricing options in which the underlying price can move to only one of two possible new prices.

Binomial tree A diagram representing price movements of the underlying in a binomial model.

Block order An order to sell or buy in a quantity that is large relative to the liquidity ordinarily available from dealers in the security or in other markets.

Bond A long-term debt security with contractual obligations regarding interest payments and redemption.

Bond option An option in which the underlying is a bond; primarily traded in over-the-counter markets.

Bond-yield-plus-risk-premium method An approach to estimating the required return on equity which specifies that required return as a bond yield plus a risk premium.

Bottom-up Focusing on company-specific fundamentals or factors such as revenues, earnings, cash flow, or new product development.

Bourse A French term often used to refer to a stock market.

Box spread An option strategy that combines a bull spread and a bear spread having two different exercise prices, which produces a risk-free payoff of the difference in the exercise prices.

Broad market indexes An index that is intended to measure the performance of an entire asset class. For example, the S&P 500 Index, Wilshire 5000, and Russell 3000 indexes for U.S. common stocks.

Broker An agent of a trader in executing trades.

Brokered markets Markets in which transactions are largely effected through a search-brokerage mechanism away from public markets.

Brokers See Futures commission merchants.

Bubbles Episodes in which asset market prices move to extremely high levels in relation to estimated intrinsic value.

Buffering With respect to style index construction, rules for maintaining the style assignment of a stock consistent with a previous assignment when the stock has not clearly moved to a new style.

Build-up approach Synonym for the risk premium approach.

Bull spread An option strategy that involves buying a call with a lower exercise price and selling a call with a higher exercise price. It can also be executed with puts.

Bullet portfolio A portfolio made up of maturities that are very close to the investment horizon.

Business cycle Fluctuations in GDP in relation to long-term trend growth, usually lasting 9–11 years.

Business risk The equity risk that comes from the nature of the firm's operating activities.

Butterfly spread An option strategy that combines two bull or bear spreads and has three exercise prices.

Buy side Investment management companies and other investors that use the services of brokerages.

Buy-side analysts Analysts employed by an investment manager or institutional investor.

Buy-side traders Professional traders that are employed by investment managers and institutional investors.

Calendar rebalancing Rebalancing a portfolio to target weights on a periodic basis; for example, monthly, quarterly, semiannually, or annually.

Calendar-and-percentage-of-portfolio rebalancing Monitoring a portfolio at regular frequencies, such as quarterly. Rebalancing decisions are then made based upon percentage-of-portfolio principles.

Call An option that gives the holder the right to buy an underlying asset from another party at a fixed price over a specific period of time.

Call option A contract giving the right to buy an asset at a specific price on or before a specified date.

Calmar ratio The compound annualized rate of return over a specified time period divided by the absolute value of maximum drawdown over the same time period.

Cap A combination of interest rate call options designed to hedge a borrower against rate increases on a floating-rate loan.

Cap rate With respect to options, the exercise interest rate for a cap.

Capital adequacy ratio A measure of the adequacy of capital in relation to assets.

Capital allocation line A graph line that describes the combinations of expected return and standard deviation of return available to an investor from combining an optimal portfolio of risky assets with a risk-free asset.

Capital flows forecasting approach An exchange rate forecasting approach that focuses on expected capital flows, particularly long-term flows such as equity investment and foreign direct investment.

Capital market expectations (CME) Expectations concerning the risk and return prospects of asset classes.

Caplet Each component call option in a cap.

Capped swap A swap in which the floating payments have an upper limit.

Caps A combination of interest rate call options designed to provide protection against interest rate increases.

Carried interest A private equity fund manager's incentive fee; the share of the private equity fund's profits that the fund manager is due once the fund has returned the outside investors' capital.

Carry Another term for owning an asset, typically used to refer to commodities. (See also Carry market and Cost of carry.)

Carry market A situation where the forward price is such that the return on a cash-and-carry is the risk-free rate.

Cash balance plan A defined-benefit plan whose benefits are displayed in individual recordkeeping accounts.

Cash flow at risk A variation of VAR that measures the risk to a company's cash flow, instead of its market value; the minimum cash flow loss expected to be exceeded with a given probability over a specified time period.

Cash flow matching An asset/liability management approach that provides the future funding of a liability stream from the coupon and matured principal payments of the portfolio. A type of dedication strategy.

Cash price or spot price The price for immediate purchase of the underlying asset.

Cash settlement A procedure used in certain derivative transactions that specifies that the long and short parties engage in the equivalent cash value of a delivery transaction.

Cause-and-effect relationship A relationship in which the occurrence of one event brings about the occurrence of another event.

Cautious investors Investors who are generally averse to potential losses.

Cell-matching technique (stratified sampling) A portfolio construction technique used in indexing that divides the benchmark index into cells related to the risk factors affecting the index and samples from index securities belonging to those cells.

Centralized risk management or companywide risk management When a company has a single risk management group that monitors and controls all of the risk-taking activities of the organization.

Centralization permits economies of scale and allows a company to use some of its risks to offset other risks. (See also Enterprise risk management.)

Chain-linking A process for combining periodic returns to produce an overall time-weighted rate of return.

Cheapest to deliver A bond in which the amount received for delivering the bond is largest compared with the amount paid in the market for the bond.

Cherry-picking When a bankrupt company is allowed to enforce contracts that are favorable to it while walking away from contracts that are unfavorable to it.

Claw-back provision With respect to the compensation of private equity fund managers, a provision that specifies that money from the fund manager be returned to investors if, at the end of a fund's life, investors have not received back their capital contributions and contractual share of profits.

Clearinghouse An entity associated with a futures market that acts as middleman between the contracting parties and guarantees to each party the performance of the other.

Closed-book markets Markets in which a trader does not have real-time access to all quotes in a security.

Closeout netting In a bankruptcy, a process by which multiple obligations between two counterparties are consolidated into a single overall value owed by one of the counterparties to the other.

Coincident economic indicators Economic indicators of current economic activity.

Coincident indicators A set of economic variables whose values reach peaks and troughs at about the same time as the aggregate economy.

Collar An option strategy involving the purchase of a put and sale of a call in which the holder of an asset gains protection below a certain level, the exercise price of the put, and pays for it by giving up gains above a certain level, the exercise price of the call. Collars also can be used to provide protection against rising interest rates on a floating-rate loan by giving up gains from lower interest rates.

Collateral return (or collateral yield) The component of the return on a commodity futures contract that comes from the assumption that the full value of the underlying futures contract is invested to earn the risk-free interest rate.

Collateralized debt obligation A securitized pool of fixed-income assets.

Combination matching (or horizon matching) A cash flow matching technique; a portfolio is duration-matched with a set of liabilities with the added constraint that it also be cash-flow matched in the first few years, usually the first five years.

Commingled real estate funds (CREFs) Professionally managed vehicles for substantial commingled (i.e., pooled) investment in real estate properties.

Commitment period The period of time over which committed funds are advanced to a private equity fund.

Commodities Articles of commerce such as agricultural goods, metals, and petroleum; tangible assets that are typically relatively homogeneous in nature.

Commodity forward A contract in which the underlying asset is oil, a precious metal, or some other commodity.

Commodity futures Futures contracts in which the underlying is a traditional agricultural, metal, or petroleum product.

Commodity option An option in which the asset underlying the futures is a commodity, such as oil, gold, wheat, or soybeans.

Commodity spread Offsetting long and short positions in closely related commodities. (See also Crack spread and Crush spread.)

Commodity swap A swap in which the underlying is a commodity such as oil, gold, or an agricultural product.

Commodity trading advisors Registered advisors to managed futures funds.

Completeness fund A portfolio that, when added to active managers' positions, establishes an overall portfolio with approximately the same risk exposures as the investor's overall equity benchmark.

Confidence band With reference to a quality control chart for performance evaluation, a range in which the manager's value-added returns are anticipated to fall a specified percentage of the time.

Confidence interval An interval that has a given probability of containing the parameter it is intended to estimate.

Confirming evidence trap The bias that leads individuals to give greater weight to information that supports an existing or preferred point of view than to evidence that contradicts it.

Consistent growth A growth investment substyle that focuses on companies with consistent growth having a long history of unit-sales growth, superior profitability, and predictable earnings.

Constant maturity swap or CMT swap A swap in which the floating rate is the rate on a security known as a constant maturity treasury or CMT security.

Constant maturity treasury or CMT A hypothetical U.S. Treasury note with a constant maturity. A CMT exists for various years in the range of 2 to 10.

Constraints 1) Restricting conditions; 2) Relating to an investment policy statement, limitations on the investor's ability to take full or partial advantage of particular investments. Such constraints are either internal (such as a client's specific liquidity needs, time horizon, and unique circumstances) or external (such as tax issues and legal and regulatory requirements).

Contango A condition in the futures markets in which the costs of holding an asset exceed the benefits, leaving the futures price more than the spot price.

Contingent claims Derivatives in which the payoffs occur if a specific event occurs; generally referred to as options.

Contingent immunization A fixed-income strategy in which immunization serves as a fall-back strategy if the actively managed portfolio does not grow at a certain rate.

Continuous auction markets Auction markets where orders can be executed at any time during the trading day.

Continuous time Time thought of as advancing in extremely small increments.

Contrarian A value investment substyle focusing on stocks that have been beset by problems.

Convenience yield A nonmonetary return to ownership of an asset or commodity.

Conversion factor An adjustment used to facilitate delivery on bond futures contracts in which any of a number of bonds with different characteristics are eligible for delivery.

Convexity A measure of how interest rate sensitivity changes with a change in interest rates.

Convexity adjustment An estimate of the change in price that is not explained by duration.

Cooling degree day The greater of (i) 6 degrees Fahrenheit minus the average daily temperature, and (ii) zero.

Core-plus A fixed-income mandate that permits the portfolio manager to add instruments with relatively high return potential to core holdings of investment-grade debt.

Core-satellite A way of thinking about allocating money that seeks to define each investment's place in the portfolio in relation to specific investment goals or roles.

Core-satellite portfolio A portfolio in which certain investments (often indexed or semiactive) are viewed as the core and the balance are viewed as satellite investments fulfilling specific roles.

Corner portfolio Adjacent corner portfolios define a segment of the minimum-variance frontier within which portfolios hold identical assets and the rate of change of asset weights in moving from one portfolio to another is constant.

Corner portfolio theorem In a sign-constrained mean–variance optimization, the result that the asset weights of any minimum-variance portfolio are a positive linear combination of the corresponding weights in the two adjacent corner portfolios that bracket it in terms of expected return (or standard deviation of return).

Corporate governance The system of internal controls and procedures used to define and protect the rights and responsibilities of various stakeholders.

Corporate venturing Investments by companies in promising young companies in the same or a related industry.

Cost of carry The costs of holding an asset.

Cost of carry model A model for pricing futures contracts in which the futures price is determined by adding the cost of carry to the spot price.

Country beta A measure of the sensitivity of a specified variable (e.g., yield) to a change in the comparable variable in another country.

Covariance A measure of the extent to which the returns on two assets move together.

Coverage Benchmark coverage is defined as the proportion of a portfolio's market value that is contained in the benchmark.

Covered call An option strategy involving the holding of an asset and sale of a call on the asset.

Covered interest arbitrage A transaction executed in the foreign exchange market in which a currency is purchased (sold) and a forward contract is sold (purchased) to lock in the exchange rate for future delivery of the currency. This transaction should earn the risk-free rate of the investor's home country.

Crack spread The difference between the price of crude oil futures and that of equivalent amounts of heating oil and gasoline.

Credit default swap A swap used to transfer credit risk to another party. A protection buyer pays the protection seller in return for the right to receive a payment from the seller in the event of a specified credit event.

Credit derivative A contract in which one party has the right to claim a payment from another party in the event that a specific credit event occurs over the life of the contract.

Credit event An event affecting the credit risk of a security or counterparty.

Credit forwards A type of credit derivative with payoffs based on bond values or credit spreads.

Credit protection seller With respect to a credit derivative, the party that accepts the credit risk of the underlying financial asset.

Credit risk or default risk The risk of loss caused by a counterparty's or debtor's failure to make a timely payment or by the change in value of a financial instrument based on changes in default risk.

Credit spread forward A forward contract used to transfer credit risk to another party; a forward contract on a yield spread.

Credit spread option An option based on the yield spread between two securities that is used to transfer credit risk.

Credit spread risk The risk that the spread between the rate for a risky bond and the rate for a default risk-free bond may vary after the purchase of the risky bond.

Credit swap A type of swap transaction used as a credit derivative in which one party makes periodic payments to the other and receives the promise of a payoff if a third party defaults.

Credit VAR A variation of VAR related to credit risk; it reflects the minimum loss due to credit exposure with a given probability during a period of time.

Credited rates Rates of interest credited to a policyholder's reserve account.

Credit-linked notes Fixed-income securities in which the holder of the security has the right to withhold payment of the full amount due at maturity if a credit event occurs.

Cross hedging With respect to hedging bond investments using futures, hedging when the bond to be hedged is not identical to the bond underlying the futures contract. With respect to currency hedging, a hedging technique that uses two currencies other than the home currency.

Cross-default provision A provision stipulating that if a borrower defaults on any outstanding credit obligations, the borrower is considered to be in default on all obligations.

Cross-product netting Netting the market values of all contracts, not just derivatives, between parties.

Crush spread The difference between the price of a quantity of soybeans and that of the soybean meal and oil that can be produced by those soybeans.

Currency exposure The sensitivity of the asset return, measured in the investor's domestic currency, to a movement in the exchange rate.

Currency forward A forward contract in which the underlying is a foreign currency.

Currency option An option that allows the holder to buy (if a call) or sell (if a put) an underlying currency at a fixed exercise rate, expressed as an exchange rate.

Currency overlay In currency risk management, the delegation of the management of currency risk in an international portfolio to a currency specialist.

Currency return The percentage change in the spot exchange rate stated in terms of home currency per unit of foreign currency.

Currency risk The risk associated with the uncertainty about the exchange rate at which proceeds in the foreign currency can be converted into the investor's home currency.

Currency swap A swap in which each party makes interest payments to the other in different currencies.

Currency-hedged instruments Investment in nondomestic assets in which currency exposures are neutralized.

Current credit risk (or jump-to-default risk) The risk of credit-related events happening in the immediate future; it relates to the risk that a payment currently due will not be paid.

Cushion spread The difference between the minimum acceptable return and the higher possible immunized rate.

Custom security-based benchmark A custom benchmark created by weighting a manager's research universe using the manager's unique weighting approach.

Cyclical stocks The shares of companies whose earnings have above-average sensitivity to the business cycle.

Daily settlement See Marking to market.

Data-mining bias Bias that results from repeatedly "drilling" or searching a dataset until some statistically significant pattern is found.

Day traders Traders that rapidly buy and sell stocks in the hope that the stocks will continue to rise or fall in value for the seconds or minutes they are prepared to hold a position. Day traders hold a position open somewhat longer than a scalper but close all positions at the end of the day.

Dealer (or market maker) A business entity that is ready to buy an asset for inventory or sell an asset from inventory to provide the other side of an order.

Decentralized risk management A system that allows individual units within an organization to manage risk. Decentralization results in duplication of effort but has the advantage of having people closer to the risk be more directly involved in its management.

Decision price (also called arrival price or strike price) The prevailing price when the decision to trade is made.

Decision risk The risk of changing strategies at the point of maximum loss.

Dedication strategies Specialized fixed-income strategies designed to accommodate specific funding needs of the investor.

Deep in the money Options that are far in-the-money.

Deep out of the money Options that are far out-of-the-money.

Default risk The risk of loss if an issuer or counterparty does not fulfill its contractual obligations.

Default risk premium Compensation for the possibility that the issue of a debt instrument will fail to make a promised payment at the contracted time and in the contracted amount.

Default swap A contract in which the swap buyer pays a regular premium; in exchange, if a default in a specified bond occurs, the swap seller pays the buyer the loss due to the default.

Defaultable debt Debt with some meaningful amount of credit risk.

Deferred swap A swap with terms specified today, but for which swap payments begin at a later date than for an ordinary swap.

Defined-benefit plan A pension plan that specifies the plan sponsor's obligations in terms of the benefit to plan participants.

Defined-contribution plan A pension plan that specifies the sponsor's obligations in terms of contributions to the pension fund rather than benefits to plan participants.

Deflation A decrease in the general level of prices; an increase in the purchasing power of a unit of currency.

Delay costs (or slippage) Implicit trading costs that arise from the inability to complete desired trades immediately due to order size or market liquidity.

Delivery A process used in a deliverable forward contract in which the long pays the agreed-upon price to the short, which in turn delivers the underlying asset to the long.

Delivery option The feature of a futures contract giving the short the right to make decisions about what, when, and where to deliver.

Delta (δ) Ratio of change in the option price to a small change in the price of the underlying asset. Also equal to the derivative of the option price with respect to the asset price.

Delta hedge An option strategy in which a position in an asset is converted to a risk-free position with a position in a specific number of options. The number of options per unit of the underlying changes through time, and the position must be revised to maintain the hedge.

Delta-normal method   A measure of VAR equivalent to the analytical method but that refers to the use of delta to estimate the option's price sensitivity.

Demand deposit   A deposit that can be drawn upon without prior notice, such as a checking account.

Demutualizing   The process of converting an insurance company from stock to mutual form.

Derivative   A financial instrument that offers a return based on the return of some other underlying asset.

Derivatives dealers   The commercial and investment banks that make markets in derivatives. Also referred to as market makers.

Descriptive statistics   Methods for effectively summarizing data to describe important aspects of a dataset.

Deteriorating fundamentals sell discipline   A sell discipline involving ongoing review of holdings in which a share issue is sold or reduced if the portfolio manager believes that the company's business prospects will deteriorate.

Diff swap   A swap in which the payments are based on the difference between interest rates in two countries but payments are made in only a single currency.

Differential returns   Returns that deviate from a manager's benchmark.

Diffusion index   An index that measures how many indicators are pointing up and how many are pointing down.

Direct commodity investment   Commodity investment that involves cash market purchase of physical commodities or exposure to changes in spot market values via derivatives, such as futures.

Direct market access   Platforms sponsored by brokers that permit buy-side traders to directly access equities, fixed income, futures, and foreign exchange markets, clearing via the broker.

Direct quotation   Quotation in terms of domestic currency/foreign currency.

Discount interest   A procedure for determining the interest on a loan or bond in which the interest is deducted from the face value in advance.

Discounted cash flow (DCF) models   Valuation models that express the idea that an asset's value is the present value of its (expected) cash flows.

Discrete time   Time thought of as advancing in distinct finite increments.

Disintermediation   To withdraw funds from financial intermediaries for placement with other financial intermediaries offering a higher return or yield. Or, to withdraw funds from a financial intermediary for the purposes of direct investment, such as withdrawing from a mutual fund to make direct stock investments.

Distressed debt arbitrage   A distressed securities investment discipline that involves purchasing the traded bonds of bankrupt companies and selling the common equity short.

Distressed securities   Securities of companies that are in financial distress or near bankruptcy; the name given to various investment disciplines employing securities of companies in distress.

Diversification effect   In reference to VAR across several portfolios (for example, across an entire firm), this effect equals the difference between the sum of the individual VARs and total VAR.

Dividend recapitalization   A method by which a buyout fund can realize the value of a holding; involves the issuance of debt by the holding to finance a special dividend to owners.

Dollar duration   A measure of the change in portfolio value for a 100 bps change in market yields.

Downgrade risk   The risk that one of the major rating agencies will lower its rating for an issuer, based on its specified rating criteria.

Downside deviation   A measure of volatility using only rate of return data points below the investor's minimum acceptable return.

Downside risk   Risk of loss or negative return.

Due diligence   Investigation and analysis in support of an investment action or recommendation, such as the scrutiny of operations and management and the verification of material facts.

Duration   A measure of the approximate sensitivity of a security to a change in interest rates (i.e., a measure of interest rate risk).

Dynamic approach   With respect to strategic asset allocation, an approach that accounts for links between optimal decisions at different points in time.

Dynamic hedging   A strategy in which a position is hedged by making frequent adjustments to the quantity of the instrument used for hedging in relation to the instrument being hedged.

EAFE index   A stock index for Europe, Australia, and the Far East published by Morgan Stanley Capital International.

Earnings at risk (EAR)   A variation of VAR that reflects the risk of a company's earnings instead of its market value.

Earnings momentum   A growth investment substyle that focuses on companies with earnings momentum (high quarterly year-over-year earnings growth).

Econometrics   The application of quantitative modeling and analysis grounded in economic theory to the analysis of economic data.

Economic exposure   The risk associated with changes in the relative attractiveness of products and services offered for sale, arising out of the competitive effects of changes in exchange rates.

Economic indicators Economic statistics provided by government and established private organizations that contain information on an economy's recent past activity or its current or future position in the business cycle.

Economic risk As used in currency risk management, the risk that arises when the foreign currency value of a foreign investment reacts systematically to an exchange rate movement.

Economic surplus The market value of assets minus the present value of liabilities.

Effective duration Duration adjusted to account for embedded options.

Effective spread Two times the distance between the actual execution price and the midpoint of the market quote at the time an order is entered; a measure of execution costs that captures the effects of price improvement and market impact.

Efficient frontier The graph of the set of portfolios that maximize expected return for their level of risk (standard deviation of return); the part of the minimum-variance frontier beginning with the global minimum-variance portfolio and continuing above it.

Electronic communications networks (ECNs) Computer-based auctions that operate continuously within the day using a specified set of rules to execute orders.

Emerging market debt The sovereign debt of nondeveloped countries.

Endogenous variable A variable whose values are determined within the system.

Endowments Long-term funds generally owned by operating non-profit institutions such as universities and colleges, museums, hospitals, and other organizations involved in charitable activities.

Enhanced derivatives products companies (or special purpose vehicles) A type of subsidiary separate from an entity's other activities and not liable for the parent's debts. They are often used by derivatives dealers to control exposure to ratings downgrades.

Enterprise risk management An overall assessment of a company's risk position. A centralized approach to risk management sometimes called firmwide risk management.

Equal probability rebalancing Rebalancing in which the manager specifies a corridor for each asset class as a common multiple of the standard deviation of the asset class's returns. Rebalancing to the target proportions occurs when any asset class weight moves outside its corridor.

Equal weighted In an equal-weighted index, each stock in the index is weighted equally.

Equitized Given equity market systematic risk exposure.

Equitizing cash A strategy used to replicate an index. It is also used to take a given amount of cash and turn it into an equity position while maintaining the liquidity provided by the cash.

Equity forward A contract calling for the purchase of an individual stock, a stock portfolio, or a stock index at a later date at an agreed-upon price.

Equity options Options on individual stocks; also known as stock options.

Equity risk premium Compensation for the additional risk of equity compared with debt.

Equity swap A swap in which the rate is the return on a stock or stock index.

Equity-indexed annuity A type of life annuity that provides a guarantee of a minimum fixed payment plus some participation in stock market gains, if any.

ESG risk The risk to a company's market valuation resulting from environmental, social, and governance factors.

Eurobond A bond underwritten by a multinational syndicate of banks and placed mainly in countries other than the country of the issuer; sometimes called an international bond.

Eurodollar A dollar deposited outside the United States.

European option An option that can be exercised only at expiration. Also referred to as European-style exercise.

Eurozone The region of countries using the euro as a currency.

Ex post alpha (or Jensen's alpha) The average return achieved in a portfolio in excess of what would have been predicted by CAPM given the portfolio's risk level; an after-the-fact measure of excess risk-adjusted return.

Excess currency return The expected currency return in excess of the forward premium or discount.

Exchange A regulated venue for the trading of investment instruments.

Exchange for physicals (EFP) A permissible delivery procedure used by futures market participants, in which the long and short arrange a delivery procedure other than the normal procedures stipulated by the futures exchange.

Exchange fund A fund into which several investors place their different share holdings in exchange for shares in the diversified fund itself.

Execution uncertainty Uncertainty pertaining to the timing of execution, or if execution will even occur at all.

Exercise or exercising the option The process of using an option to buy or sell the underlying.

Exercise rate or strike rate The fixed rate at which the holder of an interest rate option can buy or sell the underlying.

Exogenous shocks Events from outside the economic system that affect its course. These could be short-lived political events, changes in government policy, or natural disasters, for example.

Exogenous variable A variable whose values are determined outside the system.

Expiration date The date on which a derivative contract expires.

Explicit transaction costs The direct costs of trading such as broker commission costs, taxes, stamp duties, and fees paid to exchanges; costs for which the trader could be given a receipt.

Externality Those consequences of a transaction (or process) that do not fall on the parties to the transaction (or process).

Factor covariance matrix The covariance matrix of factors.

Factor push A simple stress test that involves pushing prices and risk factors of an underlying model in the most disadvantageous way to estimate the impact of factor extremes on the portfolio's value.

Factor sensitivities (also called factor betas or factor loadings) In a multifactor model, the responsiveness of the dependent variable to factor movements.

Factor-model-based benchmark A benchmark that is created by relating one or more systematic sources of returns (factors or exposures) to returns of the benchmark.

Fallen angels Debt that has crossed the threshold from investment grade to high yield.

Family offices Entities, typically organized and owned by a family for its benefit, that assume responsibility for services such as financial planning, estate planning, and asset management.

Federal funds rate The interest rate on overnight loans of reserves (deposits) between U.S. Federal Reserve System member banks.

Fee cap A limit on the total fee paid regardless of performance.

Fiduciary A person or entity standing in a special relation of trust and responsibility with respect to other parties.

Fiduciary call A combination of a European call and a risk-free bond that matures on the option expiration day and has a face value equal to the exercise price of the call.

Financial capital As used in the text, an individual investor's investable wealth; total wealth minus human capital. Consists of assets that can be traded such as cash, stocks, bonds, and real estate.

Financial equilibrium models Models describing relationships between expected return and risk in which supply and demand are in balance.

Financial futures Futures contracts in which the underlying is a stock, bond, or currency.

Financial risk Risks derived from events in the external financial markets, such as changes in equity prices, interest rates, or currency exchange rates.

Fiscal policy Government activity concerning taxation and governmental spending.

Fixed annuity A type of life annuity in which periodic payments are fixed in amount.

Fixed-income forward A forward contract in which the underlying is a bond.

Fixed-rate payer The party to an interest rate swap that is obligated to make periodic payments at a fixed rate.

Floating supply of shares (or free float) The number of shares outstanding that are actually available to investors.

Floating-rate loan A loan in which the interest rate is reset at least once after the starting date.

Floating-rate payer The party to an interest rate swap that is obligated to make periodic payments based on a benchmark floating rate.

Floor A combination of interest rate options designed to provide protection against interest rate decreases.

Floor broker An agent of the broker who, for certain exchanges, physically represents the trade on the exchange floor.

Floor traders or locals Market makers that buy and sell by quoting a bid and an ask price. They are the primary providers of liquidity to the market.

Floored swap A swap in which the floating payments have a lower limit.

Floorlet Each component put option in a floor.

Foreign bond A bond issued by a foreign company on the local market and in the local currency (e.g., Yankee bonds in the United States, Bulldog bonds in the United Kingdom, or Samurai bonds in Japan).

Formal tools Established research methods amenable to precise definition and independent replication of results.

Forward contract An agreement between two parties in which one party, the buyer, agrees to buy from the other party, the seller, an underlying asset at a later date for a price established at the start of the contract.

Forward curve The set of forward or futures prices with different expiration dates on a given date for a given asset.

Forward discount (or forward premium) The forward rate less the spot rate, divided by the spot rate; called the forward discount if negative, and forward premium if positive.

Forward hedging Hedging that involves the use of a forward contract between the foreign asset's currency and the home currency.

Forward price or forward rate The fixed price or rate at which the transaction scheduled to occur at the expiration of a forward contract will take place. This price is agreed on at the initiation date of the contract.

Forward rate agreement (FRA) A forward contract calling for one party to make a fixed interest payment and the other to make an interest payment at a rate to be determined at the contract expiration.

Forward strip Another name for the forward curve.

Forward swap A forward contract to enter into a swap.

Foundations Typically, grant-making institutions funded by gifts and investment assets.

Fourth market A term occasionally used for direct trading of securities between institutional investors; the fourth market would include trading on electronic crossing networks.

Front office The revenue generating functions at an investment firm such as those pertaining to trading and sales.

Front-run To trade ahead of the initiator, exploiting privileged information about the initiator's trading intentions.

Full replication When every issue in an index is represented in the portfolio, and each portfolio position has approximately the same weight in the fund as in the index.

Fully funded plan A pension plan in which the ratio of the value of plan assets to the present value of plan liabilities is 100 percent or greater.

Functional (or multifunctional) duration The key rate duration.

Fund of funds A fund that invests in a number of underlying funds.

Fundamental law of active management The relation that the information ratio of a portfolio manager is approximately equal to the information coefficient multiplied by the square root of the investment discipline's breadth (the number of independent, active investment decisions made each year).

Funded status The relationship between the value of a plan's assets and the present value of its liabilities.

Funding ratio A measure of the relative size of pension assets compared to the present value of pension liabilities. Calculated by dividing the value of pension assets by the present value of pension liabilities. Also referred to as the funded ratio or funded status.

Funding risk The risk that liabilities funding long asset positions cannot be rolled over at reasonable cost.

Futures commission merchants (FCMs) Individuals or companies that execute futures transactions for other parties off the exchange.

Futures contract An enforceable contract between a buyer (seller) and an established exchange or its clearinghouse in which the buyer (seller) agrees to take (make) delivery of something at a specified price at the end of a designated period of time.

Futures exchange A legal corporate entity whose shareholders are its members. The members of the exchange have the privilege of executing transactions directly on the exchange.

Futures price The price at which the parties to a futures contract agree to exchange the underlying.

Gain-to-loss ratio The ratio of positive returns to negative returns over a specified period of time.

Gamma A numerical measure of the sensitivity of delta to a change in the underlying's value.

Global custodian An entity that effects trade settlement, safekeeping of assets, and the allocation of trades to individual custody accounts.

Global investable market A practical proxy for the world market portfolio consisting of traditional and alternative asset classes with sufficient capacity to absorb meaningful investment.

Global Investment Performance Standards™ (GIPS®) A global industry standard for the ethical presentation of investment performance results promulgated by the Association for Investment Management and Research.

Global minimum-variance portfolio The portfolio on the minimum-variance frontier with smallest variance of return.

Gold standard currency system A currency regime under which currency could be freely converted into gold at established rates.

Gordon (constant) growth model A version of the dividend discount model for common share value that assumes a constant growth rate in dividends.

Government structural policies Government policies that affect the limits of economic growth and incentives within the private sector.

Grinold–Kroner model An expression for the expected return on a share as the sum of an expected income return, an expected nominal earnings growth return, and an expected repricing return.

Gross domestic product (GDP) Total value of a country's output produced by residents within the country's physical borders during a given time period.

Growth in total factor productivity A component of trend growth in GDP that results from increased efficiency in using capital inputs; also known a technical progress.

Growth investment style With reference to equity investing, an investment style focused on investing in high-earnings-growth companies.

Guaranteed investment contract A debt instrument issued by insurers, usually in large denominations, that pays a guaranteed, generally fixed interest rate for a specified time period.

Heating degree day The greater of (i) the average daily temperature minus 6 degrees Fahrenheit, and (ii) zero.

Hedge funds A historically loosely regulated, pooled investment vehicle that may implement various investment strategies.

Hedge ratio The relationship of the quantity of an asset being hedged to the quantity of the derivative used for hedging.

Hedged return The foreign asset return in local currency terms plus the forward discount (premium).

Hedging A general strategy usually thought of as reducing, if not eliminating, risk.

High yield A value investment substyle that focuses on stocks offering high dividend yield with prospects of maintaining or increasing the dividend.

High-water mark A specified net asset value level that a fund must exceed before performance fees are paid to the hedge fund manager.

High-yield investing A distressed securities investment discipline that involves investment in high-yield bonds perceived to be undervalued.

Historical method A method of estimating VAR that uses data from the returns of the portfolio over a recent past period and compiles this data in the form of a histogram.

Historical simulation method The application of historical price changes to the current portfolio.

Holdings-based style analysis An approach to style analysis that categorizes individual securities by their characteristics and aggregates results to reach a conclusion about the overall style of the portfolio at a given point in time.

Homogenization Creating a contract with standard and generally accepted terms, which makes it more acceptable to a broader group of participants.

Human capital The present value of expected future labor income.

Hybrid markets Combinations of market types, which offer elements of batch auction markets and continuous auction markets, as well as quote-driven markets.

Hypothetical events A type of scenario analysis used in stress testing that involves the evaluation of performance given events that have never happened in the markets or market outcomes to which we attach a small probability.

Illiquidity premium Compensation for the risk of loss relative to an investment's fair value if an investment needs to be converted to cash quickly.

Immunization An asset/liability management approach that structures investments in bonds to match (offset) liabilities' weighted-average duration; a type of dedication strategy.

Immunization target rate of return The assured rate of return of an immunized portfolio, equal to the total return of the portfolio assuming no change in the term structure.

Immunized time horizon The time horizon over which a portfolio's value is immunized; equal to the portfolio duration.

Implementation shortfall The difference between the money return on a notional or paper portfolio and the actual portfolio return.

Implementation shortfall strategy (or arrival price strategy) A strategy that attempts to minimize trading costs as measured by the implementation shortfall method.

Implicit transaction costs The indirect costs of trading including bid–ask spreads, the market price impacts of large trades, missed trade opportunity costs, and delay costs.

Implied repo rate The rate of return from a cash-and-carry transaction implied by the futures price relative to the spot price.

Implied volatility The volatility that option traders use to price an option, implied by the price of the option and a particular option-pricing model.

Implied yield A measure of the yield on the underlying bond of a futures contract implied by pricing it as though the underlying will be delivered at the futures expiration.

Incremental VAR A measure of the incremental effect of an asset on the VAR of a portfolio by measuring the difference between the portfolio's VAR while including a specified asset and the portfolio's VAR with that asset eliminated.

Index amortizing swap An interest rate swap in which the notional principal is indexed to the level of interest rates and declines with the level of interest rates according to a predefined schedule. This type of swap is frequently used to hedge securities that are prepaid as interest rates decline, such as mortgage-backed securities.

Index option　An option in which the underlying is a stock index.

Indexing　A common passive approach to investing that involves holding a portfolio of securities designed to replicate the returns on a specified index of securities.

Indirect commodity investment　Commodity investment that involves the acquisition of indirect claims on commodities, such as equity in companies specializing in commodity production.

Individualist investors　Investors who have a self-assured approach to investing and investment decision making.

Inferential statistics　Methods for making estimates or forecasts about a larger group from a smaller group actually observed.

Inflation　An increase in the general level of prices; a decrease in the purchasing power of a unit of currency.

Inflation hedge　An asset whose returns are sufficient on average to preserve purchasing power during periods of inflation.

Inflation premium　Compensation for expected inflation.

Information coefficient　The correlation between forecast and actual returns.

Information ratio　The mean excess return of the account over the benchmark (i.e., mean active return) relative to the variability of that excess return (i.e., tracking risk); a measure of risk-adjusted performance.

Information-motivated traders　Traders that seek to trade on information that has limited value if not quickly acted upon.

Infrastructure funds　Funds that make private investment in public infrastructure projects in return for rights to specified revenue streams over a contracted period.

Initial margin requirement　The margin requirement on the first day of a transaction as well as on any day in which additional margin funds must be deposited.

Initial public offering　The initial issuance of common stock registered for public trading by a formerly private corporation.

Input uncertainty　Uncertainty concerning whether the inputs are correct.

Inside ask (or market ask)　The lowest available ask price.

Inside bid (or market bid)　The highest available bid price.

Inside bid–ask spread (also called market bid–ask spread, inside spread, or market spread)　Market ask price minus market bid price.

Inside quote (or market quote)　Combination of the highest available bid price with the lowest available ask price.

Institutional investors　Corporations or other legal entities that ultimately serve as financial intermediaries between individuals and investment markets.

Insuring　The process of setting a minimum level for the future value of a portfolio by taking positions in various derivatives (e.g., options).

Interest rate call　An option in which the holder has the right to make a known interest payment and receive an unknown interest payment.

Interest rate cap or cap　A series of call options on an interest rate, with each option expiring at the date on which the floating loan rate will be reset, and with each option having the same exercise rate. A cap in general can have an underlying other than an interest rate.

Interest rate collar　A combination of a long cap and a short floor, or a short cap and a long floor. A collar in general can have an underlying other than an interest rate.

Interest rate floor or floor　A series of put options on an interest rate, with each option expiring at the date on which the floating loan rate will be reset, and with each option having the same exercise rate. A floor in general can have an underlying other than the interest rate.

Interest rate forward　See Forward rate agreement.

Interest rate management effect　With respect to fixed-income attribution analysis, a return component reflecting how well a manager predicts interest rate changes.

Interest rate option　An option in which the underlying is an interest rate.

Interest rate parity　A formula that expresses the equivalence or parity of spot and forward rates, after adjusting for differences in the interest rates.

Interest rate put　An option in which the holder has the right to make an unknown interest payment and receive a known interest payment.

Interest rate risk　Risk related to changes in the level of interest rates.

Interest rate swap　A contract between two parties (counterparties) to exchange periodic interest payments based on a specified notional amount of principal.

Interest spread　With respect to banks, the average yield on earning assets minus the average percent cost of interest-bearing liabilities.

Internal rate of return   The growth rate that will link the ending value of the account to its beginning value plus all intermediate cash flows; money-weighted rate of return is a synonym.

In-the-money   Options that, if exercised, would result in the value received being worth more than the payment required to exercise.

In-the-money option   An option that has a positive value if exercised immediately. For example, a call when the strike price is below the current price of the underlying asset, or a put when the strike price is above the current price of the underlying asset.

Intrinsic value or exercise value   The value obtained if an option is exercised based on current conditions.

Inventory cycle   A cycle measured in terms of fluctuations in inventories, typically lasting 2–4 years.

Inverse floater   A floating-rate note or bond in which the coupon is adjusted to move opposite to a benchmark interest rate.

Investment objectives   Desired investment outcomes, chiefly pertaining to return and risk.

Investment policy statement (IPS)   A written document that sets out a client's return objectives and risk tolerance over a relevant time horizon, along with applicable constraints such as liquidity needs, tax considerations, regulatory requirements, and unique circumstances.

Investment skill   The ability to outperform an appropriate benchmark consistently over time.

Investment strategy   An investor's approach to investment analysis and security selection.

Investment style   A natural grouping of investment disciplines that has some predictive power in explaining the future dispersion in returns across portfolios.

Investment style indexes   Indices that represent specific portions of an asset category. For example, subgroups within the U.S. common stock asset category such as large-capitalization growth stocks.

Investor's benchmark   The benchmark an investor uses to evaluate performance of a given portfolio or asset class.

J factor risk   The risk associated with a judge's track record in adjudicating bankruptcies and restructuring.

J-curve   The expected pattern of interim returns over the life of a successful venture capital fund in which early returns are negative as the portfolio of companies burns cash but later returns accelerate as companies are exited.

Key rate duration   A method of measuring the interest rate sensitivities of a fixed-income instrument or portfolio to shifts in key points along the yield curve.

Lagging economic indicators   Economic indicators of recent past economic activity.

Lagging indicators   A set of economic variables whose values reach peaks and troughs after the aggregate economy.

Law of one price   The condition in a financial market in which two financial instruments or combinations of financial instruments can sell for only one price. Equivalent to the principle that no arbitrage opportunities are possible.

Leading economic indicator   A variable that varies with the business cycle but at a fairly consistent time interval before a turn in the business cycle.

Leading indicators   A set of economic variables whose values reach peaks and troughs in advance of the aggregate economy.

Legal and regulatory factors   External factors imposed by governmental, regulatory, or oversight authorities that constrain investment decision-making.

Legal/contract risk   The possibility of loss arising from the legal system's failure to enforce a contract in which an enterprise has a financial stake; for example, if a contract is voided through litigation.

Leverage-adjusted duration gap   A leverage-adjusted measure of the difference between the durations of assets and liabilities which measures a bank's overall interest rate exposure.

Leveraged floating-rate note or leveraged floater   A floating-rate note or bond in which the coupon is adjusted at a multiple of a benchmark interest rate.

Liability   As used in the text, a financial obligation.

Life annuity   An annuity that guarantees a monthly income to the annuitant for life.

Limit down   A limit move in the futures market in which the price at which a transaction would be made is at or below the lower limit.

Limit move   A condition in the futures markets in which the price at which a transaction would be made is at or beyond the price limits.

Limit order   An instruction to execute an order when the best price available is at least as good as the limit price specified in the order.

Limit up   A limit move in the futures market in which the price at which a transaction would be made is at or above the upper limit.

Linear programming   Optimization in which the objective function and constraints are linear.

Liquidity   The ability to trade without delay at relatively low cost and in relatively large quantities.

Liquidity event   An event giving rise to a need for cash.

Liquidity requirement   A need for cash in excess of new contributions (for pension plans and endowments, for example) or savings (for individuals) at a specified point in time.

Liquidity risk Any risk of economic loss because of the need to sell relatively less liquid assets to meet liquidity requirements; the risk that a financial instrument cannot be purchased or sold without a significant concession in price because of the market's potential inability to efficiently accommodate the desired trading size.

Liquidity-motivated traders Traders that are motivated to trade based upon reasons other than an information advantage. For example, to release cash proceeds to facilitate the purchase of another security, adjust market exposure, or fund cash needs.

Locked limit A condition in the futures markets in which a transaction cannot take place because the price would be beyond the limits.

Locked up Said of investments that cannot be traded at all for some time.

Lock-up period A minimum initial holding period for investments during which no part of the investment can be withdrawn.

Logical participation strategies Protocols for breaking up an order for execution over time. Typically used by institutional traders to participate in overall market volumes without being unduly visible.

London Interbank Offer Rate (LIBOR) The Eurodollar rate at which London banks lend dollars to other London banks; considered to be the best representative rate on a dollar borrowed by a private, high-quality borrower.

Long The buyer of a derivative contract. Also refers to the position of owning a derivative.

Longevity risk The risk of outliving one's financial resources.

Long-term equity anticipatory securities (LEAPS) Options originally created with expirations of several years.

Low P/E A value investment substyle that focuses on shares selling at low prices relative to current or normal earnings.

Lower bound The lowest possible value of an option.

M2 A measure of what a portfolio would have returned if it had taken on the same total risk as the market index.

Macaulay duration The percentage change in price for a percentage change in yield. The term, named for one of the economists who first derived it, is used to distinguish the calculation from modified duration. (See also Modified duration.)

Macro attribution Performance attribution analysis conducted on the fund sponsor level.

Macro expectations Expectations concerning classes of assets.

Maintenance margin requirement The margin requirement on any day other than the first day of a transaction.

Managed futures Pooled investment vehicles, frequently structured as limited partnerships, that invest in futures and options on futures and other instruments.

Manager continuation policies Policies adopted to guide the manager evaluations conducted by fund sponsors. The goal of manager continuation policies is to reduce the costs of manager turnover while systematically acting on indications of future poor performance.

Manager monitoring A formal, documented procedure that assists fund sponsors in consistently collecting information relevant to evaluating the state of their managers' operations; used to identify warning signs of adverse changes in existing managers' organizations.

Manager review A detailed examination of a manager that currently exists within a plan sponsor's program. The manager review closely resembles the manager selection process, in both the information considered and the comprehensiveness of the analysis. The staff should review all phases of the manager's operations, just as if the manager were being initially hired.

Mandate A set of instructions detailing the investment manager's task and how his performance will be evaluated.

Margin The amount of money that a trader deposits in a margin account. The term is derived from the stock market practice in which an investor borrows a portion of the money required to purchase a certain amount of stock. In futures markets, there is no borrowing so the margin is more of a down payment or performance bond.

Market bid The best available bid; highest price any buyer is currently willing to pay.

Market fragmentation A condition whereby a market contains no dominant group of sellers (or buyers) that are large enough to unduly influence the market.

Market impact (or price impact) The effect of the trade on transaction prices.

Market integration The degree to which there are no impediments or barriers to capital mobility across markets.

Market microstructure The market structures and processes that affect how the manager's interest in buying or selling an asset is translated into executed trades (represented by trade prices and volumes).

Market model A regression equation that specifies a linear relationship between the return on a security (or portfolio) and the return on a broad market index.

Market on open (close) order A market order to be executed at the opening (closing) of the market.

Market order An instruction to execute an order as soon as possible in the public markets at the best price available.

Market oriented With reference to equity investing, an intermediate grouping for investment disciplines that cannot be clearly categorized as value or growth.

Market resilience Condition where discrepancies between market prices and intrinsic values tend to be small and corrected quickly.

Market risk The risk associated with interest rates, exchange rates, and equity prices.

Market segmentation The degree to which there are some meaningful impediments to capital movement across markets.

Market timing Increasing or decreasing exposure to a market or asset class based on predictions of its performance; with reference to performance attribution, returns attributable to shorter-term tactical deviations from the strategic asset allocation.

Market-adjusted implementation shortfall The difference between the money return on a notional or paper portfolio and the actual portfolio return, adjusted using beta to remove the effect of the return on the market.

Market-not-held order A variation of the market order designed to give the agent greater discretion than a simple market order would allow. "Not held" means that the floor broker is not required to trade at any specific price or in any specific time interval.

Marking to market A procedure used primarily in futures markets in which the parties to a contract settle the amount owed daily. Also known as the daily settlement.

Mass affluent An industry term for a segment of the private wealth marketplace that is not sufficiently wealthy to command certain individualized services.

Matrix prices Prices determined by comparisons to other securities of similar credit risk and maturity; the result of matrix pricing.

Matrix pricing An approach for estimating the prices of thinly traded securities based on the prices of securities with similar attributions, such as similar credit rating, maturity, or economic sector.

Maturity premium Compensation for the increased sensitivity of the market value of debt to a change in market interest rates as maturity is extended.

Maturity variance A measure of how much a given immunized portfolio differs from the ideal immu-

nized portfolio consisting of a single pure discount instrument with maturity equal to the time horizon.

Maximum loss optimization A stress test in which we would try to optimize mathematically the risk variable that would produce the maximum loss.

Mega-cap buy-out funds A class of buyout funds that take public companies private.

Methodical investors Investors who rely on "hard facts."

Micro attribution Performance attribution analysis carried out on the investment manager level.

Micro expectations Expectations concerning individual assets.

Middle-market buy-out funds A class of buyout funds that purchase private companies whose revenues and profits are too small to access capital from the public equity markets.

Midquote The halfway point between the market bid and ask prices.

Minimum-variance frontier The graph of the set of portfolios with smallest variances of return for their levels of expected return.

Minimum-variance hedge ratio The hedge ratio that is expected to minimize the variance of the rate of return on the hedged portfolio.

Missed trade opportunity costs Unrealized profit/loss arising from the failure to execute a trade in a timely manner.

Model risk The risk that a model is incorrect or misapplied; in investments, it often refers to valuation models.

Model uncertainty Uncertainty concerning whether a selected model is correct.

Modern portfolio theory (MPT) The analysis of rational portfolio choices based on the efficient use of risk.

Modified duration An adjustment of the duration for the level of the yield. Contrast with Macaulay duration.

Monetary policy Government activity concerning interest rates and the money supply.

Money markets Markets for fixed-income securities with maturities of one year or less.

Moneyness The relationship between the price of the underlying and an option's exercise price.

Money-weighted rate of return Same as the internal rate of return; the growth rate that will link the ending value of the account to its beginning value plus all intermediate cash flows.

Monitoring To systematically keep watch over investor circumstances (including wealth and constraints), market and economic changes, and the portfolio itself so that the client's current objectives and constraints continue to be satisfied.

Monte Carlo simulation method An approach to estimating VAR that produces random outcomes to examine what might happen if a particular risk is faced. This method is widely used in the sciences as well as in business to study a variety of problems.

Mortality risk The risk of loss of human capital in the event of premature death.

Multifactor model A model that explains a variable in terms of the values of a set of factors.

Multifactor model technique With respect to construction of an indexed portfolio, a technique that attempts to match the primary risk exposures of the indexed portfolio to those of the index.

Multiperiod Sharpe ratio A Sharpe ratio based on the investment's multiperiod wealth in excess of the wealth generated by the risk-free investment.

Mutuals With respect to insurance companies, companies that are owned by their policyholders, who share in the company's surplus earnings.

Natural liquidity An extensive pool of investors who are aware of and have a potential interest in buying and/or selling a security.

Net interest margin With respect to banks, net interest income (interest income minus interest expense) divided by average earning assets.

Net interest spread With respect to the operations of insurers, the difference between interest earned and interest credited to policyholders.

Net worth The difference between the market value of assets and liabilities.

Netting When parties agree to exchange only the net amount owed from one party to the other.

Nominal default-free bonds Conventional bonds that have no (or minimal) default risk.

Nominal gross domestic product (nominal GDP) A money measure of the goods and services produced within a country's borders.

Nominal risk-free interest rate The sum of the real risk-free interest rate and the inflation premium.

Nominal spread The spread of a bond or portfolio above the yield of a Treasury of equal maturity.

Nondeliverable forwards (NDFs) Cash-settled forward contracts, used predominately with respect to foreign exchange forwards.

Nonfinancial risk Risks that arise from sources other than the external financial markets, such as changes in accounting rules, legal environment, or tax rates.

Nonparametric Involving minimal probability-distribution assumptions.

Nonstationarity A property of a data series that reflects more than one set of underlying statistical properties.

Normal backwardation The condition in futures markets in which futures prices are lower than expected spot prices.

Normal contango The condition in futures markets in which futures prices are higher than expected spot prices.

Normal portfolio A portfolio with exposure to sources of systematic risk that are typical for a manager, using the manager's past portfolios as a guide.

Notional amount The dollar amount used as a scale factor in calculating payments for a forward contract, futures contract, or swap.

Notional principal amount The amount specified in a swap that forms the basis for calculating payment streams.

Objective function A quantitative expression of the objective or goal of a process.

Off-market FRA A contract in which the initial value is intentionally set at a value other than zero and therefore requires a cash payment at the start from one party to the other.

Offsetting A transaction in exchange-listed derivative markets in which a party re-enters the market to close out a position.

Open market operations The purchase or sale by a central bank of government securities, which are settled using reserves, to influence interest rates and the supply of credit by banks.

Open outcry auction market Public auction where representatives of buyers and sellers meet at a specified location and place verbal bids and offers.

Operations risk or operational risk The risk of loss from failures in a company's systems and procedures (for example, due to computer failures or human failures) or events completely outside of the control of organizations (which would include "acts of God" and terrorist actions).

Opportunistic participation strategies Passive trading combined with the opportunistic seizing of liquidity.

Opportunity cost sell discipline A sell discipline in which the investor is constantly looking at potential stocks to include in the portfolio and will replace an existing holding whenever a better opportunity presents itself.

Optimization With respect to portfolio construction, a procedure for determining the best portfolios according to some criterion.

Optimizer A heuristic, formula, algorithm, or program that uses risk, return, correlation, or other variables to determine the most appropriate asset allocation or asset mix for a portfolio.

Option   A financial instrument that gives one party the right, but not the obligation, to buy or sell an underlying asset from or to another party at a fixed price over a specific period of time. Also referred to as contingent claims.

Option price, option premium, or premium   The amount of money a buyer pays and seller receives to engage in an option transaction.

Option-adjusted spread (OAS)   The current spread over the benchmark yield minus that component of the spread that is attributable to any embedded optionality in the instrument.

Options on futures (futures options)   Options on a designated futures contract.

Options on physicals   With respect to options, exchange-traded option contracts that have cash instruments rather than futures contracts on cash instruments as the underlying.

Order-driven markets   Markets in which transaction prices are established by public limit orders to buy or sell a security at specified prices.

Ordinary life insurance (also whole life insurance)   A type of life insurance policy that involves coverage for the whole of the insured's life.

Orphan equities investing   A distressed securities investment discipline that involves investment in orphan equities that are perceived to be undervalued.

Orphan equity   Investment in the newly issued equity of a company emerging from reorganization.

Out-of-the-money option   An option that has no value if exercised immediately. For example, a call when the strike price is above the current price of the underlying asset, or a put when the strike price is below the current price of the underlying asset.

Output gap   The difference between the value of GDP estimated as if the economy were on its trend growth path (potential output) and the actual value of GDP.

Overall trade balance   The sum of the current account (reflecting exports and imports) and the financial account (consisting of portfolio flows).

Overconfidence trap   The tendency of individuals to overestimate the accuracy of their forecasts.

Overnight index swap (OIS)   A swap in which the floating rate is the cumulative value of a single unit of currency invested at an overnight rate during the settlement period.

Over-the-counter (OTC)   A market for securities made up of dealers. It is not an organized exchange, and trading usually takes place by telephone or other electronic means.

Pairs trade (or pairs arbitrage)   A basic long–short trade in which an investor is long and short equal currency amounts of two common stocks in a single industry.

Panel method   A method of capital market expectations setting that involves using the viewpoints of a panel of experts.

Partial correlation   In multivariate problems, the correlation between two variables after controlling for the effects of the other variables in the system.

Partial fill   Execution of a purchase or sale for fewer shares than was stipulated in the order.

Participate (do not initiate) order   A variant of the market-not-held order. The broker is deliberately low-key and waits for and responds to the initiatives of more active traders.

Passive investment approach   An approach to portfolio construction in which portfolio composition does not react to changes in capital market expectations; includes indexing and buy-and-hold investing.

Passive management   A buy-and-hold approach to investing in which an investor does not make portfolio changes based upon short-term expectations of changing market or security performance.

Passive traders   Traders that seek liquidity in their rebalancing transactions, but are much more concerned with the cost of trading.

Payer swaption   A swaption that allows the holder to enter into a swap as the fixed-rate payer and floating-rate receiver.

Payment netting   A means of settling payments in which the amount owed by the first party to the second is netted with the amount owed by the second party to the first; only the net difference is paid.

Payoff   The value of an option at expiration.

Pension funds   Funds consisting of assets set aside to support a promise of retirement income.

Pension surplus   Pension assets at market value minus the present value of pension liabilities.

Percentage-of-portfolio rebalancing   Rebalancing is triggered based on set thresholds stated as a percentage of the portfolio's value.

Percentage-of-volume strategy   A logical participation strategy in which trading takes place in proportion to overall market volume (typically at a rate of 5–20 percent) until the order is completed.

Perfect markets   Markets without any frictional costs.

Performance appraisal   The evaluation of portfolio performance; a quantitative assessment of a manager's investment skill.

Performance attribution   A comparison of an account's performance with that of a designated benchmark and the identification and quantification of sources of differential returns.

Performance evaluation The measurement and assessment of the outcomes of investment management decisions.

Performance guarantee A guarantee from the clearinghouse that if one party makes money on a transaction, the clearinghouse ensures it will be paid.

Performance measurement A component of performance evaluation; the relatively simple procedure of calculating an asset's or portfolio's rate of return.

Performance netting risk For entities that fund more than one strategy and have asymmetric incentive fee arrangements with the portfolio managers, the potential for loss in cases where the net performance of the group of managers generates insufficient fee revenue to fully cover contractual payout obligations to all portfolio managers with positive performance.

Performance-based fee Fees specified by a combination of a base fee plus an incentive fee for performance in excess of a benchmark's.

Periodic (or batch) auction markets Auction markets where multilateral trading occurs at a single price at a prespecified point in time.

Permanent income hypothesis The hypothesis that consumers' spending behavior is largely determined by their long-run income expectations.

Personality typing The determination of an investor's personality type.

Plain vanilla swap An interest rate swap in which one party pays a fixed rate and the other pays a floating rate, with both sets of payments in the same currency.

Plan sponsor An enterprise or organization—such as a business, labor union, municipal or state government, or not-for-profit organization—that sets up a pension plan.

Pledging requirement With respect to banks, a required collateral use of assets.

Point estimate A single-valued estimate of a quantity, as opposed to an estimate in terms of a range of values.

Policy portfolio A synonym of strategic asset allocation; the portfolio resulting from strategic asset allocation considered as a process.

Policyholder reserves With respect to an insurance company, an amount representing the estimated payments to policyholders, as determined by actuaries, based on the types and terms of the various insurance policies issued by the company.

Political risk (or geopolitical risk) The risk of war, government collapse, political instability, expropriation, confiscation, or adverse changes in taxation.

Portable Moveable. With reference to a pension plan, one in which a plan participant can move his or her share of plan assets to a new plan, subject to certain rules, vesting schedules, and possible tax penalties and payments.

Portable alpha A strategy involving the combining of multiple positions (e.g., long and short positions) so as to separate the alpha (unsystematic risk) from beta (systematic risk) in an investment.

Portfolio implementation decision The decision on how to execute the buy and sell orders of portfolio managers.

Portfolio management process An integrated set of steps undertaken in a consistent manner to create and maintain an appropriate portfolio (combination of assets) to meet clients' stated goals.

Portfolio optimization The combining of assets to efficiently achieve a set of return and risk objectives.

Portfolio segmentation The creation of subportfolios according to the product mix for individual segments or lines of business.

Portfolio selection/composition decision The decision in which the manager integrates investment strategies with capital market expectations to select the specific assets for the portfolio.

Portfolio trade (also known as program trade or basket trade) A trade in which a number of securities are traded as a single unit.

Position a trade To take the other side of a trade, acting as a principal with capital at risk.

Position trader A trader who typically holds positions open overnight.

Positive active position An active position for which the account's allocation to a security is greater than the corresponding weight of the same security in the benchmark.

Post-trade transparency Degree to which completed trades are quickly and accurately reported to the public.

Potential credit risk The risk associated with the possibility that a payment due at a later date will not be made.

Potential output The value of GDP if the economy were on its trend growth path.

Preferred return With respect to the compensation of private equity fund managers, a hurdle rate.

Pre-investing The strategy of using futures contracts to enter the market without an immediate outlay of cash.

Prepackaged bankruptcy A bankruptcy in which the debtor seeks agreement from creditors on the terms of a reorganization before the reorganization filing.

Prepaid swap A contract calling for payment today and delivery of the asset or commodity at multiple specified times in the future.

Present (price) value of a basis point (PVBP) The change in the bond price for a 1 basis point change in yield. Also called basis point value (BPV).

Present value distribution of cash flows A list showing what proportion of a portfolio's duration is attributable to each future cash flow.

Pretrade transparency Ability of individuals to quickly, easily, and inexpensively obtain accurate information about quotes and trades.

Price discovery Adjustment of transaction prices to balance supply and demand.

Price improvement Execution at a price that is better than the price quoted at the time of order placement.

Price limits Limits imposed by a futures exchange on the price change that can occur from one day to the next.

Price risk The risk of fluctuations in market price.

Price uncertainty Uncertainty about the price at which an order will execute.

Price weighted With respect to index construction, an index in which each security in the index is weighted according to its absolute share price.

Priced risk Risk for which investors demand compensation.

Primary risk factors With respect to valuation, the major influences on pricing.

Prime brokerage A suite of services that is often specified to include support in accounting and reporting, leveraged trade execution, financing, securities lending (related to short-selling activities), and start-up advice (for new entities).

Principal trade A trade with a broker in which the broker commits capital to facilitate the prompt execution of the trader's order to buy or sell.

Private equity Ownership interests in non-publicly-traded companies.

Private equity funds Pooled investment vehicles investing in generally highly illiquid assets; includes venture capital funds and buyout funds.

Private exchange A method for handling undiversified positions with built-in capital gains in which shares that are a component of an index are exchanged for shares of an index mutual fund in a privately arranged transaction with the fund.

Private placement memorandum A document used to raise venture capital financing when funds are raised through an agent.

Profit-sharing plans A defined-contribution plan in which contributions are based, at least in part, on the plan sponsor's profits.

Projected benefit obligation (PBO) A measure of a pension plan's liability that reflects accumulated service in the same manner as the ABO but also projects future variables, such as compensation increases.

Prospect theory The analysis of decision making under risk in terms of choices among prospects.

Protective put An option strategy in which a long position in an asset is combined with a long position in a put.

Proxy hedging Hedging that involves the use of a forward contract between the home currency and a currency that is highly correlated with the foreign asset's currency.

Prudence trap The tendency to temper forecasts so that they do not appear extreme; the tendency to be overly cautious in forecasting.

Psychological profiling The determination of an investor's psychological characteristics relevant to investing, such as his or her personality type.

Public good A good that is not divisible and not excludable (a consumer cannot be denied it).

Purchasing power parity The theory that movements in an exchange rate should offset any difference in the inflation rates between two countries.

Pure sector allocation return A component of attribution analysis that relates relative returns to the manager's sector-weighting decisions. Calculated as the difference between the allocation (weight) of the portfolio to a given sector and the portfolio's benchmark weight for that sector, multiplied by the difference between the sector benchmark's return and the overall portfolio's benchmark return, summed across all sectors.

Put An option that gives the holder the right to sell an underlying asset to another party at a fixed price over a specific period of time.

Put option A contract giving the right to sell an asset at a specified price, on or before a specified date.

Put–call parity An equation expressing the equivalence (parity) of a portfolio of a call and a bond with a portfolio of a put and the underlying, which leads to the relationship between put and call prices

Put–call–forward parity The relationship among puts, calls, and forward contracts.

Quality control charts A graphical means of presenting performance appraisal data; charts illustrating the performance of an actively managed account versus a selected benchmark.

Quality option (or swap option) With respect to Treasury futures, the option of which acceptable Treasury issue to deliver.

Quoted depth The number of shares available for purchase or sale at the quoted bid and ask prices.

Quote-driven markets (dealer markets) Markets that rely on dealers to establish firm prices at which securities can be bought and sold.

Rate duration A fixed-income instrument's or portfolio's sensitivity to a change in key maturity, holding constant all other points along the yield curve.

Ratio spread An option strategy in which a long position in a certain number of options is offset by a short position in a certain number of other options on the same underlying, resulting in a risk-free position.

Real estate Interests in land or structures attached to land.

Real estate investment trusts (REITs) Publicly traded equities representing pools of money invested in real estate properties and/or real estate debt.

Real option An option involving decisions related to tangible assets or processes.

Real risk-free interest rate The single-period interest rate for a completely risk-free security if no inflation were expected.

Rebalancing Adjusting the actual portfolio to the current strategic asset allocation because of price changes in portfolio holdings. Also: revisions to an investor's target asset class weights because of changes in the investor's investment objectives or constraints, or because of changes in capital market expectations; or to mean tactical asset allocation.

Rebalancing ratio A quantity involved in reestablishing the dollar duration of a portfolio to a desired level, equal to the original dollar duration divided by the new dollar duration.

Re-base With reference to index construction, to change the time period used as the base of the index.

Recallability trap The tendency of forecasts to be overly influenced by events that have left a strong impression on a person's memory.

Receiver swaption A swaption that allows the holder to enter into a swap as the fixed-rate receiver and floating-rate payer.

Recession A broad-based economic downturn, conventionally defined as two successive quarterly declines in GDP.

Reference entity An entity, such as a bond issuer, specified in a derivatives contract.

Regime A distinct governing set of relationships.

Regulatory risk The risk associated with the uncertainty of how a transaction will be regulated or with the potential for regulations to change.

Reinvestment risk The risk of reinvesting coupon income or principal at a rate less than the original coupon or purchase rate.

Relative economic strength forecasting approach An exchange rate forecasting approach that suggests that a strong pace of economic growth in a country creates attractive investment opportunities, increasing the demand for the country's currency and causing it to appreciate.

Relative return objective A return objective stated as a return relative to the portfolio benchmark's total return.

Relative strength indicators A price momentum indicator that involves comparing a stock's performance during a specific period either to its own past performance or to the performance of some group of stocks.

Remaindermen Beneficiaries of a trust; having a claim on the residue.

Replacement value The market value of a swap.

Repurchase agreement A contract involving the sale of securities such as Treasury instruments coupled with an agreement to repurchase the same securities at a later date.

Repurchase yield The negative of the expected percent change in number of shares outstanding, in the Grinold–Kroner model.

Required return (or return requirement) With reference to the investment policy statement, a return objective relating to level of return that will be adequate to satisfy a need.

Resampled efficient frontier The set of resampled efficient portfolios.

Resampled efficient portfolio An efficient portfolio based on simulation.

Residue With respect to trusts, the funds remaining in a trust when the last income beneficiary dies.

Retired-lives The portion of a pension fund's liabilities associated with retired workers.

Return objective An investor objective that addresses the required or desired level of returns.

Returns-based benchmarks Benchmarks that are constructed using (1) a series of a manager's account returns and (2) the series of returns on several investment style indexes over the same period. These return series are then submitted to an allocation algorithm that solves for the combination of investment style indexes that most closely tracks the account's returns.

Returns-based style analysis An approach to style analysis that focuses on characteristics of the overall portfolio as revealed by a portfolio's realized returns.

Reverse optimization A technique for reverse engineering the expected returns implicit in a diversified market portfolio.

Rho   The sensitivity of the option price to the risk-free rate.

Risk allocation   The decomposition of the risk of a portfolio into the various risk exposures taken by a manager.

Risk aversion   The degree of an investor's inability and unwillingness to take risk.

Risk budget   The desired total quantity of risk; the result of risk budgeting.

Risk budgeting   The establishment of objectives for individuals, groups, or divisions of an organization that takes into account the allocation of an acceptable level of risk.

Risk exposure   A source of risk. Also, the state of being exposed or vulnerable to a risk.

Risk governance   The process of setting overall policies and standards in risk management.

Risk management   The process of identifying the level of risk an entity wants, measuring the level of risk the entity currently has, taking actions that bring the actual level of risk to the desired level of risk, and monitoring the new actual level of risk so that it continues to be aligned with the desired level of risk.

Risk objective   An investor objective that addresses risk.

Risk premium approach   An approach to forecasting the return of a risky asset that views its expected return as the sum of the risk-free rate of interest and one or more risk premiums.

Risk profile   A detailed tabulation of the index's risk exposures.

Risk tolerance   The capacity to accept risk; the level of risk an investor (or organization) is willing and able to bear.

Risk tolerance function   An assessment of an investor's tolerance to risk over various levels of portfolio outcomes.

Risk-neutral probabilities   Weights that are used to compute a binomial option price. They are the probabilities that would apply if a risk-neutral investor valued an option.

Risk-neutral valuation   The process by which options and other derivatives are priced by treating investors as though they were risk neutral.

Roll return (or roll yield)   The component of the return on a commodity futures contract that comes from rolling long futures positions forward through time.

Rolling return   The moving average of the holding-period returns for a specified period (e.g., a calendar year) that matches the investor's time horizon.

Sample estimator   A formula for assigning a unique value (a point estimate) to a population parameter.

Sandwich spread   An option strategy that is equivalent to a short butterfly spread.

Savings–investment imbalances forecasting approach   An exchange rate forecasting approach that explains currency movements in terms of the effects of domestic savings–investment imbalances on the exchange rate.

Scalper   A trader who offers to buy or sell futures contracts, holding the position for only a brief period of time. Scalpers attempt to profit by buying at the bid price and selling at the higher ask price.

Scenario analysis   A risk management technique involving the examination of the performance of a portfolio under specified situations. Closely related to stress testing.

Seats   Memberships in a derivatives exchange.

Secondary offering   An offering after the initial public offering of securities.

Sector/quality effect   In a fixed-income attribution analysis, a measure of a manager's ability to select the "right" issuing sector and quality group.

Security selection   Skill in selecting individual securities within an asset class.

Security selection effect   In a fixed-income attribution analysis, the residual of the security's total return after other effects are accounted for; a measure of the return due to ability in security selection.

Segmentation   With respect to the management of insurance company portfolios, the notional subdivision of the overall portfolio into sub-portfolios each of which is associated with a specified group of insurance contracts.

Sell side   Broker/dealers that sell securities and make recommendations for various customers, such as investment managers and institutional investors.

Sell-side analysts   Analysts employed by brokerages.

Semiactive management (also called enhanced indexing or risk-controlled active management)   A variant of active management. In a semiactive portfolio, the manager seeks to outperform a given benchmark with tightly controlled risk relative to the benchmark.

Semiactive, risk-controlled active, or enhanced index approach   An investment approach that seeks positive alpha while keeping tight control over risk relative to the portfolio's benchmark.

Semivariance   A measure of downside risk. The average of squared deviations that fall below the mean.

Settlement date or payment date   The designated date at which the parties to a trade must transact.

Settlement netting risk The risk that a liquidator of a counterparty in default could challenge a netting arrangement so that profitable transactions are realized for the benefit of creditors.

Settlement period The time between settlement dates.

Settlement price The official price, designated by the clearinghouse, from which daily gains and losses will be determined and marked to market.

Settlement risk When settling a contract, the risk that one party could be in the process of paying the counterparty while the counterparty is declaring bankruptcy.

Sharpe ratio A measure of risk-adjusted performance that compares excess returns to the total risk of the account, where total risk is measured by the account's standard deviation of returns.

Short The seller of a derivative contract. Also refers to the position of being short a derivative.

Shortfall risk The risk that portfolio value will fall below some minimum acceptable level during a stated time horizon; the risk of not achieving a specified return target.

Shrinkage estimation Estimation that involves taking a weighted average of a historical estimate of a parameter and some other parameter estimate, where the weights reflect the analyst's relative belief in the estimates.

Shrinkage estimator The formula used in shrinkage estimation of a parameter.

Sign-constrained optimization An optimization that constrains asset class weights to be nonnegative and to sum to 1.

Single-payment loan A loan in which the borrower receives a sum of money at the start and pays back the entire amount with interest in a single payment at maturity.

Situational profiling The categorization of individual investors by stage of life or by economic circumstance.

Smart routing The use of algorithms to intelligently route an order to the most liquid venue.

Smoothing rule With respect to spending rates, a rule that averages asset values over a period of time in order to dampen the spending rate's response to asset value fluctuation.

Socially responsible investing (ethical investing) An approach to investing that integrates ethical values and societal concerns with investment decisions.

Soft dollars (also called soft dollar arrangements or soft commissions) The use of commissions to buy services other than execution services.

Sortino ratio A performance appraisal ratio equal to the mean return in excess of a stated minimum acceptable return divided by downside deviation.

Sovereign risk A form of credit risk in which the borrower is the government of a sovereign nation.

Spontaneous investors Investors who constantly readjust their portfolio allocations and holdings.

Spot return (or price return) The component of the return on a commodity futures contract that comes from changes in the underlying spot prices via the cost-of-carry model.

Spread An option strategy involving the purchase of one option and sale of another option that is identical to the first in all respects except either exercise price or expiration.

Spread duration The sensitivity of a non-Treasury security's price to a widening or narrowing of the spread over Treasuries.

Spread risk Risk related to changes in the spread between Treasuries and non-Treasuries.

Stack and roll A hedging strategy in which an existing stack hedge with maturing futures contracts is replaced by a new stack hedge with longer dated futures contracts.

Stack hedge Hedging a stream of obligations by entering futures contracts with a single maturity, with the number of contracts selected so that changes in the present value of the future obligations are offset by changes in the value of this "stack" of futures contracts.

Stale price bias Bias that arises from using prices that are stale because of infrequent trading.

Standard deviation The positive square root of variance.

Stated return desire A stated desired level of returns.

Static approach With respect to strategic asset allocation, an approach that does not account for links between optimal decisions in future time periods.

Static spread (or zero-volatility spread) The constant spread above the Treasury spot curve that equates the calculated price of the security to the market price.

Stationary A series of data for which the parameters that describe a return-generating process are stable.

Status quo trap The tendency for forecasts to perpetuate recent observations—that is, to predict no change from the recent past.

Sterling ratio The compound annualized rate of return over a specified time period divided by the average yearly maximum drawdown over the same time period less an arbitrary 10 percent.

Stock companies With respect to insurance companies, companies that have issued common equity shares.

Stock index futures Futures contracts on a specified stock index.

Storage costs or carrying costs The costs of holding an asset, generally a function of the physical characteristics of the underlying asset.

Straddle An option strategy involving the purchase of a put and a call with the same exercise price. A straddle is based on the expectation of high volatility of the underlying.

Straight-through processing Systems that simplify transaction processing through the minimization of manual and/or duplicative intervention in the process from trade placement to settlement.

Strangle A variation of a straddle in which the put and call have different exercise prices.

Strap An option strategy involving the purchase of two calls and one put.

Strategic asset allocation 1) The process of allocating money to IPS-permissible asset classes that integrates the investor's return objectives, risk tolerance, and investment constraints with long-run capital market expectations. 2) The result of the above process, also known as the policy portfolio.

Stratified sampling (representative sampling) A sampling method that guarantees that subpopulations of interest are represented in the sample.

Stress testing A risk management technique in which the risk manager examines the performance of the portfolio under market conditions involving high risk and usually high correlations across markets. Closely related to scenario analysis.

Strike spread A spread used to determine the strike price for the payoff of a credit option.

Strip An option strategy involving the purchase of two puts and one call.

Strip hedge Hedging a stream of obligations by offsetting each individual obligation with a futures contract matching the maturity and quantity of the obligation.

Structural level of unemployment The level of unemployment resulting from scarcity of a factor of production.

Structured note A variation of a floating-rate note that has some type of unusual characteristic such as a leverage factor or in which the rate moves opposite to interest rates.

Style drift Inconsistency in style.

Style index A securities index intended to reflect the average returns to a given style.

Stylized scenario A type of analysis often used in stress testing. It involves simulating the movement in at least one interest rate, exchange rate, stock price, or commodity price relevant to the portfolio.

Sunshine trades Public display of a transaction (usually high-volume) in advance of the actual order.

Surplus The difference between the value of assets and the present value of liabilities. With respect to an insurance company, the net difference between the total assets and total liabilities (equivalent to policyholders' surplus for a mutual insurance company and stockholders' equity for a stock company).

Surplus efficient frontier The graph of the set of portfolios that maximize expected surplus for given levels of standard deviation of surplus.

Survey method A method of capital market expectations setting that involves surveying experts.

Survivorship bias Bias that arises in a data series when managers with poor track records exit the business and are dropped from the database whereas managers with good records remain; when a data series as of a given date reflects only entities that have survived to that date.

Swap An agreement between two parties to exchange a series of future cash flows.

Swap rate The interest rate applicable to the pay-fixed-rate side of an interest rate swap.

Swap spread The difference between the fixed rate on an interest rate swap and the rate on a Treasury note with equivalent maturity; it reflects the general level of credit risk in the market.

Swap tenor The lifetime of a swap.

Swap term Another name for swap tenor.

Swaption An option to enter into a swap.

Symmetric cash flow matching A cash flow matching technique that allows cash flows occurring both before and after the liability date to be used to meet a liability; allows for the short-term borrowing of funds to satisfy a liability prior to the liability due date.

Synthetic call The combination of puts, the underlying, and risk-free bonds that replicates a call option.

Synthetic forward contract The combination of the underlying, puts, calls, and risk-free bonds that replicates a forward contract.

Synthetic index fund An index fund position created by combining risk-free bonds and futures on the desired index.

Synthetic put The combination of calls, the underlying, and risk-free bonds that replicates a put option.

Tactical asset allocation Asset allocation that involves making short-term adjustments to asset class weights based on short-term predictions of relative performance among asset classes.

Tactical rebalancing A variation of calendar rebalancing that specifies less frequent rebalancing when markets appear to be trending and more frequent rebalancing when they are characterized by reversals.

Tail value at risk (or conditional tail expectation) The VAR plus the expected loss in excess of VAR, when such excess loss occurs.

Target covariance matrix A component of shrinkage estimation; allows the analyst to model factors that are believed to influence the data over periods longer than observed in the historical sample.

Target semivariance The average squared deviation below a target value.

Target value The value that the portfolio manager seeks to ensure; the value that the life insurance company has guaranteed the policyholder.

Tax concerns Concerns related to an investor's tax position.

Tax efficiency The proportion of the expected pre-tax total return that will be retained after taxes.

Tax premium Compensation for the effect of taxes on the after-tax return of an asset.

Tax risk The uncertainty associated with tax laws.

Taylor rule A rule linking a central bank's target short-term interest rate to the rate of growth of the economy and inflation.

Tenor The original time to maturity on a swap.

Term life insurance A type of life insurance policy that provides coverage for a specified length of time and accumulates little or no cash values.

Termination date The date of the final payment on a swap; also, the swap's expiration date.

Theta The rate at which an option's time value decays.

Tick The smallest possible price movement of a security.

Time deposit A deposit requiring advance notice prior to a withdrawal.

Time horizon The time period associated with an investment objective.

Time to expiration The time remaining in the life of a derivative, typically expressed in years.

Time value decay The loss in the value of an option resulting from movement of the option price toward its payoff value as the expiration day approaches.

Time value or speculative value The difference between the market price of the option and its intrinsic value, determined by the uncertainty of the underlying over the remaining life of the option.

Time-period bias Bias that occurs when results are time-period specific.

Time-series estimators Estimators that are based on lagged values of the variable being forecast;

often consist of lagged values of other selected variables.

Time-weighted average price (TWAP) strategy A logical participation strategy that assumes a flat volume profile and trades in proportion to time.

Time-weighted rate of return The compound rate of growth over a stated evaluation period of one unit of money initially invested in the account.

Time-weighted return A rate of return measure that captures the rate of return per unit of currency initially invested.

Timing option With respect to certain futures contracts, the option that results from the ability of the short position to decide when in the delivery month actual delivery will take place.

Top-down With respect to investment approaches, the allocation of money first to categories such as asset classes, countries, or industry followed by the selection of individual securities within category.

Total future liability With respect to defined-benefit pension plans, the present value of accumulated and projected future service benefits, including the effects of projected future compensation increases.

Total rate of return A measure of the increase in the investor's wealth due to both investment income (for example, dividends and interest) and capital gains (both realized and unrealized).

Total return The rate of return taking into account capital appreciation/depreciation and income. Often qualified as follows: Nominal returns are unadjusted for inflation; real returns are adjusted for inflation; pretax returns are returns before taxes; post-tax returns are returns after taxes are paid on investment income and realized capital gains.

Total return analysis Analysis of the expected effect of a trade on the portfolio's total return, given an interest rate forecast.

Total return swap A swap in which one party agrees to pay the total return on a security. Often used as a credit derivative, in which the underlying is a bond.

Tracking risk (also called tracking error, tracking error volatility, or active risk) The condition in which the performance of a portfolio does not match the performance of an index that serves as the portfolio's benchmark.

Trade blotter A device for entering and tracking trade executions and orders to trade.

Trade settlement Completion of a trade wherein purchased financial instruments are transferred to the buyer and the buyer transfers money to the seller.

Trading activity   In fixed-income attribution analysis, the effect of sales and purchases of bonds over a given period; the total portfolio return minus the other components determining the management effect in an attribution analysis.

Transaction exposure   The risk associated with a foreign exchange rate on a specific business transaction such as a purchase or sale.

Transcription errors   Errors in gathering and recording data.

Translation exposure   The risk associated with the conversion of foreign financial statements into domestic currency.

Translation risk   Risk arising from the translation of the value of an asset or flow from a foreign currency to the domestic currency.

Transparency   Availability of timely and accurate market and trade information.

Treasury spot curve   The term structure of Treasury zero coupon bonds.

Treynor ratio (or reward-to-volatility)   A measure of risk-adjusted performance that relates an account's excess returns to the systematic risk assumed by the account.

Turnover   A measure of the rate of trading activity in a portfolio.

Twist   With respect to the yield curve, a movement in contrary directions of interest rates at two maturities; a nonparallel movement in the yield curve.

Type I error   With respect to manager selection, keeping (or hiring) managers with zero value-added. (Rejecting the null hypothesis when it is correct.)

Type II error   With respect to manager selection, firing (or not hiring) managers with positive value-added. (Not rejecting the null hypothesis when it is incorrect.)

Unconstrained optimization   Optimization that places no constraints on asset class weights except that they sum to 1. May produce negative asset weights, which implies borrowing or shorting of assets.

Underfunded plan   A pension plan in which the ratio of the value of plan assets to the present value of plan liabilities is less than 100 percent.

Underlying   An asset that trades in a market in which buyers and sellers meet, decide on a price, and the seller then delivers the asset to the buyer and receives payment. The underlying is the asset or other derivative on which a particular derivative is based. The market for the underlying is also referred to as the spot market.

Underwriting (profitability) cycle   A cycle affecting the profitability of insurance companies' underwriting operations.

Undisclosed limit order (reserve, hidden, or iceberg order)   A limit order that includes an instruction not to show more than some maximum quantity of the unfilled order to the public at any one time.

Unhedged return   A foreign asset return stated in terms of the investor's home currency.

Unique circumstances   Internal factors (other than a liquidity requirement, time horizon, or tax concern) that may constrain portfolio choices.

Unitary hedge ratio   A hedge ratio equal to 1.

Universal life insurance   A type of life insurance policy that provides for premium flexibility, an adjustable face amount of death benefits, and current market interest rates on the savings element.

Unrelated business income   With respect to the U.S. tax code, income that is not substantially related to a foundation's charitable purposes.

Unstructured modeling   Modeling without a theory on the underlying structure.

Uptick rules   Trading rules that specify that a short sale must not be on a downtick relative to the last trade at a different price.

Urgency of the trade   The importance of certainty of execution.

Valuation   The process of determining the value of an asset or service.

Valuation reserve   With respect to insurance companies, an allowance, created by a charge against earnings, to provide for losses in the value of the assets.

Value   The amount for which one can sell something, or the amount one must pay to acquire something.

Value at risk (VAR)   A probability-based measure of loss potential for a company, a fund, a portfolio, a transaction, or a strategy over a specified period of time.

Value investment style   With reference to equity investing, an investment style focused on paying a relatively low share price in relation to earnings or assets per share.

Value weighted (or market-capitalization weighted)   With respect to index construction, an index in which each security in the index is weighted according to its market capitalization.

Value-motivated traders   Traders that act on value judgments based on careful, sometimes painstaking research. They trade only when the price moves into their value range.

Variable annuity   A life annuity in which the periodic payment varies depending on stock prices.

Variable life insurance (unit-linked life insurance)   A type of ordinary life insurance in which death benefits and cash values are linked to the investment performance of a policyholder-selected pool of investments held in a so-called separate account.

Variable prepaid forward A monetization strategy that involves the combination of a collar with a loan against the value of the underlying shares. When the loan comes due, shares are sold to pay off the loan and part of any appreciation is shared with the lender.

Variable universal life (or flexible-premium variable life) A type of life insurance policy that combines the flexibility of universal life with the investment choice flexibility of variable life.

Variance The expected value of squared deviations from the random variable's mean; often referred to as volatility.

Variation margin Additional margin that must be deposited in an amount sufficient to bring the balance up to the initial margin requirement.

Vega A measure of the sensitivity of an option's price to changes in the underlying's volatility.

Venture capital The equity financing of new or growing private companies.

Venture capital firms Firms representing dedicated pools of capital for providing equity or equity-linked financing to privately held companies.

Venture capital fund A pooled investment vehicle for venture capital investing.

Venture capital trusts An exchange-traded, closed-end vehicle for venture capital investing.

Venture capitalists Specialists who seek to identify companies that have good business opportunities but need financial, managerial, and strategic support.

Vested With respect to pension benefits or assets, said of an unconditional ownership interest.

Vintage year With reference to a private equity fund, the year it closed.

Vintage year effects The effects on returns shared by private equity funds closed in the same year.

Volatility Represented by the Greek letter sigma (σ), the standard deviation of price outcomes associated with an underlying asset.

Volatility clustering The tendency for large (small) swings in prices to be followed by large (small) swings of random direction.

Volume-weighted average price (VWAP) The average price at which a security traded during the day, where each trade price is weighted by the fraction of the day's volume associated with the trade.

Volume-weighted average price strategy A logical participation strategy that involves breaking up an order over time according to a prespecified volume profile.

Wealth relative The ending value of one unit of money invested at specified rates of return.

Weather derivative A derivative contract with a payment based on a weather-related measurement, such as heating or cooling degree days.

Wild card option A provision allowing a short futures contract holder to delay delivery of the underlying.

Within-sector selection return In attribution analysis, a measure of the impact of a manager's security selection decisions relative to the holdings of the sector benchmark.

Worst-case scenario analysis A stress test in which we examine the worst case that we actually expect to occur.

Yield beta A measure of the sensitivity of a bond's yield to a general measure of bond yields in the market that is used to refine the hedge ratio.

Yield curve The relationship between yield and time to maturity.

Yield curve risk Risk related to changes in the shape of the yield curve.

Yield spread The difference between the yield on a bond and the yield on a default-free security, usually a government note, of the same maturity. The yield spread is primarily determined by the market's perception of the credit risk on the bond.

Yield to worst The yield on a callable bond that assumes a bond is called at the earliest opportunity.

Zero-cost collar A transaction in which a position in the underlying is protected by buying a put and selling a call with the premium from the sale of the call offsetting the premium from the purchase of the put. It can also be used to protect a floating-rate borrower against interest rate increases with the premium on a long cap offsetting the premium on a short floor.

Zero-premium collar A hedging strategy involving the simultaneous purchase of puts and sale of call options on a stock. The puts are struck below and the calls are struck above the underlying's market price.

$4\frac{5}{8}$ $4\frac{11}{16}$ $-\frac{3}{8}$

$5\frac{1}{2}$ $5\frac{1}{2}$ $-$

$20\frac{5}{8}$ $21\frac{3}{16}$ $-\frac{1}{16}$

$17\frac{3}{8}$ $18\frac{1}{8}$ $+$ $\frac{7}{8}$

$6\frac{1}{2}$ $6\frac{1}{2}$ $-$ $\frac{1}{2}$

$7\frac{1}{4}$ $6\frac{1}{2}$ $3\frac{1}{32}$ $-$

$\frac{15}{16}$ $\frac{1}{8}$

1 $\frac{9}{16}$ $\frac{9}{16}$

$1\frac{1}{32}$

$7\frac{15}{16}$ $7\frac{13}{16}$ $7\frac{15}{16}$

$2\frac{5}{8}$ $2\frac{11}{32}$ $2\frac{1}{2}$ $+$

$2\frac{3}{4}$ $2\frac{1}{4}$ $2\frac{1}{4}$

327 $1\frac{3}{8}$ $1\frac{1}{4}$ $+$

$6\frac{1}{8}$ $12\frac{1}{16}$ $11\frac{3}{8}$

87 $33\frac{3}{4}$ 33 $33\frac{1}{4}$ $-$

602 $25\frac{5}{8}$ $24\frac{9}{16}$ $25\frac{3}{4}$ $+$

633 12 $11\frac{5}{8}$ $11\frac{7}{8}$ $+$

16 $10\frac{1}{2}$ $10\frac{1}{2}$ $10\frac{1}{2}$ $-$

78 $15\frac{7}{8}$ $15\frac{13}{16}$ $15\frac{7}{8}$ $-$

4508 $9\frac{1}{16}$ $8\frac{1}{4}$ $8\frac{1}{2}$ $-$

$11\frac{1}{4}$ $10\frac{1}{8}$

Page numbers followed by n refer to footnotes. Most footnotes are numbered; some are lettered.

constant growth free cash flow to equity model, V3: 139–141

constant-mix strategies: Perold-Sharpe analysis, V5: 369–370

constant profit margin, V3: 150

constant-proportion strategy (CPPI): Perold-Sharpe analysis, V5: 370–371

constant relative risk aversion (CRRA), V3: 252n60

constraints
legal and regulatory environment, V2: 176–179
liquidity, V2: 169–171
taxes, V2: 172–176
time horizon, V2: 171–172
unique circumstances, V2: 179

consultants
in case study of conflict of interest, V1: 173–177
for evaluating investment managers, V4: 147

consulting assignment, additional compensation arrangements, Standard IV(B), V1: 149

consumer boycotts: as incentives for social responsibility, V4: 236

consumer decisions, V2: 51

consumer income after tax, V3: 64

Consumer Price Index (CPI), V2: 329

Consumer Price Index for All Urban Consumers (CPI-U). See U.S. Consumer Price Index for All Urban Consumers (CPI-U)

consumers
economic growth trends, V3: 71
expectations, surveys of, V3: 126
spending of, and business cycle, V3: 64

consumption spending, V2: 214–215, 220

contango and commodities investing, V4: 300, 399

contingent claims risk: extensions of classical immunization theory for fixed-income portfolios, V3: 348

contingent immunization: extensions of classical immunization theory for fixed-income portfolios, V3: 346

continuous auction markets, V5: 293

continuously linked settlement (CLS), V5: 18

contracting institutions, V4: 227

contractual protections: creating, V4: 235

contrarians, V2: 142
as substyle of value investing, V4: 111

control, V2: 237

convenience yield
and commodity returns, V4: 302–303
and commodity storage costs, V4: 410–411

conventional strategy, V2: 43

conversion factors of the Chicago Board of Trade (CBOT), V4: 15–16

convertible arbitrage, V4: 310

convertible bonds, example of communication with clients, Standard V(B), V1: 151

convertible debentures, example of knowledge of the law, Standard I(A), V1: 18

convexity, V4: 52–53
fixed-income portfolios
adjusting risk profiles for, V3: 325
classical immunization theory for, V3: 348
and measurement of market risk, V5: 24
vs. maturity, in global bond portfolios, structural analysis for, V3: 389n5

core-plus fixed-income portfolios, V4: 39

core-satellite investing: alternative investments, V4: 261

core-satellite portfolios in equity investing, V4: 142–145

corner portfolios, V3: 207–211, 208n32

corner portfolio theorem, V3: 208

corn forward markets: seasonality futures example, V4: 415–418

corporate bonds: bond portfolio risk and, V5: 95

corporate charter defenses against takeovers, V4: 216

corporate debt, defaultable debt, forecasting returns, V3: 94

corporate executives: responsibilities of, V4: 231n137

corporate finance
dividend decisions, V2: 129–131
managerial irrationality, V2: 131–131
security issuance, capital structure and investment, V2: 127–129

corporate governance
boards of directors
behavior of, V4: 196–199
codes of governance for, V4: 202–204
makeup of, V4: 199–202
corporate laws, V4: 202, 204
debt and, V4: 223–226

decline of, V4: 220
international codes for, V4: 203
international policies on, V4: 226–229
introduction, V4: 177–179
investor activism
active monitoring, V4: 204–205, 210–212
company ownership structure, V4: 206–210
managerial compensation
explicit, V4: 191
forms of, V4: 184–185
implicit, V4: 190–192
monetary, V4: 185–190
managerial performance
active monitoring, V4: 192–194
dysfunctional, V4: 181–184
product-market competition, V4: 194–195
moral hazards, V4: 179–181
new form of, V4: 221
risk governance and, V5: 10
runaway compensation, V4: 182
shareholder vs. stakeholder, V4: 230–231, 234–236
stakeholder society, V4: 231–234, 237–240

corporate net profits, V3: 148–149

corporate risk, V2: 382
managing, V2: 311–312

corporate venturing: as private equity investing, V4: 281

correlations
inconsistency of estimates, V3: 13, 13na
misinterpretation of, forecasts, challenges in, V3: 21–22
in times of stress, with international assets, V3: 201, 201n27

corridor band
factors affecting optimal, V5: 364–365
rebalancing and, V5: 363

cost enhancements, lowering, fixed-income portfolios, indexing strategies in, V3: 330

cost-of-carry models, V4: 296

cost of living allowance (COLA): pension liabilities and, V3: 309

costs-are-not-important trading focus, V5: 315, 317

counterparties and commodity swaps, V4: 372–374

counterparty risk, V2: 255

country beta value and foreign bond duration, V4: 32

country classification of markets, V4: 172–173

financial capital: strategic asset allocation for individual investors, V3: 250–252

financial conditions index, V3: 127

financial crises, shocks, exogenous, V3: 76–77

financial/indirect ownership in real estate investing, V4: 262

financial leverage ratio (total assets/equity), V3: 137, 138

financial market equilibrium models, capital market expectations, formulating, V3: 42–51

financial markets: investor protection, V4: 227–228

Financial Modernization Act, V2: 344

financial risk, V5: 12
  in case study of allocation of block trades, V1: 185

financial strategies, V2: 260

Financial Times and London Stock Exchange (FTSE)
  FTSE 100, V4: 106
  FTSE All-World ex-U.S. Index, V4: 169
  FTSE EPRA/Global Real Estate Index, V4: 265
  FTSE indexes, V4: 124–125, 172
  FTSE World Developed ex-North America Index, V4: 169

Financial Times (United Kingdom), V4: 166

firewalls
  material nonpublic information and, V1: 40–41, 200
  between research and investment banking, V1: 23

firms
  compliance with knowledge of the law, V1: 18
  GIPS, V6: 279

firm's code of ethics. *See also* Asset Manager Code (AMC) of Professional Conduct
  adopting CFA Code and Standards, V1: 9–10
  voluntary code of conduct, V1: 191–193

fiscal policy
  business cycle analysis, V3: 69
  business cycle phases, V3: 56, 58
  economic growth trends, V3: 74
  emerging markets, V3: 80
  monetary policy, V3: 69

Fisher, Kenneth, V2: 39

fixed annuities: longevity risk in, V3: 256

fixed expenses: depreciation and, V3: 152

fixed horizon: extensions of classical immunization theory for fixed-income portfolios, V3: 346

fixed income: taxes and inflation rates, V2: 221

fixed-income arbitrage, V4: 310

fixed-income markets: DCF models, V3: 37–38

fixed-income portfolio, example of suitability, V1: 145

fixed-income portfolio management
  bond market index, managing funds against
    benchmark bond index, selection of, V3: 320–323
    risk, tracking, V3: 327–330
    risk profiles, V3: 323–327
  combination strategies, V4: 6
  derivatives-enabled investing
    bond variance vs. bond duration, V4: 14
    credit risk instruments, V4: 23–28
    interest rate futures, V4: 14–20
    interest rate options, V4: 21–23
    interest rate risk, V4: 11–13
    interest rate swaps, V4: 20–21
    measuring risk, V4: 13–14
  framework for, V3: 316–318
  international bond investing
    active vs. passive management, V4: 30–32
    breakeven spread analysis, V4: 37–38
    currency risk, V4: 32–37
    emerging market debt, V4: 39–41
    overview, V4: 29–30
  introduction, V3: 316
  leverage, V4: 6–11
  liabilities, managing funds against
    cash flow matching strategies, V3: 354–358
    dedication strategies, V3: 335–354
  managers for, V4: 41–45
  managing funds against a bond market index, V3: 318–335
    active strategies, V3: 333–334
    enhanced indexing strategies, V3: 330–332
    monitoring/adjusting portfolio, V3: 335
    strategies for, V3: 319–320, 319n2
  summary, V3: 359–360; V4: 46–47

fixed-income portfolio managers, selecting, V4: 41–45

fixed-income premium, V3: 38–41

fixed-income securities material: bond portfolio risk and, V5: 88n3

fixed-interest portfolio duration: swap strategies and, V5: 225–228

fixed interest rates
  dual-currency bond risk and, V5: 239n19
  interest rate risk and, V5: 83–84

fixed planning horizon, V2: 288–291

fixed-rate loan: converting to floating-rate loan, V5: 222–225

fixed-rate payers: interest rate swaps for, V4: 20

flash reports and fair dealing, V1: 56

flat claims: creditor protection, V4: 235

flexible-premium variable life, V2: 337n20

flip-over provisions, V4: 217n93

float adjustments in international index construction, V4: 170

floating-rate loan
  conversion to fixed-rate loan, V5: 222–225
  dual-currency bond risk and, V5: 239n19
  interest rate cap with, V5: 188–192
  interest rate collar with, V5: 195–199
  interest rate floor with, V5: 192–195

floating-rate payers: interest rate swaps for, V4: 20

float-weighted indexes in passive portfolio management, V4: 91–92

floor: floating-rate loan and, V5: 192–195

floor broker: market-not-held order and, V5: 284

floorlets: floating-rate loan and, V5: 192–193

FOF. *See* funds of funds (FOF)

Forbes magazine, V4: 313

forecasting
  almost right defense, V2: 76
  ceteris paribus defense, V2: 76
  challenges in: capital market expectations, V3: 13–24
  debasing, V2: 79–80
  ego defense mechanism, V2: 74–78
  folly of, V2: 65–68
  hasn't happened yet defense, V2: 76
  if only defense, V2: 75
  investment professionals and, V2: 69–73
  overconfidence and, V2: 68–73, 279
  reason for use of, V2: 78–79
  single prediction defense, V2: 76
  unskilled and unaware, V2: 73–74

foreign competition, V3: 151

foreign currency management, case study, V1: 160–162

foreign currency risk
  risk of foreign currency payment, V5: 124–126